Mercedes-Benz A-Class
Owners Workshop Manual

Peter T. Gill

Models covered *(4748 - 288)*

A140, A160, A170, A190 & A210 Hatchback (W168 series), including special/limited editions
Petrol: 1.4 litre (1397cc), 1.6 litre (1598cc), 1.9 litre (1898cc) & 2.1 litre (2084cc)
Turbo-Diesel: 1.7 litre (1689cc)

ABCDE
FGHIJ
KLMNO
PQRST

A book in the **Haynes Owners Workshop Manual Series**

ISBN 978 1 84425 748 5

British Library Cataloguing in Publication Data
A catalogue record for this book is available from the British Library.

Printed in the USA

Haynes Publishing
Sparkford, Yeovil, Somerset BA22 7JJ, England

Haynes North America, Inc
861 Lawrence Drive, Newbury Park, California 91320, USA

Haynes Publishing Nordiska AB
Box 1504, 751 45 UPPSALA, Sverige

Contents

LIVING WITH YOUR MERCEDES-BENZ A-CLASS

Contents

Advanced driving

Many people see the words 'advanced driving' and believe that it won't interest them or that it is a style of driving beyond their own abilities. Nothing could be further from the truth. Advanced driving is straightforward safe, sensible driving - the sort of driving we should all do every time we get behind the wheel.

An average of 10 people are killed every day on UK roads and 870 more are injured, some seriously. Lives are ruined daily, usually because somebody did something stupid. Something like 95% of all accidents are due to human error, mostly driver failure. Sometimes we make genuine mistakes - everyone does. Sometimes we have lapses of concentration. Sometimes we deliberately take risks.

For many people, the process of 'learning to drive' doesn't go much further than learning how to pass the driving test because of a common belief that good drivers are made by 'experience'.

Learning to drive by 'experience' teaches three driving skills:

- ☐ Quick reactions. (Whoops, that was close!)
- ☐ Good handling skills. (Horn, swerve, brake, horn).
- ☐ Reliance on vehicle technology. (Great stuff this ABS, stop in no distance even in the wet...)

Drivers whose skills are 'experience based' generally have a lot of near misses and the odd accident. The results can be seen every day in our courts and our hospital casualty departments.

Advanced drivers have learnt to control the risks by controlling the position and speed of their vehicle. They avoid accidents and near misses, even if the drivers around them make mistakes.

The key skills of advanced driving are **concentration,** effective all-round **observation, anticipation** and **planning.** When **good vehicle handling** is added to these skills, all driving situations can be approached and negotiated in a safe, methodical way, leaving nothing to chance.

Concentration means applying your mind to safe driving, completely excluding anything that's not relevant. Driving is usually the most dangerous activity that most of us undertake in our daily routines. It deserves our full attention.

Observation means not just looking, but seeing and seeking out the information found in the driving environment.

Anticipation means asking yourself what is happening, what you can reasonably expect to happen and what could happen unexpectedly. (One of the commonest words used in compiling accident reports is 'suddenly'.)

Planning is the link between seeing something and taking the appropriate action. For many drivers, planning is the missing link.

If you want to become a safer and more skilful driver and you want to enjoy your driving more, contact the Institute of Advanced Motorists at www.iam.org.uk, phone 0208 996 9600, or write to IAM House, 510 Chiswick High Road, London W4 5RG for an information pack.

Working on your car can be dangerous. This page shows just some of the potential risks and hazards, with the aim of creating a safety-conscious attitude.

General hazards

Scalding

• Don't remove the radiator or expansion tank cap while the engine is hot.
• Engine oil, automatic transmission fluid or power steering fluid may also be dangerously hot if the engine has recently been running.

Burning

• Beware of burns from the exhaust system and from any part of the engine. Brake discs and drums can also be extremely hot immediately after use.

Crushing

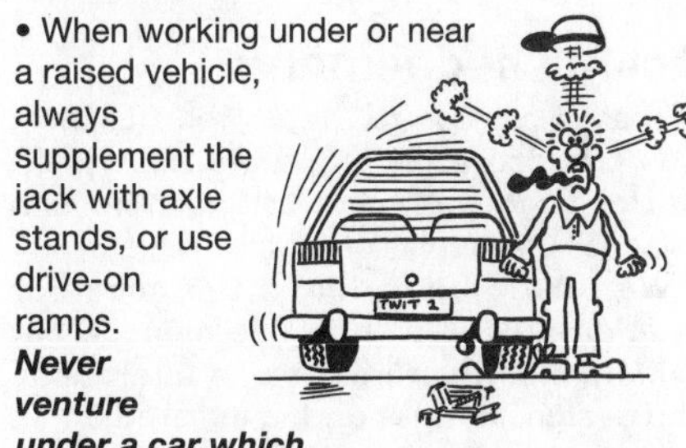

• When working under or near a raised vehicle, always supplement the jack with axle stands, or use drive-on ramps. ***Never venture under a car which is only supported by a jack.***
• Take care if loosening or tightening high-torque nuts when the vehicle is on stands. Initial loosening and final tightening should be done with the wheels on the ground.

Fire

• Fuel is highly flammable; fuel vapour is explosive.
• Don't let fuel spill onto a hot engine.
• Do not smoke or allow naked lights (including pilot lights) anywhere near a vehicle being worked on. Also beware of creating sparks (electrically or by use of tools).
• Fuel vapour is heavier than air, so don't work on the fuel system with the vehicle over an inspection pit.
• Another cause of fire is an electrical overload or short-circuit. Take care when repairing or modifying the vehicle wiring.
• Keep a fire extinguisher handy, of a type suitable for use on fuel and electrical fires.

Electric shock

• Ignition HT voltage can be dangerous, especially to people with heart problems or a pacemaker. Don't work on or near the ignition system with the engine running or the ignition switched on.
• Mains voltage is also dangerous. Make sure that any mains-operated equipment is correctly earthed. Mains power points should be protected by a residual current device (RCD) circuit breaker.

Fume or gas intoxication

• Exhaust fumes are poisonous; they often contain carbon monoxide, which is rapidly fatal if inhaled. Never run the engine in a confined space such as a garage with the doors shut.
• Fuel vapour is also poisonous, as are the vapours from some cleaning solvents and paint thinners.

Poisonous or irritant substances

• Avoid skin contact with battery acid and with any fuel, fluid or lubricant, especially antifreeze, brake hydraulic fluid and Diesel fuel. Don't syphon them by mouth. If such a substance is swallowed or gets into the eyes, seek medical advice.
• Prolonged contact with used engine oil can cause skin cancer. Wear gloves or use a barrier cream if necessary. Change out of oil-soaked clothes and do not keep oily rags in your pocket.
• Air conditioning refrigerant forms a poisonous gas if exposed to a naked flame (including a cigarette). It can also cause skin burns on contact.

Asbestos

• Asbestos dust can cause cancer if inhaled or swallowed. Asbestos may be found in gaskets and in brake and clutch linings. When dealing with such components it is safest to assume that they contain asbestos.

Special hazards

Hydrofluoric acid

• This extremely corrosive acid is formed when certain types of synthetic rubber, found in some O-rings, oil seals, fuel hoses etc, are exposed to temperatures above 400°C. The rubber changes into a charred or sticky substance containing the acid. *Once formed, the acid remains dangerous for years. If it gets onto the skin, it may be necessary to amputate the limb concerned.*
• When dealing with a vehicle which has suffered a fire, or with components salvaged from such a vehicle, wear protective gloves and discard them after use.

The battery

• Batteries contain sulphuric acid, which attacks clothing, eyes and skin. Take care when topping-up or carrying the battery.
• The hydrogen gas given off by the battery is highly explosive. Never cause a spark or allow a naked light nearby. Be careful when connecting and disconnecting battery chargers or jump leads.

Air bags

• Air bags can cause injury if they go off accidentally. Take care when removing the steering wheel and/or facia. Special storage instructions may apply.

Diesel injection equipment

• Diesel injection pumps supply fuel at very high pressure. Take care when working on the fuel injectors and fuel pipes.

Warning: Never expose the hands, face or any other part of the body to injector spray; the fuel can penetrate the skin with potentially fatal results.

Remember...

DO

• Do use eye protection when using power tools, and when working under the vehicle.

• Do wear gloves or use barrier cream to protect your hands when necessary.

• Do get someone to check periodically that all is well when working alone on the vehicle.

• Do keep loose clothing and long hair well out of the way of moving mechanical parts.

• Do remove rings, wristwatch etc, before working on the vehicle – especially the electrical system.

• Do ensure that any lifting or jacking equipment has a safe working load rating adequate for the job.

DON'T

• Don't attempt to lift a heavy component which may be beyond your capability – get assistance.

• Don't rush to finish a job, or take unverified short cuts.

• Don't use ill-fitting tools which may slip and cause injury.

• Don't leave tools or parts lying around where someone can trip over them. Mop up oil and fuel spills at once.

• Don't allow children or pets to play in or near a vehicle being worked on.

Models have been produced with a wide range of engines, including 1.4, 1.6, 1.9 and 2.1 litre petrol versions, as well as a turbo-charged 1.7 litre diesel engine. All engines use either 'indirect' or 'direct' fuel injection, and are fitted with a wide range of emission control systems. All the engines are of a well-proven design and, provided regular maintenance is carried out, are unlikely to give trouble.

All models are available in a 5-door Hatchback body style, with a short or long wheelbase option.

Fully-independent front and rear suspension is fitted, with the front suspension components attached to a subframe assembly; the rear suspension uses trailing arms.

A five-speed manual gearbox is fitted, with a five-speed automatic gearbox available as an option for some models.

A wide range of standard and optional equipment is available within the model range to suit most tastes, including an anti-lock braking system, climate control and air conditioning.

Your Mercedes-Benz A-Class Manual

The aim of this manual is to help you get the best value from your vehicle. It can do so in several ways. It can help you decide what work must be done (even should you choose to get it done by a garage). It will also provide information on routine maintenance and servicing, and give a logical course of action and diagnosis when random faults occur. However, it is hoped that you will use the manual by tackling the work yourself. On simpler jobs it may even be quicker than booking the car into a garage and going there twice, to leave and collect it. Perhaps most important, a lot of money can be saved by avoiding the costs a garage must charge to cover its labour and overheads.

The manual has drawings and descriptions to show the function of the various components so that their layout can be understood. Tasks are described and photographed in a clear step-by-step sequence.

References to the 'left' and 'right' of the vehicle are in the sense of a person in the driver's seat facing forward.

Acknowledgements

Thanks are due to Draper Tools Limited, who provided some of the workshop tools, and to all those people at Sparkford who helped in the production of this manual.

We take great pride in the accuracy of information given in this manual, but vehicle manufacturers make alterations and design changes during the production run of a particular vehicle of which they do not inform us. No liability can be accepted by the authors or publishers for loss, damage or injury caused by any errors in, or omissions from, the information given.

The following pages are intended to help in dealing with common roadside emergencies and breakdowns. You will find more detailed fault finding information at the back of the manual, and repair information in the main chapters.

If your car won't start and the starter motor doesn't turn

- ☐ If it's a model with automatic transmission, make sure the selector is in P or N.
- ☐ Remove the battery cover and make sure that the battery terminals are clean and tight.
- ☐ Switch on the headlights and try to start the engine. If the headlights go very dim when you're trying to start, the battery is probably flat. Get out of trouble by jump starting (see next page) using a friend's car.

If your car won't start even though the starter motor turns as normal

- ☐ Is there fuel in the tank?
- ☐ Is there moisture on electrical components under the bonnet? Switch off the ignition, then wipe off any obvious dampness with a dry cloth. Spray a water-repellent aerosol product (WD-40 or equivalent) on ignition and fuel system electrical connectors like those shown in the photos. (Note that diesel engines don't usually suffer from damp.)

Check the condition and security of the battery connections.

Check the fuses in the fusebox located in the battery compartment inside the vehicle.

Check the wiring to the ignition coil at the front of the engine (petrol models only).

Check that the ECM wiring is secure.

Check that the fuel lines are secure and no air in the system (diesel model shown).

Jump starting

When jump-starting a car using a booster battery, observe the following precautions:

✔ Before connecting the booster battery, make sure that the ignition is switched off.

✔ Ensure that all electrical equipment (lights, heater, wipers, etc) is switched off.

✔ Take note of any special precautions printed on the battery case.

✔ Make sure that the booster battery is the same voltage as the discharged one in the vehicle.

✔ If the battery is being jump-started from the battery in another vehicle, the two vehicles MUST NOT TOUCH each other.

✔ Make sure that the transmission is in neutral (or PARK, in the case of automatic transmission).

Jump starting will get you out of trouble, but you must correct whatever made the battery go flat in the first place. There are three possibilities:

1 The battery has been drained by repeated attempts to start, or by leaving the lights on.

2 The charging system is not working properly (alternator drivebelt slack or broken, alternator wiring fault or alternator itself faulty).

3 The battery itself is at fault (electrolyte low, or battery worn out).

1 Connect one end of the red jump lead to the positive (+) terminal of the flat battery

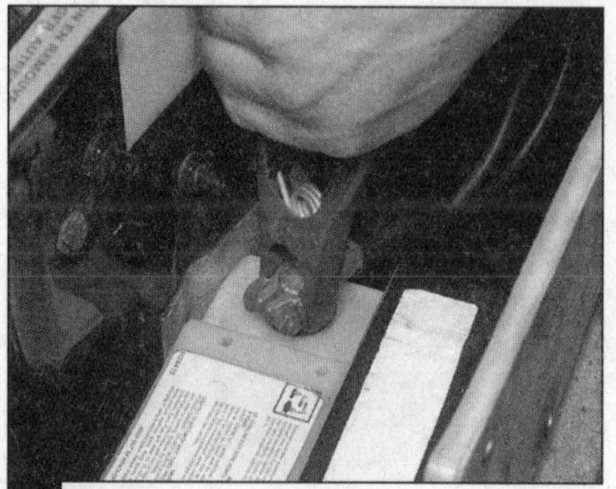

2 Connect the other end of the red lead to the positive (+) terminal of the booster battery.

3 Connect one end of the black jump lead to the negative (-) terminal of the booster battery

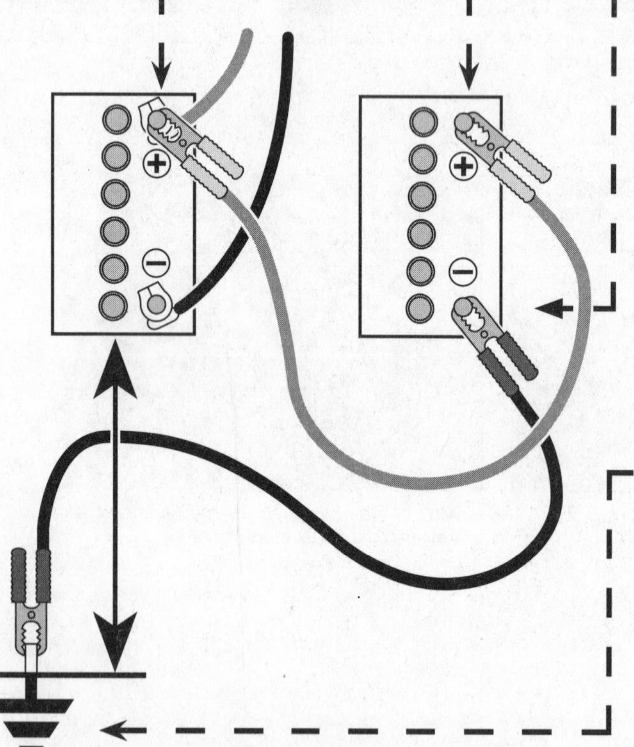

4 Connect the other end of the black jump lead to a bolt or bracket on the engine block, well away from the battery, on the vehicle to be started.

5 Make sure that the jump leads will not come into contact with the fan, drive-belts or other moving parts of the engine.

6 Start the engine using the booster battery and run it at idle speed. Switch on the lights, rear window demister and heater blower motor, then disconnect the jump leads in the reverse order of connection. Turn off the lights etc.

Wheel changing

Warning: Do not change a wheel in a situation where you risk being hit by other traffic. On busy roads, try to stop in a lay-by or a gateway. Be wary of passing traffic while changing the wheel – it is easy to become distracted by the job in hand.

Preparation

- ☐ When a puncture occurs, stop as soon as it is safe to do so.
- ☐ Park on firm level ground, if possible, and well out of the way of other traffic.
- ☐ Use hazard warning lights if necessary.
- ☐ If you have one, use a warning triangle to alert other drivers of your presence.
- ☐ Apply the handbrake and engage first or reverse gear (or P on models with automatic transmission).
- ☐ Chock the wheel diagonally opposite the one being removed – a couple of large stones will do for this.
- ☐ If the ground is soft, use a flat piece of wood to spread the load under the jack.

Changing the wheel

Note: *Some of the details shown here will vary according to model.*

1 The spare wheel and tools are stored in the luggage compartment. Raise the floor covering, and lift out the jack and wheel changing tools.

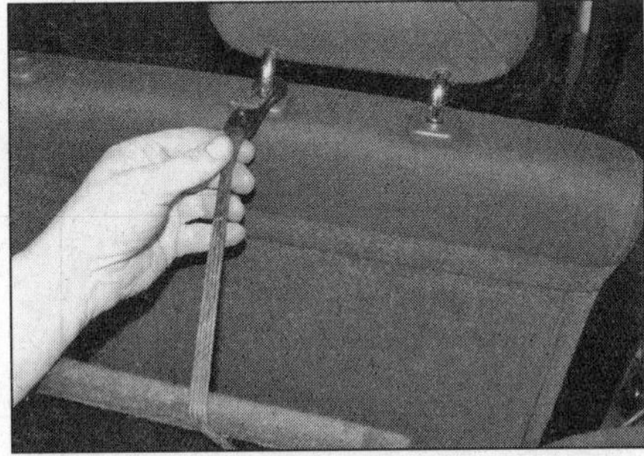

2 Use the strap to hold the floor cover up.

3 Use the wheel brace to slacken each wheel bolt by half a turn.

4 Unscrew the plastic retainer and remove the spare wheel.

5 Locate the jack on firm ground below the reinforced point on the sill (don't jack the vehicle at any other point of the sill), then turn the jack handle clockwise until the wheel is raised clear of the ground.

6 Unscrew the wheel bolts and remove the wheel.

7 Fit the spare wheel, and screw in the bolts. Lightly tighten the bolts with the wheel brace then lower the vehicle to the ground.

8 Securely tighten the wheel bolts in the sequence shown then refit the wheel trim/ hub cap. Stow the punctured wheel back in the spare wheel well. Note that the wheel bolts should be tightened to the specified torque at the earliest possible opportunity.

Finally . . .

- ☐ Remove the wheel chocks.
- ☐ Stow the jack and tools with the spare wheel in the luggage compartment.
- ☐ Check the tyre pressure on the wheel just fitted. If it is low, or if you don't have a pressure gauge with you, drive slowly to the nearest garage and inflate the tyre to the correct pressure.

Note: *If a temporary 'space-saver' spare wheel has been fitted, special conditions apply to its use. This type of spare wheel is only intended for use in an emergency, and should not remain fitted any longer than it takes to get the punctured wheel repaired. While the temporary wheel is in use, ensure it is inflated to the correct pressure, do not exceed 50 mph, and avoid harsh acceleration, braking or cornering.*

Identifying leaks

Puddles on the garage floor or drive, or obvious wetness under the bonnet or underneath the car, suggest a leak that needs investigating. It can sometimes be difficult to decide where the leak is coming from, especially if the engine bay is very dirty already. Leaking oil or fluid can also be blown rearwards by the passage of air under the car, giving a false impression of where the problem lies.

Warning: Most automotive oils and fluids are poisonous. Wash them off skin, and change out of contaminated clothing, without delay.

The smell of a fluid leaking from the car may provide a clue to what's leaking. Some fluids are distinctively coloured.
It may help to clean the car carefully and to park it over some clean paper overnight as an aid to locating the source of the leak.
Remember that some leaks may only occur while the engine is running.

Sump oil

Engine oil may leak from the drain plug...

Oil from filter

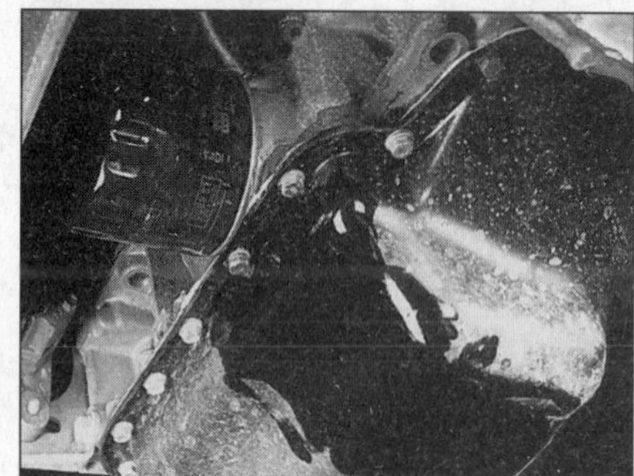

...or from the base of the oil filter.

Gearbox oil

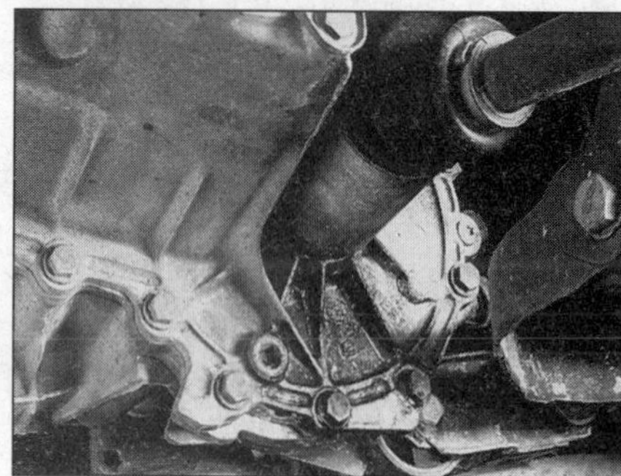

Gearbox oil can leak from the seals at the inboard ends of the driveshafts.

Antifreeze

Leaking antifreeze often leaves a crystalline deposit like this.

Brake fluid

A leak occurring at a wheel is almost certainly brake fluid.

Power steering fluid

Power steering fluid may leak from the pipe connectors on the steering rack.

Towing

When all else fails, you may find yourself having to get a tow home – or of course you may be helping somebody else. Long-distance recovery should only be done by a garage or breakdown service. For shorter distances, DIY towing using another car is easy enough, but observe the following points:

- ☐ Use a proper tow-rope – they are not expensive. The vehicle being towed must display an ON TOW sign in its rear window.
- ☐ Always turn the ignition key to the 'On' position when the vehicle is being towed, so that the steering lock is released, and the direction indicator and brake lights work.
- ☐ Only attach the tow-rope to the towing eyes provided. The towing eye is supplied as part of the toolkit stored in the luggage compartment. To fit the eye, remove the vent/cover from the bumper. Screw the eye into position, and tighten using the wheel brace handle.
- ☐ Before being towed, release the handbrake and select neutral on the transmission. On models with automatic transmission, do not exceed 30 mph and do not tow for more than 30 miles. If in doubt, do not tow, or transmission damage may result.
- ☐ Note that greater-than-usual pedal pressure will be required to operate the brakes, since the vacuum servo unit is only operational with the engine running.
- ☐ Because the power steering will not be operational, greater-than-usual steering effort will be required.
- ☐ The driver of the car being towed must keep the tow-rope taut at all times to avoid snatching.
- ☐ Make sure that both drivers know the route before setting off.
- ☐ Only drive at moderate speeds and keep the distance towed to a minimum. Drive smoothly and allow plenty of time for slowing down at junctions.

Introduction

There are some very simple checks which need only take a few minutes to carry out, but which could save you a lot of inconvenience and expense.

These *Weekly checks* require no great skill or special tools, and the small amount of time they take to perform could prove to be very well spent, for example:

□ Keeping an eye on tyre condition and pressures, will not only help to stop them wearing out prematurely, but could also save your life.

□ Many breakdowns are caused by electrical problems. Battery-related faults are particularly common, and a quick check on a regular basis will often prevent the majority of these.

□ If your car develops a brake fluid leak, the first time you might know about it is when your brakes don't work properly. Checking the level regularly will give advance warning of this kind of problem.

□ If the oil or coolant levels run low, the cost of repairing any engine damage will be far greater than fixing the leak, for example.

Underbonnet check points

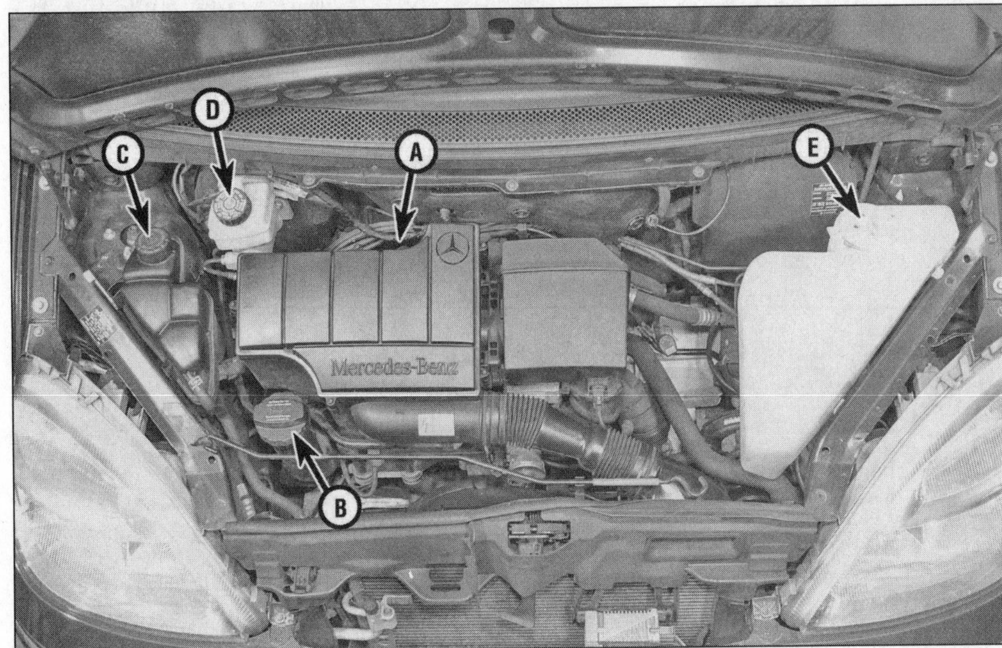

◀ 1.6 litre petrol

A *Engine oil level dipstick*
B *Engine oil filler cap*
C *Coolant expansion tank*
D *Brake/clutch fluid reservoir*
E *Screen washer fluid reservoir*

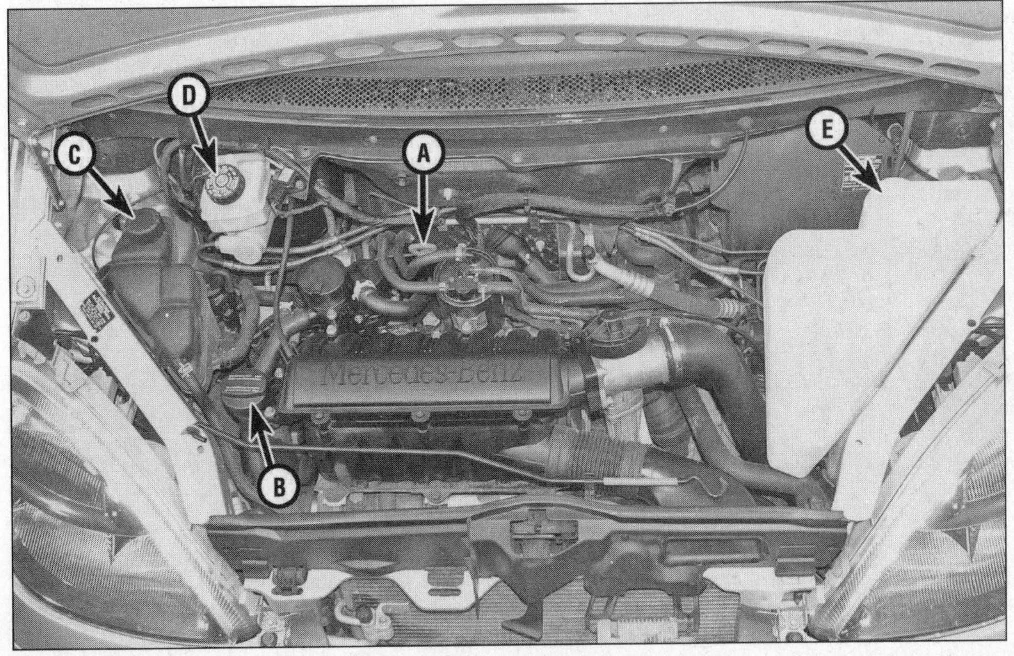

◀ Diesel engine

A *Engine oil level dipstick*
B *Engine oil filler cap*
C *Coolant expansion tank*
D *Brake/clutch fluid reservoir*
E *Screen washer fluid reservoir*

Engine oil level

Before you start

✔ Make sure that the car is on level ground.

✔ Check the oil level before the car is driven, or at least 5 minutes after the engine has been switched off.

If the oil is checked immediately after driving the vehicle, some of the oil will remain in the upper engine components, resulting in an inaccurate reading on the dipstick.

The correct oil

Modern engines place great demands on their oil. It is very important that the correct oil for your car is used (see *Lubricants and fluids*).

Car care

● If you have to add oil frequently, you should check whether you have any oil leaks. Place some clean paper under the car overnight, and check for stains in the morning. If there are no leaks, then the engine may be burning oil.

● Always maintain the level between the upper and lower dipstick marks. If the level is too low, severe engine damage may occur. Oil seal failure may result if the engine is overfilled by adding too much oil.

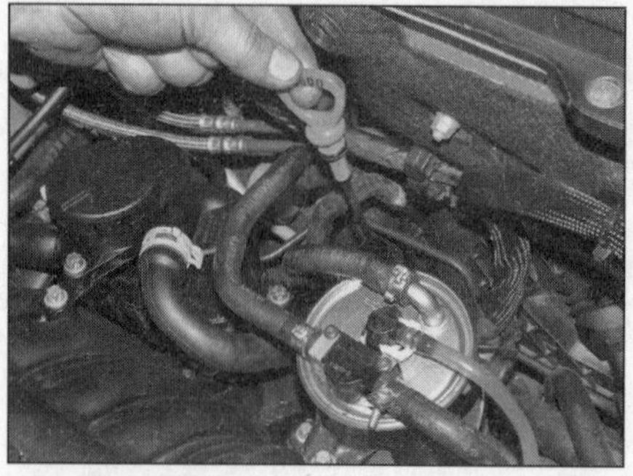

1 The dipstick is coloured red for easy identification (see *Underbonnet check points* for exact location). Withdraw the dipstick, and then use a clean rag or paper towel to wipe the oil from it. Insert the clean dipstick into the tube as far as it will go, then withdraw it again.

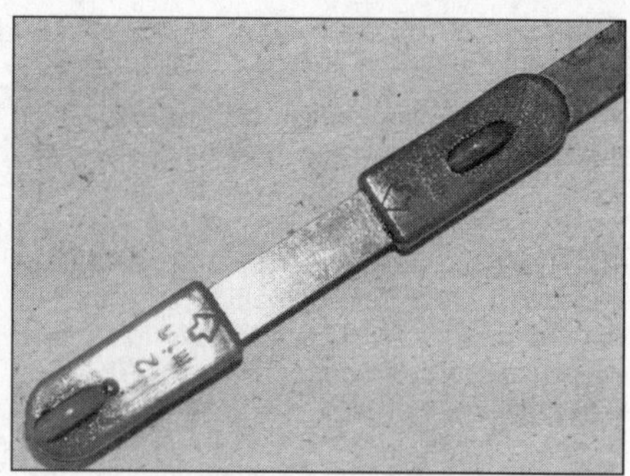

2 Note the level on the end of the dipstick, which should be between the upper (MAX) and lower (MIN) mark.

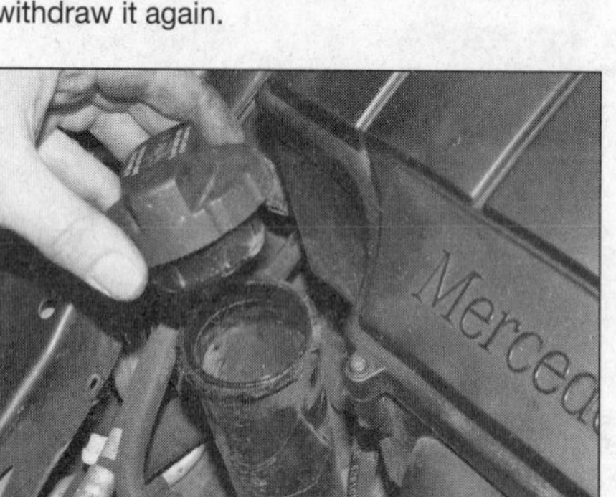

3 Oil is added through the filler cap aperture. Unscrew the cap.

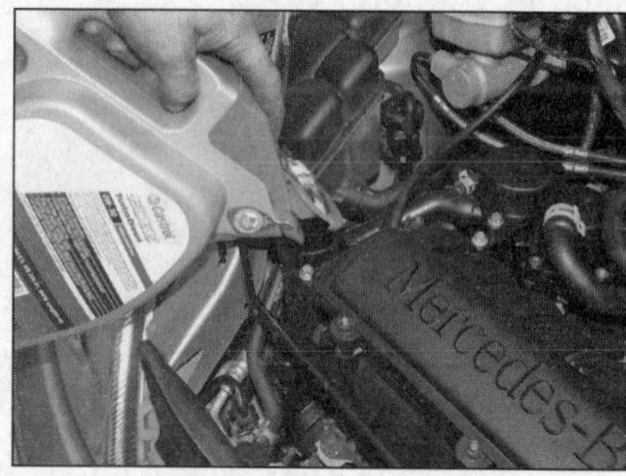

4 Place some cloth rags around the filler cap aperture, then top-up the level. A funnel may help to reduce spillage. Add the oil slowly, checking the level on the dipstick frequently. Avoid overfilling (see *Car care*).

Coolant level

Warning: Do not attempt to remove the expansion tank pressure cap when the engine is hot, as there is a very great risk of scalding. Do not leave open containers of coolant about, as it is poisonous.

Car care

● With a sealed-type cooling system, adding coolant should not be necessary on a regular basis. If frequent topping-up is required, it is likely there is a leak. Check the radiator, all hoses and joint faces for signs of staining or wetness, and rectify as necessary.

● It is important that antifreeze is used in the cooling system all year round, not just during the winter months. Don't top up with water alone, as the antifreeze will become diluted.

1 The coolant level varies with the temperature of the engine. When the engine is cold, the coolant level should be between the top and bottom of the level mark on the side of the tank (arrowed).

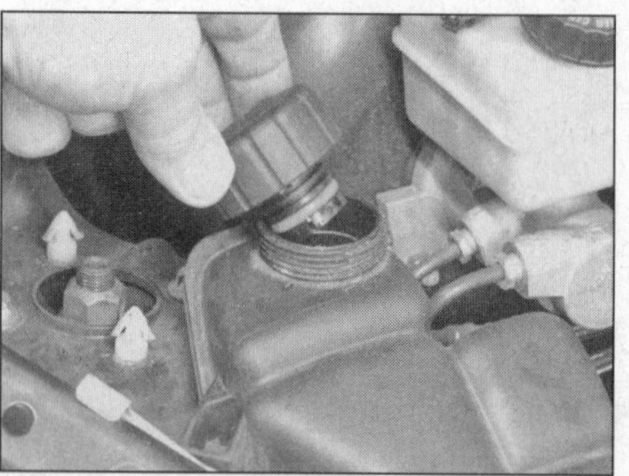

2 If topping-up is necessary, wait until the engine is cold. Slowly unscrew the cap to release any pressure present in the cooling system, and remove the cap.

3 Add a mixture of water and the specified antifreeze (see *Lubricants and fluids*) to the expansion tank until the coolant level is halfway up the level mark. Refit the cap and tighten it securely.

Brake (and clutch) fluid level

Note: *On manual transmission models, the fluid reservoir also supplies the clutch master cylinder with fluid.*

Before you start

✔ Make sure that the car is on level ground.

✔ Cleanliness is of great importance when dealing with the braking system, so take care to clean around the reservoir cap before topping-up. Use only clean brake fluid.

Safety first!

● If the reservoir requires repeated topping-up, this is an indication of a fluid leak somewhere in the system, which should be investigated immediately.

● If a leak is suspected, the car should not be driven until the braking system has been checked. Never take any risks where brakes are concerned.

Warning: Brake fluid can harm your eyes and damage painted surfaces, so use extreme caution when handling and pouring it. Do not use fluid which has been standing open for some time, as it absorbs moisture from the air, which can cause a dangerous loss of braking effectiveness.

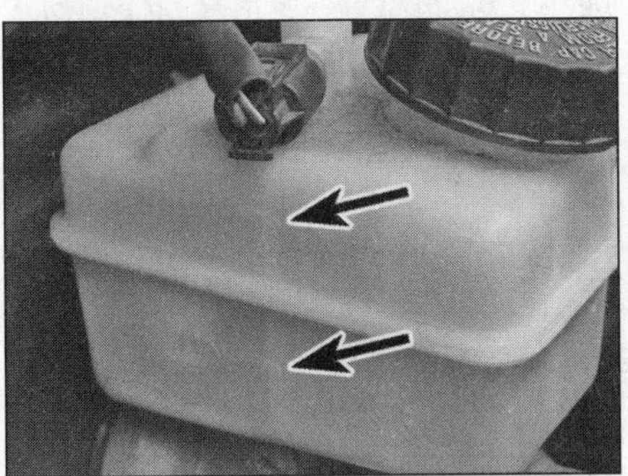

1 The MIN and MAX marks are indicated on the reservoir. The fluid level must be kept between the marks at all times. If topping-up is necessary, first wipe clean the area around the filler cap to prevent dirt entering the hydraulic system.

2 Unscrew and remove the reservoir cap.

3 Carefully add fluid, taking care not to spill it onto the surrounding components (use a funnel). Use only the specified fluid (see *Lubricants and fluids*); mixing different types can cause damage to the system. On completion, securely refit the cap and wipe away any spilt fluid.

Washer fluid level

● Screenwash additives not only keep the windscreen clean during bad weather, they also prevent the washer system freezing in cold weather – which is when you are likely to need it most. Don't top-up using plain water, as the screenwash will become diluted, and will freeze in cold weather.

Warning: On no account use engine coolant antifreeze in the screen washer system – this may damage the paintwork.

1 The screenwash fluid reservoir is located on the left-hand side (as seen from the driver's seat) of the engine compartment, behind the headlight. Pull up the filler cap to release it from the reservoir.

2 When topping-up the reservoir, a screenwash additive should be added in the quantities recommended on the bottle.

Tyre condition and pressure

It is very important that tyres are in good condition, and at the correct pressure - having a tyre failure at any speed is highly dangerous. Tyre wear is influenced by driving style - harsh braking and acceleration, or fast cornering, will all produce more rapid tyre wear. As a general rule, the front tyres wear out faster than the rears. Interchanging the tyres from front to rear ("rotating" the tyres) may result in more even wear. However, if this is completely effective, you may have the expense of replacing all four tyres at once!

Remove any nails or stones embedded in the tread before they penetrate the tyre to cause deflation. If removal of a nail does reveal that the tyre has been punctured, refit the nail so that its point of penetration is marked. Then immediately change the wheel, and have the tyre repaired by a tyre dealer.

Regularly check the tyres for damage in the form of cuts or bulges, especially in the sidewalls. Periodically remove the wheels, and clean any dirt or mud from the inside and outside surfaces. Examine the wheel rims for signs of rusting, corrosion or other damage. Light alloy wheels are easily damaged by "kerbing" whilst parking; steel wheels may also become dented or buckled. A new wheel is very often the only way to overcome severe damage.

New tyres should be balanced when they are fitted, but it may become necessary to re-balance them as they wear, or if the balance weights fitted to the wheel rim should fall off. Unbalanced tyres will wear more quickly, as will the steering and suspension components. Wheel imbalance is normally signified by vibration, particularly at a certain speed (typically around 50 mph). If this vibration is felt only through the steering, then it is likely that just the front wheels need balancing. If, however, the vibration is felt through the whole car, the rear wheels could be out of balance. Wheel balancing should be carried out by a tyre dealer or garage.

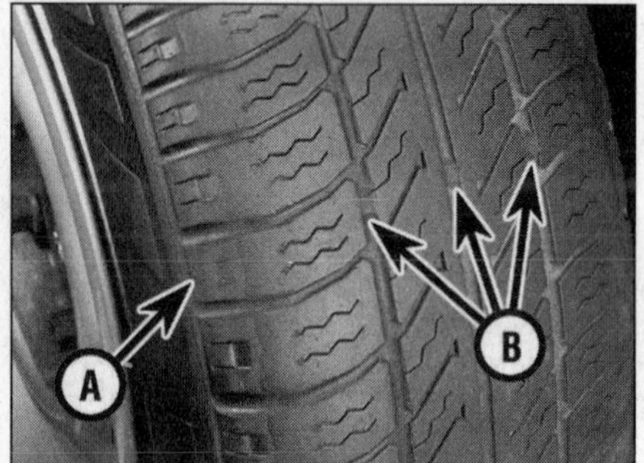

1 ***Tread Depth - visual check***
The original tyres have tread wear safety bands (B), which will appear when the tread depth reaches approximately 1.6 mm. The band positions are indicated by a triangular mark on the tyre sidewall (A).

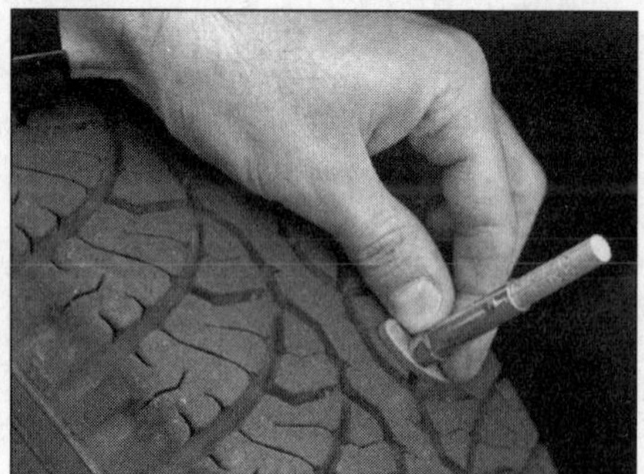

2 ***Tread Depth - manual check***
Alternatively, tread wear can be monitored with a simple, inexpensive device known as a tread depth indicator gauge.

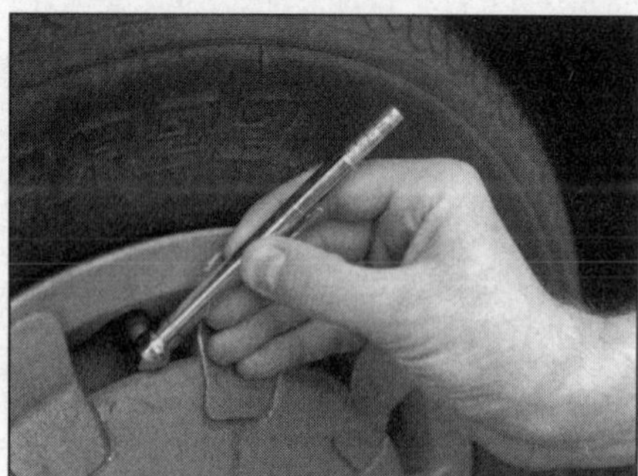

3 ***Tyre Pressure Check***
Check the tyre pressures regularly with the tyres cold. Do not adjust the tyre pressures immediately after the vehicle has been used, or an inaccurate setting will result.

Tyre tread wear patterns

Shoulder Wear

Underinflation (wear on both sides)
Under-inflation will cause overheating of the tyre, because the tyre will flex too much, and the tread will not sit correctly on the road surface. This will cause a loss of grip and excessive wear, not to mention the danger of sudden tyre failure due to heat build-up.
Check and adjust pressures
Incorrect wheel camber (wear on one side)
Repair or renew suspension parts
Hard cornering
Reduce speed!

Centre Wear

Overinflation
Over-inflation will cause rapid wear of the centre part of the tyre tread, coupled with reduced grip, harsher ride, and the danger of shock damage occurring in the tyre casing.
Check and adjust pressures

If you sometimes have to inflate your car's tyres to the higher pressures specified for maximum load or sustained high speed, don't forget to reduce the pressures to normal afterwards.

Uneven Wear

Front tyres may wear unevenly as a result of wheel misalignment. Most tyre dealers and garages can check and adjust the wheel alignment (or "tracking") for a modest charge.
Incorrect camber or castor
Repair or renew suspension parts
Malfunctioning suspension
Repair or renew suspension parts
Unbalanced wheel
Balance tyres
Incorrect toe setting
Adjust front wheel alignment
Note: *The feathered edge of the tread which typifies toe wear is best checked by feel.*

Battery

Caution: Before carrying out any work on the vehicle battery, read the precautions given in 'Safety first!' at the start of this manual.

✔ Make sure that the battery tray is in good condition, and that the clamp is tight. Corrosion on the tray, retaining clamp and the battery itself can be removed with a solution of water and baking soda. Thoroughly rinse all cleaned areas with water. Any metal parts damaged by corrosion should be covered with a zinc-based primer, then painted.

✔ Periodically (approximately every three months), check the charge condition of the battery as described in Chapter 5A.

✔ If the battery is flat, and you need to jump start your vehicle, see *Roadside Repairs*.

1 The battery is located under the floor in the driver's side footwell, next to the fuse and relay box. Lift the floor cover and the insulation, to gain access to the battery terminals. The exterior of the battery should be inspected periodically for damage such as a cracked case or cover.

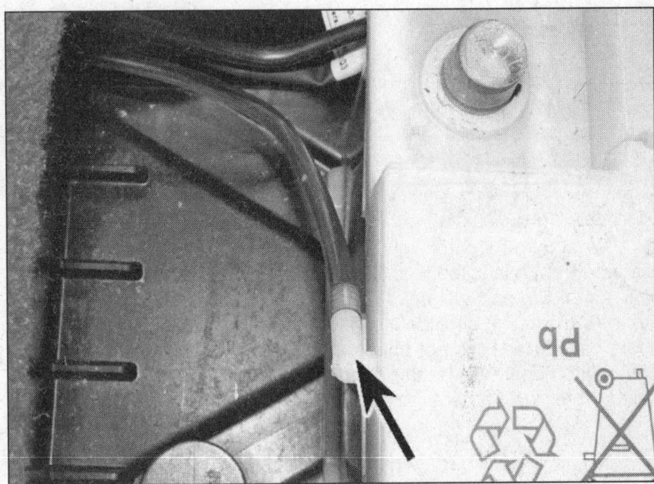

2 Check the ventilation tube is fitted to the side of the battery securely.

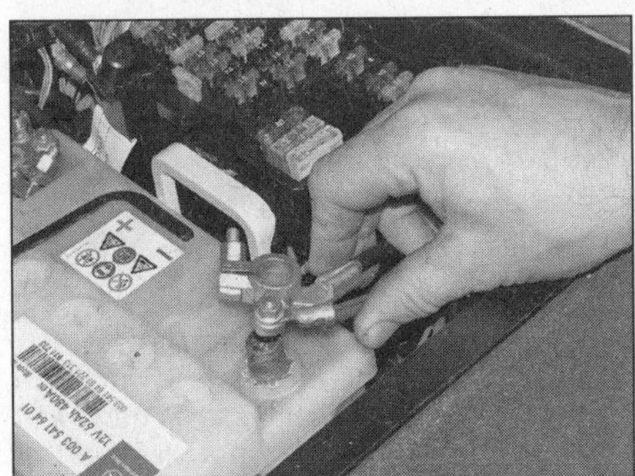

3 Check the security and condition of all the battery and fuse connections. The exterior of the battery should be inspected periodically for damage such as a cracked case or cover.

4 If corrosion (white, fluffy deposits) is evident, remove the cables from the battery terminals (refer to *Disconnecting the battery* in Reference), clean them with a small wire brush, then refit them. Automotive stores sell a tool for cleaning the battery post . . .

5 . . . as well as the battery cable clamps.

Electrical systems

✔ Check all external lights and the horn. Refer to the appropriate Sections of Chapter 12 for details if any of the circuits are found to be inoperative.

✔ Visually check all accessible wiring connectors, harnesses and retaining clips for security, and for signs of chafing or damage.

If you need to check your brake lights and indicators unaided, back up to a wall or garage door and operate the lights. The reflected light should show if they are working properly.

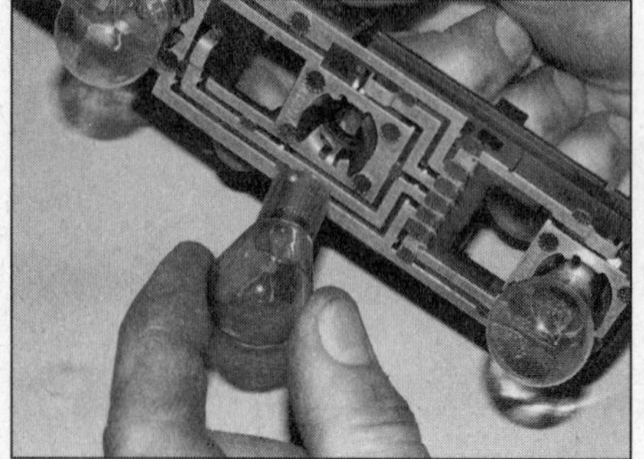

1 If a single indicator light, brake light or headlight has failed, it is likely that a bulb has blown and will need to be renewed. Refer to Chapter 12 for details. If both brake lights have failed, it is possible that the brake light switch operated by the brake pedal has failed. Refer to Chapter 9 for details.

2 If more than one indicator light or headlight has failed, it is likely that either a fuse has blown or that there is a fault in the circuit (see *Electrical fault finding* in Chapter 12). The fuses are in the fusebox beneath a cover on the right-hand end of the facia panel. Use a small screwdriver to prise off the cover. The circuits protected by the fuses are shown on the inside of the cover. Additional fuses and fusible links are in the fusebox located under the driver's side floor panel with the battery.

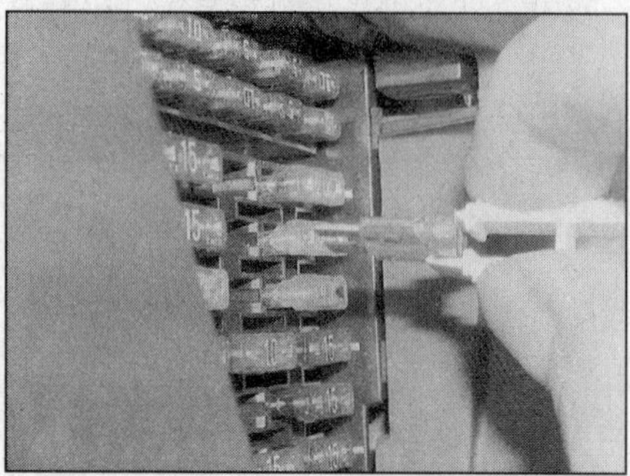

3 To renew a blown fuse, pull it from its location in the fusebox, using the plastic pliers provided. Fit a new fuse of the same rating, available from car accessory shops. It is important that you find the reason that the fuse blew (see *Electrical fault finding* in Chapter 12).

Wiper blades

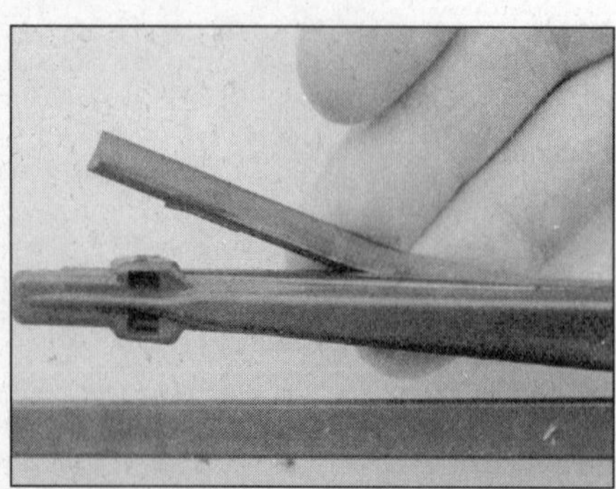

1 Check the condition of the wiper blades; if they are cracked or show any signs of deterioration, or if the glass swept area is smeared, renew them. For maximum clarity of vision, wiper blades should be renewed annually, as a matter of course.

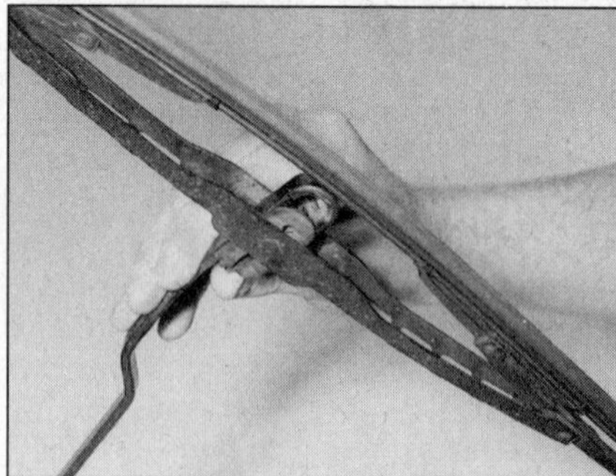

2 To remove a windscreen wiper blade, pull the arm fully away from the screen until it locks. On standard wipers, swivel the blade through 90°, press the locking tab with your fingers, and slide the blade out of the hooked end of the arm.

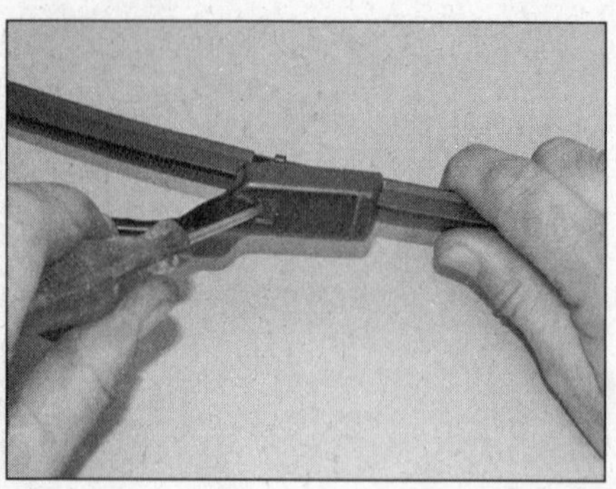

3 On aerodynamic wipers, depress the catch with a screwdriver, and pull the blade from the arm.

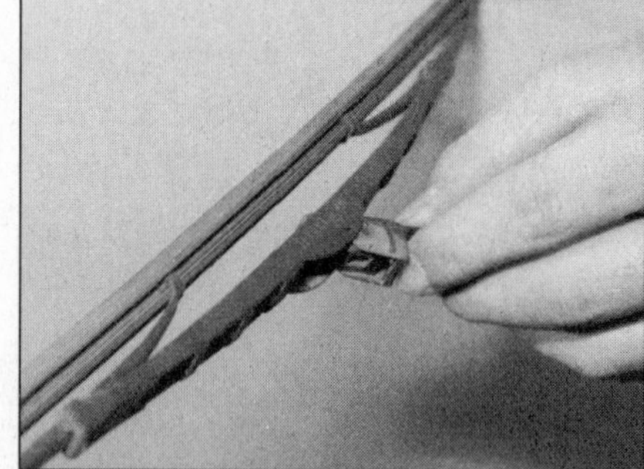

4 Where applicable, don't forget to check the tailgate wiper blade as well. To remove the blade, depress the retaining tab and slide the blade out of the hooked end of the arm.

Lubricants and fluids

Engine	Multigrade engine oil with a viscosity suited to the ambient temperature **(see illustration)** approved in accordance with MB sheets 229.1 and 229.3
Cooling system	Mercedes-Benz antifreeze agent KFM type 30 (for aluminum corrosion protection)
Power steering fluid	MB 345.0 Hydraulic fluid A 001 989 2403
Manual transmission	Gear oil MB 317 or MB 235.10 transmission oil 001 989 2603
Automatic transmission	MB 236.10 ATF 001 989 2103
Braking system	Hydraulic fluid to SAE J1703F or DOT 4

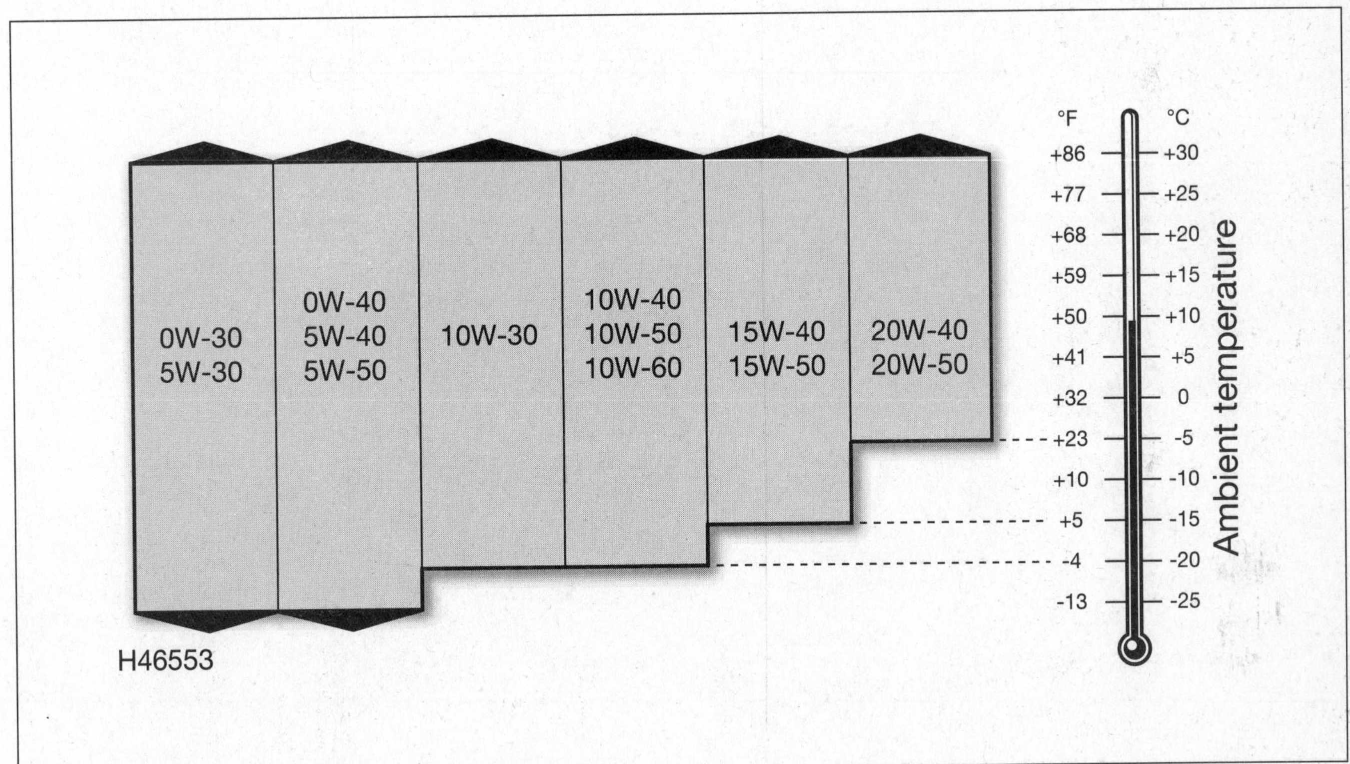

Tyre pressures

Note: *The recommended tyre pressures for each vehicle are given on a sticker attached to the inside of the fuel filler flap. The pressures given are for the original equipment tyres – the recommended pressures may vary if any other make or type of tyre is fitted; check with the tyre manufacturer or supplier for latest recommendations. The following pressures are typical.*

	Front	**Rear**
Normal load	2.0 bars (29 psi)	2.2 bars (32 psi)
Full load	2.2 bars (32 psi)	2.6 bars (38 psi)

Chapter 1 Part A: Routine maintenance and servicing – petrol models

Contents

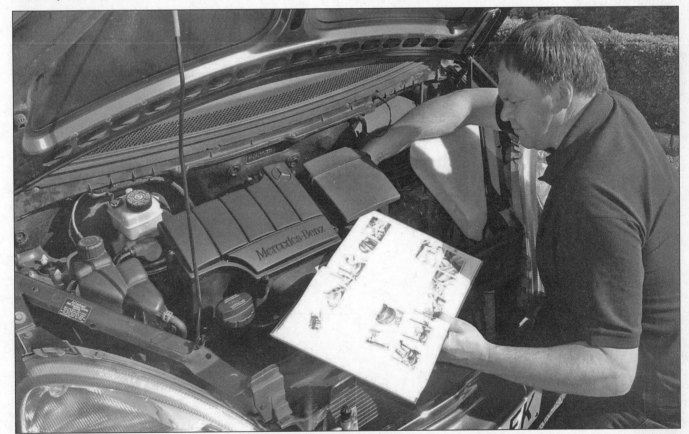

Degrees of difficulty

Easy, suitable for novice with little experience 	**Fairly easy,** suitable for beginner with some experience	**Fairly difficult,** suitable for competent DIY mechanic	**Difficult,** suitable for experienced DIY mechanic 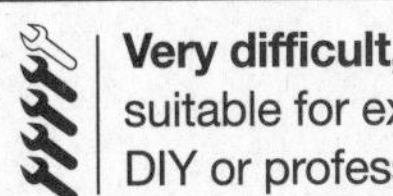	**Very difficult,** suitable for expert DIY or professional 

Lubricants and fluids

Refer to end of *Weekly checks* on page 0•17

Capacities

Engine oil – including filter	
All models	4.5 litres
Cooling system (approximate)	
Manual transmission	5.5 litres
Automatic transmission	5.7 litres
Transmission (approximate)	
Manual transmission	1.8 litres
Automatic transmission	5.5 litres
Fuel tank	
All models (including reserve of 6 litres)	54 litres

Cooling system

Antifreeze mixture:	
50% antifreeze	Protection down to -37°C
55% antifreeze	Protection down to -45°C

Note: *Refer to antifreeze manufacturer for latest recommendations.*

Ignition system

Spark plugs:	
Type	Mercedes-Benz 003 159 75 03/26
Electrode gap	1.0 mm

Brakes

Brake pad lining minimum thickness	2.0 mm
Brake shoe lining minimum thickness	2.0 mm

Torque wrench settings

	Nm	lbf ft
Manual gearbox:		
Filler plug	35	26
Drain plug	30	22
Oil filter screw cap	25	18
Roadwheel bolts	110	81
Spark plugs	25	18
Sump drain plug	25	18

The maintenance intervals in this manual are provided with the assumption that you, not the dealer, will be carrying out the work. These are the minimum intervals recommended by us for vehicles driven daily. If you wish to keep your vehicle in peak condition at all times, you may wish to perform some of these procedures more often. We encourage frequent maintenance, since it enhances the efficiency, performance and resale value of your vehicle.

When the vehicle is new, it should be serviced by a dealer service department (or other workshop recognised by the vehicle manufacturer as providing the same standard of service) in order to preserve the warranty. The vehicle manufacturer may reject warranty claims if you are unable to prove that servicing has been carried out as and when specified, using only original equipment parts or parts certified to be of equivalent quality.

All Mercedes-Benz models are equipped with ASSYST (Active Service SYSTem), which lets you know when the next service is due. The service symbol will illuminate on the instrument panel approximately one month before the next service is due. Depending on your driving style, the time between servicing can vary. A moderate style of driving with no short trips and at a medium engine speed can increase the time between servicing. The different type of symbols that illuminate will indicate which type of service is due: one spanner being a minor service (Service A) and two spanners being a major service (Service B).

After completing a service, Mercedes-Benz technicians use a special instrument to reset the service display to the next service interval, and a printout is put in the vehicle service record. The display can be reset by the owner as described in Section 4.

Every 250 miles or weekly

- [ ] Refer to Weekly checks

Every 7500 miles or 12 months, whichever comes first

- [ ] Renew the engine oil and filter (Section 3)

Note: *Frequent oil and filter changes are good for the engine. We recommend changing the oil at least once a year.*

One spanner on display (Service A)

In addition to the items listed above, carry out the following:

- [ ] Reset the service interval display (Section 4)
- [ ] Check the condition of the exhaust system and its mountings* (Section 5)
- [ ] Check the coolant antifreeze concentration (Section 6)
- [ ] Check the battery condition, security and electrolyte level (Section 7)
- [ ] Lubricate all hinges and locks (Section 8)
- [ ] Check the condition of the airbag unit(s)* (Section 9)
- [ ] Check the operation of the windscreen/tailgate washer system(s) (Section 10)

* **Note:** *These items are not specified by Mercedes-Benz as routine maintenance items.*

Two spanners on display (Service B)

In addition to the items listed above, carry out the following:

- [ ] Check the front and rear brake pad or shoe thickness (Section 11)
- [ ] Check all underbonnet components and hoses for fluid and oil leaks (Section 12)
- [ ] Check the brake hydraulic circuit for leaks and damage (Section 13)
- [ ] Check the condition of the auxiliary drivebelt (Section 14)
- [ ] Check the headlight beam adjustment (Section 15)
- [ ] Renew the pollen/combination filter element (Section 16)
- [ ] Check the condition of the driveshaft gaiters (Section 17)
- [ ] Check the steering and suspension components for condition and security (Section 18)
- [ ] Check the power steering fluid level (Section 19)
- [ ] Carry out a road test and check exhaust emissions (Section 20)

Every 2 years

Note: *These tasks are normally performed at the same time as a Service A or Service B.*

- [ ] Check the manual transmission oil level* (Section 21)
- [ ] Check the bodywork and underbody protection for damage (Section 22)
- [ ] Check the automatic transmission fluid level* (Section 23)
- [ ] Renew the brake (and clutch) fluid (Section 24)

* **Note:** *These tasks are not specified by Mercedes-Benz as routine maintenance items.*

Every 3 years

Note: *This task is normally performed at the same time as a Service A or Service B.*

- [ ] Renew the coolant (Section 25)

Note: *This work is every 15 years/155 000 miles in the Mercedes-Benz schedule for later models if the recommended Mercedes-Benz coolant antifreeze/inhibitor is used.*

Every 4 years or 30 000 to 45 000 miles

Note: *This task is normally performed at the same time as a Service A or Service B.*

- [ ] Renew the spark plugs (Section 26)

Every 4 years or 50 000 miles, whichever comes first

Note: *These tasks are normally performed at the same time as a Service A or Service B.*

- [ ] Renew the air filter element (Section 27)
- [ ] Renew the fuel filter element (Section 28)

Underbonnet view of a 1.6 litre model

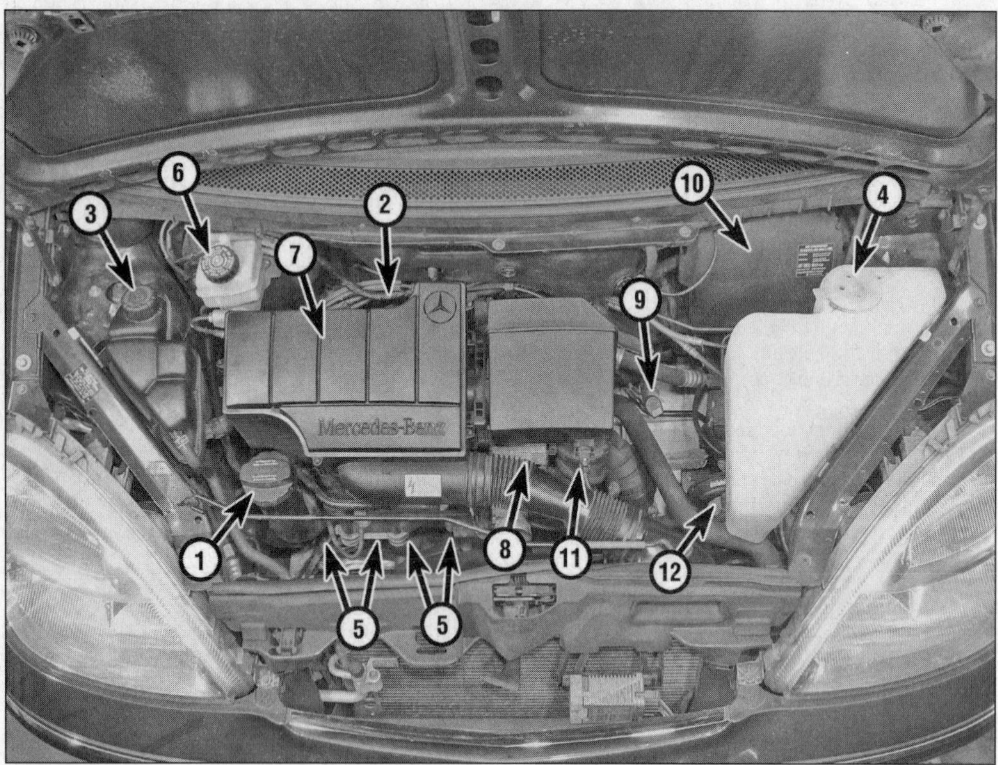

1. *Engine oil filler cap*
2. *Engine oil dipstick*
3. *Coolant expansion tank*
4. *Washer fluid reservoir*
5. *Ignition coil and spark plugs*
6. *Brake master cylinder fluid reservoir*
7. *Air filter cover*
8. *Idle speed control actuator/throttle module*
9. *Transmission oil level tube (automatic)*
10. *Electronic Control Module (ECM) cover*
11. *Air temperature sensor*
12. *Secondary air injection pump*

Front underbody view of a 1.6 litre model

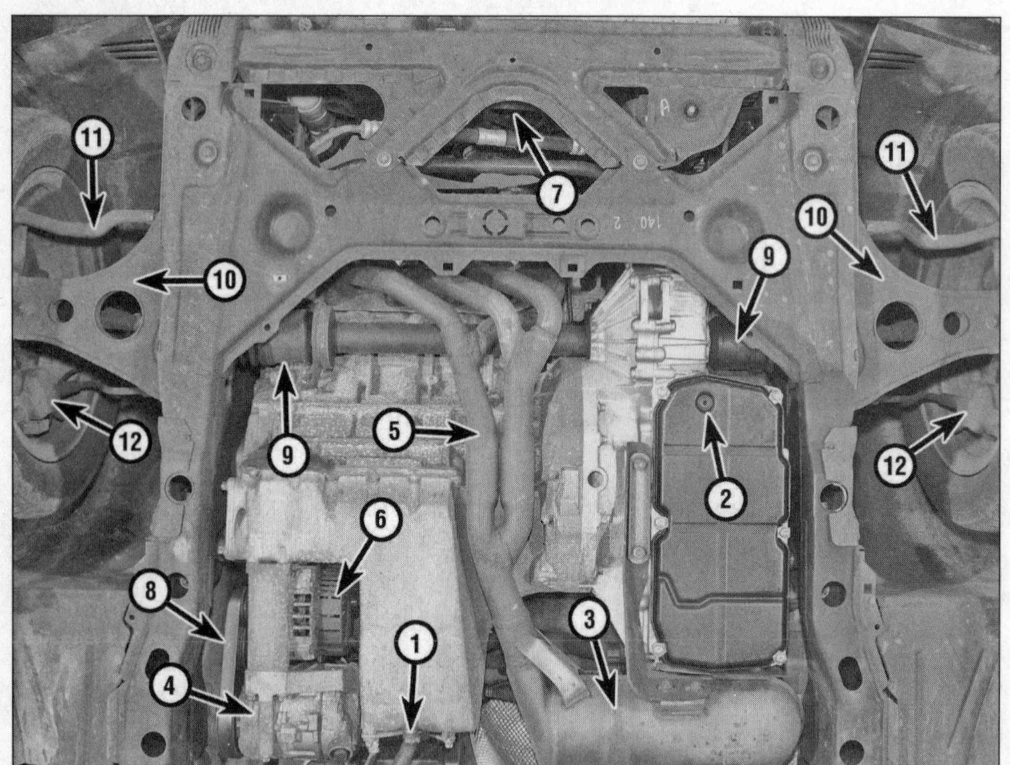

1. *Sump drain plug*
2. *Automatic transmission drain plug*
3. *Catalytic converter*
4. *Air conditioning compressor*
5. *Exhaust front pipe*
6. *Alternator*
7. *Radiator and electric cooling fans*
8. *Auxiliary drivebelt*
9. *Driveshafts*
10. *Front suspension lower arms*
11. *Steering track rods*
12. *Brake calipers*

Rear underbody view of a 1.6 litre model

1 *Fuel tank*
2 *Anti-roll bar*
3 *Fuel tank filler neck*
4 *Coil springs*
5 *Shock absorber lower mountings*
6 *Trailing arms*
7 *Brake calipers*
8 *Handbrake cable adjuster*
9 *Exhaust rear silencers and tail pipe*

Maintenance procedures

1 Introduction

This Chapter is designed to help the home mechanic maintain his/her vehicle for safety, economy, long life and peak performance.

The Chapter contains a master maintenance schedule, followed by Sections dealing specifically with each task in the schedule. Visual checks, adjustments, component renewal and other helpful items are included. Refer to the accompanying illustrations of the engine compartment and the underside of the vehicle for the locations of the various components.

Servicing your vehicle will provide a planned maintenance programme, which should result in a long and reliable service life. This is a comprehensive plan, so maintaining some items but not others, will not produce the same results.

As you service your vehicle, you will discover that many of the procedures can – and should – be grouped together, because of the particular procedure being performed, or because of the proximity of two otherwise unrelated components to one another. For example, if the vehicle is raised for any reason, the exhaust can be inspected at the same time as the suspension and steering components.

The first step in this maintenance programme is to prepare yourself before the actual work begins. Read through all the Sections relevant to the work to be carried out, then make a list and gather all the parts and tools required. If a problem is encountered, seek advice from a parts specialist, or a dealer service department.

2 Regular maintenance

1 If, from the time the vehicle is new, the routine maintenance schedule is followed closely, and frequent checks are made of fluid levels and high-wear items, as suggested throughout this manual, the engine will be kept in relatively good running condition, and the need for additional work will be minimised.

2 It is possible that there will be times when the engine is running poorly due to the lack of regular maintenance. This is even more likely if a used vehicle, which has not received regular and frequent maintenance checks, is purchased. In such cases, additional work may need to be carried out, outside of the regular maintenance intervals.

3 If engine wear is suspected, a compression test (refer to the relevant Part of Chapter 2) will provide valuable information regarding the overall performance of the main internal components. Such a test can be used as a basis to decide on the extent of the work to be carried out. If, for example, a compression test indicates serious internal engine wear, conventional maintenance as described in this Chapter will not greatly improve the performance of the engine, and may prove a waste of time and money, unless extensive overhaul work is carried out first.

4 The following series of operations are those most often required to improve the performance of a generally poor-running engine:

Primary operations

a) Clean, inspect and test the battery (See 'Weekly checks').
b) Check all the engine-related fluids (See 'Weekly checks').
c) Check the condition and tension of the auxiliary drivebelt (Section 14).
d) Renew the spark plugs (Section 26).
e) Check the condition of the air filter, and renew if necessary (Section 27).
f) Check the condition of all hoses, and check for fluid leaks (Section 12).

5 If the above operations do not prove fully effective, carry out the following secondary operations:

Secondary operations

All items listed under *Primary operations*, plus the following:

a) Check the charging system (see Chapter 5A).
b) Check the ignition system (see Chapter 5B).
c) Check the fuel system (see Chapter 4A).

Every 7500 miles or 12 months

3 Engine oil and filter renewal

1 Frequent oil and filter changes are the most important maintenance procedures, which can be undertaken by the DIY owner. As engine oil ages, it becomes diluted and contaminated, which leads to premature engine wear.

2 Before starting this procedure, gather all the necessary tools and materials. Also make sure that you have plenty of clean rags and newspapers handy, to mop-up any spills. Ideally, the engine oil should be warm, as it will drain better, and more built-up sludge will be removed with it. Take care, however, not to touch the exhaust or any other hot parts of the engine when working under the vehicle. To avoid any possibility of scalding, and to protect yourself from possible skin irritants and other harmful contaminants in used engine oils, it is advisable to wear gloves when carrying out this work. Access to the underside of the vehicle will be greatly improved if it can be raised on a lift, driven onto ramps, or jacked up and supported on axle stands (see *Jacking and vehicle support*). Whichever method is chosen, make sure that the vehicle remains level, or if it is at an angle, that the drain plug is at the lowest point. Undo the retaining screws and remove the engine undertray(s), then also remove the engine top cover where applicable. To aid the draining of the engine oil, remove the dipstick and oil filler cap before removing the drain plug.

3 Using a socket and wrench or a ring spanner, slacken the drain plug about half a turn **(see illustration)**. Position the draining container under the drain plug, and then remove the plug completely **(see Haynes Hint)**. Recover the sealing ring from the drain plug.

4 Allow some time for the old oil to drain, noting that it may be necessary to reposition the container as the oil flow slows to a trickle.

5 After all the oil has drained, wipe off the drain plug with a clean rag, and fit a new sealing washer. Clean the area around the drain plug opening, and refit the plug. Tighten the plug to the specified torque.

6 If the filter is also to be renewed, place rags around the base of the oil filter. The oil filter is an element type and is located from above in a housing on the rear of the engine.

7 To remove the renewable element type oil filter, unscrew and remove the cap complete with the filter element **(see illustration)**. Discard the O-ring seals, as new ones will be required when refitting.

8 Clean the filter housing and cap as necessary, and then fit the new sealing rings **(see illustrations)**.

9 Fit the new filter to the cap and locate it in its housing and tighten the cap to the specified torque **(see illustration)**.

10 Remove the old oil and all tools from under the car. Refit the engine undertray(s), tighten the retaining screws securely, and then lower the car to the ground. Also refit the engine top cover where applicable.

11 Fill the engine, using the correct grade and type of oil (see *Lubricants and fluids*). An oil can spout or funnel may help to reduce spillage. Pour in half the specified quantity of oil first, and then wait a few minutes for the oil to run to the sump. Continue adding oil a small quantity at a time until the level is up to the maximum mark on the dipstick. Refit the filler cap.

12 Start the engine and run it for a few minutes; check for leaks around the oil filter seal and the sump drain plug. Note that there may be a few seconds delay before the oil pressure warning light goes out when the engine is started, as the oil circulates through the engine oil galleries and the new oil filter (where fitted) before the pressure builds-up.

13 Switch off the engine, and wait a few minutes for the oil to settle in the sump once more. With the new oil circulated and the filter completely full, recheck the level on the dipstick, and add more oil as necessary.

14 Dispose of the used engine oil safely, with reference to *General repair procedures* in the *Reference* section of this manual.

3.3 Remove the engine oil drain plug from the rear of the sump

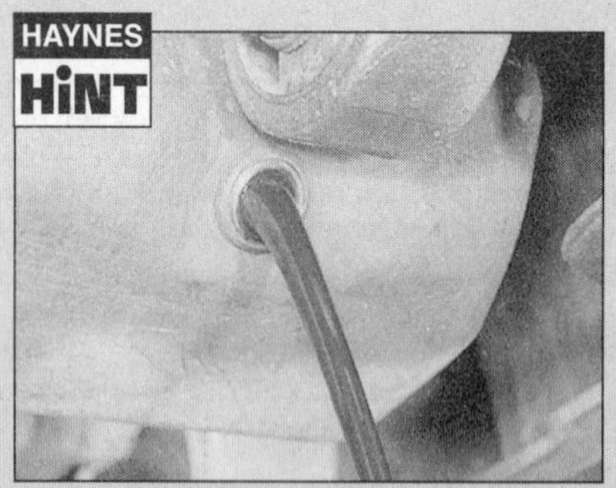

Keep the drain plug pressed into the sump while unscrewing it by hand the last couple of turns. As the plug releases, move it away sharply so the stream of oil issuing from the sump runs into the container, not up your sleeve.

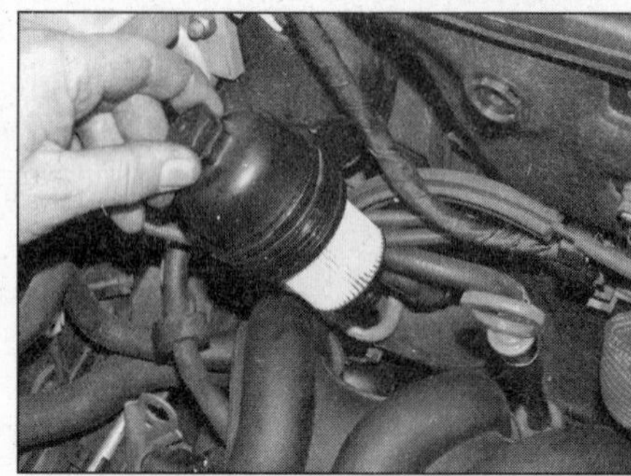

3.7 Removing the oil filter cap complete with filter

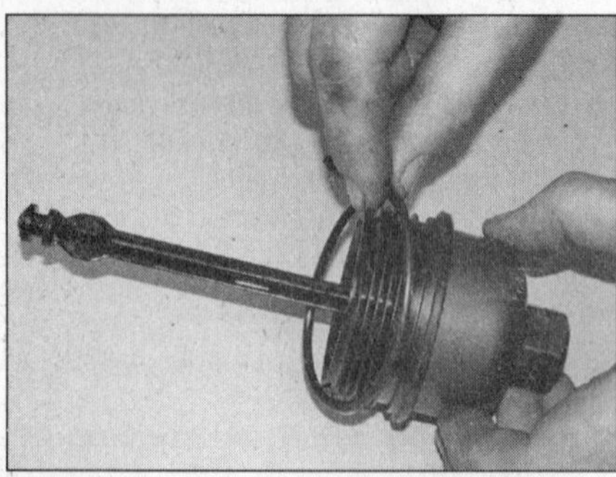

3.8a Renew the large sealing ring . . .

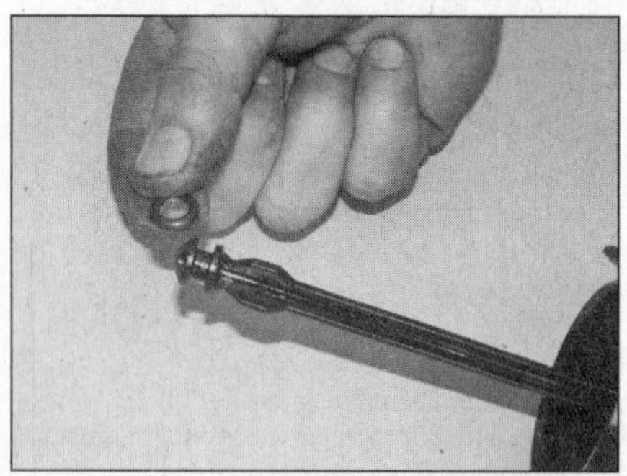

3.8b . . . and the small sealing ring

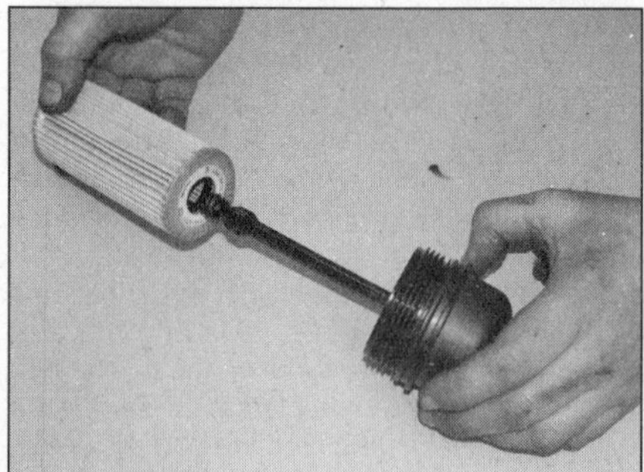

3.9 Fit the new filter to the cap

One spanner on display (Service A)

4 Resetting the service interval display

1 After all necessary maintenance work has been completed; the service interval display must be reset. Mercedes-Benz technicians use a special dedicated instrument to do this, and a printout is then put in the vehicle service record. It is possible for the owner to reset the display as described in the following paragraphs.

2 To reset the display manually:

1. *Turn the ignition switch to position II, then immediately press the 000.0 button (which is positioned to the left-hand side lower part of the of the instrument cluster) twice within one second.*
2. *Turn the ignition switch to position 0 within the next ten seconds.*
3. *Press and hold down the 000.0 button.*
4. *Turn the ignition switch to position II, the last service indication will appear in the display.*
5. *Keep the 000.0 button pressed, and the last service indication remains displayed. An audible signal will be heard after approximately ten seconds, the service indicator will now be displayed with the new value.*
6. *Release the 000.0 button.*
7. *Leave the ignition switch in position II for at least another five seconds, and the service indicator is now reset.*

5 Exhaust system check

1 With the engine cold (at least an hour after the vehicle has been driven), check the complete exhaust system from the engine to the end of the tailpipe. The exhaust system is most easily checked with the vehicle raised on a hoist, or supported on axle stands, so that the exhaust components are readily visible and accessible (see *Jacking and vehicle support*).

2 Check the exhaust pipes and connections for evidence of leaks, severe corrosion and damage. Make sure that all brackets and mountings are in good condition, and that all relevant nuts and bolts are tight. Leakage at any of the joints or in other parts of the system will usually show up as a black sooty stain in the vicinity of the leak.

3 Rattles and other noises can often be traced to the exhaust system, especially the brackets and mountings **(see illustration)**. Try to move the pipes and silencers. If the components are able to come into contact with the body or suspension parts, secure the system with new mountings. Otherwise separate the joints (if possible) and twist the pipes as necessary to provide additional clearance.

6 Antifreeze check

1 The cooling system should be filled with the recommended antifreeze and corrosion protection fluid – **do not** mix this antifreeze with any other type. Over a period of time, the concentration of fluid may be reduced due to topping-up (this can be avoided by topping-up with the correct antifreeze mixture – see Specifications) or fluid loss. If loss of coolant has been evident, it is important to make the necessary repair before adding fresh fluid.

2 With the engine **cold**, carefully remove the cap from the expansion tank. If the engine is not completely cold, place a cloth rag over the cap before removing it, and remove it slowly to allow any pressure to escape.

3 Antifreeze testers are available from car accessory shops. Draw some coolant from the expansion tank and observe how many plastic balls are floating in the checker. Usually, 2 or 3 balls must be floating for the correct concentration of antifreeze, but follow the manufacturer's instructions.

4 If the concentration is incorrect, it will be necessary to either withdraw some coolant and add antifreeze, or alternatively drain the old coolant and add fresh coolant of the correct concentration (see Section 25).

7 Battery check

1 The battery is located in the front footwell, under the carpet, in front of the driver's seat. Remove the driver's floor mat, lift up tab and turn it anti-clockwise to remove the battery cover **(see illustration)**.

2 The vehicle's main fusebox is also located under the carpet next to the battery.

7.1 Battery location

3 Check that both battery terminals and all the fuse holder connections are securely attached and are free from corrosion. **Note:** *Before disconnecting the terminals from the battery, refer to 'Disconnecting the battery' in the Reference Chapter at the end of this manual. It is always safer to remove the keys from the ignition before disconnecting the battery, to prevent any electronic components getting damaged.*

4 Check the battery casing for signs of damage or cracking and check the battery retaining-clamp is secure. If the battery casing is damaged in any way the battery must be renewed (see Chapter 5A).

5 If the vehicle is not fitted with a sealed-for-life maintenance-free battery, check the electrolyte level is between the MAX and MIN level markings on the battery casing. If topping-up is necessary, remove the battery (see Chapter 5A) from the vehicle then remove the cell caps/cover (as applicable). Using distilled water, top the electrolyte level of each cell up to the MAX level mark then securely refit the cell caps/cover. Ensure the battery has not been overfilled then refit the battery to the vehicle (see Chapter 5A).

6 Check the vent pipe on the side of the battery is connected and free from any blockage **(see illustration)**.

7 On completion of the check, refit the insulation panel and clip the battery cover securely back into position, refit the carpet.

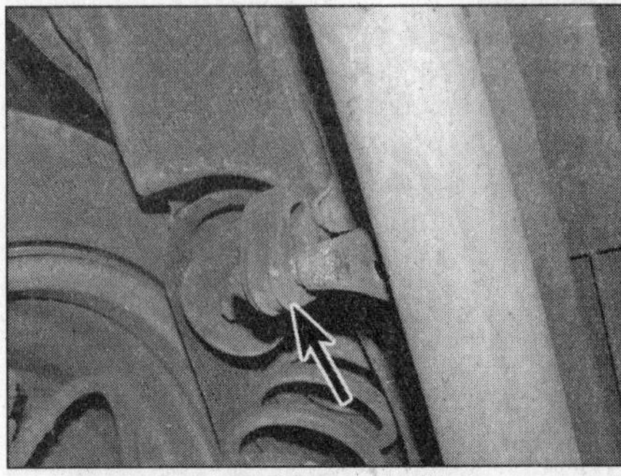

5.3 Check the rubber mountings – arrowed

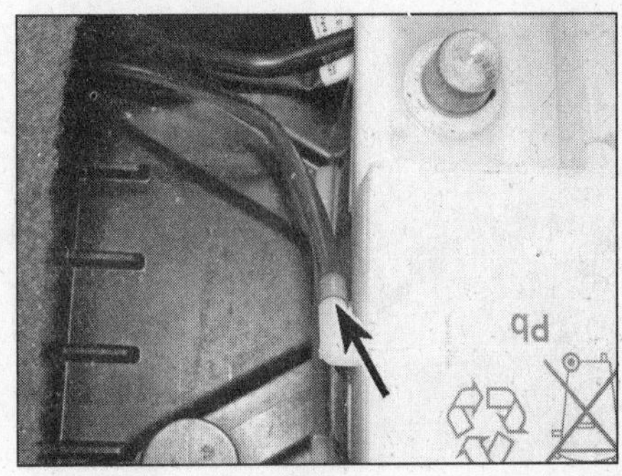

7.6 Vent pipe on the side of the battery

8 Hinge and lock lubrication

1 Lubricate the hinges of the bonnet, doors and tailgate with light general-purpose oil. Similarly, lubricate all latches, locks and lock strikers. At the same time, check the security and operation of all the locks, adjusting them if necessary (see Chapter 11).

2 Lightly lubricate the bonnet release mechanism and cable with suitable grease.

9 Airbag unit check

Inspect the exterior condition of the airbag(s) for signs of damage or deterioration. If an airbag shows signs of damage, it must be renewed (see Chapter 12). Note that it is not permissible to attach any stickers to the surface of the airbag, as this may affect the deployment of the unit.

10 Windscreen/tailgate washer system check

1 Check that each of the washer jet nozzles are clear and that each nozzle provides a strong jet of washer fluid.

2 The tailgate jet should be aimed to spray at the centre top of the screen, using a pin.

3 The windscreen washer nozzles should be aimed slightly above the centre of the screen.

4 Especially during the winter months, make sure that the washer fluid frost concentration is sufficient to prevent freezing.

Two spanners on display (Service B)

11 Brake pad and shoe check

Brake pads

1 The outer brake pads can be checked without removing the wheels, by observing the brake pads through the holes in the wheels **(see illustration)**. If necessary, remove the wheel trim. The thickness of the pad lining must not be less than the dimension given in the Specifications.

2 If the outer pads are worn near their limits, it is worthwhile checking the inner pads as well. Apply the handbrake then jack up vehicle and support it on axle stands (see *Jacking and vehicle support*). Remove the roadwheels.

3 Use a steel rule to check the thickness of the brake pads, and compare with the minimum thickness given in the Specifications **(see illustration)**.

4 For a comprehensive check, the brake pads should be removed and cleaned. The operation of the caliper can then also be checked, and the condition of the brake disc itself can be fully examined on both sides. Refer to Chapter 9.

5 If any pad's friction material is worn to the specified minimum thickness or less, *all four pads at the front or rear, as applicable, must be renewed as a set.*

11.1 The outer brake pads can be observed through the holes in the wheels

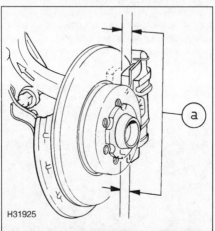

6 On completion of the check, refit the roadwheels and lower the vehicle to the ground.

Brake shoes

7 To check the rear brake shoes for wear, remove the brake drums (see Chapter 9).

12 Hose and fluid leak check

1 Visually inspect the engine joint faces, gaskets and seals for any signs of water or oil leaks. Pay particular attention to the areas around the camshaft cover, cylinder head, oil filter and sump joint faces. Bear in mind that, over a period of time, some very slight seepage from these areas is to be expected – what you are really looking for is any indication of a serious leak. Should a leak be found, renew the offending gasket or oil seal by referring to the appropriate Chapters in this manual.

2 Also check the security and condition of all the engine-related pipes and hoses. Ensure that all cable-ties or securing clips are in place and in good condition. Clips that are broken or missing can lead to chafing of the hoses, pipes or wiring, which could cause more serious problems in the future.

11.3 The thickness (a) of the brake pad linings must not be less than the specified amount

3 Carefully check the radiator hoses and heater hoses along their entire length. Renew any hose that is cracked, swollen or deteriorated. Cracks will show up better if the hose is squeezed. Pay close attention to the hose clips that secure the hoses to the cooling system components. Hose clips can pinch and puncture hoses, resulting in cooling system leaks.

4 Inspect all the cooling system components (hoses, joint faces, etc) for leaks **(see Haynes Hint)**. Where any problems of this nature are found on system components, renew the component or gasket with reference to Chapter 3.

5 Where applicable, inspect the automatic transmission fluid cooler hoses for leaks or deterioration.

6 With the vehicle raised, inspect the petrol tank and filler neck for punctures, cracks and other damage. The connection between the filler neck and tank is especially critical. Sometimes a rubber filler neck or connecting hose will leak due to loose retaining clamps or deteriorated rubber.

A leak in the cooling system will usually show up as white- or antifreeze-coloured deposits on the area adjoining the leak.

7 Carefully check all rubber hoses and metal fuel lines leading away from the petrol tank. Check for loose connections, deteriorated hoses, crimped lines, and other damage. Pay particular attention to the vent pipes and hoses, which often loop up around the filler neck and can become blocked or crimped. Follow the lines to the front of the vehicle, carefully inspecting them all the way. Renew damaged sections as necessary.
8 From within the engine compartment, check the security of all fuel hose attachments and pipe unions, and inspect the fuel hoses and vacuum hoses for kinks, chafing and deterioration.
9 Where applicable, check the condition of the power steering fluid hoses and pipes.

13 Brake hydraulic circuit check

1 Check the entire brake hydraulic circuit for leaks and damage. Start by checking the master cylinder in the engine compartment. At the same time, check the vacuum servo unit and ABS units for signs of fluid leakage.
2 Raise the front and rear of the vehicle and support it on axle stands (see *Jacking and vehicle support*). Check the rigid hydraulic brake lines for corrosion and damage.
3 At the front and rear of the vehicle, check that any flexible hydraulic hoses to the calipers are not twisted or chafing on any of the surrounding suspension components. Turn the steering on full lock to make this check. Also check that the hoses are not brittle or cracked.
4 Lower the vehicle to the ground after making the checks.

14 Auxiliary drivebelt check and renewal

1 The poly-vee drivebelt drives the alternator, coolant pump and where fitted, the air conditioning compressor **(see illustration)**.
2 On all engines, the drivebelt tension is adjusted automatically by an idler pulley, which is spring-tensioned.
3 The drivebelt can only be accessed from under the vehicle.

Checking

4 Apply the handbrake, then jack up the front of the vehicle and support it on axle stands (see *Jacking and vehicle support*). Remove the engine undertray as the belt will need to be checked from underneath the vehicle.
5 Using a socket on the crankshaft pulley bolt, turn the engine slowly clockwise so that the full length of the auxiliary drivebelt can be examined. Look for cracks, splitting and fraying on the surface of the belt; check also for signs of glazing (shiny patches) and separation of the belt plies. If required, use a mirror to check the underside of the drivebelt **(see illustration)**. If damage or wear is visible, or if there are traces of oil or grease on it, the belt should be renewed.

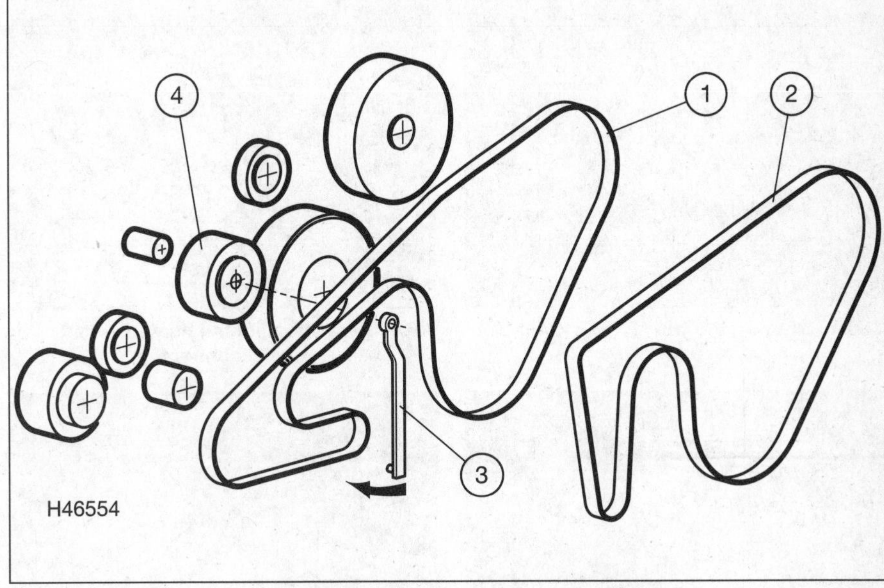

14.1 Auxiliary drivebelt routing – all models

1 With air conditioning
2 Without air conditioning
3 Tensioner spanner
4 Tensioner pulley

Renewal

6 Apply the handbrake, and then jack up the front of the vehicle and support it on axle stands (see *Jacking and vehicle support*). Remove the engine undertray.
7 Remove the right-hand front roadwheel, and then remove the inner wheel arch liner.
8 If the drivebelt is to be re-used, mark it for clockwise direction to ensure it is refitted the same way round.
9 Use a spanner to turn the tensioner central bolt clockwise to release the tension on the drivebelt **(see illustration)**.
10 While holding the tension off the belt, note how the drivebelt is routed, then remove it from around the pulleys. When belt is removed, slowly release the tensioner back to its stop.
11 With the belt removed, see Section 8 of this Chapter to inspect the condition of the belt.
12 Locate the new (if required) drivebelt on the pulleys, then release the tensioner. Check that the belt is located correctly in the grooves in the pulleys.
13 Refit the inner wheel arch liner and roadwheel, and refit the engine undertray. Lower the vehicle to the ground.

15 Headlight beam adjustment

1 Accurate adjustment of the headlight beam is only possible using optical beam-setting equipment, and this work should therefore be carried out by a Mercedes-Benz dealer or service station with the necessary facilities.
2 Basic adjustments can be carried out in an emergency, and further details are given in Chapter 12.

14.5 Checking the underside of the auxiliary drivebelt with a mirror

14.9 Use a spanner to turn the tensioner clockwise

16.2 Removing the windscreen lower trim panel

16.4 Disconnecting the heated washer jet wiring connector

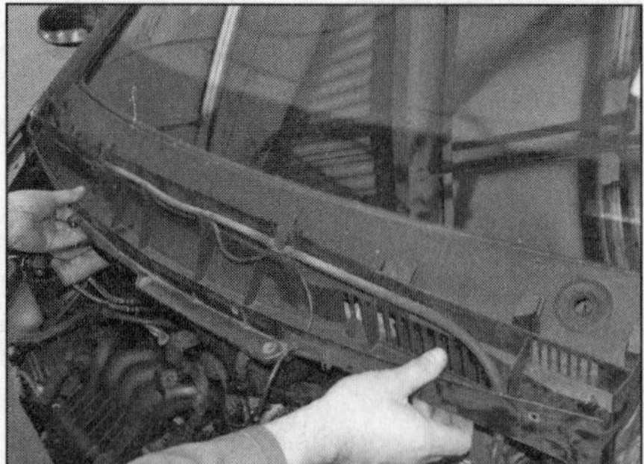
16.6 Remove the scuttle panel from the vehicle

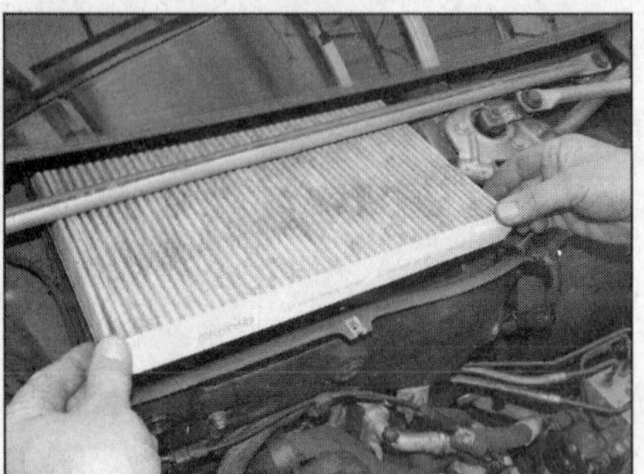
16.7 Lift the pollen filter out from the housing

16.8 Note the direction of the arrow on the front of the filter

16 Pollen/combination filter element renewal

1 The pollen filter is located in the upper part of the heater unit and is accessed from under the bonnet, below the air intake grill at the bottom of the windscreen.

2 With the bonnet open, undo the four retaining screws and withdraw the plastic grill from the lower part of the windscreen **(see illustration)**.

3 Unclip the cover from the lower part of the wiper arms and undo the retaining nuts, and then remove the wiper arms, with reference to Chapter 12.

4 Where fitted disconnect the washer jet heater wiring connector from the centre of the plastic scuttle panel **(see illustration)**.

5 Disconnect the washer jet supply hose from the connection at the washer pump.

6 Undo the five retaining screws and remove the lower plastic scuttle panel from the rear of the engine compartment **(see illustration)**.

7 Lift the pollen filter element at the front and withdraw it from the heater unit **(see illustration)**. Note the direction of the arrow on the front edge of the filter.

8 Fit the new element (with the arrow on the front edge of the filter facing downwards) **(see illustration)** and then refit the plastic scuttle panel.

9 Refit the remaining parts using a reversal of the removal procedure.

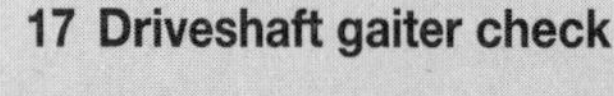

17 Driveshaft gaiter check

1 With the vehicle raised and securely supported on stands, slowly rotate the roadwheel. Inspect the condition of the outer constant velocity (CV) joint rubber gaiters, squeezing the gaiters to open out the folds. Check for signs of cracking, splits or deterioration of the rubber, which may allow the grease to escape, and lead to water and grit entry into the joint. Also check the security and condition of the retaining clips. Repeat these checks on the inner joints **(see illustration)**. If any damage or deterioration is found, the gaiters should be renewed (see Chapter 8).

2 At the same time, check the general condition of the CV joints themselves by first holding the driveshaft and attempting to rotate the wheel. Repeat this check by holding the inner joint and attempting to rotate the driveshaft. Any appreciable movement indicates wear in the joints; wear in the driveshaft splines, or a loose driveshaft-retaining nut.

18 Steering and suspension check

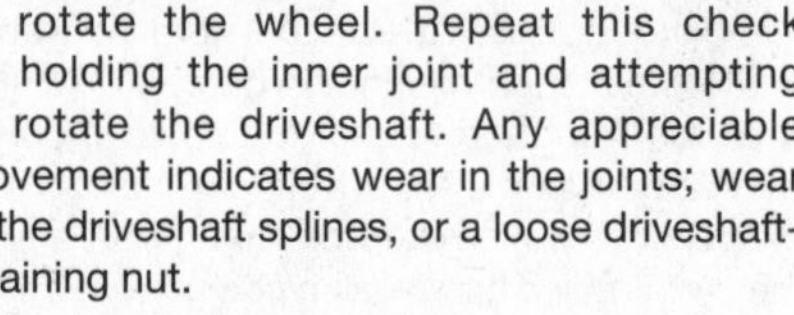

1 Raise the front and rear of the vehicle, and securely support it on axle stands (see *Jacking and vehicle support*).

2 Visually inspect the track rod end balljoint dust cover, the lower front suspension balljoint dust cover, and the steering rack-and-pinion gaiters for splits, chafing or deterioration. Any wear of these components will cause loss of lubricant, together with dirt and water entry, resulting in rapid deterioration of the balljoints or steering gear.

3 Check the power steering fluid hoses for chafing or deterioration, and the pipe and hose unions for fluid leaks. Also check for signs of fluid leakage under pressure from the steering gear rubber gaiters, which would indicate failed fluid seals within the steering gear.

4 Grasp the roadwheel at the 12 o'clock and 6 o'clock positions, and try to rock it **(see illustration)**. Very slight free play may be felt, but if the movement is appreciable, further investigation is necessary to determine the source. Continue rocking the wheel while an assistant depresses the footbrake. If the movement is now eliminated or significantly

17.1 Check the condition of the driveshaft inner and outer gaiters

18.4 Check for wear in the hub bearings by grasping the wheel and trying to rock it

reduced, it is likely that the hub bearings are at fault. If the free play is still evident with the footbrake depressed, then there is wear in the suspension joints or mountings.

5 Now grasp the wheel at the 9 o'clock and 3 o'clock positions, and try to rock it as before. Any movement felt now may again be caused by wear in the hub bearings or the steering track rod balljoints. If the inner or outer balljoint is worn, the visual movement will be obvious.

6 Using a large screwdriver or flat bar, check for wear in the suspension mounting bushes by levering between the relevant suspension component and its attachment point. Some movement is to be expected as the mountings are made of rubber, but excessive wear should be obvious. Also check the condition of any visible rubber bushes, looking for splits, cracks or contamination of the rubber.

7 With the car standing on its wheels, have an assistant turn the steering wheel back-and-forth about an eighth of a turn each way. There should be very little, if any, lost movement between the steering wheel and roadwheels. If this is not the case, closely observe the joints and mountings previously described, but in addition, check the steering column universal joints for wear, and the rack-and-pinion steering gear itself.

8 Check for any signs of fluid leakage around the front suspension struts and rear shock absorber. Should any fluid be noticed, the suspension strut or shock absorber is defective internally, and should be renewed. **Note:** *Suspension struts/shock absorbers should always be renewed in pairs on the same axle to ensure correct vehicle handling.*

9 The efficiency of the suspension strut/shock absorber may be checked by bouncing the vehicle at each corner. Generally speaking, the body will return to its normal position and stop after being depressed. If it rises and returns on a rebound, the suspension strut/shock absorber is probably suspect. Examine also the suspension strut/shock absorber upper and lower mountings for any signs of wear.

19 Power steering fluid level check

Note: *New fluid must be used when draining and refilling the steering system.*

1 Wipe clean the area around the power steering fluid reservoir, and then remove the filler cap. The cap has a dipstick, which has temperature markings when checking in cold or hot conditions.

2 Wipe clean the dipstick and refit the reservoir cap. **Note:** *When the cap is removed, take care not to allow any dirt to enter the reservoir.*

3 Remove the reservoir cap and check the fluid level on the dipstick, taking into consideration the temperature of the fluid. If necessary, top-up with the specified fluid (see *Lubricants and fluids*).

4 When the fluid level is correct, check the sealing ring on the cap and refit the cap to the top of the reservoir.

5 Frequent need for topping-up indicates that there is a leak, which should be corrected as soon as possible.

20 Road test and exhaust emissions check

Instruments and electrical equipment

1 Check the operation of all instruments and electrical equipment including the air conditioning system.

2 Make sure that all instruments read correctly, and switch on all electrical equipment in turn, to check that it functions properly.

Steering and suspension

3 Check for any abnormalities in the steering, suspension, handling or road 'feel'.

4 Drive the vehicle, and check that there are no unusual vibrations or noises that may indicate wear in the driveshafts, wheel bearings, etc.

5 Check that the steering feels positive, with no excessive 'sloppiness', or roughness, and check for any suspension noises when cornering and driving over bumps.

Drivetrain

6 Check the performance of the engine, clutch (where applicable), gearbox/transmission and driveshafts.

7 Listen for any unusual noises from the engine, clutch and gearbox/transmission.

8 Make sure the engine runs smoothly at idle, and there is no hesitation on accelerating.

9 Check that, where applicable, the clutch action is smooth and progressive, that the drive is taken up smoothly, and that the pedal travel is not excessive. Also listen for any noises when the clutch pedal is depressed.

10 On manual gearbox models, check that all gears can be engaged smoothly without noise, and that the gear lever action is smooth and not abnormally vague or 'notchy'.

11 On automatic transmission models, make sure that all gearchanges occur smoothly, without snatching, and without an increase in engine speed between changes. Check that all the gear positions can be selected with the vehicle at rest. If any problems are found, they should be referred to a Mercedes-Benz dealer.

12 Listen for a metallic clicking sound from the front of the vehicle, as the vehicle is driven slowly in a circle with the steering on full-lock. Carry out this check in both directions. If a clicking noise is heard, this indicates wear in a driveshaft joint, in which case renew the joint if necessary.

Braking system

13 Make sure that the vehicle does not pull to one side when braking, and that the wheels do not lock when braking hard.

14 Check that there is no vibration through the steering when braking.

15 Check that the handbrake operates correctly without excessive movement of the lever, and that it holds the vehicle stationary on a slope.

16 Test the operation of the brake servo unit as follows. With the engine off, depress the footbrake four or five times to exhaust the vacuum. Hold the brake pedal depressed, and then start the engine. As the engine starts, there should be a noticeable 'give' in the brake pedal as vacuum builds-up. Allow the engine to run for at least two minutes, and then switch it off. If the brake pedal is depressed now, it should be possible to detect a hiss from the servo as the pedal is depressed. After about four or five applications, no further hissing should be heard, and the pedal should feel considerably harder.

17 Under controlled emergency braking, the pulsing of the ABS unit must be felt at the footbrake pedal.

Exhaust emissions check

18 Although not part of the manufacturer's maintenance schedule, this check will normally be carried out on a regular basis according to the country the vehicle is operated in. Currently in the UK, exhaust emissions testing is included as part of the annual MOT test after the vehicle is 3 years old.

Every 2 years

21 Manual transmission oil level check

1 Park the car on a level surface. For improved access to the filler/level plug, apply the handbrake, then jack up the front of the vehicle and support it on axle stands (see *Jacking and vehicle support*), but note that the rear of the vehicle should also be raised to ensure an accurate level check. The oil level must be checked before the car is driven, or at least 5 minutes after the engine has been switched off. If the oil is checked immediately after driving the car, some of the oil will remain distributed around the transmission components, resulting in an inaccurate level reading.

2 Undo the retaining screws and remove the engine undertray. Wipe clean the area

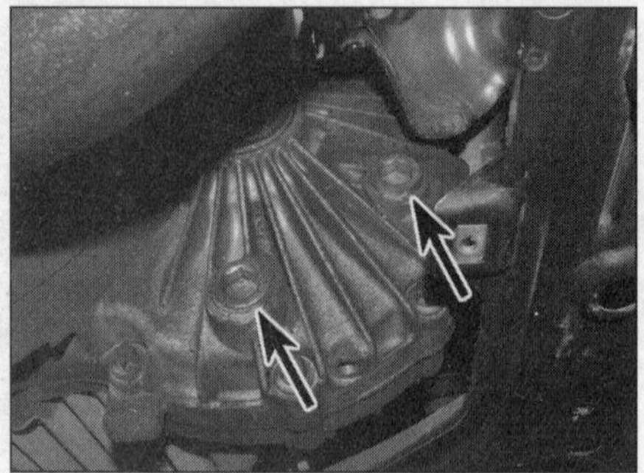

21.2 Transmission filler/level plug (upper) and drain plug (lower) locations

around the transmission filler/level plug, which is situated, on the front of the transmission casing, facing the engine **(see illustration)**.

3 The oil level should reach the lower edge of the filler/level hole. A certain amount of oil will have gathered behind the filler/level plug, and will trickle out when it is removed; this does **not** necessarily indicate that the level is correct. To ensure that a true level is established, wait until the initial trickle has stopped, then add oil as necessary until a trickle of new oil can be seen emerging. The level will be correct when the flow ceases; use only good-quality oil of the specified type.

4 If the transmission has been overfilled so that oil flows out when the filler/level plug is removed, check that the car is completely level (front-to-rear and side-to-side), and allow the surplus to drain off into a suitable container.

5 When the oil level is correct, refit the filler/level plug and tighten it to the specified torque. Wipe off any spilt oil then refit the engine undertray(s), tighten the retaining screws securely, and lower the car to the ground.

22 Bodywork and underbody protection check

Raise and support the vehicle on axle stands (see *Jacking and vehicle support*). Using an

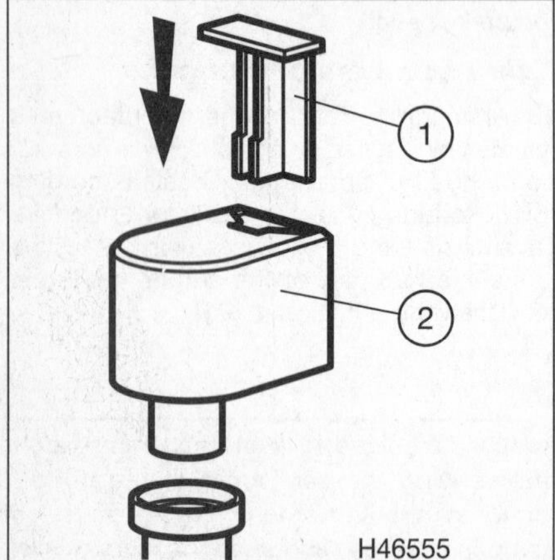

23.6 Refit the cap (2) and insert a new locking clip (1)

23.2 Locking clip (arrowed) in top of dipstick tube

electric torch or lead light, inspect the entire underside of the vehicle, paying particular attention to the wheel arches. Look for any damage to the flexible underbody coating, which may crack or flake off with age, leading to corrosion. Also check that the wheel arch liners are securely attached with any clips provided – if they come loose, dirt may get in behind the liners and defeat their purpose. If there is any damage to the underseal, or any corrosion, it should be repaired before the damage gets too serious.

Check the bodywork for stone chips and scratches. Either touch them up yourself (see Chapter 12) or have the work done by someone more experienced.

23 Automatic transmission fluid level check

Note: *There is no dipstick fitted to the transmission and one will need to be purchased (part no 168 589 01 21 00) from a Mercedes-Benz dealer to carry out this work. An accurate fluid level check can only be made with the transmission fluid at the correct temperature. If it is not possible to ascertain this temperature, it is strongly recommended that the check be made by a Mercedes-Benz dealer who will have the instrumentation to do this. At the same time they can check the transmission electronics for fault codes. Overfilling or underfilling adversely affects the function of the transmission.*

1 Make sure the transmission oil is warm

24.3 The fluid level should be between the MAX and MIN markings

and shift the gear lever through all gears to circulate the oil, then park the vehicle on level ground and engage P or N with the selector lever.

2 Using a screwdriver release the locking clip from the cap on the top of the filling pipe and remove the cap. **Note:** *A new locking clip will be needed for refitting* ***(see illustration)****.*

3 When the transmission is cold, the oil level indicator must be between marks 2 and 4 (30°C). The hot oil level must be between marks 8 and 12 (70°C to 80°C).

4 Check the transmission oil temperature (Mercedes-Benz dealers have a handheld tester) with the selector lever in one of the following lever positions: P, R, N or D.

5 Insert dipstick as far down as possible and then remove to take reading on the end of the stick. If required, top-up the fluid through the dipstick tube to the recommended level. When fluid is added to the transmission, carry out the procedure in paragraph 1 before rechecking the fluid level.

6 When the fluid level is correct, fit the cap to the top of the dipstick tube and insert a new locking clip **(see illustration)**.

7 Frequent need for topping-up indicates that there is a leak, which should be corrected as soon as possible.

24 Brake (and clutch) fluid renewal

Warning: Brake hydraulic fluid can harm your eyes and damage painted surfaces, so use extreme caution when handling and pouring it. Do not use fluid that has been standing open for some time, as it absorbs moisture from the air. Excess moisture can cause a dangerous loss of braking effectiveness.

1 The procedure is similar to that for the bleeding of the hydraulic system as described in Chapter 9, except that the brake fluid reservoir should be emptied by syphoning, using a clean poultry baster or similar before starting, and allowance should be made for the old fluid to be expelled when bleeding a section of the circuit. Since the clutch hydraulic system also uses fluid from the brake system reservoir, it should also be bled at the same time by referring to Chapter 6.

2 Working as described in Chapter 9, open the first bleed screw in the sequence, and pump the brake pedal gently until nearly all the old fluid has been emptied from the master cylinder reservoir.

3 Top-up to the MAX level with new fluid, and continue pumping until only the new fluid remains in the reservoir, and new fluid can be seen emerging from the bleed screw. Tighten the screw, and top the reservoir level up to the MAX level line **(see illustration)**.

4 Work through all the remaining bleed screws in the sequence until new fluid can be seen at all of them. Be careful to keep the master cylinder reservoir topped-up to above the MIN level at all times, or air may enter the system and greatly increase the length of the task.

5 When the operation is complete, check that all bleed screws are securely tightened, and that their dust caps are refitted. Wash off all traces of spilt fluid, and recheck the master cylinder reservoir fluid level.

6 On models with manual transmission, once the brake fluid has been changed the clutch fluid should also be renewed. Referring to Chapter 6, bleed the clutch until new fluid is seen to be emerging from the slave cylinder bleed screw, keeping the master cylinder fluid level above the MIN level line at all times to prevent air entering the system. Once the new fluid emerges, securely tighten the bleed screw then disconnect and remove the bleeding equipment. Securely refit the dust cap then wash off all traces of spilt fluid.

7 On all models, ensure the master cylinder fluid level is correct (see *Weekly checks*) and thoroughly check the operation of the brakes and (where necessary) clutch before taking the car on the road.

Every 3 years

25 Coolant renewal

Warning: Wait until the engine is cold before starting this procedure. Do not allow antifreeze to come in contact with your skin, or with the painted surfaces of the vehicle. Rinse off spills immediately with plenty of water. Never leave antifreeze lying around in an open container, or in a puddle in the driveway or on the garage floor. Children and pets are attracted by its sweet smell, but antifreeze can be fatal if ingested.

Note: *This work is performed every 15 years/ 155 000 miles in the Mercedes-Benz schedule for later models if the recommended Mercedes-Benz coolant antifreeze/inhibitor is used. However, if standard antifreeze/inhibitor is used, the work should be carried out at this recommended interval.*

Cooling system draining

1 With the engine completely cold, unscrew the expansion tank cap.

2 Firmly apply the handbrake then jack up the front of the vehicle and support it on axle stands (see *Jacking and vehicle support*). Undo the retaining screws and remove the engine undertray to gain access to the base of the radiator.

3 Position a suitable container beneath the coolant drain outlet, which is located to the bottom right-hand side of the radiator. Unscrew the drain plug (there is no need to remove it completely) and allow the coolant to drain into the container, through the outlet pipe **(see illustrations)**. If required a length of pipe can be fitted over the outlet pipe to direct the coolant flow.

4 To fully drain the system, also undo the cylinder block drain plug, which is located at the front of the cylinder block **(see illustration)**.

5 If the coolant has been drained for a reason other than renewal, then provided it is clean, it can be re-used.

6 Once all the coolant has drained, securely tighten the radiator drain plug. Where necessary, also tighten the cylinder block drain plug. Refit the undertray, and tighten the retaining screws securely.

Cooling system flushing

7 If the recommended coolant has not been used and coolant renewal has been neglected, or if the antifreeze mixture has become diluted, the cooling system may gradually lose efficiency, as the coolant passages become restricted due to rust, scale deposits, and other sediment. The cooling system efficiency can be restored by flushing the system clean.

8 The radiator should be flushed separately from the engine, to avoid excess contamination.

Radiator flushing

9 To flush the radiator, first tighten the radiator drain plug.

10 Disconnect the top and bottom hoses and any other relevant hoses from the radiator (see Chapter 3).

11 Insert a garden hose into the radiator top inlet. Direct a flow of clean water through the radiator, and continue flushing until clean water emerges from the radiator bottom outlet.

12 If after a reasonable period, the water still does not run clear, the radiator can be flushed with a good proprietary cleaning agent. It is important that their manufacturer's instructions are followed carefully. If the contamination is particularly bad, insert the hose in the radiator bottom outlet, and reverse-flush the radiator.

Engine flushing

13 To flush the engine, remove the thermostat (see Chapter 3).

14 With the bottom hose disconnected from the radiator, insert a garden hose into the coolant housing. Direct a clean flow of water through the engine, and continue flushing until clean water emerges from the radiator bottom hose.

15 When flushing is complete, refit the thermostat and reconnect the hoses (see Chapter 3).

Cooling system filling

16 Before attempting to fill the cooling system, ensure the drain plug is securely closed and make sure that all hoses are securely connected and their retaining clips are in good condition. If the recommended Mercedes-Benz coolant is not being used, ensure that a suitable antifreeze mixture is used all year round, to prevent corrosion of the engine components (see following sub-Section).

17 Remove the expansion tank filler cap and slowly fill the system with the coolant. Continue to fill the cooling system until bubbles stop appearing in the expansion tank. Help to bleed the air from the system by repeatedly squeezing the radiator bottom hose.

18 When no more bubbles appear, top the coolant level up to the MAX level mark then securely refit the cap to the expansion tank.

19 Run the engine at a fast idle speed until

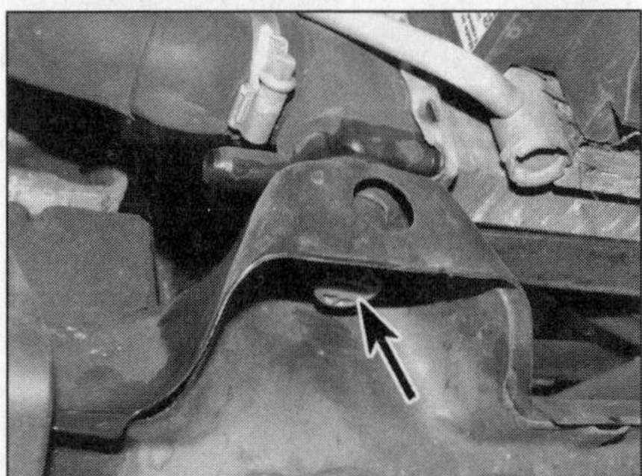

25.3a Undo the drain screw (arrowed) . . .

25.3b . . . and fit tube to drain outlet (bumper removed for clarity)

25.4 Cylinder block drain plug location – arrowed

the cooling fan cuts in. Wait for the fan to stop then switch the engine off and allow the engine to cool.

20 When the engine has cooled, check the coolant level with reference to *Weekly checks*. Top-up the level if necessary, and refit the expansion tank cap.

Antifreeze mixture

21 Antifreeze should always be renewed at the specified intervals, this is necessary not only to maintain the antifreeze properties, but also to prevent corrosion, which would otherwise occur as the corrosion inhibitors become progressively less effective.

22 Always use an ethylene-glycol based antifreeze which is suitable for use in mixed-metal cooling systems. The quantity of antifreeze and levels of protection are indicated in the Specifications.

23 Before adding antifreeze, the cooling system should be completely drained, preferably flushed, and all hoses checked for condition and security.

24 After filling with antifreeze, a label should be attached to the expansion tank, stating the type and concentration of antifreeze used, and the date installed. Any subsequent topping-up should be made with the same type and concentration of antifreeze.

Caution: Do not use engine antifreeze in the windscreen/tailgate washer system, as it will damage the vehicle paintwork. A screenwash additive should be added to the washer system in the quantities stated on the bottle.

Every 4 years or 30 000 to 45 000 miles

26 Spark plug renewal

1 The correct functioning of the spark plugs is vital for the correct running and efficiency of the engine. It is essential that the plugs fitted are appropriate for the engine (a suitable type is specified at the beginning of this Chapter). If this type is used and the engine is in good condition, the spark plugs should not need attention between scheduled renewal intervals. Spark plug cleaning is rarely necessary, and should not be attempted unless specialised equipment is available, as damage can easily be caused to the firing ends.

2 Remove the ignition coil module as described in Chapter 5B.

3 It is advisable to remove the dirt from the spark plug recesses using a clean brush, vacuum cleaner or compressed air before removing the plugs, to prevent dirt dropping into the cylinders.

4 Unscrew the plugs using a spark plug spanner, suitable box spanner or a deep socket and extension bar **(see illustration)**. Keep the socket aligned with the spark plug – if it is forcibly moved to one side, the ceramic insulator may be broken off. The use of a universal joint socket will be helpful. As each plug is removed, examine it as follows.

5 Examination of the spark plugs will give a good indication of the condition of the engine. If the insulator nose of the spark plug is clean and white, with no deposits, this is indicative of a weak mixture or too hot a plug (a hot plug transfers heat away from the electrode slowly, a cold plug transfers heat away quickly).

6 If the tip and insulator nose are covered with hard black-looking deposits, then this is indicative that the mixture is too rich. Should the plug be black and oily, and then it is likely that the engine is fairly worn, as well as the mixture being too rich.

7 If the insulator nose is covered with light tan to greyish-brown deposits, then the mixture is correct and it is likely that the engine is in good condition.

8 The spark plug electrode gap is of considerable importance as, if it is too large or too small, the size of the spark and its efficiency will be seriously impaired. On engines fitted with multi-electrode spark plugs, it is recommended that the plugs are renewed rather than attempting to adjust the gaps. On other spark plugs, the gap should be set to the value given by the manufacturer.

9 To set the gap on single electrode plugs, measure it with a feeler blade and then bend open, or closed, the outer plug electrode until the correct gap is achieved. The centre electrode should never be bent, as this may crack the insulator and cause plug failure, if nothing worse. If using feeler blades, the gap is correct when the appropriate-size blade is a firm sliding fit **(see illustrations)**.

10 Special spark plug electrode gap adjusting tools are available from most motor accessory shops, or from some spark plug manufacturers **(see illustration)**.

26.4 The spark plugs are located at the front of the engine

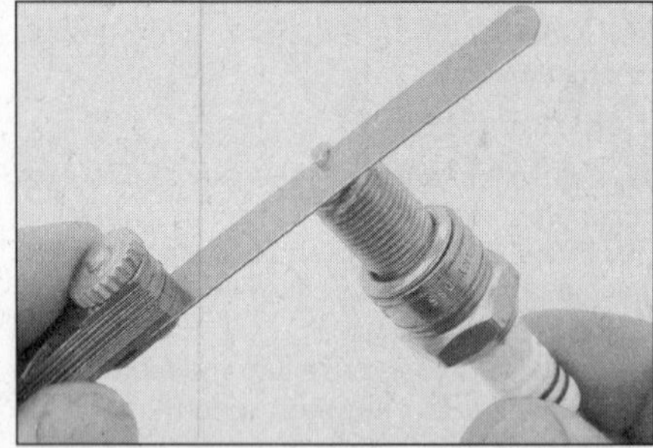

26.9a If single electrode plugs are being fitted, check the electrode gap using a feeler gauge . . .

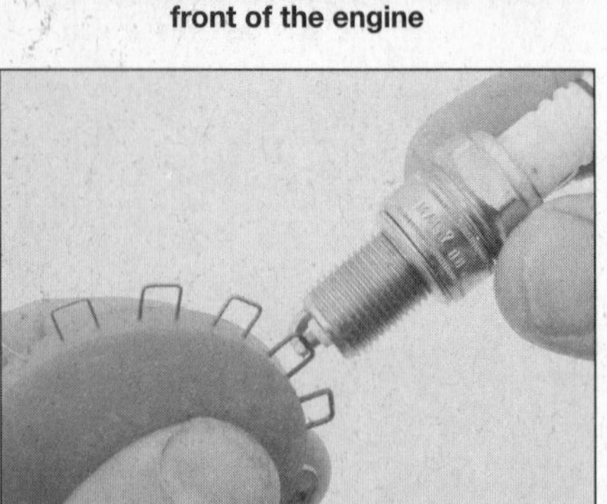

26.9b . . . or a wire gauge . . .

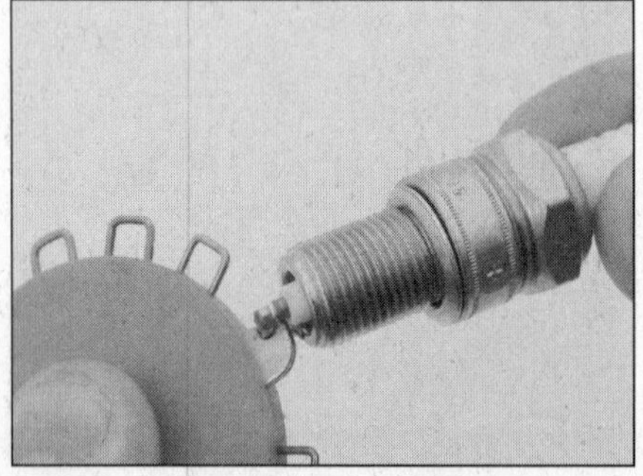

26.10 . . . and if necessary adjust the gap by bending the electrode

HAYNES HiNT

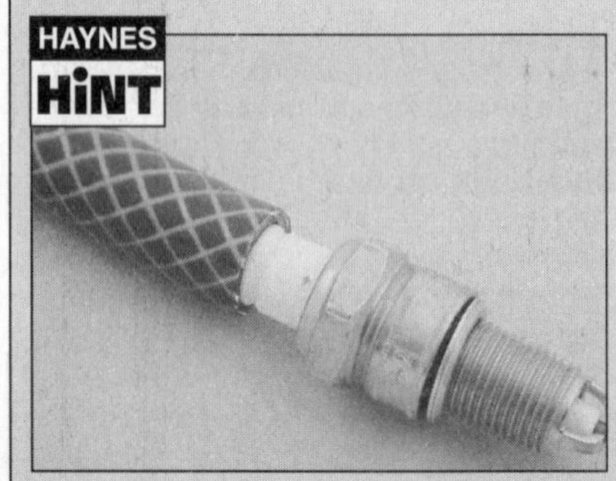

It is very often difficult to insert spark plugs into their holes without cross-threading them. To avoid this possibility, fit a short length of rubber hose over the end of the spark plug. The flexible hose acts as a universal joint to help align the plug with the plug thread, the hose will slip on the spark plug, preventing thread damage to the aluminium cylinder head.

11 Before fitting the spark plugs, check that the threaded connector sleeves are tight, and that the plug exterior surfaces and threads are clean. It's often difficult to screw in new spark plugs without cross-threading them – this can be avoided using a piece of rubber hose **(see Haynes Hint)**.

12 Remove the rubber hose (if used), and tighten the plug to the specified torque using the spark plug socket and a torque wrench. Refit the remaining spark plugs in the same manner.

13 Reconnect and refit the ignition coil module using a reversal of the removal procedure. If required refer to Chapter 5B.

Every 4 years or 50 000 miles

27 Air filter element renewal

1 The air filter element is located in the air filter housing on top of the engine.

2 Undo the retaining screws and remove the cover from the top of the air filter housing **(see illustration)**.

3 Pull back the air filter locating slide and withdraw the air filter from the housing **(see illustrations)**.

4 Fit the new filter element using a reversal of the removal procedure, making sure that the air filter is located correctly **(see illustration)**.

28 Fuel filter element renewal

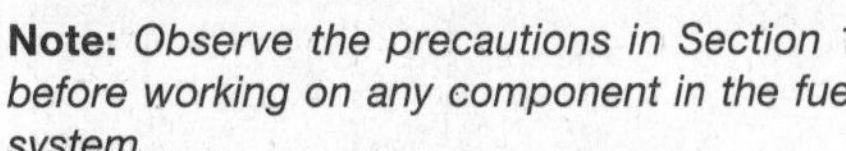

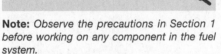

Note: *Observe the precautions in Section 1 before working on any component in the fuel system.*

1 The fuel filter is located underneath the vehicle, below the driver's side footwell, next to the battery box **(see illustration)**.

2 To gain easier access, jack up the right-hand side of the car, and support it on an axle stand (see *Jacking and vehicle support*). When positioning the axle stand, ensure that it will not inhibit access to the filter.

3 Remove the fuel cap from the fuel tank filler neck, to release the pressure in the tank.

4 Disconnect the fuel vent pipe from the fuel filter **(see illustration)**.

5 Disconnect the three fuel hoses at each end of the filter, noting their locations for refitting. Slacken the securing clips and disconnect each pipe in turn **(see illustration)**. It may be necessary to release the hoses from the clips on the underside of the car, to allow greater movement.

6 The filter is held in position by a large-diameter retaining clip on the side of the charcoal canister. Before removing the filter, look for an arrow marking, which points in the direction of fuel flow – the new filter must be fitted the same way round.

27.2 Remove the air cleaner cover . . .

27.3a . . . pull back the locating slide . . .

27.3b . . . then remove the filter element

27.4 Make sure the filter is located correctly in the housing

28.1 Fuel filter location – arrowed

28.4 Disconnecting the fuel vent pipe

28.5 Disconnecting one of the fuel lines

28.7 Unclip the filter from the mounting bracket

28.8 Direction of fuel flow – arrowed

7 Slide the filter out of position **(see illustration)**. Try to keep it as level as possible, to reduce fuel spillage. Dispose of the old filter carefully – even if the fuel inside is tipped out, the filter element will still be soaked in fuel, and will be highly flammable.

8 Offer the new filter into position; making sure it is located in the retaining clip securely. Ensure that the direction-of-flow arrow is pointing in the correct direction, as noted on removal **(see illustration)**.

9 Connect the fuel hoses to each end of the filter, in the same positions as noted on removal. Push the hoses fully onto the filter stubs, and where necessary tighten the securing clips. Where applicable, clip the fuel hoses back to the underside of the car.

10 Lower the car to the ground, refit the fuel cap to the fuel filler neck, and then start the engine. Check for signs of fuel leakage from the hoses at both ends of the filter.

Chapter 1 Part B: Routine maintenance and servicing – diesel models

Contents

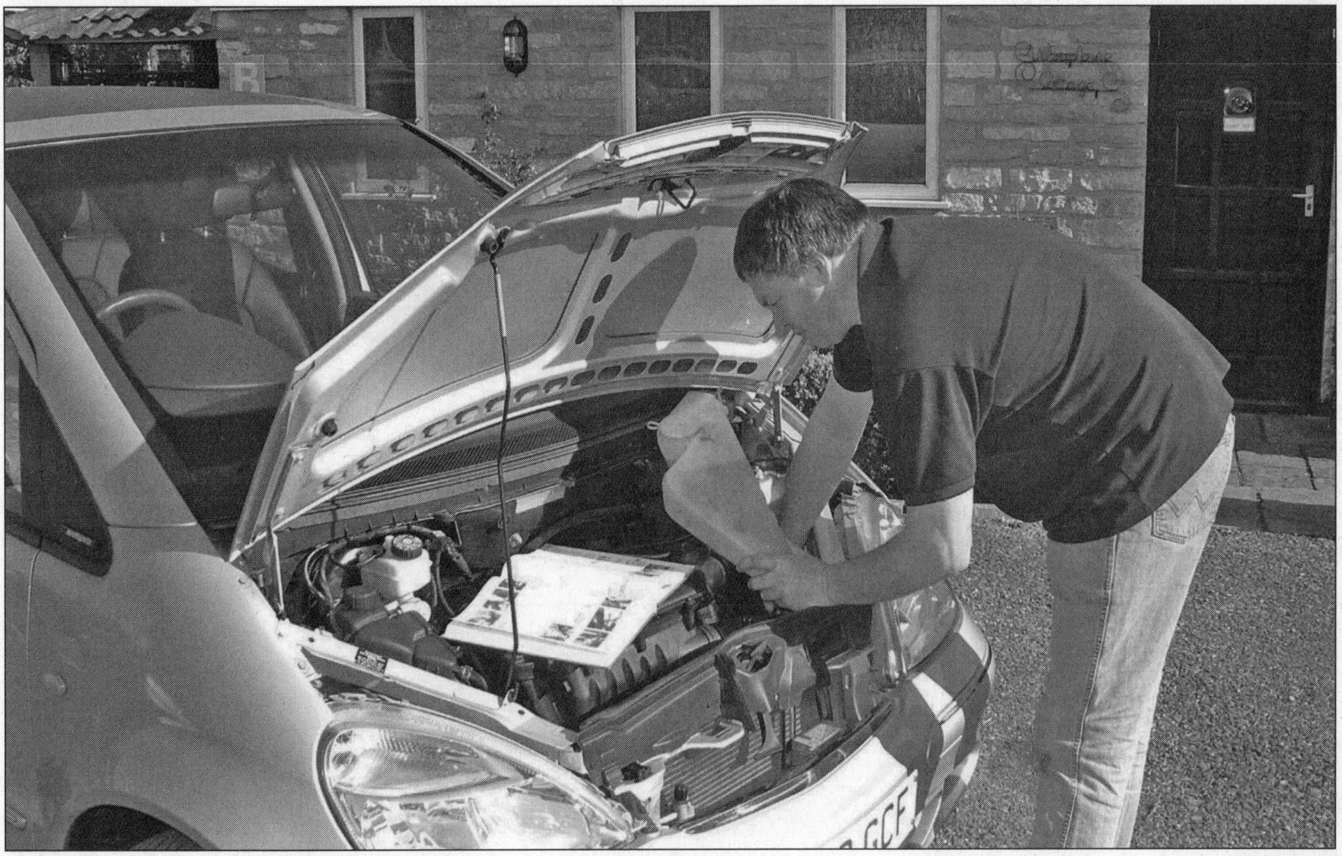

Degrees of difficulty

Easy, suitable for novice with little experience 	**Fairly easy,** suitable for beginner with some experience	**Fairly difficult,** suitable for competent DIY mechanic	**Difficult,** suitable for experienced DIY mechanic	**Very difficult,** suitable for expert DIY or professional 

Lubricants and fluids

Refer to the end of *Weekly checks* on page 0•17

Capacities

Engine oil (including filter)

All engines	5.0 litres

Cooling system

All engines	6.5 litres

Transmission

Manual transmission	1.8 litres
Automatic transmission	5.5 litres

Fuel tank (approximate)

All models	54 litres

Cooling system

Antifreeze mixture:

50% antifreeze	Protection down to -37°C
55% antifreeze	Protection down to -45°C

Note: *Refer to antifreeze manufacturer for latest recommendations.*

Brakes

Brake pad lining minimum thickness	2.0 mm
Brake shoe lining minimum thickness	2.0 mm

Torque wrench settings	Nm	lbf ft
Manual gearbox filler/level plug	30	22
Oil filter cap	25	18
Roadwheel bolts	120	89
Sump drain plug	25	18

The maintenance intervals in this manual are provided with the assumption that you, not the dealer, will be carrying out the work. These are the minimum intervals recommended by us for vehicles driven daily. If you wish to keep your vehicle in peak condition at all times, you may wish to perform some of these procedures more often. We encourage frequent maintenance, since it enhances the efficiency, performance and resale value of your vehicle.

When the vehicle is new, it should be serviced by a dealer service department (or other workshop recognised by the vehicle manufacturer as providing the same standard of service) in order to preserve the warranty. The vehicle manufacturer may reject warranty claims if you are unable to prove that servicing has been carried out as and when specified, using only original equipment parts or parts certified to be of equivalent quality.

All Mercedes-Benz models are equipped with ASSYST (Active Service SYSTem), which lets you know when the next service is due. The service symbol will illuminate on the instrument panel approximately one month before the next service is due. Depending on your driving style, the time between servicing can vary. A moderate style of driving with no short trips and at a medium engine speed can increase the time between servicing. The different type of symbols that illuminate will indicate which type of service is due: one spanner being a minor service (Service A) and two spanners being a major service (Service B).

After completing a service, Mercedes-Benz technicians use a special instrument to reset the service display to the next service interval, and a printout is put in the vehicle service record. The display can be reset by the owner as described in Section 4.

Every 250 miles or weekly

- ☐ Refer to *Weekly checks*

Every 7500 miles or 12 months, whichever comes first

- ☐ Renew the engine oil and filter (Section 3)

Note: *Frequent oil and filter changes are good for the engine. We recommend changing the oil at least once a year.*

One spanner on display (Service A)

In addition to the items listed above, carry out the following:

- ☐ Reset the service interval display (Section 4)
- ☐ Check the condition of the exhaust system and its mountings* (Section 5)
- ☐ Check the coolant antifreeze concentration (Section 6)
- ☐ Check the battery condition, security and electrolyte level (Section 7)
- ☐ Lubricate all hinges and locks (Section 8)
- ☐ Check the condition of the airbag unit(s)* (Section 9)
- ☐ Check the operation of the windscreen/tailgate washer system(s) (Section 10)

* **Note:** *These items are not specified by Mercedes-Benz as routine maintenance items.*

Two spanners on display (Service B)

In addition to the items listed above, carry out the following:

- ☐ Check the front and rear brake pad or shoe thickness (Section 11)
- ☐ Check all underbonnet components and hoses for fluid and oil leaks (Section 12)
- ☐ Check the brake hydraulic circuit for leaks and damage (Section 13)
- ☐ Check the condition of the auxiliary drivebelt (Section 14)
- ☐ Check the headlight beam adjustment (Section 15)
- ☐ Renew the pollen/combination filter element (Section 16)
- ☐ Check the condition of the driveshaft gaiters (Section 17)
- ☐ Check the steering and suspension components for condition and security (Section 18)
- ☐ Check the power steering fluid level (Section 19)
- ☐ Carry out a road test and check exhaust emissions (Section 20)

Every 2 years

Note: *These tasks are normally performed at the same time as a Service A or Service B.*

- ☐ Check the manual transmission oil level* (Section 21)
- ☐ Check the bodywork and underbody protection for damage (Section 22)
- ☐ Check the automatic transmission fluid level* (Section 23)
- ☐ Renew the brake (and clutch) fluid (Section 24)

* **Note:** *These tasks are not specified by Mercedes-Benz as routine maintenance items.*

Every 3 years

Note: *This task is normally performed at the same time as a Service A or Service B.*

- ☐ Renew the coolant (Section 25)

Note: *This work is every 15 years/155 000 miles in the Mercedes-Benz schedule for later models if the recommended Mercedes-Benz coolant antifreeze/inhibitor is used.*

Every 4 years or 50 000 miles, whichever comes first

Note: *These tasks are normally performed at the same time as a Service A or Service B.*

- ☐ Renew the air filter element (Section 26)
- ☐ Renew the fuel filter element (Section 27)

Component location – diesel models

Underbonnet view

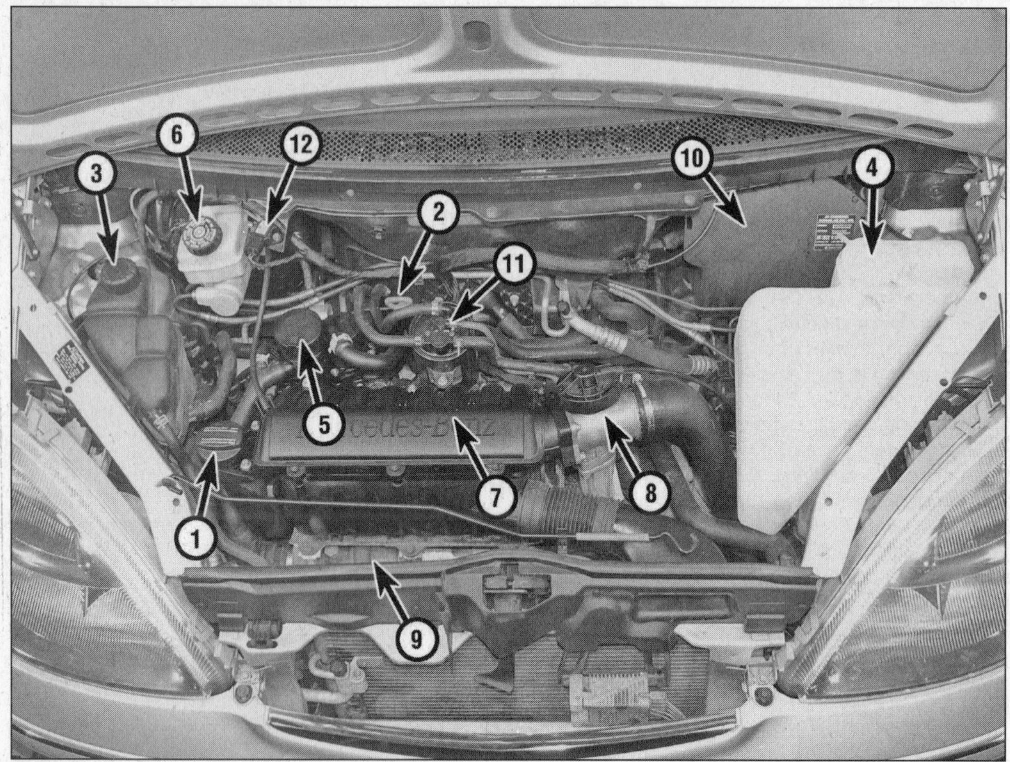

1. *Engine oil filler cap*
2. *Engine oil dipstick*
3. *Coolant expansion tank*
4. *Washer fluid reservoir*
5. *Oil separator/crankcase breather*
6. *Brake master cylinder fluid reservoir*
7. *Inlet manifold*
8. *EGR valve*
9. *Turbocharger*
10. *Electronic Control Module (ECM) cover*
11. *Fuel filter*
12. *Charge air pressure sensor*

Front underbody view

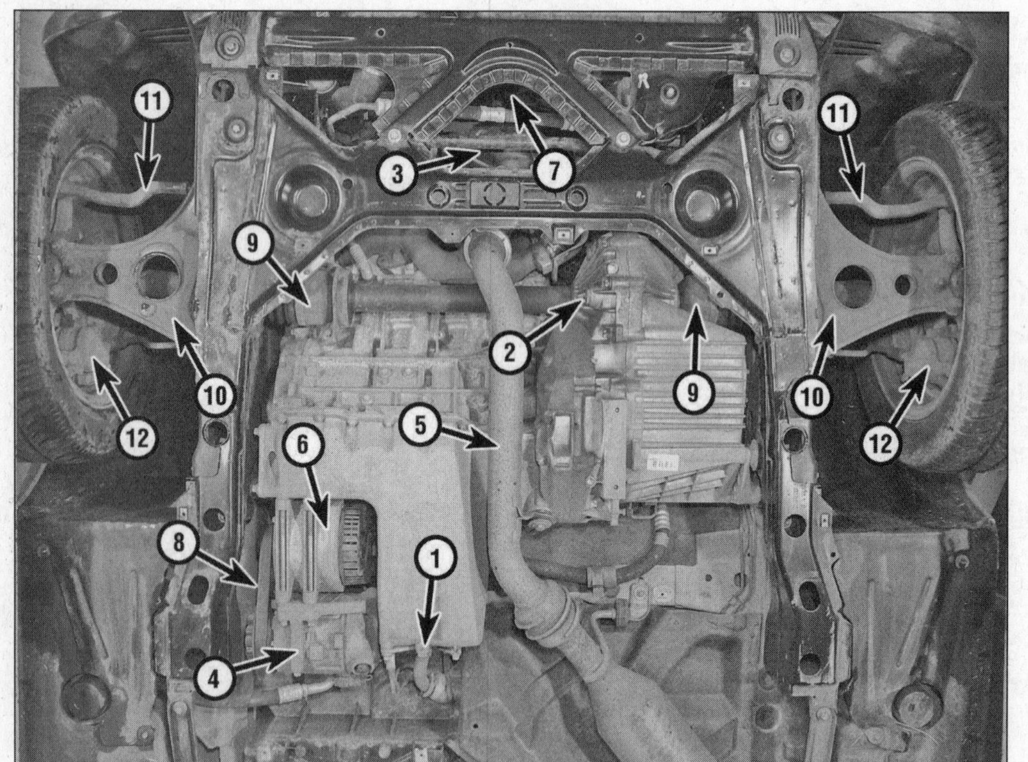

1. *Sump drain plug*
2. *Manual transmission drain plug*
3. *Catalytic converter*
4. *Air conditioning compressor*
5. *Exhaust front pipe*
6. *Alternator*
7. *Radiator and electric cooling fans*
8. *Auxiliary drivebelt*
9. *Driveshafts*
10. *Front suspension lower arms*
11. *Steering track rods*
12. *Brake calipers*

Rear underbody view

1 *Fuel tank*
2 *Anti-roll bar*
3 *Fuel tank filler neck*
4 *Coil springs*
5 *Shock absorber lower mountings*
6 *Trailing arms*
7 *Brake calipers*
8 *Handbrake cable adjuster*
9 *Exhaust rear silencers and tail pipe*

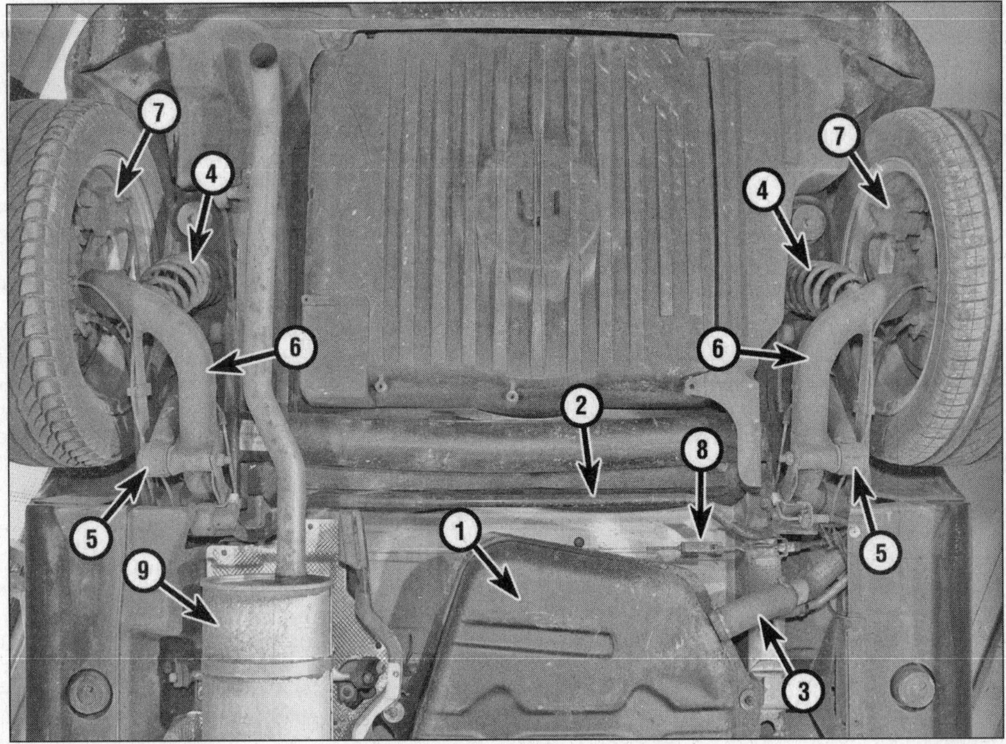

Maintenance procedures

1 Introduction

This Chapter is designed to help the home mechanic maintain his/her vehicle for safety, economy, long life and peak performance.

The Chapter contains a master maintenance schedule, followed by Sections dealing specifically with each task in the schedule. Visual checks, adjustments, component renewal and other helpful items are included. Refer to the accompanying illustrations of the engine compartment and the underside of the vehicle for the locations of the various components.

Servicing your vehicle will provide a planned maintenance programme, which should result in a long and reliable service life. This is a comprehensive plan, so maintaining some items but not others will not produce the same results.

As you service your vehicle, you will discover that many of the procedures can – and should – be grouped together, because of the particular procedure being performed, or because of the proximity of two otherwise unrelated components to one another. For example, if the vehicle is raised for any reason, the exhaust can be inspected at the same time as the suspension and steering components.

The first step in this maintenance programme is to prepare yourself before the actual work begins. Read through all the Sections relevant to the work to be carried out, then make a list and gather all the parts and tools required. If a problem is encountered, seek advice from a parts specialist, or a dealer service department.

2 Regular maintenance

1 If, from the time the vehicle is new, the routine maintenance schedule is followed closely, and frequent checks are made of fluid levels and high-wear items, as suggested throughout this manual, the engine will be kept in relatively good running condition, and the need for additional work will be minimised.

2 It is possible that there will be times when the engine is running poorly due to the lack of regular maintenance. This is even more likely if a used vehicle, which has not received regular and frequent maintenance checks, is purchased. In such cases, additional work may need to be carried out, outside of the regular maintenance intervals.

3 If engine wear is suspected, a compression test (refer to the relevant Part of Chapter 2) will provide valuable information regarding the overall performance of the main internal components. Such a test can be used as a basis to decide on the extent of the work to be carried out. If, for example, a compression test indicates serious internal engine wear, conventional maintenance as described in this Chapter will not greatly improve the performance of the engine, and may prove a waste of time and money, unless extensive overhaul work is carried out first.

4 The following series of operations are those most often required to improve the performance of a generally poor-running engine:

Primary operations

a) Clean, inspect and test the battery (See 'Weekly checks').
b) Check all the engine-related fluids (See 'Weekly checks').
c) Drain the water from the fuel filter.
d) Check the condition and tension of the auxiliary drivebelt (Section 14).
e) Check the condition of the air filter, and renew if necessary (Section 26).
f) Check the condition of all hoses, and check for fluid leaks (Section 12).

5 If the above operations do not prove fully effective, carry out the following secondary operations:

Secondary operations

All items listed under *Primary operations*, plus the following:

a) Check the charging system (see Chapter 5A).
b) Check the preheating system (see Chapter 5C).
c) Renew the fuel filter (Section 27) and check the fuel system (see Chapter 4B).

Every 7500 miles or 12 months

3 Engine oil and filter renewal

1 Frequent oil and filter changes are the most important maintenance procedures, which can be undertaken by the DIY owner. As engine oil ages, it becomes diluted and contaminated, which leads to premature engine wear.

2 Before starting this procedure, gather all the necessary tools and materials. Also make sure that you have plenty of clean rags and

3.3 Remove the engine oil drain plug from the rear of the sump

HAYNES HiNT

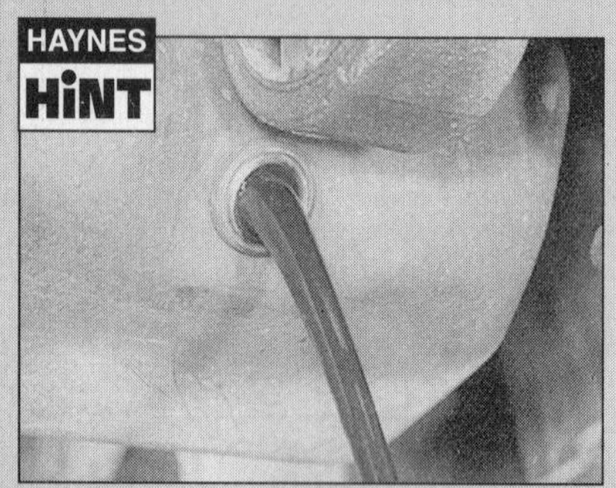

Keep the drain plug pressed into the sump while unscrewing it by hand the last couple of turns. As the plug releases, move it away sharply so the stream of oil issuing from the sump runs into the container, not up your sleeve.

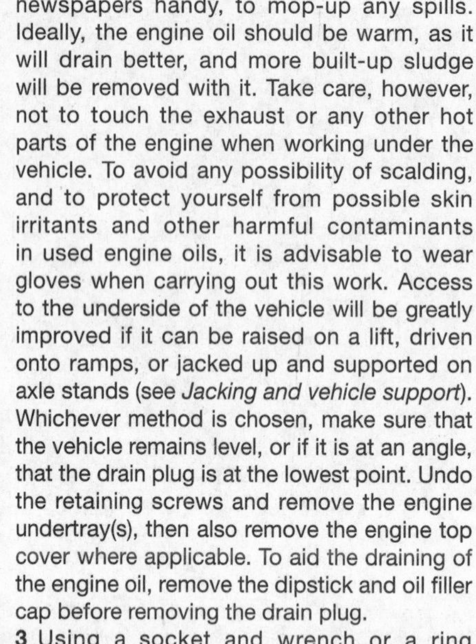

newspapers handy, to mop-up any spills. Ideally, the engine oil should be warm, as it will drain better, and more built-up sludge will be removed with it. Take care, however, not to touch the exhaust or any other hot parts of the engine when working under the vehicle. To avoid any possibility of scalding, and to protect yourself from possible skin irritants and other harmful contaminants in used engine oils, it is advisable to wear gloves when carrying out this work. Access to the underside of the vehicle will be greatly improved if it can be raised on a lift, driven onto ramps, or jacked up and supported on axle stands (see *Jacking and vehicle support*). Whichever method is chosen, make sure that the vehicle remains level, or if it is at an angle, that the drain plug is at the lowest point. Undo the retaining screws and remove the engine undertray(s), then also remove the engine top cover where applicable. To aid the draining of the engine oil, remove the dipstick and oil filler cap before removing the drain plug.

3 Using a socket and wrench or a ring spanner, slacken the drain plug about half a turn **(see illustration)**. Position the draining container under the drain plug, and then remove the plug completely **(see Haynes Hint)**. Recover the sealing ring from the drain plug.

4 Allow some time for the old oil to drain, noting that it may be necessary to reposition the container as the oil flow slows to a trickle.

5 After all the oil has drained, wipe off the

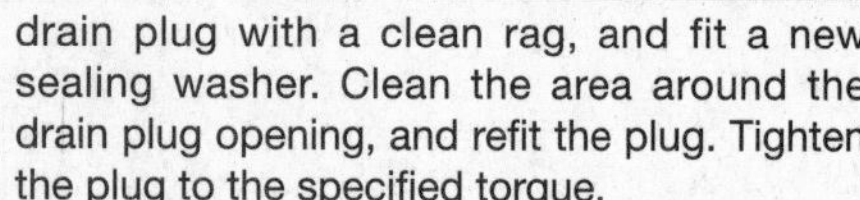

drain plug with a clean rag, and fit a new sealing washer. Clean the area around the drain plug opening, and refit the plug. Tighten the plug to the specified torque.

6 If the filter is also to be renewed, place rags around the base of the oil filter. The oil filter is an element type and is located from above in a housing on the rear of the engine.

7 To remove the oil filter, unscrew and remove the cap complete with the filter element **(see illustration)**. Discard the O-ring seals, as new ones will be required when refitting.

8 Clean the filter housing and cap as necessary, and fit the new sealing rings to the oil filter cap **(see illustrations)**.

9 To fit the new filter, locate it in its housing and refit the cap together with the new sealing rings **(see illustrations)**. Tighten the cap to the specified torque.

10 Remove the old oil and all tools from under the car. Refit the engine undertray(s), tighten the retaining screws securely, and then lower the car to the ground. Also refit the engine top cover where applicable.

11 Fill the engine, using the correct grade and type of oil (see *Lubricants and fluids*). An oil can spout or funnel may help to reduce spillage. Pour in half the specified quantity of oil first, and then wait a few minutes for the oil to run to the sump. Continue adding oil a small quantity at a time until the level is up to the maximum mark on the dipstick. Refit the filler cap.

12 Start the engine and run it for a few

3.7 Removing the oil filter cap complete with filter

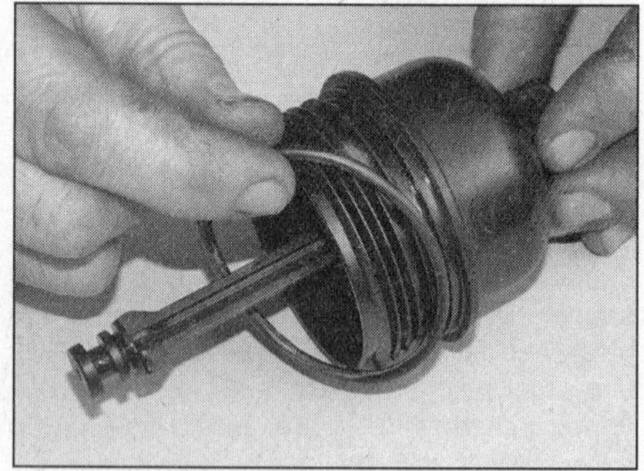

3.8a Renew the large sealing ring . . .

3.8b . . . and the small sealing ring

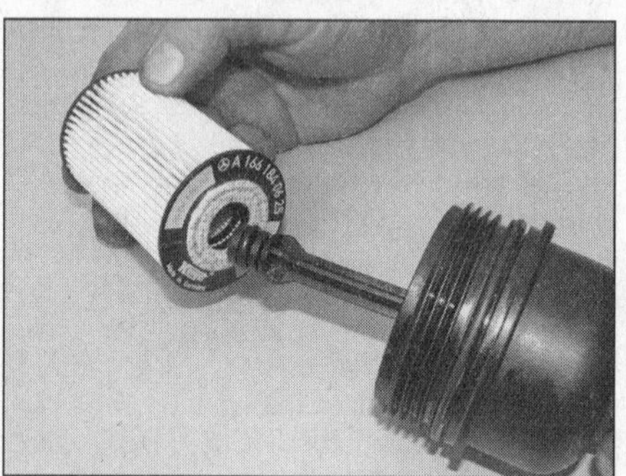

3.9a Fit the new filter to the cap . . .

3.9b . . . and refit it to the engine

minutes; check for leaks around the oil filter seal and the sump drain plug. Note that there may be a few seconds delay before the oil pressure warning light goes out when the engine is started, as the oil circulates through the engine oil galleries and the new oil filter (where fitted) before the pressure builds-up.

⚠ *Warning: On turbocharged engines, do not increase the engine speed above idling while the oil pressure light is illuminated, as considerable damage can be caused to the turbocharger.*

13 Switch off the engine, and wait a few minutes for the oil to settle in the sump once more. With the new oil circulated and the filter completely full, recheck the level on the dipstick, and add more oil as necessary.

14 Dispose of the used engine oil safely, with reference to *General repair procedures* in the *Reference* section of this manual.

One spanner on display (Service A)

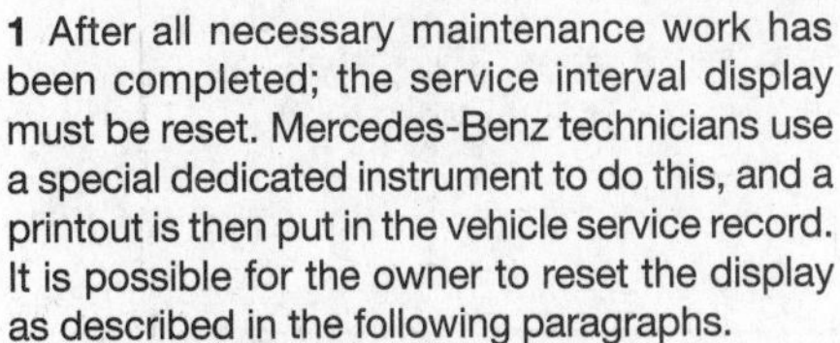

4 Resetting the service interval display

1 After all necessary maintenance work has been completed; the service interval display must be reset. Mercedes-Benz technicians use a special dedicated instrument to do this, and a printout is then put in the vehicle service record. It is possible for the owner to reset the display as described in the following paragraphs.

2 To reset the display manually:

1) *Turn the ignition switch to position II, then immediately press the 000.0 button (which is positioned to the left-hand side lower part of the of the instrument cluster) twice within one second.*
2) *Turn the ignition switch to position 0 within the next ten seconds.*
3) *Press and hold down the 000.0 button.*
4) *Turn the ignition switch to position II, the last service indication will appear in the display.*
5) *Keep the 000.0 button pressed, and the last service indication remains displayed. An audible signal will be heard after approximately ten seconds, the service indicator will now be displayed with the new value.*
6) *Release the 000.0 button.*
7) *Leave the ignition switch in position II for at least another five seconds, and the service indicator is now reset.*

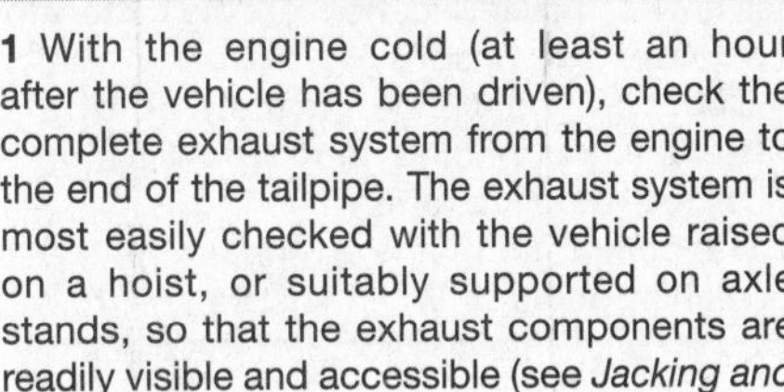

5 Exhaust system check

1 With the engine cold (at least an hour after the vehicle has been driven), check the complete exhaust system from the engine to the end of the tailpipe. The exhaust system is most easily checked with the vehicle raised on a hoist, or suitably supported on axle stands, so that the exhaust components are readily visible and accessible (see *Jacking and vehicle support*).

2 Check the exhaust pipes and connections for evidence of leaks, severe corrosion and damage. Make sure that all brackets and mountings are in good condition, and that all relevant nuts and bolts are tight. Leakage at any of the joints or in other parts of the system will usually show up as a black sooty stain in the vicinity of the leak.

3 Rattles and other noises can often be traced to the exhaust system, especially the brackets and mountings **(see illustration)**. Try to move the pipes and silencers. If the components are able to come into contact with the body or suspension parts, secure the system with new mountings. Otherwise separate the joints (if possible) and twist the pipes as necessary to provide additional clearance.

6 Antifreeze check

1 The cooling system should be filled with the recommended antifreeze and corrosion protection fluid – **do not** mix this antifreeze with any other type. Over a period of time, the concentration of fluid may be reduced due to topping-up (this can be avoided by topping-up with the correct antifreeze mixture – see Specifications) or fluid loss. If loss of coolant has been evident, it is important to make the necessary repair before adding fresh fluid.

2 With the engine **cold**, carefully remove the cap from the expansion tank. If the engine is not completely cold, place a cloth rag over the cap before removing it, and remove it slowly to allow any pressure to escape.

3 Antifreeze testers are available from car accessory shops. Draw some coolant from the expansion tank and observe how many plastic balls are floating in the checker. Usually, 2 or 3 balls must be floating for the correct concentration of antifreeze, but follow the manufacturer's instructions.

4 If the concentration is incorrect, it will be necessary to either withdraw some coolant and add antifreeze, or alternatively drain the old coolant and add fresh coolant of the correct concentration (see Section 25).

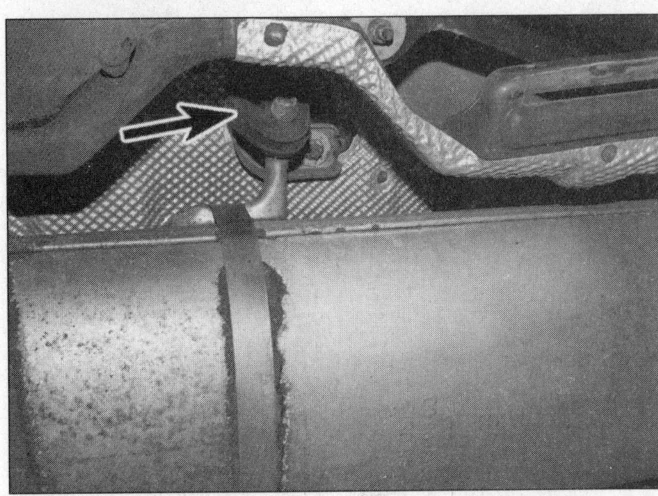

5.3 Check the exhaust rubbers – one arrowed

7.1 Battery location

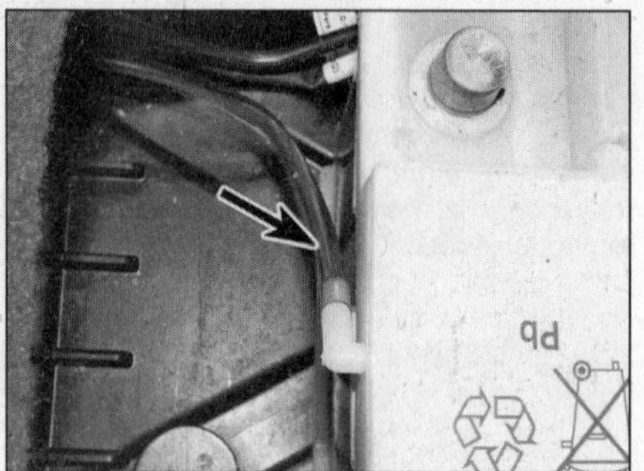

7.6 Vent pipe on the side of the battery

7 Battery check

1 The battery is located in the front footwell, under the carpet, in front of the driver's seat. Remove the driver's floor mat, lift up tab and turn it anti-clockwise to remove the battery cover **(see illustration)**.

2 The vehicle's main fusebox is also located under the carpet next to the battery.

3 Check that both battery terminals and all the fuse holder connections are securely attached and are free from corrosion. **Note:** *Before disconnecting the terminals from the battery, refer to 'Disconnecting the battery' in the Reference Chapter at the end of this manual. It is always safer to remove the keys from the ignition, before disconnecting the battery, to prevent any electronic components getting damaged.*

4 Check the battery casing for signs of damage or cracking and check the battery retaining-clamp is secure. If the battery casing is damaged in any way the battery must be renewed (see Chapter 5A).

5 If the vehicle is not fitted with a sealed-for-life maintenance-free battery, check the electrolyte level is between the MAX and MIN level markings on the battery casing. If topping-up is necessary, remove the battery (see Chapter 5A) from the vehicle then remove the cell caps/cover (as applicable). Using distilled water, top the electrolyte level of each cell up to the MAX level mark then securely refit the cell caps/cover. Ensure the battery has not been overfilled then refit the battery to the vehicle (see Chapter 5A).

6 Check the vent pipe on the side of the battery is connected and free from any blockage **(see illustration)**.

7 On completion of the check, refit the insulation panel and clip the battery cover securely back into position, refit the carpet.

8 Hinge and lock lubrication

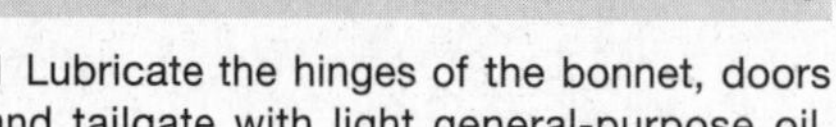

1 Lubricate the hinges of the bonnet, doors and tailgate with light general-purpose oil. Similarly, lubricate all latches, locks and lock strikers. At the same time, check the security and operation of all the locks, adjusting them if necessary (see Chapter 11).

2 Lightly lubricate the bonnet release mechanism and cable with suitable grease.

9 Airbag unit check

Inspect the exterior condition of the airbag(s) for signs of damage or deterioration. If an airbag shows signs of damage, it must be renewed (see Chapter 12). Note that it is not permissible to attach any stickers to the surface of the airbag, as this may affect the deployment of the unit.

10 Windscreen/tailgate washer system check

1 Check that each of the washer jet nozzles are clear and that each nozzle provides a strong jet of washer fluid.

2 The tailgate jet should be aimed to spray at the centre of the screen, using a pin.

3 The windscreen washer nozzles should be aimed slightly above the centre of the screen.

4 Especially during the winter months, make sure that the washer fluid frost concentration is sufficient to prevent freezing.

Two spanners on display (Service B)

11 Brake pad and shoe check

Brake pads

1 The outer brake pads can be checked without removing the wheels, by observing the brake pads through the holes in the wheels **(see illustration)**. If necessary, remove the wheel trim. The thickness of the pad lining must not be less than the dimension given in the Specifications.

2 If the outer pads are worn near their limits, it is worthwhile checking the inner pads as well. Apply the handbrake then jack up vehicle and support it on axle stands (see *Jacking and vehicle support*). Remove the roadwheels.

3 Use a steel rule to check the thickness of the brake pads, and compare with the minimum thickness given in the Specifications **(see illustration)**.

4 For a comprehensive check, the brake

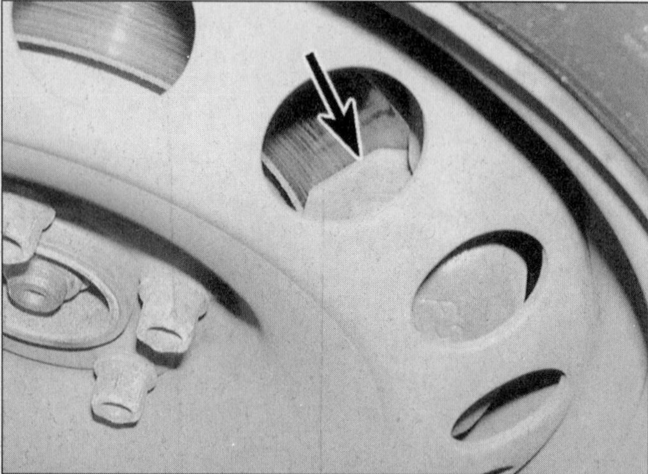

11.1 The outer brake pads can be observed through the holes in the wheels

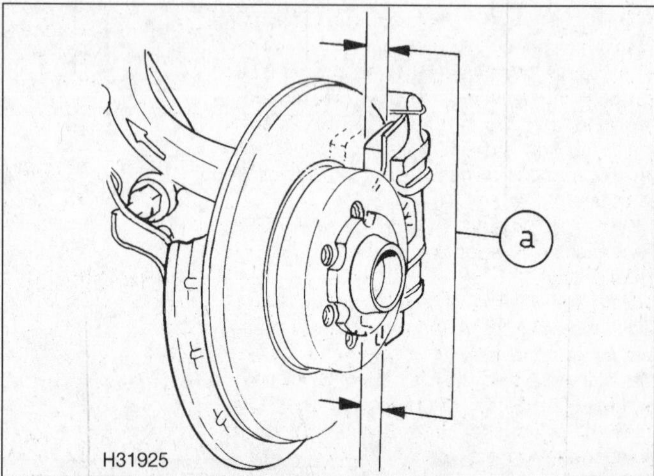

11.3 The thickness (a) of the brake pad linings must not be less than the specified amount

pads should be removed and cleaned. The operation of the caliper can then also be checked, and the condition of the brake disc itself can be fully examined on both sides. Refer to Chapter 9.

5 If any pad's friction material is worn to the specified minimum thickness or less, *all four pads at the front or rear, as applicable, must be renewed as a set.*

6 On completion of the check, refit the road-wheels and lower the vehicle to the ground.

Brake shoes

7 To check the rear brake shoes for wear, remove the brake drums (see Chapter 9).

12 Hose and fluid leak check

1 Visually inspect the engine joint faces, gaskets and seals for any signs of water or oil leaks. Pay particular attention to the areas around the camshaft cover, cylinder head, oil filter and sump joint faces. Bear in mind that, over a period of time, some very slight seepage from these areas is to be expected – what you are really looking for is any indication of a serious leak. Should a leak be found, renew the offending gasket or oil seal by referring to the appropriate Chapters in this manual.

2 Also check the security and condition of all the engine-related pipes and hoses. Ensure that all cable-ties or securing clips are in place and in good condition. Clips that are broken or missing can lead to chafing of the hoses, pipes or wiring, which could cause more serious problems in the future.

3 Carefully check the radiator hoses and heater hoses along their entire length. Renew any hose which is cracked, swollen or deteriorated. Cracks will show up better if the hose is squeezed. Pay close attention to the hose clips that secure the hoses to the cooling system components. Hose clips can pinch and puncture hoses, resulting in cooling system leaks.

4 Inspect all the cooling system components (hoses, joint faces, etc) for leaks **(see Haynes Hint)**. Where any problems of this nature are found on system components, renew the component or gasket with reference to Chapter 3.

5 Where applicable, inspect the automatic transmission fluid cooler hoses for leaks or deterioration.

6 With the vehicle raised, inspect the fuel tank and filler neck for punctures, cracks and other damage. The connection between the filler neck and tank is especially critical. Sometimes a rubber filler neck or connecting hose will leak due to loose retaining clamps or deteriorated rubber.

7 Carefully check all rubber hoses and metal fuel lines leading away from the tank. Check for loose connections, deteriorated hoses, crimped lines, and other damage. Pay particular attention to the vent pipes and hoses, which often loop up around the filler neck and can become blocked or crimped. Follow the lines to the front of the vehicle, carefully inspecting them all the way. Renew damaged sections as necessary.

8 From within the engine compartment, check the security of all fuel hose attachments and pipe unions, and inspect the fuel hoses and vacuum hoses for kinks, chafing and deterioration.

9 Check the condition of the power steering fluid hoses and pipes.

13 Brake hydraulic circuit check

1 Check the entire brake hydraulic circuit for leaks and damage. Start by checking the master cylinder in the engine compartment. At the same time, check the vacuum servo unit and ABS units for signs of fluid leakage.

2 Raise the front and rear of the vehicle and support it on axle stands (see *Jacking and vehicle support*). Check the rigid hydraulic brake lines for corrosion and damage.

3 At the front and rear of the vehicle, check that any flexible hydraulic hoses to the calipers are not twisted or chafing on any of the surrounding suspension components. Turn the steering on full lock to make this check. Also check that the hoses are not brittle or cracked.

4 Lower the vehicle to the ground after making the checks.

14 Auxiliary drivebelt check and renewal

1 The poly-vee drivebelt drives the alternator, coolant pump and where fitted, the air conditioning compressor.

2 On all engines, the drivebelt tension is adjusted automatically by an idler pulley, which is spring-tensioned.

3 The drivebelt can only be accessed from under the vehicle.

14.5 Checking the underside of the belt with a mirror

A leak in the cooling system will usually show up as white- or antifreeze-coloured deposits on the area adjoining the leak.

Checking

4 Apply the handbrake, then jack up the front of the vehicle and support it on axle stands (see *Jacking and vehicle support*). Remove the engine undertray as the belt will need to be checked from underneath the vehicle.

5 Using a socket on the crankshaft pulley bolt, turn the engine slowly clockwise so that the full length of the auxiliary drivebelt can be examined. Look for cracks, splitting and fraying on the surface of the belt; check also for signs of glazing (shiny patches) and separation of the belt plies. If required, use a mirror to check the underside of the drivebelt **(see illustration)**. If damage or wear is visible, or if there are traces of oil or grease on it, the belt should be renewed.

Renewal

6 Apply the handbrake, and then jack up the front of the vehicle and support it on axle stands (see *Jacking and vehicle support*). Remove the engine undertray.

7 Remove the right-hand front roadwheel, and then remove the inner wheel arch liner.

8 If the drivebelt is to be re-used, mark it for clockwise direction to ensure it is refitted the same way round.

9 Use a spanner to turn the tensioner central bolt clockwise to release the tension on the drivebelt **(see illustration)**.

10 While holding the tension off the belt,

14.9 Turn the spanner (arrowed) clockwise to release the tension

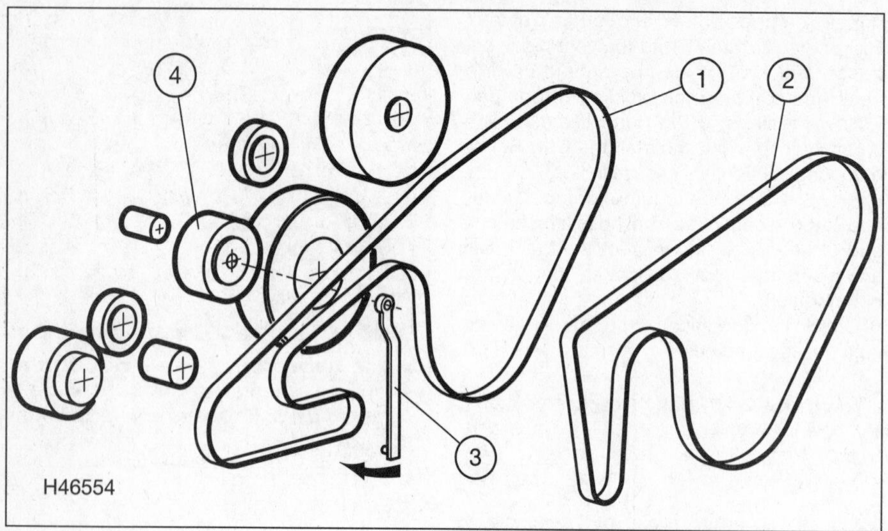

14.11 Auxiliary drivebelt routing

1 With air conditioning
2 Without air conditioning
3 Tensioner spanner
4 Tensioner pulley

note how the drivebelt is routed, then remove it from around the pulleys. When belt is removed, slowly release the tensioner back to its stop.

11 Locate the new (if required) drivebelt on the pulleys, then release the tensioner. Check that the belt is located correctly in the grooves in the pulleys **(see illustration)**.

12 Refit the inner wheel arch liner and roadwheel, and refit the engine undertray. Lower the vehicle to the ground.

15 Headlight beam adjustment

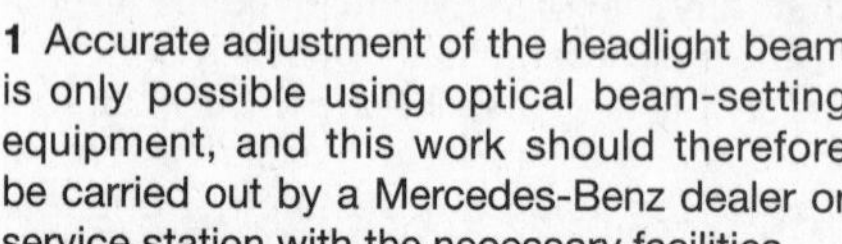

1 Accurate adjustment of the headlight beam is only possible using optical beam-setting equipment, and this work should therefore be carried out by a Mercedes-Benz dealer or service station with the necessary facilities.

2 Basic adjustments can be carried out in an emergency, and further details are given in Chapter 12.

16 Pollen/combination filter element renewal

1 The pollen filter is located in the upper part of the heater unit and is accessed from under the bonnet, below the air intake grill at the bottom of the windscreen.

2 With the bonnet open, undo the four retaining screws and withdraw the plastic grill from the lower part of the windscreen **(see illustration)**.

3 Unclip the cover from the lower part of the wiper arms and undo the retaining nuts, and then remove the wiper arms, with reference to Chapter 12.

4 Where fitted disconnect the washer jet heater wiring connector from the centre of the plastic scuttle panel **(see illustration)**.

5 Disconnect the washer jet supply hose from the connection at the washer pump.

6 Undo the five retaining screws and remove the lower plastic scuttle panel from the rear of the engine compartment **(see illustration)**.

7 Lift the pollen filter element at the front and withdraw it from the heater unit **(see illustration)**. Note the direction of the arrow on the front edge of the filter.

8 Fit the new element (with the arrow on the front edge of the filter facing upwards) **(see illustration)** and then refit the plastic scuttle panel.

9 Refit the remaining parts using a reversal of the removal procedure.

17 Driveshaft gaiter check

1 With the vehicle raised and securely supported on stands, slowly rotate the roadwheel. Inspect the condition of the outer constant velocity (CV) joint rubber gaiters, squeezing the gaiters to open out the folds. Check for signs of cracking, splits or deterioration of the rubber, which may allow the grease to escape, and lead to water and grit entry into the joint. Also check the

16.2 Removing the windscreen lower trim panel

16.4 Disconnecting the heated washer jet wiring connector

16.6 Remove the scuttle panel from the vehicle

16.7 Lift the pollen filter out from the housing

16.8 Note the direction of the arrow on the front of the filter

security and condition of the retaining clips. Repeat these checks on the inner joints **(see illustration)**. If any damage or deterioration is found, the gaiters should be renewed (see Chapter 8).

2 At the same time, check the general condition of the CV joints themselves by first holding the driveshaft and attempting to rotate the wheel. Repeat this check by holding the inner joint and attempting to rotate the driveshaft. Any appreciable movement indicates wear in the joints, wear in the driveshaft splines, or a loose driveshaft retaining nut.

17.1 Check the condition of the driveshaft inner and outer gaiters – arrowed

18 Steering and suspension check

1 Raise the front and rear of the vehicle, and securely support it on axle stands (see *Jacking and vehicle support*).

2 Visually inspect the track rod end balljoint dust cover, the lower front suspension balljoint dust cover, and the steering rack-and-pinion gaiters for splits, chafing or deterioration. Any wear of these components will cause loss of lubricant, together with dirt and water entry, resulting in rapid deterioration of the balljoints or steering gear.

3 Check the power steering fluid hoses for chafing or deterioration, and the pipe and hose unions for fluid leaks. Also check for signs of fluid leakage under pressure from the steering gear rubber gaiters, which would indicate failed fluid seals within the steering gear.

4 Grasp the roadwheel at the 12 o'clock and 6 o'clock positions, and try to rock it **(see illustration)**. Very slight free play may be felt, but if the movement is appreciable, further investigation is necessary to determine the source. Continue rocking the wheel while an assistant depresses the footbrake. If the movement is now eliminated or significantly reduced, it is likely that the hub bearings are at fault. If the free play is still evident with the footbrake depressed, then there is wear in the suspension joints or mountings.

5 Now grasp the wheel at the 9 o'clock and 3 o'clock positions, and try to rock it as before. Any movement felt now may again be caused by wear in the hub bearings or the steering track rod balljoints. If the inner or outer balljoint is worn, the visual movement will be obvious.

6 Using a large screwdriver or flat bar, check for wear in the suspension mounting bushes by levering between the relevant suspension component and its attachment point. Some movement is to be expected as the mountings are made of rubber, but excessive wear should be obvious. Also check the condition of any visible rubber bushes, looking for splits, cracks or contamination of the rubber.

7 With the car standing on its wheels, have an assistant turn the steering wheel back-and-forth about an eighth of a turn each way. There should be very little, if any, lost movement between the steering wheel and roadwheels. If this is not the case, closely observe the joints and mountings previously described, but in addition, check the steering column universal joints for wear, and the rack-and-pinion steering gear itself.

8 Check for any signs of fluid leakage around the front suspension struts and rear shock absorber. Should any fluid be noticed, the suspension strut or shock absorber is defective internally, and should be renewed. **Note:** *Suspension struts/shock absorbers should always be renewed in pairs on the same axle to ensure correct vehicle handling.*

9 The efficiency of the suspension strut/shock absorber may be checked by bouncing the vehicle at each corner. Generally speaking, the body will return to its normal position and stop after being depressed. If it rises and returns on a rebound, the suspension strut/shock absorber is probably suspect. Examine also the suspension strut/shock absorber upper and lower mountings for any signs of wear.

19 Power steering fluid level check

Note: *New fluid must be used when draining and refilling the steering system.*

1 Wipe clean the area around the power steering fluid reservoir, and then remove the filler cap. The cap has a dipstick, which has temperature markings when checking in cold or hot conditions.

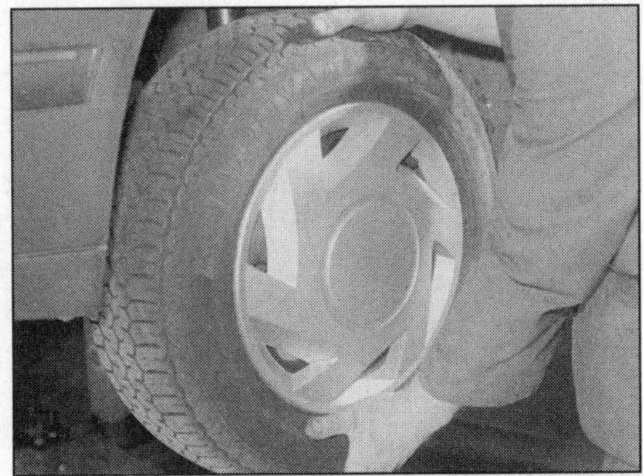

18.4 Check for wear in the hub bearings by grasping the wheel and trying to rock it

2 Wipe clean the dipstick and refit the reservoir cap. **Note:** *When the cap is removed, take care not to allow any dirt to enter the reservoir.*

3 Remove the reservoir cap and check the fluid level on the dipstick, taking into consideration the temperature of the fluid. If necessary, top-up with the specified fluid (see *Lubricants and fluids*).

4 When the fluid level is correct, check the sealing ring on the cap and refit the cap to the top of the reservoir.

5 Frequent need for topping-up indicates that there is a leak, which should be corrected as soon as possible.

20 Road test and exhaust emissions check

Instruments and electrical equipment

1 Check the operation of all instruments and electrical equipment including the air conditioning system.

2 Make sure that all instruments read correctly, and switch on all electrical equipment in turn, to check that it functions properly.

Steering and suspension

3 Check for any abnormalities in the steering, suspension, handling or road 'feel'.

4 Drive the vehicle, and check that there are no unusual vibrations or noises, which may indicate wear in the driveshafts, wheel bearings, etc.

5 Check that the steering feels positive, with no excessive 'sloppiness', or roughness, and check for any suspension noises when cornering and driving over bumps.

Drivetrain

6 Check the performance of the engine, clutch (where applicable), gearbox/transmission and driveshafts.

7 Listen for any unusual noises from the engine, clutch and gearbox/transmission.

8 Make sure the engine runs smoothly at idle, and there is no hesitation on accelerating.

9 Check that, where applicable, the clutch action is smooth and progressive, that the drive is taken up smoothly, and that the pedal travel is not excessive. Also listen for any noises when the clutch pedal is depressed.

10 On manual gearbox models, check that all gears can be engaged smoothly without noise, and that the gear lever action is smooth and not abnormally vague or 'notchy'.

11 On automatic transmission models, make sure that all gearchanges occur smoothly, without snatching, and without an increase in engine speed between changes. Check that all the gear positions can be selected with the vehicle at rest. If any problems are found, they should be referred to a Mercedes-Benz dealer.

12 Listen for a metallic clicking sound from the front of the vehicle, as the vehicle is driven slowly in a circle with the steering on full-lock. Carry out this check in both directions. If a clicking noise is heard, this indicates wear in a driveshaft joint, in which case renew the joint if necessary.

Braking system

13 Make sure that the vehicle does not pull to one side when braking, and that the wheels do not lock when braking hard.

14 Check that there is no vibration through the steering when braking.

15 Check that the handbrake operates correctly without excessive movement of the lever, and that it holds the vehicle stationary on a slope.

16 Test the operation of the brake servo unit as follows. With the engine off, depress the footbrake four or five times to exhaust the vacuum. Hold the brake pedal depressed, and then start the engine. As the engine starts, there should be a noticeable 'give' in the brake pedal as vacuum builds-up. Allow the engine to run for at least two minutes, and then switch it off. If the brake pedal is depressed now, it should be possible to detect a hiss from the servo as the pedal is depressed. After about four or five applications, no further hissing should be heard, and the pedal should feel considerably harder.

17 Under controlled emergency braking, the pulsing of the ABS unit must be felt at the footbrake pedal.

Exhaust emissions check

18 Although not part of the manufacturer's maintenance schedule, this check will normally be carried out on a regular basis according to the country the vehicle is operated in. Currently in the UK, exhaust emissions testing is included as part of the annual MOT test after the vehicle is 3 years old.

Every 2 years

21 Manual transmission oil level check

1 Park the car on a level surface. For improved access to the filler/level plug, apply the handbrake, then jack up the front of the vehicle and support it on axle stands (see *Jacking and vehicle support*), but note that the rear of the vehicle should also be raised to ensure an accurate level check. The oil level must be checked before the car is driven, or at least 5 minutes after the engine has been switched off. If the oil is checked immediately after driving the car, some of the oil will remain distributed around the transmission components, resulting in an inaccurate level reading.

2 Undo the retaining screws and remove the engine undertray. Wipe clean the area around the transmission filler/level plug, which is situated, on the front of the transmission casing, facing the engine **(see illustration)**.

3 The oil level should reach the lower edge of the filler/level hole. A certain amount of oil will have gathered behind the filler/level plug, and will trickle out when it is removed; this does **not** necessarily indicate that the level is correct. To ensure that a true level is established, wait until the initial trickle has stopped, then add oil as necessary until a trickle of new oil can be seen emerging. The level will be correct when the flow ceases; use only good-quality oil of the specified type.

21.2 Transmission filler/level plug (upper) and drain plug (lower) locations

4 If the transmission has been overfilled so that oil flows out when the filler/level plug is removed, check that the car is completely level (front-to-rear and side-to-side), and allow the surplus to drain off into a suitable container.

5 When the oil level is correct, refit the filler/level plug and tighten it to the specified torque. Wipe off any spilt oil then refit the engine undertray(s), tighten the retaining screws securely, and lower the car to the ground.

22 Bodywork and underbody protection check

Raise and support the vehicle on axle stands (see *Jacking and vehicle support*). Using an electric torch or lead light, inspect the entire underside of the vehicle, paying particular attention to the wheel arches. Look for any damage to the flexible underbody coating, which may crack or flake off with age, leading to corrosion. Also check that the wheel arch liners are securely attached with any clips provided – if they come loose, dirt may get in behind the liners and defeat their purpose. If there is any damage to the underseal, or any corrosion, it should be repaired before the damage gets too serious.

23.2 Locking clip (arrowed) in top of dipstick tube

Check the bodywork for stone chips and scratches. Either touch them up yourself (see Chapter 12) or have the work done by someone more experienced.

23 Automatic transmission fluid level check

Note: *There is no dipstick fitted to the transmission and one will need to be purchased (part no 168 589 01 21 00) from a Mercedes-Benz dealer to carry out this work. An accurate fluid level check can only be made with the transmission fluid at the correct temperature. If it is not possible to ascertain this temperature, it is strongly recommended that the check be made by a Mercedes-Benz dealer who will have the instrumentation to do this. At the same time they can check the transmission electronics for fault codes. Overfilling or underfilling adversely affects the function of the transmission.*

1 Make sure the transmission oil is warm and shift the gear lever through all gears to circulate the oil, then park the vehicle on level ground and engage P or N with the selector lever.

2 Using a screwdriver release the locking clip from the cap on the top of the filling pipe and remove the cap. **Note:** *A new locking clip will be needed for refitting* ***(see illustration).***

3 When the transmission is cold, the oil level indicator must be between marks 2 and 4 (30°C). The hot oil level must be between marks 8 and 12 (70°C to 80°C).

4 Check the transmission oil temperature (Mercedes-Benz dealers have a handheld tester) with the selector lever in one of the following lever positions: P, R, N or D.

5 Insert dipstick as far down as possible and then remove to take reading on the end of the stick. If required, top-up the fluid through the dipstick tube to the recommended level. When fluid is added to the transmission, carry out the procedure in paragraph 1 before rechecking the fluid level.

6 When the fluid level is correct, fit the cap to the top of the dipstick tube and insert a new locking clip **(see illustration)**.

7 Frequent need for topping-up indicates that there is a leak, which should be corrected as soon as possible.

24 Brake (and clutch) fluid renewal

Warning: Brake hydraulic fluid can harm your eyes and damage painted surfaces, so use extreme caution when handling and pouring it. Do not use fluid that has been standing open for some time, as it absorbs moisture from the air. Excess moisture can cause a dangerous loss of braking effectiveness.

1 The procedure is similar to that for the bleeding of the hydraulic system as described in Chapter 9, except that the brake fluid reservoir should be emptied by syphoning, using a clean poultry baster or similar before starting, and allowance should be made for the old fluid to be expelled when bleeding a section of the circuit. Since the clutch hydraulic system also uses fluid from the brake system reservoir, it should also be bled at the same time by referring to Chapter 6.

2 Working as described in Chapter 9, open the first bleed screw in the sequence, and pump the brake pedal gently until nearly all the old fluid has been emptied from the master cylinder reservoir.

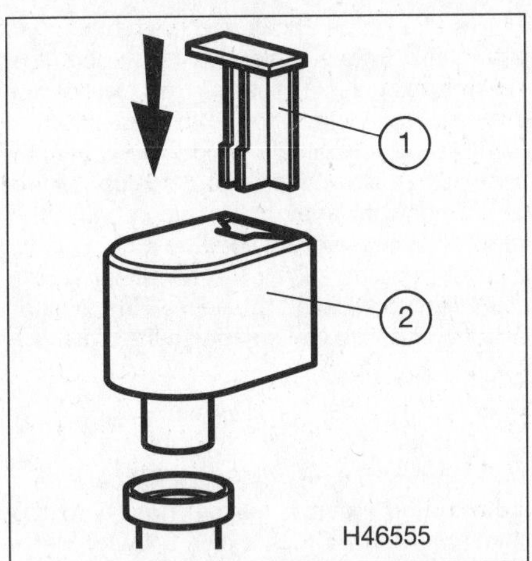

23.6 Refit the cap (2) and insert a new locking clip (1)

3 Top-up to the MAX level with new fluid, and continue pumping until only the new fluid remains in the reservoir, and new fluid can be seen emerging from the bleed screw. Tighten the screw, and top the reservoir level up to the MAX level line **(see illustration)**.

4 Work through all the remaining bleed screws in the sequence until new fluid can be seen at all of them. Be careful to keep the master cylinder reservoir topped-up to above the MIN level at all times, or air may enter the system and greatly increase the length of the task.

5 When the operation is complete, check that all bleed screws are securely tightened, and that their dust caps are refitted. Wash off all

24.3 The fluid level should be between the MAX and MIN markings

traces of spilt fluid, and recheck the master cylinder reservoir fluid level.

6 On models with a manual transmission unit, once the brake fluid has been changed the clutch fluid should also be renewed. Referring to Chapter 6, bleed the clutch until new fluid is seen to be emerging from the slave cylinder bleed screw, keeping the master cylinder fluid level above the MIN level line at all times to prevent air entering the system. Once the new fluid emerges, securely tighten the bleed screw then disconnect and remove the bleeding equipment. Securely refit the dust cap then wash off all traces of spilt fluid.

7 On all models, ensure the master cylinder fluid level is correct (see *Weekly checks*) and thoroughly check the operation of the brakes and (where necessary) clutch before taking the car on the road.

Every 3 years

25 Coolant renewal

Note: *This work is every 15 years/155 000 miles in the Mercedes-Benz schedule for later models if the recommended Mercedes-Benz coolant antifreeze/inhibitor is used. However, if standard antifreeze/inhibitor is used, the work should be carried out at the recommended interval.*

Warning: Wait until the engine is cold before starting this procedure. Do not allow antifreeze to come in contact with your skin, or with the painted surfaces of the vehicle. Rinse off spills immediately with plenty of water. Never leave antifreeze lying around in an open container, or in a puddle in the driveway or on the garage floor. Children and pets are attracted by its sweet smell, but antifreeze can be fatal if ingested.

Cooling system draining

1 With the engine completely cold, unscrew the expansion tank cap.

2 Firmly apply the handbrake then jack up the front of the vehicle and support it on axle stands (see *Jacking and vehicle support*). Undo the retaining screws and remove the engine undertray to gain access to the base of the radiator.

3 Position a suitable container beneath the coolant drain outlet, which is located to the bottom right-hand side of the radiator. Unscrew the drain plug (there is no need to remove it completely) and allow the coolant to drain into the container, through the outlet pipe **(see illustrations)**. If required a length of pipe can be fitted over the outlet pipe to direct the coolant flow.

4 To fully drain the system, also undo the cylinder block drain plug, which is located at the front of the cylinder block **(see illustration)**.

25.3a Slacken the drain screw (arrowed) . . .

25.3b . . . and fit tube to drain outlet (bumper removed for clarity)

25.4 Cylinder block drain plug location – arrowed

5 If the coolant has been drained for a reason other than renewal, then provided it is clean, it can be re-used.

6 Once all the coolant has drained, securely tighten the radiator drain plug. Where necessary, also tighten the cylinder block drain plug. Refit the undertray, and tighten the retaining screws securely.

Cooling system flushing

7 If the recommended Mercedes-Benz coolant has not been used and coolant renewal has been neglected, or if the antifreeze mixture has become diluted, the cooling system may gradually lose efficiency, as the coolant passages become restricted due to rust, scale deposits, and other sediment. The cooling system efficiency can be restored by flushing the system clean.

8 The radiator should be flushed separately from the engine, to avoid excess contamination.

Radiator flushing

9 To flush the radiator, first tighten the radiator drain plug.

10 Disconnect the top and bottom hoses and any other relevant hoses from the radiator (see Chapter 3).

11 Insert a garden hose into the radiator top inlet. Direct a flow of clean water through the radiator, and continue flushing until clean water emerges from the radiator bottom outlet.

12 If after a reasonable period, the water still does not run clear, the radiator can be flushed with a good proprietary cleaning agent. It is important that their manufacturer's instructions are followed carefully. If the contamination is particularly bad, insert the hose in the radiator bottom outlet, and reverse-flush the radiator.

Engine flushing

13 To flush the engine, remove the thermostat (see Chapter 3).

14 With the bottom hose disconnected from the radiator, insert a garden hose into the coolant housing. Direct a clean flow of water through the engine, and continue flushing until clean water emerges from the radiator bottom hose.

15 When flushing is complete, refit the thermostat and reconnect the hoses (see Chapter 3).

Cooling system filling

16 Before attempting to fill the cooling system, ensure the drain plug is securely closed and make sure that all hoses are connected and are securely retained by their clips. If the recommended Mercedes-Benz coolant is not being used, ensure that a suitable antifreeze mixture is used all year round, to prevent corrosion of the engine components (see following sub-Section).

17 Remove the expansion tank filler cap and slowly fill the system with the coolant. Continue to fill the cooling system until bubbles stop appearing in the expansion tank. Help to bleed the air from the system by repeatedly squeezing the radiator bottom hose.

18 When no more bubbles appear, top the coolant level up to the MAX level mark then securely refit the cap to the expansion tank.

19 Run the engine at a fast idle speed until the cooling fan cuts in. Wait for the fan to stop then switch the engine off and allow the engine to cool.

20 When the engine has cooled, check the coolant level with reference to *Weekly checks*. Top-up the level if necessary, and refit the expansion tank cap.

Antifreeze mixture

21 If the recommended Mercedes-Benz coolant is not being used, the antifreeze should always be renewed at the specified intervals. This is necessary not only to maintain the antifreeze properties, but also to prevent corrosion, which would otherwise occur as the corrosion inhibitors become progressively less effective.

22 Always use an ethylene-glycol based antifreeze which is suitable for use in mixed-metal cooling systems. The quantity of antifreeze and levels of protection are indicated in the Specifications.

23 Before adding antifreeze, the cooling system should be completely drained, preferably flushed, and all hoses checked for condition and security.

24 After filling with antifreeze, a label should be attached to the expansion tank, stating the type and concentration of antifreeze used, and the date installed. Any subsequent topping-up should be made with the same type and concentration of antifreeze.

Caution: Do not use engine antifreeze in the windscreen/tailgate washer system, as it will damage the vehicle paintwork. A screenwash additive should be added to the washer system in the quantities stated on the bottle.

Every 4 years or 50 000 miles

26 Air filter element renewal

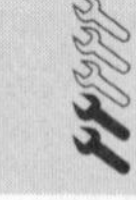

1 The air filter element is located in the air filter housing on top of the engine.

2 To make access easier, unclip the windscreen washer reservoir from the inner wing panel and move it to one side.

3 Slacken the retaining clip and disconnect the air intake hose **(see illustration)**.

4 Rotate the cover on the end of the air filter housing anti-clockwise and remove **(see illustration)**.

5 Withdraw the filter element from the housing **(see illustration)**.

6 Remove any debris that may have collected inside the air cleaner.

7 Fit a new air filter element into position, ensuring that it is located correctly. **Note:** *On models after June 2000 the air filter and air filter housing end cover where modified. When*

26.3 Disconnect the air intake hose

26.4 Rotate the end cover . . .

26.5 . . . and withdraw the air filter

27.2 Disconnect the fuel inlet pipe . . .

27.3 . . . and the fuel outlet pipe . . .

27.4a . . . undo the securing screws . . .

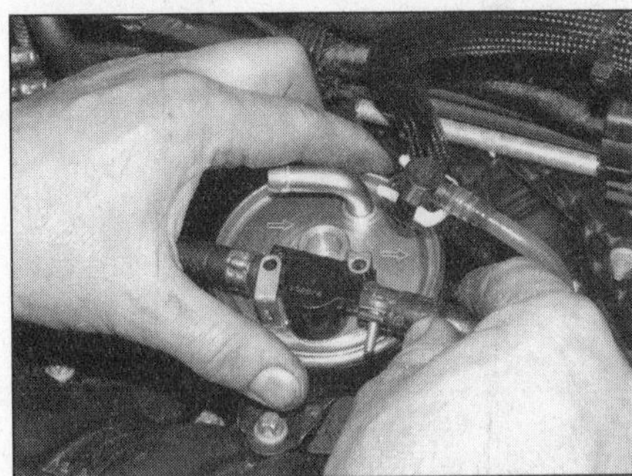
27.4b . . . and release the hose connection from the filter

27.5 Withdraw the filter from the mounting bracket

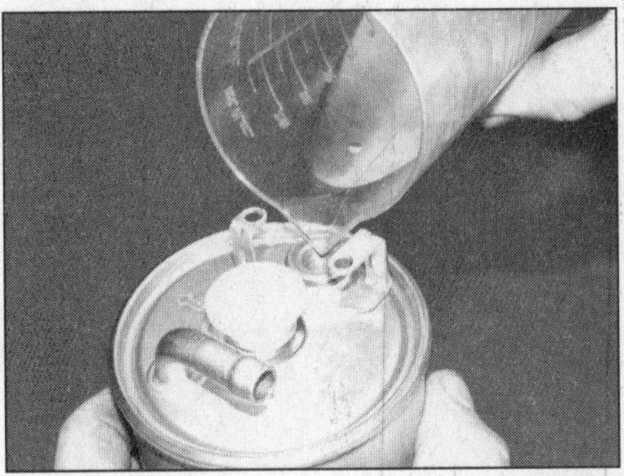
27.6 Topping-up the filter with clean fuel

fitting a new filter, make sure the modified end cover is fitted.

8 Refit the end cover, turning it clockwise to lock into position, making sure that the air filter is located correctly.

9 Refitting is the reversal of the removal procedure.

27 Fuel filter renewal

1 The fuel filter is mounted on the inlet manifold at the rear of the cylinder head. Place rags around the filter to absorb any fuel that may be spilt.

2 Release the securing clip and disconnect the fuel inlet pipe on the top of the fuel filter **(see illustration)**. Note the direction arrows on the top of the filter.

3 Slide out the white locking clip and disconnect the low-pressure fuel outlet pipe from the top of the fuel filter **(see illustration)**.

4 Undo the two retaining screws and remove the hose connection from the fuel filter housing **(see illustrations)**.

5 Slacken the pinch-bolt at the rear of the fuel filter, and then slide the filter out from the mounting bracket **(see illustration)**. Discard the fuel filter safely.

6 Refit the new fuel filter using a reversal of the removal procedure. To help with restarting the vehicle, top the fuel filter up with clean fuel before refitting the hoses **(see illustration).**

7 Make sure the fuel hoses are fitted in the correct positions as noted on removal.

8 With all fuel lines securely connected, start and run the engine at idle, then check around the fuel filter for fuel leaks. **Note:** *It may take a few seconds of cranking before the engine starts.*

Notes

Chapter 2 Part A:
Petrol engine in-car repair procedures

Contents

Degrees of difficulty

Easy, suitable for novice with little experience 	**Fairly easy,** suitable for beginner with some experience	**Fairly difficult,** suitable for competent DIY mechanic	**Difficult,** suitable for experienced DIY mechanic	**Very difficult,** suitable for expert DIY or professional 

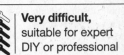

Specifications

General

Type	Four-cylinder in-line, chain-driven single (SOHC) overhead camshaft, four stroke, liquid-cooled
Engine capacities:	
A140	1397 cc
A160	1598 cc
A190	1898 cc
A210	2084 cc
Manufacturer's engine codes*:	
1397 cc	166.940
1598 cc	166.960
1898 cc	166.990
2084 cc	166.995
Maximum power output:	
1397 cc	60 kW at 5000 rpm
1598 cc	75 kW at 5500 rpm
1898 cc	92 kW at 5500 rpm
2084 cc	103 kW @ 5500 rpm
Maximum torque output:	
1397 cc	130 Nm at 3750 rpm
1598 cc	150 Nm at 4000 rpm
1898 cc	180 Nm at 5500 rpm
2084 cc	205 Nm @ 4000 rpm
Bore:	
1397 cc and 1598 cc	80.00 mm
1898 cc and 2084 cc	84.00 mm
Stroke:	
1397 cc	69.50 mm
1598 cc	75.50 mm
1898 cc	85.60 mm
2084 cc	94.00 mm
Compression ratio:	
1397 cc 1598 cc and 2048 cc	11.0 : 1
1898 cc	10.8 : 1
Firing order	1 – 3 – 4 – 2
No 1 cylinder location	Crankshaft pulley end
Direction of crankshaft rotation	Clockwise (when viewed from right-hand side of vehicle)

* **Note:** *See 'Vehicle identification' at the end of this manual for the location of engine code markings.*

Lubrication system

Oil pump type	Chain-driven from crankshaft
Minimum oil pressure (oil temperature 90°C):	
At 1000 rpm	1.5 bar
At 3000 rpm	4.0 bar
At 5750 rpm	4.5 bar

Cylinder head bolts

Length when new	183 mm
Maximum length (renew bolt if longer)	186 mm

Connecting rod bolts

Length when new	38.0 mm
Maximum length (renew bolt if longer)	38.4 mm

Torque wrench settings

	Nm	lbf ft
Big-end bearing caps bolts*:		
Stage 1	5	4
Stage 2	15	11
Stage 3	Angle-tighten a further 90°	
Camshaft cover	8	6
Camshaft housing to cylinder head	14	10
Camshaft position sensor	8	6
Camshaft sprocket bolts:		
Stage 1	20	15
Stage 2	Angle-tighten a further 60°	
Coolant pump pulley	8	6
Crankshaft oil seal housing	8	6
Crankshaft pulley bolt:		
Stage 1	200	148
Stage 2	Angle-tighten a further 90°	
Cylinder head bolts to cylinder block:		
Stage 1	35	26
Stage 2	Angle-tighten a further 90°	
Stage 3	Angle-tighten a further 90°	
Cylinder head bolts to timing chain cover	20	15
Crankshaft speed sender	8	6
Driveplate bolts (new)*:		
Stage 1	45	33
Stage 2	Angle-tighten a further 90°	
Engine mountings:		
Front mountings:		
Bolt to engine mounting bracket	55	41
Nut to subframe	40	30
Rear mountings:		
Bolt to engine mounting bracket	25	18
Bolt to subframe	25	18
Nut to subframe	25	18
Exhaust manifold to cylinder head	40	30
Flywheel bolts (new)*:		
Stage 1	45	33
Stage 2	Angle-tighten a further 90°	
Knock sensor	20	15
Main bearing cap bolts:*		
Stage 1	29	21
Stage 2	Angle-tighten a further 90°	
Oil filter cap	25	18
Oil level and temperature sender	8	6
Oil level/pressure sensor-to-sump bolts	8	6
Oil pump to cylinder block	14	10
Sump	14	10
Sump oil drain plug	25	18
Thermostat housing	8	6
Timing chain tensioner	8	6
Timing cover:		
Cover bolts to cylinder head	20	15
Cover bolts to cylinder block	8	6

** Use thread-locking compound.*

1 General information

How to use this Chapter

This Part of Chapter 2 describes those repair procedures that can reasonably be carried out on the engine while it remains in the vehicle. If the engine has been removed from the vehicle and is being dismantled as described in Part C, any preliminary dismantling procedures can be ignored.

Note that while it may be possible physically to overhaul certain items while the engine is in the vehicle, such tasks are not usually carried out as separate operations, and usually require the execution of several additional procedures (not to mention the cleaning of components and of oilways); for this reason, all such tasks are classed as major overhaul procedures, and are described in Part C of this Chapter.

Engine description

The engine is a single overhead camshaft (SOHC), in-line four-cylinder unit, which is mounted transversely at the front of the vehicle, with the transmission bolted to the left-hand end of the engine. It has a multipoint fuel injection system.

The cylinder block, cylinder head and camshaft housing are all cast in aluminium alloy. The cylinder bores are machined in the cylinder block. The crankshaft has five main bearings, and thrustwashers are fitted to number 3 main bearing to control crankshaft endfloat.

Camshaft drive is by chain from the crankshaft, and the chain is tensioned by a hydraulic tensioner. The valves are closed by coil springs and the camshafts actuate the valves by roller-type rocker arms and hydraulic tappets. This is an eight-valve engine with 2 valves per cylinder.

The flywheel is located on a flange at the left-hand end of the crankshaft.

The main bearings and the big-end bearings are of shell type, whilst the connecting rod small-end bearings are of the bronze bush type, being pressed into the connecting rod and reamed to suit.

The oil pump is chain-driven from the front of the crankshaft. Oil is drawn from the sump through a strainer and circulated through an externally-mounted filter to the various engine components.

Operations with engine in car

The following work can be carried out with the engine in the vehicle:

a) Compression pressure – testing.
b) Timing chain – renewal.
c) Timing chain tensioner – removal and refitting.
d) Camshaft and roller/rocker arms – removal and refitting.
e) Cylinder head – removal and refitting.*
f) Cylinder head – decarbonising.
g) Engine/transmission mountings – inspection and renewal.

** Cylinder head dismantling procedures are detailed in Chapter 2C.*

2 Compression test – description and interpretation

1 When engine performance is down, or if misfiring occurs which cannot be attributed to the ignition or fuel systems, a compression test can provide diagnostic clues as to the engine's condition. If the test is performed regularly, it can give warning of trouble before any other symptoms become apparent.

2 The engine must be fully warmed-up to normal operating temperature, the battery must be fully charged, and the spark plugs together with the ignition coil module must be removed as described in Chapter 1A. The aid of an assistant will also be required.

3 Remove the fuel pump relay from the fusebox, next to the battery, under the driver's side floor panel **(see illustration)**.

4 Fit a compression tester to the No 1 cylinder spark plug hole – the type of tester which screws into the plug thread is to be preferred.

5 Have the assistant hold the throttle wide open and crank the engine on the starter motor; after one or two revolutions, the compression pressure should build-up to a maximum figure and then stabilise. Record the highest reading obtained, and then repeat the test on the remaining three cylinders, recording the pressure in each.

6 The compression should build-up quickly in a healthy engine; low compression on the first stroke, followed by gradually increasing pressure on successive strokes, indicates worn piston rings.

7 A low compression reading on the first stroke, which does not build-up during successive strokes, indicates leaking valves or a blown head gasket (a cracked head could also be the cause). Deposits on the underside of the valve heads can also cause low compression.

2.3 Fuel pump relay (arrowed) – this location may vary, see Chapter 12

8 Due to the variety of testers available, and the fluctuation in starter motor speed when cranking the engine, different readings are often obtained when carrying out the compression test. For this reason, specific compression pressure readings are not quoted by Mercedes-Benz. However, the most important factor is that the compression pressures are uniform in all four cylinders, and that is what the test is mainly concerned with.

9 If the pressure in any cylinder is considerably lower than the others, carry out the following test to isolate the cause. Introduce a teaspoonful of clean oil into that cylinder through its spark plug hole and repeat the test.

10 If the addition of oil temporarily improves the compression pressure, this indicates that bore or piston wear is responsible for the pressure loss. No improvement suggests that leaking or burnt valves, or a blown head gasket, may be to blame.

11 A low reading from two adjacent cylinders is almost certainly due to the head gasket having blown between them; the presence of coolant in the engine oil will confirm this.

12 If one cylinder is about 20 percent lower than the others and the engine has a slightly rough idle; a worn camshaft lobe could be the cause.

13 On completion of the test, refit the spark plugs and ignition coil module. Refit the fuel pump relay. Note that carrying out this test by removing the relay may result In one or more fault codes being stored by the engine management system. These codes can be erased by a Mercedes-Benz dealer or specialist with the right equipment.

3 Engine assembly and valve timing marks – general information and usage

1 Top dead centre (TDC) is the highest point in its travel up-and-down its cylinder bore that each piston reaches as the crankshaft rotates. While each piston reaches TDC both at the top of the compression stroke and again at the top of the exhaust stroke, for the purpose of timing the engine, TDC refers to the No 1 piston position at the top of its compression stroke.

2 No 1 piston and cylinder are at the right-hand (timing chain) end of the engine. Note that the crankshaft rotates clockwise when viewed from the right-hand side of the vehicle.

3 Switch off the ignition and all electrical consumers, and remove the ignition key. Remove all four spark plugs as described in Chapter 1A.

4 Apply the handbrake, then jack up the front of the vehicle and support it on axle stands (see *Jacking and vehicle support*). Remove the right-hand front roadwheel.

5 Undo the retaining screws, release any securing clips and remove the inner wheel arch liners **(see illustrations)**. Note the

3.5a Disconnect the wiring connectors . . .

3.5b . . . and remove the inner wheel arch liner

3.7 TDC timing mark on engine cover – arrowed

3.8 Align mark (A) with pointers (B) on the bearing cap

3.9a Disconnect the wiring connector . . .

wiring connectors for the ABS and brake pad warning light will need to be disconnected before the liner can be removed.

6 Remove the camshaft cover as described in Section 4.

7 Turn the engine with an Allen key socket on the crankshaft pulley bolt until the TDC markings on the front pulley align with the TDC mark on the timing chain cover **(see illustration)**.

8 In this position the alignment mark on the camshaft sprocket should be in line with the markings on No 1 camshaft bearing cap **(see illustration).** The camshaft lobes on No 1 cylinder should be facing upwards, the engine is now at TDC on No 1 piston.

9 A further check, if required, is to disconnect the wiring connector from the TDC sensor, which is positioned to the transmission end of the cylinder head, directly above the flywheel. Undo the retaining bolt and withdraw the sensor from the cylinder block. Note that it may be necessary to disconnect the air intake hose to access the TDC sensor. Insert a locking tool into the TDC sensor hole so that it locates in the edge of the flywheel; a locking tool can be made up of a deep socket and 6 mm bolt **(see illustrations).**

10 Refitting of components, is the reversal of the removal procedure with reference to the relevant Chapters.

4 Camshaft cover – removal and refitting

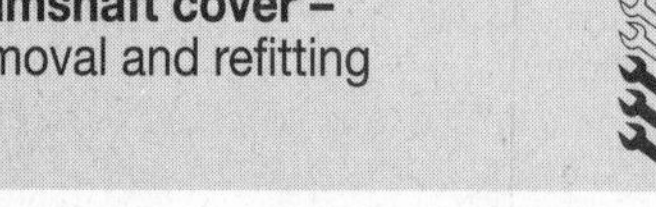

Removal

1 Remove the air cleaner housing and intake manifold as described in Chapter 4A.

2 Disconnect the wiring connector from the camshaft position sensor on the timing chain end of the camshaft cover **(see illustration)**.

3 Disconnect the crankcase breather hose from the transmission end of the camshaft cover.

4 Where fitted, disengage the secondary air

3.9b . . . and remove the retaining screw from the TDC sensor

3.9c Homemade tool, using a deep socket and a 6 mm bolt sticking out of the end

4.2 Disconnect the camshaft position sensor

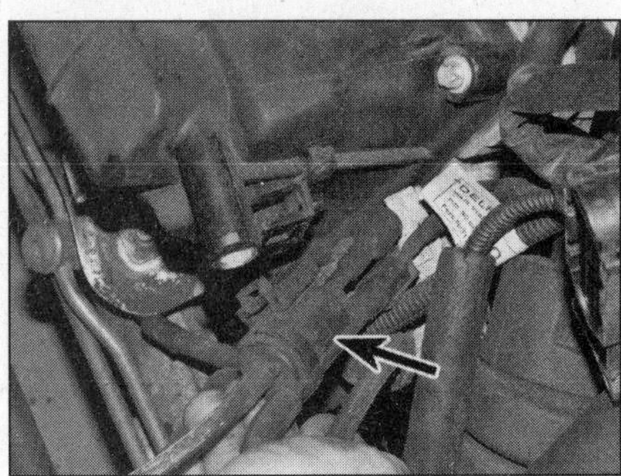

4.4 Secondary air pump switchover valve – arrowed

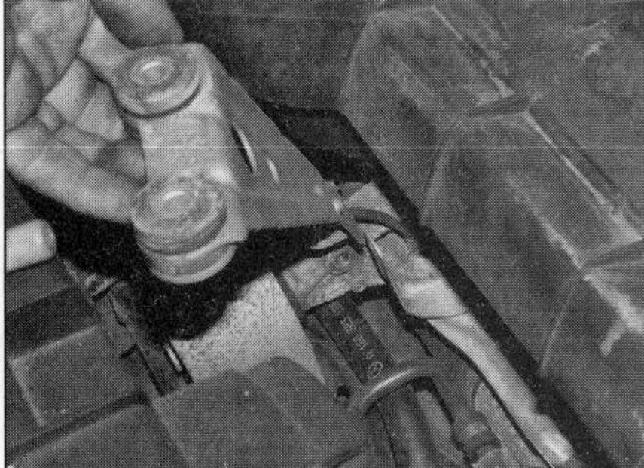

4.5 Remove the mounting bracket

4.6 Remove the mounting bracket – arrowed

pump switchover valve from the camshaft cover **(see illustration)**.

5 Undo the retaining bolt and remove the mounting bracket from the front right-hand corner of the camshaft cover, noting its fitted position **(see illustration)**.

6 Undo the retaining bolts from the front left-hand corner of the camshaft cover and remove the mounting bracket, noting its fitted position **(see illustration)**.

7 Working your way around the outside of the camshaft cover, undo the remaining bolts, and lift the cover from the cylinder head **(see illustration)**. Make sure that any mounting bracket positions are noted for refitting. Retrieve the rubber gasket and discard it, a new one will be required for refitting.

Refitting

8 Refitting is the reversal of removal. Fit new rubber gasket to the camshaft cover, making sure it is located securely **(see illustration)**.

5 Timing chain and tensioner – removal and refitting

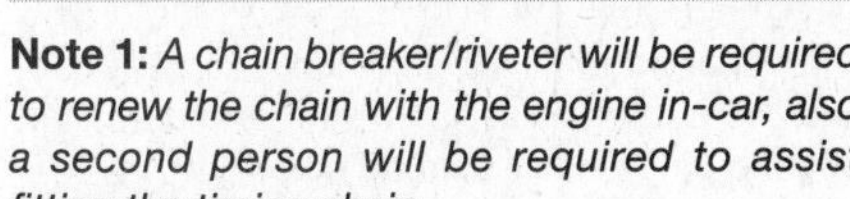

Note 1: *A chain breaker/riveter will be required to renew the chain with the engine in-car, also a second person will be required to assist fitting the timing chain.*

Note 2: *If the chain needs to be renewed as a complete assembly, then the engine will need to be removed, as there is not enough room for the removal of the timing chain cover (see Chapter 2C).*

1 Set the engine to TDC as described in Section 3.

2 Unclip the coolant expansion tank and move it to one side, making sure the hoses do not get damaged.

3 Remove the camshaft cover as described in Section 4.

4 Mark the fitted position of the timing chain tensioner, as it has to be fitted the correct way around. Undo the two retaining bolts evenly as it is spring-loaded, and then withdraw it from the cylinder head **(see illustration)**. Remove the gasket/seal and discard, a new one will be required for refitting.

5 With the engine still in the TDC position, use a couple of cable ties to keep the timing chain on the camshaft sprocket. Put some clean rag into the timing chain recess to prevent anything dropping down into the engine **(see illustration)**.

6 Use the chain breaker to press out one of the timing chain pins and split the timing chain **(see illustrations)**.

7 Connect the new timing chain to the old chain and press the chain link pin back into position **(see illustration)**. **Note:** *Make sure the new chain is connected to the front part*

4.7 Removing the camshaft cover

4.8 Make sure the rubber gasket is located correctly

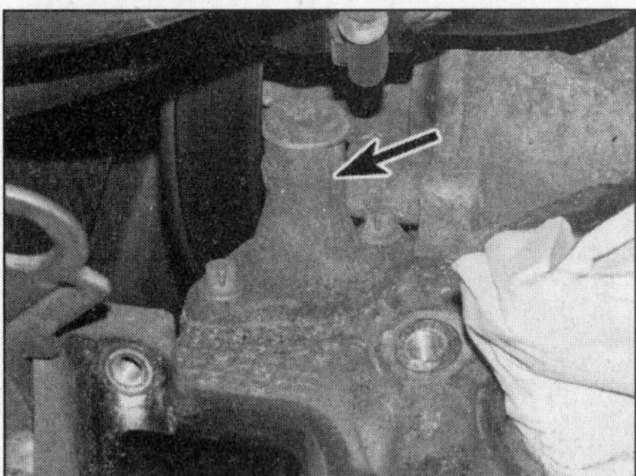

5.4 Timing chain adjuster – arrowed

5.5 Fasten cable ties around the chain and put clean rag in timing chain recess

5.6a Using a chain breaker . . .

5.6b . . . to push out the chain pin

5.7 Connect the new chain to the old chain

5.8a Keep a tight hold of the timing chain . . .

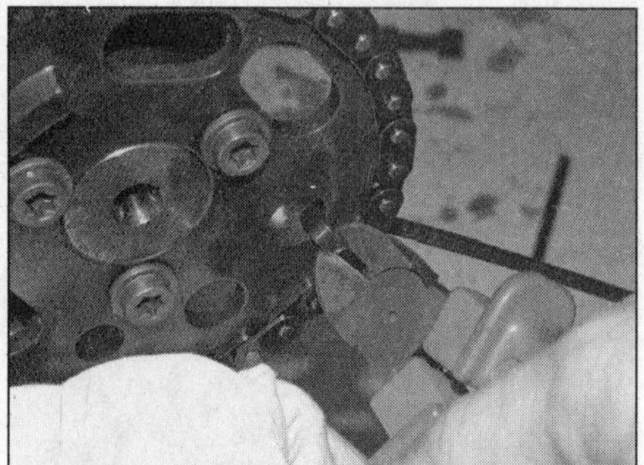

5.8b . . . and remove the cable ties

5.9 Keep the timing chain fitted around the sprocket

5.11a Use the chain breaker again . . .

5.11b . . . and disconnect the old chain from the new one

of the chain, as the engine has to be turned clockwise, in the direction of rotation, to feed the chain around the sprockets.

8 With the new chain connected securely to the old chain, take a firm hold of both ends of the chain and remove the cable ties from the camshaft sprocket **(see illustrations)**. Remove the clean rag from around the timing chain before turning the engine.

9 With the aid of an assistant, turn the engine in the direction of rotation. Keeping the timing chain taut, feed it around the crankshaft sprocket, until the new chain comes all the way around to the camshaft sprocket **(see illustration)**.

10 Cable tie both ends of the timing chain back to the camshaft sprocket, and refit the clean rag back into the timing chain recess.

11 Use the chain breaker to press out the timing chain pin and split the old timing chain from the new timing chain **(see illustrations)**. **Note:** *Make sure the chain is pulled tight on the lower section of the engine, and the upper section slack to allow for the fitting of the chain tensioner.*

12 Check that the TDC marks on the crankshaft pulley and timing chain cover are aligned, and the marks on the camshaft and camshaft bearing cap are still aligned correctly.

13 Fit the new timing chain link, using the timing chain riveter to connect the two ends of the chain securely **(see illustrations)**. Always read the instructions that come with the chain riveter, as there are many different types available. The link pins need to be riveted securely, to prevent the chain coming apart.

14 Remove the clean rag from the timing chain recess, and fit the timing chain tensioner complete with new gasket, making sure it is fitted the correct way around as noted on removal **(see illustrations)**. With the tensioner now fitted, check the timing marks are still in line.

15 Rotate the engine two complete turns and check the timing marks come back in alignment.

16 Refit the camshaft cover with reference to Section 4.

17 Refit the coolant expansion tank, making sure the hoses are routed correctly.

5.13a Fit the new chain link . . .

5.13b . . . and secure it in place with the riveter tool

5.14a Fit the tensioner with a new gasket

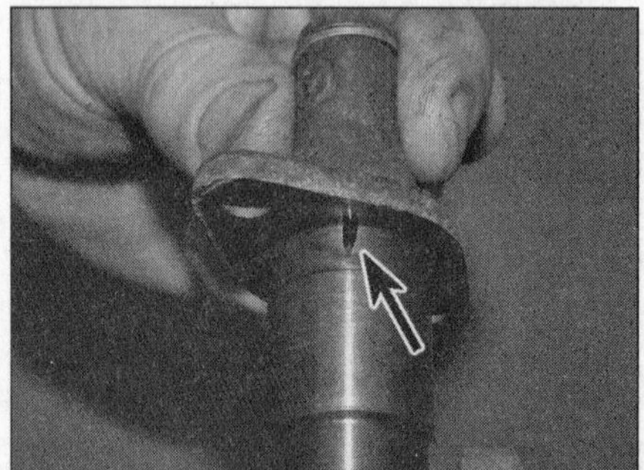

5.14b Make sure the oilway (arrowed) is fitted as noted on removal

6.4 Use a spanner to counterhold the camshaft

6.5 Secure the chain with a couple of cable ties

6.7 Keep the chain taut when removing the sprocket

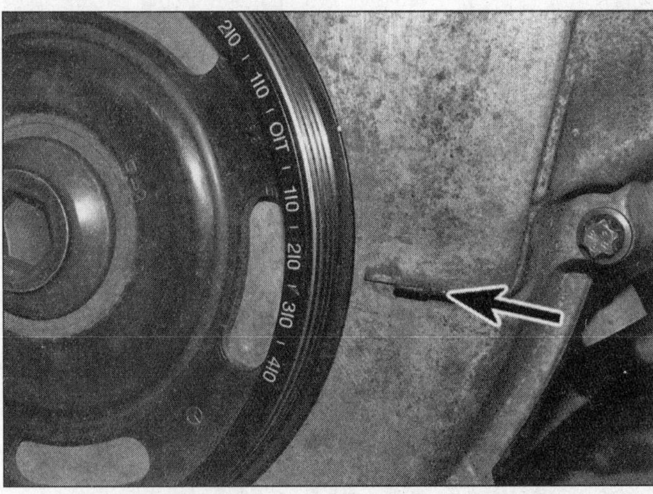

6.8 Timing mark on engine cover – arrowed

6.9 Make sure the markings (arrowed) are noted for refitting

6 Camshaft housing, camshaft and rocker arms – removal, inspection and refitting

Removal

1 Remove the camshaft cover as described in Section 4.

2 Unclip the coolant expansion tank and move it to one side, making sure the hoses do not get damaged.

3 Set the engine to TDC as described in Section 3.

4 While holding the camshaft in position, using a spanner on the hexagon part of the shaft, loosen the sprocket retaining bolts **(see illustration)**. Make sure the markings on the camshaft and housing are still aligned at TDC.

5 Using a couple of cable ties; secure the timing chain to the camshaft sprocket, so that it will stay in position for refitting **(see illustration)**.

6 Mark the fitted position of the timing chain tensioner, undo the two retaining bolts evenly as it is spring-loaded, then withdraw it from the cylinder head. Remove the gasket/seal and discard, a new one will be required for refitting.

7 The retaining bolts can now be removed and the sprocket withdrawn from the end of the camshaft. Keeping the timing chain taut, to prevent it coming off the crankshaft sprocket, secure the chain and sprocket to one side **(see illustration)**.

8 For the remaining removal procedure the pistons must be positioned halfway down their bores as a precaution against the valves touching them. Turn the crankshaft 20° anti-clockwise so that all of the pistons are slightly down their bores **(see illustration)**.

9 Progressively unscrew the mounting bolts and remove the camshaft bearing caps from the top of the camshaft housing. Check for markings on the bearing caps (they should be on the intake side), as they will need to be refitted in their original positions **(see illustration)**. If no markings are found on the bearing caps, then mark them with some paint.

10 With all the bearing caps removed, lift the camshaft from the camshaft/rocker arm housing.

11 The camshaft housing, complete with rocker arms, can now be lifted from the cylinder head **(see illustration)**. If it is tight, use a mallet or rubber hammer to tap the housing in several places in order to release it from the locating dowels.

12 With the housing on the bench, note the fitted position of the rocker shafts and remove the circlips from each end of the housing **(see illustration)**.

6.11 Removing the camshaft housing

6.12 Remove the circlip from the end of the housing

6.13a Withdraw the shaft (arrowed) . . .

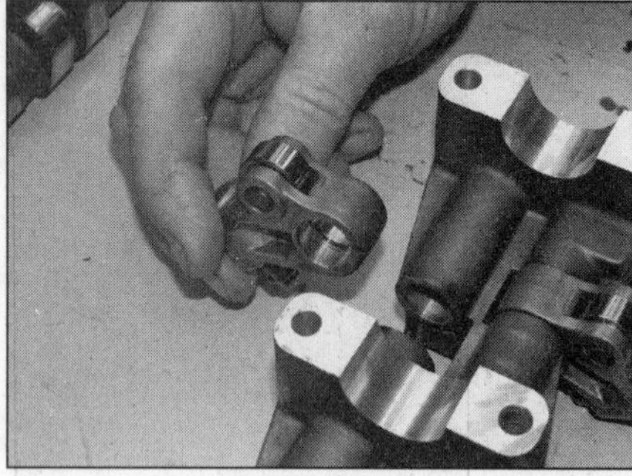

6.13b . . . and remove the roller/rocker arm

13 Obtain a suitable box with compartments for each of the roller/rocker arms, so that they can be identified for their correct position. Remove the rocker shafts from the housing and place the roller/rocker arms in the box, making sure they are identified for location to ensure correct refitting **(see illustrations)**.

Inspection

14 Thoroughly clean the camshafts and housing, making sure that the cylinder head upper mating surface and camshaft cover are clean.

Caution: Where applicable, make sure that any TDC alignment marks are not removed from the end of the camshaft and the housing.

15 Visually inspect camshaft for evidence of wear on the surfaces of the lobes and journals. Normally their surfaces should be smooth and have a dull shine; look for scoring, erosion or pitting and areas that appear highly polished, indicating excessive wear. Accelerated wear will occur once the hardened exterior of the camshaft has been damaged, so always renew worn items.

16 If the machined surfaces of the camshaft appear discoloured or blued, it is likely that it has been overheated at some point, probably due to inadequate lubrication.

17 If a new camshaft is required, make sure the correct shaft is fitted, as they are colour-coded for each model.

a) 1.4 litre engine (166.940) – white.
b) 1.6 litre engine (166.960) – reddish/pink.
c) 1.9 litre engine (166.990) – blue.
d) 2.1 litre engine (166.995) – green.

18 To measure the camshaft endfloat, temporarily locate it back in position on the housing with the bearing caps in place. Anchor a DTI gauge to the end of the housing and align the gauge probe with the camshaft axis **(see illustration)**. Push the camshaft to one end of the housing as far as it will travel, then rest the DTI gauge probe on the end of the camshaft, and zero the gauge display. Push the camshaft as far as it will go to the other end of the housing, and record the gauge reading. Verify the reading by pushing the camshaft back to its original position and checking that the gauge indicates zero again.

19 See your local Mercedes-Benz dealer to check if the measurement is within limit, as it was not available during the time of writing. Wear outside of this limit is unlikely to be confined to any one component, so renewal of the camshafts and housing must be considered.

20 Inspect the roller/rockers for obvious signs of wear or damage, and renew if necessary **(see illustration)**. Check that the oil holes in the rocker arms and rocker shafts are free from obstructions.

Refitting

21 Lubricate the roller/rocker arms and assemble the housing making sure that all the rockers and rocker shafts are fitted back to their original positions, as noted on removal. Fit new circlips to the end of the rocker shafts.

22 When assembled, refit the roller/rocker arm housing to the cylinder head, making sure all the rocker arms are pointing in the correct position.

23 Lubricate the camshaft journals and bearing surfaces in the camshaft housing, then locate the camshaft in position.

24 Set the camshaft to its TDC position, and refit the camshaft bearing caps in their original position as noted on removal. Progressively tighten the bolts, starting in the centre and working outwards in a spiral fashion.

25 Turn the engine 20° clockwise back to the TDC position.

26 Refit the timing chain and camshaft sprocket back onto the end of the camshaft with new bolts; making sure the TDC markings are still aligned. Tighten the new retaining bolts to the specified torque setting while holding them stationary as for removal.

27 Refit the timing chain tensioner, making sure that it is fitted correctly as noted on removal and tighten the bolts evenly to the specified torque. **Note:** *There is an oil feed hole to the tensioner, when fitting the new gasket, make sure the oil holes are aligned* ***(see illustration 5.14a and 5.14b).***

28 Remove the cable ties from the timing chain and sprocket, and then rotate the engine two full turns, and check that the TDC marks are re-aligned. See Section 3 for further information on checking the timing marks.

29 Refit the camshaft cover as described in Section 4.

30 Refit the coolant expansion tank, making sure the hoses are routed correctly.

7 Cylinder head – removal, inspection and refitting

Note: *The cylinder head must be removed with the engine cold. A new cylinder head gasket will be required on refitting, also new cylinder head bolts may be needed if they have stretched beyond specifications – see text.*

Removal

1 Drain the cooling system and engine oil, as described in Chapter 1A.

2 Remove the spark plugs as described in Chapter 1A.

3 Remove the camshaft cover as described in Section 4 of this Chapter.

4 Remove the exhaust manifold as described in Chapter 4C.

5 Disconnect the hoses from the shut-off valve, on the left-hand end of the cylinder head **(see illustrations)**.

6.18 Checking the camshaft endfloat using a DTI gauge

6.20 Inspect the roller/rocker arm for wear

7.5a Disconnect the hoses . . .

7.5b . . . from the shut-off valve

7.6a Disconnect the wiring connector . . .

7.6b . . . and the hoses

6 Disconnect the wiring connector and coolant hoses from the thermostat housing on the left-hand rear of the cylinder head **(see illustrations)**. If required, remove the thermostat housing as described in Chapter 3.
7 Remove the camshaft housing, rockers and camshaft as described in Section 6.
8 Using a trolley jack, support the engine from underneath, undo the retaining bolts and remove the engine mounting from the front right-hand end of the cylinder head **(see illustration)**.
9 Progressively slacken the cylinder head bolts in the **reverse** order to that given for tightening in paragraph 24. Remove the cylinder head bolts. **Note:** *The bolts may need to be renewed if they have stretched. See paragraph 17 – obtain new ones if required.*
10 With all the bolts removed, lift the cylinder head from the block, if the cylinder head is stuck, tap it with a soft-faced mallet to break the joint. **Do not** insert a lever into the gasket joint.
11 Lift the cylinder head gasket from the block.

Inspection

12 Dismantling and inspection of the cylinder head is covered in Chapter 2C.
13 The mating faces of the cylinder head and block must be perfectly clean before refitting the head.
14 Use a scraper to remove all traces of gasket and carbon, also clean the tops of the pistons. Take particular care with the aluminium surfaces, as the soft metal is easily damaged.
15 Make sure that debris is not allowed to enter the oil and water passages – this is particularly important for the oil circuit, as carbon could block the oil supply to the camshaft and crankshaft bearings. Using adhesive tape and paper, seal the water, oil and bolt holes in the cylinder block. To prevent carbon entering the gap between the pistons and bores, smear a little grease in the gap. After cleaning a piston, rotate the crankshaft so that the piston moves down the bore, and then wipe out the grease and carbon with a cloth rag. Clean the other piston crowns in the same way.
16 Check the head and block for nicks, deep scratches and other damage. If slight, they may be removed carefully with a file. More serious damage may be repaired by machining, but this is a specialist job. If warpage of the cylinder head is suspected, use a straight-edge to check it for distortion, as described in Part C of this Chapter.
17 Check the length of the cylinder head bolts, by measuring from the underside of the head **(see illustration)**; use new cylinder head bolts if the length is greater than the dimension listed in the Specifications at the beginning of this Chapter.

Refitting

18 If not already done, before refitting the cylinder head, the pistons must be positioned halfway down their bores as a precaution against the valves touching them. To do this turn the crankshaft 45° anti-clockwise.
19 Ensure that the cylinder head bolt holes in the cylinder block are clean and free of oil. Syringe or soak up any oil left in the bolt holes. This is most important in order that the correct bolt tightening torque can be applied, and to prevent the possibility of the block being cracked by hydraulic pressure when the bolts are tightened.
20 Apply sealant to the joint between the cylinder head and the timing chain cover **(see illustration)**.
21 Ensure that the cylinder head locating dowels are in place in the cylinder block, and then fit a new cylinder head gasket over the dowels. Ensure that it is fitted the correct way up, as noted on removal. Where applicable, the OBEN/TOP marking should also be uppermost. Note that Mercedes-Benz recommend that the gasket is only removed from its packaging immediately prior to fitting
22 Lower the cylinder head into position on the gasket, ensuring that it engages correctly over the dowels. Also align the lower chain guide with the locating pin inside the cylinder head **(see illustration)**.

7.8 Remove the front engine mounting – arrowed

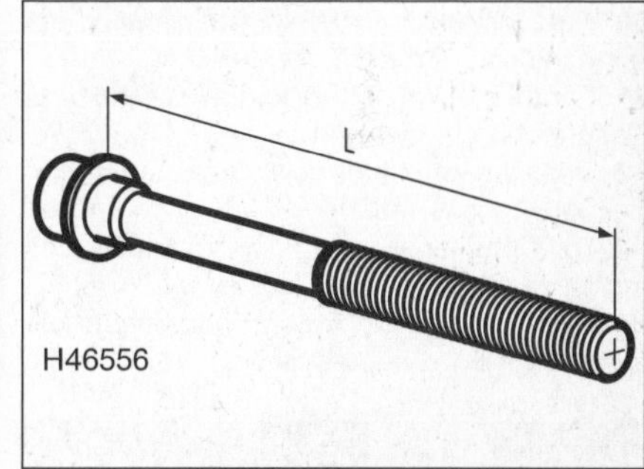

7.17 Check the length of the cylinder head bolts

7.20 Apply sealant to the arrowed areas

7.22 Locating pin for chain guide – arrowed

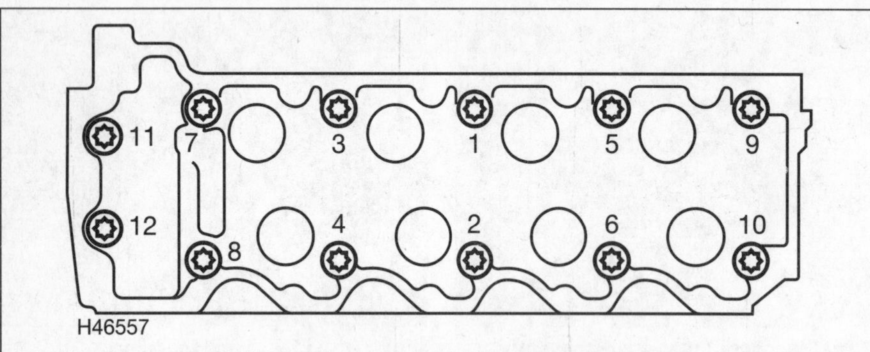

7.24 Tightening sequence for cylinder head bolts

23 Insert the new cylinder bolts and tighten them as far as possible by hand.

24 Working in sequence, tighten all the cylinder head bolts to the specified Stage 1 torque **(see illustration)**.

25 Again working in sequence, tighten all the cylinder head bolts through the specified Stage 2 angle.

26 Finally, tighten all the cylinder head bolts, in sequence, through the specified Stage 3 angle.

27 Refit the engine mounting to the front of the cylinder head, when secure, lower the trolley jack and remove it from under the engine.

28 Refit the rocker arms, camshaft and housing as described in Section 6.

29 Fit the coolant hoses to the thermostat housing and also the wiring connector. If required refer to Chapter 3 for further information.

30 Refit the hoses to the shut-off valve on the left-hand end of the cylinder head.

31 Refit the exhaust manifold as described In Chapter 4C.

32 Refit the camshaft cover as described in Section 4.

33 Refit the spark plugs and ignition coil module as described in Chapter 1A.

34 Refill the cooling system and engine oil, as described in Chapter 1A

8 Engine/transmission mountings - inspection and renewal

Inspection

1 If improved access is required, jack up the front of the vehicle, and support it securely on axle stands (see *Jacking and vehicle support*). Remove the both front road wheels and inner wheel arch liners.

2 Check the mounting rubbers to see if they are cracked **(see illustration)**, hardened or separated from the metal at any point; renew the mounting if any such damage or deterioration is evident.

3 Check that all the mountings are securely tightened; use a torque wrench to check if possible.

4 Using a large screwdriver or a crowbar, check for wear in the mounting by carefully levering against it to check for free play. Where this is not possible, enlist the aid of an assistant to move the engine/transmission back-and-forth, or from side-to-side, whilst you observe the mounting. While some free play is to be expected, even from new components, excessive wear should be obvious. If excessive free play is found, check first that the fasteners are correctly secured, and then renew any worn components as described in the following paragraphs.

Renewal

5 To give easier access, remove the air filter and housing as described in Chapter 1A.

6 Where fitted, undo the retaining bolts and remove the engine undertray(s).

7 Attach a hoist and lifting tackle to the engine lifting brackets on the cylinder head, and raise the hoist to just take the weight of the engine and transmission. Alternatively the engine can be supported on a trolley jack under the engine/transmission. Use a block of wood between the engine/transmission and the head of the jack, to prevent any damage to the transmission.

Front mountings

8 Carry out the procedures from paragraph 5 to 7.

9 Slacken and remove the bolt that secures the engine mounting to the engine-mounting bracket **(see illustration).**

10 From under the vehicle slacken and remove the nut that secures the engine mounting to the subframe.

11 Withdraw the mounting from the engine compartment. If required, carry out the same procedure for the mounting on the other side.

12 Refitting is a reversal of removal; tighten all fixings to the specified torque.

Rear mountings

13 Carry out the procedures from paragraph 5 to 7.

14 From under the vehicle slacken and remove the nut that secures the engine mounting to the subframe.

15 Slacken and remove the bolt that secures the engine mounting to the engine-mounting bracket **(see illustration).**

16 Slacken and remove the bolt that secures the engine mounting to the subframe.

17 Withdraw the mounting from the engine compartment. If required, carry out the same procedure for the mounting on the other side.

18 Refitting is a reversal of removal; tighten all fixings to the specified torque.

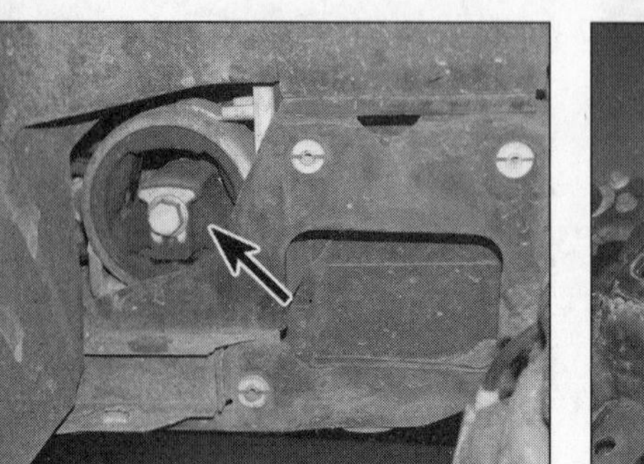

8.2 Check the rubber part (arrowed) of the engine mountings

8.9 Remove the mounting bolt - arrowed

8.15 Remove the mounting bolt - arrowed

Chapter 2 Part B: Diesel engine in-car repair procedures

Contents

Degrees of difficulty

Easy, suitable for novice with little experience	**Fairly easy,** suitable for beginner with some experience	**Fairly difficult,** suitable for competent DIY mechanic	**Difficult,** suitable for experienced DIY mechanic	**Very difficult,** suitable for expert DIY or professional

Specifications

General

Type .... Four-cylinder in-line, chain-driven double overhead camshafts (DOHC), liquid-cooled
Engine capacity .... 1689 cc
Manufacturer's engine codes*:
A160 .... 668.940 and 668.941
A170 .... 668.940 and 668.942
Maximum power outputs*:
A160 .... 55 kW at 3600 rpm
A170:
668.940 .... 66 kW at 4200 rpm
668.942 .... 70 kW at 4200 rpm
Maximum torque outputs*:
A160 .... 160 Nm at 1500 to 2800 rpm
A170 .... 180 Nm at 1600 to 3600 rpm
Bore .... 80.0 mm
Stroke .... 84.0 mm
Compression ratio .... 19.0 : 1
Firing order .... 1 – 3 – 4 – 2
No 1cylinder location .... Timing chain end
Direction of crankshaft rotation .... Clockwise (when viewed from right-hand side of vehicle)

* **Note:** *See 'Vehicle identification' at the end of this manual for the location of engine code markings.*

Lubrication system

Oil pump type .... Gear type, chain-driven from crankshaft
Oil pressure (oil temperature 80°C):
At 1200 rpm .... 1.2 bar
At 2000 rpm .... 2.0 bar
At 2800 rpm .... 2.8 bar

Cylinder head bolts

Length when new .... 186 mm
Maximum length (renew bolt if longer) .... 188 mm

Connecting rod bolts

Length when new .... 38.0 mm
Maximum length (renew bolt if longer) .... 38.4 mm

Torque wrench settings	Nm	lbf ft
Auxiliary drivebelt tensioner/roller mounting unit	20	15
Big-end bearing caps bolts*:		
Stage 1	5	4
Stage 2	15	11
Stage 3	Angle-tighten a further 90°	
Brake vacuum pump to end cover	14	10
Camshaft bearing cap bolts	9	7
Camshaft cover nuts/bolts	8	6
Camshaft sprocket bolts	18	13
Coolant drain plug in block	10	7
Coolant pump bolts	8	6
Coolant pump pulley bolts	8	6
Crankshaft oil seal housing bolts	8	6
Crankshaft pulley bolt:		
Stage 1	200	148
Stage 2	Angle-tighten a further 90°	
Cylinder head bolts to cylinder block (Nos 1 to 10)*:		
Stage 1	35	26
Stage 2	Angle-tighten a further 90°	
Stage 3	Angle-tighten a further 90°	
Cylinder head bolts to timing chain cover (Nos 11 and 12)	20	15
Cylinder head end cover bolts	9	7
Driveplate:		
Stage 1	45	33
Stage 2	Angle-tighten a further 90°	
Engine mountings:		
Front mountings:		
Bolt to engine mounting bracket	55	41
Nut to subframe	40	30
Rear mountings:		
Bolt to engine mounting bracket	25	18
Bolt to subframe	25	18
Nut to subframe	25	18
Flywheel:		
Stage 1	45	33
Stage 2	Angle-tighten a further 90°	
Fuel high-pressure pump to end cover	14	10
Fuel predelivery pump to end cover	9	7
Injector mounting bracket bolts:		
Stage 1	7	5
Stage 2	Angle-tighten a further 90°	
Stage 3	Angle-tighten a further 90°	
Main bearing cap bolts*:		
Stage 1	40	30
Stage 2	Angle-tighten a further 90°	
Main bearing caps 2, 3 and 4 side bolts*:		
Stage 1	20	15
Stage 2	Angle-tighten a further 90°	
Oil dipstick guide tube	8	6
Oil drain plug	25	18
Oil filter housing-to-cylinder block bolts	14	10
Oil filter cover	25	18
Oil level/pressure sensor-to-sump bolts	8	6
Oil pump securing bolts	14	10
Sump:		
Sump-to-cylinder block bolts	14	10
Sump-to-transmission bolts	20	15
Thermostat housing	9	7
Timing chain cover bolts	8	6
Timing chain tensioner	80	59
Turbocharger:		
To exhaust manifold	21	15
Oil drain line union nut	9	7
Oil feed/supply line union nut	30	22
Support bracket	30	22
Heat shield	9	7

* **Note:** *Use new bolts*

1 General information

How to use this Chapter

This Part of Chapter 2 describes those repair procedures that can reasonably be carried out on the engine while it remains in the vehicle. If the engine has been removed from the vehicle and is being dismantled as described in Part C, any preliminary dismantling procedures can be ignored.

Note that while it may be possible physically to overhaul certain items while the engine is in the vehicle, such tasks are not usually carried out as separate operations, and usually require the execution of several additional procedures (not to mention the cleaning of components and of oilways); for this reason, all such tasks are classed as major overhaul procedures, and are described in Part C of this Chapter.

Engine description

Engines are referred to by type, and are identified and referred to by the manufacturer's code letters. A listing of all engines covered, together with their code letters, is given in the Specifications at the start of this Chapter.

The engine is a water-cooled, double overhead camshafts (DOHC), in-line four-cylinder units, with aluminium-alloy cylinder block and cylinder head. All are mounted transversely at the front of the vehicle, with the transmission bolted to the left-hand end of the engine.

The crankshaft is of five-bearing type, and thrustwashers are fitted to the centre main bearing to control crankshaft endfloat.

Drive for the inlet camshaft is by a timing chain from the crankshaft, the exhaust camshaft is then gear driven from the inlet camshaft. Each camshaft is mounted at the top of the cylinder head, and is secured by bearing caps. The valves are closed by coil springs, and run in guides pressed into the cylinder head. The camshaft actuates the valves through roller rocker arms and hydraulic tappets.

The gear-type oil pump is driven by a chain from a sprocket on the crankshaft. Oil is drawn from the sump through a strainer, and then forced through an externally-mounted, renewable filter via a heat exchanger. From there, it is distributed to the cylinder head, where it lubricates the camshaft journals and hydraulic tappets, and also to the crankcase, where it lubricates the main bearings, connecting rod big-ends, gudgeon pins and cylinder bores. Oil jets are fitted to the base of each cylinder – these spray oil onto the underside of the pistons to improve cooling.

All engines are fitted with a brake servo vacuum pump driven by the camshaft on the timing chain end of the cylinder head. The fuel pump is driven by the camshaft on the transmission end of the cylinder head.

On all engines, engine coolant is circulated by a pump, driven by the auxilliary belt. For details of the cooling system, refer to Chapter 3.

Operations with engine in car

The following operations can be performed without removing the engine:

a) Compression pressure – testing.
b) Camshaft cover – removal and refitting.
c) Timing chain and tensioner – removal, refitting and adjustment.
d) Camshaft oil seals – renewal.
e) Camshafts, roller rocker arms and hydraulic tappets – removal, inspection and refitting.
f) Cylinder head – removal and refitting.
g) Engine/transmission mountings – inspection and renewal.

** Cylinder head dismantling procedures are detailed in Chapter 2C.*

2 Compression and leakdown tests – description and interpretation

Compression test

Note: *A compression tester suitable for use with diesel engines will be required for this test.*

1 When engine performance is down, or if misfiring occurs which cannot be attributed to the ignition or fuel systems, a compression test can provide diagnostic clues as to the engine's condition. If the test is performed regularly, it can give warning of trouble before any other symptoms become apparent.

2 The engine must be fully warmed-up to normal operating temperature, the battery must be fully-charged, and you will require the aid of an assistant.

3 Disconnect the wiring to the injectors. **Note:** *As a result of the wiring being disconnected, faults will be stored in the ECU memory. These must be erased after the compression test.*

4 Remove the glow plugs, then fit a compression tester to the No 1 cylinder glow (heater) plug hole. The type of tester, which screws into the plug thread, is preferred.

5 Have your assistant crank the engine for several seconds on the starter motor. After one or two revolutions, the compression pressure should build-up to a maximum figure and then stabilise. Record the highest reading obtained.

6 Repeat the test on the remaining cylinders, recording the pressure in each.

7 The cause of poor compression is less easy to establish on a diesel engine than on a petrol engine. The effect of introducing oil into the cylinders (wet testing) is not conclusive, because there is a risk that the oil will sit in the recess on the piston crown, instead of passing to the rings. However, the following can be used as a rough guide to diagnosis.

8 All cylinders should produce very similar pressures. Any difference greater than that specified indicates the existence of a fault. Note that the compression should build-up quickly in a healthy engine. Low compression on the first stroke, followed by gradually increasing pressure on successive strokes, indicates worn piston rings. A low compression reading on the first stroke, which does not build-up during successive strokes, indicates leaking valves or a blown head gasket (a cracked head could also be the cause).

9 A low reading from two adjacent cylinders is almost certainly due to the head gasket having blown between them and the presence of coolant in the engine oil will confirm this.

10 On completion, remove the compression tester, and refit the glow plugs.

11 Reconnect the wiring to the injectors. If required, have a Mercedes-Benz dealer erase any fault codes from the ECU memory.

Leakdown test

12 A leakdown test measures the rate at which compressed air fed into the cylinder is lost. It is an alternative to a compression test, and in many ways it is better, since the escaping air provides easy identification of where pressure loss is occurring (piston rings, valves or head gasket).

13 The equipment required for leakdown testing is unlikely to be available to the home mechanic. If poor compression is suspected, have the test performed by a suitably-equipped garage.

3 Engine assembly and valve timing marks – general information and usage

1 Top dead centre (TDC) is the highest point in its travel up-and-down its cylinder bore that each piston reaches as the crankshaft rotates. While each piston reaches TDC both at the top of the compression stroke and again at the top of the exhaust stroke, for the purpose of timing the engine, TDC refers to the No 1 piston position at the top of its compression stroke.

2 No 1 piston and cylinder are at the right-hand (timing chain) end of the engine. Note that the crankshaft rotates clockwise when viewed from the right-hand side of the vehicle.

3 Switch off the ignition and all electrical consumers, and remove the ignition key. Remove all four glow (heater) plugs.

4 Apply the handbrake, then jack up the front of the vehicle and support it on axle stands (see *Jacking and vehicle support*). Remove the right-hand front roadwheel.

5 Undo the retaining screws, release any securing clips and remove the inner wheel arch liners **(see illustrations)**. Note that the wiring connectors for the ABS and brake pad warning light will need to be disconnected before the liner can be removed.

6 Remove the camshaft cover as described in Section 4.

3.5a Disconnect the wiring connectors . . .

3.5b . . . and remove the inner wheel arch liner

3.7 TDC timing mark on engine cover – arrowed

3.8 Fit the two 6 mm pins (arrowed) in the position showed

3.9a Disconnect the wiring connector . . .

7 Turn the engine with an Allen key socket on the crankshaft pulley bolt until the TDC markings on the front pulley align with the TDC mark on the timing chain cover **(see illustration)**.

8 In this position the alignment holes in the camshaft sprockets should be at 3 o'clock position (looking from the driver's side), in this position slide two 6 mm pins into the two alignment holes in the camshaft sprockets **(see illustration).** The camshaft lobes on No 1 cylinder should be facing upwards; the engine is now at TDC on No 1 piston.

9 A further check, if required, is to disconnect the wiring connector from the TDC sensor, which is positioned to the transmission end of the cylinder head, directly above the flywheel. Undo the retaining bolt and withdraw the sensor from the cylinder block. Note it may be necessary to disconnect the air intake hose to access the TDC sensor. Insert a locking tool into the TDC sensor hole so that it locates in the edge of the flywheel, a locking tool can be made up of a deep socket and 6 mm bolt **(see illustrations).**

10 Refitting of components, is the reversal of the removal procedure with reference to the relevant Chapters.

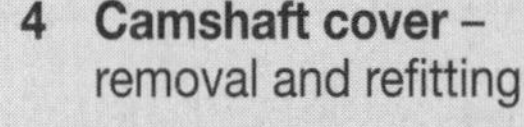

4 Camshaft cover – removal and refitting

Removal

1 Remove the injectors as described in Chapter 4B.

2 Undo the retaining bolts and remove the oil filler neck from the right-hand end of the cylinder head **(see illustration)**. Discard the oil seal, as a new one will be required for refitting.

3.9b . . . and remove the retaining screw from the TDC sensor

3.9c Homemade tool, using a deep socket and a 6 mm bolt sticking out of the end

4.2 Undo the three bolts – arrowed

4.4a Disconnect the fuel pipe . . .

4.4b . . . undo the retaining bolts and withdraw the rail

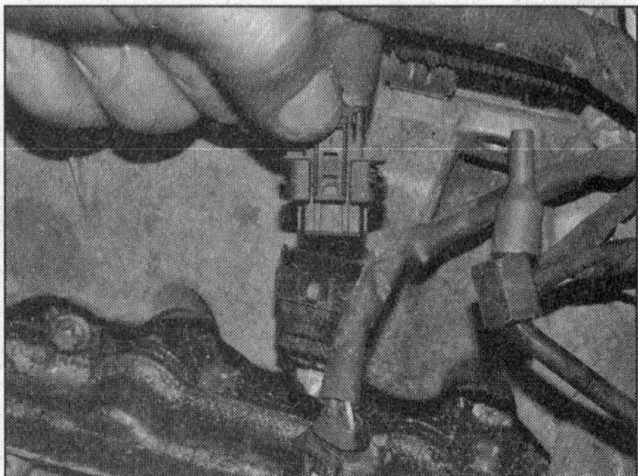
4.5 Disconnect the wiring connector from the camshaft sensor

On models up to 31/08/00, disconnect the breather/vent hose from the top of the filler neck.

3 On models up to 28/02/01, disconnect the wiring connector from the fuel shut-off valve on the left-hand end of the cylinder head. Disconnect the fuel pipe, undo the retaining bolts and remove it from the top of the fuel predelivery pump.

4 Disconnect the fuel pipe, undo the retaining bolts and move the fuel rail to one side **(see illustrations)**

5 Disconnect the wiring connector from the camshaft sensor on the top of the camshaft cover **(see illustration)**.

6 Undo the turbocharger oil feed pipe connection from the rear of the cylinder block, undo the mounting bolt from the top of the camshaft cover and move it to one side **(see illustrations)**.

7 Unclip the glow plug wiring loom from the clips along the top of the camshaft cover **(see illustration)**.

8 Undo the retaining bolts and remove the turbocharger support bracket.

9 Slacken the retaining clip and disconnect the EGR pipe, removing it from the engine **(see illustration)**.

10 Cover the ends of the fuel pipes to prevent dirt ingress, and then unclip the fuel pipe from along the top of the camshaft cover and move to one side **(see illustration)**.

11 Unscrew the camshaft cover retaining bolts and lift the cover away. If it sticks, do not attempt to lever it off – instead free it by working around the cover and tapping it lightly with a soft-faced mallet **(see illustration)**.

12 Recover the camshaft cover rubber gaskets, noting the fitted position, and renew gaskets on refitting.

13 Clean the mating surfaces of the cylinder head and camshaft cover thoroughly, removing all traces of oil and old gasket – take care to avoid damaging the surfaces as you do this.

Refitting

14 Refit the camshaft cover by following the removal procedure in reverse, noting the following points:

a) *Tighten the camshaft cover retaining nuts/bolts progressively to the specified torque.*
b) *Fit new rubber gaskets, masking sure they are located correctly.*
c) *Follow the procedure in Chapter 4B for refitting the injectors.*

4.6a Slacken the oil feed pipe connection – arrowed . . .

4.6b . . . and the retaining bolt – arrowed

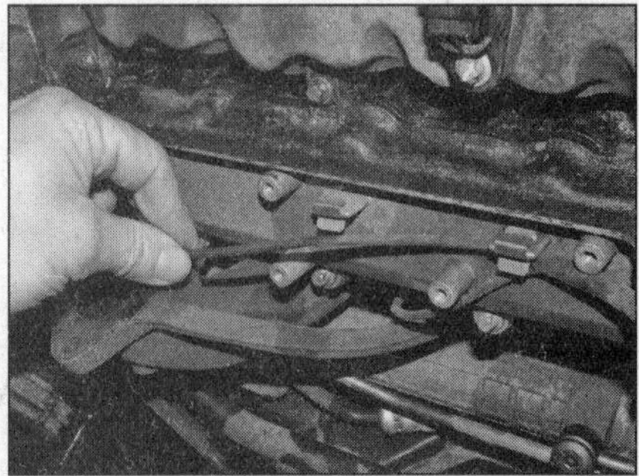
4.7 Unclip the wiring from the retaining clips

4.9 Remove the EGR pipe

4.10 Move the fuel pipes to one side

4.11 Remove the camshaft cover

5.4 Removing the timing chain tensioner

5.5a Secure the chain with a cable tie . . .

5.5b . . . and put some clean rag in the timing chain recess

5 Timing chain and tensioner – removal and refitting

Note 1: *A chain breaker/riveter will be required to renew the chain with the engine in-car, also a second person will be required to assist fitting the timing chain.*

Note 2: *If the chain needs to be renewed as a complete assembly, then the engine will need to be removed, as there is not enough room for the removal of the timing chain cover (see Chapter 2C).*

1 Set the engine to TDC as described in Section 3.

2 Unclip the coolant expansion tank and move it to one side, making sure the hoses do not get damaged.

3 Remove the camshaft cover as described in Section 4.

4 Slacken and remove the timing chain tensioner from the rear of the engine, and then withdraw it from the cylinder head **(see illustration)**. Remove the gasket/seal and discard, a new one will be required for refitting.

5 With the engine still in the TDC position, use a couple of cable ties to keep the timing chain on the camshaft sprocket. Put some clean rag into the timing chain recess to prevent anything dropping down into the engine **(see illustrations)**.

6 Use the chain breaker to press out one of the timing chain pins and split the timing chain **(see illustrations)**.

7 Connect the new timing chain to the old chain and press the chain link pin back into position **(see illustration)**. **Note:** *Make sure the new chain is connected to the front part of the chain, as the engine has to be turned clockwise, in the direction of rotation to feed the chain around the sprockets.*

8 With the new chain connected securely to the old chain, take a firm hold of both ends of the chain and remove the cable ties from the camshaft sprocket **(see illustrations)**. Remove the clean rag from around the timing chain before turning the engine.

9 Remove the two 6 mm alignment pins from the camshaft sprockets.

10 With the aid of an assistant, turn the engine in the direction of rotation. Keeping the timing chain taut, feed it around the crankshaft sprocket, until the new chain comes all the way around to the camshaft sprocket **(see illustration)**.

11 Cable tie both ends of the timing chain back to the camshaft sprocket, and refit the clean rag back into the timing chain recess.

12 Use the chain breaker to press out the timing chain pin and split the old timing chain from the new timing chain **(see illustrations)**. **Note:** *Make sure the chain is pulled tight on*

5.6a Using a chain breaker . . .

5.6b . . . to push out the chain pin

5.7 Connect the new chain to the old chain

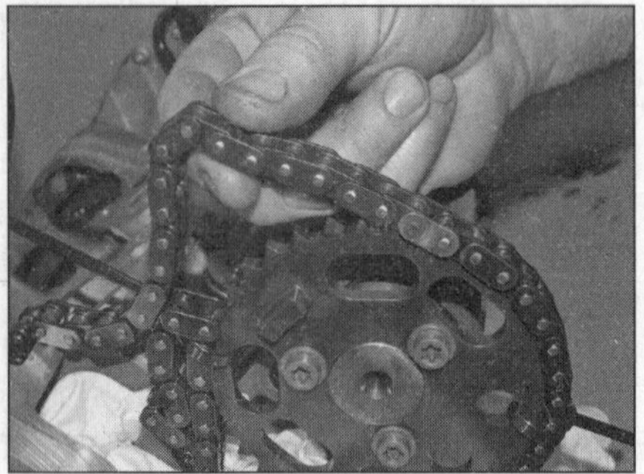

5.8a Keep a tight hold of the timing chain . . .

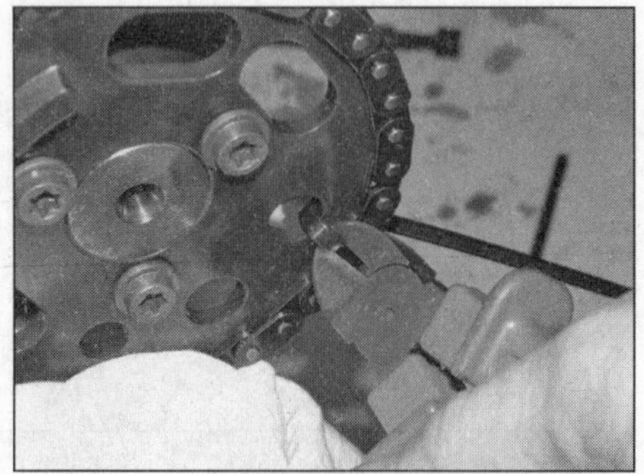

5.8b . . . and remove the cable ties

5.10 Keep the timing chain fitted around the sprocket

the lower section of the engine, and the upper section slack to allow for the fitting of the chain tensioner.

13 Check that the TDC marks on the crankshaft pulley and timing chain cover are aligned, and the alignment holes in the camshaft sprockets. In this position slide two 6 mm pins into the two alignment holes in the camshaft sprockets **(see illustration 3.8)**

14 Fit the new timing chain link, using the timing chain riveter to connect the two ends of the chain securely **(see illustrations)**. Always read the instructions that come with the chain riveter, as there are many different types available. The link pins need to be riveted securely, to prevent the chain coming apart.

15 Remove the clean rag from the timing chain recess, and fit the timing chain tensioner complete with new seal. With the tensioner now fitted, check the timing marks are still in line.

16 Rotate the engine, by hand, two complete turns and check the timing marks come back in alignment.

17 Refit the camshaft cover with reference to Section 4.

18 Refit the coolant expansion tank, making sure the hoses are routed correctly.

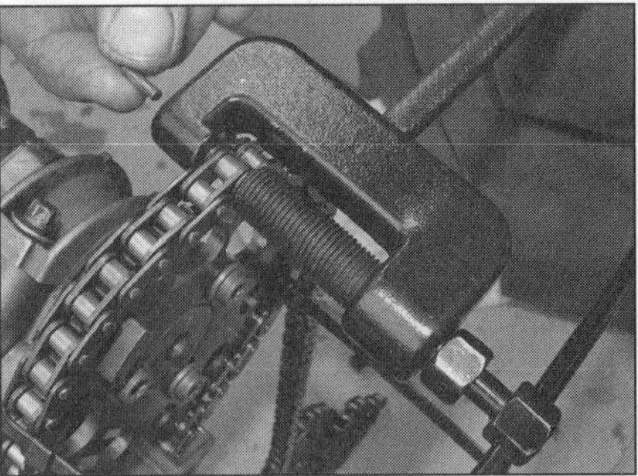

5.12a Use the chain breaker again . . .

5.12b . . . and disconnect the old chain from the new one

5.14a Fit the new chain link . . .

5.14b . . . and secure it in place with the riveter tool

6 Camshaft, roller rocker arms and hydraulic tappets – removal, inspection and refitting

Note: *New oil seal will be required for the vacuum pump and sealant for the cylinder head end covers.*

Removal

1 Set number one cylinder to TDC as described in Section 3.

2 Remove the camshaft cover as described in Section 4

3 Disconnect the vacuum hose, undo the retaining bolts, and withdraw the vacuum pump from the timing chain end of the cylinder head **(see illustration)**. Retrieve the sealing ring and discard; a new one will be required for refitting.

4 Undo the retaining bolts and remove the vacuum pump mounting bracket/upper cover from the end of the cylinder head **(see illustration)**. If it is tight, do not attempt to lever it off – instead free it by working around the cover and tapping it lightly with a soft-faced mallet.

5 Remove the predelivery and high-pressure fuel pump from the transmission end of the cylinder head, as described in Chapter 4B.

6 Undo the retaining bolts and remove the pump mounting bracket/upper cover from the end of the cylinder head **(see illustration)**. If it is tight, do not attempt to lever it off – instead free it by working around the cover and tapping it lightly with a soft-faced mallet.

7 Lock the crankshaft in position to prevent the engine from turning.

8 Mark the timing chain in relation to the camshaft sprocket and secure it in position with a couple of cable ties **(see illustration)**.

9 Slacken and remove the timing chain tensioner from the rear of the engine, and then withdraw it from the cylinder head **(see illustration)**. Remove the gasket/seal and discard, a new one will be required for refitting.

10 Undo the retaining bolts and remove the camshaft sprocket complete with timing

6.3 Removing the vacuum pump . . .

6.4 . . . and the end plate/mounting bracket

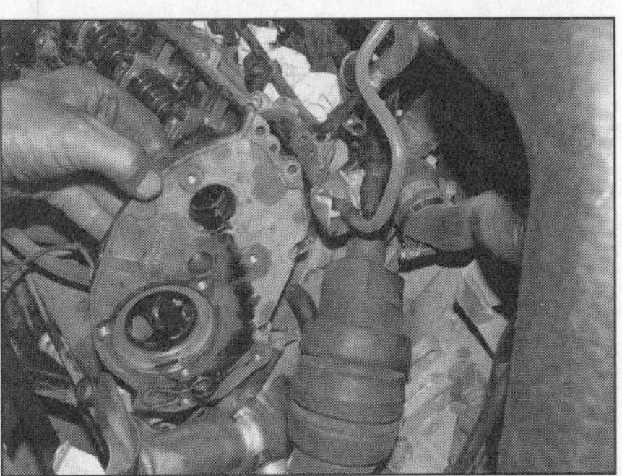

6.6 Removing the fuel pump mounting plate

6.8 Secure the chain with a cable tie

6.9 Removing the tensioner

6.10a Counterhold the camshaft with a spanner

6.10b Remove the sprocket from the camshaft

chain from the end of the camshaft **(see illustrations)**. Fasten the sprocket and timing chain to one side, keeping the timing chain taut. Note the position of the locating dowel in the sprocket, if the dowel is loose, remove it and keep it safe for refitting.

11 Check the camshaft bearing caps for identification markings **(see illustration)**. The bearing caps are normally stamped 1 to 4 on the inlet camshaft and 5 to 8 on the exhaust camshaft. If no marks are present, make suitable marks using a scriber or punch. The caps should be numbered from 1 (inlet) and 5 (exhaust), starting at the timing chain end of the engine. Note on which side of the bearing caps the marks are made to ensure that they are refitted the correct way round.

12 Working progressively, in a diagonal sequence, slacken the nuts securing the bearing caps. Note that as the nuts are slackened, the valve springs will push the camshaft up. Once the nuts securing the bearing caps have been fully slackened, lift off the bearing caps.

13 Carefully lift the camshaft from the cylinder head, keeping it level and supported at both ends as it is removed so that the journals and lobes are not damaged **(see illustration)**.

14 Lift the roller rocker arms, complete with hydraulic tappets, from their position in the cylinder head, and store them in a clean container **(see illustration)**. Make a note of the position of each one, as they must be refitted in their original locations on reassembly – accelerated wear leading to early failure will result if the rocker arms are interchanged.

Inspection

15 With the camshafts removed, examine the bearing caps and the bearing locations in the cylinder head for signs of obvious wear or pitting. If evident, a new cylinder head will probably be required. Also check that the oil supply holes in the cylinder head are free from obstructions.

16 Visually inspect the camshaft for evidence of wear on the surfaces of the lobes and journals. Normally their surfaces should be smooth and have a dull shine; look for scoring, erosion or pitting and areas that appear highly polished, indicating excessive wear. Accelerated wear will occur once the hardened exterior of the camshaft has been damaged, so always renew worn items. **Note:** *If these symptoms are visible on the tips of the camshaft lobes, check the corresponding tappet, as it will probably be worn as well.*

17 If the machined surfaces of the camshaft appear discoloured or blued, it is likely that it has been overheated at some point, probably due to inadequate lubrication. This may have distorted the shaft, so check with a Mercedes-Benz dealer workshop or suitably-equipped automotive repair facility to check condition.

18 Inspect the roller rocker arms and hydraulic tappets **(see illustration)** for obvious signs of wear or damage, and renew if necessary. Check that any oil holes are free from obstructions.

6.11 Camshaft bearing cap marking – arrowed

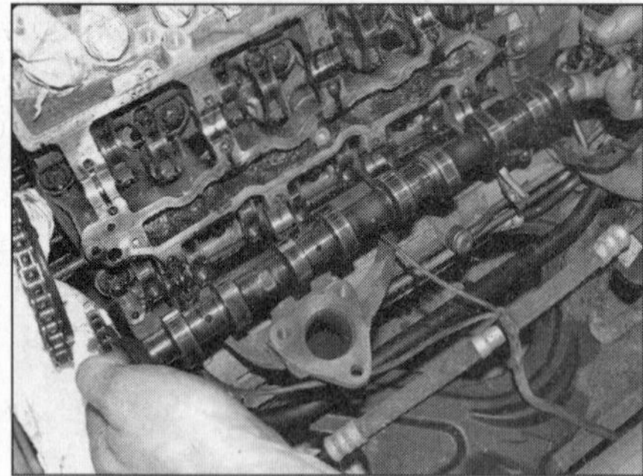
6.13 Lift the camshaft from the cylinder head

6.14 Remove the rocker arm and hydraulic tappet

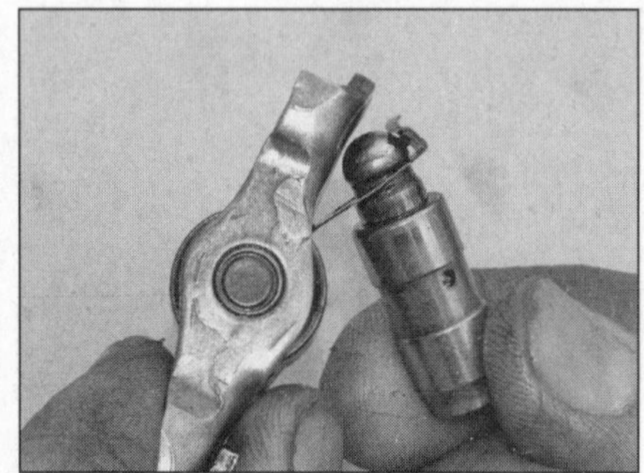
6.18 Check for wear on the rocker arms and tappet

Refitting

19 Smear some clean engine oil onto the sides of the roller rocker arms, and offer them into position in their original positions in the cylinder head. Push them down until they contact the valves, and then lubricate the camshaft lobe contact surfaces.

20 Lubricate the camshaft and cylinder head bearing journals with clean engine oil.

21 Carefully lower the camshafts into position in the cylinder head, making sure that they are still in the TDC position, as noted on removal.

22 Oil the upper surfaces of the camshaft bearing journals and then fit the bearing caps. Ensure that they are fitted the right way round and in the correct locations, and then progressively tighten the retaining bolts (one turn at a time) in a diagonal sequence to the specified torque. Note that as the bolts are tightened, the camshaft will be forced down against the pressure of the valve springs.

23 With both camshafts in the TDC position, refit the inlet camshaft sprocket complete with timing chain to the end of the inlet camshaft. If required, refit the locating dowel to the end of the camshaft. Tighten the sprocket retaining bolts to their specified torque setting.

24 Refit the timing chain tensioner and tighten to the specified torque setting.

25 The cable ties can now be removed from the timing chain/camshaft sprocket.

26 Refit the fuel pump mounting bracket/ upper cover to the transmission end of the cylinder head. Apply sealant with a bead of 1.5 to 2.0 mm to the mounting bracket and tighten the retaining bolts **(see illustration)**. **Note:** *The cover must be fitted within 10 minutes of applying the sealant.*

27 Refit the predelivery and high-pressure fuel pump, with reference to Chapter 4B.

28 Refit the vacuum pump mounting bracket/ upper cover to the timing chain end of the cylinder head. Apply sealant with a bead of 1.5 to 2.0 mm to the mounting bracket and tighten the retaining bolts **(see illustration)**. **Note:** *The cover must be fitted within 10 minutes of applying the sealant.*

29 Refit the brake vacuum pump to the cylinder head, fit new sealing ring and tighten retaining bolts to the specified torque setting. Reconnect the vacuum hose.

30 Refit the camshaft cover as described in Section 4

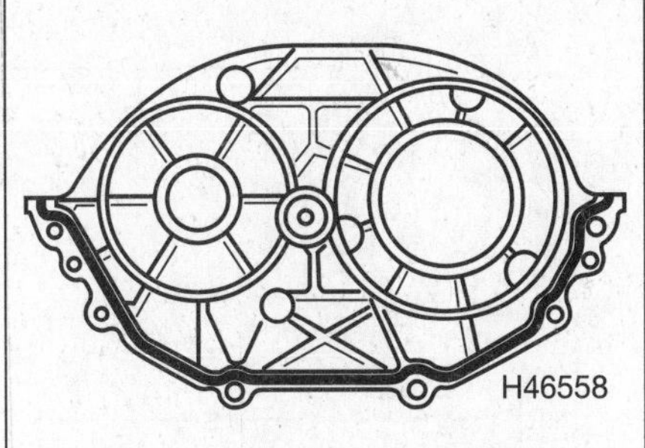

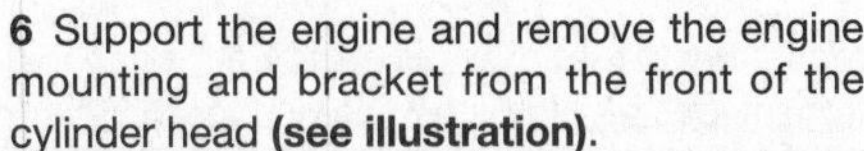

6.26 Apply the sealant as shown

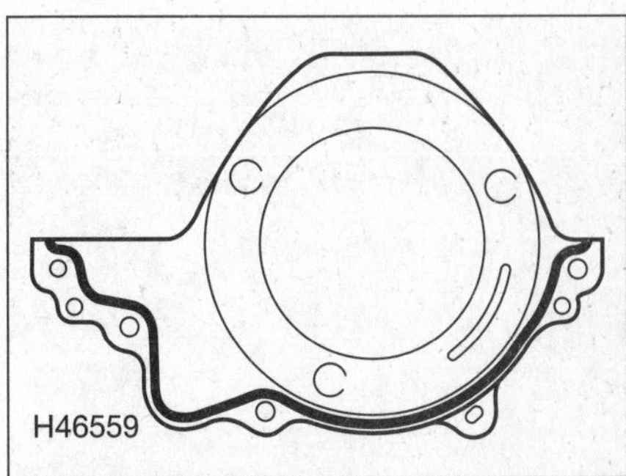

6.28 Apply the sealant as shown

7 Cylinder head – removal, inspection and refitting

Note: *The cylinder head must be removed with the engine cold. A new cylinder head gasket will be required on refitting, also new cylinder head bolts may be needed If they have stretched beyond specifications – see text.*

Removal

1 Disconnect the battery earth cable as described in Chapter 5A.

2 Remove the undertray from below the engine compartment.

3 Drain the cooling system and engine oil, as described in Chapter 1B.

4 Remove camshafts and rocker arms as described in Section 6.

5 Disconnect any coolant hoses which are still attached to the cylinder head.

6 Support the engine and remove the engine mounting and bracket from the front of the cylinder head **(see illustration)**.

7 Disconnect the exhaust front pipe as described in Chapter 4D.

8 Note the locations of any electrical wiring, and then disconnect methodically and move to one side.

9 Progressively slacken the cylinder head bolts in the **reverse** order to that given for tightening in paragraph 24, noting the two bolts located in the timing chain recess **(see illustration)**. Check around the cylinder head, making sure that nothing remains connected, and then lift the cylinder head from the engine block. Seek assistance if possible, as it is a heavy assembly, especially if it is being removed complete with the exhaust manifold.

10 Remove the gasket from the top of the block, noting any locating dowels. If the dowels are a loose fit, remove them and store them with the cylinder head (noting its fitted position) for safekeeping. Do not discard the gasket yet – it will be needed for identification purposes. If desired, the exhaust manifold can be removed from the cylinder head with reference to Chapter 4D.

Inspection

11 Dismantling and inspection of the cylinder head is covered in Chapter 2C.

12 The mating faces of the cylinder head and block must be perfectly clean before refitting the head.

13 Use a scraper to remove all traces of gasket and carbon, also clean the tops of the pistons. Take particular care with the aluminium surfaces, as the soft metal is easily damaged.

14 Make sure that debris is not allowed to enter the oil and water passages – this is particularly important for the oil circuit, as carbon could block the oil supply to the camshaft and crankshaft bearings. Using adhesive tape and paper, seal the water, oil and bolt holes in the cylinder block. To prevent carbon entering the gap between the pistons and bores, smear a little grease in the gap. After cleaning a piston, rotate the crankshaft so that the piston moves down the bore, and then wipe out the grease and carbon with a cloth rag. Clean the other piston crowns in the same way.

15 Check the head and block for nicks, deep scratches and other damage. If slight, they may be removed carefully with a file. More serious damage may be repaired by machining, but this is a specialist job. If warpage of the cylinder head is suspected, use a straight-edge to check it for distortion, as described in Part C of this Chapter.

16 Check the length of the cylinder head bolts by measuring from the underside of the head **(see illustration)**; use new cylinder head bolts if the length is greater than the dimension listed in the Specifications at the beginning of this Chapter.

Refitting

17 Ensure that the cylinder head bolt holes in the crankcase are clean and free of oil. Syringe or soak up any oil left in the bolt holes. This is most important in order that the correct bolt tightening torque can be applied, and

7.6 Front engine mounting – arrowed

7.9 Two smaller bolts (arrowed) in the end of the cylinder head

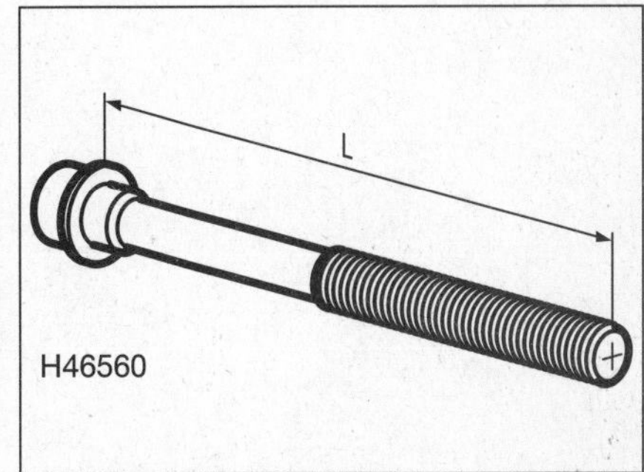

7.16 Check the length of the cylinder head bolts

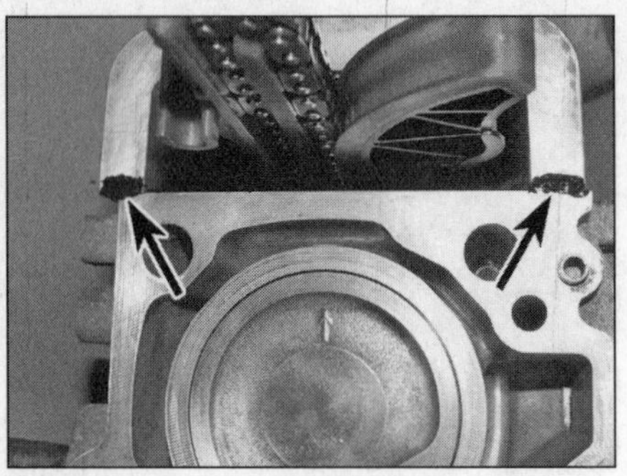
7.20 Apply sealant to the arrowed areas

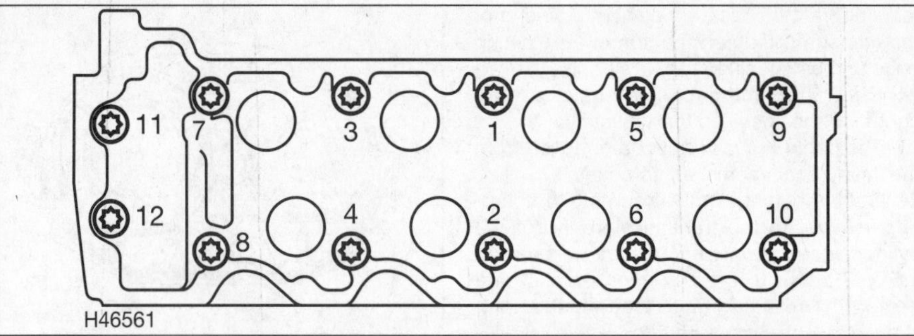

7.24 Tightening sequence for cylinder head bolts

to prevent the possibility of the block being cracked by hydraulic pressure when the bolts are tightened.

18 Turn the crankshaft anti-clockwise all the pistons at an equal height, approximately halfway down their bores from the TDC position (see Section 3). This will eliminate any risk of piston-to-valve contact as the cylinder head is refitted.

19 If required, refit the exhaust manifold with reference to Chapter 4D.

20 Apply sealant to the joint between the cylinder head and the timing chain cover **(see illustration)**.

21 Ensure that the cylinder head locating dowels are in place in the cylinder block, and then fit the new cylinder head gasket over the dowels. Ensure that it is fitted the correct way up, as noted on removal. Where applicable, the OBEN/TOP marking should also be uppermost. Note that Mercedes-Benz recommend that the gasket is only removed from its packaging immediately prior to fitting.

22 Lower the cylinder head into position on the gasket, ensuring that it engages correctly over the dowels. Also align the timing chain guides inside the cylinder head.

23 Insert the new cylinder head bolts and screw them in as far as possible by hand.

24 Working progressively, in sequence, tighten all the cylinder head bolts to the specified Stage 1 torque **(see illustration)**.

25 Again working progressively, in sequence, tighten all the cylinder head bolts to the specified Stage 2 angle.

26 Finally, tighten all the cylinder head bolts, in sequence, through the specified Stage 3 angle.

27 Refit the engine mounting to the front of the cylinder head, when secure, lower the trolley jack and remove it from under the engine.

28 Refit the camshafts, roller rocker arms and hydraulic adjusters as described in Section 6.

29 Fit the coolant hoses to the thermostat housing and also the wiring connector. If required refer to Chapter 3 for further information.

30 The remainder of the refitting procedure is a reversal of the removal procedure, bearing in mind the following points.

a) Refit the camshaft cover with reference to Section 4.

b) Reconnect the exhaust and turbo with reference to Chapter 4D.

c) Refill the cooling system and engine oil as described in Chapter 1B.

8 Engine/transmission mountings – inspection and renewal

Proceed as described in Chapter 2A.

Chapter 2 Part C:
Engine removal and overhaul procedures

Contents

Degrees of difficulty

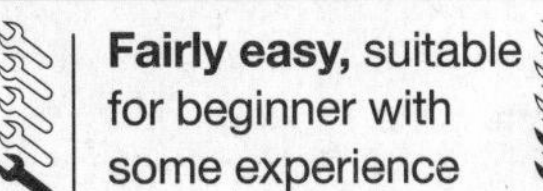

Easy, suitable for novice with little experience	**Fairly easy,** suitable for beginner with some experience	**Fairly difficult,** suitable for competent DIY mechanic	**Difficult,** suitable for experienced DIY mechanic	**Very difficult,** suitable for expert DIY or professional

Specifications

Engine codes*

Petrol engines:	
1.4 litre	166.940
1.6 litre	166.960
1.9 litre	166.990
2.1 litre	166.995
Diesel engine	668.940, 668.941 and 668.942

*** Note:** *See 'Vehicle identification' at the end of this manual for the location of engine code markings.*

Cylinder head

Maximum cylinder head gasket face distortion	0.08 mm

Connecting rod bolts

Thread diameter	7 mm
Length when new	38 mm
Maximum length (renew bolt if longer)	38.4 mm

Oil pressure readings

	rpm	bar
Petrol engines:		
Oil pressure at 90°C	700	1.0
	1000	1.5
	3000	4.0
	5750	4.5
Oil pressure at 120°C	700	0.5
	1000	0.8
	3000	2.5
	5750	3.0
Diesel engines (oil pressure at 80°C)	760	0.7
	1200	1.2
	2800	2.8
	4400	3.0

Piston rings	New	Wear limit
End gaps:		
Top compression ring	0.22 to 0.42 mm	1.5 mm
Lower compression ring	0.20 to 0.40 mm	1.0 mm
Oil scraper ring	0.20 to 0.40 mm	1.0 mm
Ring-to-groove clearance:		
Top compression ring	0.12 to 0.16 mm	0.20 mm
Lower compression ring	0.05 to 0.09 mm	0.15 mm
Oil scraper ring	0.03 to 0.07 mm	0.10 mm

Pistons

Diameter (standard):	
Petrol engines:	
1.4 and 1.6 litre engines	79.970 to 79.976 mm
1.9 and 2.1 litre engines	83.970 to 83.976 mm
Diesel engine	79.970 to 79.976 mm
Running clearance:	
New	0.017 to 0.043 mm
Wear limit	0.12 mm
Piston (gudgeon) pin clearance:	
In connecting rod	0.018 to 0.024 mm
In piston	0.004 to 0.015 mm

Crankshaft

Petrol engines:	
Crankshaft bearing journal (standard size)	54.950 to 54.975 mm
Crankshaft journal width at bearing	23.55 to 23.59 mm
Big-end bearing journal (standard size)	45.940 to 45.965 mm
Big-end bearing journal width	22.90 to 23.10 mm
Main bearing play (when new):	
Radial movement	0.023 to 0.048 mm
Axial movement	0.100 to 0.261 mm
Running clearances (main and big-end bearings)	0.031 to 0.073 mm
Endfloat	0.30 mm
Diesel engines:	
Crankshaft bearing journal (standard size)	54.940 to 54.965 mm
Crankshaft journal width at bearing	23.55 to 23.59 mm
Big-end bearing journal (standard size)	45.940 to 45.965 mm
Big-end bearing journal width	22.90 to 23.10 mm
Main bearing play (when new):	
Radial movement	0.032 to 0.064 mm
Axial movement	0.100 to 0.261 mm
Running clearances (main and big-end bearings)	0.031 to 0.073 mm
Endfloat	0.30 mm
Crankshaft machining tolerances (all engines):	
Maximum taper of main bearing journals	0.010 mm
Maximum taper of big-end crankpins	0.015 mm
Maximum out-of-round of journals	0.005 mm
Maximum run-out of main journals (with journals 1 and 5 in V-blocks):	
Journals 2 and 4	0.07 mm
Journal 3	0.10 mm

Valves

Valve stem diameter:	
Inlet	5.960 to 5.990 mm
Exhaust	6.955 to 7.045 mm
Valve seat width	1.7 to 1.9 mm
Valve seat angle	45°

Torque wrench settings

Refer to Chapter 2A or 2B as applicable.

1 General information

Included in this Part of Chapter 2 are details of removing the engine from the car and general overhaul procedures for the cylinder head, cylinder block and all other engine internal components.

The information given ranges from advice concerning preparation for an overhaul and the purchase of new parts, to detailed step-by-step procedures covering removal, inspection, renovation and refitting of engine internal components.

All instructions are based on the assumption that the engine has been removed from the car (except cylinder head overhaul). For information concerning in-car engine repair, as well as the removal and refitting of those external components necessary for full overhaul, refer to the relevant in-car repair procedure section (Chapters 2A or 2B) and to Section 5 of this Chapter. Ignore any preliminary dismantling operations described in the relevant in-car repair sections that are no longer relevant once the engine has been removed from the car.

Apart from torque wrench settings, which are given at the beginning of the relevant in-car repair procedure in Chapters 2A or 2B, all specifications relating to engine overhaul are given at the beginning of this Part of Chapter 2.

2 Engine overhaul – general information

It is not always easy to determine when, or if, an engine should be completely overhauled, as a number of factors must be considered.

High mileage is not necessarily an indication that an overhaul is needed, while low mileage does not preclude the need for an overhaul. Frequency of servicing is probably the most important consideration. An engine, which has had regular and frequent oil and filter changes, as well as other required maintenance, should give many thousands of miles of reliable service. Conversely, a neglected engine may require an overhaul very early in its life.

Excessive oil consumption is an indication that piston rings, valve seals and/or valve guides are in need of attention. Make sure that oil leaks are not responsible before deciding that the rings and/or guides are worn. Perform a compression (or leakdown) test, as described in Part A or B of this Chapter (as applicable), to determine the likely cause of the problem.

The oil pressure will need to be checked by a Mercedes-Benz dealer or by a specialist with the correct equipment to carry out this procedure. If it is extremely low, the main and big end bearings, and/or the oil pump, are probably worn.

Loss of power, rough running, knocking or metallic engine noises, excessive valve gear noise, and high fuel consumption may also point to the need for an overhaul, especially if they are all present at the same time. If a complete service does not remedy the situation, major mechanical work is the only solution.

An engine overhaul involves restoring all internal parts to the specification of a new engine. During an overhaul, the pistons and the piston rings are renewed. New main and big-end bearings are generally fitted; if necessary, the crankshaft may be renewed to restore the journals. The valves are also serviced as well, since they are usually in less-than-perfect condition at this point. While the engine is being overhauled, other components, such as the starter and alternator, can be overhauled as well. The end result should be an as-new engine that will give many trouble-free miles. **Note:** *Critical cooling system components such as the hoses, thermostat and coolant pump should be renewed when an engine is overhauled. The radiator should be checked carefully, to ensure that it is not clogged or leaking. Also, it is a good idea to renew the oil pump whenever the engine is overhauled.*

Before beginning the engine overhaul, read through the entire procedure, to familiarise yourself with the scope and requirements of the job. Overhauling an engine is not difficult if you follow carefully all of the instructions, have the necessary tools and equipment, and pay close attention to all specifications. It can, however, be time-consuming. Plan on the car being off the road for a minimum of two weeks, especially if parts must be taken to an engineering works for repair or reconditioning. Check on the availability of parts and make sure that any necessary special tools and equipment are obtained in advance. Most work can be done with typical hand tools, although a number of precision measuring tools are required for inspecting parts to determine if they must be renewed. Often the engineering works will handle the inspection of parts and offer advice concerning reconditioning and renewal. **Note:** *Always wait until the engine has been completely dismantled, and until all components (especially the cylinder block and the crankshaft) have been inspected, before deciding what service and repair operations must be performed by an engineering works. The condition of these components will be the major factor to consider when determining whether to overhaul the original engine, or to buy a reconditioned unit. Do not, therefore, purchase parts or have overhaul work done on other components until they have been thoroughly inspected.* As a general rule, time is the primary cost of an overhaul, so it does not pay to fit worn or sub-standard parts.

As a final note, to ensure maximum life and minimum trouble from a reconditioned engine, everything must be assembled with care, in a spotlessly clean environment.

3 Engine/transmission removal – preparation and precautions

The engine on the Mercedes-Benz A-Class is removed complete with transmission and lowered on the subframe out from under the vehicle. The engine and transmission can then be split by using an engine hoist to lift the engine and transmission from the subframe and suspension. To carry out the removal of some of the ancillary components the subframe can be lowered complete with engine to access the upper components, see Section 4. If you have decided that the engine must be removed for overhaul or major repair work, several preliminary steps should be taken.

Locating a suitable place to work is extremely important. Adequate workspace, along with storage space for the vehicle, will be needed. If a workshop or garage is not available, at the very least a solid, level, clean work surface is required.

If possible, clear some shelving close to the work area and use it to store the engine components and ancillaries as they are removed and dismantled. In this manner, the components stand a better chance of staying clean and undamaged during the overhaul. Laying out components in groups together with their fixings bolts, screws, etc, will save time and avoid confusion when the engine is refitted.

Clean the engine compartment and engine before beginning the removal procedure; this will help visibility and help to keep tools clean.

The help of an assistant is essential; there are certain instances when one person cannot safely perform all of the operations required to remove the engine from the vehicle. Safety is of primary importance, considering the potential hazards involved in this kind of operation. A second person should always be in attendance to offer help in an emergency. If this is the first time you have removed an engine, advice and aid from someone more experienced would also be beneficial.

Plan the operation ahead of time. Before starting work, obtain (or arrange for the hire of) all of the tools and equipment you will need. Access to the following items will allow the task of removing and refitting the engine to be completed safely and with relative ease: a hoist and lifting tackle, trolley jacks – rated in excess of the weight of the engine, complete sets of spanners and sockets as described at the rear of this manual, wooden blocks, and plenty of rags and cleaning solvent for mopping-up spilled oil, coolant and fuel. A selection of different-sized plastic storage bins will also prove useful for keeping dismantled components grouped together. If any of the equipment must be hired, make sure that you arrange for it in advance, and perform all of the operations possible without it beforehand; this may save you time and money.

Plan on the vehicle being out of use for quite a while, especially if you intend to carry out an engine overhaul. Read through the whole of this Section and work out a strategy based on your own experience, and the tools, time and workspace available to you. Some of the overhaul processes may have to be carried out by a Mercedes-Benz dealer or an engineering works – these establishments often have busy schedules, so it would be prudent to consult them before removing or dismantling the engine, to get an idea of the amount of time required to carry out the work.

When removing the engine from the vehicle, be methodical about the disconnection of external components. Labeling cables and hoses as they are removed will greatly assist the refitting process.

4.7a Disconnect the wiring connectors – arrowed . . .

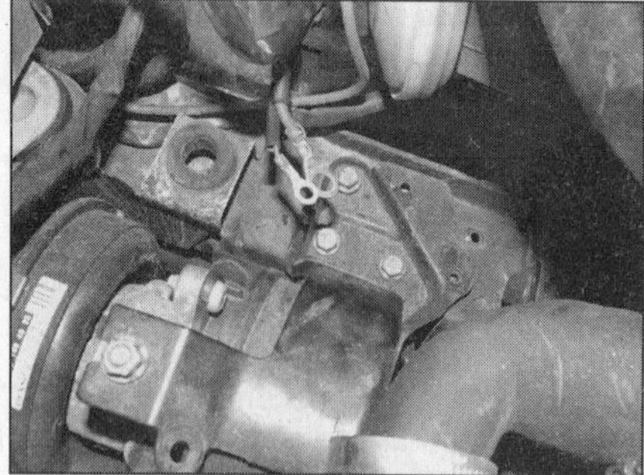
4.7b . . . and remove the connection block

4.8 Undo steering bolt – arrowed

Always be extremely careful when removing the engine from the engine compartment. Serious injury can result from careless actions. If help is required, it is better to wait until it is available than risk personal injury and/or damage components by continuing alone. By planning ahead and taking your time, a job of this nature, although major, can be accomplished successfully and without incident.

4 Engine and transmission – lowering, removal and refitting

Note: *To carry out some procedures, such as starter motor and coolant pump removal, it is possible to lower the engine/transmission assembly complete with front subframe by approximately 60 mm to make access easier.*

Lowering

1 Apply the handbrake, then jack up the front of the vehicle and support it on axle stands (see *Jacking and vehicle support*).

2 Remove both front roadwheels, inner wheel arch liners and engine undertrays.

3 Switch off the ignition and all electrical consumers, and remove the ignition key.

4 Disconnect the battery earth cable with reference to Chapter 5A.

5 Remove the engine top cover/air filter housing and all associated air ducting with reference to Chapter 4A or 4B.

6 Release the retaining clip and remove the windscreen washer fluid reservoir and move it to one side, with reference to Chapter 12.

7 Disconnect the positive wire and control wire for the power steering pump on the left-hand side of the subframe and remove the connection block **(see illustrations)**.

8 Undo the retaining bolt and disconnect the steering shaft coupling **(see illustration)**, make a note of its fitted position, with reference to Chapter 10.

9 Undo the retaining bolt(s) and disconnect the front exhaust pipe from the catalytic converter, with reference to Chapters 4A or 4B. Trace the wiring from the oxygen sensors and disconnect the wiring connector, releasing the wiring from any retaining clips **(see illustration)**. Note there are two sensors fitted.

10 Unclip the wiring harness from the top of the sump.

11 Undo the securing bolt and remove the retaining clip from the refrigerant line at the right-hand rear of the subframe **(see illustration)**.

12 Slacken (do not completely remove at this point) the upper mounting bolts from both right- and left-hand side suspension mountings **(see illustration)**.

13 Undo the front brake caliper mounting bolts and move the calipers to one side. Fasten the calipers up using cable ties to prevent brake hoses being damaged **(see illustration)**.

14 Make sure the trolley jacks are safely positioned under the front subframe. It may be necessary to support the engine from the top with an engine hoist and using a couple of trolley jacks under the front subframe to control lowering the engine and subframe.

15 Undo the mounting bolts and remove the metal strut plates from the rear of the subframe to the floor housing **(see illustration)**.

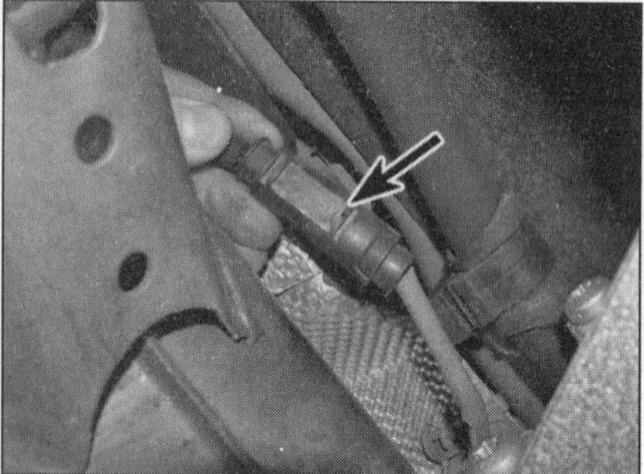
4.9 Disconnect the oxygen wiring connector – arrowed

4.11 Undo the retaining clip bolt – arrowed

4.12 Slacken the bolts – arrowed

4.13 Secure the brake caliper with a cable tie

4.15 Undo the bolts from the rear of the subframe

16 With the engine hoist and trolley jacks in position, work your way around the subframe and remove the eight subframe mounting bolts **(see illustration)**.

Warning: Make sure the subframe/engine is safely supported and the trolley jacks correctly positioned, before removing the mounting bolts. If required use axle stands to initially support the subframe.

17 Remove the upper strut mounting bolts and then carefully lower the engine/transmission assembly complete with subframe approximately 60 mm **(see illustration)**. As the engine is lowered, check around the engine compartment, to make sure that all cables, hoses, wiring, etc, are not going to get damaged.

18 Insert threaded rod into six of the subframe mounting bolt holes (three each side). Fit a nut between the chassis and the subframe and lock it into position to support the threaded rod. Fit a large washer and nut to the bottom of the threaded rod and thread it up to the lower part of the subframe **(see illustration)**. Carry this procedure out on all six lengths of threaded rod.

19 With the six lengths of threaded rod in position and the subframe equally adjusted to the 60 mm lower position the trolley jacks, if required, can be removed from under the subframe.

20 There is now more space to work on any components that are on the rear of the cylinder block, such as the starter motor, coolant pump, oil level/pressure switch, etc.

21 Refitting is the reversal of the removal procedure, with reference to the relevant Chapters.

Removal

Note: *Mercedes-Benz technicians have special tools and engine lowering equipment to carry out this work. An engine hoist or a couple of trolley jacks are required, capable of supporting the engine and front subframe. Renew all hose retaining clips on refitting*

Warning: If required, have the air conditioning system discharged by a suitably-qualified specialist before attempting to remove the compressor.

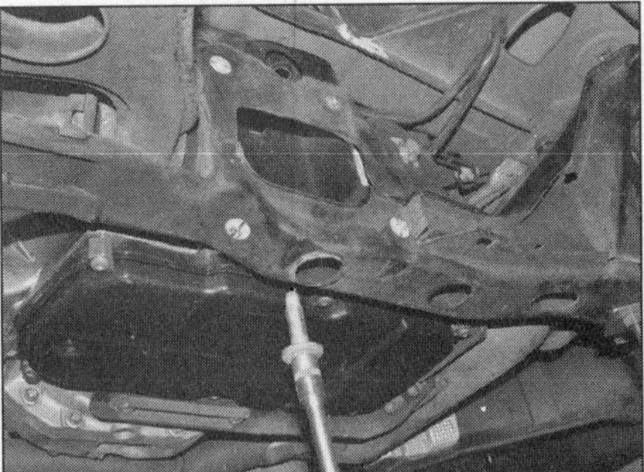
4.16 Removing the subframe bolts

4.17 Engine and subframe supported on three trolley jacks

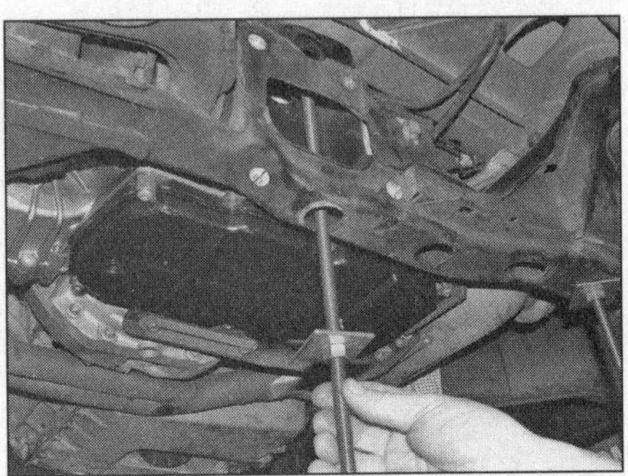
4.18a Insert the threaded rod . . .

4.18b . . . and lock a nut under the vehicle body

22 The engine and transmission assembly is lowered from the engine compartment on the front subframe, and then withdrawn from under the car.

23 Apply the handbrake, then jack up the front of the vehicle and support it on axle stands (see *Jacking and vehicle support*). Remove both front roadwheels and inner wheel arch liners. **Note:** *The vehicle needs to be at a height so that the engine and subframe can be withdrawn from under the vehicle.*

24 Switch off the ignition and all electrical consumers, and remove the ignition key.

25 Disconnect the battery earth cable with reference to Chapter 5A.

26 Drain the cooling system as described in Chapter 1A or 1B.

27 Drain engine oil and transmission oil with reference to Chapter 1A or 1B.

28 Release the retaining clip and remove the windscreen washer fluid reservoir and move it to one side, with reference to Chapter 12.

29 Remove the engine top cover/air filter housing and all associated air ducting with reference to Chapter 4A or 4B.

30 Disconnect the fuel lines from the fuel rail/diesel filter with reference to Chapter 4A or 4B.

31 Disconnect the wiring connector and coolant hose(s) from the thermostat housing **(see illustrations)**.

32 Disconnect the lower coolant hose from the heater matrix at the rear of the engine compartment **(see illustration)**.

33 On models from 01/06/99, disconnect the coolant hoses and remove the coolant expansion tank from the mounting bracket on the inner wing panel **(see illustration)**.

34 On automatic models, disconnect the two oil lines from the left-hand side of the radiator

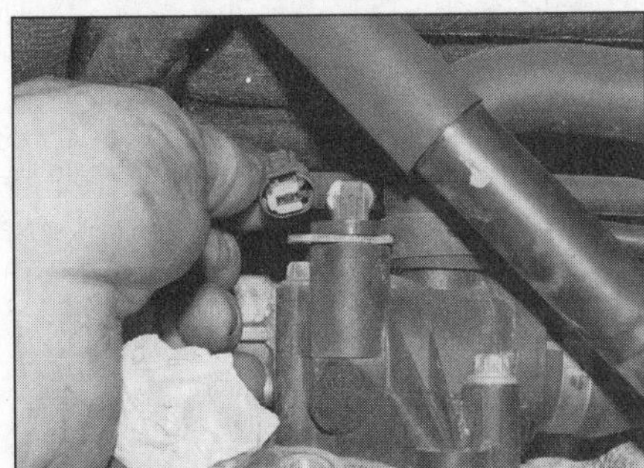
4.31a Disconnect the wiring connector . . .

4.31b . . . and the coolant hoses

4.32 Disconnect the heater hose

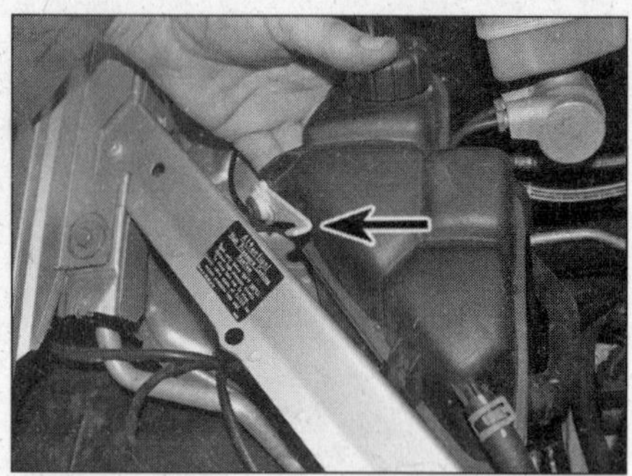
4.33 Release the locking lever – arrowed

4.34 Disconnect the hoses – arrowed

4.35 Undo cable retaining bolt – arrowed

4.36a Release the locking collar (arrowed) for the breather hose

4.36b Pull off the vacuum hose to disconnect

4.37 Disconnect the wiring connector from the ECM

(see illustration). Plug the ends of the pipes to prevent dirt ingress.

Petrol models

35 Undo the retaining bolt and disconnect the earth cable from the right-hand front engine mounting **(see illustration).**

36 Disconnect the breather pipe and vacuum hose from the front left-hand end of the inlet manifold **(see illustrations).**

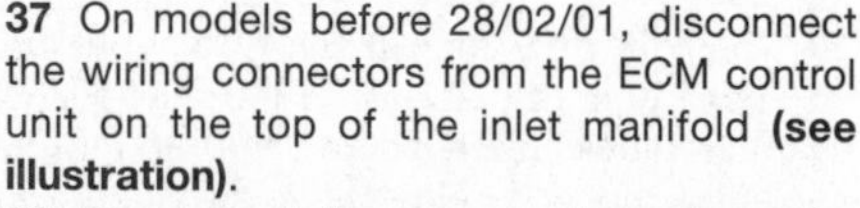
37 On models before 28/02/01, disconnect the wiring connectors from the ECM control unit on the top of the inlet manifold **(see illustration).**

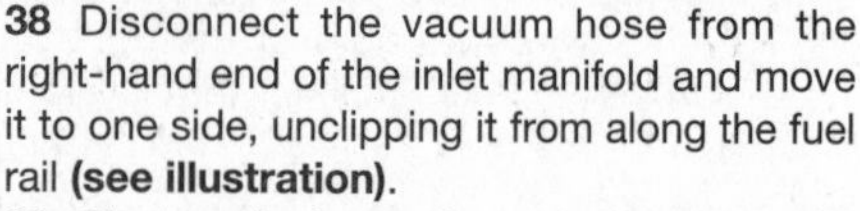
38 Disconnect the vacuum hose from the right-hand end of the inlet manifold and move it to one side, unclipping it from along the fuel rail **(see illustration).**

39 Slacken the hose clip and disconnect the coolant hose from the right-hand rear of the cylinder head **(see illustration)**

40 On models from 01/03/01, disconnect the hose from the secondary air pump **(see illustration).**

Diesel models

41 Undo the retaining screws, and then unclip the cover at the rear of the engine compartment and disconnect the engine wiring loom from the timer relay and diesel injection (CDI) control modules **(see illustrations).**

4.38 Disconnect the vacuum hose

4.39 Disconnect the coolant hose

4.40 Disconnect the air hose

4.41a Remove the ECU cover . . .

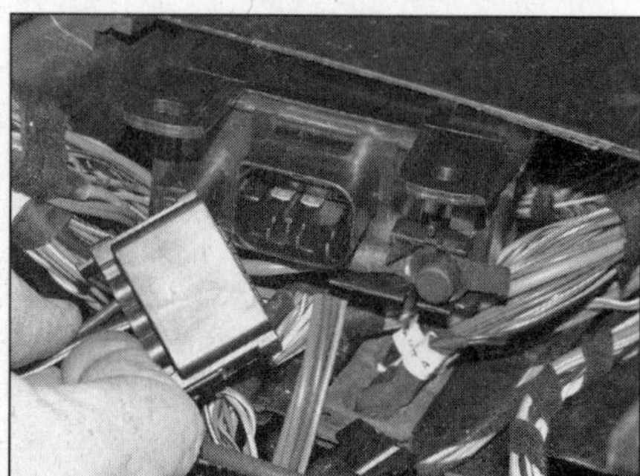
4.41b . . . and disconnect the wiring from the timer relay

42 Remove the front bumper as described in Chapter 11.

43 Where fitted, remove the intercooler as described in Chapter 4B.

44 Disconnect the vacuum pipes from the turbocharger and EGR valve **(see illustrations)**.

45 Disconnect the vacuum pipe from the brake vacuum pump, which is located on the right-and end of the cylinder head.

46 Slacken the retaining clips and disconnect the induction hose from the turbocharger **(see illustration)**.

47 Remove the turbocharger as described in Chapter 4D.

All models

48 Undo the retaining bolts and disconnect the steering shaft coupling **(see illustration 4.8)**, with reference to Chapter 10.

49 Disconnect the positive wire and control wire for the power steering pump on the left-hand side of the subframe and remove the connection block **(see illustrations 4.7a and 4.7b)**.

50 Disconnect the gearchange cables from the transmission with reference to Chapter 7A or 7B.

51 Slacken (do not completely remove at this point) the upper mounting bolts from both right and left hand side suspension mountings **(see illustration 4.12)**.

52 Undo the front brake caliper mounting bolts and move the calipers to one side. Fasten the calipers up using cable ties to prevent brake hoses being damaged **(see illustration 4.13)**.

53 Undo the retaining bolt(s) and disconnect the front exhaust pipe from the catalytic converter, with reference to Chapters 4C or 4D.

54 Trace the wiring from the oxygen sensors and disconnect the wiring connector, releasing the wiring from any retaining clips **(see illustration 4.9)**.

55 On manual models, remove the retaining clip and disconnect the clutch hose from the clutch slave cylinder with reference to Chapter 6.

56 Where applicable, refer to Chapter 3 and unbolt the air conditioning compressor from the rear of the sump, without disconnecting the refrigerant lines. Suspend the compressor to the underside of the vehicle, taking care not to damage any pipes and wiring **(see illustration)**.

57 Undo the securing bolt and remove the retaining clip from the refrigerant line at the right-hand rear of the subframe.

58 Make sure the trolley jacks and framework are safely positioned under the front subframe. It may be necessary to support the engine from the top with an engine hoist and using a couple of trolley jacks under the front subframe to control lowering the engine and subframe from under the vehicle. Note that a framework that fits on top of the heads of the jacks to support the front subframe will need to be made.

4.44a Disconnect the vacuum pipe – arrowed

59 Undo the mounting bolts and remove the metal strut plates from the rear of the subframe to the floor housing **(see illustration 4.15)**.

60 With the engine hoist and trolley jacks in position, work your way around the subframe and remove the eight subframe mounting bolts **(see illustration 4.16)**.

Warning: Make sure the subframe/engine is safely supported and the trolley jacks correctly positioned, before removing the mounting bolts. If required use axle stands to initially support the subframe.

61 Disconnect the wiring connectors from the starter motor and alternator, then make a final check to ensure that all relevant wiring, hoses and pipes have been disconnected. **Note:** *It may be necessary to lower the engine/subframe slightly, to access the wiring connectors, refer to Chapter 5A.*

62 Remove the upper strut mounting bolts and then carefully lower the engine/transmission assembly complete with subframe **(see illustration 4.17)**, and withdraw forwards from the front of the car.

Refitting

63 Reconnection and refitting are a reversal of removal, bearing in mind the following points:

a) On automatic transmission models, when fitting the torque converter, make sure that it engages correctly.

b) Ensure that any brackets noted before removal are in place on the engine-to-transmission bolts.

c) Tighten all fixings to the specified torque, where given.

4.44b Disconnect the EGR vacuum pipe

d) Where applicable, have the air conditioning system recharged with refrigerant by a suitably-qualified professional.

e) Ensure that all wiring, hoses and pipes are correctly reconnected and routed as noted before removal.

f) Ensure that the fuel lines are correctly reconnected.

g) On completion, refill the cooling system, engine oil and transmission oil as described in Chapter 1A or 1B.

5 Engine overhaul – preliminary information

It is much easier to dismantle and work on the engine if it is mounted on a portable engine stand. These stands can often be hired from a tool hire shop. Before the engine is mounted on a stand, the flywheel should be removed, so that the stand bolts can be tightened into the end of the cylinder block/crankcase. **Note:** *Do not measure cylinder bore dimensions with the engine mounted on this type of stand*

If a stand is not available, it is possible to dismantle the engine with it blocked up on a sturdy workbench, or on the floor. Be very careful not to tip or drop the engine when working without a stand.

If you intend to obtain a reconditioned engine, all ancillaries must be removed first, so that they can be transferred to the new engine (just as they will if you are doing a complete engine overhaul yourself). These components

4.46 Slacken the retaining clip at the turbocharger

4.56 Using cable ties (arrowed) to secure the compressor to one side

6.4 Removing the crankshaft pulley bolt

include the following (it may be necessary to transfer additional components, such as the oil level dipstick/tube assembly, oil filter housing, etc, depending on which components are supplied with the reconditioned engine:

Petrol engines

a) Alternator and starter motor (Chapter 5A).
b) The ignition system components including all sensors and spark plugs (Chapters 1A and 5B).
c) The fuel injection system components (Chapter 4A).
d) All electrical switches, actuators and sensors, and the engine wiring harness (Chapters 3, 4A and 5B).
e) Inlet and exhaust manifolds (Chapters 4A and 4C).
f) Engine mountings (Chapter 2A).
g) Clutch components (Chapter 6).
h) Oil separator (where applicable).

Diesel engines

a) Alternator and starter motor (Chapter 5A).
b) The glow plug/preheating system components (Chapter 5C).
c) All fuel system components, including fuel injectors, all sensors and actuators (Chapter 4B).
d) The brake vacuum pump (Chapter 9).
e) All electrical switches, actuators and sensors, and the engine wiring harness (Chapter 3, 4B and 5C).
f) Inlet and exhaust manifolds/turbocharger (Chapters 4B and 4D).
g) Engine mountings (Chapter 2B).
h) Clutch components (Chapter 6).

7.3 Removing the pulley

All engines

Note: *When removing the external components from the engine, pay close attention to details that may be helpful or important during refitting. Note the fitted position of gaskets, seals, spacers, pins, washers, bolts, mounting brackets and other small components.*

If you are obtaining a short engine (the engine cylinder block/crankcase, crankshaft, pistons and connecting rods, all fully assembled), then the cylinder head, sump, oil pump, timing chain (together with tensioner and covers), auxiliary drivebelt (together with its tensioner), coolant pump, thermostat housing, coolant outlet elbows, oil filter housing and, where applicable, oil cooler will also have to be removed.

If you are planning a full overhaul, the engine can be dismantled in the order given below:

a) Inlet and exhaust manifolds (see the relevant part of Chapter 4).
b) Timing chain, sprockets and tensioner (see the relevant part of Chapter 2).
c) Cylinder head (see the relevant part of Chapter 2).
d) Flywheel/driveplate (see the relevant part of Chapter 2).
e) Sump (see Section 11).
f) Oil pump (see Section 12).
g) Piston/connecting rod assemblies (see Section 13).
h) Crankshaft (see Section 14).

6 Crankshaft pulley – removal and refitting

Note: *The crankshaft pulley bolt must be renewed whenever removed.*

Removal

1 Remove the engine and subframe assembly and then undo the engine mountings and lift the engine from the subframe, as described in Section 4.

2 If not already done, mark the auxiliary drivebelt for normal rotation to ensure correct refitting, and note its routing for ease of refitting. Remove the drivebelt as described in Chapter 1A.

3 The engine must now be held stationary while the crankshaft pulley bolt is loosened. Remove the starter motor and prevent the engine from turning by using a wide-bladed screwdriver engaged with the ring gear teeth on the flywheel/driveplate.

4 Unscrew and remove the bolt and withdraw the pulley from the end of the crankshaft, making sure the Woodruff key is located securely in the end of the crankshaft **(see illustration)**. The bolt must be renewed whenever removed. It is recommended that the timing cover oil seal be renewed at the same time, with reference to Section 15.

Refitting

5 Thoroughly clean the end of the crankshaft and timing cover.

6 If required, fit the new timing cover oil seal as described in Section 15.

7 Make sure the Woodruff key is located correctly in the end of the crankshaft and refit the pulley, tightening the bolt in the two stages given in Specifications. Use the same method of stopping the engine from turning as on removal.

8 Refit the auxiliary drivebelt as described in Chapter 1A.

9 Refit the engine and subframe as described in Section 4.

7.8 Undo the two bolts – arrowed

7 Timing chain and cover – removal and refitting

Note: *Sealant will be required for the jointing faces of the camshaft cover, timing cover and sump (Mercedes-Benz recommended sealant number – A 003 989 98 20 or equivalent).*

Timing chain cover

Removal

1 Remove the engine and subframe assembly and then undo the engine mountings and lift the engine from the subframe, as described in Section 4.

2 If not already done, mark the auxiliary drivebelt for normal rotation to ensure correct refitting, and note its routing for ease of refitting. Remove the drivebelt as described in Chapter 1A.

3 Unscrew the retaining bolts and remove the coolant pump pulley from the drive flange **(see illustration)**.

4 Remove the camshaft cover as described in Chapters 2A or 2B.

5 Remove the sump as described in Section 11.

6 Remove the crankshaft pulley as described in Section 6.

7 Where applicable, disconnect the crankcase breather hose from the side of the timing chain cover.

8 Undo the two upper retaining bolts securing the timing cover to the cylinder head **(see illustration)**.

9 Progressively unscrew and remove all of the following retaining bolts to the cylinder block, noting their locations as they are of different

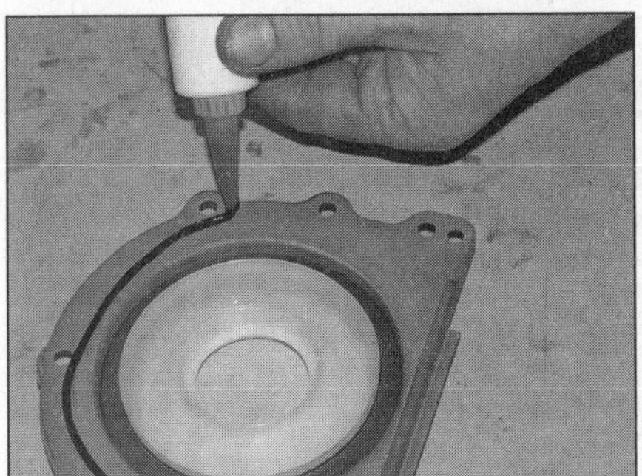
7.10 Applying sealant to the cover

7.20 Using a spanner to counterhold the camshaft

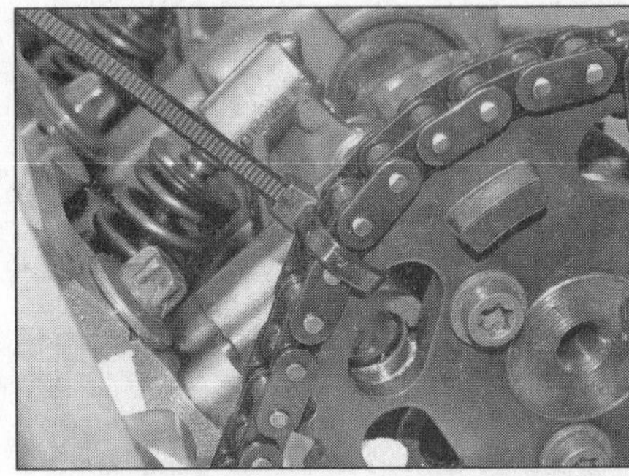
7.21 Cable tie the chain to the sprocket

lengths, then remove the timing cover from the engine. If necessary, tap the cover lightly to release it, and then withdraw the cover from the location dowels. It is recommended that the timing cover oil seal be renewed at the same time, with reference to Section 15.

Refitting

10 Ensure that the cylinder block mating face of the timing cover is free from all traces of old sealant, oil and grease, and then apply a 1.5 to 2.5 mm thick bead of silicone sealant (A 003 989 98 20 or equivalent) to the timing cover **(see illustration)**. Note that the sealant should be run around the inside of the bolt holes **(see illustration 6.28 in Chapter 2B)** and the timing cover must be fitted within 10 minutes of applying the sealant. Also apply some sealant under the front edge of the cylinder head, where the top of the timing cover meets. See note at the beginning of this Section.
11 If required, fit the new timing cover oil seal as described in Section 15.
12 Locate the cover onto the engine, and then insert the bolts in their correct positions as noted on removal. Tighten them progressively to the specified torques.
13 Refit the sump (Section 11) and crankshaft pulley (Section 6).
14 Refit the camshaft cover as described in Chapters 2A or 2B.
15 Refit the coolant pump pulley and tighten the bolts.
16 Refit the auxiliary drivebelt with reference to Chapter 1A.
17 Refit the engine to the subframe and back into the vehicle as described in Section 4.

Timing chain

Removal

18 Remove the timing chain cover as described above.
19 Set the engine to TDC as described in Chapter 2A or 2B, Section 3.
20 While holding the camshaft in position, using a spanner on the hexagon part of the shaft, loosen the sprocket retaining bolt(s) **(see illustration)**. Make sure the markings on the camshaft and housing are still aligned at TDC.
21 Using a couple of cable ties, secure the timing chain to the camshaft sprocket, so that it will stay in position for refitting **(see illustration)**.

7.22 Note the fitted position of the tensioner – arrowed

7.23 Removing the camshaft sprocket

22 Mark the fitted position of the timing chain tensioner, as it has to be fitted the correct way around. Undo the two retaining bolts evenly as it is spring-loaded, and then withdraw it from the cylinder head **(see illustration)**. Remove the gasket/seal and discard, a new one will be required for refitting.
23 The retaining bolts can now be removed and the sprocket withdrawn from the end of the camshaft **(see illustration)**.
24 Unhook the timing chain from around the crankshaft sprocket and withdraw it complete with camshaft sprocket out from the top of the cylinder head.

Refitting

25 Refitting the reversal of the removal procedure. Refer to Chapter 2A or 2B, Section 3, for setting up the timing marks.

8.4 Remove the thermostat housing

8 Cylinder head – dismantling

Note: *A valve spring compressor tool will be required for this operation.*

Petrol engines

1 With the cylinder head removed (see Chapter 2A), proceed as follows.
2 If not already removed, remove the inlet and exhaust manifolds as described in Chapter 4A and 4C.
3 Remove the camshaft and roller rocker arms, as described in the relevant part of Chapter 2A.
4 If desired, unbolt the thermostat housing from the rear of the cylinder head, and recover the seal **(see illustration)**.
5 Unbolt any remaining auxiliary brackets and/or engine lifting brackets from the cylinder head as necessary, noting their locations to aid refitting.
6 Turn the cylinder head over, and rest it on one side.
7 Using a valve spring compressor, compress each valve spring in turn until the split collets can be removed. If, when the valve spring compressor is screwed down, the spring cap refuses to free and expose the split collets, gently tap the top of the tool, directly over the spring cap, with a light hammer, this will free the retainer **(see illustration)**.
8 Release the pressure on the valve spring compressor, and lift off the spring cap, spring and seating washer **(see illustrations)**.

8.7 Compressing the valve spring with compression tool

8.8a Lift off the spring cap and spring . . .

8.8b . . . and then remove the seating washer

8.9 Using a removal tool to remove the valve stem oil seal

8.10 Removing a valve

9 Using a pair of pliers, or a removal tool, carefully extract the valve stem oil seal from the top of the valve guide **(see illustration)**.

10 Withdraw the valve from the gasket side of the cylinder head **(see illustration)**.

11 It is essential that each valve is stored together with its collets, cap, spring and spring seat. The valves should be kept in their correct sequences, unless they are so badly worn that they are to be renewed.

Diesel engines

12 With the cylinder head removed (see Chapter 2B), proceed as follows.

13 If not already removed, remove the inlet and exhaust manifolds as described in Chapters 4B and 4D.

14 Remove the camshaft and hydraulic tappets, as described in Chapter 2B.

15 Remove the glow plugs.

16 Remove the fuel injectors, with reference to Chapter 4B.

17 Unbolt any remaining auxiliary brackets and/or engine lifting brackets from the cylinder head as necessary, noting their locations to aid refitting.

18 Proceed as described in paragraphs 6 to 11.

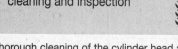

9 Cylinder head and valves - cleaning and inspection

1 Thorough cleaning of the cylinder head and valve components, followed by a detailed inspection, will enable you to decide how much valve service work must be carried out during engine overhaul. **Note:** *If the engine has been severely overheated, it is best to assume that the cylinder head is warped - check carefully for signs of this.*

Cleaning

2 Using a suitable degreasing agent, remove all traces of oil deposits from the cylinder head, paying particular attention to the camshaft bearing surfaces, hydraulic tappet bores, valve guides and oilways. Scrape off any traces of old gasket from the mating surfaces, taking care not to score or gouge them. If using emery paper, do not use a grade of less than 100.

3 Turn the head over and, using a blunt blade, scrape any carbon deposits from the combustion chambers and ports. Finally, wash the entire head casting with a suitable solvent to remove the remaining debris.

9.7 Measuring the distortion of the cylinder head gasket surface

4 Clean the valve heads and stems using a fine wire brush (or a power-operated wire brush). If the valve is covered with heavy carbon deposits, scrape off the majority of the deposits with a blunt blade first, then use the wire brush. Thoroughly clean the remainder of the components using solvent and allow them to dry completely. Discard the oil seals, as new ones must be fitted when the cylinder head is reassembled.

Inspection

Cylinder head

5 Examine the head casting closely to identify any damage or cracks that may have developed. Cracks can often be identified from evidence of coolant or oil leakage. Pay particular attention to the areas around the valve seats and spark plug/fuel injector holes. Moderately pitted and scorched valve seats can be repaired by lapping the valves in during reassembly, as described later in this Chapter.

6 Badly worn or damaged valve seats may be restored by recutting where permitted, only minimal reworking being possible. If in any doubt as to the condition of the seats, consult your local engineering specialist.

7 Measure any distortion of the gasket surfaces using a straight-edge and a set of feeler blades. Take one measurement longitudinally on the manifold mating surface(s). Take several measurements across the head gasket surface, to assess the level of distortion in all planes **(see illustration)**.

8 Compare the measurements with the figures in the Specifications.

9 If the cylinder head is distorted beyond the specified limit, it may be possible to have it machined by an engineering works. If the head is distorted beyond the specified limit, the head must be renewed.

Camshaft

10 Inspection of the camshaft is covered in Parts A and B of this Chapter, as applicable.

Valves and associated components

11 Examine each valve closely for signs of wear. Inspect the valve stems for wear ridges, scoring or variations in diameter; measure their diameters at several points along their lengths with a micrometer to check **(see illustration)**.

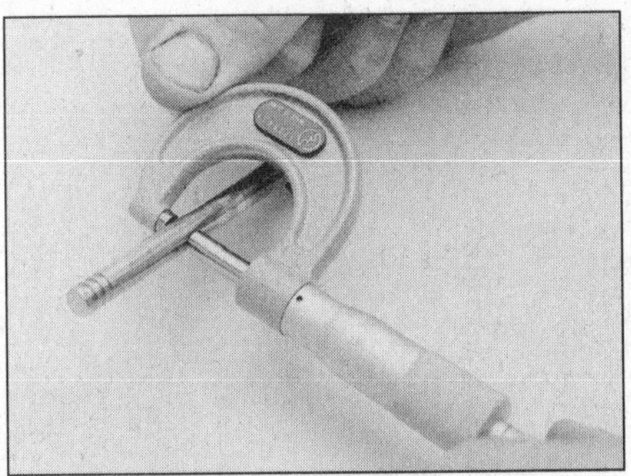

9.11 **Measure the diameter of the valve stems using a micrometer**

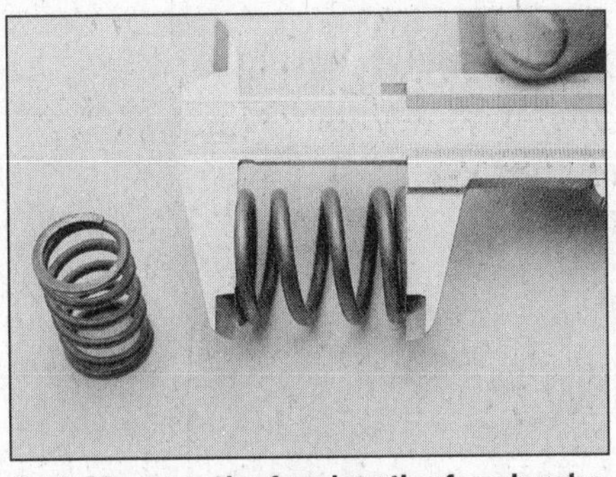

9.14 **Measure the free length of each valve spring**

9.15 **Checking the squareness of a valve spring**

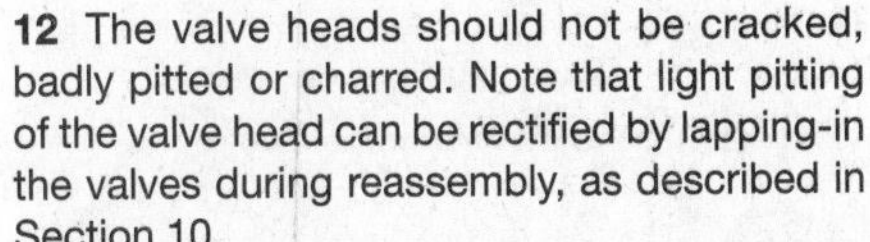

12 The valve heads should not be cracked, badly pitted or charred. Note that light pitting of the valve head can be rectified by lapping-in the valves during reassembly, as described in Section 10.

13 Check that the valve stem end face is free from excessive pitting or indentation; this could be caused by defective rocker arms.

14 Using vernier calipers, measure the free length of each of the valve springs. As a manufacturer's figure is not quoted, the only way to check the length of the springs is by comparison with a new component. Note that valve springs are usually renewed during a major engine overhaul **(see illustration)**.

15 Stand each spring on its end on a flat surface, against an engineer's square **(see illustration)**. Check the squareness of the spring visually, and renew it if it appears distorted.

16 Renew the valve stem oil seals regardless of their apparent condition.

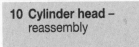

10 Cylinder head – reassembly

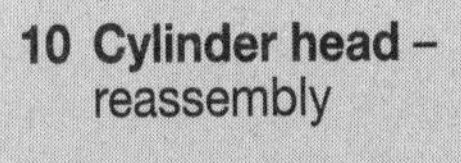

Note: *A valve spring compressor tool will be required for this operation.*

Petrol engines

1 To achieve a gas-tight seal between the valves and their seats, it will be necessary to lap-in (or grind-in) the valves. To complete this process you will need a quantity of fine/coarse grinding paste and a grinding tool – this can either be of the rubber sucker type, or the automatic type which is driven by a rotary power tool.

2 Smear a small quantity of *fine* grinding paste on the sealing face of the valve head. Turn the cylinder head over so that the combustion chambers are facing upwards and insert the valve into the correct guide. Attach the grinding tool to the valve head and using a backward/forward rotary action, grind the valve head into its seat. Periodically lift the valve and rotate it to redistribute the grinding paste **(see illustration)**.

3 Continue this process until the contact between valve and seat produces an unbroken, matt grey ring of uniform width, on both faces. Repeat the operation on the remaining valves.

4 If the valves and seats are so badly pitted that coarse grinding paste must be used, bear in that there is a maximum permissible reworking dimension for the valves and seats (see your local engineering specialist). If this minimum dimension is exceeded due to excessive lapping-in, the hydraulic tappets may not operate correctly, and the cylinder head must be renewed.

5 Assuming the repair is feasible, work as described previously, but use coarse grinding paste initially, to achieve a dull finish on the valve face and seat. Wash off the coarse paste with solvent and repeat the process using fine grinding paste to obtain the correct finish.

6 When all the valves have been ground in, remove all traces of grinding paste from the cylinder head and valves using solvent, and allow the head and valves to dry completely.

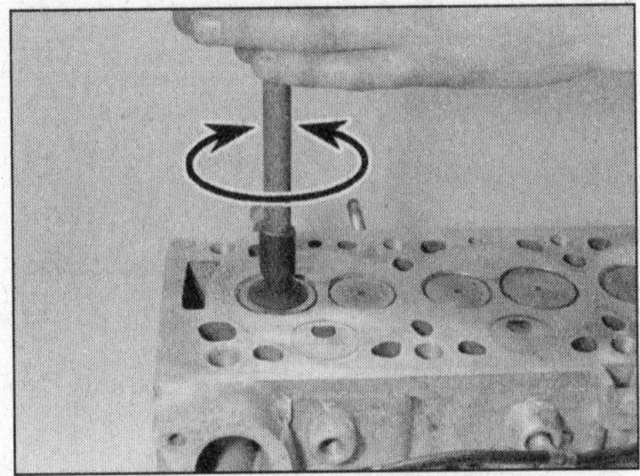

10.2 Grinding-in a valve

10.8b Fitting a protective sleeve over the valve stem before fitting the stem seal – petrol shown

7 Turn the cylinder head on its side.

8 Working on one valve at a time, lubricate the valve stem with clean engine oil, and insert the valve into its guide. Fit one of the protective plastic sleeves supplied with the new valve stem oil seals over the end of the valve stem – this will protect the oil seal as it is being fitted **(see illustrations)**.

9 Dip a new valve stem seal in clean engine oil, and carefully push it over the valve stem and onto the top of the valve guide – take care not to damage the stem seal as it is fitted. Use a suitable long-reach socket or a valve stem seal-fitting tool to press the seal firmly into position **(see illustrations)**. Remove the protective sleeve from the valve stem.

10 Where applicable, fit the spring seating washer onto the cylinder head, and then locate

10.8a Lubricate the valve stem with clean engine oil – petrol shown

10.9a Carefully slide the seal over the protective sleeve . . .

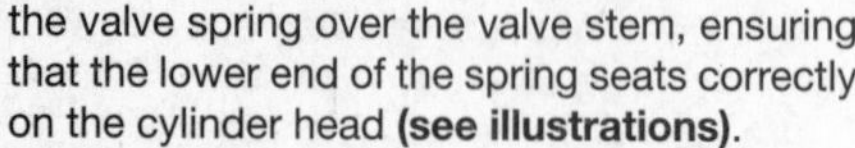

10.9b . . . and use a long-reach socket to fit a valve stem oil seal

10.10a Fitting a valve spring seating washer . . .

10.10b . . . and then the valve spring

the valve spring over the valve stem, ensuring that the lower end of the spring seats correctly on the cylinder head **(see illustrations)**.

11 Fit the upper spring seat over the top of the spring, then using a valve spring compressor, compress the spring until the upper seat is pushed beyond the collet grooves in the valve stem. Refit the split collets. Gradually release the spring compressor, checking that the collets remain correctly seated as the spring extends. When correctly seated, the upper spring seat should force the collets securely into the grooves in the end of the valve stem.

12 Repeat this process for the remaining sets of valve components, ensuring that all components are refitted to their original locations. To settle the components after installation, strike the end of each valve stem with a mallet, using a block of wood to protect the stem from damage. Check before progressing any further that the split collets remain firmly seated in the grooves in the end of the valve stem.

13 Refit any auxiliary brackets and/or engine lifting brackets to their original locations, as noted before removal.

14 Where applicable, refit the coolant housing to the rear of the cylinder head, using a new seal.

15 Refit the camshaft and roller/rocker arms as described in Chapter 2A.

16 Refit the inlet and exhaust manifolds as described in Chapters 4A and 4C.

Diesel engines

17 Proceed as described in paragraphs 1 to 13.

18 Refit the fuel injectors, with reference to Chapter 4B.

19 Refit the glow plugs.

20 Refit the camshafts and rocker arms, as described in Chapter 2B.

21 Refit the inlet and exhaust manifolds (and turbocharger, where applicable), as described in Chapters 4B and 4D.

11 Sump – removal and refitting

Removal

1 Drain the engine oil as described in Chapter 1A or 1B.

2 Remove the engine and subframe assembly, and then undo the engine mountings and lift the engine from the subframe, as described in Section 4.

3 If not already done, mark the auxiliary drivebelt for normal rotation to ensure correct refitting, and note its routing for ease of refitting. Remove the drivebelt as described in Chapter 1A or 1B.

4 Undo the retaining bolt and withdraw the dipstick guide tube from the cylinder block **(see illustrations)**. Remove and discard the O-ring seal at the lower end of the dipstick tube, a new one will be required for refitting. Disconnect the wiring connector from the oil level/temperature sensor on the sump **(see illustration)**.

5 Release the retaining clip and disconnect the crankcase breather pipe from the sump **(see illustration)**.

6 Undo the retaining bolts and remove the auxiliary drivebelt tensioners/rollers mounting bracket from the timing chain end of the sump **(see illustration)**.

11.4a Undo the retaining bolt – arrowed . . .

11.4b . . . and withdraw the dipstick guide tube

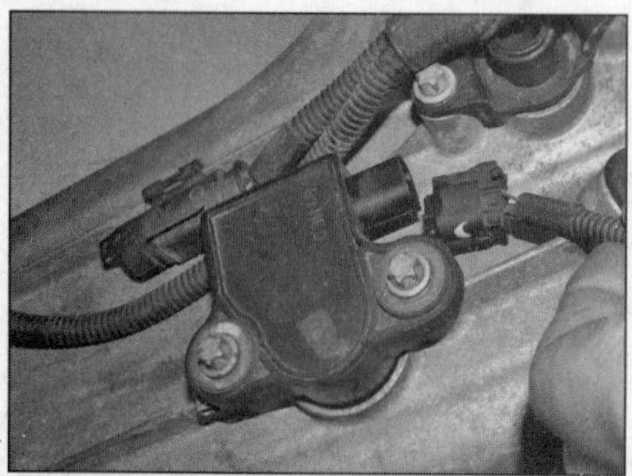

11.4c Disconnect the wiring connector

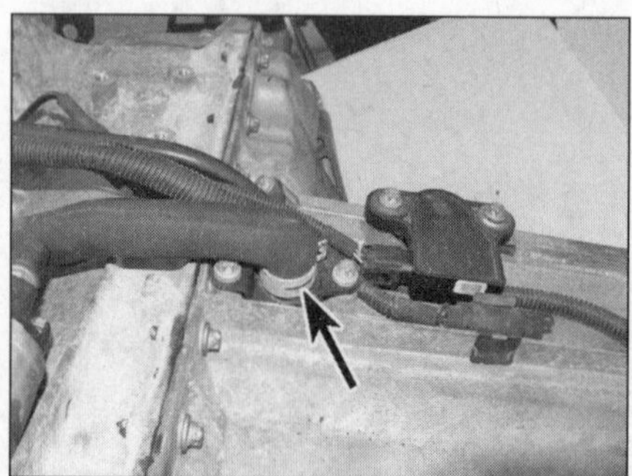

11.5 Release the retaining clip (arrowed) from the breather pipe

11.6 Removing the mounting bracket

7 With the hoist/lifting tackle attached to the engine lifting brackets on the cylinder head, raise the hoist to just take the weight of the engine.

8 Unscrew and remove the bolts securing the sump to the cylinder block, and then withdraw the sump.

9 If necessary, release the sump by tapping with a soft-faced mallet.

Refitting

10 Commence refitting by thoroughly cleaning the mating faces of the sump and cylinder block. Ensure that all traces of old sealant are removed.

11 Ensure that the cylinder block mating face of the sump is free from all traces of old sealant, oil and grease, and then apply a 1.5 to 2.5 mm thick bead of silicone sealant (A 003 989 98 20 or equivalent) to the sump **(see illustration)**. Note that the sealant should be run around the inside of the bolt holes in the sump. The sump must be fitted within 10 minutes of applying the sealant.

12 Offer the sump up to the cylinder block, then refit the retaining bolts, and progressively tighten them in diagonal sequence to the specified torque.

13 Refit the auxiliary drivebelt tensioners/rollers mounting bracket to the timing chain end of the sump.

14 Refit the auxiliary drivebelt as described in Chapter 1A or 1B.

15 Refit the crankcase breather pipe to the sump and tighten the retaining clip.

16 Reconnect the wiring connector to the oil level/temperature sender on the sump.

17 Fit new O-ring seal and refit the dipstick guide tube to the cylinder block **(see illustration)**.

18 Refit the engine to the subframe and back into the vehicle as described in Section 4.

19 On completion, refill the engine with oil and check for oil leaks, with reference to Chapter 1A or 1B.

12 Oil pump, drive chain and sprockets – removal, inspection and refitting

Removal

1 Remove the sump as described in Section 11. It is not necessary to remove the timing cover unless renewing the chain.

2 Undo the retaining bolts and remove the cover from the oil pump drive sprocket **(see illustration)**.

3 Unscrew the mounting bolts and withdraw the oil pump from the cylinder block and disengage the sprocket from the oil pump drive chain **(see illustration)**. Remove and discard the O-ring oil seal, a new one will be required for refitting.

4 If it is required to remove the oil pump chain, remove the timing chain and timing cover as described in Section 7. Unhook the chain from around the crankshaft sprocket and remove.

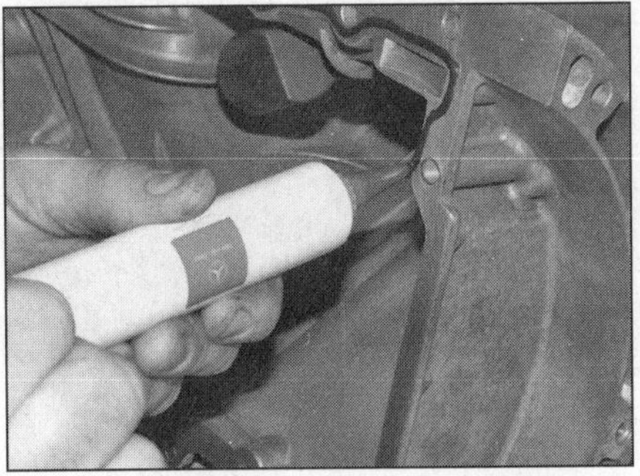

11.11 Applying sealant to the sump

Inspection

5 Thoroughly clean all components, then examine the oil pump drive chain for excessive wear. Also check the sprocket teeth for wear.

6 If the engine has covered a high mileage, the chain and sprockets should be renewed as a matter of course.

Refitting

7 Fit new O-ring seal and then engage the oil pump sprocket with the chain and locate the oil pump on the cylinder block and the chain around the crankshaft sprocket **(see illustration)**, insert the mounting bolts and tighten them to the specified torque.

8 Refit the timing chain with reference to Section 7.

9 Refit the cover over the oil pump sprocket and tighten the retaining bolt.

10 Refit the sump with reference to Section 11.

12.2 Removing the sprocket cover

12.7 Fit new O-ring seal to the oil pump

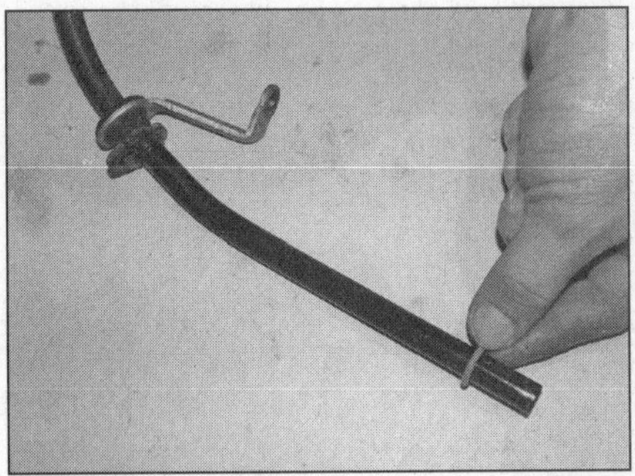

11.17 Fit new O-ring seal to the guide tube

13 Piston/connecting rod assemblies – removal

1 Remove the cylinder head, as described in Chapter 2A or 2B.

2 Remove the sump and oil baffle plate, and oil pump, as described in Sections 11 and 12 of this Chapter.

3 Inspect the tops of the cylinder bores for ridges at the point where the pistons reach top dead centre. These must be removed otherwise the pistons may be damaged when they are pushed out of their bores. Use a scraper or ridge reamer to remove the ridges. Such a ridge indicates excessive wear of the cylinder bore.

4 Check the connecting rods and big-end caps for identification markings. Both connecting rods and caps should be marked with the cylinder number on the exhaust

12.3 Removing the oil pump from the drive chain

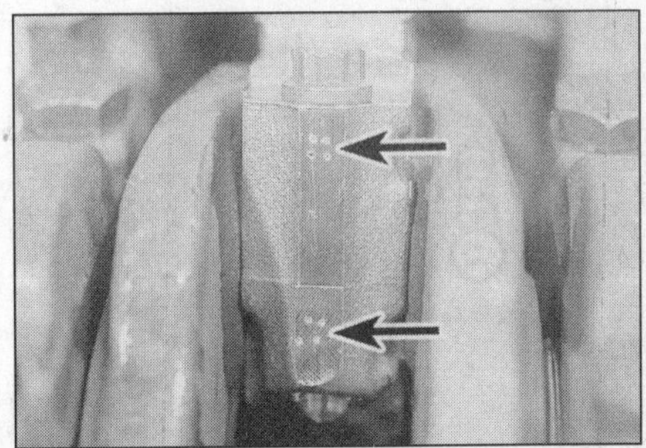

13.4 If required, mark the caps and connecting rods with cylinder numbers – arrowed

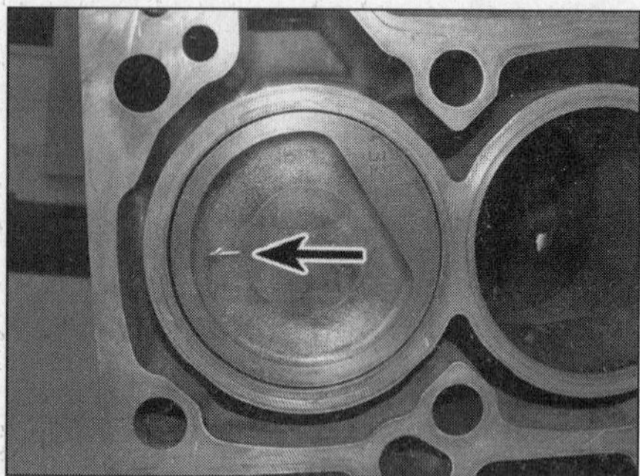
13.5 Note direction of arrow on top of piston

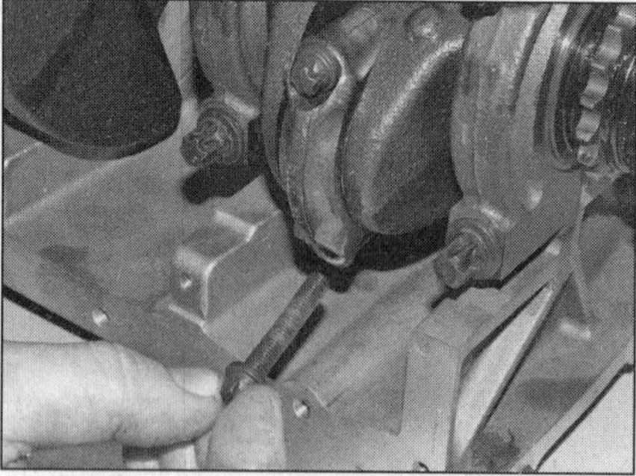
13.7a Remove the retaining bolts . . .

13.7b . . . and withdraw the big-end caps

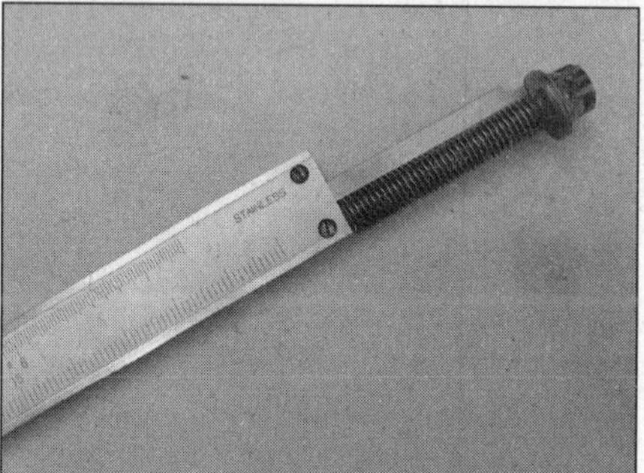
13.7c Measure the length of the bolts

manifold side of each assembly. Note that No 1 cylinder is at the timing chain end of the engine. If no marks are present, using a hammer and centre-punch, paint or similar, mark each connecting rod and big-end bearing cap with its respective cylinder number – note on which side of the connecting rods and caps the marks are made **(see illustration)**.

5 Similarly, check the piston crowns for direction markings. An arrow on each piston crown should point towards the timing chain end of the engine **(see illustration)**. On some engines, this mark may be obscured by carbon build-up, in which case the piston crown should be cleaned to check for a mark. In some cases, the direction arrow may have worn off, in which case a suitable mark should be made on the piston crown using a scriber – do not deeply score the piston crown, but ensure that the mark is easily visible.

6 Turn the crankshaft to bring Nos 1 and 4 pistons to bottom dead centre.

7 Unscrew the bolts from No 1 piston big-end bearing cap. Lift off the cap, and recover the bottom half bearing shell. If the bearing shells are to be re-used, tape the cap and bearing shell together. Note that if the bearing shells are to be re-used, they must be fitted to the original connecting rod and cap **(see illustrations)**. **Note:** *The length of the bolts will need to be checked, with the figures given in the Specifications at the beginning of this Chapter. New bolts will be required if the bolts are too long* ***(see illustration)***.

8 Using a hammer handle, push the piston up through the bore, and remove it from the top of the cylinder block. Recover the upper bearing shell, and tape it to the connecting rod for safe-keeping.

9 Loosely refit the big-end cap to the connecting rod, and secure with the bolts – this will help to keep the components in their correct order.

10 Remove No 4 piston assembly in the same way.

11 Turn the crankshaft as necessary to bring Nos 2 and 3 pistons to bottom dead centre, and remove them in the same way.

14 Crankshaft – removal

Note: *If no work is to be done on the pistons and connecting rods, there is no need to push the pistons out of the cylinder bores. The pistons should just be pushed far enough up the bores so that they are positioned clear of the crankshaft journals.*

1 Remove the timing chain and crankshaft sprocket, sump and oil baffle plate, oil pump and pick-up pipe, flywheel/driveplate, and the crankshaft oil seal housings.

2 Remove the pistons and connecting rods, or disconnect them from the crankshaft, as described in Section 13 (see Note at the beginning of this Section).

3 Check the crankshaft endfloat as described in Section 19, then proceed as follows.

4 The main bearing caps should be numbered 1 to 5 from the timing chain end of the engine. If the bearing caps are not marked, mark them accordingly using a centre-punch. Note the orientation of the markings to ensure correct refitting.

5 Slacken and remove the main bearing cap bolts, and lift off each cap **(see illustration)**. **Note:** *On diesel models, there are side bolts through the crankcase, securing caps 2, 3 and 4; these will need to be removed before the bearing caps can be removed.* If the caps appear to be stuck, tap them with a soft-faced mallet to free them from the cylinder block. Recover the lower bearing shells, and tape them to their caps for safe-keeping.

6 Recover the lower crankshaft endfloat control thrustwasher halves from either side of the No 3 main bearing cap, noting their orientation **(see illustration)**.

7 Lift the crankshaft from the cylinder block **(see illustration)**. Take care, as the crankshaft is heavy. Recover the upper bearing shells from the cylinder block, and tape them to their respective caps for safe-keeping. Similarly, recover the upper crankshaft endfloat control thrustwasher halves, noting their orientation.

14.5 Removing the main bearing cap – petrol engine shown

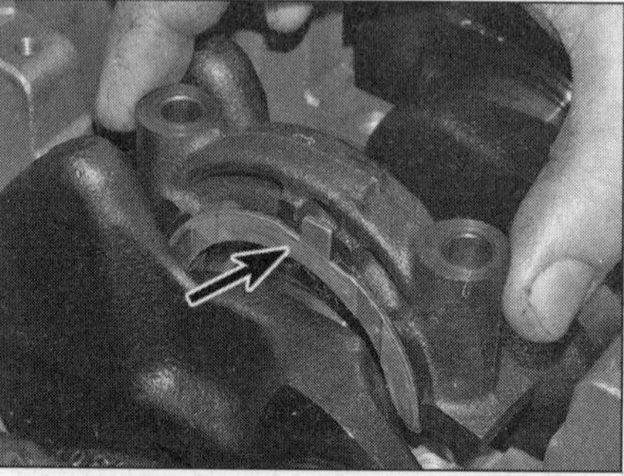
14.6 Thrustwasher (one side shown) – arrowed

14.7 Removing the crankshaft

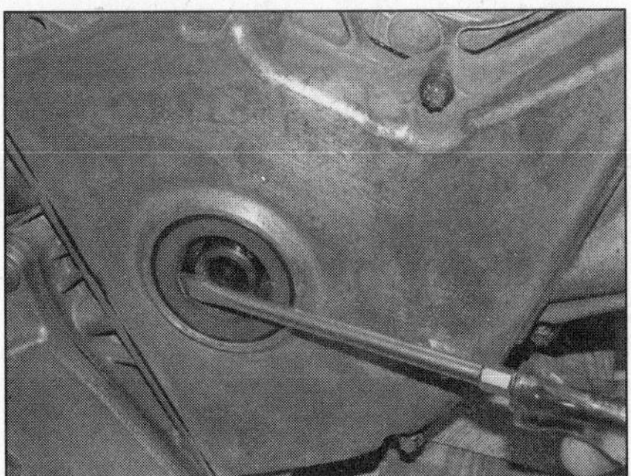

15.3a Using a screwdriver to lever out the seal . . .

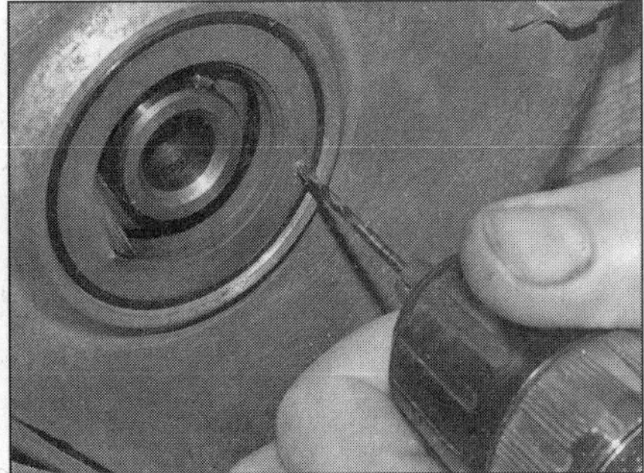

15.3b . . . or drill the seal and fit a screw . . .

15.3c . . . and pull the seal out from the cover

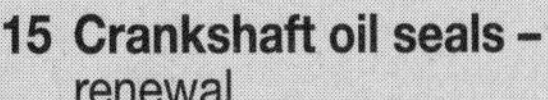

15 Crankshaft oil seals – renewal

Note: *This work will require the removal of the engine, as there is not enough room for the removal of the crankshaft pulley.*

Timing chain end oil seal

1 Remove the engine and subframe assembly, and then undo the engine mountings and lift the engine from the subframe, as described in Section 4.

2 Remove the crankshaft pulley as described in Section 6. Note the fitted depth of the oil seal in the timing cover, this should be flush with the surface face of the timing cover. If required, it can be pressed evenly further into the casing, but no further than 0.7 mm.

3 Carefully lever the old seal out of the timing cover using a suitable flat-bladed screwdriver, taking care not to damage the cover or crankshaft. Alternatively, punch or drill two small holes opposite each other in the seal, then screw a self-tapping screw into each and pull on the screws with pliers to extract the seal **(see illustrations)**.

4 Clean the cover recess and crankshaft end journal.

5 Using a special drift (or large socket), drive the oil seal back into position in the timing cover **(see illustrations)**. Alternatively, the seal can be tapped into position using a suitable tubular drift, such as a socket, which bears only on the hard outer edge of the seal.

15.5a Fit the new seal into the cover . . .

15.5b . . . and using a drift to keep it square, tap it into the cover

Note that the sealing lips must face inwards.

6 Refit the crankshaft pulley as described in Section 6.

Flywheel/driveplate end oil seal

Note: *The flywheel end oil seal is integral with the oil seal housing and should be renewed whenever it is removed.*

7 Remove the flywheel/driveplate as described in Section 16.

8 Unscrew the retaining bolts and remove the oil seal/housing from the cylinder block. Discard the bolts as new ones must used on refitting.

9 Remove the locating dowels from the cylinder block and replace any that are damaged. The dowels need to be removed from the cylinder block, to allow for refitting the new seal.

10 New oil seal/housings are supplied with a plastic sleeve on the inside of the seal to aid refitting of the seal over the end of the crankshaft. DO NOT remove the plastic fitting sleeve until the oil seal housing is in its fitted position.

11 Ensure that the cylinder block mating face of the oil seal housing is free from all traces of old sealant, oil and grease, and then apply a 1.5 to 2.5 mm thick bead of silicone sealant (A 003 989 98 20 or equivalent) to the oil seal housing **(see illustration)**. Note that the sealant should be run around the inside of the bolt holes in the oil seal housing. It must be fitted within 10 minutes of applying the sealant. Also apply sealant, at the area where the sump, oil seal housing and cylinder block meet.

12 Fit the new oil seal housing over the crankshaft and onto the cylinder block, keeping the plastic sleeve in position **(see illustration)**.

13 Refit the locating dowels into the cylinder block, once the oil seal housing is positioned correctly, and then using a drift tap them into place **(see illustrations)**.

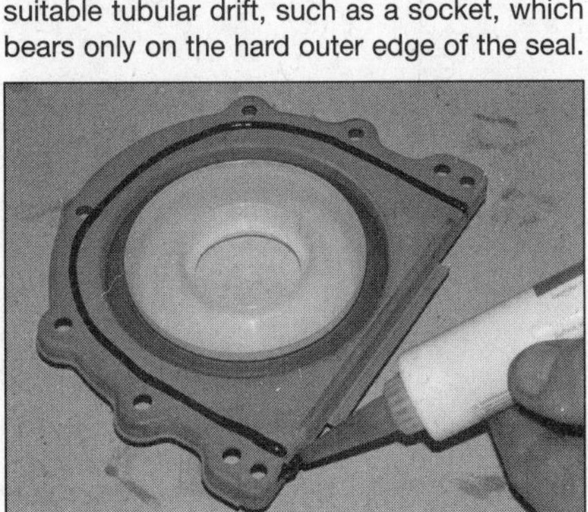

15.11 Apply sealant to the seal housing, also along the lower edge

15.12 Fitting the seal housing with plastic sleeve in position

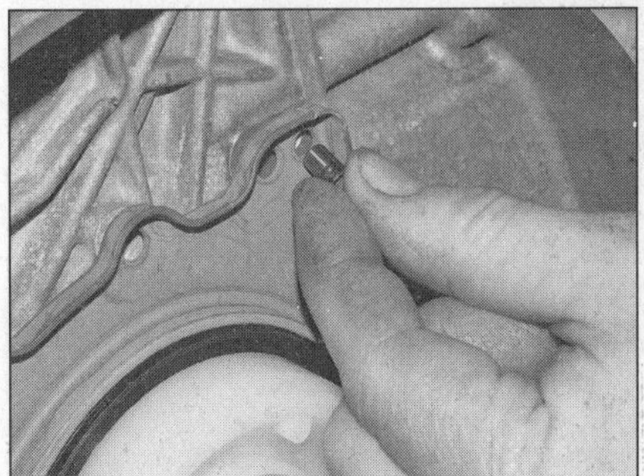

15.13a Fit the dowels back into position . . .

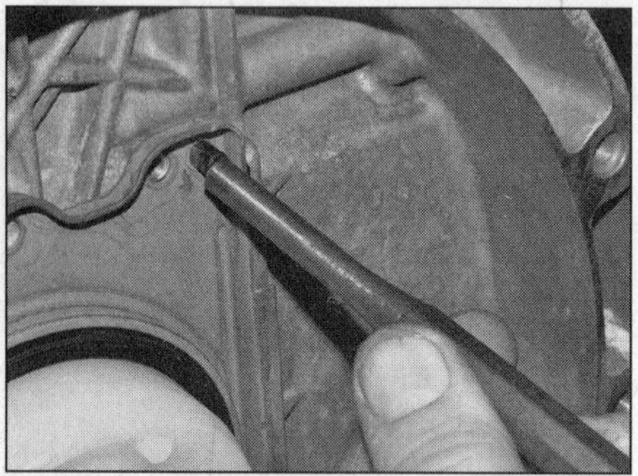

15.13b . . . using a drift to tap them into place

14 Fit the new retaining bolts and tighten them to the specified torque setting.

15 Remove the plastic fitting sleeve from the new oil seal housing **(see illustration)**.

16 Refit the flywheel/driveplate with reference to Section 16.

16 Flywheel/driveplate - removal, inspection and refitting

Removal

1 Remove the engine and subframe assembly from the vehicle, and then separate the engine from the transmission, as described in Section 4.

2 The flywheel/driveplate bolts are offset to ensure correct fitment. Unscrew the bolts while holding the flywheel/driveplate stationary. Temporarily insert a bolt in the

15.15 Removing the plastic sleeve

cylinder block, and use a screwdriver to hold the flywheel/driveplate, or make up a holding tool **(see illustrations)**. Discard the bolts, as new ones must be used on refitting.

3 On automatic transmission models, remove the centre plate from the driveplate **(see illustration)**.

4 Lift the flywheel/driveplate from the crankshaft **(see illustration)**.

Inspection

5 Check the flywheel/driveplate for wear and damage. Examine the starter ring gear for excessive wear to the teeth; if evident, the flywheel/driveplate must be renewed complete, as the ring gear is not supplied separately.

6 On manual transmission models, if the clutch contact surface is worn excessively, it may be possible to have it reground by a specialist.

16.2a Socket and 6 mm bolt in TDC hole . . .

16.2b . . . used to lock the flywheel/driveplate - auto shown

Refitting

7 Refitting is a reversal of removal, bearing in mind the following points.

a) Use new bolts when refitting the flywheel or driveplate, and coat the threads of the bolts with locking fluid before inserting them.

b) Tighten the securing bolts to the specified torque.

17 Cylinder block/crankcase - cleaning and inspection

Cleaning

1 Remove all external components and electrical switches/sensors from the block, including mounting brackets, the coolant pump and the oil filter housing **(see illustration)**, etc. For complete cleaning, the core plugs should ideally be removed. Drill a small hole in the plugs, and then insert a self-tapping screw into the hole. Extract the plugs by pulling on the screw with a pair of grips, or by using a slide hammer.

2 Scrape all traces of gasket and sealant from the cylinder block/crankcase, taking care not to damage the sealing surfaces.

3 Remove all oil gallery plugs (where fitted). The plugs are usually very tight - they may have to be drilled out, and the holes retapped. Use new plugs when the engine is reassembled.

4 If the casting is extremely dirty, it should be steam-cleaned. After this, clean all oil holes and galleries one more time. Flush all internal passages with warm water until the water runs clear. Dry thoroughly, and apply a light film of oil to all mating surfaces and cylinder bores, to prevent rusting. If you have access to compressed air, use it to speed up the drying process, and to blow out all the oil holes and galleries.

Warning: Wear eye protection when using compressed air.

5 If the castings are not very dirty, you can do an adequate cleaning job with hot, soapy water and a stiff brush. Take plenty of time,

16.3 Removing the centre plate - automatic transmission

16.4 Removing the driveplate - automatic shown

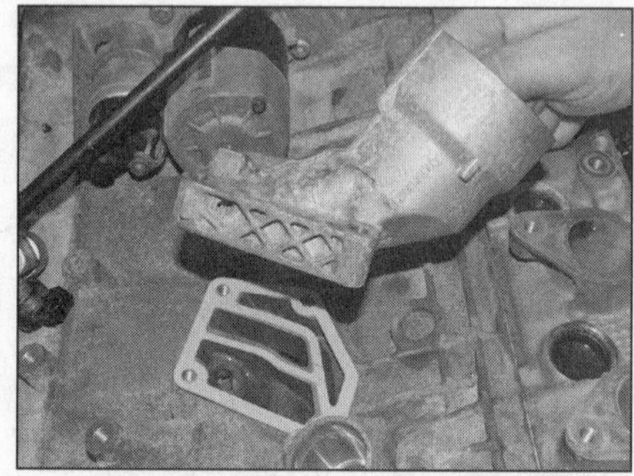

17.1 Removing the oil filter housing

and do a thorough job. Regardless of the cleaning method used, be sure to clean all oil holes and galleries very thoroughly, and to dry all components well. Protect the cylinder bores as described above, to prevent rusting.

6 Where applicable, check the piston cooling oil spray jets for damage, and renew if necessary. Check the oil spray hole and the oil passages for blockage.

7 All threaded holes must be clean, to ensure accurate torque readings during reassembly. To clean the threads, run the correct-size tap into each of the holes to remove rust, corrosion, thread sealant or sludge, and to restore damaged threads **(see illustration)**. If possible, use compressed air to clear the holes free of debris produced by this operation. **Note:** *Take extra care to remove all cleaning liquid from blind tapped holes, as the casting may be cracked by hydraulic action if a bolt is threaded into a hole containing liquid.*

8 After coating the mating surfaces of the new core plugs with suitable sealant, fit them to the cylinder block. Make sure that they are driven in straight and seated correctly, or leakage could result.

9 Apply suitable sealant to the new oil gallery plugs, and insert them into the holes in the block. Tighten them securely.

10 If the engine is not going to be reassembled immediately, cover it with a large plastic bag to keep it clean; protect all mating surfaces and the cylinder bores, to prevent rusting.

Inspection

11 Visually check the castings for cracks and corrosion. Look for stripped threads in the threaded holes. If there has been any history of internal coolant leakage, it may be worthwhile having an engine overhaul specialist check the cylinder block/crankcase for cracks with special equipment. If defects are found, have them repaired, if possible, or renew the assembly.

12 Check each cylinder bore for scuffing and scoring.

13 If in any doubt as the condition of the cylinder block have the block/bores inspected and measured by an engine-reconditioning specialist. They will be able to advise on whether the block is serviceable, whether a rebore is necessary, and supply the appropriate pistons and rings.

14 If the bores are in reasonably good condition and not excessively worn, then it may only be necessary to renew the piston rings.

15 If this is the case, the bores should be honed, to allow the new rings to bed-in correctly and provide the best possible seal. Consult an engine-reconditioning specialist

16 On diesel engines, if the oil/water pump housing was removed, it can be refitted at this stage if wished. Use a new gasket, and before fully tightening the bolts, align the housing faces with those of the engine block.

17 The cylinder block/crankcase should now be completely clean and dry, with all components checked for wear or damage, and repaired or overhauled as necessary.

18 Apply a light coating of engine oil to the mating surfaces and cylinder bores to prevent rust forming.

19 Refit as many ancillary components as possible, for safe-keeping. If reassembly is not to start immediately, cover the block with a large plastic bag to keep it clean, and protect the machined surfaces as described above to prevent rusting.

18 Piston/connecting rod assemblies – cleaning and inspection

Cleaning

1 Before the inspection process can begin, the piston/connecting rod assemblies must be cleaned, and the original piston rings removed from the pistons.

2 The rings should have smooth, polished working surfaces, with no dull or carbon-coated sections (showing that the ring is not sealing correctly against the bore wall, so allowing combustion gases to blow by) and no traces of wear on their top and bottom surfaces. The end gaps should be clear of carbon, but not polished (indicating a too-small end gap), and all the rings (including the elements of the oil control ring) should be free to rotate in their grooves, but without excessive up-and-down movement. If the rings appear to be in good condition, they are probably fit for further use; check the end gaps (in an unworn part of the bore) as described in Section 22.

3 If any of the rings appears to be worn or damaged, or has an end gap significantly different from the specified value, the usual course of action is to renew all of them as a set. **Note:** *While it is usual to renew piston rings when an engine is overhauled, they may be re-used if in acceptable condition. If re-using the rings, make sure that each ring is marked during removal to ensure that it is refitted correctly.*

4 Carefully expand the old rings over the top of the pistons. The use of two or three old feeler blades will be helpful in preventing the rings dropping into empty grooves **(see illustration)**. Be careful not to scratch the piston with the ends of the ring. The rings are brittle, and will snap if they are spread too far. They are also very sharp – protect your hands and fingers. Note that the third ring incorporates an expander.

18.4 Old feeler blades can be used to prevent piston rings from dropping into empty grooves

17.7 To clean the cylinder block threads, run the correct size tap into the holes

5 Keep each set of rings with its piston if the old rings are to be re-used. Note which way up each ring is fitted to ensure correct refitting.

6 Scrape away all traces of carbon from the top of the piston. A hand-held wire brush (or a piece of fine emery cloth) can be used, once the majority of the deposits have been scraped away.

7 Remove the carbon from the ring grooves in the piston, using an old ring. Break the ring in half to do this (be careful not to cut your fingers – piston rings are sharp). Be careful to remove only the carbon deposits – do not remove any metal, and do not nick or scratch the sides of the ring grooves.

8 Once the deposits have been removed, clean the piston/connecting rod assembly with paraffin or a suitable solvent, and dry thoroughly. Make sure that the oil return holes in the ring grooves are clear.

Inspection

9 If the pistons and cylinder bores are not damaged or worn excessively, and if the cylinder block does not need to be rebored, the original pistons can be refitted. Using a micrometer, measure the diameter of all four pistons at a point 10 mm from the bottom of the skirt, at right angles to the gudgeon pin axis **(see illustration)**. Compare the measurements with those listed in the Specifications. Note

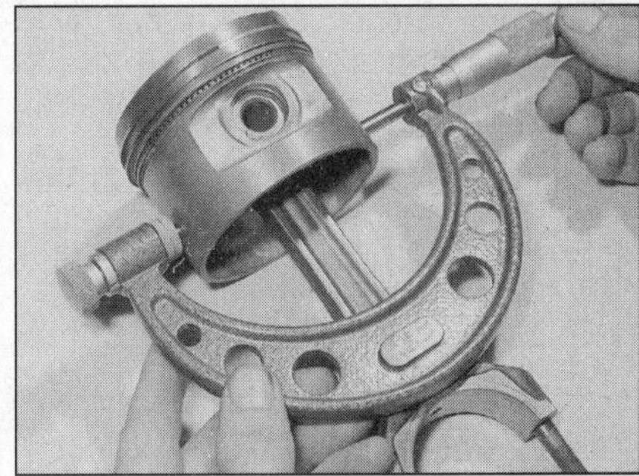

18.9 Using a micrometer to measure the diameter of a piston

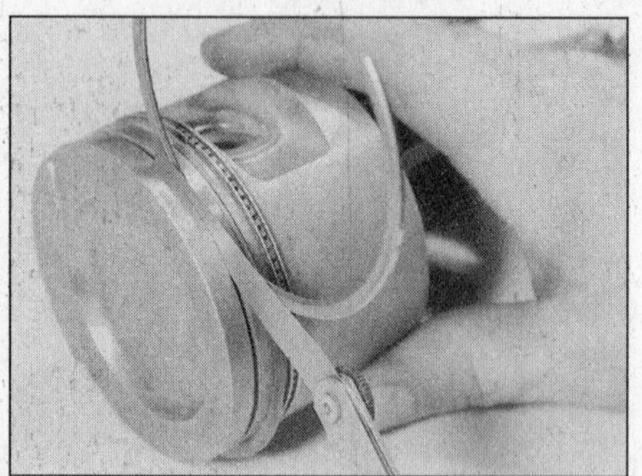

18.18 Measuring the piston ring-to-groove clearance using a feeler blade

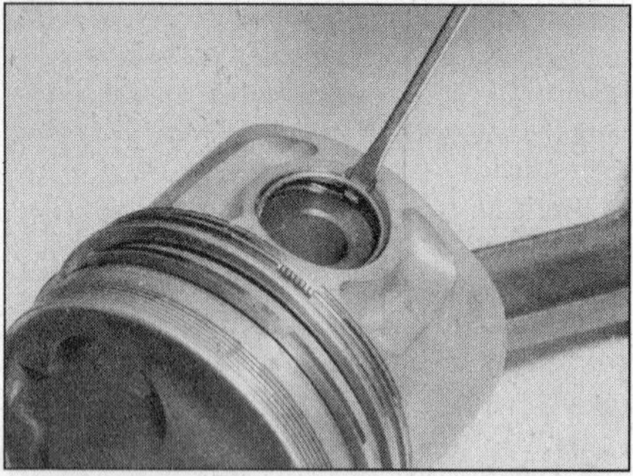

18.22a Use a small flat-bladed screwdriver to prise out the circlip . . .

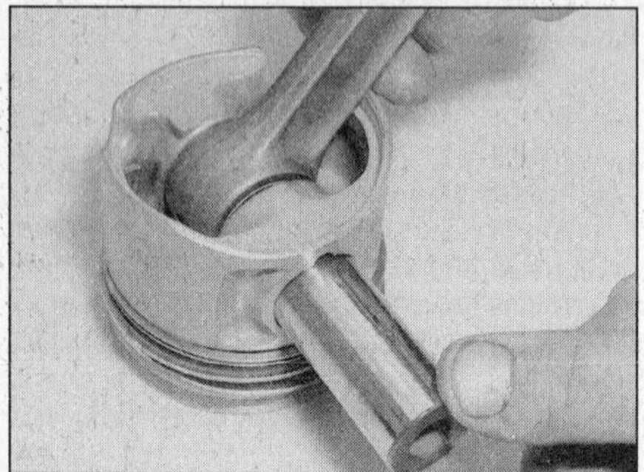

18.22b . . . then push out the gudgeon pin and separate the piston and connecting rod

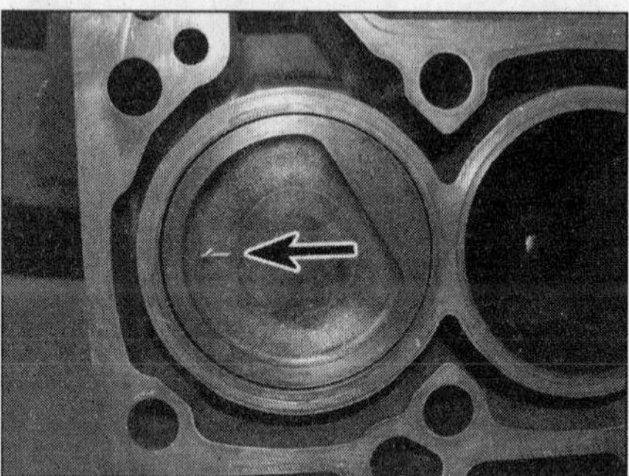

18.25 The piston crown is marked with an arrow which must point towards the timing chain end of the engine

that the piston size grades are stamped on the piston crowns.

10 If the piston diameter is incorrect for its particular size, then it must be renewed. **Note:** *If the cylinder block was rebored during a previous overhaul, oversize pistons may already have been fitted.*

11 Normal piston wear shows up as even vertical wear on the piston thrust surfaces, and slight looseness of the top ring in its groove. New piston rings should always be used when the engine is reassembled.

12 Carefully inspect each piston for cracks around the skirt, around the gudgeon pin holes, and at the piston ring 'lands' (between the ring grooves).

13 Look for scoring and scuffing on the piston skirt, holes in the piston crown, and burned areas at the edge of the crown. If the skirt is scored or scuffed, the engine may have been suffering from overheating, and/or abnormal combustion, which caused excessively high operating temperatures. The cooling and lubrication systems should be checked thoroughly.

14 Scorch marks on the sides of the pistons show that blow-by has occurred.

15 A hole in the piston crown, or burned areas at the edge of the piston crown, indicates that abnormal combustion (pre-ignition, knocking, or detonation) has been occurring.

16 If any of the above problems exist, the causes must be investigated and corrected, or the damage will occur again. The causes may include incorrect ignition/injection pump timing, inlet air leaks or incorrect air/fuel mixture (petrol engines), or a faulty fuel injector (diesel engines).

17 Corrosion of the piston, in the form of pitting, indicates that coolant has been leaking into the combustion chamber and/ or the crankcase. Again, the cause must be corrected, or the problem may persist in the rebuilt engine.

18 Locate a new piston ring in the appropriate groove and measure the ring-to-groove clearance using a feeler blade **(see illustration)**. Note that the rings are of different widths, so use the correct ring for the groove. Compare the measurements with those listed; if the clearances are outside of the tolerance band, then the piston must be renewed. Confirm this by checking the width of the piston ring with a micrometer.

19 New pistons can be purchased from a Mercedes-Benz dealer.

20 Examine each connecting rod carefully for signs of damage, such as cracks around the big-end and small-end bearings. Check that the rod is not bent or distorted. Damage is highly unlikely, unless the engine has been seized or badly overheated. Detailed checking of the connecting rod assembly can only be carried out by a Mercedes-Benz dealer or engine repair specialist with the necessary equipment.

21 The gudgeon pins are of the floating type, secured in position by two circlips. The pistons and connecting rods can be separated as follows.

22 Using a small flat-bladed screwdriver, prise out the circlips, and push out the gudgeon pin **(see illustrations)**. Hand pressure should be sufficient to remove the pin. Identify the piston and rod to ensure correct reassembly. Discard the circlips – new ones *must* be used on refitting. If the gudgeon pin proves difficult to remove, heat the piston to 60°C with hot water – the resulting expansion will then allow the two components to be separated.

23 Examine the gudgeon pin and connecting rod small-end bearing for signs of wear or damage. It should be possible to push the gudgeon pin through the connecting rod bush by hand, without noticeable play. Wear can be cured by renewing both the pin and bush. Bush renewal, however, is a specialist job – press facilities are required, and the new bush must be reamed accurately.

24 Examine all components, and obtain any new parts from your Mercedes-Benz dealer. If new pistons are purchased, they will be supplied complete with gudgeon pins and circlips. Circlips can also be purchased individually.

25 The orientation of the piston with respect to the connecting rod must be correct when the two are reassembled. The piston crown is marked with an arrow (which may be obscured by carbon deposits); this must point towards the timing chain end of the engine when the piston is installed **(see illustration)**. The connecting rod and its bearing cap both have recesses machined into them on one side, close to their mating surfaces – these recesses must both face the same way as the arrow on the piston crown (ie, towards the timing chain end of the engine) when correctly installed. Reassemble the two components to satisfy this requirement.

26 Apply a smear of clean engine oil to the gudgeon pin. Slide it into the piston and through the connecting rod small-end. Check that the piston pivots freely on the rod, then secure the gudgeon pin in position with two new circlips. Ensure that each circlip is correctly located in its groove in the piston.

27 Repeat the cleaning and inspection process for the remaining pistons and connecting rods.

19 Crankshaft – checking endfloat and inspection

Checking endfloat

1 If the crankshaft endfloat is to be checked, this must be done when the crankshaft is still installed in the cylinder block/crankcase, but is free to move (see Section 14).

2 Check the endfloat using a dial gauge in contact with the end of the crankshaft. Push the crankshaft fully one way, and then zero the gauge. Push the crankshaft fully the other way, and check the endfloat. The result can be compared with the specified amount, and will give an indication as to whether new thrustwasher halves are required **(see**

19.2 Measuring crankshaft endfloat using a dial gauge

19.3 Measuring crankshaft endfloat using feeler blades

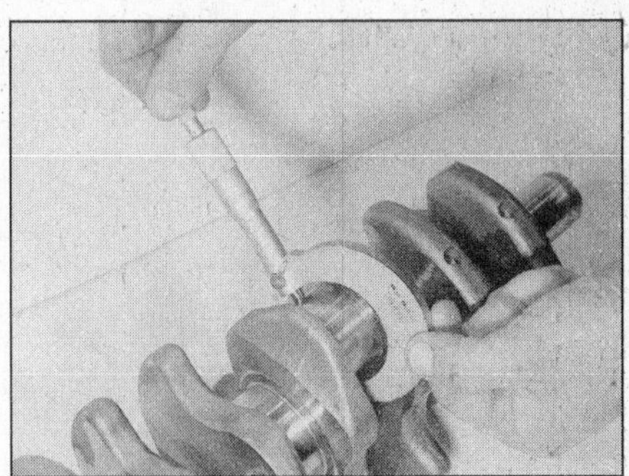
19.10 Use a micrometer to measure the diameter of each crankshaft bearing journal

illustration). Note that all thrustwashers must be of the same thickness.

3 If a dial gauge is not available, feeler blades can be used. First push the crankshaft fully towards the flywheel end of the engine, and then use feeler blades to measure the gap between the web of No 3 crankpin and the thrustwasher halves **(see illustration)**.

Inspection

4 Clean the crankshaft using paraffin or a suitable solvent, and dry it, preferably with compressed air if available. Be sure to clean the oil holes with a pipe cleaner or similar probe, to ensure that they are not obstructed.

Warning: Wear eye protection when using compressed air.

5 Check the main and big-end bearing journals for uneven wear, scoring, pitting and cracking.

6 Big-end bearing wear is accompanied by distinct metallic knocking when the engine is running (particularly noticeable when the engine is pulling from low speed) and some loss of oil pressure.

7 Main bearing wear is accompanied by severe engine vibration and rumble – getting progressively worse as engine speed increases – and again by loss of oil pressure.

8 Check the bearing journal for roughness by running a finger lightly over the bearing surface. Any roughness (which will be accompanied by obvious bearing wear) indicates that the crankshaft requires regrinding (where possible) or renewal.

9 If the crankshaft has been reground, check for burrs around the crankshaft oil holes (the holes are usually chamfered, so burrs should not be a problem unless regrinding has been carried out carelessly). Remove any burrs with a fine file or scraper, and thoroughly clean the oil holes as described previously.

10 Using a micrometer, measure the diameter of the main and big-end bearing journals, and compare the results with the Specifications **(see illustration)**. By measuring the diameter at a number of points around each journal's circumference, you will be able to determine whether or not the journal is out-of-round. Take the measurement at each end of the journal, near the webs, to determine if the journal is tapered.

11 Check the oil seal contact surfaces at each end of the crankshaft for wear and damage. If the seal has worn a deep groove in the surface of the crankshaft, consult an engine overhaul specialist; repair may be possible, but otherwise a new crankshaft will be required.

12 If the crankshaft journals have not already been reground, it may be possible to have the crankshaft reconditioned, and to fit undersize shells (see Section 23). If no undersize shells are available and the crankshaft has worn beyond the specified limits, it will have to be renewed. Consult your Mercedes-Benz dealer or engine specialist for further information on parts availability.

20 Main and big-end bearings – inspection

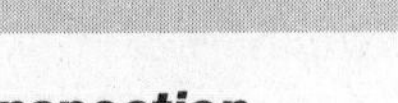

Inspection

1 Even though the main and big-end bearings should be renewed during the engine overhaul, the old bearings should be retained for close examination, as they may reveal valuable information about the condition of the engine **(see illustration)**.

2 Bearing failure can occur due to lack of lubrication, the presence of dirt or other foreign particles, overloading the engine, or corrosion. Regardless of the cause of bearing failure, the cause must be corrected before the engine is reassembled, to prevent it from happening again.

3 When examining the bearing shells, remove them from the cylinder block/crankcase, the main bearing caps, the connecting rods and the connecting rod big-end bearing caps. Lay them out on a clean surface in the same general position as their location in the engine. This will enable you to match any bearing problems with the corresponding crankshaft journal. *Do not* touch any shell's internal bearing surface with your fingers while checking it, or the delicate surface may be scratched.

4 Dirt and other foreign matter get into the engine in a variety of ways. It may be left in the engine during assembly, or it may pass through filters or the crankcase ventilation system. It may get into the oil, and from there into the bearings. Metal chips from machining operations and normal engine wear are often present. Abrasives are sometimes left in engine components after reconditioning, especially when parts are not thoroughly cleaned using the proper cleaning methods. Whatever the source, these foreign objects often end up embedded in the soft bearing material, and are easily recognised. Large particles will not embed in the bearing, but will score or gouge the bearing and journal. The best prevention for this cause of bearing failure is to clean all parts thoroughly, and keep everything spotlessly-clean during engine assembly. Frequent and regular engine oil and filter changes are also recommended.

5 Lack of lubrication (or lubrication breakdown) has a number of interrelated causes. Excessive heat (which thins the oil), overloading (which squeezes the oil from the bearing face) and oil leakage (from excessive bearing clearances, worn oil pump or high engine speeds) all contribute to lubrication breakdown. Blocked oil passages, which usually are the result of misaligned oil holes in

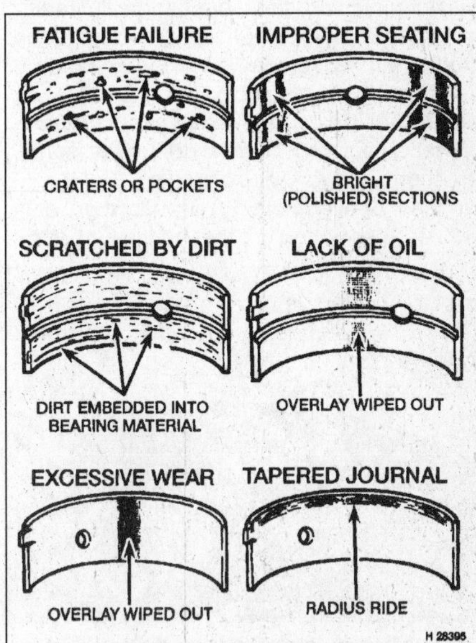

20.1 Typical bearing failures

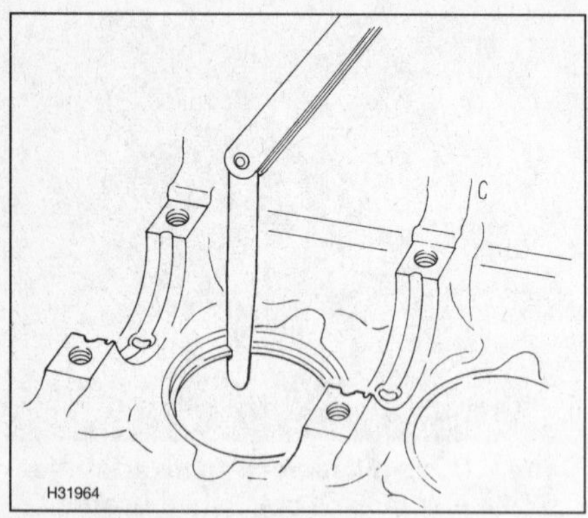

22.4 Checking a piston ring end gap using a feeler blade

a bearing shell, will also oil-starve a bearing, and destroy it. When lack of lubrication is the cause of bearing failure, the bearing material is wiped or extruded from the steel backing of the bearing. Temperatures may increase to the point where the steel backing turns blue from overheating.

6 Driving habits can have a definite effect on bearing life. Full-throttle, low-speed operation (labouring the engine) puts very high loads on bearings, tending to squeeze out the oil film. These loads cause the bearings to flex, which produces fine cracks in the bearing face (fatigue failure). Eventually, the bearing material will loosen in pieces, and tear away from the steel backing.

7 Short-distance driving leads to corrosion of bearings, because insufficient engine heat is produced to drive off the condensed water and corrosive gases. These products collect in the engine oil, forming acid and sludge. As the oil is carried to the engine bearings, the acid attacks and corrodes the bearing material.

8 Incorrect bearing installation during engine assembly will lead to bearing failure as well. Tight-fitting bearings leave insufficient bearing running clearance, and will result in oil starvation. Dirt or foreign particles trapped behind a bearing shell result in high spots on the bearing, which lead to failure.

9 *Do not* touch any shell's internal bearing surface with your fingers during reassembly as there is a risk of scratching the delicate surface, or of depositing particles of dirt on it.

10 As mentioned at the beginning of this Section, the bearing shells should be renewed as a matter of course during engine overhaul. To do otherwise is false economy.

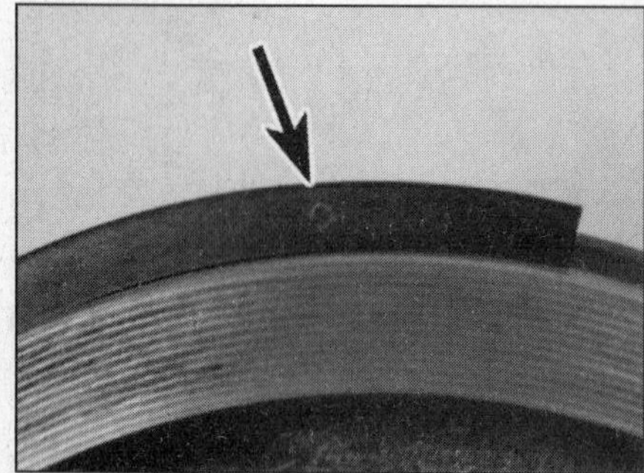

22.9 Marking (arrowed) on the top surface of the piston ring

Bearing selection

11 Main and big-end bearings for the engines described in this Chapter are available in standard sizes and a range of undersizes to suit reground crankshafts.

12 The running clearances will need to be checked when the crankshaft is refitted with its new bearings (see Sections 23 and 24).

21 Engine overhaul – reassembly sequence

Before reassembly begins, ensure that all new parts have been obtained, and that all necessary tools are available. Read through the entire procedure to familiarise yourself with the work involved, and to ensure that all items necessary for reassembly of the engine are at hand.

In addition to all normal tools and materials, thread-locking compound will be needed. A suitable tube of liquid sealant will also be required for the joint faces that are fitted without gaskets.

In order to save time and avoid problems, engine reassembly can be carried out in the following order, referring to Part A or B of this Chapter unless otherwise stated. Where applicable, use new gaskets and seals when refitting the various components.

a) Crankshaft (Section 23).
b) Piston/connecting rod assemblies (Section 24).
c) Oil pump (Section 12).
d) Sump (Section 11).
e) Flywheel/driveplate (Section 16).
f) Cylinder head.
g) Timing chain, tensioner and sprockets.
h) Engine external components.

At this stage, all engine components should be absolutely clean and dry, with all faults repaired. The components should be laid out (or in individual containers) on a completely clean work surface.

22 Piston rings – refitting

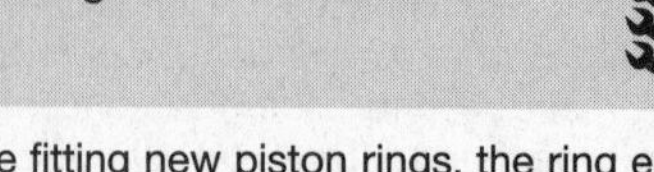

1 Before fitting new piston rings, the ring end gaps must be checked as follows.

2 Lay out the piston/connecting rod assemblies and the new piston ring sets, so that the ring sets will be matched with the same piston and cylinder during the end gap measurement and subsequent engine reassembly.

3 Insert the top ring into the first cylinder, and push it down the bore using the top of the piston. This will ensure that the ring remains square with the cylinder walls. Position the ring approximately 15.0 mm from the bottom of the cylinder bore, at the lower limit of ring travel. Note that the top and second compression rings are different.

4 Measure the end gap using feeler blades, and compare the measurements with the figures given in the Specifications **(see illustration)**.

5 If the gap is too small (unlikely if genuine Mercedes-Benz parts are used), it must be enlarged, or the ring ends may contact each other during engine operation, causing serious damage. Ideally, new piston rings providing the correct end gap should be fitted. As a last resort, filing the ring ends very carefully with a fine file can increase the end gap. Mount the file in a vice equipped with soft jaws, slip the ring over the file with the ends contacting the file face, and slowly move the ring to remove material from the ends. Take care, as piston rings are sharp, and are easily broken.

6 With new piston rings, it is unlikely that the end gap will be too large. If the gaps are too large, check that you have the correct rings for your engine and for the particular cylinder bore size.

7 Repeat the checking procedure for each ring in the first cylinder, and then for the rings in the remaining cylinders. Remember to keep rings, pistons and cylinders matched up.

8 Once the ring end gaps have been checked and if necessary corrected, the rings can be fitted to the pistons.

9 Fit the piston rings using the same technique as for removal. Fit the bottom (oil control) ring first, and work up. Note that a two- or three-section oil control ring may be fitted; where a two-section ring is fitted, first insert the wire expander, then fit the ring. Ensure that the rings are fitted the correct way up – the top surface of the rings is normally marked TOP **(see illustration)**. Offset the piston ring gaps by 120° from each other. **Note:** *Always follow any instructions supplied with the new piston ring sets – different manufacturers may specify different procedures. Do not mix up the top and second compression rings, as they have different cross-sections.*

23 Crankshaft – refitting and main bearing clearance check

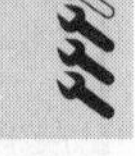

Main bearing clearance check

1 The running clearance check can be carried out using the original bearing shells. However, it is preferable to use a new set, since the results obtained will be more conclusive. If new shells are being fitted, ensure that all traces of the protective grease are cleaned off using paraffin.

2 Clean the backs of the bearing shells, and the bearing locations in both the cylinder block/crankcase and the main bearing caps.

3 With the cylinder block positioned on a clean work surface, with the crankcase

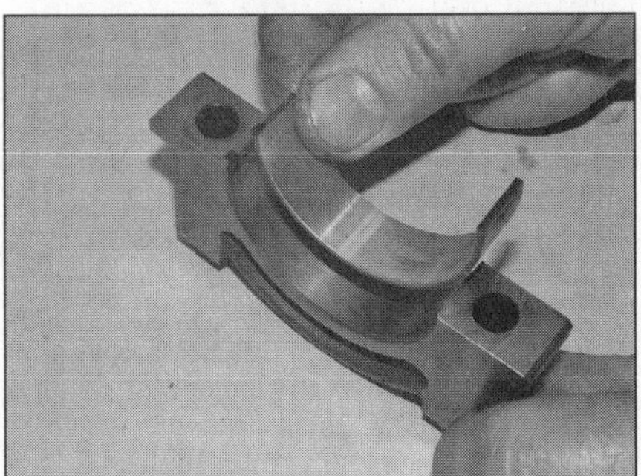
23.3 Fitting the bearing shell to the cap

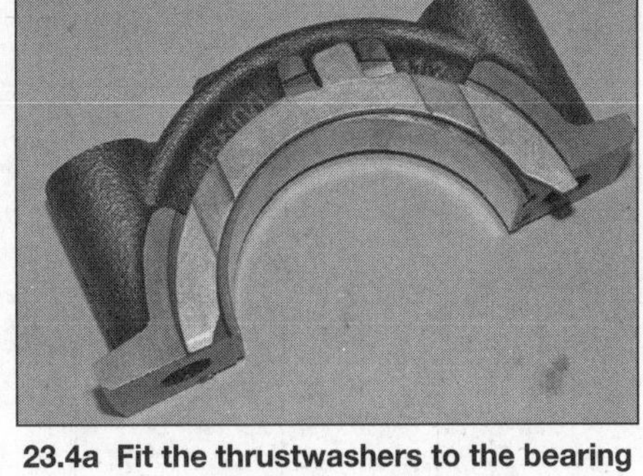
23.4a Fit the thrustwashers to the bearing cap . . .

23.4b . . . and fit the bearing cap into place

uppermost, press the bearing shells into their locations, ensuring that the tab on each shell engages in the notch in the cylinder block or bearing cap, and that the oil holes in the cylinder block and bearing shell are aligned **(see illustration)**. Take care not to touch any shell's bearing surface with your fingers. If the original bearing shells are being used for the check, ensure that they are refitted in their original locations.

4 Fit the crankshaft endfloat control thrustwasher halves either side of the No 3 bearing location **(see illustrations)**. Use a small quantity of grease to hold them in place. Ensure that the thrustwashers are seated correctly in the machined recesses, with the oil grooves facing outwards.

5 The running clearance can be checked, although this will be difficult to achieve without a range of internal micrometers or internal/external expanding calipers.

6 Refit the main bearing caps to the cylinder block/crankcase, with bearing shells in place. With the original cap retaining bolts tightened to the specified torque, measure the internal diameter of each assembled pair of bearing shells. If the diameter of each corresponding crankshaft journal is measured and then subtracted from the bearing internal diameter, the result will be the main bearing running clearance.

Final crankshaft refitting

7 Carefully lift the crankshaft out of the cylinder block once more, and wipe off the surfaces of the bearing shells in the crankcase and bearing caps.

8 Where applicable, refit the crankshaft speed/position sensor wheel, and tighten the securing bolts securely. Make sure that the sensor wheel is correctly orientated as noted before removal. Liberally coat the bearing shells in the crankcase with clean engine oil of the appropriate grade **(see illustration)**. Make sure that the bearing shells are still correctly seated in their locations.

9 Lower the crankshaft into position so that No 1 cylinder crankpin is at BDC, ready for fitting No 1 piston. Ensure that the crankshaft endfloat control thrustwasher halves, either side of the No 3 main bearing location, remain in position. Where applicable, take care not to damage the crankshaft speed/position sensor wheel as the crankshaft is lowered into position.

10 Lubricate the lower bearing shells in the main bearing caps with clean engine oil. Make sure that the crankshaft endfloat control thrustwasher halves are still correctly seated either side of No 3 bearing cap **(see illustration)**.

11 Fit the main bearing caps in the correct order and orientation – No 1 bearing cap must be at the timing chain end of the engine and the bearing shell tab locating recesses in the crankcase and bearing caps must be adjacent to each other **(see illustration)**. Insert the bearing cap bolts (using new bolts where necessary), and hand-tighten them only.

12 Working from the centre bearing cap outwards, tighten the bearing cap bolts to their specified torque. On engines where two Stages are given for the torque, tighten all bolts to the Stage 1 torque, then go round again, and tighten all bolts through the Stage 2 angle **(see illustrations)**.

13 Check that the crankshaft rotates freely by

23.8 Lubricate the bearing shells in the block

23.10 Lubricate the shells in the end cap

23.11 Refitting a main bearing cap

23.12a Tighten the main bearing cap bolts to the specified torque . . .

23.12b . . . then through the specified angle

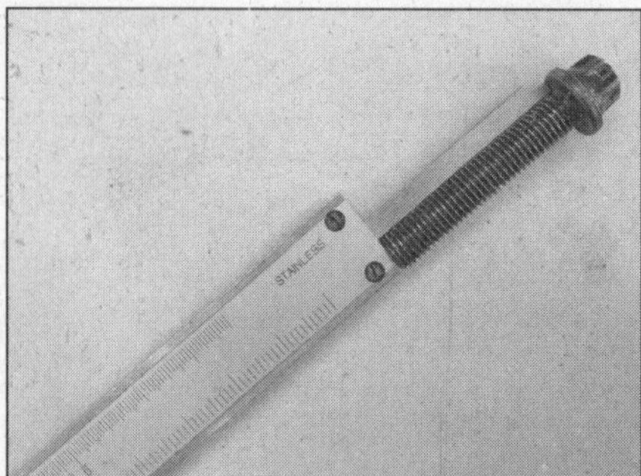

24.7 Checking the length of the big-end bolt

24.9a Lubricate the cylinder bores . . .

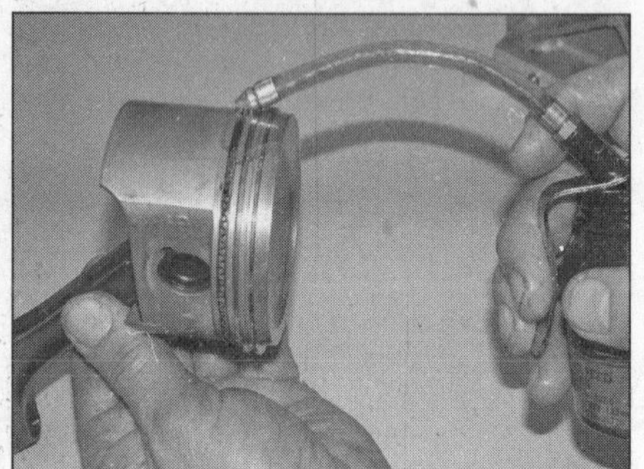

24.9b . . . the pistons/rings . . .

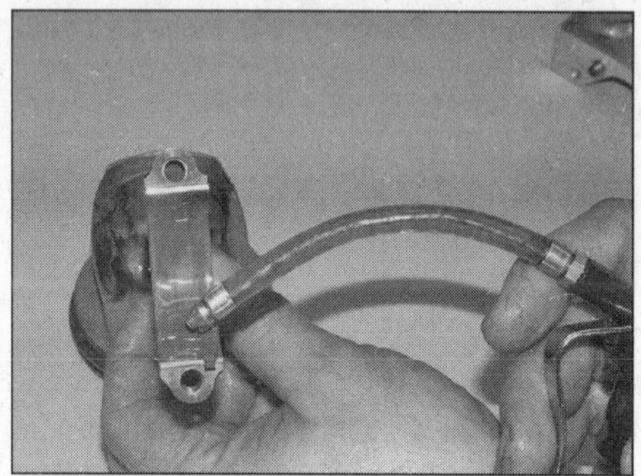

24.9c . . . and the bearing shells, with clean engine oil

turning it by hand. If resistance is felt, recheck the bearing running clearances, as described previously.

14 Check the crankshaft endfloat as described at the beginning of Section 19. If the thrust surfaces of the crankshaft have been checked and new thrustwashers have been fitted, then the endfloat should be within specification.

15 Refit the pistons and connecting rods or reconnect them to the crankshaft as described in Section 24.

16 Refit the crankshaft oil seal housings, flywheel/driveplate, oil pump, sump and oil baffle plate, and the crankshaft sprocket and timing chain.

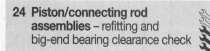

24 Piston/connecting rod assemblies – refitting and big-end bearing clearance check

Note: *A piston ring compressor tool will be required for this operation.*

Big-end bearing clearance check

1 The running clearance check can be carried out using the original bearing shells. However, it is preferable to use a new set, since the results obtained will be more conclusive.

2 Clean the backs of the bearing shells, and the bearing locations in both the connecting rods and the big-end bearing caps.

3 Press the bearing shells into their locations, ensuring that the tab on each shell engages in the notch in the connecting rod or cap. Take care not to touch any shell's bearing surface with your fingers. If the original bearing shells are being used for the check, ensure that they are refitted in their original locations.

4 The running clearance can be checked, although this will be difficult to achieve without a range of internal micrometers or internal/external expanding calipers.

5 Refit the big-end bearing cap to the connecting rod, using the marks made or noted on removal to ensure that they are fitted the correct way around, with the bearing shells in place. With the original cap retaining bolts correctly tightened, use an internal micrometer or vernier caliper to measure the internal diameter of each assembled pair of bearing shells. If the diameter of each corresponding crankshaft journal is measured, and then subtracted from the bearing internal diameter, the result will be the big-end bearing running clearance.

24.13 Using a hammer handle to tap the piston into its bore

Piston/connecting rods refitting

6 Note that the following procedure assumes that the crankshaft main bearing caps are in place. Where applicable, refit the piston cooling oil spray jets to the bottom of the cylinder block, and tighten the securing bolts securely.

7 The length of the big-end bolts will need to be checked, with the figures given in the Specifications at the beginning of this Chapter. Where applicable, fit new bolts to the connecting rods **(see illustration)**.

8 Ensure that the bearing shells are correctly fitted, as described at the beginning of this Section. If new shells are being fitted, ensure that all traces of the protective grease are cleaned off using paraffin. Wipe dry the shells and connecting rods with a lint-free cloth.

9 Lubricate the cylinder bores, the pistons, piston rings and upper bearing shells with clean engine oil **(see illustrations)**. Lay out each piston/connecting rod assembly in order on a clean work surface.

10 Start with piston/connecting rod assembly No 1. Make sure that the piston rings are still spaced as described in Section 22, and then clamp them in position with a piston ring compressor tool.

11 Insert the piston/connecting rod assembly into the top of cylinder No 1. Lower the big-end in first, guiding it to protect the cylinder bores. Where oil jets are located at the bottoms of the bores, take particular care not to damage them when guiding the connecting rods onto the crankpins.

12 Ensure that the orientation of the piston in its cylinder is correct – the piston crown, connecting rod and big-end bearing cap have markings, which must point towards the timing chain end of the engine when the piston is installed in the bore – refer to Section 18 for details.

13 Using a block of wood or hammer handle against the piston crown, tap the assembly into the cylinder until the piston crown is flush with the top of the cylinder **(see illustration)**.

14 Ensure that the bearing shell is still correctly installed in the connecting rod, and then liberally lubricate the crankpin and both bearing shells with clean engine oil.

15 Taking care not to mark the cylinder bores, tap the piston/connecting rod assembly down the bore and onto the crankpin. Oil the bolt threads, and the undersides of the heads.

16 Fit the big-end bearing cap, tightening its retaining bolts finger-tight at first. Make sure the bearing caps are fitted correctly as noted on removal.

17 Tighten the retaining bolts to the specified torque and angle, in the three stages given in the Specifications **(see illustration)**.

18 Refit the remaining three piston/connecting rod assemblies in the same way.

19 Rotate the crankshaft by hand. Check that it turns freely; some stiffness is to be expected if new parts have been fitted, but there should be no binding or tight spots.

20 Refit the oil pump, sump and oil baffle plate as described previously in this Chapter, and the cylinder head, as described in Chapter 2A or 2B.

25 Engine – initial start-up after overhaul and reassembly

1 Refit the remainder of the engine components in the order listed in Section 5 of this Chapter.
2 Refit the engine to the vehicle as described in the relevant Section of this Chapter. Double-check the engine oil and coolant levels, and make a final check that everything has been reconnected. Make sure that there are no tools or rags left in the engine compartment. Where necessary, reconnect the battery leads with reference to *Disconnecting the battery* at the rear of this manual.

Petrol models

3 Remove the spark plugs, referring to Chapter 1A for details.
4 The engine must be immobilised such that it can be turned over using the starter motor without starting – disable the fuel pump by unplugging the fuel pump power relay from the relay board with reference to Chapter 12, and also disable the ignition system by disconnecting the wiring from the DIS module or coils, as applicable.
Caution: To prevent damage to the catalytic converter, it is important to disable the fuel system.
5 Turn the engine using the starter motor until the oil pressure warning lamp goes out. If the lamp fails to extinguish after several seconds of cranking, check the engine oil level and oil filter security. Assuming these are correct, check the security of the oil pressure switch wiring – do not progress any further until you are satisfied that oil is being pumped around the engine at sufficient pressure.
6 Refit the spark plugs, and reconnect the wiring to the fuel pump relay and DIS module or coils, as applicable.

Diesel models

7 Disconnect the injector harness wiring plug at the rear of the engine compartment – refer to Chapter 4B for details.
8 Turn the engine using the starter motor until the oil pressure warning lamp goes out.
9 If the lamp fails to extinguish after several seconds of cranking, check the engine oil level and oil filter security. Assuming these are correct, check the security of the oil pressure switch cabling – do not progress any further until you are satisfied that oil is being pumped around the engine at sufficient pressure.
10 Reconnect the injector wiring plug.

All models

11 Start the engine, but be aware that as fuel system components have been disturbed, the cranking time may be a little longer than usual.

24.17 Tightening the big-end bearing cap bolts to a specified angle

12 While the engine is idling, check for fuel, water and oil leaks. Don't be alarmed if there are some odd smells and the occasional plume of smoke as components heat up and burn off oil deposits.
13 Assuming all is well; keep the engine idling until hot water is felt circulating through the top hose.
14 After a few minutes, recheck the oil and coolant levels, and top-up as necessary.
15 There is no need to retighten the cylinder head bolts once the engine has been run following reassembly.
16 If new pistons, rings or crankshaft bearings have been fitted, the engine must be treated as new, and run-in for the first 600 miles. *Do not* operate the engine at full-throttle, or allow it to labour at low engine speeds in any gear. It is recommended that the engine oil and filter are changed at the end of this period.

Chapter 3
Cooling, heating and air conditioning systems

Contents

Degrees of difficulty

Easy, suitable for novice with little experience	**Fairly easy,** suitable for beginner with some experience	**Fairly difficult,** suitable for competent DIY mechanic	**Difficult,** suitable for experienced DIY mechanic	**Very difficult,** suitable for expert DIY or professional 

Specifications

General

System type	Sealed cooling system with auxiliary belt driven coolant pump. The system also has a thermostat and an electrically-operated fan; which is operated by the electronic control unit (ECU), via information from the temperature sensor

Cooling system

Antifreeze mixture:	
50% antifreeze	Protection down to -37°C
55% antifreeze	Protection down to -45°C

Cooling system pressure cap

Opening pressure	1.4 bar

Thermostat

Type	Wax element
Begins to open	89°C
Fully open	101°C

Torque wrench settings

	Nm	lbf ft
Automatic transmission pipes to radiator	25	18
Coolant pump to crankcase	8	6
Coolant pump pulley:		
Petrol engine	8	6
Diesel engine	10	7
Radiator	5	4
Reinforcement support bar:		
Front end bolts	23	17
A-pillar bolts	11	8
Thermostat housing bolts:		
Petrol engine	8	6
Diesel engine	9	7

2.3a Remove the retaining clips (A) screw type and (B) spring type . . .

2.3b . . . and pull off the hoses

1 General information and precautions

A pressurised cooling system is used, with a pump, an aluminium crossflow radiator, electric cooling fan, a thermostat and a heater matrix, as well as the interconnecting hoses. On automatic transmission models, oil feed pipes from the transmissoin are connected to the left-hand side of the radiator.

The system functions as follows. Coolant is circulated through the cylinder block and head passages by the coolant pump which is driven by the auxiliary drivebelt. The coolant cools the cylinder bores, combustion surfaces and valves of the engine.

When the engine is cold, the thermostat is closed and the coolant only circulates around the engine and the heater matrix in the passenger compartment, however, when the engine reaches a predetermined temperature, the thermostat opens and the coolant passes through the radiator for additional cooling. The coolant enters the top of the radiator and is cooled, as it circulates down through the cooling tubes, by the inrush of air when the car is in forward motion. Airflow is supplemented by the action of the electric cooling fan when necessary. Upon leaving the bottom of the radiator, the coolant returns to the engine and the cycle is repeated.

Refer to Section 10 for information on the air conditioning system.

Precautions

Warning: Do not attempt to remove the expansion tank filler cap or disturb any part of the cooling system while the engine is hot, as there is a high risk of scalding. If the expansion tank filler cap must be removed before the engine and radiator have fully cooled (even though this is not recommended) the pressure in the cooling system must first be relieved. Cover the cap with a thick layer of cloth, to avoid scalding, and slowly unscrew the filler cap until a hissing sound can be heard. When the hissing has stopped, indicating that the pressure has reduced, slowly unscrew the filler cap until it can be removed; if more hissing sounds are heard, wait until they have stopped before unscrewing the cap completely. At all times keep well away from the filler cap opening.

- Do not allow antifreeze to come into contact with skin or painted surfaces of the vehicle. Rinse off spills immediately with plenty of water. Never leave antifreeze lying around in an open container or in a puddle in the driveway or on the garage floor. Children and pets are attracted by its sweet smell. Antifreeze can be fatal if ingested.
- If the engine is hot, the electric cooling fan may start rotating even if the engine is not running, so be careful to keep hands, hair and loose clothing well clear when working in the engine compartment.
- Refer to Section 10 for additional precautions to be observed when working on models with air conditioning.

2 Cooling system hoses - disconnection and renewal

Note: *Refer to the warnings given in Section 1 of this Chapter before proceeding.*

1 If the checks described in the relevant part of Chapter 1 reveal a faulty hose, it must be renewed as follows.

2 First drain the cooling system as described in Chapter 1A or 1B. If the coolant is not due for renewal, it may be re-used if it is collected in a clean container.

3 To disconnect a hose, use a pair of pliers to release the spring clamps (or a screwdriver to slacken screw-type clamps), then move them along the hose, clear of the union **(see illustrations)**. Carefully work the hose free from its stub. The hoses can be removed with relative ease when new - on an older vehicle, they may be stuck.

4 In order to disconnect the radiator inlet and outlet hoses, apply pressure to hold the hose on to the relevant union, pull out the spring clip and pull the hose from the union. Note that the radiator inlet and outlet unions are fragile; do not use excessive force when attempting to remove the hoses. If a hose proves to be difficult to remove, try to release it by rotating the hose ends before attempting to free it.

5 When fitting a hose, first slide the clips onto the hose, and then work the hose into position. If clamp type clips were originally fitted, it is a good idea to use screw type clips when refitting the hose. If the hose is stiff, use a little soapy water as a lubricant, or soften the hose by soaking it in hot water.

6 Work the hose into position, checking that it is correctly routed, and then slide each clip along the hose until it passes over the flared end of the relevant union, before securing it in position with the retaining clip.

7 Prior to refitting a radiator inlet or outlet hose, renew the connection O-ring regardless of condition. The connections are a push-fit over the radiator unions.

8 Refill the cooling system as described in Chapter 1A or 1B.

9 Check thoroughly for leaks as soon as possible after disturbing any part of the cooling system.

3 Radiator - removal, inspection and refitting

Removal

1 Switch off the ignition and all electrical consumers.

2 Drain the cooling system as described in Chapter 1A or 1B.

Petrol models

3 Remove the front bumper as described in Chapter 11.

4 Remove the air cleaner housing as described in Chapter 4A.

5 Disconnect the wiring from the cooling fan connector and detach the fan shroud, complete with fan from the radiator, as described in Section 5.

6 Disconnect the coolant hoses from the radiator; ease them off carefully to prevent damage to the radiator **(see illustrations)**. If hoses are tight, twist them before pulling them off, to break the seal.

7 On models with automatic transmission, disconnect the oil cooler lines from the left-hand side of the radiator. Plug the ends of the oil lines to prevent dirt ingress **(see illustration)**.

8 Release the retaining clamps and rubber mountings from the top edge of the radiator.

9 On models with air conditioning, unclip the condenser from the radiator, and then fasten it to one side **(see illustration)**.

10 Check around the radiator for any pipes or bolts, and then lift out from the front of the engine compartment. Check the rubber grommets at the bottom of the radiator and check condition for refitting.

Diesel models

11 On models from 01/06/99, detach the coolant expansion reservoir from the inner wing and move it to one side **(see illustration)**.

12 Detach the windscreen washer reservoir from the inner wing panel and move it to one side.

13 Remove the plastic trim from across the front panel and unclip the air intake cowl from the front crossmember **(see illustration)**.

14 Release the retaining clamps and rubber mountings from the top edge of the radiator **(see illustration)**.

15 Remove the front bumper as described in Chapter 11.

16 Undo the retaining bolts, and remove the left-hand headlight unit, disconnect the wiring connectors as it is removed, with reference to Chapter 12.

17 Unclip any hoses or wiring from along the upper reinforcement support bar **(see illustration)**.

3.6a Unscrew the top hose retaining clip . . .

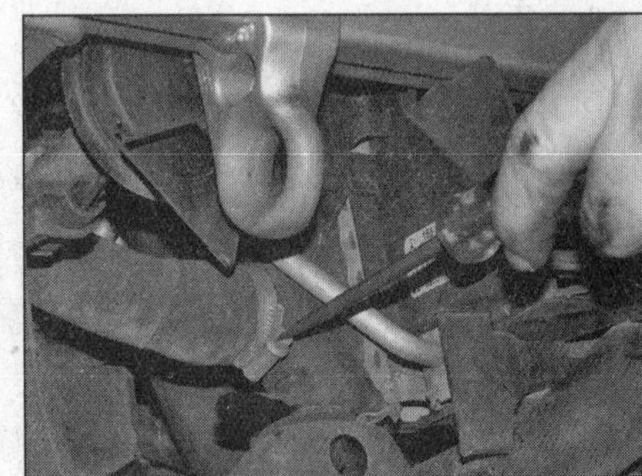

3.6b . . . and the bottom hose retaining clip

3.7 Disconnecting the oil cooler pipes

3.9 Release the retaining clip

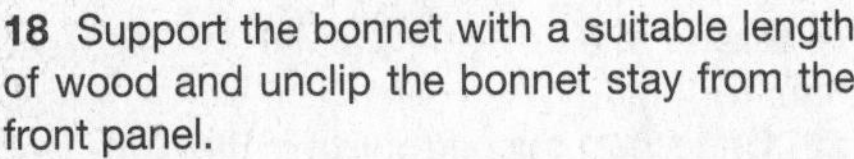

18 Support the bonnet with a suitable length of wood and unclip the bonnet stay from the front panel.

19 Unbolt the reinforcement support bar from across the front of the vehicle and move it to one side, leaving the bonnet cable/lock still attached **(see illustrations)**.

20 Disconnect the coolant hoses from the radiator; ease them off carefully to prevent damage to the radiator **(see illustration 3.6a**

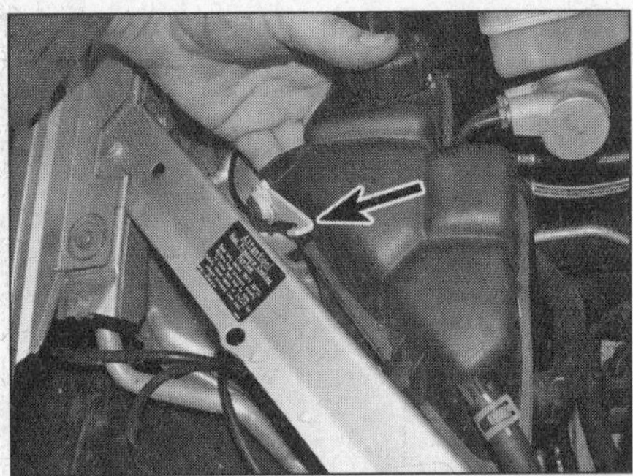

3.11 Release the locking lever – arrowed

3.13 Unclip the air intake from the front crossmember

3.14 Withdraw the upper radiator mountings

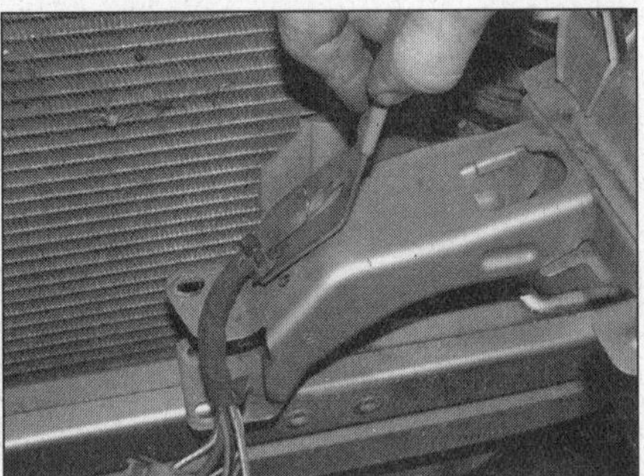

3.17 Releasing the wiring retaining clips

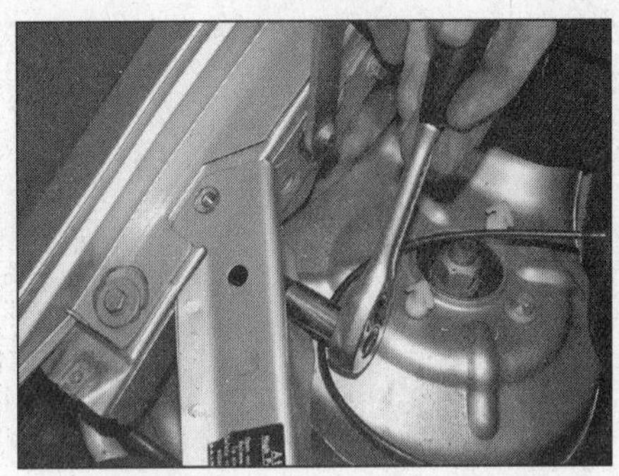

3.19a Undo the retaining bolts . . .

3.19b . . . and remove the front crossmember

3.22 Undo the mounting bolt – arrowed

3.24 Carefully lift out the fan and shroud

3.25 Withdraw the radiator out from the engine compartment

and 3.6b). If hoses are tight, twist them before pulling them off, to break the seal.

21 On models with automatic transmission, disconnect the oil cooler lines from the left-hand side of the radiator. Plug the ends of the oil lines to prevent dirt ingress **(see illustration 3.7)**.

22 Undo the mounting bolt from the right-hand side of the radiator **(see illustration)**.

23 On models with air conditioning, unclip the condenser from the radiator **(see illustration 3.9)**.

24 Disconnect the wiring from the cooling fan connector and detach the fan shroud complete with fan from the radiator **(see illustration)**.

25 Check around the radiator for any pipes or bolts, and then lift it out from the front of the engine compartment **(see illustration)**. Check the rubber grommets at the bottom of the radiator and check condition for refitting.

Inspection

26 If the radiator has been removed due to suspected blockage, reverse flush it as described in the relevant part of Chapter 1.

27 Clean dirt and debris from the radiator fins, using an airline (in which case, wear eye protection) or a soft brush. Be careful, as the fins are sharp and easily damaged.

28 If necessary, a radiator specialist can perform a 'flow test' on the radiator, to establish whether an internal blockage exists.

29 A leaking radiator must be referred to a specialist for permanent repair. Do not attempt to weld or solder a leaking radiator, as damage may result.

30 Check the radiator mounting rubbers, and renew if necessary.

Refitting

31 Refitting is a reversal of removal. On completion, refill the cooling system using the correct type of antifreeze as described in the relevant part of Chapter 1.

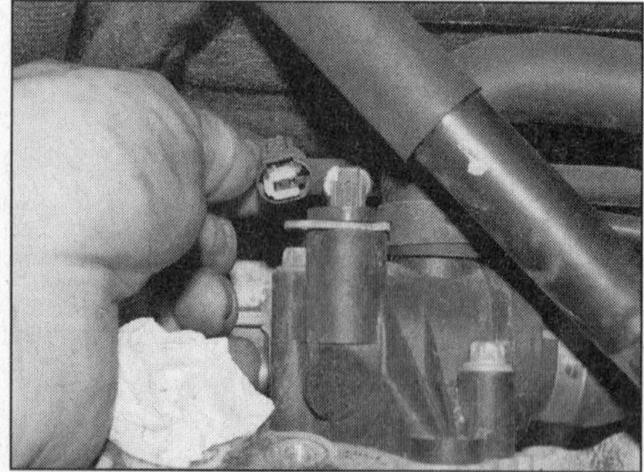
4.3 Disconnect the temperature sensor wiring connector

4.4 Remove the hoses from the thermostat housing

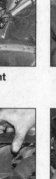

4.5a Undo the retaining bolts (arrowed) . . .

4.5b . . . and remove the thermostat housing

4 Thermostat – removal, testing and refitting

Note: *The thermostat is integrated as part of the thermostat housing and can only be renewed as a complete assembly.*

Removal

1 The thermostat is located in a housing at the left-hand rear end of the cylinder head.

2 Drain the cooling system as described in Chapter 1A or 1B.

3 Disconnect the wiring connector from the temperature sensor in the thermostat housing **(see illustration)**.

4 Disconnect the coolant hoses from the thermostat housing **(see illustration)**. There are two hoses on petrol engines and three hoses on diesel engines.

5 Undo the retaining bolts, and remove the thermostat housing (noting the locations of any brackets secured by the bolts), and then remove the thermostat housing from the cylinder head. Recover the rubber seal (petrol models) or gasket (diesel models) and discard; a new one will be required on refitting **(see illustrations)**.

Testing

6 A rough test of the thermostat may be made by suspending it with a piece of string in a container full of water, but not touching the container. Heat the water to bring it to the boil – the thermostat must open by the time the water boils. If not, renew it.

7 If a thermometer is available, the precise opening temperature of the thermostat may be determined, and compared with the figures given in the Specifications. The opening temperature is also usually marked on the thermostat.

8 A thermostat that fails to close as the water cools down, must also be renewed.

Refitting

9 Refitting is a reversal of removal, bearing in mind the following points.

*a) Refit the thermostat housing using a new rubber seal or gasket **(see illustration)**.*

b) Refill the cooling system with the correct type and quantity of coolant as described in Chapter 1A or 1B.

5 Electric cooling fan – testing, removal and refitting

Testing

1 The cooling fan is supplied with current through the ignition switch, control unit, temperature sensor, the relays and fuses/fusible link (see Chapter 12). The circuit is activated by the engine management control unit (ECU), which activates it according to the engine coolant temperature sensor.

2 If a fan does not appear to work, first check the fuses, fusible links and relays (see Chapter 12). If they are good, run the engine until normal operating temperature is reached, then allow it to idle. If the fan does not cut-in within a few minutes, the cause may be the temperature sender (where applicable), which can be checked by a Mercedes-Benz dealer using specialist diagnostic equipment.

3 The motors can be checked by disconnecting the motor wiring connector, and connecting a 12 volt supply directly to the motor terminals. If the motor is faulty, it must be renewed, as no spares are available.

4 If the fan still fails to operate, check the cooling fan circuit wiring (Chapter 12). Check each wire for continuity and ensure that all connections are clean and free of corrosion.

5 If no other fault can be found, then it is likely that the control unit is faulty. Testing of the unit should be entrusted to a Mercedes-Benz dealer or specialist; if the unit is faulty it must be renewed.

Removal

6 Disconnect the battery negative lead and position it away from the terminal. **Note:** *Before disconnecting the battery, refer to 'Disconnecting the battery' in the reference section at the rear of this manual.*

7 On petrol models, remove the air intake cowl/scoop from the front crossmember, and

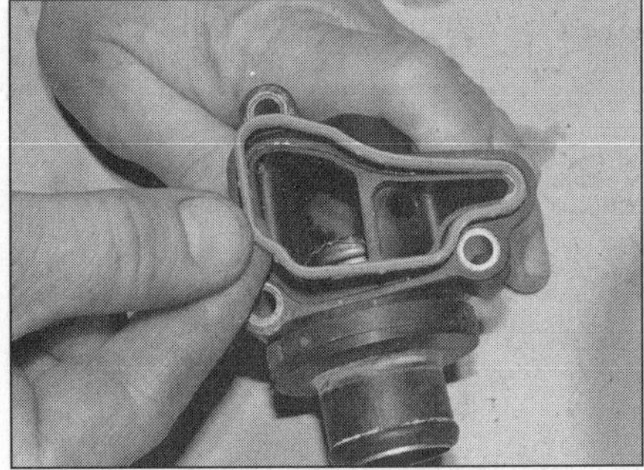

4.9 Fit new rubber seal to housing

disconnect the vacuum pipe from the front of the inlet manifold **(see illustrations)**.

8 On diesel models, remove the air intake assembly as described in Chapter 4B.

9 Disconnect the wiring plug for the cooling fan motor.

10 Lift the fan shroud assembly upwards to disengage it from the guides on the radiator and remove from the engine compartment **(see illustration)**.

11 To remove the fan and motor from the shroud, first disconnect and release the wiring from any retaining clips, then unscrew the Torx bolts and remove the fan motor from the shroud. **Note:** *One of the Torx bolts acts as a locking bolt to prevent the fan-retaining block from turning.*

Refitting

12 Refitting is a reversal of removal.

6 Coolant temperature sensor – testing, removal and refitting

1 The coolant temperature sensor is located in the thermostat housing at the left-hand rear of the cylinder head.

Testing

2 The sensor contains a thermistor, which consists of an electronic component whose electrical resistance decreases at a predetermined rate as its temperature rises. When the coolant is cold, the sensor resistance is high, current flow through the gauge is reduced, and the gauge needle points towards the 'cold' end of the scale. No resistance-to-temperature values are available. Therefore the only method of accurately checking the sensor is with dedicated diagnostic equipment, and should be entrusted to a Mercedes-Benz dealer or specialist. If the sensor is faulty, it must be renewed.

Removal and refitting

3 Disconnect the wiring connector from the sensor **(see illustration)**, located in the thermostat housing at the left-hand rear of the cylinder head.

4 Partially drain the cooling system to below the level of the sensor (as described in Chapter 1A or 1B).

5 To remove the temperature sensor from the thermostat housing, release the

5.7a Unclip the air scoop from the front of the crossmember . . .

5.7b . . . and then disconnect the air intake hose

5.7c Release the vacuum pipe from the inlet manifold

5.10 Carefully lift out the fan and shroud

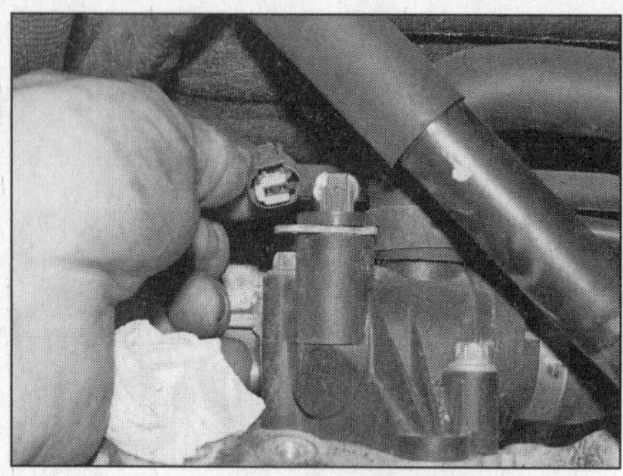
6.3 Disconnect the temperature sensor wiring connector

6.5a Withdraw the retaining clip . . .

6.5b . . . and remove the sensor

retaining clip and withdraw the sensor **(see illustrations)**. Discard the sealing ring, as a new one will be required for refitting.

6 Refitting is a reversal of removal. Bearing in mind the following points.

a) Refit the sensor with a new O-ring.

b) Refill the cooling system as described in Chapter 1A or 1B, or top-up as described in 'Weekly checks'.

7 Coolant pump – removal and refitting

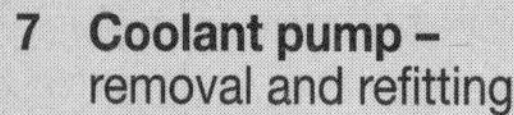

Note: *The engine will need to be lowered on the subframe to carry out this procedure.*

Removal

1 Drain the cooling system as described in Chapter 1A or 1B.

2 With reference to Chapter 2C, lower the engine and front subframe to access the coolant pump, which is situated at the front/ timing chain end of the engine.

3 Before removing the auxiliary drivebelt, loosen the coolant pump pulley bolts, then remove the drivebelt as described in Chapter 1A or 1B.

4 Unscrew the bolts and remove the pulley from the coolant pump **(see illustration)**.

5 Unscrew the mounting bolts and remove the coolant pump from the cylinder block **(see illustrations)**. Recover the shaped rubber seal and discard, a new one will be required for refitting.

Refitting

6 Refitting is a reversal of removal, bearing in mind the following points.

a) Clean the mating surfaces thoroughly before fitting the pump.

*b) Fit new coolant pump rubber seal **(see illustration)**.*

c) Refit the engine and front subframe with reference to Chapter 2C.

d) Refill the cooling system as described in Chapter 1A or 1B.

7.4 Remove the coolant pump pulley

7.5a Undo the retaining bolts . . .

7.5b . . . and remove the coolant pump

7.6 Fit new rubber seal

8 Heating and ventilation system – general information

1 The heating/ventilation system consists of either a four- (early models) or five-speed (later models) blower motor (housed in the passenger compartment), face-level vents in the centre and at each end of the facia, and air ducts to the front and rear footwells.

2 The control unit is located in the facia, and the controls operate flap valves to deflect and mix the air flowing through the various parts of the heating/ventilation system. The flap valves are contained in the air distribution housing, which acts as a central distribution unit, passing air to the various ducts and vents.

3 Cold air enters the system through the grille at the rear of the engine compartment. A pollen filter (combination filter) is fitted to filter out dust, soot, pollen and spores from the air entering the vehicle.

4 The airflow, which can be boosted by the blower, flows through the various ducts, according to the settings of the controls. Stale air is expelled through ducts at the rear of the vehicle. If warm air is required, the cold air is passed through the heater matrix, which is heated by the engine coolant.

5 If necessary, the outside air supply can be closed off, allowing the air inside the vehicle to be recirculated. This can be useful to prevent unpleasant odours entering from outside the vehicle, but should only be used briefly, as the recirculated air quality inside the vehicle will soon deteriorate.

9 Heating/ventilation system components – removal and refitting

Heater/ventilation control unit

1 Disconnect the battery negative lead and position it away from the terminal. **Note:** *Before disconnecting the battery, refer to*

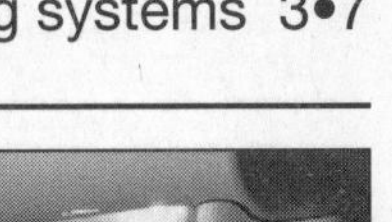

9.13 Unclip the storage compartment

9.14a Undo the two retaining screws – arrowed . . .

9.14b . . . and remove the front switch panel

9.15 Disconnect the wiring connectors

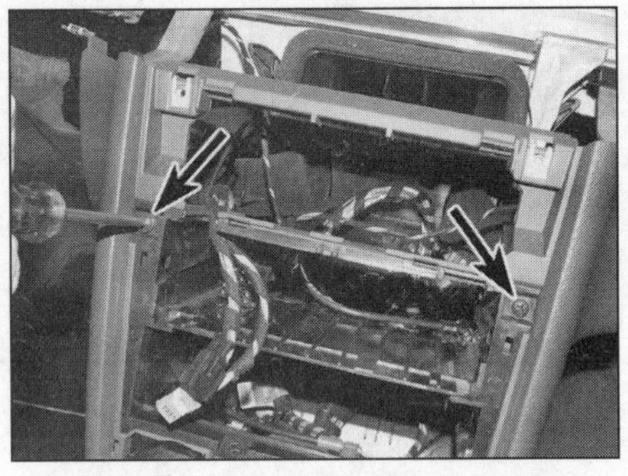
9.16a Undo the two retaining screws – arrowed . . .

9.16b . . . and withdraw the reinforcement panel

'Disconnecting the battery' in the reference section at the rear of this manual.

2 Remove the radio as described in Chapter 12.

Models up to 28/02/01

3 Remove the trim panels from around the side air vents and along the facia panel with reference to Chapter 11.

4 Undo the retaining screw from inside the radio aperture, at the top centre.

5 Unclip the storage compartment, and pull it out from the facia panel.

6 Undo the four retaining screws (two at the top and two at the bottom), and remove the centre cover from the facia panel.

7 As the cover is removed, disconnect the wiring connector from the rear of the hazard warning light switch.

8 Release the retaining clips and unclip the row of switches from the rear of the cover.

9 Undo the two retaining screws (one at each side) and unclip the heater control unit from the rear of the cover.

10 Disconnect the wiring block connector(s) from the back of the heater control unit. On models without air conditioning, there is one wiring block connector and, on models with air conditioning, there are two connectors.

11 Note the location of the heater control cables, and then release the retaining clamps and disconnect them from the back of the heater control unit. On models without air conditioning, there are four control cables and, on models with air conditioning, there are two control cables.

12 Remove the heater control unit from the facia, and if required, the heater control slide button can be removed from the control unit.

Models from 01/03/01

13 Unclip the storage compartment, and pull it out from the facia panel **(see illustration)**.

14 Undo the two retaining screws from inside the aperture, at the top of the heater switch control unit **(see illustrations)**.

15 As the cover is removed, disconnect the wiring connector from the rear of the group of switches **(see illustration)**.

16 Undo the two retaining screws and remove the reinforcement panel from inside the radio aperture, above the heater control unit **(see illustrations)**.

17 Release the retaining clips at the lower part of the heater control unit, push backwards and unclip the control unit from the facia panel **(see illustrations)**.

18 Note the location of the heater control cables, and then release the retaining clamps and disconnect them from the back of the heater control unit. On models without air conditioning, there are three control cables and, on models with air conditioning, there are two control cables (see paragraph 23).

19 Disconnect the two wiring block connectors from the back of the heater control unit **(see illustrations)**.

20 The heater control unit can now be removed from the facia panel.

All models

21 Refitting is a reversal of removal, noting the following points:

9.17a Release the retaining clips . . .

9.17b . . . and remove the heater control panel

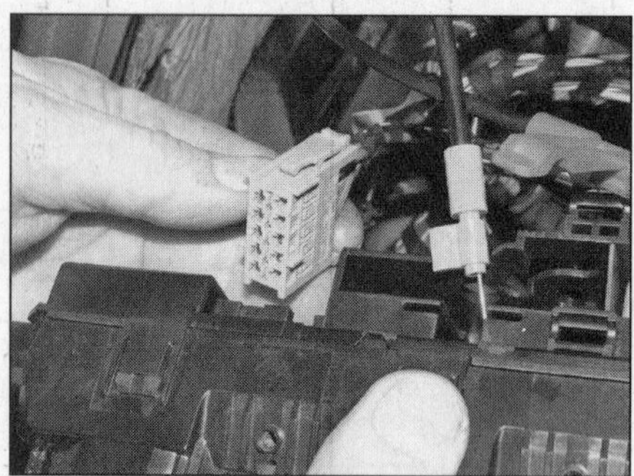

9.19a Disconnect the wiring connectors . . .

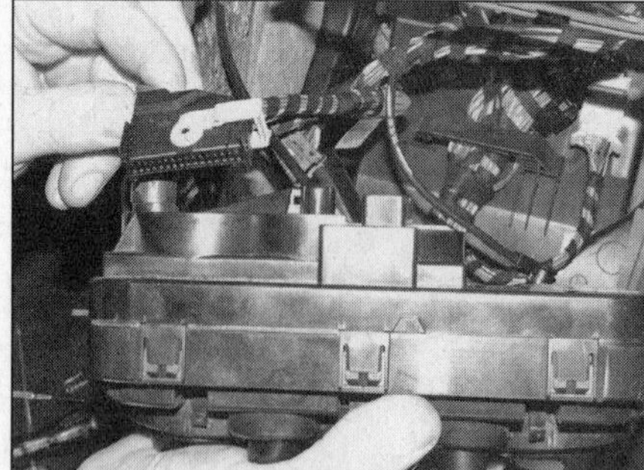

9.19b . . . from the back of the control panel

9.23a Release the upper outer cable . . .

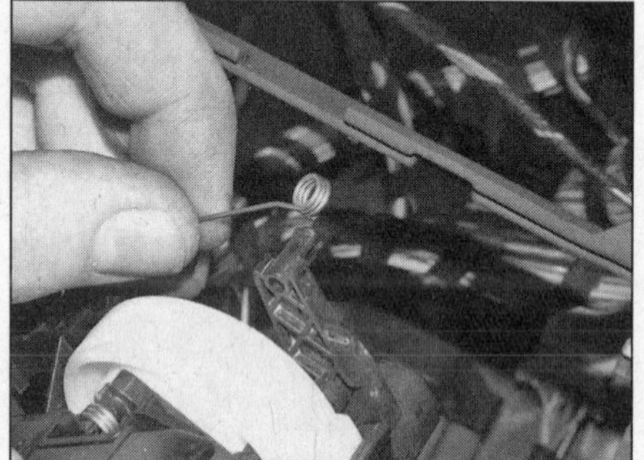

9.23b . . . and unclip the inner cable . . .

9.23c . . . and then the other cable can then be unclipped

a) Ensure the control knobs are positioned correctly and the cables are secure.

b) Check the operation of the heater control switches before the facia centre cover is refitted.

c) Use the relevant Chapters for refitting, where applicable.

Heater control cables

22 Remove the heater/ventilation control unit from the facia as described previously.

23 Reach into the facia and release the outer cables, and then disconnect the inner cable from the control panel **(see illustrations)**.

24 Remove the trim from the left-hand side of the heater as described in Chapter 11.

25 Disconnect the inner and outer cables from the temperature flap and heater unit **(see illustrations)**.

26 Refitting is a reversal of removal, but check that the control knobs can be turned easily after fitting.

Fresh/recirculating air flap positioning motor

27 Remove the trim from the right-hand side of the heater as described in Chapter 11.

28 Disconnect the wiring connector from the top of the motor.

29 Undo the retaining screws, and then remove the motor from the heater housing disconnecting the linkage rod as it is removed **(see illustration)**.

30 Refitting is a reversal of removal. Note that if the motor is renewed, its basic settings may need to be reprogrammed by a Mercedes-Benz dealer using specialist equipment

Heater blower motor

31 Open the bonnet and remove the pollen/dust filter as described in Chapter 1A or 1B.

32 Disconnect the wiper linkage rod and move it to one side.

33 Release the three retaining clips, and remove the pollen filter plastic framework from the top of the blower motor housing **(see illustrations)**.

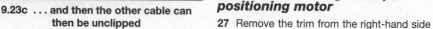

9.25a Heater cable on left-hand side of heater housing

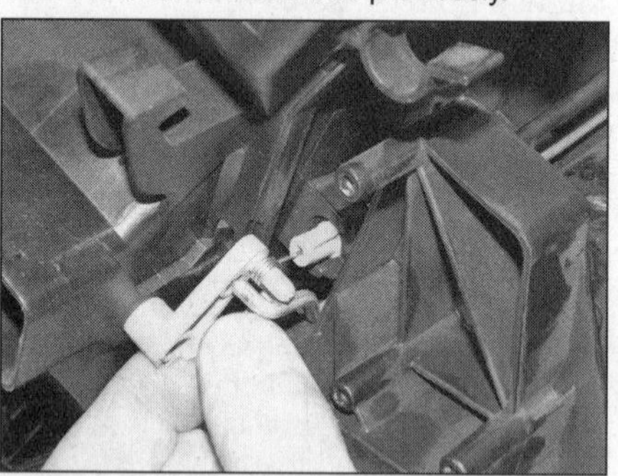

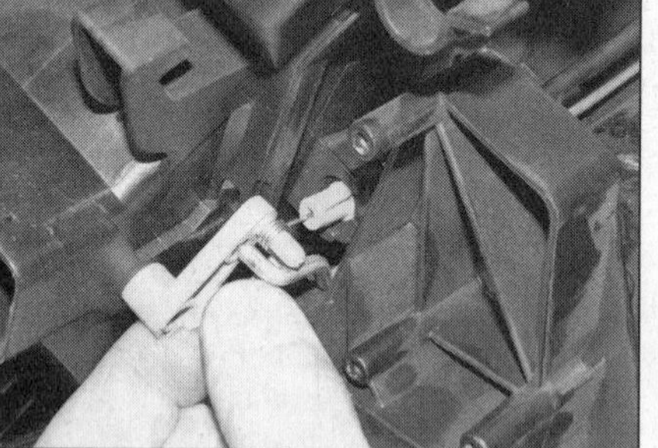

9.25b Disconnecting cable at right-hand rear of heater housing

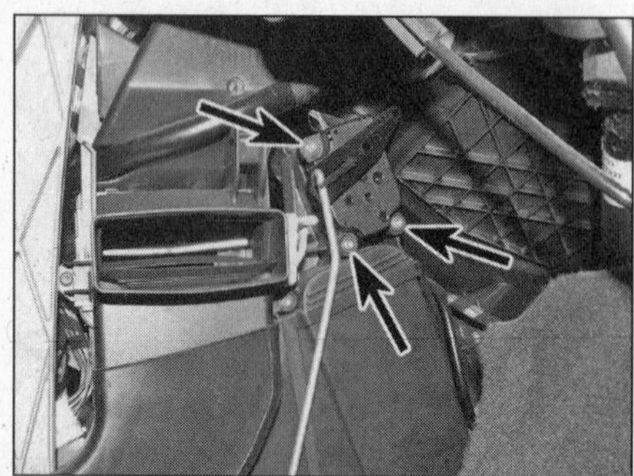

9.29 Undo the retaining screws – arrowed

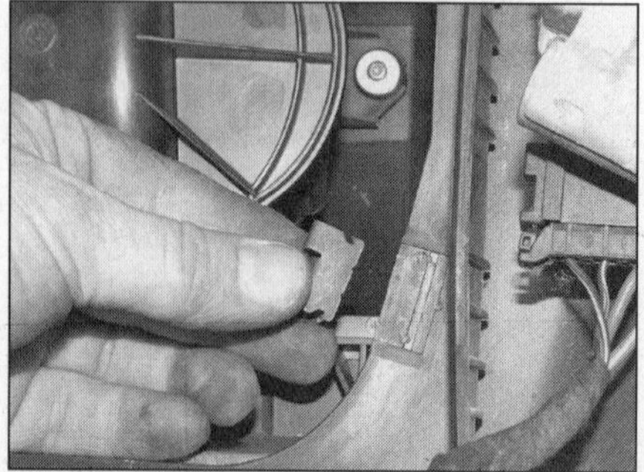

9.33a Release the retaining clips . . .

9.33b . . . and remove the filter framework

34 Undo the retaining screws, and remove the cover from the top of the heater blower motor **(see illustration)**.
35 Disconnect the wiring connector, undo the retaining bolts, and remove the heater blower motor from the housing **(see illustrations)**.
36 Refitting is a reversal of removal.

Heater blower motor series resistor

37 Switch off the ignition and all electrical consumers.
38 Pull back the carpet in the driver's side footwell and disconnect the wiring connector from the heater blower resistor **(see illustration)**.
Caution: The resistor may be very hot if the heater has recently been in use.
39 On models up to 28/02/01, the resistor can now be pulled out of its location.
40 On models from 01/03/01, slide the resistor to the right and then pull it out from its location.
41 Refitting is the reverse of removal.

Heater housing unit

Without air conditioning

42 Drain the cooling system as described in Chapter 1A or 1B.
43 Remove the facia panel as described in Chapter 11.
44 Working at the rear of the engine compartment, disconnect the two heater hoses from the heater matrix **(see illustration)**. Place a container beneath the hoses, to catch any coolant that is still left in the hoses. Note the location of the hoses for correct refitting.
45 Inside the car, place cloth rags or similar on the floor beneath the heater unit, to catch any excess coolant as the heater housing is withdrawn from inside the vehicle.
46 Unclip the air ducts from the top and sides of the heater housing.
47 Check around the heater housing and note the location and routing of any wiring or cables, if required, disconnect them from the heater unit. Also note the location of plastic cable ties to ensure correct refitting.
48 Unscrew and remove the four heater unit mounting bolts.
49 Undo the mounting bolts and remove the supporting strut from the right-hand side of the heater unit **(see illustration)**.

9.34 Remove the upper housing

9.35a Disconnect the wiring connector . . .

9.35b . . . and remove the retaining bolts – arrowed

9.38 Heater blower resistor – arrowed

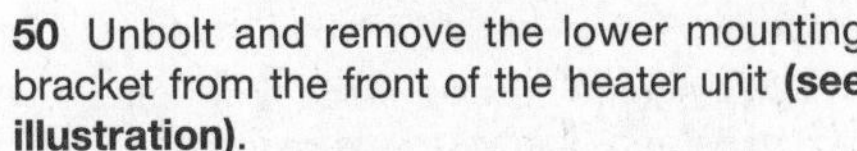

50 Unbolt and remove the lower mounting bracket from the front of the heater unit **(see illustration)**.
51 Carefully pull the heater unit from the bulkhead, taking care not to damage or bend the matrix tubes on the bulkhead. The help of an assistant may be required. Be prepared for coolant spillage as the assembly is removed from inside the car.
52 Refitting is a reversal of removal, but top-up the coolant with reference to *Weekly Checks* at the beginning of this Manual.

With air conditioning

Warning: Refer to the precautions given in Section 10.

53 It is not possible to remove the unit without opening the refrigerant circuit to the evaporator, therefore this task must be entrusted to a Mercedes-Benz dealer or an air conditioning specialist. With the refrigerant evacuated, the procedure is as described for models without air conditioning, except for the following.
Caution: The air conditioning compressor is driven permanently by the auxiliary drivebelt, and is not fitted with a magnetic clutch. It is not recommended that the engine is started without refrigerant being present in the system, as the compressor may overheat causing internal damage. Note also that if the refrigerant circuit is not opened within 10 minutes of evacuation, slight pressure may develop due to re-evaporation.

a) Where fitted, remove the cover from the expansion valve by unscrewing the nut and releasing the clips.
b) Unscrew the nut securing the refrigerant lines to the evaporator on the bulkhead at the rear of the engine compartment, and detach them. Recover the seals and

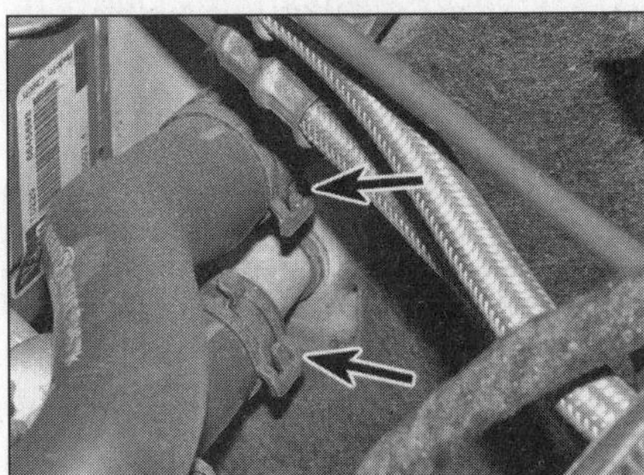

9.44 Heater hose retaining clips – arrowed

9.49 Support strut lower mounting bolt – arrowed

9.50 Heater unit lower front mounting bracket – arrowed

9.55a Undo the housing retaining screws (only four shown)

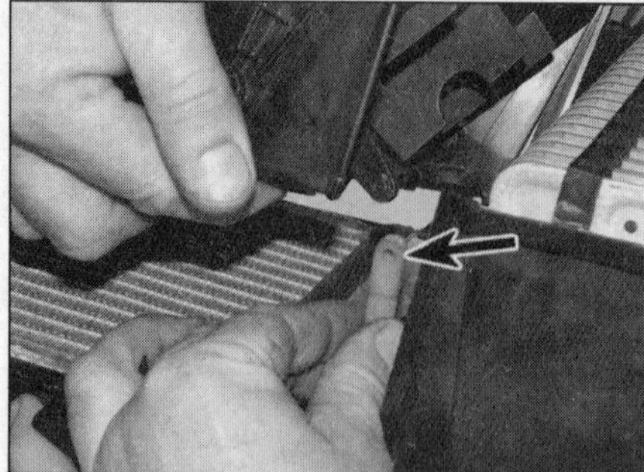

9.55b Release the air flap linkage – arrowed

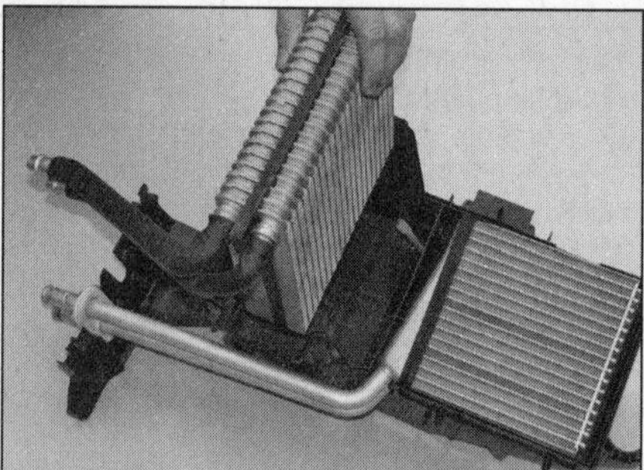

9.57 Withdraw the heater matrix from the housing

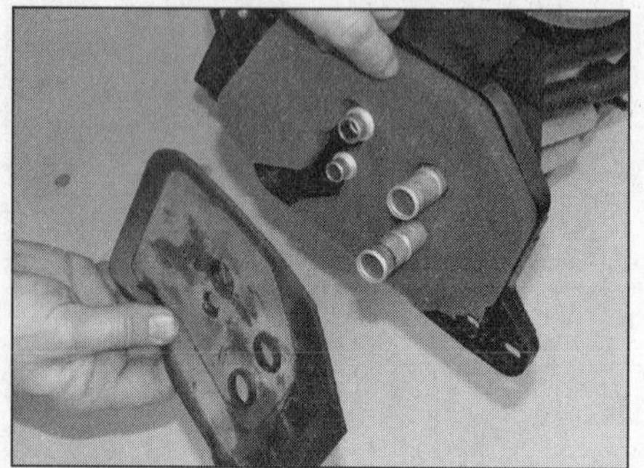

9.62a Remove the rubber and foam mounting pad . . .

9.62b . . . and withdraw the evaporator

9.66 Undo the retaining bolts – arrowed

plug the lines and evaporator openings to prevent entry of foreign matter and water vapour. Discard the seals as new ones must be used on refitting ***(see illustration)****.*

c) *Remove the footrest and condensation water drainage hose from the driver's side of the heater unit.*
d) *Top-up the coolant level with reference to 'Weekly Checks' at the beginning of this Manual.*

Heater matrix

54 Remove the heater housing unit from the facia as described previously.

55 Working your way around the housing, undo the retaining screws and remove the heater blower housing from the front of the heater unit. **Note:** *Unclip any wiring from the retaining clips around the heater unit, noting their fitted position.*

56 Working your way around the housing, undo the retaining screws and remove the upper half of the housing from the lower part. As the upper section of the housing is removed, detach the air flap linkage.

57 The heater matrix can now be withdrawn from the heater housing unit **(see illustration)**. Recover the gasket/seal, if damaged this will need to be renewed on refitting.

58 Refitting is a reversal of removal, noting the following.

a) *Make sure the gasket/seal is fitted correctly around the perimeter of the matrix.*
b) *Check the heater matrix pipe spacer is correctly located.*
c) *When reconnecting the coolant pipes, make sure the hoses are secure.*
d) *Check that the rubber grommet in the bulkhead is correctly located in its hole.*
e) *Top-up the coolant level with reference to 'Weekly Checks' at the beginning of this Manual.*

Air conditioning evaporator

Warning: Refer to the precautions given in Section 10.

59 Have the refrigerant evacuated from the air conditioning system by a Mercedes-Benz dealer or refrigeration specialist.

Caution: The air conditioning compressor is driven permanently by the auxiliary drivebelt, and is not fitted with a magnetic clutch. It is not recommended that the engine is started without refrigerant being present in the system, as the compressor may overheat causing internal damage. Note also that if the refrigerant circuit is not opened within 10 minutes of evacuation, slight pressure may develop due to re-evaporation.

60 Remove the heater housing unit as described earlier in this Section.

61 Dismantle the unit as shown and remove the heater matrix as described earlier in this Section.

62 Remove the evaporator from the housing together with the refrigerant lines and rubber grommet **(see illustrations)**.

63 Refitting is a reversal of removal, but fit new seals and have the system recharged by a Mercedes-Benz dealer or refrigeration specialist.

Air conditioning condenser

Warning: Refer to the precautions given in Section 10.

64 The condenser is attached to the front of the radiator. Have the refrigerant evacuated from the air conditioning system by a Mercedes-Benz dealer or refrigeration specialist.

Caution: The air conditioning compressor is driven permanently by the auxiliary drivebelt, and is not fitted with a magnetic clutch. It is not recommended that the engine is started without refrigerant being present in the system, as the compressor may overheat causing internal damage. Note also that if the refrigerant circuit is not opened within 10 minutes of evacuation, slight pressure may develop due to re-evaporation.

65 Remove the radiator as described in Section 3 of this Chapter.

66 Undo the screws and disconnect the refrigerant lines from the condenser **(see illustration)**. Recover the seals and plug the lines and condenser openings to prevent entry of foreign matter and water vapour.

67 Carefully withdraw the condenser upwards, taking care not to damage its fins.

68 Refitting is a reversal of removal, but fit new seals and have the system recharged by a Mercedes-Benz dealer or refrigeration specialist.

10 Air conditioning system – general information and precautions

General information

Air conditioning is fitted as standard to most models, and is available as manually-operated or can also be automatically-operated. The system works in conjunction with the heating and air conditioning systems to maintain a selected vehicle interior.

The air conditioning system enables the temperature of incoming air to be lowered, and dehumidifies the air, which makes for rapid demisting and increased comfort. The cooling side of the system works in the same way as a domestic refrigerator. Refrigerant gas is drawn into a belt-driven compressor and passes into a condenser mounted in front of the radiator, where it loses heat and becomes liquid. The liquid passes through an expansion valve to an evaporator, where it changes from liquid under high pressure to gas under low pressure. This change is accompanied by a drop in temperature, which cools the evaporator. The refrigerant returns to the compressor and the cycle begins again.

Air blown through the evaporator passes to the air distribution unit, where it is mixed with hot air blown through the heater matrix to achieve the desired temperature in the passenger compartment.

The heating side of the system works in the same way as on models without air conditioning.

The operation of the system is controlled electronically by coolant temperature switches, and pressure switches which are screwed into the compressor high-pressure line. Any problems with the system should be referred to a Mercedes-Benz dealer or an air conditioning specialist.

The only operation which can be carried out easily without discharging the refrigerant is the renewal of the compressor drivebelt, which is covered in the relevant part of Chapter 1 **(see Tool tip)**. Removal of the evaporator and condenser requires the evacuation of the refrigerant. If necessary the compressor can be unbolted and moved aside, without disconnecting its flexible hoses, after removing the drivebelt **(see illustration)**.

Many car accessory shops sell one-shot air conditioning recharge aerosols. These generally contain refrigerant, compressor oil, leak sealer and system conditioner. Some also have a dye to help pinpoint leaks.

Warning: These products must only be used as directed by the manufacturer, and do not remove the need for regular maintenance.

Precautions

- When an air conditioning system is fitted, it is necessary to observe special precautions whenever dealing with any part of the system, its associated components and any items which require disconnection of the system. If for any reason the system must be disconnected, entrust this task to your Mercedes-Benz dealer or an air conditioning specialist.
- Do not operate the air conditioning system if it is known to be short of refrigerant, as this may damage the compressor.

Warning: The refrigeration circuit contains a refrigerant and it is therefore dangerous to disconnect any part of the system without specialised knowledge and equipment. The refrigerant is potentially dangerous and should only be handled by qualified persons. If it is splashed onto the skin it can cause frostbite. It is not itself poisonous, but in the presence of a naked flame (including a cigarette) it forms a poisonous gas. Uncontrolled discharging of the refrigerant is dangerous and potentially damaging to the environment.

10.6 Air conditioning compressor – arrowed

11 Climate control components – removal and refitting

Ambient temperature sender

1 The ambient temperature sender is located behind the front bumper to the lower right-hand side of the radiator.

2 Remove the front bumper as described in Chapter 11.

3 Disconnect the wiring connecter from the temperature sender and remove it from the mounting bracket **(see illustration)**.

4 Refitting is a reversal of removal. Make sure the wiring is fully connected to prevent entry of water.

Evaporator sensor

5 The evaporator sensor is located to the left-hand front of the heater unit.

6 Switch off the ignition and all electrical consumers.

7 Remove the lower part of the facia panel from the passenger side of the vehicle, as described in Chapter 11.

8 Disconnect the wiring plug and withdraw the sensor from the heater unit **(see illustration)**.

9 Refitting is a reversal of removal.

Humidity sensor

10 The humidity sensor is located below the pollen filter, inside the blower motor housing **(see illustration)**.

11.3 Disconnecting the wiring from the air temperature sensor

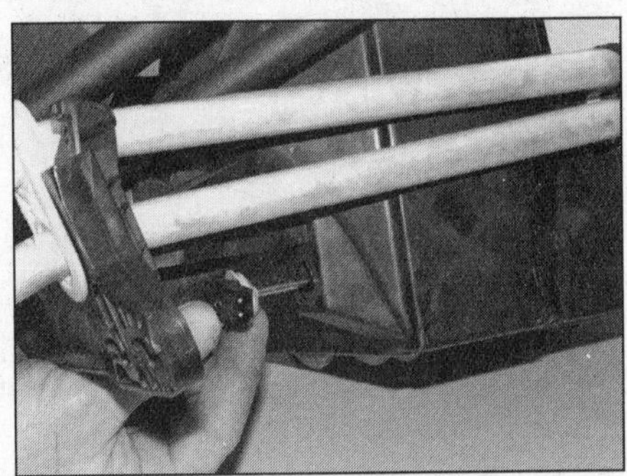

11.8 Evaporator sensor location

11.10 Humidity sensor location

11.19a Undo the retaining screws – arrowed . . .

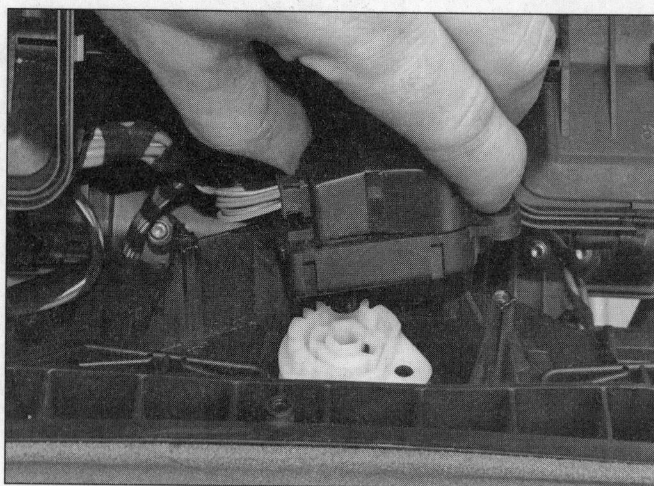

11.19b . . . and remove the stepper motor

11 Switch off the ignition and all electrical consumers.

12 Open the bonnet and remove the pollen filter as described in Chapters 1A or 1B.

13 Turn the sensor anti-clockwise, and withdraw it from the housing.

14 Disconnect the wiring connector from the sensor. **Note:** *The wiring to the sensor is very short, take care that the wiring does not slip back into the blower motor housing.*

15 Refitting is a reversal of removal.

Air stepper motor

16 The air stepper motor (for fresh air recirculation) is located in the top of the heater housing unit.

17 Remove the instrument panel as described in Chapter 12.

18 Unclip the air ducts from the top of the heater housing.

19 Undo the two retaining bolts and withdraw the stepper motor from the top of the heater unit **(see illustrations)**. Disconnect the wiring plug as it is removed.

20 Refitting is a reversal of removal.

Chapter 4 Part A:
Petrol engine fuel systems

Contents

Degrees of difficulty

Easy, suitable for novice with little experience

Fairly easy, suitable for beginner with some experience

Fairly difficult, suitable for competent DIY mechanic

Difficult, suitable for experienced DIY mechanic

Very difficult, suitable for expert DIY or professional

Specifications

System type

All engines	Bosch MSM multipoint fuel injection

Fuel system data

Fuel pump type	Electric, immersed in fuel tank
Regulated fuel pressure	2.5 bar
Engine idle speed	Non-adjustable, electronically-controlled
Idle CO content	0.5% max (non-adjustable, electronically-controlled)
Injector electrical resistance (typical)	12 to 17 ohms

Torque wrench settings

	Nm	lbf ft
Fuel rail mounting bolts	10	7
Fuel rail mounting bolts	15	11
Fuel tank mounting nuts	30	22
Idle speed control (ICS) actuator mounting bolts	7	5
Inlet manifold to cylinder head	25	18
Knock sensors	20	15
Oxygen sensors	55	41
Throttle housing/module mounting bolts	10	7

1 General information and precautions

General information

The systems described in this Chapter are all self-contained engine management systems, which control both the fuel injection and ignition. This Chapter deals with the fuel system components only – see Chapter 4C for information on the exhaust and emission control systems, and to Chapter 5B for details of the ignition system.

The fuel injection system consists of a fuel tank, an electric fuel lift pump/level sender unit, a fuel filter, fuel supply and return lines, a throttle housing/module, four electronic fuel injectors, and an Electronic Control Module (ECM) together with its associated sensors, actuators and wiring. The fuel injection system is an indirect injection system where the injectors inject fuel into the inlet manifold upstream of the inlet valves. This system uses a fuel rail and injectors fitted to the inlet manifold.

The fuel pump is immersed in the fuel inside the tank, and delivers a constant supply of fuel through a filter to the fuel rail. The fuel pressure regulator maintains a constant fuel pressure to the fuel injectors, and returns excess fuel to the tank through the return line. This constant flow system also helps to reduce fuel temperature, and prevents vaporisation. The pressure regulator is located on the end of the fuel rail.

The fuel injectors are opened and closed by an Electronic Control Module (ECM), which calculates the injection timing and duration according to engine speed, crankshaft/camshaft position, throttle position and rate of opening, inlet manifold depression, inlet air temperature, coolant temperature, roadspeed and exhaust gas oxygen content information, received from sensors mounted on and around the engine.

Inlet air is drawn into the engine through the air cleaner, which contains a renewable paper filter element. The inlet air temperature is regulated by a sensor mounted in the air filter intake trunking, which sends information to the ECM.

The temperature and pressure of the air entering the throttle housing is measured by a sensor mounted on the inlet manifold. This information is used by the ECM to fine-tune the fuelling requirements for different operating conditions.

The exhaust gas oxygen content is constantly monitored by the ECM by oxygen sensors (also known as lambda sensors), one before the catalytic converter, and one after – this improves sensor response time and accuracy, and the ECM compares the signals from each sensor to confirm that the converter is working correctly. The ECM uses the information from the sensors to modify the injection timing and duration to maintain the optimum air/fuel ratio. All models are fitted with a catalytic converter – see Chapter 4C.

The ECM also controls the operation of the activated charcoal filter evaporative loss system – refer to Chapter 4C for further details.

It should be noted that fault diagnosis of all the engine management systems described in this Chapter is only possible with dedicated electronic test equipment. Problems with the systems operation should therefore be referred to a Mercedes-Benz dealer for assessment. Once the fault has been identified, the removal/refitting sequences detailed in the following Sections will then allow the appropriate component(s) to be renewed as required.

Precautions

Warning: Petrol is extremely flammable – great care must be taken when working on any part of the fuel system.

Warning: Avoid direct skin contact with fuel – wear protective clothing and gloves when handling fuel system components. Ensure that the work area is well-ventilated to prevent the build-up of fuel vapour.

- Do not smoke, or allow any naked flames or uncovered light bulbs near the work area. Note that gas-powered domestic appliances with pilot flames, such as heaters boilers and tumble-dryers, also present a fire hazard – bear this in mind if you are working in an area where such appliances are present. Always keep a suitable fire extinguisher close to the work area, and familiarise yourself with its operation before starting work. Wear eye protection when working on fuel systems, and wash off any fuel spilt on bare skin immediately with soap and water. Note that fuel vapour is just as dangerous as liquid fuel – possibly more so; a vessel that has been emptied of liquid fuel will still contain vapour, and can be potentially explosive.
- Many of the operations described in this Chapter involve the disconnection of fuel lines, which may cause an amount of fuel spillage. Before commencing work, refer to the above *Warning* and the information in *Safety first!* at the beginning of this manual.
- Residual fuel pressure always remains in the fuel system, long after the engine has been switched off. This pressure must be relieved in a controlled manner before work can commence on any component in the fuel system – refer to Section 7 for details.
- When working with fuel system components, pay particular attention to cleanliness – dirt entering the fuel system may cause blockages, which will lead to poor running.
- In the interests of personal safety and equipment protection, many of the procedures in this Chapter suggest that the negative lead be removed from the battery terminal. This firstly eliminates the possibility of accidental short-circuits being caused as the vehicle is being worked upon, and secondly prevents damage to electronic components (eg, sensors, actuators, ECMs) which are particularly sensitive to the power surges caused by disconnection or reconnection of the wiring harness whilst they are still 'live'. Refer to *Disconnecting the battery* at the rear of this manual.

2 Air filter and intake housing – removal and refitting

Removal

1 Open the bonnet and remove the air scoop from the front crossmember to the air intake housing **(see illustrations)**.

2 On models up to 31/08/01, where applicable, disconnect the breather hose from the base of the air intake resonator housing.

3 On models from 01/09/01, disconnect the breather hose from the base of the air intake resonator housing **(see illustration)**.

2.1a Unclip the air scoop . . .

2.1b . . . and remove the air intake ducting

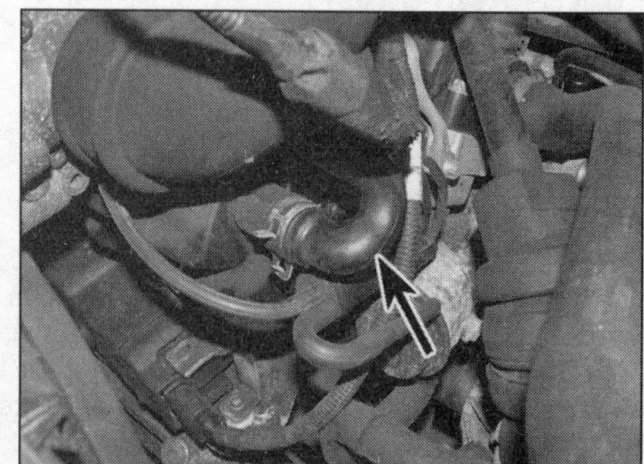

2.3 Disconnect the breather hose – arrowed

4 On models from 01/09/01, disconnect the wiring connector from the intake air temperature sensor on the resonator housing **(see illustration)**.

5 Undo the securing screws and remove the resonator cover/housing from the air intake housing **(see illustrations)**. Recover the sealing ring from around the housing and discard, a new one will be required for refitting.

6 To gain better access, remove the oil filler cap from the filler neck.

7 Slide the air cleaner housing to the timing chain side of the engine to release it from the locating guides and then remove it from the engine compartment **(see illustration)**.

8 On models up to 31/08/01, with the airflow meter/ECM detached from the air intake housing and the wiring connectors still attached, move it to one side, making sure it is safely positioned.

Refitting

9 Refitting is a reversal of removal, noting the following points:

a) On models up to 31/08/01, ensure that the engine control module is correctly refitted.

b) Fit new sealing ring to air intake housing.

c) Apply a small amount of grease on the locating guides to aid refitting.

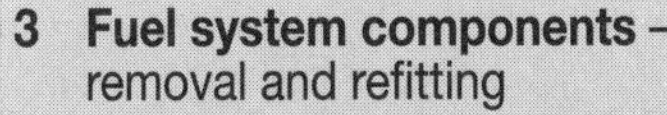

3 Fuel system components – removal and refitting

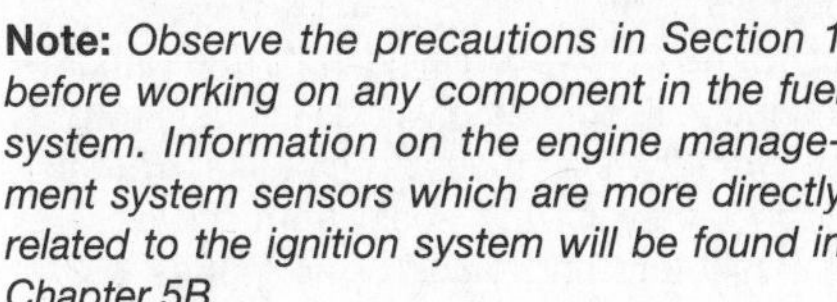

Note: *Observe the precautions in Section 1 before working on any component in the fuel system. Information on the engine management system sensors which are more directly related to the ignition system will be found in Chapter 5B.*

Idle speed control (ICS) actuator

Models up to 31/08/01

1 Remove air filter and intake housing as described previously in Section 2.

2 Disconnect the wiring connector(s) from the airflow meter/ECM and remove it from the engine compartment.

3 Refitting is a reversal of removal.

Models from 01/09/01

4 Remove air filter and intake housing as described previously in Section 2.

5 Disconnect the wiring connector from the idle speed control actuator **(see illustration)**.

6 Unscrew and remove the through-bolts, then lift the idle speed control actuator from the inlet manifold **(see illustrations)**. Recover the O-ring seal and discard, a new one will be required for refitting.

7 Refitting is a reversal of removal, noting the following:

2.4 Disconnect the air temperature sensor

2.5b . . . and remove the air intake housing

a) Use a new throttle housing-to-inlet manifold seal ***(see illustration)****.*

b) Tighten the throttle housing through-bolts evenly to the specified torque.

c) Ensure that all hoses and electrical connectors are refitted securely.

3.5 Disconnect the control unit

3.6b . . . and remove the speed control actuator

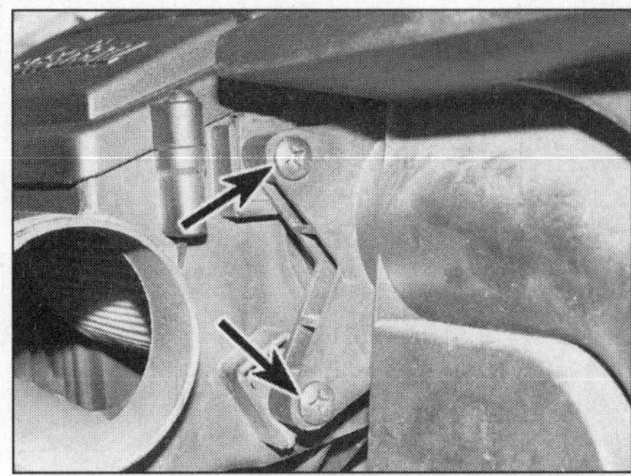

2.5a Undo the retaining screws (two shown) . . .

2.7 Slide the air cleaner housing out of the locating holes

Air temperature/pressure sensor

Models up to 31/08/01

8 The air temperature/pressure sensor is located inside the ECM on the idle speed actuator and cannot be removed separately.

3.6a Undo the retaining bolts – arrowed . . .

3.7 Fit new rubber sealing ring

3.10 Disconnect the wiring connector from the air temperature sensor

3.14 Disconnect the wiring connector from the air pressure sensor

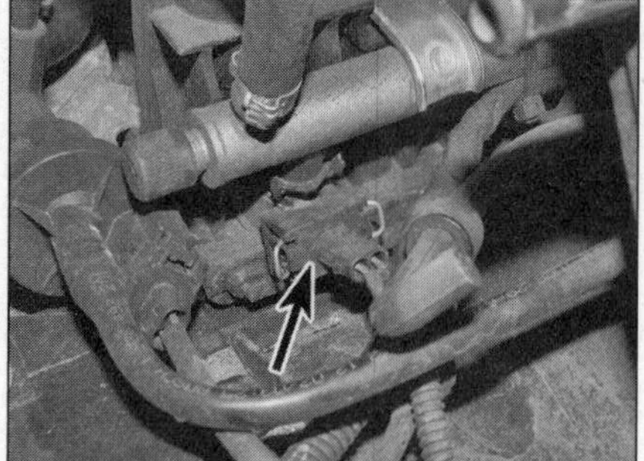

3.18a Disconnect the wiring connectors from . . .

3.18b . . . all four fuel injectors – arrowed

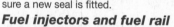

3.20a Disconnect the fuel pipe – arrowed . . .

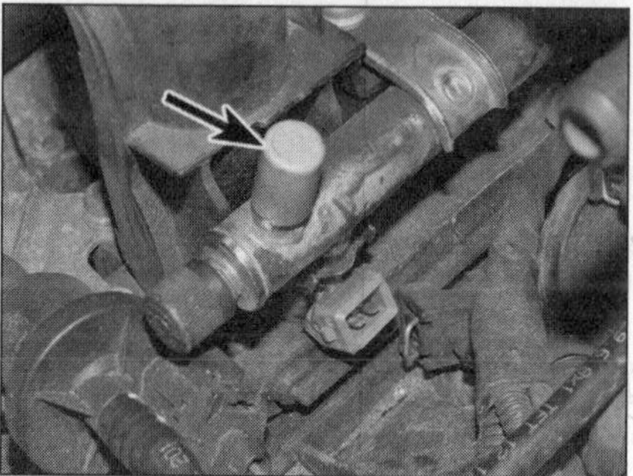

3.20b . . . and fit a cap (arrowed) to prevent dirt ingress

Air temperature sensor

Models from 01/09/01

9 The air temperature sensor is located on the air filter resonator housing.

10 Disconnect the wiring connector from the sensor **(see illustration)**.

11 Press each side of the sensor to release the securing clips and pull the sensor from the housing. Recover the seal and discard, as a new one must be used on refitting.

12 Refitting is a reversal of removal, making sure a new seal is fitted.

Air pressure sensor

Models from 01/09/01

13 The air pressure sensor is located on the top of the inlet manifold.

14 Disconnect the wiring connector from the sensor **(see illustration)**.

15 Undo the two retaining screws and remove the sensor from the inlet manifold. Recover the seal and discard, as a new one must be used on refitting.

16 Refitting is a reversal of removal, making sure a new seal is fitted.

Fuel injectors and fuel rail

Note: *Observe the precautions in Section 1 before working on any component in the fuel system. If a faulty injector is suspected, before removing the injectors, it is worth trying the effect of one of the proprietary injector-cleaning treatments. These can be added to the petrol in the tank, and are intended to clean the injectors as you drive.*

17 Remove air filter and intake housing as described previously in Section 2.

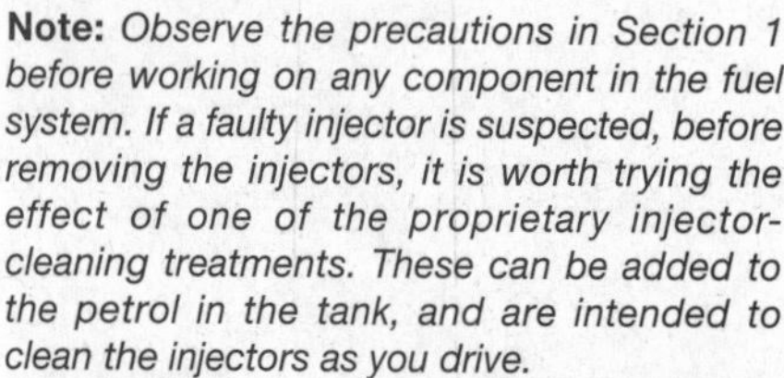

18 Disconnect the wiring connectors from the four injectors located along the fuel rail and release the wiring loom from its retaining clips **(see illustrations)**. Note the fitted position of the wiring loom, to aid refitting.

19 Refer to Section 7 of this chapter to release the fuel pressure that is still in the fuel line.

20 Using a rag around the fuel line, slacken the retaining clip and disconnect the fuel pipe from the end of the fuel rail **(see illustrations)**. Plug the end of the line to prevent entry of dust and dirt.

21 Undo the two retaining bolts and withdraw the fuel rail, complete with injectors, upwards out from the inlet manifold **(see illustrations)**. Recover the O-ring seals from the ends of the injectors and discard, new ones will be required for refitting.

22 To remove the injectors from the fuel rail, remove the securing clips and withdraw them from the rail **(see illustrations)**. Discard the O-ring seals, as new ones will be required for refitting.

23 Refitting is a reversal of removal, but thoroughly clean the fuel injector seatings, and fit new injector seals **(see illustrations)**. Lubricate the seals for easier assembly.

3.21a Left-hand mounting bolt – arrowed . . .

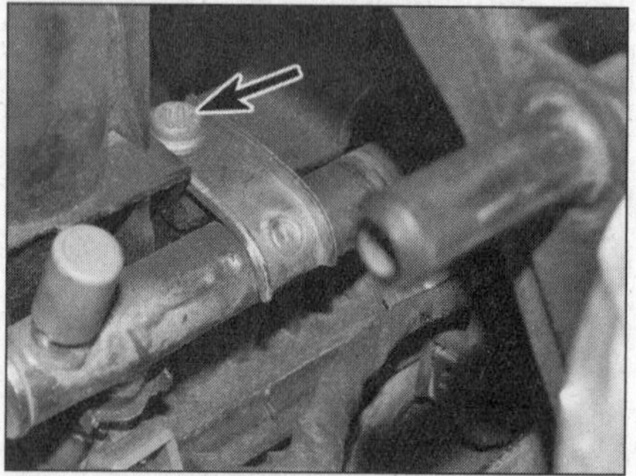

3.21b . . . and right-hand fuel rail mounting bolt – arrowed

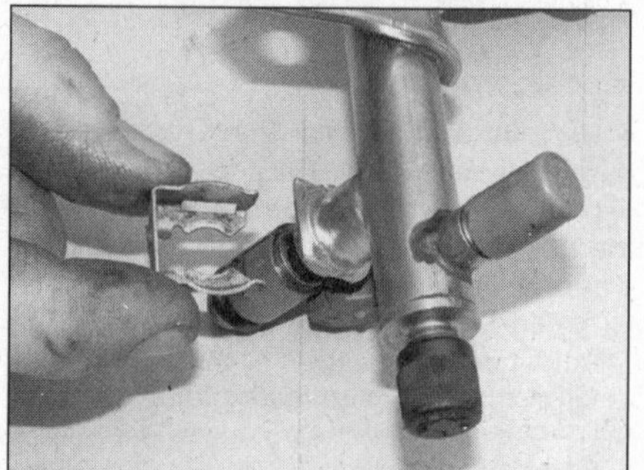

3.22a Remove the retaining clip . . .

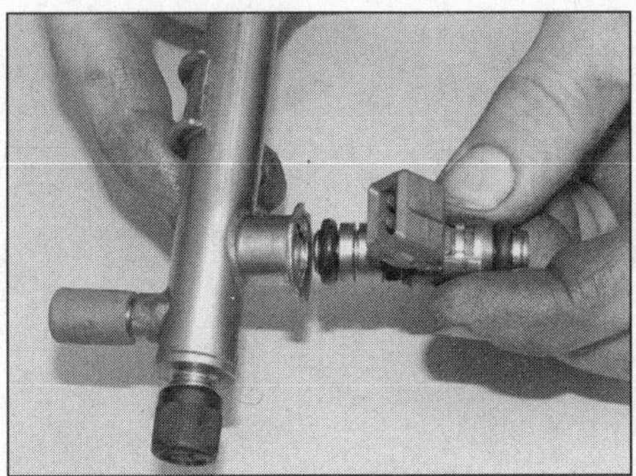

3.22b . . . and withdraw the injector from the rail

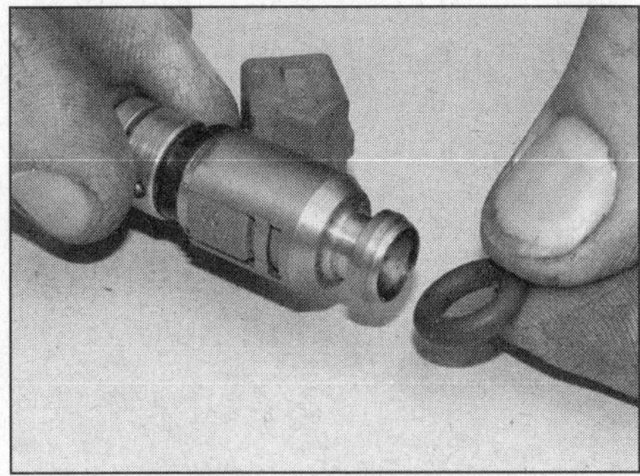

3.23a Fit new injector seal . . .

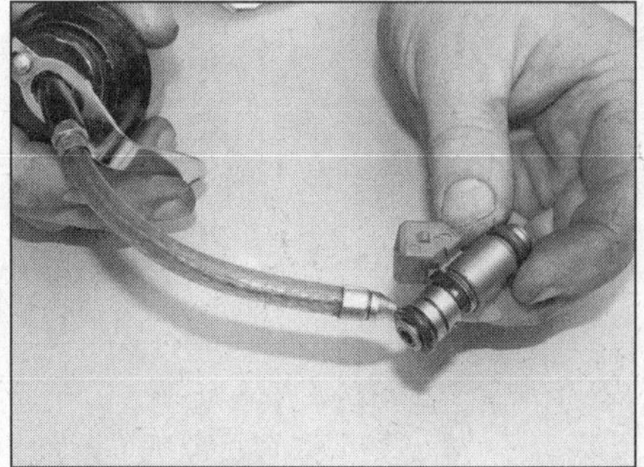

3.23b . . . and lubricate to aid refitting

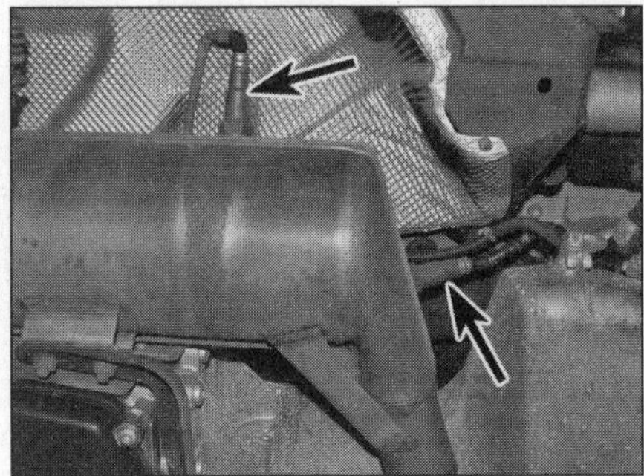

3.25 Location of oxygen sensors – arrowed

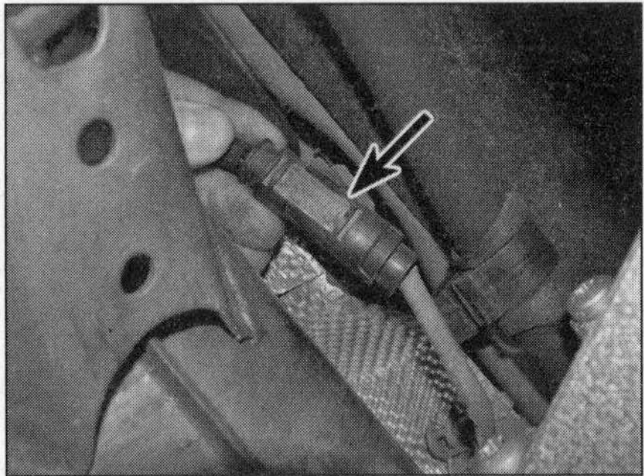

3.26a Disconnect the wiring connector – arrowed . . .

3.26b . . . and the second sensor wiring on the rear of the sump

Coolant temperature sensor

24 Refer to Chapter 3.

Oxygen (lambda) sensors

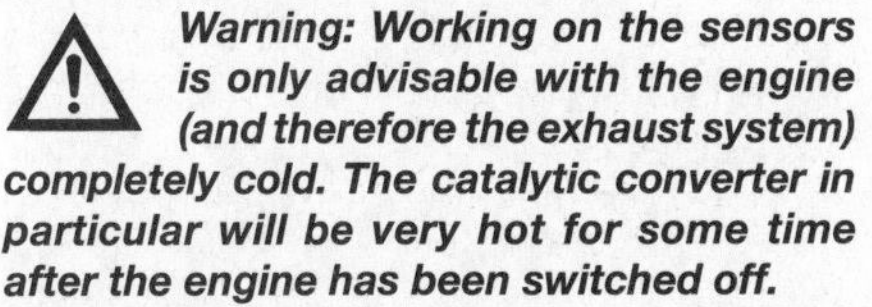

Warning: Working on the sensors is only advisable with the engine (and therefore the exhaust system) completely cold. The catalytic converter in particular will be very hot for some time after the engine has been switched off.

25 All models have one sensor threaded into the exhaust manifold side of the catalytic converter, and a second sensor mounted in the side of the catalytic converter. Refer to Chapter 4C for more details **(see illustration)**.

26 Working from the sensor, trace the wiring harness from the oxygen sensor back to the connector, and disconnect it. Unclip the sensor wiring from any retaining clips, noting how it is routed **(see illustrations)**.

27 Access to the sensors will only be possible from under the vehicle. Jack up the front of the car, and support it on axle stands (see *Jacking and vehicle support*).

28 Unscrew and remove the sensor, taking care to avoid damaging the sensor probe as it is removed. **Note:** *As a flying lead remains connected to the sensor after it has been disconnected, if the correct-size spanner is not available, a slotted socket will be required to remove the sensor.*

29 Apply a small amount of high-temperature anti-seize grease to the sensor threads – avoid contaminating the probe tip.

30 Refit the sensor, tightening it to the correct torque. Reconnect the wiring **(see illustration)**.

Crankshaft position sensor

31 Crankshaft position sensor is mounted at the top/front of the cylinder block, next to the transmission bellhousing. Move the coolant hose to one side to access the sensor **(see illustration)**.

3.30 Sensor connection (shown out of car for clarity)

3.33a Undo the retaining screw . . .

32 Disconnect the wiring connector from the sensor.

33 Unscrew the retaining bolt and withdraw the sensor from the cylinder block **(see illustrations)**.

34 Refitting is a reversal of removal.

3.31 Location of crankshaft position sensor – arrowed

3.33b . . . and withdraw the sensor

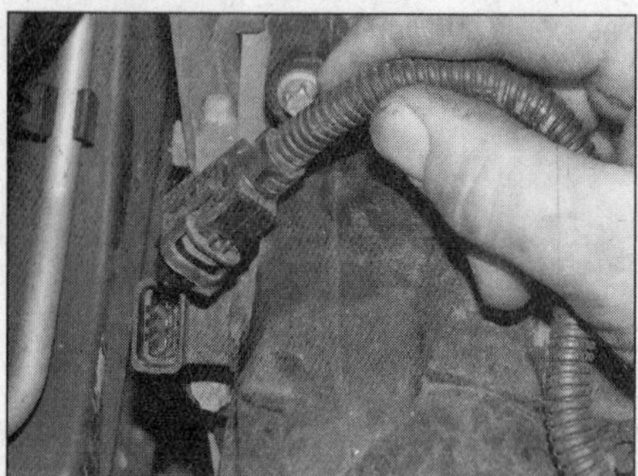
3.36 Disconnect the wiring connector

3.37 Removing the camshaft position sensor

3.40 Throttle position sensor – arrowed

3.46 Remove the plastic cover . . .

3.47 . . . disconnect the wiring connectors . . .

3.48 . . . and withdraw the ECM

Camshaft position sensor

35 The camshaft position sensor is located on the timing chain end of the camshaft cover.

36 Disconnect the wiring **(see illustration)**.

37 Undo the screw and remove the sensor **(see illustration)**. Recover the O-ring seal.

38 Refitting is a reversal of removal, but fit a new O-ring seal.

Fuel pressure regulator

39 The fuel pressure regulator is part of the fuel sender unit and is located inside the fuel tank, refer to Section 5.

Throttle pedal/position sensor

40 All models are fitted with a 'fly-by-wire' throttle where the position sensor is integral with the accelerator pedal **(see illustration)**.

41 Undo the bolts securing the throttle pedal to the bulkhead and remove it, disconnecting the wiring connector as it is removed.

42 Refitting is a reversal of removal.

Clutch pedal switch

43 Refer to Chapter 6.

Electronic Control Module (ECM)

Caution: Always wait at least 30 seconds after switching off the ignition before disconnecting the wiring from the ECM. When the wiring is disconnected, all the learned values are erased, although any contents of the fault memory are retained. After reconnecting the wiring, the basic settings must be reinstated by a Mercedes-Benz dealer using a special test instrument. Note also that if the ECM is renewed, it may need to be set up with diagnostic equipment by a Mercedes-Benz dealer.

44 Disconnect the battery negative lead and position it away from the terminal. **Note:** *Refer to 'Disconnecting the battery' at the rear of this manual first.*

45 The ECM is located behind a plastic panel to the left-hand end of the engine compartment bulkhead.

46 Undo the retaining screws and remove the plastic cover **(see illustration)**.

47 Release the securing clips and disconnect the wiring connectors from the electronic control module **(see illustration)**.

48 Withdraw the electronic control module from its location in the bulkhead **(see illustration)**.

49 Refitting is a reversal of removal. Noting the comments made in the *Caution* above – the ECM may need to be set at a Mercedes-Benz dealer.

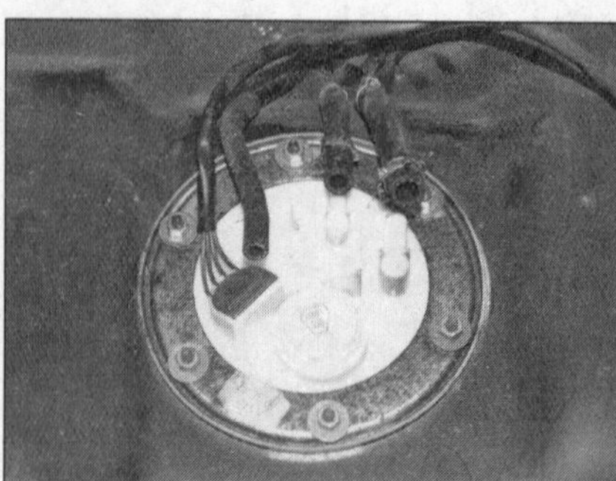
5.4 Disconnect the fuel pipes, noting their fitted position

Fuel pump

50 The fuel pump is part of the fuel sender unit and is located inside the fuel tank refer to Section 5.

4 Fuel filter – renewal

Refer to Chapter 1A.

5 Fuel pump and gauge sender unit – removal and refitting

Note: *Observe the precautions in Section 1 before working on any component in the fuel system.*

General information

1 The fuel pump and gauge sender unit are combined in one assembly, which is mounted in the top of the fuel tank. Access to the fuel pump and gauge sender is by removing the fuel tank.

Removal

2 Ensure that the vehicle is parked on a level surface, then disconnect the battery negative lead and position it away from the terminal. **Note:** *Refer to 'Disconnecting the battery' at the rear of this manual first.*

3 Remove the fuel tank as described in Section 6

4 Release the securing clips and remove the two fuel pipes from the fuel pump/sender unit,

5.5 Remove the plastic hose protector

5.6a Remove the retaining plate . . .

5.6b . . . and withdraw the fuel pump

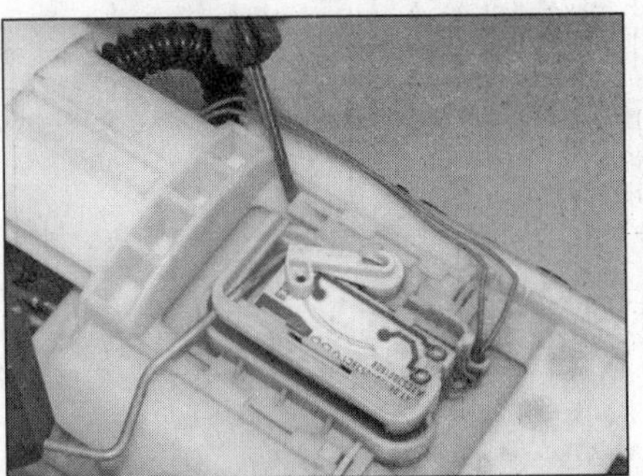

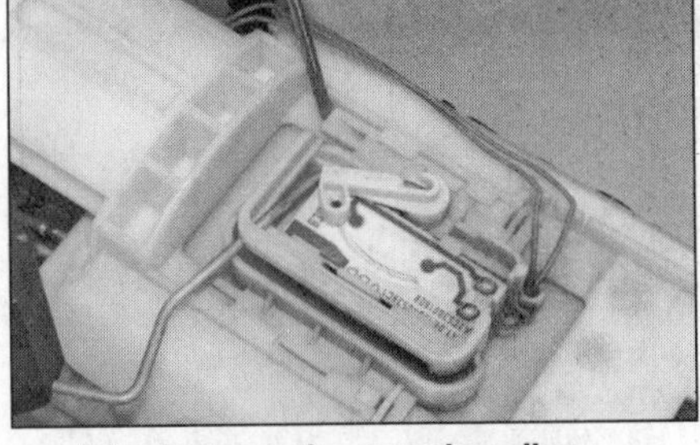

5.8a Release the securing clips . . .

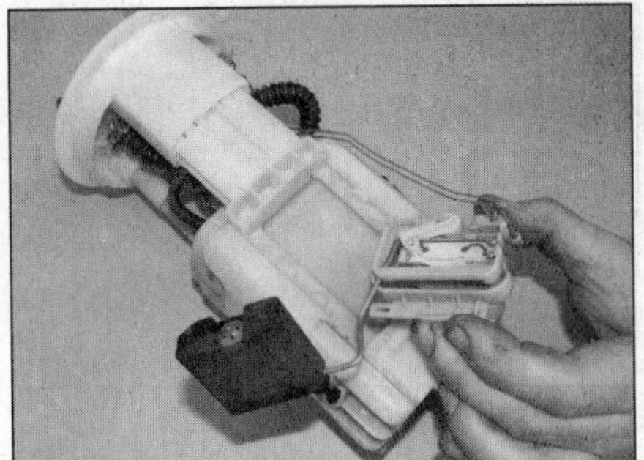

5.8b . . . unclip the sender unit . . .

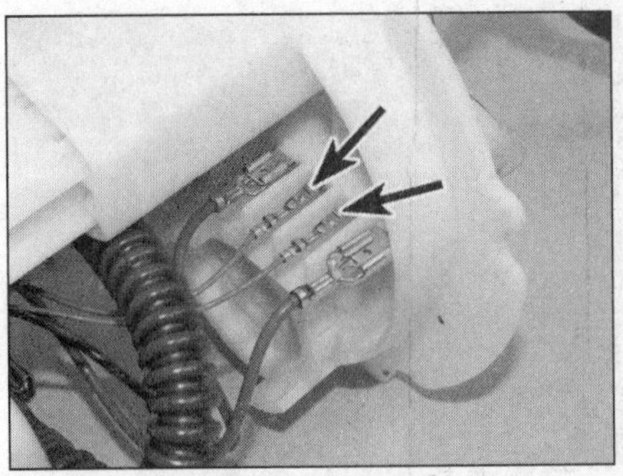

5.8c . . . and disconnect the wiring connectors – arrowed

also disconnect the vent pipe **(see illustration)**. Note their fitted position to aid refitting.

5 Hold the fuel lines to one side and unclip the plastic hose protector from the top of the fuel pump/sender unit **(see illustration)**.

6 Unscrew the retaining nuts, remove the retaining plate and withdraw the fuel pump/sender unit from the fuel tank, noting its fitted position **(see illustrations)**. Check the condition of the sealing ring, renew if required.

7 With the pump/sender unit removed from the car, lay it on an absorbent card or rag. Inspect the float at the end of the sender unit swinging-arm for punctures and fuel ingress, also check the wiper track on the sender unit – renew the unit if it appears damaged.

8 If required, the sender unit can be separated from the assembly, as follows. Disconnect the two small (green) wires, noting their fitted positions, then release the retaining clips and unclip the unit from the pump/sender body **(see illustrations)**.

9 Inspect the rubber seal from the fuel tank aperture for signs of fatigue – renew it if necessary **(see illustration)**.

Refitting

10 Refit the lift pump/sender unit by following the removal procedure in reverse, noting the following points:

a) Take care not to bend the float arm as the unit is refitted.

b) Smear the outside of tank aperture rubber seal with clean fuel or lubricating spray, to ease fitting. Locate the seal on the fuel pump/sender unit before fitting.

c) Refit the fuel pump/sender unit in the position noted on removal.

d) Reconnect the fuel hoses to the correct ports, ensuring that they are fitted securely.

e) On completion, check that all associated pipes are securely fitted, then run the engine and check for fuel leaks.

6 Fuel tank – removal and refitting

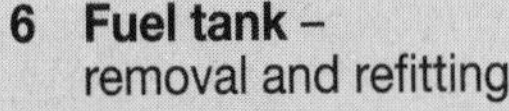

Note: *Observe the precautions in Section 1 before working on any component in the fuel system.*

Removal

1 Before the tank can be removed, it must be drained of as much fuel as possible. As no drain plug is provided, it is preferable to carry out this operation with the tank almost empty.

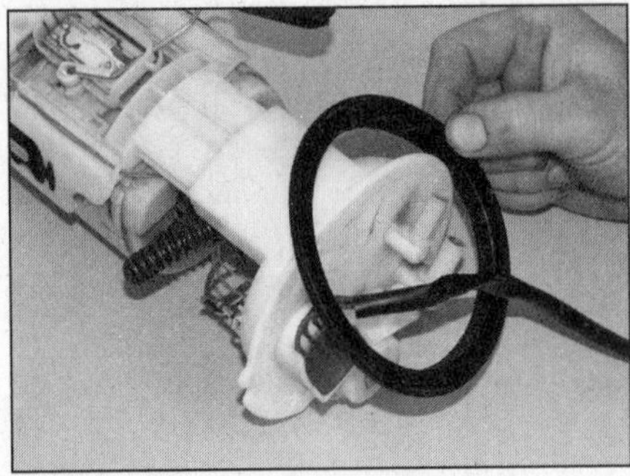

5.9 Check the rubber seal

2 Open the fuel filler flap, and unscrew the fuel filler cap – leave the cap loosely in place.

3 Disconnect the battery negative lead and position it away from the terminal. **Note:** *Refer to 'Disconnecting the battery' at the rear of this manual first.* Using a hand pump or syphon, remove any remaining fuel from the bottom of the tank.

4 To gain better access, jack up the vehicle, and support it on axle stands (see *Jacking and vehicle support*). Undo the retaining bolts and remove the centre section of undertray from under the vehicle.

5 Remove the exhaust middle section with reference to Chapter 4C

6 Disconnect the filler hose and vent hose from the side of the fuel tank **(see illustration)**. **Note:** *Cover the access holes in the fuel tank, to prevent any fuel that is left in the tank from leaking.*

7 Disconnect the fuel pipes and the charcoal

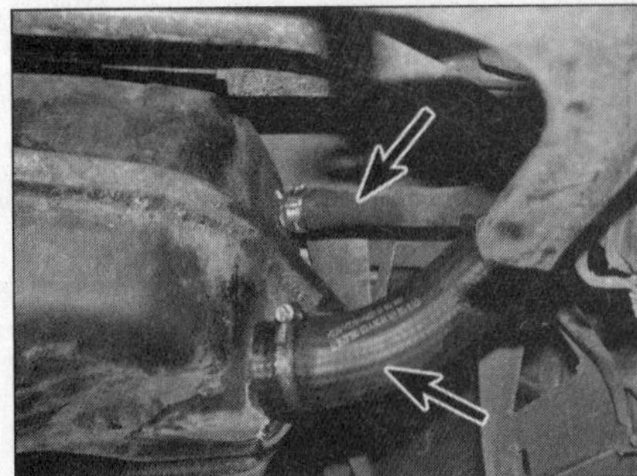

6.6 Disconnect the hoses – arrowed

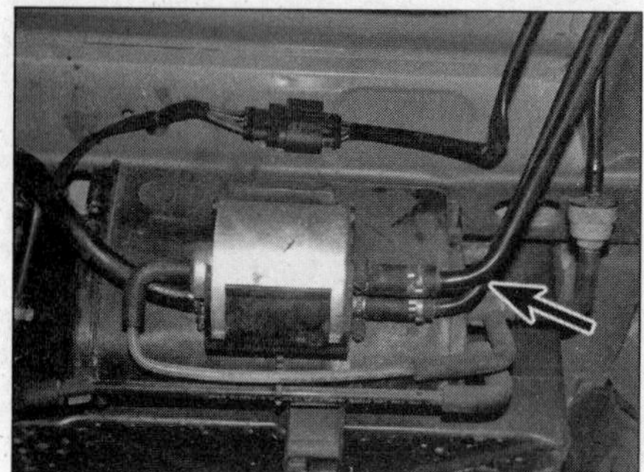

6.7a Disconnect the fuel pipes – arrowed . . .

6.7b . . . and disconnect the vent pipe

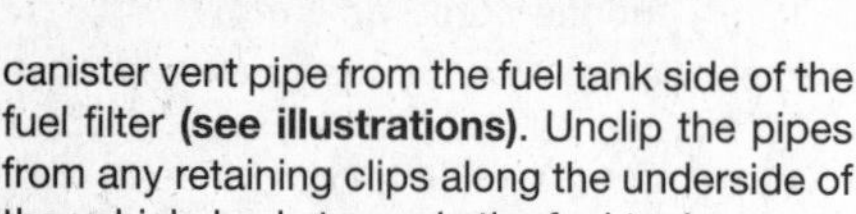

6.8 Disconnect the wiring connector

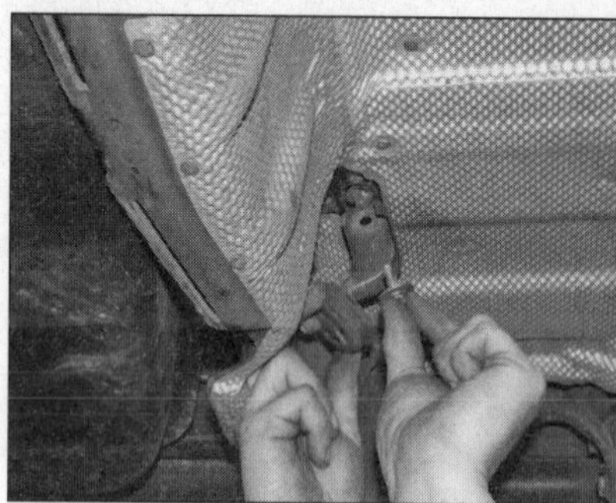

6.9 Removing the exhaust bracket

canister vent pipe from the fuel tank side of the fuel filter **(see illustrations)**. Unclip the pipes from any retaining clips along the underside of the vehicle body towards the fuel tank.

8 Disconnect the wiring connector from above the fuel filter **(see illustration)**, and unclip the wiring from any retaining clips along the underside of the vehicle body towards the fuel tank.

9 Undo the retaining bolt and remove the exhaust mounting bracket from the exhaust heat shield **(see illustration)**.

10 Undo the retaining nut and pull down the exhaust heat shield from the fuel tank side mounting stud **(see illustrations)**.

11 Position a trolley jack under the centre of the tank. Insert a block of wood between the jack head and the tank to prevent damage to the tank surface. Raise the jack until it just takes the weight of the tank.

12 Working your way around the edge of the fuel tank unscrew the mounting bolts **(see illustration)**.

13 Lower the jack and fuel tank, keeping it balanced, and then carefully withdraw the fuel tank from the underside of the vehicle.

14 If the tank is contaminated with sediment or water, remove the fuel pump/sender unit (see Section 5) and swill the tank out with clean fuel. If the tank is damaged or badly corroded, it should be renewed. However, in certain cases it may be possible to have small leaks or minor damage repaired. Seek the advice of a suitable specialist before attempting to repair the fuel tank.

Refitting

15 Refitting is the reverse of the removal procedure, noting the following points:

a) When lifting the tank back into position, make sure the mounting points are correctly positioned, and take care to ensure none of the hoses get trapped between the tank and vehicle body.

b) Ensure that all pipes and hoses are correctly routed, are not kinked, and are securely held in position with their retaining clips.

c) Tighten the tank retaining nuts to the specified torque.

d) On completion, refill the tank with fuel, and exhaustively check for signs of leakage prior to taking the vehicle out on the road.

7 Fuel injection system – depressurisation

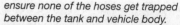

Note: *Observe the precautions in Section 1 before working on any component in the fuel system.*

Warning: The following procedure will merely relieve the pressure in the fuel system – remember that fuel will still be present in the system components and take precautions accordingly before disconnecting any of them.

1 The fuel system referred to in this Section is defined as the tank-mounted fuel pump/sender unit, the fuel filter, the fuel injectors, and the metal pipes and flexible hoses of the fuel lines between these components. All these contain fuel which will be under pressure while the engine is running and/or while the ignition is switched on. The pressure will remain for some time after the ignition has been switched off, and must be relieved before any of these components are disturbed for servicing work. Ideally, the engine should be allowed to cool completely before work commences.

2 Refer to Chapter 12 and remove the fuel pump relay. Alternatively, identify and remove the fuel pump fuse from the fusebox. With the fuel pump disabled; crank the engine for about ten seconds. The engine may fire and run for a while, but let it continue running until it stops. The fuel injectors should have opened enough times during cranking to considerably reduce the line fuel pressure, and reduce the risk of fuel spraying out when a fuel line is disturbed.

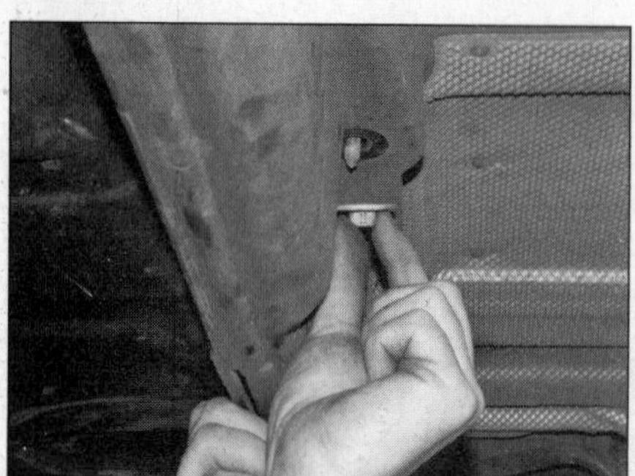

6.10a Undo the retaining nuts . . .

6.10b . . and remove the heat shield

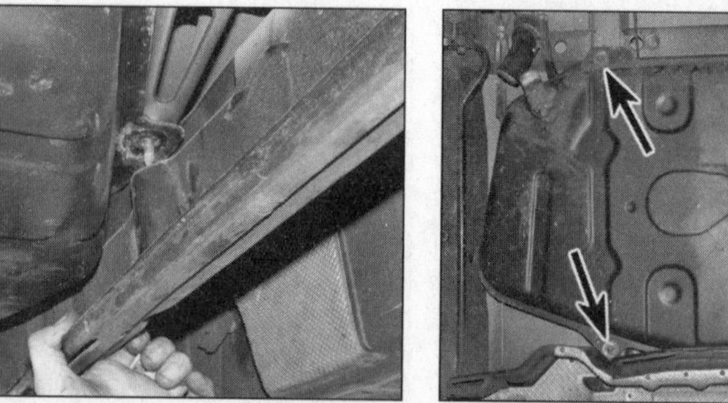

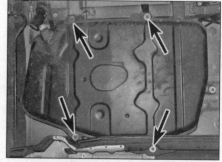

6.12 Fuel tank mounting bolts

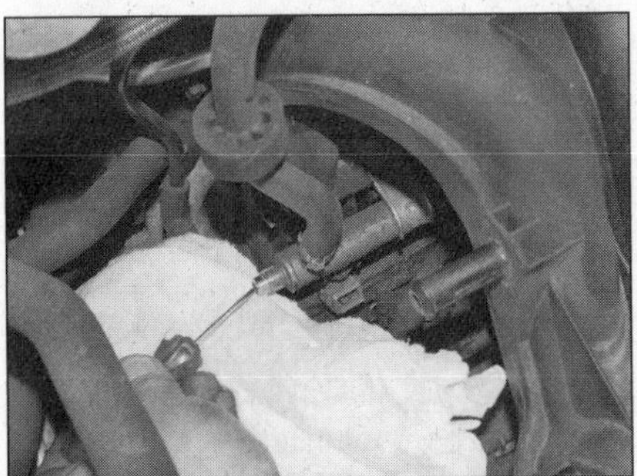

7.4 Releasing the fuel pressure from the fuel rail

3 Disconnect the battery negative lead and position it away from the terminal. **Note:** *Refer to 'Disconnecting the battery' at the rear of this manual first.*

4 If working on the fuel rail and injectors, remove the plastic cap from the valve in the end of the fuel rail, place rags around the area and release the pressure in the rail using a small screwdriver **(see illustration).**

5 Place a suitable container beneath the relevant connection/union to be disconnected, and have a large rag ready to soak up any escaping fuel not being caught by the container.

6 Slowly open the connection to avoid a sudden release of pressure, and position the rag around the connection to catch any fuel spray that may be expelled. Once the pressure has been released, disconnect the fuel line. Insert plugs to minimise fuel loss and prevent the entry of dirt into the fuel system.

7 After working on the fuel system, reconnect the wiring/fuse/relay as applicable. Have the engine management fault code memory checked by a Mercedes-Benz dealer for codes inserted when disconnecting the wiring.

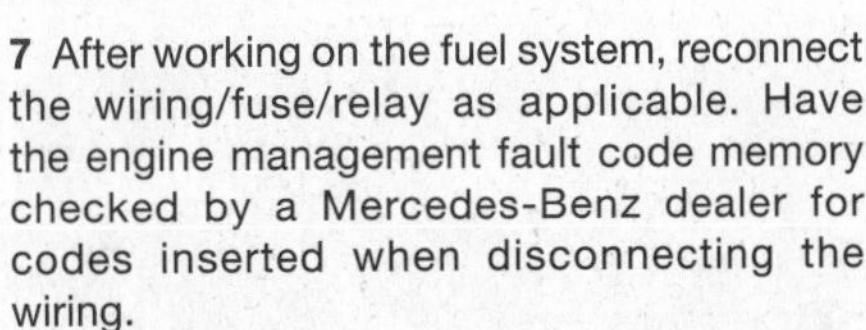

8 Inlet manifold – removal and refitting

Removal

1 Disconnect the battery negative lead and position it away from the terminal. **Note:** *Refer to 'Disconnecting the battery' at the rear of this manual first.*

2 Remove air filter and intake housing as described previously in Section 2.

3 Undo the retaining bolt from the dipstick tube at the rear of the inlet manifold **(see illustration).**

4 With reference to Section 3, remove the idle speed control actuator from the inlet manifold.

5 Disconnect the vacuum hose from the right-hand side of the inlet manifold **(see illustration).**

6 Disconnect the brake vacuum hose from the front left-hand side of the inlet manifold **(see illustration).**

7 Disconnect the vacuum hose from the left-hand side front of the inlet housing **(see illustration).**

8 Undo the retaining bolts and remove the mounting bracket from the front right-hand side of the inlet manifold **(see illustration).**

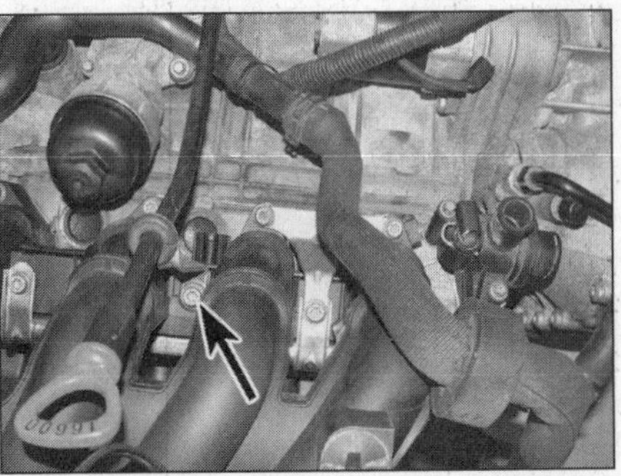

8.3 Undo the dipstick bracket retaining bolt – arrowed

9 On models from 01/03/01, disconnect the wiring plug from the inlet air pressure sensor on the front of the inlet manifold **(see illustration).**

10 Remove the fuel rail and injectors as described in Section 3. However, if the manifold is being removed as part of another procedure (such as cylinder head or engine removal), the fuel rail can be left in place.

11 Progressively loosen the bolts and withdraw the manifold from the cylinder head **(see illustration)**. Note the lengths of the bolts as they are removed, as there are varying lengths. Recover the seals and discard – all should be renewed when refitting the manifold.

12 Disconnect the breather hose from the rear of the inlet manifold as the manifold is removed.

8.5 Disconnect the vacuum hose

8.6 Releasing the brake vacuum hose

8.7 Disconnect vacuum hose

8.8 Remove the mounting bracket – arrowed

8.9 Disconnect the wiring connector

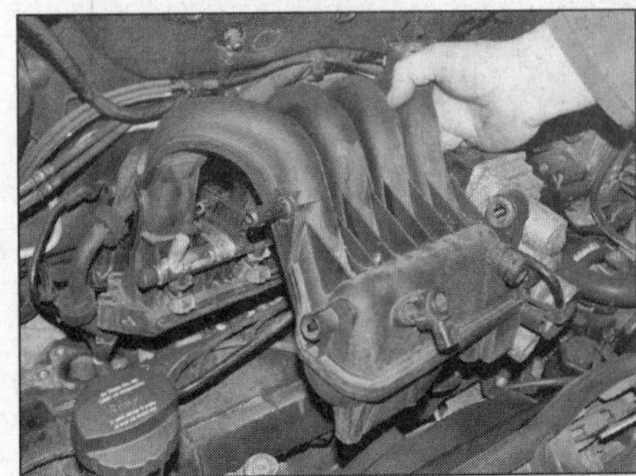

8.11 Removing the inlet manifold

8.13 Fit new manifold rubber seals

9.2 Diagnostic connector location – arrowed

Refitting

13 Refitting is a reversal of removal, noting the following points:

*a) Fit new inlet manifold seals **(see illustration).***

b) Tighten the retaining bolts to the specified torque.

c) It is very important that there are no air leaks at the joint.

d) Refit the air filter intake housing with reference to Section 2.

9 Fuel injection system – testing and adjustment

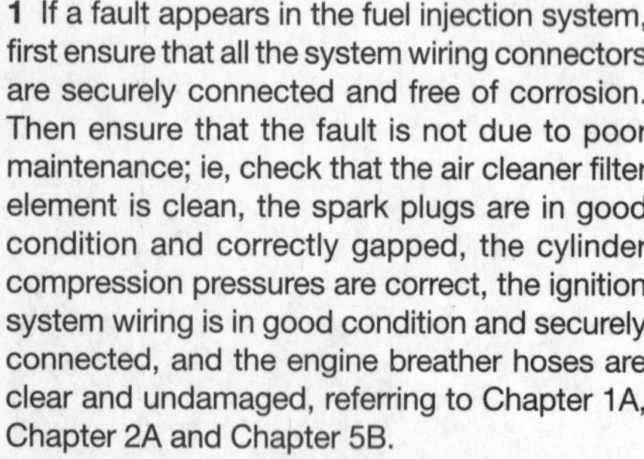

1 If a fault appears in the fuel injection system, first ensure that all the system wiring connectors are securely connected and free of corrosion. Then ensure that the fault is not due to poor maintenance; ie, check that the air cleaner filter element is clean, the spark plugs are in good condition and correctly gapped, the cylinder compression pressures are correct, the ignition system wiring is in good condition and securely connected, and the engine breather hoses are clear and undamaged, referring to Chapter 1A, Chapter 2A and Chapter 5B.

2 If these checks fail to reveal the cause of the problem, the vehicle should be taken to a suitably-equipped Mercedes-Benz dealer for testing. A diagnostic connector is incorporated in the engine management system wiring harness, into which dedicated electronic test equipment can be plugged (the connector is located under the driver's side lower facia panel by the bonnet release lever – unclip and remove the cover for access **(see illustration)**. The test equipment is capable of 'interrogating' the engine management system ECM electronically and accessing its internal fault log (reading fault codes).

3 Fault codes can only be extracted from the ECM using a dedicated fault code reader. A Mercedes-Benz dealer will obviously have such a reader, but they are also available from other suppliers. It is unlikely to be cost-effective for the private owner to purchase a fault code reader, but a well-equipped local garage or auto-electrical specialist will have one.

4 Using this equipment, faults can be pinpointed quickly and simply, even if their occurrence is intermittent. Testing all the system components individually in an attempt to locate the fault by elimination is a time-consuming operation that is unlikely to be fruitful (particularly if the fault occurs dynamically), and carries a high risk of damage to the ECM's internal components.

5 Experienced home mechanics equipped with an accurate tachometer and a carefully-calibrated exhaust gas analyser may be able to check the exhaust gas CO content and the engine idle speed; if these are found to be out of specification, then the vehicle must be taken to a suitably-equipped Mercedes-Benz dealer for assessment. Neither the air/fuel mixture (exhaust gas CO content) nor the engine idle speeds are manually adjustable; incorrect test results indicate the need for maintenance (possibly, injector cleaning) or a fault within the fuel injection system.

10 Cruise control system – general information

1 Certain models may be equipped with a cruise control system, in which the driver can set a chosen speed, which the system will then try to maintain regardless of gradients, etc.

2 Once the desired speed has been set, the system is entirely under the control of the engine management ECM, which regulates the speed with the throttle housing.

3 The system is deactivated if the clutch or brake pedals are pressed, signaled by the clutch pedal switch or the brake stop-light switch (Chapter 9).

4 The cruise control switch is the upper control lever on the left-hand side of the steering column, which can be removed as described in Chapter 12.

5 Any problems with the system which are not caused by wiring faults or failure of the components mentioned in this Section should be referred to a Mercedes-Benz dealer. In the event of a problem occurring, it is advisable to first take the car to a suitably-equipped dealer for electronic fault diagnosis, using a fault code reader – refer to Section 9.

Chapter 4 Part B:
Diesel engine fuel system

Contents

Degrees of difficulty

Easy, suitable for novice with little experience

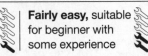

Fairly easy, suitable for beginner with some experience

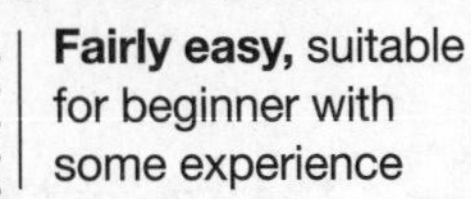

Fairly difficult, suitable for competent DIY mechanic

Difficult, suitable for experienced DIY mechanic

Very difficult, suitable for expert DIY or professional

Specifications

General

Fuel injection system	Common rail diesel injection (CDI)
Firing order	1-3-4-2

High-pressure fuel pump

Fuel pressure	3.5 bar

Torque wrench settings

Torque wrench settings	Nm	lbf ft
Air mixing chamber to inlet manifold	9	7
EGR pipe flange to air mixing chamber	9	7
Fuel filter to inlet manifold	9	7
Up to 08/03/2000	20	15
From 09/03/2000 to 04/02/2002	22	16
From 05/02/2002 to 24/09/2003	20	15
From 25/09/2003	23	17
Fuel leak-off banjo bolt	20	15
Fuel predelivery pump mounting bolts	9	7
Fuel pressure regulator retaining bolts:		
Stage 1	3	2
Stage 2	5	4
Fuel rail pressure sensor:		
Yellow union (up to production no 86512)	35	26
Grey union (from production no 86513)	22	16
Fuel rail to camshaft cover	9	7
High-pressure fuel pipe union nuts:		
High-pressure fuel pump mounting bolts	14	10
Injector clamp mounting bracket bolts:*		
Stage 1	7	5
Stage 2	Angle-tighten a further 90°	
Stage 3	Angle-tighten a further 90°	
Inlet manifold to cylinder head	14	10
Oil filler neck to inlet manifold	9	7

** Use new fasteners*

1 General information and precautions

General information

All engines covered by this Manual are fitted with the same common rail diesel-injection (CDI) fuel system, with a fuel tank, an engine-bay mounted fuel filter, a high-pressure fuel pump, a predelivery pump, a common rail with pressure sensor, four fuel injectors, and fuel supply and return lines.

The fuel is delivered by a predelivery pump driven off the transmission end of the inlet camshaft and the main fuel pump driven off the transmission end of the exhaust camshaft. A 'roller rocker' assembly with hydraulic tappet is mounted below the camshafts. The precise timing of the injection is controlled by the engine management ECM and a solenoid on each injector.

The direct-injection fuelling system is controlled electronically by a diesel engine management system, comprising an Electronic Control Module (ECM) and its associated sensors, actuators and wiring. In addition, the ECM manages the operation of the Exhaust Gas Recirculation (EGR) emission control system (Chapter 4D), the turbocharger boost pressure control system (Chapter 4D) and the glow plug control system (Chapter 5C).

It should be noted that fault diagnosis of the diesel engine management system is only possible with dedicated electronic test equipment. Problems with the system's operation should therefore be referred to a Mercedes-Benz dealer or suitably-equipped specialist for assessment. Once the fault has been identified, the removal/refitting sequences detailed in the following Sections will then allow the appropriate component(s) to be renewed as required.

Precautions

Many of the operations described in this Chapter involve the disconnection of fuel lines, which may cause an amount of fuel spillage. Before commencing work, refer to the warnings below and the information in Safety first! at the beginning of this manual.

Warning: When working on any part of the fuel system, avoid direct contact skin contact with diesel fuel – wear protective clothing and gloves when handling fuel system components. Ensure that the work area is well-ventilated to prevent the build-up of diesel fuel vapour.

- Fuel injectors operate at extremely high pressures and the jet of fuel produced at the nozzle is capable of piercing skin, with potentially fatal results. When working with pressurised injectors, take care to avoid exposing any part of the body to the fuel spray. It is recommended that a diesel fuel systems specialist should carry out any pressure testing of the fuel system components.
- Under no circumstances should diesel fuel be allowed to come into contact with coolant hoses – wipe off accidental spillage immediately. Hoses that have been contaminated with fuel for an extended period should be renewed.
- Diesel fuel systems are particularly sensitive to contamination from dirt, air and water. Pay particular attention to cleanliness when working on any part of the fuel system, to prevent the ingress of dirt. Thoroughly clean the area around fuel unions before disconnecting them. Only use lint-free cloths and clean fuel for component cleansing.
- Store dismantled components in sealed containers to prevent contamination and the formation of condensation.

2 Air cleaner assembly – general information

1 The air cleaner is located inside the transmission end of the inlet manifold. Remove the air filter as described in Chapter 1B.

2 Remove the inlet manifold as described in Section 5.

3 Diesel engine management system – component removal and refitting

Throttle pedal/position sensor

1 All models are fitted with a 'fly-by-wire' throttle where the position sensor is integral with the accelerator pedal **(see illustration)**.

2 Undo the bolts securing the throttle pedal to the bulkhead and remove it, disconnecting the wiring connector as it is removed.

3 Refitting is a reversal of removal.

Coolant temperature sensor

4 Refer to Chapter 3.

Crankshaft position sensor

5 Crankshaft position sensor is mounted at the top/front of the cylinder block, next to the transmission bellhousing. It may be necessary to move the coolant hose to one side to access the sensor **(see illustration)**.

6 Disconnect the wiring connector from the sensor.

7 Unscrew the retaining bolt and withdraw the sensor from the cylinder block **(see illustrations)**.

8 Refitting is a reversal of removal.

Electronic Control Module (ECM)

Caution: Always wait at least 30 seconds after switching off the ignition before disconnecting the wiring from the ECM. When the wiring is disconnected, all the learned values are erased, although any contents of the fault memory are retained. After reconnecting the wiring, the basic settings must be reinstated by a Mercedes-Benz dealer using a special test instrument. Note also that if the ECM is renewed, it may need to be set up with diagnostic equipment by a Mercedes-Benz dealer.

3.1 Throttle position sensor location – arrowed

3.5 Crankshaft position sensor location – arrowed

3.7a Remove the retaining screw . . .

3.7b . . . and withdraw the sensor

3.11 Removing the ECM plastic cover

3.12 Disconnect the wiring connectors

3.13 Remove the ECM

9 Disconnect the battery negative lead and position it away from the terminal. **Note:** *Refer to 'Disconnecting the battery' at the rear of this manual first.*

10 The ECM is located behind a plastic panel to the left-hand end of the engine compartment bulkhead.

11 Undo the retaining screws and remove the plastic cover **(see illustration).**

12 Release the securing clips and disconnect the wiring connectors from the electronic control module **(see illustration).**

13 Withdraw the electronic control module from its location in the bulkhead **(see illustration).**

14 Refitting is a reversal of removal. Noting the comments made in the *Caution* above – the ECM may need to be set at a Mercedes-Benz dealer.

Clutch pedal switch

15 Refer to Chapter 6.

Airflow mixing chamber (with exhaust gas recirculation)

16 The airflow mixing chamber is located at the left-hand side of the inlet manifold.

17 Slacken the retaining clip and disconnect the charge air intake pipe **(see illustration).**

18 Disconnect the vacuum pipe from the EGR valve **(see illustration).**

19 Slacken and remove the two retaining bolts from the EGR pipe on the bottom of the airflow mixing chamber **(see illustration).** Discard the gasket as a new one will be required on refitting.

20 Slacken and remove the four retaining bolts from the airflow mixing chamber to the inlet manifold **(see illustration).** Discard the O-ring seal as a new one will be required on refitting.

21 Refitting is a reversal of removal. Renew the O-ring seal in the end of the inlet manifold and the gasket for the EGR pipe **(see illustration).**

Inlet air temperature sensor

Before charge air intercooler

22 The air temperature sensor is located on the air pipe in the right-hand side of the inlet manifold, and is removed after disconnecting the wiring connector and unscrewing the retaining screws. Check and if necessary renew the gasket before refitting and tightening the screws **(see illustrations).**

3.17 Disconnect the air intake pipe

3.18 Disconnecting the vacuum pipe

3.19 Undo the two retaining bolts – arrowed

3.20 Removing the airflow mixing chamber

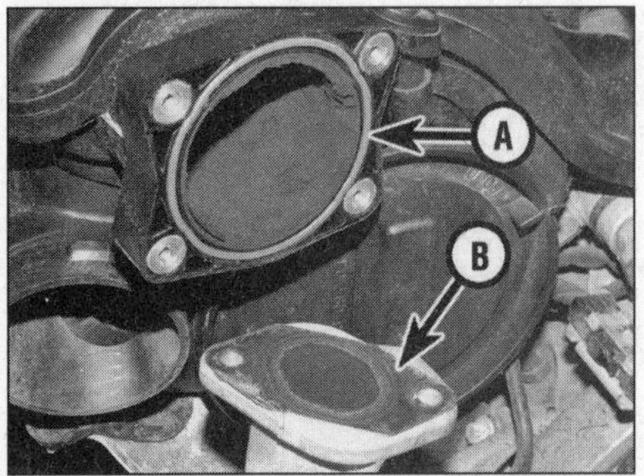

3.21 Renew the seal (A) and gasket (B)

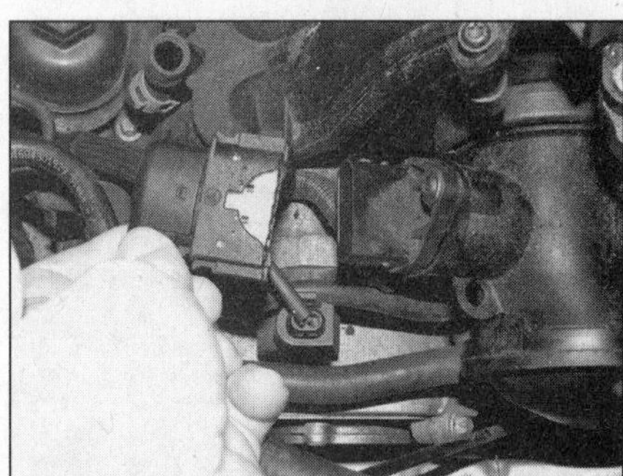
3.22a Disconnect the wiring connector . . .

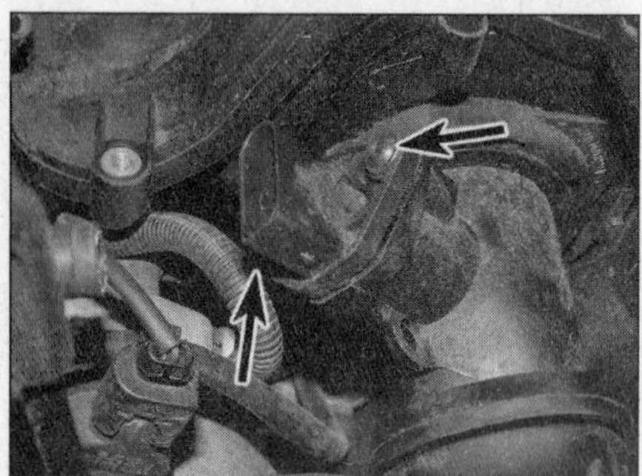

3.22b ... and undo the retaining screws

3.23 Air temperature sensor location – arrowed

3.24 Disconnecting the wiring connector from the fuel pressure regulator

3.25 Disconnecting the wiring connector from the fuel pressure sensor

After charge air intercooler

23 The air temperature sensor is located on the air pipe, which comes out of the intercooler on the front left-hand side of the vehicle. To make access easier, unclip and move the windscreen washer reservoir to one side. Disconnect the wiring connector, release the two securing clips and pull the sensor out from the air inlet pipe **(see illustration)**.

Fuel pressure regulator

Note: *Observe the precautions in Section 1 before working on any component in the fuel system.*

24 The fuel pressure regulator is located on the right-hand end of the fuel rail, and is removed after disconnecting the wiring and unscrewing the two retaining screws. Discard the two sealing rings, as new ones will be required for refitting **(see illustration)**. Make sure the seals are clean and free from any dirt before refitting; Mercedes-Benz use a special grease (BR00.45-Z-1036-06A) to lubricate the seals when fitting.

Fuel rail pressure sensor

Note: *Observe the precautions in Section 1 before working on any component in the fuel system.*

25 The fuel rail pressure sensor is located on the left-hand end of the fuel rail, and is removed after disconnecting the wiring and unscrewing the sensor from the end of the fuel rail. Use a spanner on the end of the fuel rail to counterhold, while slackening the pressure sensor **(see illustration)**. Make sure the threads are clean and free from any dirt before refitting; lubricate threads when refitting. Tighten to the specified torque setting; the production number can be found on a plate on the fuel rail.

Fuel electric shut-off valve

Models up to 28/02/01

Note: *Observe the precautions in Section 1 before working on any component in the fuel system.*

26 The fuel shut-off valve is located at the left-hand side of the cylinder head, on top of the predelivery pump, see Section 10.

27 Release the retaining clip and disconnect the fuel pipe from the side of the shut-off valve.

28 Disconnect the wiring connector from the shut-off valve.

29 Undo the two retaining bolts and withdraw the shut-off valve from the top of the delivery pump. Discard the seal, as a new one will be required on refitting.

30 Refitting is a reversal of removal. Renew the O-ring seal between the shut-off valve and the predelivery pump.

4 Fuel rail and injectors – removal and refitting

Warning: Exercise extreme caution when working on the fuel injectors. Never expose the hands or any part of the body to injector spray, as the high working pressure can cause the fuel to penetrate the skin, with possibly fatal results. You are strongly advised to have any work that involves testing the injectors under pressure carried out by a dealer or fuel injection specialist. Refer to the precautions given in Section 1 of this Chapter before proceeding.

Note: *Take care not to allow dirt into the fuel rail, injectors or fuel pipes during this procedure. Keep the fuel pipes and injectors identified for position to ensure correct refitting. As the fuel pipes are removed, plug the ends of the pipes, injectors and fuel rail to prevent dirt ingress.*

Fuel rail

Removal

1 Remove the inlet manifold as described in Section 5.

2 Disconnect the wiring connectors from each end of the fuel rail **(see illustrations)**.

4.2a Disconnect the wiring connector from the pressure sensor . . .

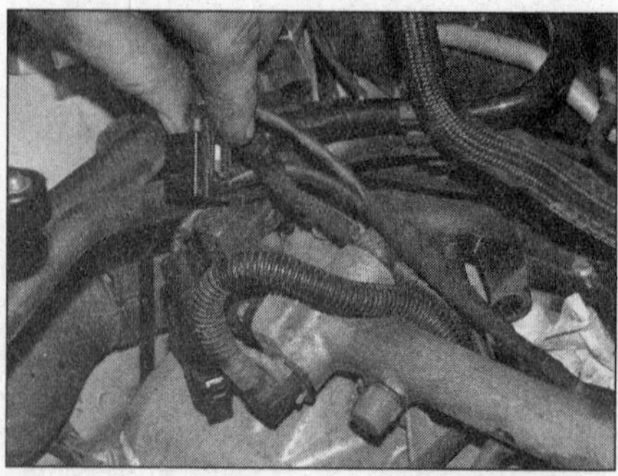

4.2b . . . and from the pressure valve

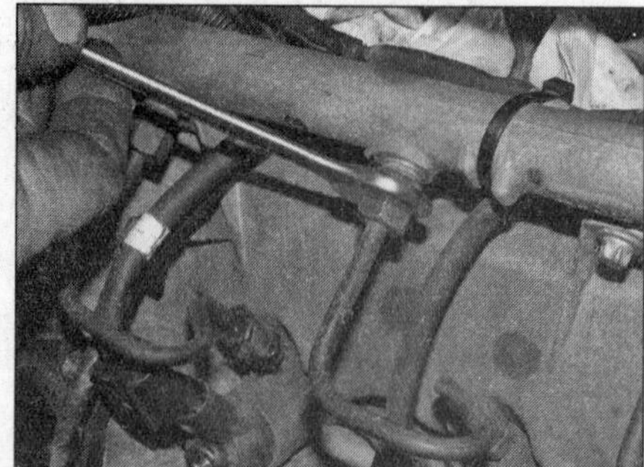

4.3a Undo the fuel pipe union . . .

4.3b . . . and disconnect the fuel pipe . . .

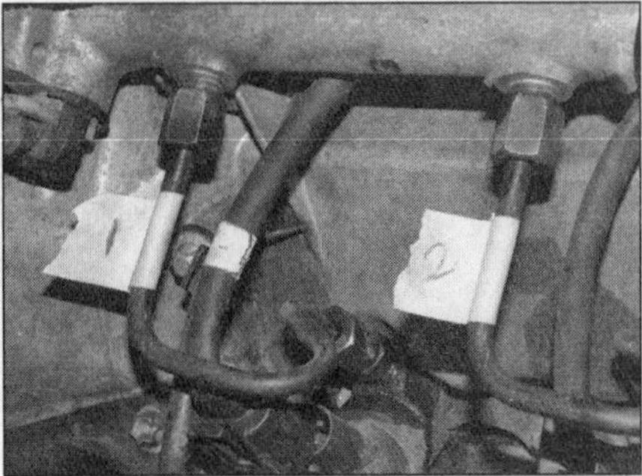

4.3c . . . label pipes for refitting . . .

4.3d . . . and cap the ends to prevent dirt ingress

4.4 Removing the fuel feed pipe

4.5 Remove the fuel return pipe

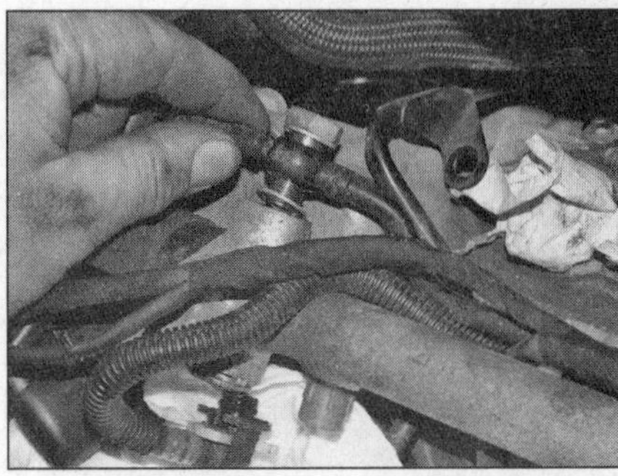
4.6 Remove the fuel leak-off pipe

3 Working your way along the fuel rail, slacken and remove the injector fuel pipes from the fuel rail. Make a note of their fitted position, as they will need to be refitted in the same position on refitting **(see illustrations)**.

4 Slacken and remove the fuel feed pipe from the left-hand end of the fuel rail **(see illustration)**.

5 Release the securing clip and remove the fuel return pipe from the right-hand end of the fuel rail **(see illustration)**. Discard sealing ring, as a new one will be required for refitting.

6 Slacken and remove the fuel leak-off pipe from the right-hand end of the fuel rail **(see illustration)**. Discard the sealing washers, as a new ones will be required for refitting.

7 Release the retaining clips and unclip the fuel lines from along the fuel rail, and move them to one side. Note their fitted position to aid refitting.

8 Undo the three retaining bolts and withdraw the fuel rail from the top of the camshaft cover **(see illustrations)**.

Refitting

9 Refitting is a reversal of removal, using new O-ring seals/washers where applicable. Tighten the mounting bolts and union nuts to the specified torque.

Fuel injectors

Note: *Injectors deteriorate with prolonged use, and it is reasonable to expect them to need reconditioning after 60 000 miles or so. Accurate testing, overhaul and calibration of the injectors must be left to a specialist. Do not drop the injectors or allow the needles at their tips to become damaged. The injectors are precision-made to fine limits, and must not be handled roughly.*

Caution: The injector clamping bracket retaining bolt can be tight and thread damage or bolt breaking can occur. Bolt repair or Helicoil may be required; this may need to be done by a specialist. A puller will also be required for pulling the injectors out from the cylinder head.

4.8a Undo the retaining bolts – arrowed . . .

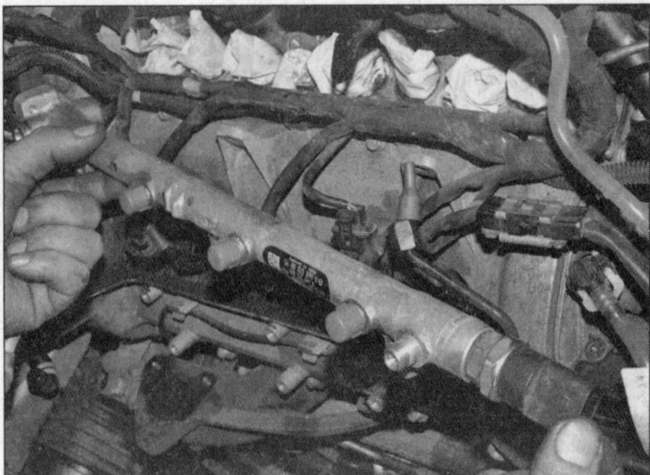
4.8b . . . and remove the fuel rail

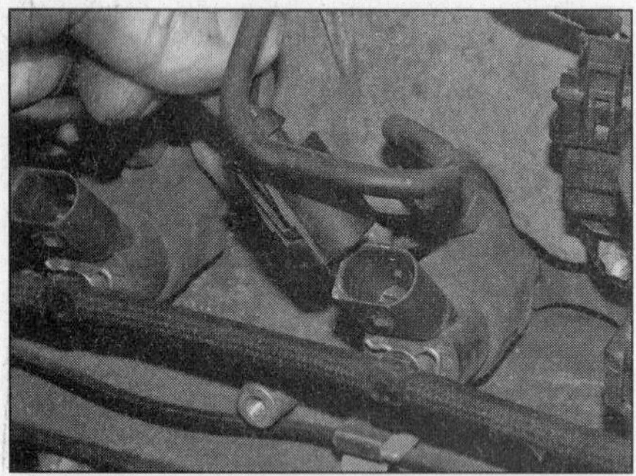
4.12 Disconnect the wiring connectors from the injectors

4.13 Removing the heat shield

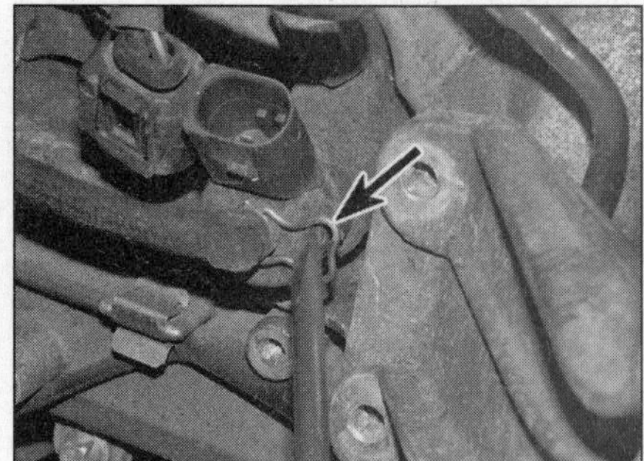
4.14a Release the retaining clip – arrowed . . .

4.14b . . . then pull out of the injectors . . .

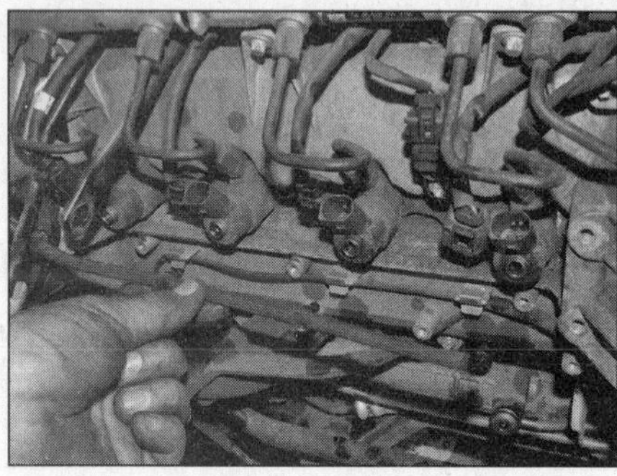
4.14c . . . and remove the fuel leak-off pipe

4.15 Remove the injector retaining bolt

Removal

10 Remove the inlet manifold as described in Section 5.

11 Remove the exhaust front pipe and turbocharger as described in Chapter 4D.

12 Disconnect the wiring connectors from each of the fuel injectors **(see illustration)**.

13 Undo the retaining bolts and remove the heat shield from the front of the cylinder head **(see illustration)**.

4.16a Fit a puller on the injector . . .

4.16b . . . and withdraw the pair of injectors

5.1a Unclip the air scoop . . .

5.1b . . . and remove the air ducting

14 Release the securing clips and disconnect the fuel leak-off pipes from the top of the four injectors **(see illustrations)**. Discard the securing clips, as new ones will be required on refitting.

15 Slacken and remove the injector clamp mounting bracket retaining bolts (see *Caution* above), from between the injectors **(see illustration)**. Discard the mounting bolts, as new ones will be required when refitting.

16 Using a slide hammer/puller withdraw the injectors from the cylinder head, withdraw the pair of injectors (1 and 2 or 3 and 4) evenly, as the clamp mounting bracket is located between the injectors **(see illustrations)**. Recover the sealing rings and discard. New ones must be used for refitting

Refitting

17 Refitting is a reversal of removal, using new sealing rings. Fit new clamp mounting bracket retaining bolts and tighten them to the specified torque.

5 Inlet manifold – removal and refitting

Removal

1 Open the bonnet and remove the air scoop from the front crossmember to the air intake housing **(see illustrations)**.

2 Remove the airflow mixing chamber as described in Section 3 of this Chapter.

5.3a Undo the retaining bolts – arrowed . . .

5.3b . . . and move the fuel filter to one side

5.4 Disconnect the vacuum pipe

5.5a Disconnect the breather pipes . . .

5.5b . . . from the crankcase breather

5.6 Disconnect the wiring connector

3 Undo the three fuel filter mounting bracket retaining bolts and move the filter to the rear of the engine compartment, leaving the fuel pipes connected **(see illustrations)**.

4 Disconnect the charge pressure sensor vacuum pipe from the end of the inlet manifold **(see illustration).**

5 Release the securing clips and disconnect the crankcase breather hoses from the top of the oil seperator **(see illustrations)**.

6 Disconnect the wiring connector from the intake air temperature sensor **(see illustration)**.

7 Undo the three oil seperator mounting bracket retaining bolts and remove it from the engine, disconnecting the breather pipe(s) from the base of the separator as it is removed **(see illustration)**.

8 Slacken and remove the oil filler neck mounting bolts from the end of the inlet manifold **(see illustration)**.

9 Undo the three heat shield retaining bolts from along the front edge of the inlet manifold **(see illustration)**.

10 Working your way around the inlet manifold, slacken and remove the retaining bolts, note the position of any brackets or wiring clips for refitting. Recover the rubber O-rings (8) and discard, as a new ones must be used on refitting **(see illustration)**.

Refitting

11 Refitting is a reversal of removal, using new gaskets/O-ring seals where applicable. Tighten the mounting bolts to the specified torque.

6 Fuel filter – renewal

Note: *Observe the precautions in Section 1 before working on any component in the fuel system.*

Refer to Chapter 1B.

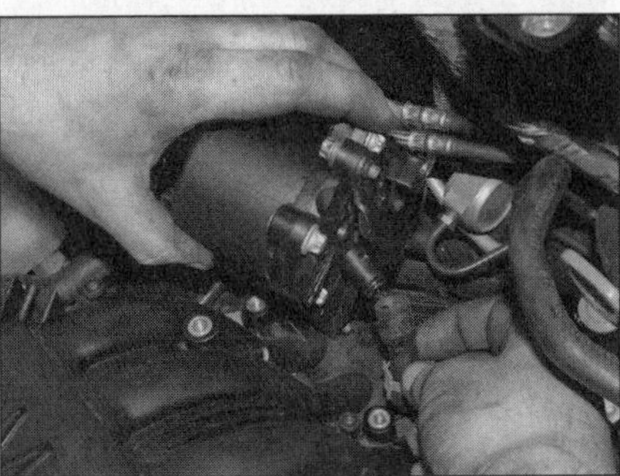
5.7 Removing the crankcase breather

5.8 Undo the filler neck bolts – arrowed

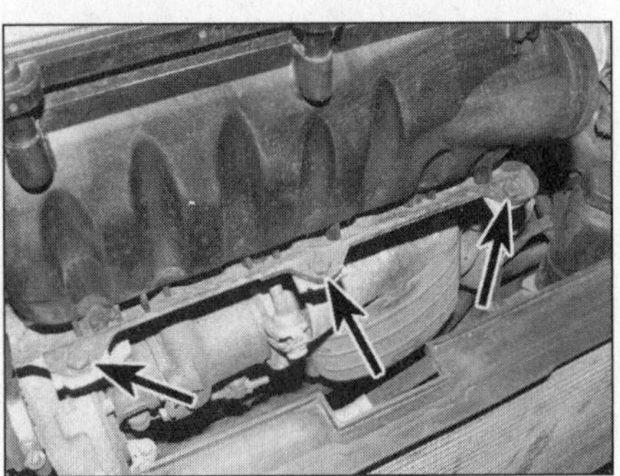
5.9 Undo the heat shield bolts – arrowed

5.10 Remove the inlet manifold

9.1 High-pressure fuel pump location – arrowed

9.3b . . . and move the fuel pipe to one side

7 Fuel gauge sender unit – removal and refitting

Note: *Observe the precautions in Section 1 before working on any component in the fuel system.*

Warning: Avoid direct skin contact with fuel – wear protective clothing and gloves when handling fuel system components. Ensure that the work area is well ventilated, to prevent the build-up of fuel vapour.

1 The fuel gauge sender unit is mounted in the top of the fuel tank and requires the removal of the fuel tank to access it. The unit protrudes into the fuel tank, and its removal involves exposing the contents of the tank to the atmosphere.

2 Refer to the procedures in Chapter 4A for removal and refitting procedures.

8 Fuel tank – removal and refitting

Note: *Observe the precautions in Section 1 before working on any component in the fuel system.*

1 Refer to the procedures in Chapter 4A. The procedure is the same for petrol models, but note the fuel pipe connections and wiring connector are not located in the same position.

9.2 Slackening the lower union nut

9.6 Removing the fuel pump from the cylinder head

9 High-pressure fuel pump – removal and refitting

Note: *Observe the precautions in Section 1 before working on any component in the fuel system.*

Removal

1 The high-pressure fuel pump is located on the left-hand end of the exhaust camshaft, bolted to the cylinder head end cover **(see illustration)**.

2 Place rags around the fuel line and slacken the union nut on the lower part of the fuel pressure pump **(see illustration)**.

3 Undo the retaining bolt from the fuel pipe securing bracket and move the fuel pipe to one side **(see illustrations)**.

4 Clean around the fuel feed and fuel return pipes and then undo the retaining bolt and remove the fuel pipe retaining bracket.

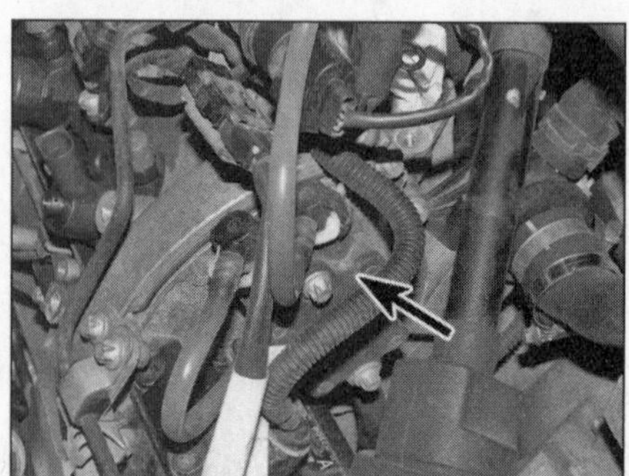

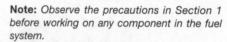

10.1 Predelivery fuel pump location – arrowed

9.3a Undo the bracket retaining bolt – arrowed . . .

5 Disconnect the fuel feed hose and the return hose from the fuel pump and drain any fuel from the hoses into a suitable container, noting their fitted position. Discard the seals, as new ones will be required for refitting. Plug the end of the fuel lines and fuel pump connections to prevent dirt ingress.

6 Unscrew the three mounting bolts and remove the fuel pump from the cylinder head end cover **(see illustration)**. Recover the sealing ring and discard, as a new one must be used on refitting. There are no serviceable parts within the pump; if the pump is faulty, it must be renewed.

Refitting

7 Refitting is a reversal of removal, but use a new sealing ring and tighten the mounting bolts to the specified torque. Ensure the pump pinion engages correctly with the drive slot in the camshaft.

10 Predelivery fuel pump – removal and refitting

Note: *Observe the precautions in Section 1 before working on any component in the fuel system.*

Removal

1 The predelivery fuel pump is located on the left-hand end of the inlet camshaft, bolted to the cylinder head end cover **(see illustration)**. Place rags around the fuel pump to catch any spilt fuel from the fuel lines as they are removed.

2 On models up to 28/02/01, remove the electric fuel shut-off valve as described in Section 3 of this Chapter. Undo the retaining bolts and slide the shut-off valve, mounting bracket out from the slot in the top of the predelivery pump.

3 Release the retaining clip(s) and disconnect the fuel pipe(s) from the top of the predelivery fuel pump **(see illustration)**. **Note:** *On models up to 28/02/01, there is only one pipe fitted to the top of the predelivery pump. On models from 01/03/01, there are two fuel pipes fitted.*

4 Unscrew the two mounting bolts and

remove the predelivery fuel pump from the cylinder head end cover **(see illustration)**. Recover the sealing ring and discard, as a new one must be used on refitting. There are no serviceable parts within the pump; if the pump is faulty, it must be renewed.

Refitting

5 Refitting is a reversal of removal, but use a new sealing ring and tighten the mounting bolts to the specified torque. Before refitting, fill the pump with clean fuel while rotating the shaft. When fitting, ensure the pump pinion engages correctly with the drive slot in the camshaft.

10.3 Disconnect the fuel lines from the top of the pump

10.4 Removing the predelivery pump

Chapter 4 Part C: Emission control and exhaust systems – petrol engines

Contents

Degrees of difficulty

Easy, suitable for novice with little experience 	Fairly easy, suitable for beginner with some experience	Fairly difficult, suitable for competent DIY mechanic	Difficult, suitable for experienced DIY mechanic	Very difficult, suitable for expert DIY or professional 

Specifications

Emission control applications

Type . . . . Catalytic converter in front pipe, two oxygen sensors and secondary air injection

Torque wrench settings	Nm	lbf ft
Catalytic converter to intermediate pipe	25	18
Exhaust manifold nuts*	40	30
Oxygen sensors	55	41

** Use new nuts*

1 General information

Emission control systems

All petrol models are designed to use unleaded petrol, and are controlled by engine management systems that are programmed to give the best compromise between driveability, fuel consumption and exhaust emission production. In addition, a number of systems are fitted that help to minimise other harmful emissions. A crankcase emission control system is fitted, which reduces the release of pollutants from the engine's lubrication system, and a catalytic converter is fitted which reduces exhaust gas pollutant. An evaporative loss emission control system is fitted which reduces the release of gaseous hydrocarbons from the fuel tank.

Crankcase emission control

To reduce the emission of unburned hydrocarbons from the crankcase into the atmosphere, the engine is sealed and the blow-by gases and oil vapour are drawn from inside the crankcase, through a wire-mesh oil separator, into the inlet tract to be burned by the engine during normal combustion.

Under conditions of high manifold depression, the gases will be sucked positively out of the crankcase. Under conditions of low manifold depression, the gases are forced out of the crankcase by the (relatively) higher crankcase pressure. If the engine is worn, the raised crankcase pressure (due to increased blow-by) will cause some of the flow to return under all manifold conditions.

Exhaust emission control

To minimise the amount of pollutants, which escape into the atmosphere, all petrol models are fitted with a catalytic converter in the exhaust system. The fuelling system is of the closed-loop type, in which an oxygen (lambda) sensor in the exhaust system provides the engine management system ECM with constant feedback, enabling the ECM to adjust the air/fuel mixture to optimise combustion.

The oxygen sensor has a built-in heating element, controlled by the ECM through the oxygen sensor relay, to quickly bring the sensor's tip to its optimum operating temperature. The sensor's tip is sensitive to oxygen, and sends a voltage signal to the ECM that varies according to the amount of oxygen in the exhaust gas. If the inlet air/fuel mixture is too rich, the exhaust gases are low in oxygen so the sensor sends a low-voltage signal, the voltage rising as the mixture weakens and the amount of oxygen rises in the exhaust gases. Peak conversion efficiency of all major pollutants occurs if the inlet air/fuel mixture is maintained at the chemically correct ratio for the complete combustion of petrol of 14.7 parts (by weight) of air to 1 part of fuel (the stoichiometric ratio). The sensor output voltage alters in a large step at this point, the ECM using the signal change as a reference point and correcting the inlet air/fuel mixture accordingly by altering the fuel injector pulse width.

Most models have two sensors, one before and one after the main catalytic converter. This enables more efficient monitoring of the exhaust gas, allowing a faster response time. The overall efficiency of the converter itself can also be checked. Details of the oxygen sensor removal and refitting are given in Chapter 4A.

A secondary air system is fitted to most

1.10 Exhaust rubber mounting – arrowed

models, to reduce cold-start emissions when the catalytic converter is still warming-up. The system is an electric air pump, fed with air from the air cleaner, and a system of valves. When the engine is cold, air is pumped into the exhaust manifold, and mixes with the exhaust gas, in order to prolong combustion of any unburnt exhaust gases. The process also helps to bring the catalytic converter to its working temperature more quickly. When the engine coolant temperature is high enough, and the converter is operating normally, the system is switched off by the engine management ECM.

Evaporative emission control

To minimise the escape of unburned hydrocarbons into the atmosphere, an evaporative loss emission control system is fitted to all petrol models. The fuel tank filler cap is sealed and a charcoal canister that is mounted underneath the vehicle below the driver's side footwell, next to the battery box. The charcoal canister collects the petrol vapours which are released from the fuel contained in the fuel tank. It stores them until they can be drawn from the canister (under the control of the fuel injection/ignition system ECM) via the purge valve(s) into the inlet tract, where the engine then burns them during normal combustion.

To ensure that the engine runs correctly when it is cold and/or idling and to protect the catalytic converter from the effects of an over-rich mixture, the purge control valve(s) are not opened by the ECM until the engine has warmed-up, and the engine is under load; the valve solenoid is then modulated on and off to allow the stored vapour to pass into the inlet tract.

Exhaust systems

On most models, the exhaust system is split into two parts, the exhaust manifold/front pipe and the intermediate pipe/silencer/tailpipe. The catalytic converter is incorporated into the exhaust manifold/front pipe. The system is supported by various metal brackets screwed to the vehicle floor, with rubber vibration dampers fitted to suppress noise **(see illustration).**

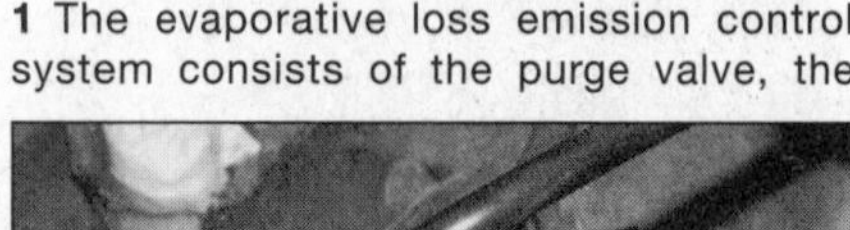

2 Evaporative loss emission control system – information and component renewal

1 The evaporative loss emission control system consists of the purge valve, the activated charcoal filter canister and a series of connecting vacuum hoses.

Purge valve

2 The purge valve is located on the right-hand side of the inlet manifold, below the brake master cylinder **(see illustration).**

3 Ensure that the ignition is switched off, and then unplug the wiring connector from the purge valve **(see illustration).**

4 Disconnect the vacuum hoses and withdraw it from the engine compartment.

5 Refitting is a reversal of removal.

Charcoal canister

6 The charcoal canister is located underneath the vehicle below the driver's side footwell, next to the battery box **(see illustration).**

7 Unclip the fuel filter from the retaining clip on the side of the charcoal canister housing.

8 Undo the retaining bolt from the lower part of the charcoal canister, and then slide it to one side and unclip it from the vehicle body.

9 Disconnect the vent hoses from the canister as it is being removed.

10 Refitting is a reversal of removal.

3 Crankcase emission system – general information

1 The crankcase emission control system consists of hoses connecting the crankcase to the air cleaner, inlet manifold and camshaft cover. The oil separator is part of the top half of the camshaft cover.

2 The system requires no attention other than to check at regular intervals that the hoses, valve and oil separator are free of blockages and in good condition.

4 Secondary air injection system – information and component renewal

1 The secondary air injection system consists of an electrically-operated air pump (fed with air from the air cleaner), a relay for the air pump, a vacuum-operated aspirator shut-off valve, a solenoid switchover valve to regulate the vacuum supply, and pipework to feed the air into the exhaust manifold. For more information on the principles of operation, refer to Section 1.

2 To improve access to the air pump, shut-off valve and solenoid valve, release the securing clip and move windscreen washer reservoir to one side.

Air pump

3 The air pump is mounted on a bracket attached to the left-hand inner wing panel.

4 Disconnect the air hose to the shut-off valve **(see illustration).**

5 Disconnect the wiring connector from the air pump **(see illustration).**

2.2 Purge valve location – arrowed

2.3 Disconnect the wiring connector

2.6 Charcoal canister location – arrowed

4.4 Disconnecting the air hose

4.5 Disconnect the air pump wiring connector

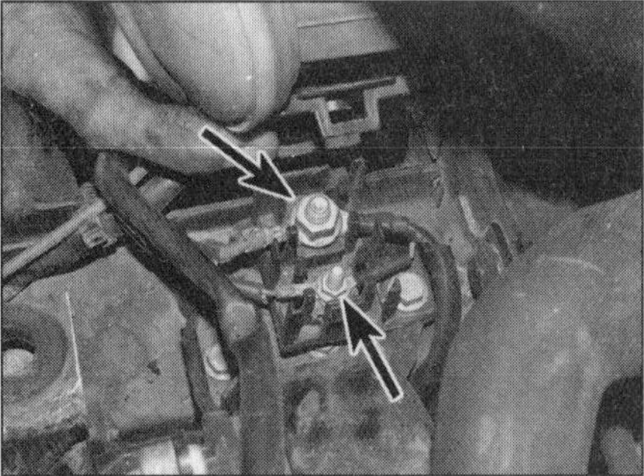
4.6a Disconnect the wiring connectors – arrowed . . .

4.6b . . . and undo the retaining bolt

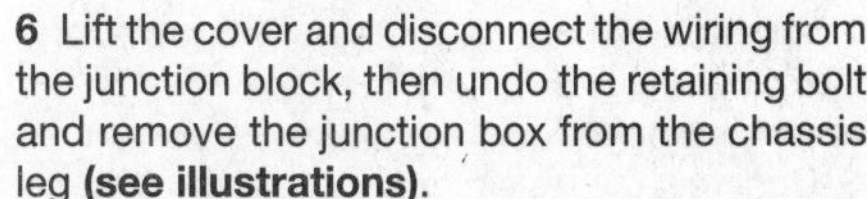
6 Lift the cover and disconnect the wiring from the junction block, then undo the retaining bolt and remove the junction box from the chassis leg **(see illustrations)**.

7 Unscrew the pump mounting bracket bolts and remove the air pump out from the engine compartment **(see illustrations)**.

8 If required, the mounting bracket can be removed from the air pump by slackening the three retaining nuts and sliding the pump out from the mounting bracket.

9 Refitting is a reversal of removal.

Air pump relay

10 Refer to Chapter 12 for more details on location of air pump relay and fuses.

Aspirator shut-off valve

11 The shut-off valve is mounted on the left-hand (transmission) end of the cylinder head **(see illustration)**.

12 Disconnect the vacuum hose from the top of the shut-off valve **(see illustration)**.

13 Disconnect the air hose to the electric air pump **(see illustration 4.4)**.

14 Remove the two valve mounting bolts from below the valve, and lift the valve off its mounting flange. Recover the gasket.

15 Refitting is a reversal of removal. Use a new gasket **(see illustration)**.

Solenoid switchover valve

16 The solenoid valve is mounted on the left-hand (transmission) end of the camshaft cover **(see illustration)**.

17 Release the retaining clip and slide the solenoid valve out from the mounting bracket on the end of the camshaft cover **(see illustration)**.

4.7a Undo the retaining bolts . . .

4.7b . . . and remove the air pump

18 Disconnect the wiring connector from the solenoid valve.

19 Disconnect the two vacuum pipes from the solenoid valve, note which ports the pipes are fitted to, to avoid confusion when refitting.

20 Refitting is a reversal of removal, making sure that the vacuum pipes are fitted in their correct positions, as noted on removal.

4.11 Shut-off valve location – arrowed

4.12 Disconnect the vacuum pipe

4.15 Renew the gasket on refitting

4.16 Switchover valve location – arrowed

4.17 Release the valve from the mounting bracket

5.3a Oxygen sensors – arrowed

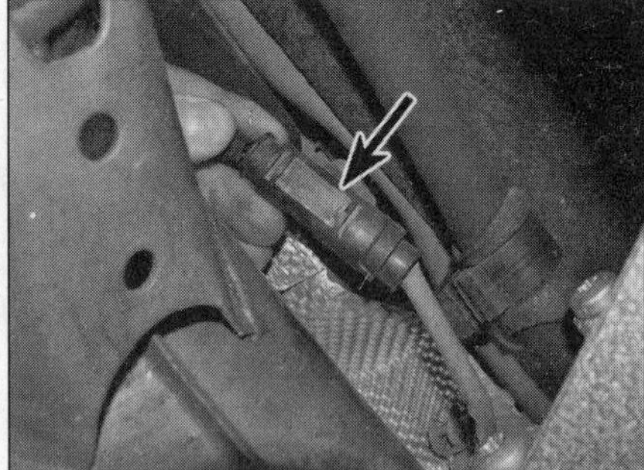
5.3b Disconnect the wiring connector – arrowed

5.4 Support bracket retaining bolts and nuts – arrowed

5 Exhaust manifold/front pipe/catalytic converter – removal and refitting

Warning: *Allow ample time for the exhaust system to cool before starting work. In particular, note that the catalytic converter runs at very high temperatures. If there is any chance that the system may still be hot, wear suitable gloves. When removing the exhaust sections, take care not to damage the oxygen sensors if they are not removed from their locations.*

Note: *The catalytic converter is incorporated into the exhaust manifold/front pipe assembly. Renew any self-locking nuts and gaskets on refitting.*

Removal

1 Apply the handbrake, then jack up the front of the vehicle and support it on axle stands (see *Jacking and vehicle support*).

2 The exhaust manifold is located on the front of the cylinder head. For access to the exhaust front pipe, first remove the engine undertrays from the front of the vehicle.

3 Locate the oxygen sensors and trace the wiring back to the connectors and disconnect **(see illustrations)**. Unclip the oxygen sensor wiring from any clips or brackets, noting how it is routed for refitting.

4 Undo the retaining bolts and nuts, then remove the support bracket from the front edge of the catalytic converter **(see illustration)**.

5 Undo the retaining bolts/nuts and disconnect the catalytic converter from the intermediate exhaust pipe **(see illustration)**. Check the condition of the gasket ring and renew if required.

6 Unscrew the nuts and withdraw the exhaust manifold/catalytic converter from the cylinder head **(see illustrations)**. Discard the nuts, as new ones must be used on refitting.

7 Undo the mounting bracket bolt and remove the gasket/heat shield from the manifold studs **(see illustration)**, discard as a new one will be required for refitting.

Refitting

8 Refitting is a reversal of the removal procedure, but fit new gaskets and locking nuts, tighten all nuts and bolts to the specified torque where given. **Note:** *The manifold gasket is part of the manifold heat shield.*

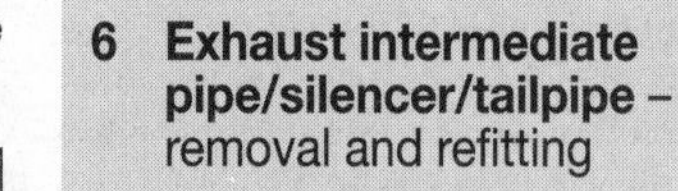
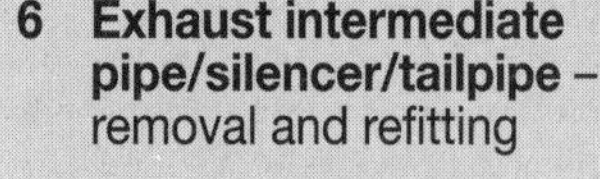

6 Exhaust intermediate pipe/silencer/tailpipe – removal and refitting

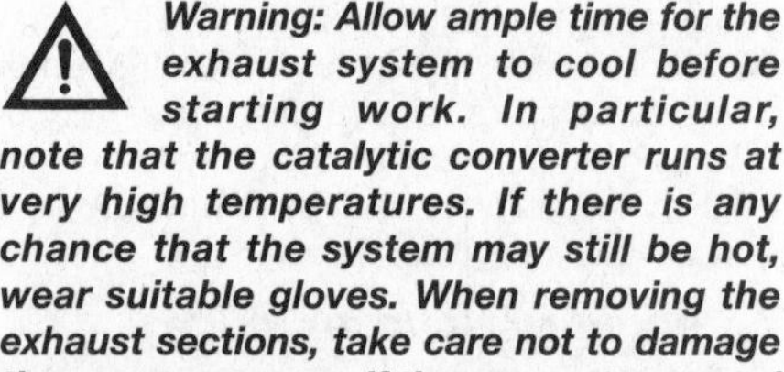

Warning: *Allow ample time for the exhaust system to cool before starting work. In particular, note that the catalytic converter runs at very high temperatures. If there is any chance that the system may still be hot, wear suitable gloves. When removing the exhaust sections, take care not to damage the oxygen sensors if they are not removed from their locations.*

Removal

1 The original Mercedes-Benz system fitted in the factory is in two sections: the front section and the rear section. A catalytic converter is fitted to all models, and is located in the front pipe. The rear section has a silencer halfway along its length.

2 Apply the handbrake, then jack up the rear of the vehicle and support it on axle stands (see *Jacking and vehicle support*). For access to the front exhaust clamp, it may be necessary to first remove the engine undertrays.

3 Undo the retaining bolts/nuts and disconnect the intermediate exhaust pipe from the catalytic converter **(see illustration 5.5)**. Check the condition of the gasket ring and renew if required.

4 Support the front of the pipe, then working

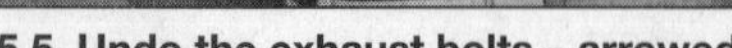
5.5 Undo the exhaust bolts – arrowed

5.6a Undo the manifold retaining nuts . . .

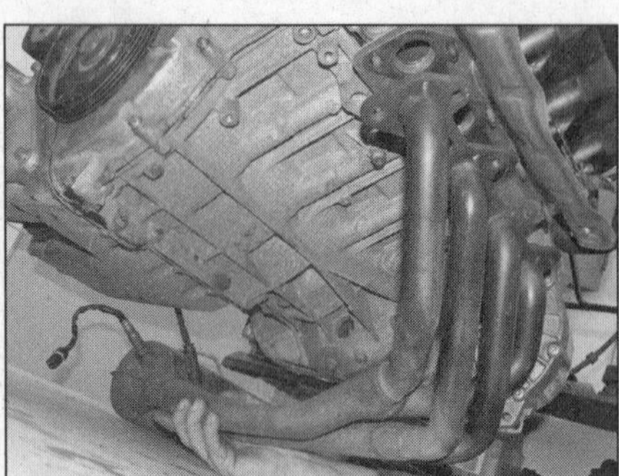
5.6b . . . and remove the exhaust front pipe/catalytic converter

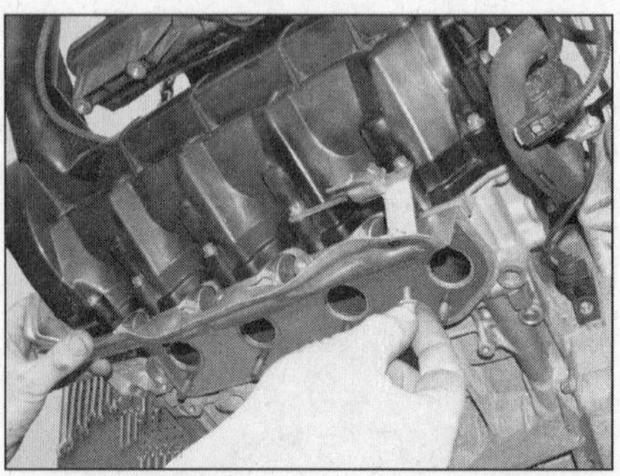
5.7 Unbolt the heat shield/gasket from the cylinder head

your way to the rear of the vehicle and unhook the rubber mountings, from their mounting brackets **(see illustrations)**. When the pipe is free, lower it to the ground and remove it from under the car.

Refitting

5 Refitting is the reversal of the removal sequence, noting the following points:

a) Ensure that all traces of corrosion have been removed from the flanges or pipe ends, and renew all necessary gaskets.
b) If necessary, renew any damaged or worn clamps.
c) Inspect the rubber mountings for signs of damage or deterioration, and renew as necessary.
d) If using exhaust assembly paste, make sure this is only applied to joints downstream (after) of the catalyst.
e) Prior to tightening the exhaust system mountings and clamps, ensure that all rubber mountings are correctly located and that there is adequate clearance between the exhaust system and vehicle underbody. Try to ensure that no unnecessary twisting stresses are applied to the pipes – move the pipes relative to each other at the clamps to relieve this.

7 Catalytic converter – general information and precautions

1 The catalytic converter is a reliable and simple device which needs no maintenance in itself, but there are some facts of which an owner should be aware if the converter is to function properly for its full service life:

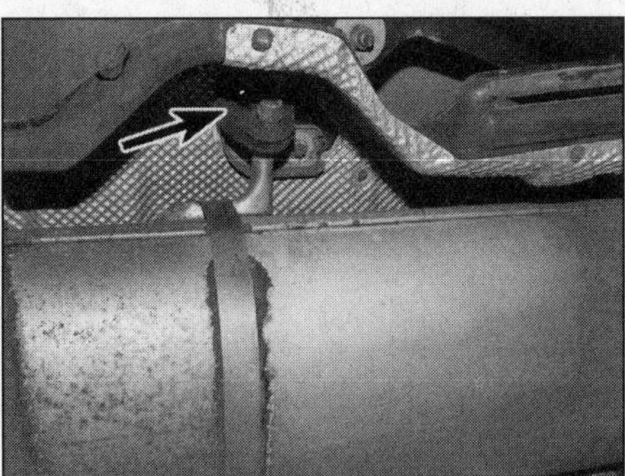

6.4a Exhaust silencer rubber mounting – arrowed . . .

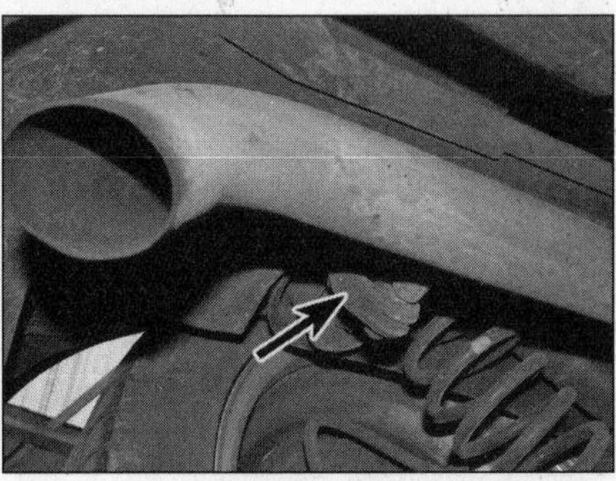

6.4b . . . and tail pipe rubber mounting – arrowed

a) DO NOT use leaded or lead-replacement petrol in a car equipped with a catalytic converter – the lead (or other additives) will coat the precious metals, reducing their converting efficiency and will eventually destroy the converter.
b) Always keep the ignition and fuel systems well maintained in accordance with the manufacturer's schedule (see Chapter 1A).
c) If the engine develops a misfire, do not drive the car at all (or at least as little as possible) until the fault is cured.
d) DO NOT push- or tow-start the car – this will soak the catalytic converter in unburned fuel, causing it to overheat when the engine does start.
e) DO NOT switch off the ignition at high engine speeds – ie, do not 'blip' the throttle immediately before switching off the engine.
f) DO NOT use fuel or engine oil additives – these may contain substances harmful to the catalytic converter.
g) DO NOT continue to use the car if the engine burns oil to the extent of leaving a visible trail of blue smoke.
h) Remember that the catalytic converter operates at very high temperatures. DO NOT, therefore, park the car in dry undergrowth, over long grass or piles of dead leaves after a long run.
i) Remember that the catalytic converter is FRAGILE – do not strike it with tools during servicing work, and take care handling it when removing it from the car for any reason.
j) In some cases, a sulphurous smell (like that of rotten eggs) may be noticed from the exhaust. This is common to many catalytic converter-equipped cars, and has more to do with the sulphur content of the brand of fuel being used than the converter itself.
k) The catalytic converter, used on a well-maintained and well-driven car, should last for between 50 000 and 100 000 miles – if the converter is no longer effective, it must be renewed.

Chapter 4 Part D: Emission control and exhaust systems – diesel engines

Contents

Degrees of difficulty

Easy, suitable for novice with little experience 	**Fairly easy,** suitable for beginner with some experience	**Fairly difficult,** suitable for competent DIY mechanic	**Difficult,** suitable for experienced DIY mechanic	**Very difficult,** suitable for expert DIY or professional 

Specifications

Emission control applications

Type	Two catalytic converters, one in downpipe at front of engine and one in intermediate pipe under front of vehicle, and EGR system

Torque wrench settings

Torque wrench settings	Nm	lbf ft
Exhaust manifold retaining nuts:*		
Up to 07/12/2000	21	15
From 08/12/2000	30	22
Exhaust manifold cylinder head stud:		
Up to 07/12/2000	11	8
From 08/12/2000	9	7
Turbocharger oil return pipe flange bolts	9	7
Turbocharger oil supply union banjo bolt	30	22
Turbocharger support strut bolt	21	15
Turbocharger to exhaust manifold	21	15

** Use new nuts/bolts*

1 General information

Emission control systems

All diesel-engined models have a crankcase emission control system, and in addition are fitted with a catalytic converter. All diesel engines are fitted with an Exhaust Gas Recirculation (EGR) system to reduce exhaust emissions.

Crankcase emission control

To reduce the emission of unburned hydrocarbons from the crankcase into the atmosphere, the engine is sealed and the blow-by gases and oil vapour are drawn from inside the crankcase, through a wire mesh oil separator, into the inlet tract to be burned by the engine during normal combustion.

Under conditions of high manifold depression, the gases will be sucked positively out of the crankcase. Under conditions of low manifold depression, the gases are forced out of the crankcase by the (relatively) higher crankcase pressure. If the engine is worn, the raised crankcase pressure (due to increased blow-by) will cause some of the flow to return under all manifold conditions. All diesel engines have a pressure-regulating valve, to control the flow of gases from the crankcase.

Exhaust emission control

Two catalytic converters are fitted in the exhaust system of all diesel-engine models. This has the effect of removing a large proportion of the gaseous hydrocarbons, carbon monoxide and particulates present in the exhaust gas.

An Exhaust Gas Recirculation (EGR) system is fitted; this reduces the level of nitrogen oxides produced during combustion by introducing a proportion of the exhaust gas back into the inlet manifold under certain engine operating conditions. The system is controlled electronically by the diesel engine management ECM.

Exhaust systems

The exhaust system consists of the exhaust manifold, catalytic converter and front pipe, main section with catalytic converter and silencer, and bolt-on tailpiece. The turbocharger is bolted to the top of the exhaust manifold, and is driven by the exhaust gases.

The system is supported by various metal brackets screwed to the vehicle floor, with rubber vibration dampers fitted to suppress noise.

2.1 Crankcase breather location – arrowed

2.3a Disconnect the breather hoses . . .

2.3b . . . from the oil separator

2 Crankcase emission system – general information

1 The crankcase emission control system consists of an oil separator with hoses connecting the crankcase to the air cleaner and inlet manifold. The oil separator is located at the right-hand rear of the engine compartment bolted to the inlet manifold **(see illustration)**.

2 The system requires no attention other than to check at regular intervals that the hoses and oil separator are free of blockages and in good condition.

3 To remove the oil separator, first release the securing clips and disconnect the crankcase breather hoses from the top of the oil seperator **(see illustrations)**.

4 Undo the three oil separator mounting bracket retaining bolts and remove it from the engine, disconnecting the breather pipe(s) from the base of the separator as it is removed **(see illustration)**. Note the position of the breather pipes for refitting.

5 To clean out the oil separator, unclip the cap and withdraw the diaphragm, spring and filter. Clean out the filter and oil separator housing and re-assemble **(see illustrations)**.

6 Note the position of any sealing rings or gaskets and renew if required **(see illustrations)**.

3 Exhaust Gas Recirculation (EGR) system – component removal

1 The EGR system consists of the EGR valve, which directs exhaust gas from the exhaust manifold to the inlet manifold, and a control valve, which actuates the system according to engine load and speed.

2 This is a vacuum-operated EGR system that has a solenoid control valve, which opens vacuum from the inlet manifold to the EGR valve actuator, when the solenoid is energised by the engine management ECU.

3 The EGR valve is located on the airflow mixing chamber, which is attached to the left-hand (transmission) end of the inlet manifold. See Chapter 4B, Section 3, for the removal and refitting procedure.

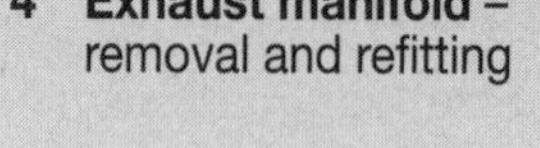

4 Exhaust manifold – removal and refitting

Removal

1 Remove the catalytic converter from the front of the engine as described in Section 9.

2.4 Undo the bolts and remove the oil separator

2.5a Unclip the plastic cover . . .

2.5b . . . remove the spring . . .

2.5c . . . and remove the filter

2.6a Check the rubber sealing ring . . .

2.6b . . . and rubber sealing gasket

4.2a Remove the clamp . . .

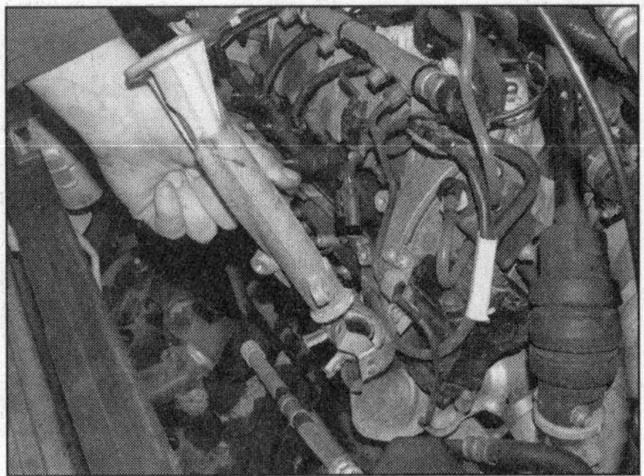

4.2b . . . and remove the EGR pipe

4.3 Turbocharger mounting bolts – arrowed

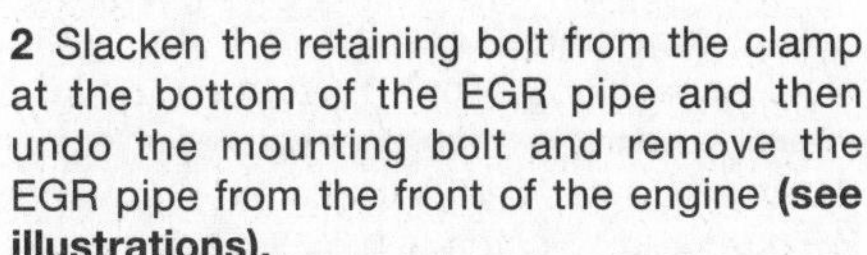

2 Slacken the retaining bolt from the clamp at the bottom of the EGR pipe and then undo the mounting bolt and remove the EGR pipe from the front of the engine **(see illustrations).**

3 Undo the three retaining bolts and disconnect the turbocharger from the exhaust manifold **(see illustration).**

4 Undo the three retaining bolts and disconnect the turbocharger from charge air hose **(see illustration).**

5 Undo the two retaining bolts from the turbocharger oil return pipe on the cylinder block **(see illustration)**, then undo the two retaining bolts from the connection under the turbocharger and withdraw the oil return pipe. Be prepared to catch any oil spillage as the pipe is removed. Discard the gaskets as new ones will be required when refitting.

6 Slacken and remove the exhaust manifold retaining nuts and withdraw the manifold out from the front of the engine. Hold the turbo in position as the manifold is removed. Discard the retaining nuts as new ones will be needed for refitting.

Refitting

7 Refitting is removal procedure in reverse, noting the following points:

a) Renew all gaskets and manifold retaining nuts.
b) Inspect the condition of the manifold studs in cylinder head, renew if required.
c) Tighten all nuts and bolts to the specified torque, where given.
d) Check engine oil level, top-up if required.

5 Turbocharger – general information and precautions

General information

The turbocharger increases engine efficiency by raising the pressure in the inlet manifold above atmospheric pressure. Instead of the air simply being sucked into the cylinders, it is forced in.

Energy for the operation of the turbocharger comes from the exhaust gas. The gas flows through a specially-shaped housing (the turbine housing) and in so doing, spins the turbine wheel. The turbine wheel is attached to a shaft, at the end of which is another vaned wheel, known as the compressor wheel. The compressor wheel spins in its own housing, and compresses the inducted air on the way to the inlet manifold.

4.4 Undo the mounting bolts – arrowed

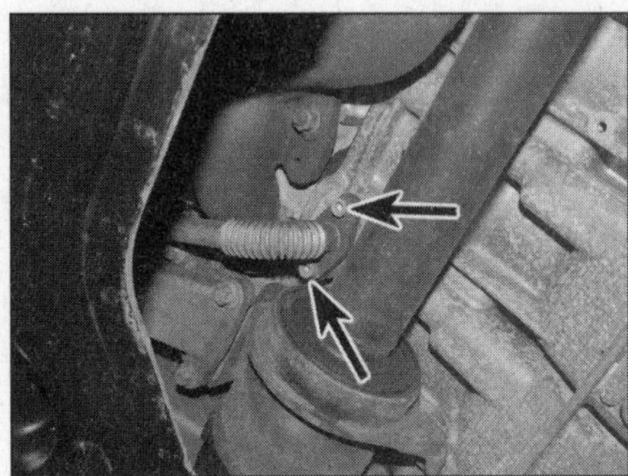

4.5 Oil return pipe mounting bolts – arrowed

Between the turbocharger and the inlet manifold, the compressed air passes through an intercooler. The purpose of the intercooler is to remove from the inducted air some of the heat gained in being compressed. Because cooler air is denser, removal of this heat further increases engine efficiency.

Boost pressure (the pressure in the inlet manifold) is limited by a wastegate, which diverts the exhaust gas away from the turbine wheel in response to a pressure-sensitive actuator.

The turbo shaft is pressure-lubricated by an oil feed pipe from the engine oil filter mounting. The shaft 'floats' on a cushion of oil. Oil is returned to the sump through a return pipe that connects to the sump.

Precautions

The turbocharger operates at extremely high speeds and temperatures. Certain precautions must be observed to avoid premature failure of the turbo, or injury to the operator.

- Do not operate the turbo with any parts exposed – foreign objects falling onto the rotating vanes could cause excessive damage and (if ejected) personal injury.
- Cover the turbocharger air inlet ducts to prevent debris entering, and clean using lint-free cloths only.
- Do not race the engine immediately after start-up, especially if it is cold. Give the oil a few seconds to circulate.
- Observe the recommended intervals for oil and filter changing, and use a reputable oil of the specified quality. Neglect of oil changing, or use of inferior oil, can cause carbon formation on the turbo shaft and subsequent failure. Thoroughly clean the area around all oil pipe unions before disconnecting them to prevent the ingress of dirt. Store dismantled components in a sealed container to prevent contamination.

6 Turbocharger – removal and refitting

Warning: Allow ample time for the exhaust system to cool before starting work. In particular, note that the catalytic converter runs at very high temperatures. If there is any chance that the system may still be hot, wear suitable gloves.

Removal

1 Apply the handbrake, then jack up the front of the vehicle and support it on axle stands (see *Jacking and vehicle support*). Remove the engine compartment undertrays.

2 Slacken the air intake hose securing clip, pull out the plastic retaining clip and move the air intake housing to one side **(see illustrations).**

3 Remove the inlet manifold **(see illustration),** as described Chapter 4B, Section 5.

6.2a Slacken the retaining clip . . .

6.2b . . . withdraw the retaining clip . . .

6.2c . . . and remove the air intake housing

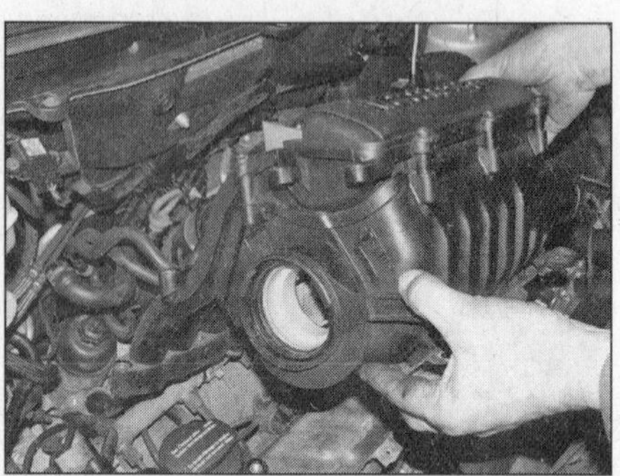

6.3 Remove the inlet manifold

6.4 Undo the retaining clamp bolt – arrowed

4 Undo the retaining bolt and release the clamp from around the joint where the catalytic converter joins the turbocharger **(see illustration)**.

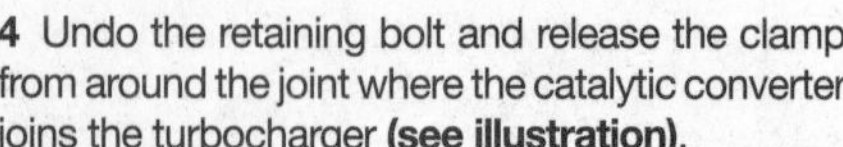

5 Undo the upper mounting bolt and move the catalytic converter away from the turbocharger **(see illustration)**.

6 Disconnect the vacuum pipe from the turbocharger vacuum unit **(see illustration)**.

7 Undo the three retaining bolts and disconnect the turbocharger from charge air hose **(see illustration)**.

8 Undo the two retaining bolts from the turbocharger oil return pipe on the cylinder block **(see illustration)**, then undo the two retaining bolts from the connection under the turbocharger and withdraw the oil return pipe**.** Be prepared to catch any oil spillage as the pipe is removed. Discard the gaskets as new ones will be required when refitting.

9 Slacken and remove the oil feed pipe to the top of the turbocharger **(see illustration)**. Discard the sealing washers as new ones will be required on refitting.

10 Undo the retaining bolt and disconnect the support strap from the top of the turbocharger. If required, carefully bend the small heat shield above the turbocharger upwards.

11 Undo the three retaining bolts and disconnect the turbocharger from the exhaust manifold, lift the turbocharger out from the engine compartment **(see illustration).** Take care not to damage the radiator; put a piece of plywood in front of the radiator to prevent any damage.

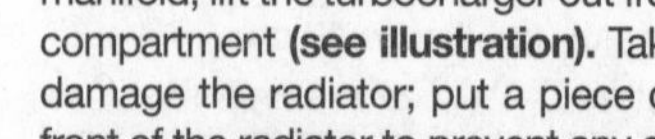

6.5 Undo the catalytic converter mounting bolt – arrowed

6.6 Disconnect the vacuum pipe – arrowed

6.7 Undo the turbocharger bolts – arrowed

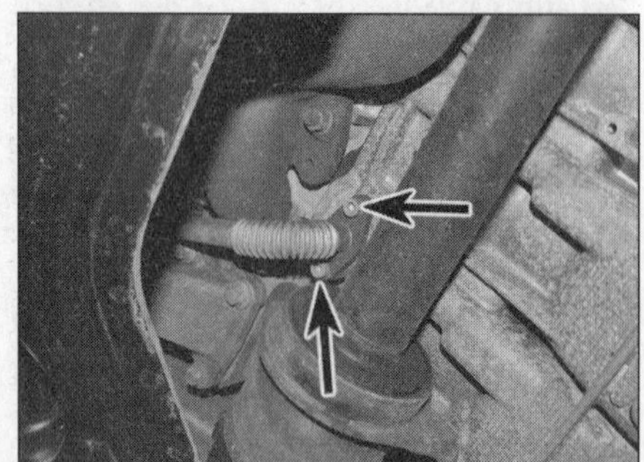

6.8 Oil return pipe mounting bolts – arrowed

6.9 Removing the oil feed banjo bolt

6.11 Removing the turbocharger from the engine compartment

7.1 Charge air pressure sensor – arrowed

8.2a Twist the collar to disconnect the hose . . .

8.2b . . . and undo the retaining bolt to remove the hose

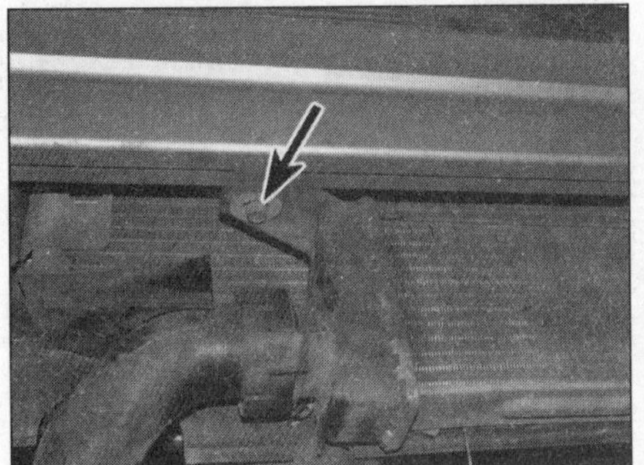

8.3a Undo the right-hand mounting bolt – arrowed . . .

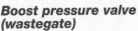

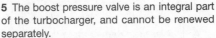

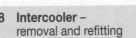

Refitting

12 Refit the turbocharger by following the removal procedure in reverse, noting the following points:

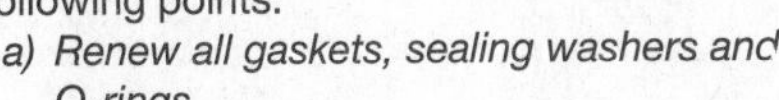

a) *Renew all gaskets, sealing washers and O-rings.*
b) *Before reconnecting the oil supply pipe, fill the turbocharger with fresh oil using an oil can.*
c) *Tighten all nuts and bolts to the specified torque, where given.*
d) *Ensure that the air hose clips are securely tightened, to prevent air leaks.*
e) *When the engine is started after refitting, allow it to idle for approximately one minute to give the oil time to circulate around the turbine shaft bearings.*
f) *Check for signs of oil or coolant leakage from the relevant unions, top-up if required.*

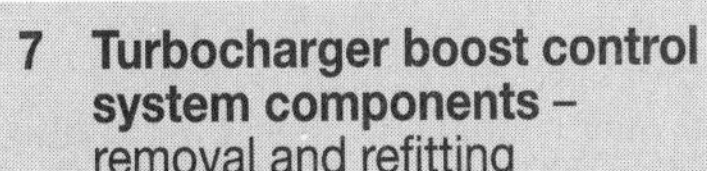

7 Turbocharger boost control system components – removal and refitting

Charge air pressure sensor

1 The charge air pressure sensor is fitted at the rear of the engine compartment, on the right-hand side, next to the brake fluid reservoir **(see illustration)**.

2 Disconnect the wiring connector, then undo the retaining bolt and remove the sensor from its location.

3 Disconnect the vacuum pipes from the sensor.

8.3b . . . and left-hand mounting bolt – arrowed

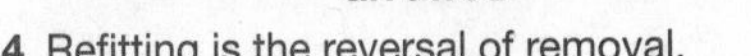

4 Refitting is the reversal of removal.

Boost pressure valve (wastegate)

5 The boost pressure valve is an integral part of the turbocharger, and cannot be renewed separately.

8 Intercooler – removal and refitting

Removal

1 The intercooler is mounted at the front of the vehicle, in front of the lower part of the cooling system radiator. Remove the front bumper as described in Chapter 11.

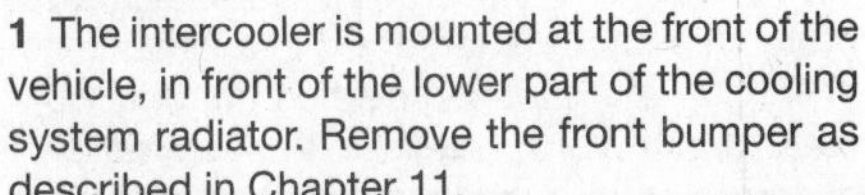

2 Twist the collar on the charge air hose and disconnect it from the left-hand side of the intercooler, undo the retaining bolt and move the air charge hose to one side **(see illustrations)**.

3 Slacken and remove the two intercooler upper mounting bolts from the front crossmember **(see illustrations)**.

4 Twist the collar on the right-hand charge air hose and disconnect the intercooler from the vehicle **(see illustration)**.

Refitting

5 Refitting is the reversal of removal. Renew the O-ring seals in both charge air hose collars before refitting. Make sure the collars are fitted correctly and lock in place.

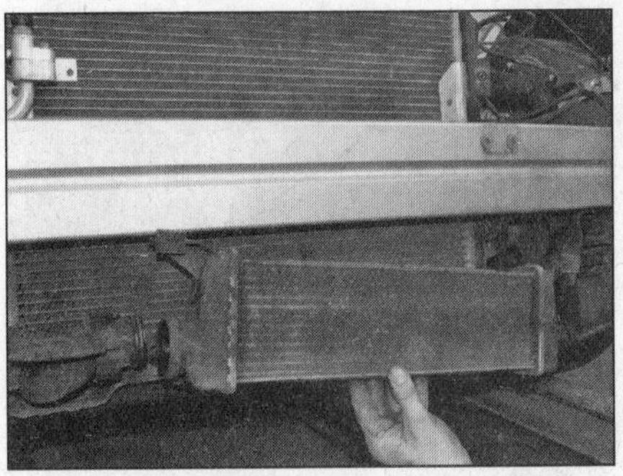

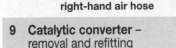

8.4 Remove the intercooler from the right-hand air hose

9 Catalytic converter – removal and refitting

Warning: Allow ample time for the exhaust system to cool before starting work. In particular, note that the catalytic converter runs at very high temperatures. If there is any chance that the system may still be hot, wear suitable gloves.

At front of engine

1 Remove the inlet manifold as described Chapter 4B, Section 5.

2 Undo the retaining bolts and remove the heat shield from across the top of the manifold **(see illustration)**.

3 Remove the fan and shroud from the rear of the radiator as described in Chapter 3.

9.2 Removing the heat shield

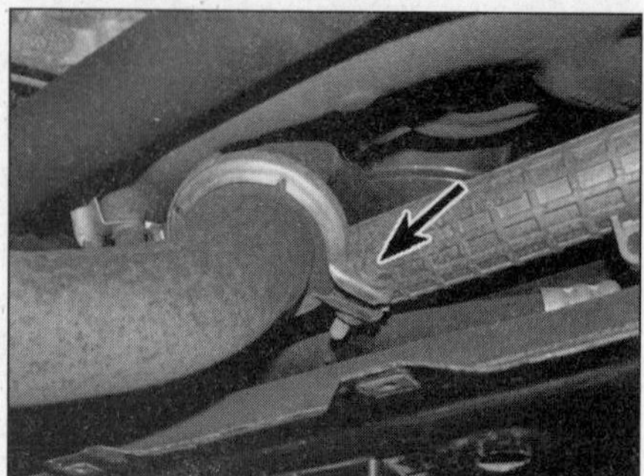

9.4 Undo the exhaust clamp bolt – arrowed

9.6b . . . and the upper mounting bolt . . .

4 Undo the retaining bolt and release the clamp from around the joint at the bottom of the catalytic converter **(see illustration)**.

5 Undo the retaining bolt and release the clamp from around the joint at the top of the catalytic converter **(see illustration)**.

6 Undo the two mounting bolts and withdraw the catalytic converter from the front of the engine **(see illustrations)**. Take care not to damage the radiator as it is removed; put a piece of plywood in front of the radiator to prevent any damage.

7 Refit the catalytic converter by following the removal procedure in reverse, renew gaskets, where required.

Under vehicle

8 The under-vehicle catalytic converter is part of the intermediate/rear exhaust section, see Section 10 for further information.

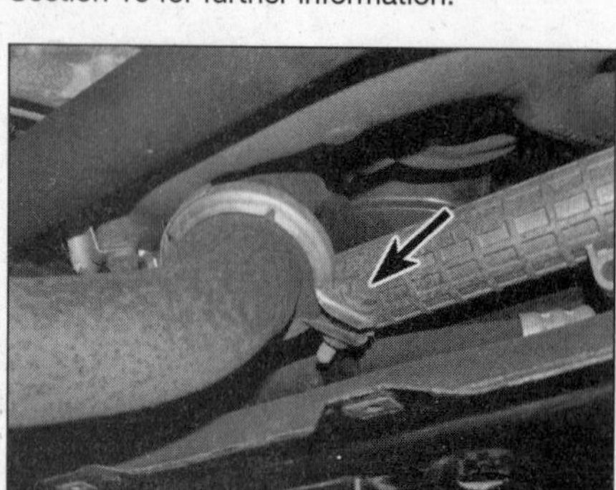

10.3 Undo the exhaust clamp securing bolt – arrowed

9.5 Remove the catalytic converter retaining clamp

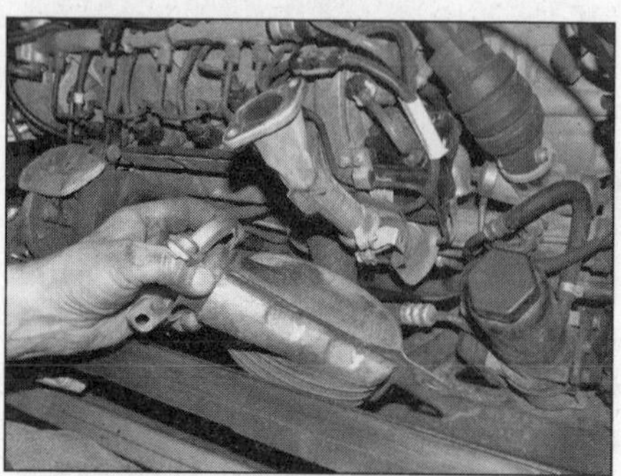

9.6c . . . then remove the catalytic converter

10 Exhaust system – component renewal

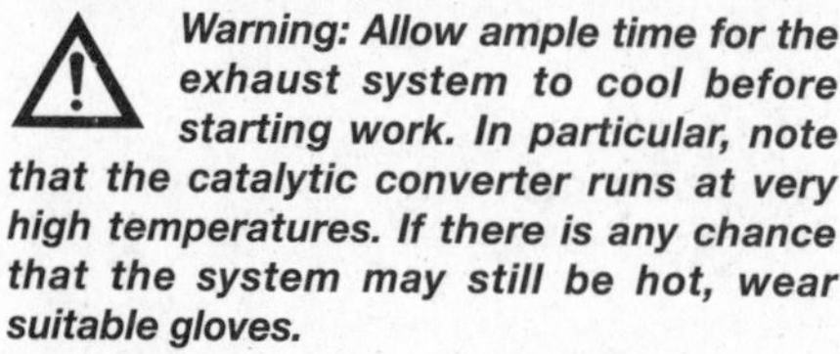

Warning: Allow ample time for the exhaust system to cool before starting work. In particular, note that the catalytic converter runs at very high temperatures. If there is any chance that the system may still be hot, wear suitable gloves.

Removal

1 The original Mercedes-Benz exhaust system fitted in the factory is in two sections. The front pipe is a short section from the front catalytic converter back to the second part of the exhaust system, which incorporates a second catalytic converter and a silencer.

10.5 Undo the mounting bracket retaining bolt – arrowed

9.6a Remove the lower mounting bolt . . .

If the rear catalytic converter or the silencer needs renewing, the exhaust can be cut at a certain point, so that an individual piece can be fitted.

2 To remove part of the system, first jack up the front or rear of the car and support it on axle stands (see *Jacking and vehicle support)*. Alternatively, position the car over an inspection pit or on car ramps.

Front pipe

3 Undo the retaining bolt and release the clamp from around the joint at the bottom of the catalytic converter **(see illustration)**.

4 Release the retaining clip and disconnect the front pipe from the rear section of exhaust pipe.

5 Undo the bolt from the mounting bracket on the lower part of the engine sump **(see illustration)**.

6 Release the front pipe withdraw from under the car.

Rear pipe, including catalytic converter and silencer

7 If the factory-fitted Mercedes-Benz exhaust centre/rear section is being worked on, then it can be removed in one section. If the exhaust centre/rear section has been changed before, then there may be a clamp connection just before the rear silencer.

8 Release the retaining clip and disconnect the front pipe from the rear section of exhaust pipe **(see illustration 10.3)**.

9 Support the front of the pipe, then working your way to the rear of the vehicle and unhook the rubber mountings, from there mounting brackets. When the pipe is free, lower it to the ground and remove it from under the car.

10 If a new section of pipe is purchased (silencer or catalytic converter), hold it up against the original pipe that has been removed, and mark for cutting to the correct length. On short wheel base vehicles, the original pipe should be cut 170 mm in front of the rear silencer. On long wheel base models, the original pipe should be cut 330 mm in front of the rear silencer. A pipe cutter will be required to make a clean cut in the exhaust pipe.

Refitting

11 Each section is refitted by a reversal of

the removal sequence, noting the following points:

a) *Ensure that all traces of corrosion have been removed from the flanges or pipe ends, and renew all necessary gaskets.*
b) *The design of the clamps used between the exhaust sections means that they play a greater role in ensuring a gas-tight seal – fit new clamps if they are in less than perfect condition.*
c) *When fitting the clamps, use the markings on the pipes as a guide to the clamp's correct fitted position.*
d) *Inspect the mountings for signs of damage or deterioration, and renew as necessary.*
e) *If using exhaust assembly paste, make sure this is only applied to joints downstream of the catalyst.*
f) *Prior to tightening the exhaust system mountings and clamps, ensure that all rubber mountings are correctly located and that there is adequate clearance between the exhaust system and vehicle underbody.*

11 Catalytic converter – general information and precautions

1 The catalytic converter fitted to diesel models is simpler than that fitted to petrol models, but it still needs to be treated with respect to avoid problems. The converter is a reliable and simple device which needs no maintenance in itself, but there are some facts of which an owner should be aware if the converter is to function properly for its full service life:

a) *DO NOT use fuel or engine oil additives – these may contain substances harmful to the catalytic converter.*
b) *DO NOT continue to use the car if the engine burns (engine) oil to the extent of leaving a visible trail of blue smoke.*
c) *Remember that the catalytic converter is FRAGILE – do not strike it with tools during servicing work, and take care handling it when removing it from the car for any reason.*
d) *The catalytic converter, used on a well-maintained and well-driven car, should last for between 50 000 and 100 000 miles – if the converter is no longer effective, it must be renewed.*

Notes

Chapter 5 Part A: Starting and charging systems

Contents

Degrees of difficulty

Easy, suitable for novice with little experience 	**Fairly easy,** suitable for beginner with some experience	**Fairly difficult,** suitable for competent DIY mechanic	**Difficult,** suitable for experienced DIY mechanic	**Very difficult,** suitable for expert DIY or professional 

Specifications

General

System type	12 volt, negative earth

Battery

Type	Low maintenance or maintenance free sealed for life
Ratings	35 to 100 Ah (depending on model and market)
Charge condition:	
Poor	12.5 volts
Normal	12.6 volts
Good	12.7 volts

Alternator

Rating:	
Petrol engines	90 Ah @ 2200 rpm
Diesel engines	150 Ah @ 2100 rpm

Torque wrench settings

	Nm	lbf ft
Alternator mounting bolts	20	15
Starter mounting bolts	20	15

1 General information and precautions

General information

The engine electrical system consists of the charging and starting systems. Because of their engine-related functions, these are covered separately from the body electrical devices such as the lights, instruments, etc (which are covered in Chapter 12). On petrol engine models refer to Part B of this Chapter for information on the ignition system, and on diesel models refer to Part C for the preheating system.

The electrical system is of the 12 volt negative earth type.

The battery is of the low maintenance or maintenance-free (sealed for life) type and is charged by the alternator, which is belt-driven from the crankshaft pulley.

The starter motor is of the pre-engaged type, with an integral solenoid. On starting, the solenoid moves the drive pinion into engagement with the flywheel ring gear before the starter motor is energised. Once the engine has started, a one-way clutch prevents the motor armature being driven by the engine until the pinion disengages from the flywheel.

Further details of the various systems are given in the relevant Sections of this Chapter. While some repair procedures are given, the usual course of action is to renew the component concerned.

Precautions

Warning: It is necessary to take extra care when working on the electrical system to avoid damage to semi-conductor devices (diodes and transistors), and to avoid the risk of personal injury.

In addition to the precautions given in *Safety first!* observe the following when working on the system:

- ***Always remove rings, watches, etc, before working on the electrical system.*** Even with the battery disconnected, capacitive discharge could occur if a component's live terminal is earthed through a metal object. This could cause a shock or nasty burn.
- ***Do not reverse the battery connections.*** Components such as the alternator, electronic control units, or any other components having semi-conductor circuitry could be irreparably damaged.
- ***Never disconnect the battery terminals, the alternator, any electrical wiring or any test instruments when the engine is running.***

• Do not allow the engine to turn the alternator when the alternator is not connected.

• Never test for alternator output by flashing the output lead to earth.

• Always ensure that the battery negative lead is disconnected when working on the electrical system.

• If the engine is being started using jump leads and a slave battery, connect the batteries ***positive-to-positive*** and ***negative-to-negative*** (see *Jump starting* at the beginning of the manual). This also applies when connecting a battery charger.

• Before using electric-arc welding equipment on the car, ***disconnect the battery, alternator and components such as the electronic control modules*** (where applicable) to protect them from the risk of damage.

Caution: Certain audio units fitted as standard equipment by Mercedes-Benz have a built-in security code to deter thieves. If the power source to the unit is cut, the anti-theft system will activate. Even if the power source is immediately reconnected, the unit will not function until the correct security code has been entered. Therefore, if you do not know the correct security code for the unit, do not disconnect the battery negative terminal or remove the audio unit from the vehicle. Refer to your Mercedes-Benz dealer for further information on whether the unit fitted to your car has a security code. Refer to 'Disconnecting the battery' in the Reference section at the rear of this manual.

2 Battery – testing and charging

Testing

Standard and low-maintenance battery

1 If the vehicle covers a small annual mileage, it is worthwhile checking the specific gravity of the electrolyte every three months to determine the state of charge of the battery. Remove the battery (see Section 3) then remove the cell caps/cover (as applicable) and use a hydrometer to make the check, comparing the results with the following table. Note that the specific gravity readings assume an electrolyte temperature of 15°C; for every 10°C below 15°C subtract 0.007. For every 10°C above 15°C add 0.007. If the electrolyte level of any cell is low, top it up to the MAX level mark with distilled water.

	Above 15°C	Below 15°C
Fully-charged	*1.210 to 1.230*	*1.270 to 1.290*
70% charged	*1.170 to 1.190*	*1.230 to 1.250*
Discharged	*1.050 to 1.070*	*1.110 to 1.130*

2 If the battery condition is suspect, first check the specific gravity of electrolyte in each cell. A variation of 0.040 or more between any cells indicates loss of electrolyte or deterioration of the internal plates.

3 If the specific gravity variation is 0.040 or more, the battery should be renewed. If the cell variation is satisfactory but the battery is discharged, it should be recharged as described later in this Section.

Maintenance-free battery

4 In cases where a sealed for life maintenance-free battery is fitted, topping-up and testing of the electrolyte in each cell is not possible. The condition of the battery can therefore only be tested using a battery condition indicator or a voltmeter.

5 Certain models may be fitted with a maintenance-free battery with a built-in charge condition indicator. The indicator is located in the top of the battery casing, and indicates the condition of the battery from its colour. If the indicator shows green, then the battery is in a good state of charge. If the indicator turns darker, eventually to black, then the battery requires charging, as described later in this Section. If the indicator shows clear/yellow, then the electrolyte level in the battery is too low to allow further use, and the battery should be renewed. **Do not** attempt to charge, load or jump start a battery when the indicator shows clear/yellow.

All battery types

6 If testing the battery using a voltmeter, connect the voltmeter across the battery and note the voltage. The test is only accurate if the battery has not been subjected to any kind of charge for the previous six hours. If this is not the case, switch on the headlights for 30 seconds, then wait four to five minutes before testing the battery after switching off the headlights. All other electrical circuits must be switched off, so check that the doors and tailgate are fully shut when making the test.

7 If the voltage reading is less than 12.2 volts, then the battery is discharged, whilst a reading of 12.2 to 12.4 volts indicates a partially discharged condition. The battery should be recharged as described later in this Section.

Charging

Note: *The following is intended as a guide only. Always refer to the manufacturer's recommendations (often printed on a label attached to the battery) before charging a battery.*

8 If the battery is to be recharged, we recommend that you use a low current battery charger. Note that it is **not** necessary to disconnect the battery leads when using a low current battery charger. If the battery is disconnected (eg, if it is to be removed and recharged on the bench), note that certain 'learned' values will be lost from the engine management ECM memory, requiring the car to be driven over a short distance after refitting the battery. Also, when the battery is reconnected, the warning lights for the ESP and electro-mechanical steering will light up and stay on. They will extinguish if you drive briefly in a straight line at a speed of 9 to 13 mph.

Standard and low maintenance battery

9 Charge the battery at a rate equivalent to 10% of the battery capacity (eg, for a 45 Ah battery charge at 4.5 A) and continue to charge the battery at this rate until no further rise in specific gravity is noted over a four-hour period.

10 Alternatively, a trickle charger charging at the rate of 1.5 amps can safely be used overnight.

11 Specially rapid boost charges, which are claimed to restore the power of the battery in 1 to 2 hours, are not recommended, as they can cause serious damage to the battery plates through overheating.

12 While charging the battery, note that the temperature of the electrolyte should never exceed 38°C.

Maintenance-free battery

13 This battery type takes considerably longer to fully recharge than the standard type, the time taken being dependent on the extent of discharge, but it can take anything up to three days.

14 The battery should be removed from the car, and a constant voltage type charger is required, to be set, when connected, to 13.9 to 14.9 volts with a charger current below 25 amps. Using this method, the battery should be useable within three hours, giving a voltage reading of 12.5 volts, but this is for a partially-discharged battery and, as mentioned, full charging can take far longer.

15 If the battery is to be charged from a fully discharged state (condition reading less than 12.2 volts), have it recharged by your local automotive electrician, as the charge rate is higher and constant supervision during charging is necessary.

3 Battery – removal and refitting

Note: *If the vehicle has a security-coded radio, make sure that you have the code number before disconnecting the battery. If necessary, a 'code-saver' or 'memory-saver' can be used to preserve the radio code and any other relevant memory values whilst the battery is disconnected (see 'Disconnecting the battery' in the Reference Section).*

Removal

1 The battery is located inside the vehicle under the driver's side footwell, where an insulator cover and carpet are fitted over the top.

2 Release the locking clip, lift out the carpet access panel cover and foam insulator **(see illustrations)**.

3 Loosen the clamp nut and disconnect the

3.2a Release the locking clip . . .

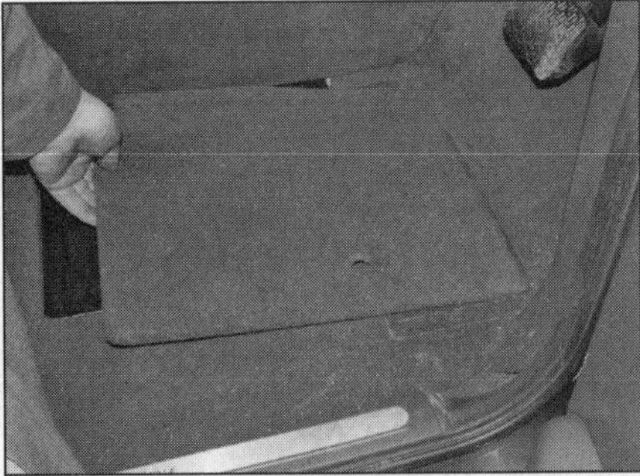

3.2b . . . lift the carpet access panel . . .

3.2c . . . and remove the foam insulator

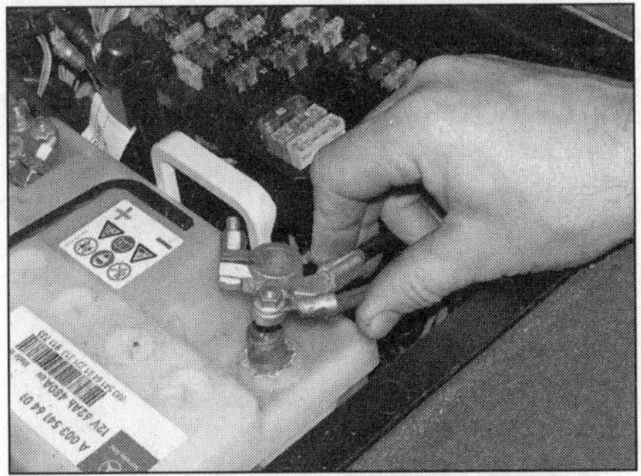

3.3 Disconnect the battery terminal

3.4a Undo the two bolts – arrowed . . .

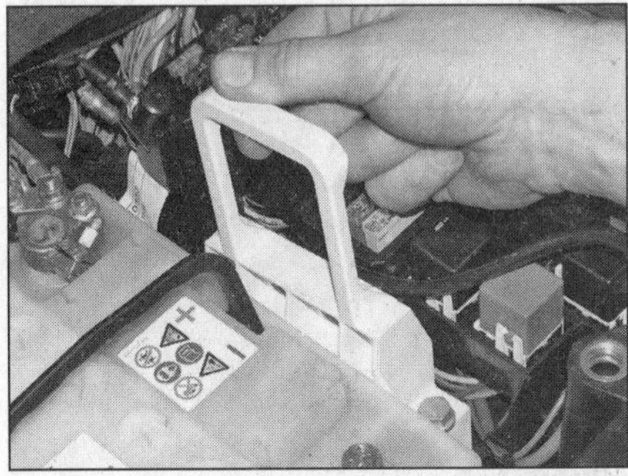

3.4b . . . and remove the retaining bracket

battery negative (-) then positive (+) leads from the terminals **(see illustration).**

4 Unscrew the retaining bolts and pull out the battery retaining bracket **(see illustrations).**

5 Then battery can then be lifted out from the plastic insulator box, disconnect the vent pipe from the battery as it is being removed **(see illustration)**.

Refitting

6 Refit the battery by following the removal procedure in reverse. Tighten the clamp bolt securely and make sure the vent pipe is secure.

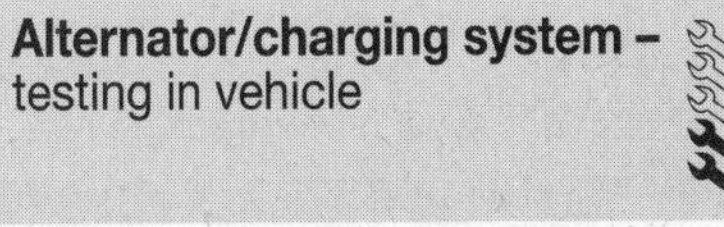

4 Alternator/charging system – testing in vehicle

Note: *Refer to Section 1 of this Chapter before starting work.*

1 If the charge warning light fails to illuminate when the ignition is switched on, first check the alternator wiring connections for security. If the light still fails to illuminate, check the continuity of the warning light feed wire from the alternator to the bulbholder. If all is satisfactory, the alternator is at fault and should be renewed or taken to an auto-electrician for testing and repair.

2 Similarly, if the charge warning light comes on with the ignition, but is then slow to go out when the engine is started, this may indicate an impending alternator problem. Check all the items listed in the preceding paragraph, and refer to an auto-electrical specialist if no obvious faults are found.

3 If the charge warning light illuminates when the engine is running, stop the engine and check that the auxiliary drivebelt is not broken (see Chapter 1A or 1B) and that the alternator connections are secure. If all is so far satisfactory, check the alternator brushes and slip-rings as described in Section 6. If the fault persists, the alternator should be renewed, or taken to an auto-electrician for testing and repair.

4 If the alternator output is suspect even though the warning light functions correctly, the regulated voltage may be checked as follows.

5 Connect a voltmeter across the battery terminals, and start the engine.

6 Increase the engine speed until the voltmeter reading remains steady; the reading should be approximately 12 to 13 volts, and no more than 14 volts.

7 Switch on as many electrical accessories (eg, the headlights, heated rear window and heater blower) as possible, and check that the alternator maintains the regulated voltage at around 13 to 14 volts.

3.5 Vent pipe (arrowed) on side of battery

8 If the regulated voltage is not as stated, this may be due to worn brushes, weak brush springs, a faulty voltage regulator, a faulty diode, a severed phase winding or worn or damaged slip-rings. The brushes and slip-rings may be checked (see Section 6), but if the fault persists, the alternator should be renewed or taken to an auto-electrician.

5 Alternator – removal and refitting

Removal

1 Disconnect the battery negative lead and position it away from the terminal. **Note:** *Before disconnecting the battery, refer to 'Disconnecting the battery' in the reference section at the rear of this manual.*

2 Remove the auxiliary drivebelt from the alternator pulley (see Chapter 1A or 1B). Mark the drivebelt for direction to ensure it is refitted in the same position.

3 Jack up the front of the car, and support it on an axle stand (see *Jacking and vehicle support*).

4 Undo the mounting bolts and move the air conditioning compressor to one side, without disconnecting the refrigerant pipes. Fasten the compressor to one side using cable ties **(see illustrations)**.

5.4a Undo the retaining bolts – arrowed . . .

5.4b . . . and hold the compressor to one side with cable ties – arrows

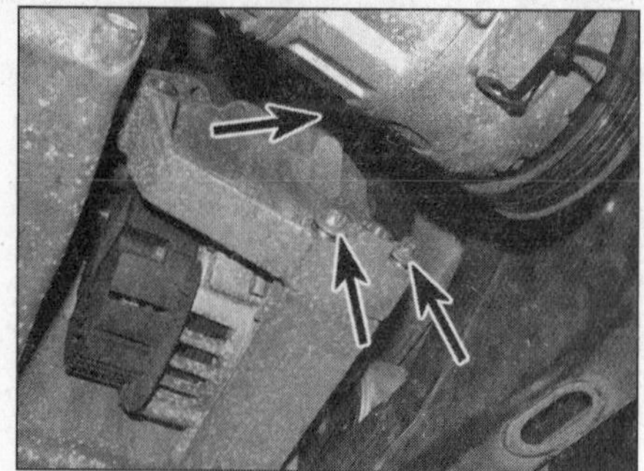

5.5a Undo the mounting bolts – arrowed . . .

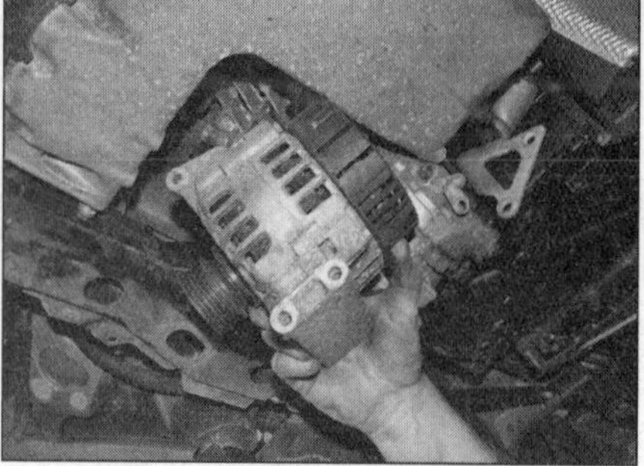

5.5b . . . and remove the alternator

6.3 Remove the rear cover

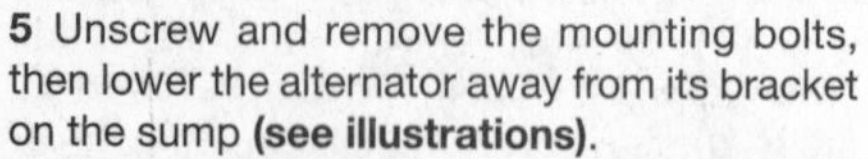

5 Unscrew and remove the mounting bolts, then lower the alternator away from its bracket on the sump **(see illustrations)**.

6 While supporting the alternator, disconnect the wiring connectors from the top of the alternator.

Refitting

7 Refitting is a reversal of removal. Refer to Chapter 1A or 1B as applicable for details of refitting and tensioning the auxiliary drivebelt. Tighten the alternator mounting bolts to the specified torque.

6 Alternator – brush holder/regulator module renewal

Removal

1 Remove the alternator, as described in Section 5.

2 Place the alternator on a clean work surface, with the pulley facing down.

3 Undo the three retaining nuts, and lift away the outer plastic cover **(see illustration)**.

4 Unscrew the three securing bolts, and remove the voltage regulator **(see illustration)**.

Inspection

5 Check the condition of the carbon brushes if they are worn, renew the regulator module.

6 Clean and inspect the surfaces of the slip-rings **(see illustration)** at the end of the alternator shaft. If they are excessively worn, or damaged, the alternator must be renewed.

6.4 Undo the retaining bolts – arrowed

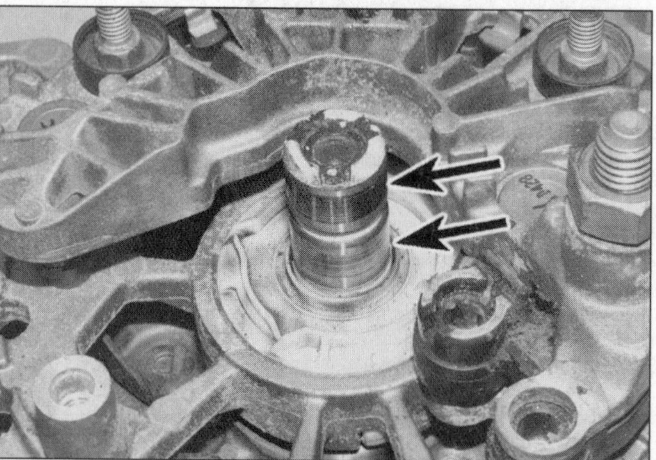

6.6 Clean and inspect the surfaces of the slip-rings

6.7a Carefully drill a hole in the cover

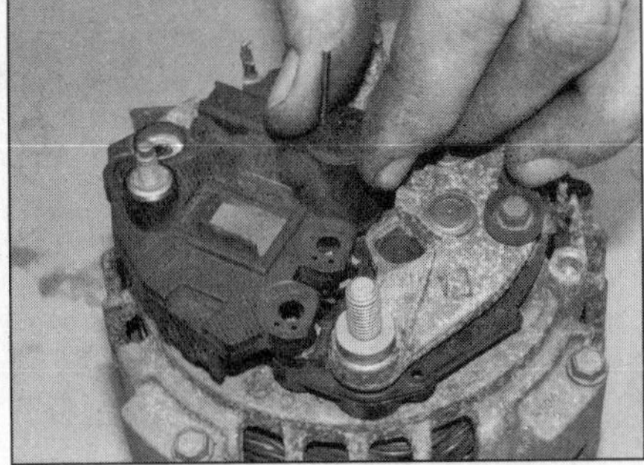

6.7b Use the drill bit to hold back the brushes . . .

6.7c . . . and slide the drill out when fitting regulator

Refitting

7 Drill a small hole in the top of the regulator housing, taking care not to damage the carbon brushes. Insert a thin rod (drill bit) into the hole to depress the carbon brushes into the housing, then refit the voltage regulator and tighten the bolts and nuts securely **(see illustrations)**. Refit the outer plastic cover. On completion, refer to Section 5 and refit the alternator.

7 Starting system – testing

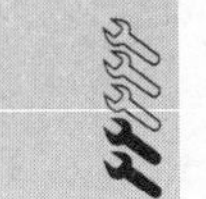

Note: *Refer to Section 1 of this Chapter before starting work.*

1 If the starter motor fails to operate when the ignition key is turned to the appropriate position, the following possible causes may be to blame:

a) The battery is faulty.
b) The electrical connections between the switch, solenoid, battery and starter motor are somewhere failing to pass the necessary current from the battery through the starter to earth.
c) The solenoid is faulty.
d) The starter motor is mechanically or electrically defective.

2 To check the battery, switch on the headlights. If they dim after a few seconds, this indicates that the battery is discharged – recharge (see Section 2) or renew the battery. If the headlights glow brightly, operate the ignition switch and observe the lights. If they dim, then this indicates that current is reaching the starter motor; therefore the fault must lie in the starter motor. If the lights continue to glow brightly (and no clicking sound can be heard from the starter motor solenoid), this indicates that there is a fault in the circuit or solenoid – see following paragraphs. If the starter motor turns slowly when operated, but the battery is in good condition, then this indicates that either the starter motor is faulty, or there is considerable resistance somewhere in the circuit.

3 If a fault in the circuit is suspected, disconnect the battery leads (including the earth connection to the body), the starter/solenoid wiring and the engine/transmission earth strap. **Note:** *Before disconnecting the battery, refer to 'Disconnecting the battery' in the Reference section at the rear of this manual.* Thoroughly clean the connections, and reconnect the leads and wiring, then use a voltmeter or test light to check that full battery voltage is available at the battery positive lead connection to the solenoid, and that the earth is sound.

4 If the battery and all connections are in good condition, check the circuit by disconnecting the wire from the solenoid blade terminal. Connect a voltmeter or test light between the wire end and a good earth (such as the battery negative terminal), and check that the wire is live when the ignition switch is turned to the start position. If it is, then the circuit is sound – if not the circuit wiring can be checked as described in Chapter 12.

5 The solenoid contacts can be checked by connecting a voltmeter or test light between the battery positive feed connection on the starter side of the solenoid, and earth. When the ignition switch is turned to the start position, there should be a reading or lighted bulb, as applicable. If there is no reading or lighted bulb, the solenoid is faulty and should be renewed.

6 If the circuit and solenoid are proved sound, the fault must lie in the starter motor. It may be possible to have the starter motor overhauled by a specialist, but check on the availability and cost of spares before proceeding, as it may prove more economical to obtain a new or exchange motor.

8 Starter motor – removal and refitting

Note: *To remove the starter motor, the engine will need to be lowered, as access to the starter motor is not possible while it is in position.*

Removal

1 Disconnect the battery negative lead **Note:** *Before disconnecting the battery, refer to 'Disconnecting the battery' in the Reference section at the rear of this manual.*

2 Apply the handbrake, then jack up the front of the vehicle and support it on axle stands (see *Jacking and vehicle support*). Remove the engine undertray.

3 Lower the engine on the front subframe as described in Chapter 2C.

4 Remove the plastic cap(s) then unscrew the nuts and disconnect the wiring connectors from the rear of the starter solenoid.

5 Unscrew and remove the two starter motor retaining bolts **(see illustration)**.

6 Remove the starter motor out of the bellhousing aperture and from the engine **(see illustration)**.

Refitting

7 Refit the starter motor by following the removal procedure in reverse. Tighten the mounting bolts to the specified torque.

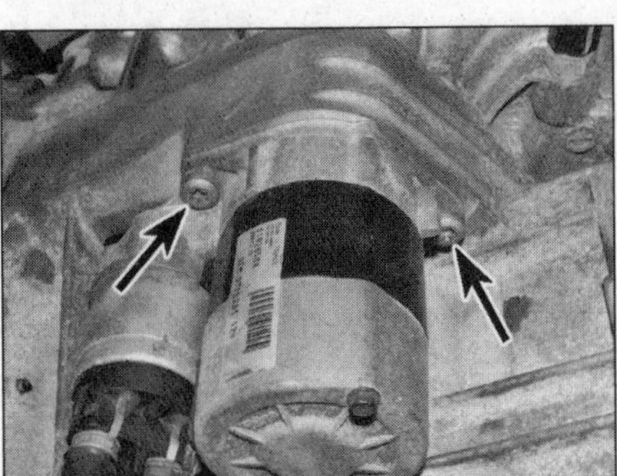

8.5 Undo the two retaining bolts – arrowed . . .

8.6 . . . and remove the starter motor

9 Starter motor – testing and overhaul

If the starter motor is thought to be defective, it should be removed from the vehicle and taken to an auto-electrician for assessment. In the majority of cases, new starter motor brushes can be fitted at a reasonable cost. However, check the cost of repairs first as it may prove more economical to purchase a new or exchange motor.

Chapter 5 Part B: Ignition system – petrol engines

Contents

Degrees of difficulty

Easy, suitable for novice with little experience

Fairly easy, suitable for beginner with some experience

Fairly difficult, suitable for competent DIY mechanic

Difficult, suitable for experienced DIY mechanic

Very difficult, suitable for expert DIY or professional

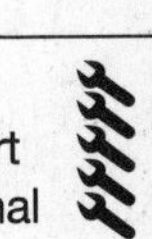

Specifications

General

System type	Bosch MSM, distributorless engine management system
Firing order	1-3-4-2 (No 1 cylinder at the timing chain end of the engine)

Ignition timing

Checking	The ignition timing is constantly altered by the engine management Electronic Control Module (ECM), and cannot be checked without specialist equipment

Ignition coil

Type	Ignition coil module

Spark plugs

See Chapter 1A Specifications

Torque wrench settings

	Nm	lbf ft
Ignition coil module mounting bolts	20	15
Knock sensor mounting bolt	20	15
Spark plugs	25	18

1 General information

The Bosch MSM system is a self-contained engine management system, which control both the fuel injection and ignition. This Chapter deals with the ignition system components only – refer to Chapter 4A for details of the fuel system components.

The ignition system fitted is of the 'distributorless' (DIS – Distributorless Ignition System) or 'static' type (there are no moving parts). Despite the many different system names and designations, as far as the ignition system fitted to the Mercedes-Benz is concerned, it has one ignition coil module with four individual coils built into it.

The ignition timing cannot be adjusted by conventional means, and the advance and retard functions are carried out by the Electronic Control Module (ECM).

The ignition system consists of the spark plugs, electronic ignition coil module, camshaft position sensor, crankshaft position sensor and the ECM together with its associated sensors and wiring.

The component layout varies slightly, but the basic operation is the same for all models: the ECM supplies a voltage to the input stage of the ignition coil, which causes the primary windings in the coil to be energised. The supply voltage is periodically interrupted by the ECM and this results in the collapse of primary magnetic field, which then induces a much larger voltage in the secondary coil, called the HT voltage. This voltage is directed to the spark plug in the cylinder currently on its ignition stroke. The spark plug electrodes form a gap small enough for the HT voltage to arc across, and the resulting spark ignites the fuel/air mixture in the cylinder. The timing of this sequence of events is critical, and is regulated solely by the ECM.

The ECM calculates and controls the ignition timing primarily according to engine speed, crankshaft position, camshaft position, and inlet airflow rate information, received from sensors mounted on and around the engine. Other parameters that affect ignition timing are throttle position and rate of opening, intake air temperature, coolant temperature and engine knock, monitored by sensors mounted on the engine. Note that most of these sensors have a dual role, in that the information they provide is equally useful in determining the fuelling requirements as in deciding the optimum ignition or firing point – therefore, removal of some of the sensors mentioned below is described in Chapter 4A.

The ECM computes engine speed and crankshaft position from toothed impulse ring attached to the engine crankshaft, with an engine speed sensor whose inductive head runs just above ring. As the crankshaft rotates, the ring 'teeth' pass the engine speed sensor, which transmits a pulse to the ECM every time a tooth passes it. At the top dead centre (TDC) position, there is one missing tooth in the ring periphery, which results in a longer pause between signals from the sensor. The ECM recognises the absence of a pulse from the engine speed sensor at this point, and uses it to establish the TDC position for No 1 piston. The time interval between pulses, and the location of the missing pulse, allow the ECM to accurately determine the position of the crankshaft and its speed. The camshaft position sensor enhances this information by detecting whether a particular piston is on an inlet or an exhaust cycle.

Information on engine load is supplied to the ECM by the inlet manifold pressure sensor, and from the throttle position sensor. The engine load is determined by computation based on the quantity of air being drawn into the engine. Further engine load information is sent to the ECM from the knock sensor. These sensors are sensitive to vibration, and detect the knocking, which occurs when the engine starts to 'pink' (pre-ignite). If pre-ignition occurs, the ECM retards the ignition timing of the cylinder that is pre-igniting in steps until the pre-ignition ceases. The ECM then advances the ignition timing of that cylinder in steps until it is restored to normal, or until pre-ignition occurs again.

Sensors monitoring coolant temperature, throttle position, camshaft position, roadspeed, and (where applicable) automatic transmission gear position and air conditioning system operation provide additional input signals to the ECM on vehicle operating conditions. From all this constantly changing data, the ECM selects, and if necessary modifies, a particular ignition advance setting from a map of ignition characteristics stored in its memory.

The ECM also uses the ignition timing to finely adjust the engine idle speed, in response to signals from the air conditioning switch (to prevent stalling), or if the alternator output voltage falls too low.

In the event of a fault in the system due to loss of a signal from one of the sensors, the ECM reverts to an emergency ('limp-home') program. This will allow the car to be driven, although engine operation and performance will be limited. A warning light on the instrument panel will illuminate if the fault is likely to cause an increase in harmful exhaust emissions.

It should be noted that comprehensive fault diagnosis of all the engine management systems described in this Chapter is only possible with dedicated electronic test equipment. In the event of a sensor failing or other fault occurring, a fault code will be stored in the ECM's fault log, which can only be extracted from the ECM using a dedicated fault code reader. A Mercedes-Benz dealer will obviously have such a reader, but they are also available from other suppliers. It is unlikely to be cost-effective for the private owner to purchase a fault code reader, but a well-equipped local garage or auto-electrical specialist will have one. Once the fault has been identified, the removal/refitting sequences detailed in the following Sections will then allow the appropriate component(s) to be renewed as required.

Ignition coil

The single coil unit fitted operates on the 'wasted spark' principle; the coil unit in fact contains four separate coils – one for each cylinder. Two coils produces an HT voltage at both outputs every time its primary coil voltage is interrupted – ie, cylinders 1 and 4 always 'fire' together, then 2 and 3 'fire' together. When this happens, one of the two cylinders concerned will be on the compression stroke (and will ignite the fuel/air mixture), while the other one is on the exhaust stroke – because the spark on the exhaust stroke has no effect, it is effectively wasted, hence the term 'wasted spark'. The ignition spark on the exhaust stroke requires very little energy, so the main energy is available for the ignition spark on the compression stroke.

2 Ignition system – testing

Warning: Voltages produced by an electronic ignition system are considerably higher than those produced by conventional ignition systems. Extreme care must be taken when working on the system with the ignition switched on; it is possible to get a substantial electric shock from a vehicle's ignition system. Persons with cardiac pacemaker devices should keep well clear of the ignition circuits, components and test equipment. Always switch off the ignition before disconnecting or connecting any component and when using a multimeter to check resistances.

1 If a fault appears in the engine management (fuel injection/ignition) system which is thought to ignition related, first ensure that the fault is not due to a poor electrical connection or poor maintenance; ie, check that the air cleaner filter element is clean, the spark plugs are in good condition and correctly gapped, that the engine breather hoses are clear and undamaged, referring to Chapter 1A for further information. If the engine is running very roughly, check the compression pressures as described in Chapters 2A.

2 If these checks fail to reveal the cause of the problem, the vehicle should be taken to a Mercedes-Benz dealer for testing. A diagnostic connector is incorporated in the engine management circuit into which a special electronic diagnostic tester can be plugged (see Chapter 4A). The tester will locate the fault quickly and simply, alleviating the need to test all the system components individually, which is a time-consuming operation that carries a high risk of damaging the ECM.

3 The only ignition system checks which can be carried out by the home mechanic are those described in Chapter 1A, relating to the spark plugs. If necessary, the system wiring and wiring connectors can be checked as described in Chapter 12 ensuring that the ECM wiring connector(s) have first been disconnected.

3 Ignition coil module – removal and refitting

Removal

1 On all models, the ignition coil module is mounted on the front of the engine.

2 Make sure the ignition is switched off (take out the key). To make access easier remove the air intake hose from the front crossmember to the idle speed actuator.

3 Unclip the protective cover from the top of the ignition coil module **(see illustration)**.

4 Disconnect the wiring connector from the end of the ignition coil module **(see illustration)**.

5 Undo the retaining bolt from the mounting bracket on the wiring connection end of the ignition coil module.

6 Undo the two retaining bolts and carefully pull the ignition coil module from the spark plugs **(see illustrations)**. Mercedes-Benz technicians use a special tool/puller to withdraw the ignition coil module evenly from the top of the spark plugs.

Refitting

7 Refitting is a reversal of the relevant removal procedure. Tighten the ignition coil module mounting bolts to the specified torque setting.

4 Ignition timing – checking and adjusting

The ignition timing is under the control of the engine management system ECM and is not manually adjustable without access to dedicated electronic test equipment. A basic setting cannot be quoted because the ignition timing is constantly being altered to control engine idle speed (see Section 1 for details).

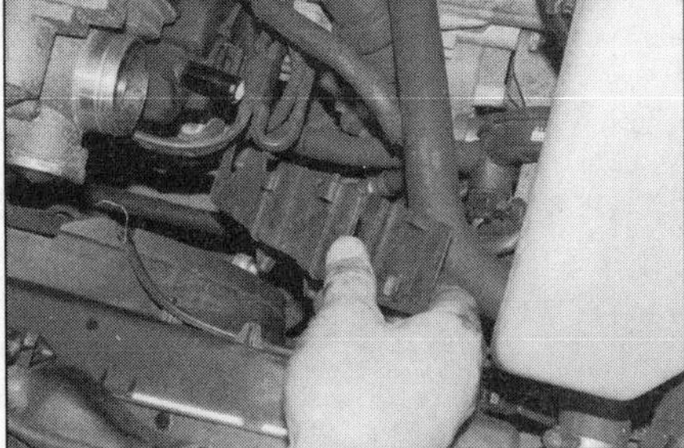

3.3 Unclip the cover from the ignition coil module

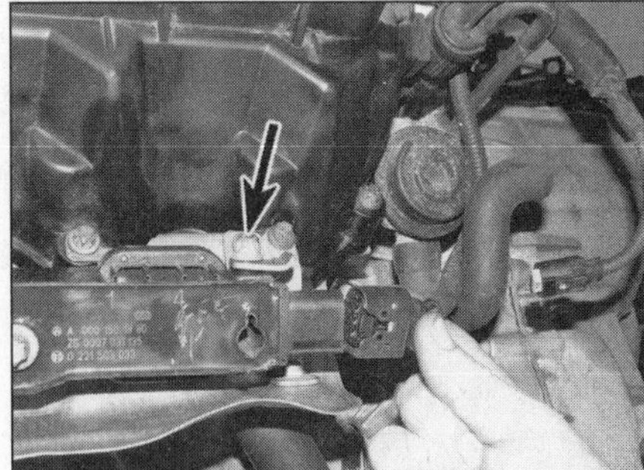

3.4 Disconnect the wiring connector and undo the bolt – arrowed

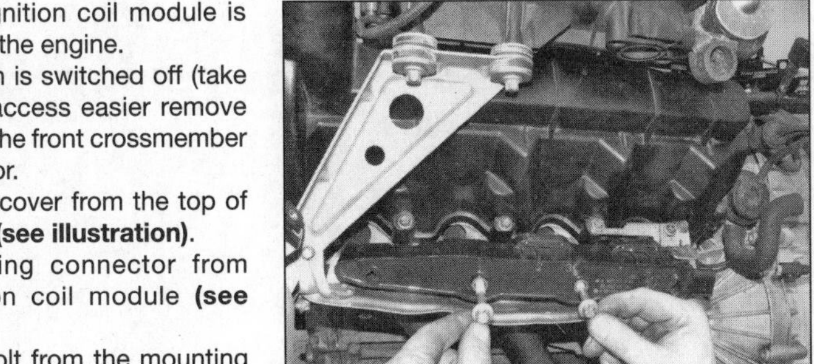

3.6a Remove the two securing bolts . . .

3.6b . . . and withdraw the coil module

5 Knock sensor – removal and refitting

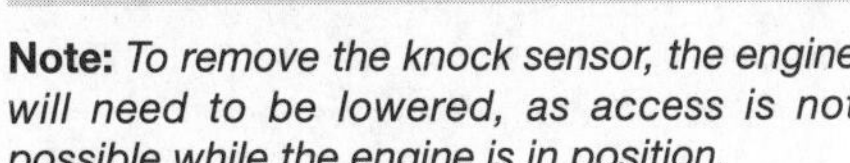

Note: *To remove the knock sensor, the engine will need to be lowered, as access is not possible while the engine is in position.*

Removal

1 The knock sensor is located on the rear lower side of the cylinder block.

2 Disconnect the battery negative lead. **Note:** *Before disconnecting the battery, refer to 'Disconnecting the battery' in the Reference section at the rear of this manual.*

3 Apply the handbrake, then jack up the front of the vehicle and support it on axle stands (see *Jacking and vehicle support*). Remove the engine undertray.

4 Lower the engine on the front subframe as described in Chapter 2C.

5 Disconnect the wiring connector from the sensor **(see illustration)**.

6 Slacken and remove the dipstick tube upper and lower mounting bolts, and twist the dipstick tube around to access the knock sensor mounting bolt **(see illustration)**.

7 Unscrew the mounting bolt and remove the sensor from the cylinder block **(see illustration)**.

Refitting

8 Refitting is the reverse of removal. Ensure the mating surfaces of the sensor and cylinder block are clean and dry and ensure the mounting bolt is tightened to the specified torque to ensure correct operation. Refer to Chapter 2C for refitting of the engine/subframe.

5.5 Disconnect the wiring connector

5.6 Dipstick tube lower mounting bolt – arrowed

5.7 Undo the retaining bolt and remove the sensor

Chapter 5 Part C:
Preheating system – diesel engines

Contents

Section number

Degrees of difficulty

Easy, suitable for novice with little experience 	**Fairly easy,** suitable for beginner with some experience 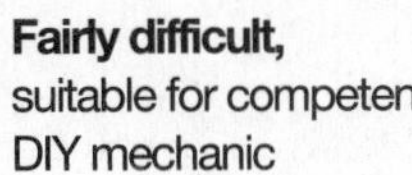	**Fairly difficult,** suitable for competent DIY mechanic	**Difficult,** suitable for experienced DIY mechanic 	**Very difficult,** suitable for expert DIY or professional 

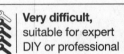

Specifications

Torque wrench setting	Nm	lbf ft
Glow plug to cylinder head	15	11

1 General information

To assist cold starting, diesel engine models are fitted with a preheating system, which consists of four glow plugs, a glow plug control unit, a facia-mounted warning light and the associated electrical wiring.

The glow plugs are miniature electric heating elements, encapsulated in a metal case with a probe at one end and electrical connection at the other. Each inlet tract has a glow plug threaded into it, which is positioned directly in line with the incoming spray of fuel. When the glow plug is energised, the fuel passing over it is heated, allowing its optimum combustion temperature to be achieved more readily in the combustion chamber.

The duration of the preheating period is governed by the ECM, which monitors the temperature of the engine through the coolant temperature sensor and alters the preheating time to suit the conditions.

A facia-mounted warning light informs the driver that preheating is taking place. The light extinguishes when sufficient preheating has taken place to allow the engine to be started, but power will still be supplied to the glow plugs for a further period until the engine is started. If no attempt is made to start the engine, the power supply to the glow plugs is switched off to prevent battery drain and glow plug burn-out. If the warning light flashes, or comes on during normal driving, this indicates a fault with the diesel engine management system, which should be investigated by a Mercedes-Benz dealer as soon as possible.

After the engine has been started, the glow plugs continue to operate for a further period of time. This helps to improve fuel combustion whilst the engine is warming-up, resulting in quieter, smoother running and reduced exhaust emissions.

2 Glow plugs – testing, removal and refitting

Warning: Under no circumstances should the glow plugs be tested outside the engine. A correctly functioning glow plug will become red-hot in a very short time. This fact should also be borne in mind when removing the glow plugs if they have recently been in use.

Testing

1 If the system malfunctions, testing is ultimately by substitution of known good units, but some preliminary checks may be made as described in the following paragraphs.

2 Before testing the system, check that the battery voltage is at least 11.5 volts, using a multimeter. Switch off the ignition.

3 If improved access is required, jack up the front of the vehicle, and support it securely on axle stands (see *Jacking and vehicle support*). Remove the engine undertrays as access from under the vehicle may be easier.

4 Disconnect the wiring plug from the coolant temperature sender at the left-hand rear of the engine (left as seen from the driver's seat) – refer to Chapter 3. Disconnecting the sender in this way simulates a cold engine, which is a requirement for the glow plug system to activate.

5 Disconnect the wiring connector from the most convenient glow plug, and connect a suitable multimeter between the wiring connector and a good earth.

6 Have an assistant switch on the ignition for approximately 20 seconds.

7 Battery voltage should be displayed – note that the voltage will drop to zero when the preheating period ends.

8 If no supply voltage can be detected at the glow plug, then either the glow plug control unit (see Section 3) or the supply wiring must be faulty. Also check that the glow plug fuse or fusible link (see Chapter 12) has not blown – if it has, this may indicate a serious wiring fault; consult a Mercedes-Benz dealer for advice.

9 To locate a faulty glow plug, first disconnect the battery negative cable and position it away from the terminal.

2.17a Disconnect the wiring connector . . .

2.17b . . . and undo the retaining nut – arrowed

2.18 Removing glow plug four (glow plug three – arrowed)

10 Disconnect the wiring connector from the glow plug terminal; note the wiring connectors go to numbers 1 and 3 cylinders. There are metal strips (busbars) which link to cylinders 2 and 4, these will need to be removed from across the top of the glow plugs.

11 Measure the electrical resistance between the glow plug terminal and the engine earth, check each one in turn to see if there are different readings given. At the time of writing, no resistance figures where given – as a guide, a resistance of more than a few ohms indicates that the plug is defective.

12 If an ammeter is available, connect it between the glow plug and its wiring connector, and measure the steady-state current consumption (ignore the initial current surge, which will be about 50% higher). As a guide, high current consumption (or no current draw at all) indicates a faulty glow plug.

13 As a final check, remove the glow plugs and inspect them visually, as described in the following paragraph.

14 Inspect each glow plug for physical damage. Burnt or eroded glow plug tips can be caused by a bad injector spray pattern. Have the injectors checked if this sort of damage is found.

Removal

Note: *Refer to the Warning at the start of this Section before proceeding.*

15 Disconnect the battery negative (earth) lead (see *Disconnecting the battery*).

16 Jack up the front of the vehicle, and support it securely on axle stands (see *Jacking and vehicle support*). Remove the engine undertrays as access from under the vehicle may be easier.

17 Disconnect the wiring connectors from the glow plugs 1 and 3, then undo the securing nuts and remove the metal straps (busbars) from glow plugs 2 and 4. Note their fitted position, to make refitting easier **(see illustrations)**.

18 Unscrew and remove the glow plugs **(see illustration)**, access to the glow plugs 2 and 3 are through the webs on the exhaust manifold.

Refitting

19 Refitting is a reversal of removal, but tighten the glow plugs to the specified torque.

3 Glow plug control unit – removal and refitting

Caution: Always wait at least 30 seconds after switching off the ignition before disconnecting the wiring from the any electronic control unit. When the wiring is disconnected, all the learned values are erased, although any contents of the fault memory are retained. After reconnecting the wiring, the basic settings may need to be reinstated by a Mercedes-Benz dealer using a special test instrument.

1 Disconnect the battery negative lead and position it away from the terminal. **Note:** *Refer to 'Disconnecting the battery' at the rear of this manual first.*

2 The glow plug control unit is located behind a plastic panel to the left-hand rear of the engine compartment bulkhead.

3 Undo the retaining screws and remove the plastic cover **(see illustration)**.

4 The glow plug control unit is the lower control unit out of the three control units behind the plastic cover. If required, remove the other electronic control modules as described in Chapter 4A **(see illustration)**.

5 Disconnect the two wiring block connectors from the glow plug control unit and then undo the securing nut and disconnect the supply cable **(see illustrations)**.

6 With the wiring disconnected, withdraw the control unit from its location in the bulkhead.

7 Refitting is a reversal of removal. Noting the comments made in the *Caution* above – the control unit may need to be set at a Mercedes-Benz dealer.

3.3 Removing the control unit cover

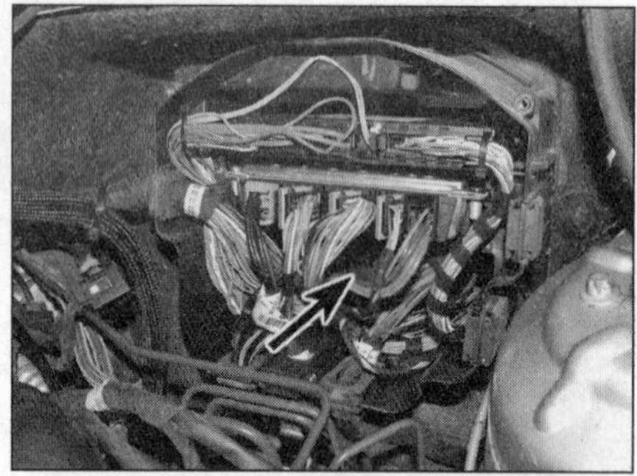
3.4 Glow plug control unit location – arrowed

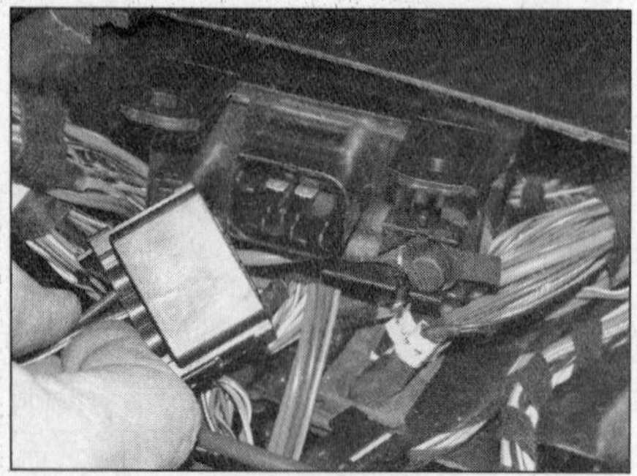
3.5a Disconnect the wiring connectors . . .

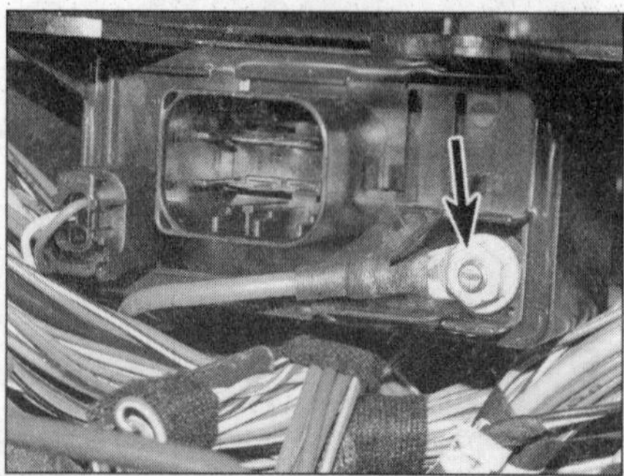
3.5b . . . and the securing nut – arrowed

Chapter 6
Clutch

Contents

Degrees of difficulty

Easy, suitable for novice with little experience 	**Fairly easy,** suitable for beginner with some experience 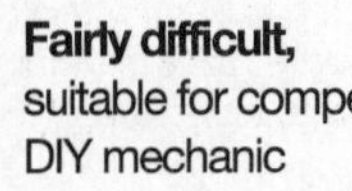	**Fairly difficult,** suitable for competent DIY mechanic	**Difficult,** suitable for experienced DIY mechanic	**Very difficult,** suitable for expert DIY or professional 

Specifications

General

Type	Single dry plate, diaphragm spring
Operation	Hydraulic with master and slave cylinders

Torque wrench settings	**Nm**	**lbf ft**
Clutch master cylinder-to-pedal bracket nut:		
Up to 31/10/2000	15	11
From 01/11/2000	8	6
Clutch pressure plate-to-flywheel bolts:*		
Single-piece flywheel	25	18
Two-piece flywheel (Dual Mass)	10	7
Clutch slave cylinder/release bearing bolts	10	7

** Use new bolts/nuts.*

1 General information

The clutch is of single dry plate type, incorporating a diaphragm spring pressure plate, and is hydraulically-operated.

The pressure plate is bolted to the rear face of the flywheel, and the friction disc is located between the pressure plate and the flywheel friction surface. The friction disc hub is splined to the transmission input shaft and is free to slide along the splines. Friction lining material is riveted to each side of the disc, and the disc hub incorporates cushioning springs to absorb transmission shocks and ensure a smooth take-up of drive.

When the clutch pedal is depressed, the slave cylinder pushrod moves the release lever forwards. The release bearing is forced onto the pressure plate diaphragm spring fingers. As the centre of the diaphragm spring is pushed in, the outer part of the spring moves out and releases the pressure plate from the friction disc. Drive then ceases to be transmitted to the transmission.

When the clutch pedal is released, the diaphragm spring forces the pressure plate into contact with the linings on the friction disc, and at the same time pushes the disc slightly forward along the input shaft splines into engagement with the flywheel. The friction disc is now firmly sandwiched between the pressure plate and flywheel. This causes drive to be taken up.

As the linings wear on the friction disc, the pressure plate rest position moves closer to

2.3 Clutch slave cylinder bleed screw – arrowed

the flywheel resulting in the 'rest' position of the diaphragm spring fingers being raised. The hydraulic system requires no adjustment since the quantity of hydraulic fluid in the circuit automatically compensates for wear every time the clutch pedal is operated.

On some models, there is an automatic clutch operating system (ACS or AKS) fitted. This system operates in the same way as the standard clutch, except it has additional parts including an automatic control module, a central control unit and various sensors fitted on the transmission and in front of the gear lever inside the vehicle. When a gear is selected, the sensors transmit an electrical signal to the clutch control module and then the central control unit then controls the remaining clutch operation. The automatic control module is part of the central control unit, and is located behind the inner wheel arch liner, on the left-hand side front of the vehicle. This system is complex and should only be attempted by your local Mercedes-Benz dealer, as it will need to be checked with diagnostic equipment.

2 Hydraulic system – bleeding

Warning: Hydraulic fluid is poisonous; thoroughly wash off spills from bare skin without delay. Seek immediate medical advice if any fluid is swallowed or gets into the eyes. Certain types of hydraulic fluid are inflammable and may ignite when brought into contact with hot components. Hydraulic fluid is also an effective paint stripper. If spillage occurs onto painted bodywork or fittings, it should be washed off immediately, using copious quantities of cold water. It is also hygroscopic (ie, it can absorb moisture from the air) which then renders it useless. Old fluid may have suffered contamination, and should never be re-used. When topping-up or renewing the fluid, always use the recommended grade, and ensure that it comes from a freshly-opened sealed container.

Note: *It is recommended that pressure-bleeding equipment be used for this operation. DO NOT use a system that pressure-fills the system while at the same time it is being pressure bled.*

1 If any part of the hydraulic system is dismantled, or if air has accidentally entered the system, the system will need to be bled. The presence of air is characterised by the pedal having a spongy feel and it results in difficulty in changing gear.

2 The design of the clutch hydraulic system does not allow bleeding to be carried out using the conventional method of pumping the clutch pedal. In order to remove all air present in the system, it is necessary to use pressure bleeding equipment. This is available from auto accessory shops at relatively low cost.

3 The pressure bleeding equipment should be connected to the brake/clutch hydraulic fluid reservoir in accordance with the manufacturer's instructions. The system is bled through the bleed screw of the clutch slave cylinder, which is located on the rear of the transmission housing **(see illustration)**. Access is best achieved by jacking up the front of the vehicle, and supporting it safely on axle stands (see *Jacking and vehicle support*). Remove the undertray for access to the transmission.

4 Bleed the system until the fluid being ejected is free from air bubbles. Close the bleed screw, then disconnect and remove the bleeding equipment.

5 Check the operation of the clutch to see that it is satisfactory. If air still remains in the system, repeat the bleeding operation.

6 Discard any fluid, which is bled from the system, even if it looks clean. Hydraulic fluid absorbs water and its re-use can cause internal corrosion of the master and slave cylinders, leading to excessive wear and failure of the seals.

7 Finally, road test the vehicle and check the operation of the clutch and the brake system, as they share the same fluid reservoir.

3.3 Remove the pushrod pin

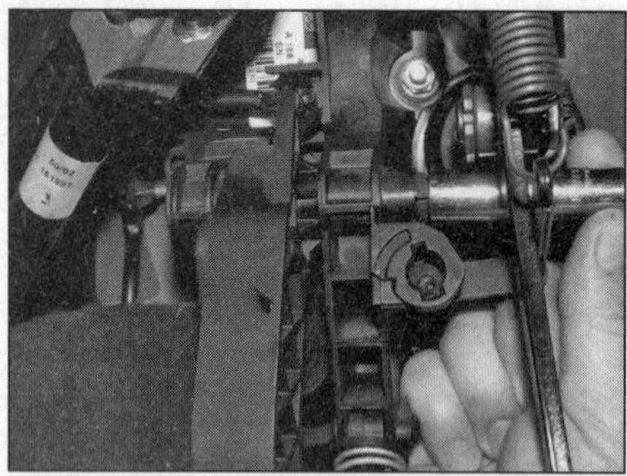
3.5a Using a socket . . .

3.5b . . . to release the locating clips – arrowed . . .

3.5c . . . and withdraw the pivot pin

3 Clutch pedal – removal and refitting

Removal

1 Move the driver's seat fully to the rear, and adjust the steering column to its highest position.

2 If required, remove the driver's side lower facia trim panel, with reference to Chapter 11.

3 Release the pushrod pin from the clutch pedal and withdraw it from the pedal assembly **(see illustration)**.

4 Check the condition of the plastic pushrod pin, if worn or damaged renew.

5 Release the pedal pivot pin from the top of the clutch pedal, by closing up the locating clips and withdrawing it from the pedal assembly **(see illustrations)**. To make removal easier, it may be necessary to release the steering column height adjuster, and move the steering column to allow the pivot pin to be withdrawn.

6 Withdraw the clutch pedal from the mounting bracket; note the position of the return spring as the pedal is removed **(see illustration)**.

7 If required, unclip the clutch pedal switch from the top of the mounting bracket **(see illustration)**.

Refitting

8 Refitting is a reversal of removal, bearing in mind the following points:

a) *Check the condition of the pivot pin and pushrod pin, renew it if worn or damaged.*
b) *Press the pushrod and pivot pins firmly into the pedal until making sure they are secure.*
c) *On completion, check the clutch pedal operation.*

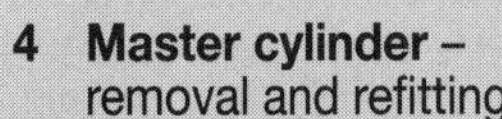

4 Master cylinder – removal and refitting

Note: *Refer to the warning at the beginning of Section 2 regarding the hazards of working with hydraulic fluid.*

Removal

1 The clutch master cylinder is located through the bulkhead, inside the car on the clutch pedal-mounting bracket. Hydraulic fluid for the unit is supplied from the brake master cylinder reservoir.

2 Before proceeding, place cloth rags on the carpet inside the car to prevent damage from spilt hydraulic fluid. Also place cloth rags around the reservoir and hoses in the engine compartment.

3 Working in the engine compartment, position a suitable container, or a wad of clean cloth, beneath the master cylinder to catch escaping hydraulic fluid. Release the clip and disconnect the fluid supply hose from the master cylinder **(see illustration)** – be prepared for fluid spillage. Plug the ends of the fluid hose to prevent dirt ingress.

4 To disconnect the reservoir connecting hose from the master cylinder, release the retaining clip and disconnect the hose. Plug the ends of the fluid hose to prevent dirt ingress.

5 Slacken the fluid metal hose connection from the master cylinder and disconnect **(see illustration).** Plug the end of the fluid pipe to prevent dirt ingress.

6 Working inside the driver's footwell, release the pushrod pin from the clutch pedal and withdraw it from the pedal assembly **(see illustration)**. Check the condition of the plastic pushrod pin, renew it if worn or damaged. See Section 3, for further information on the clutch pedal.

7 Slacken and remove the two master cylinder mounting nuts from inside the driver's footwell **(see illustration).**

8 The master cylinder can now be withdrawn from the bulkhead; use a cloth rag to catch any spilt fluid.

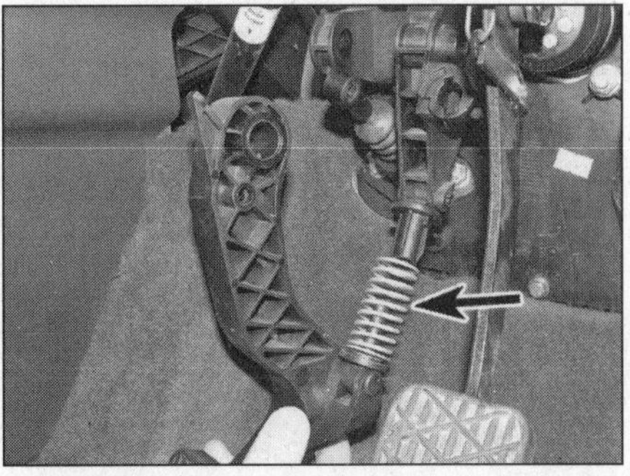

3.6 Clutch pedal return spring - arrowed

Refitting

9 Refitting is a reversal of removal, but bleed the clutch hydraulic system as described in Section 2. Check the system for leaks.

5 Slave cylinder/ release bearing – removal and refitting

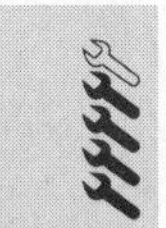

Note: *The clutch slave cylinder and thrust release bearing are integrated and can only be purchased as a complete assembly. Refer to the warning at the beginning of Section 2 regarding the hazards of working with hydraulic fluid.*

Removal

1 Remove the transmission, as described in Chapter 7A.

2 Wipe clean the outside of the slave cylinder, and then if required, slacken the union nut and disconnect the hydraulic pipe. Wipe up any spilt fluid with a clean cloth.

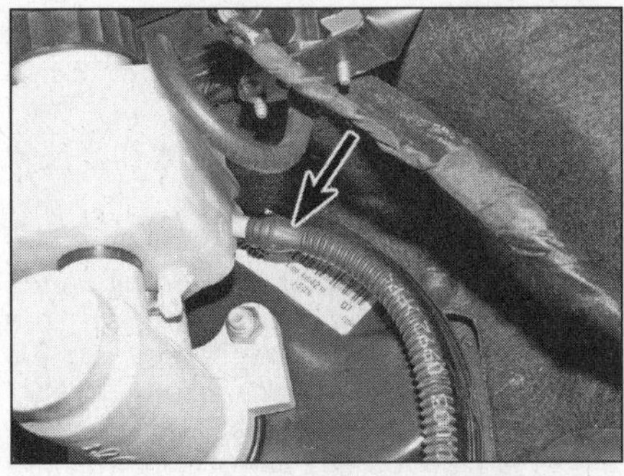

4.3 Fluid supply hose - arrowed

4.6 Remove the pushrod pin

3.7 Unclip the pedal switch

3 Unscrew the four retaining bolts and slide the slave cylinder off from the transmission input shaft **(see illustration overleaf)**. As the cylinder is withdrawn, release the fluid supply and vent pipes from the transmission housing. Whilst the cylinder is removed, take care not to allow any debris to enter the transmission unit.

4 The slave cylinder is a sealed unit and cannot be overhauled. If the cylinder seals have failed or the release bearing is noisy or rough in operation, then the complete unit must be renewed.

Refitting

5 Ensure the slave cylinder and transmission mating surfaces are clean and dry.

6 Lubricate the slave cylinder seal with a

4.5 Disconnect the pipe connection – arrowed

4.7 Master cylinder retaining nuts – arrowed

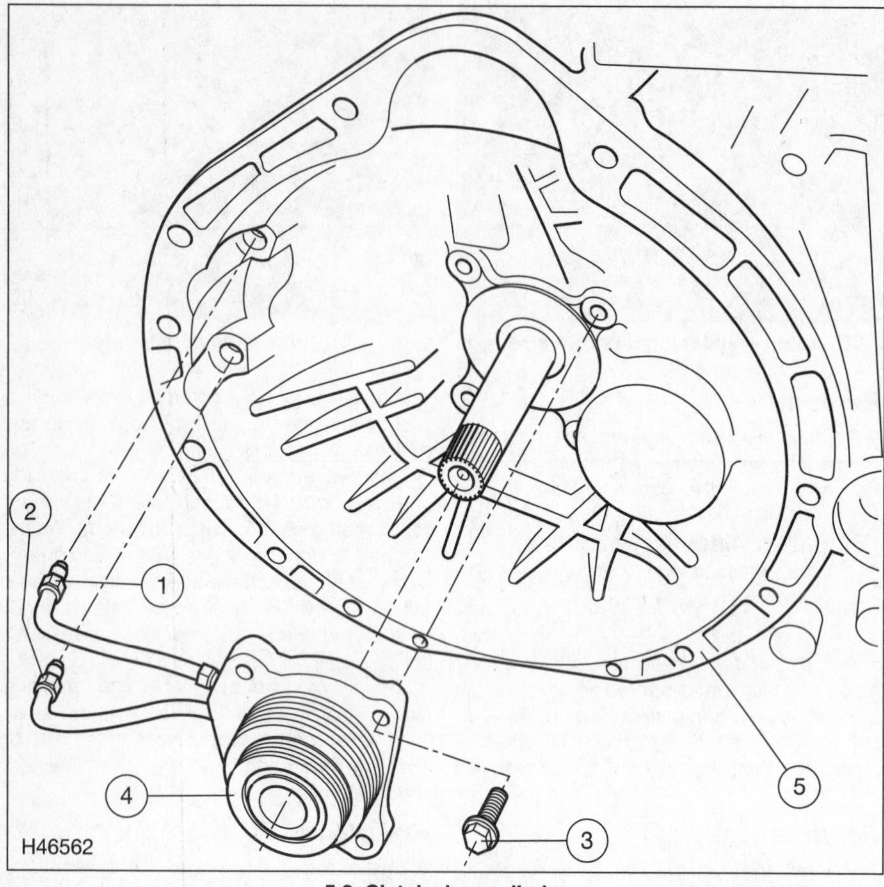

5.3 Clutch slave cylinder

1 Hydraulic fluid pipe
2 Vent pipe
3 Retaining bolts (one shown)
4 Clutch release bearing
5 Transmission

smear of transmission oil then carefully ease the cylinder along the input shaft and into position. Ensure the fluid pipes locate correctly in the transmission housing

7 Refit the slave cylinder retaining bolts and tighten them to the specified torque.

8 Where applicable, reconnect the hydraulic pipe to the slave cylinder, tightening its union nut securely.

9 Refit the transmission unit as described in Chapter 7A.

10 Bleed the slave cylinder with hydraulic fluid, as described in Section 2.

6.4 Lift the pressure plate and friction disc away from the flywheel

6 Clutch friction disc and pressure plate - removal, inspection and refitting

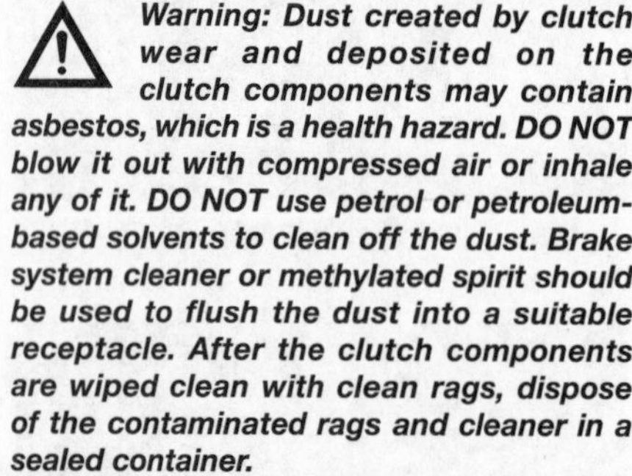

Warning: Dust created by clutch wear and deposited on the clutch components may contain asbestos, which is a health hazard. DO NOT blow it out with compressed air or inhale any of it. DO NOT use petrol or petroleum-based solvents to clean off the dust. Brake system cleaner or methylated spirit should be used to flush the dust into a suitable receptacle. After the clutch components are wiped clean with clean rags, dispose of the contaminated rags and cleaner in a sealed container.

Note: *New clutch pressure plate securing bolts will be required on refitting. It is recommended that a friction disc centralising tool be used when refitting the clutch.*

Removal

1 Access to the clutch is obtained by removing the transmission as described in Chapter 7A.

2 Mark the clutch pressure plate and flywheel in relation to each other.

3 Hold the flywheel stationary, and then unscrew the clutch pressure plate bolts progressively in diagonal sequence. With the bolts unscrewed two or three turns, check that the pressure plate is not binding on the dowel pins. If necessary, use a screwdriver to release the pressure plate.

4 Remove all the bolts, then lift the clutch pressure plate and friction disc from the flywheel **(see illustration)**.

Inspection

5 Clean the pressure plate, disc and flywheel. Do not inhale the dust, as it may contain asbestos, which is dangerous to health.

6 Examine the fingers of the diaphragm spring for wear or scoring. If the depth of wear exceeds half the thickness of the fingers, a new pressure plate assembly must be fitted.

7 Examine the pressure plate for scoring, cracking and discoloration. Light scoring is acceptable, but if excessive, a new pressure plate assembly must be fitted.

8 Examine the friction disc linings for wear and cracking, and for contamination with oil or grease. The linings are worn excessively if they are worn down to, or near, the rivets. Check the disc hub and splines for wear, by temporarily fitting it on the transmission input shaft. Renew the friction disc as necessary.

9 Examine the flywheel friction surface for scoring, cracking and discoloration (caused by overheating). If excessive, it may be possible to have the flywheel machined by an engineering works, otherwise it should be renewed.

10 Ensure that all parts are clean, and free of oil or grease, before reassembling. Apply just a small amount of high melting-point grease to the splines of the friction disc hub. Note that new pressure plates and clutch covers may be coated with protective grease. It is only permissible to clean the grease away from the friction disc lining contact area. Removal of the grease from other areas will shorten the service life of the clutch.

Refitting

11 During refitting, the clutch friction disc must be centralised in relation to the pressure plate and flywheel, to ensure the input shaft engages correctly when the transmission is refitted. Although, it is possible to use a homemade wooden mandrel, it is recommended that a centralising tool be used. There are two basic types of tool available, the early type centralises the disc to the flywheel, and the later type centralises the disc to the pressure plate.

Centralising disc to flywheel

12 Commence reassembly by locating the friction disc on the flywheel, with the raised, torsion spring side of the hub facing outwards. If necessary, use the centralising mandrel or tool to hold the disc on the flywheel **(see illustration)**.

6.12 **Locating the friction disc on the flywheel**

6.13 **Locating the clutch pressure plate over the friction disc**

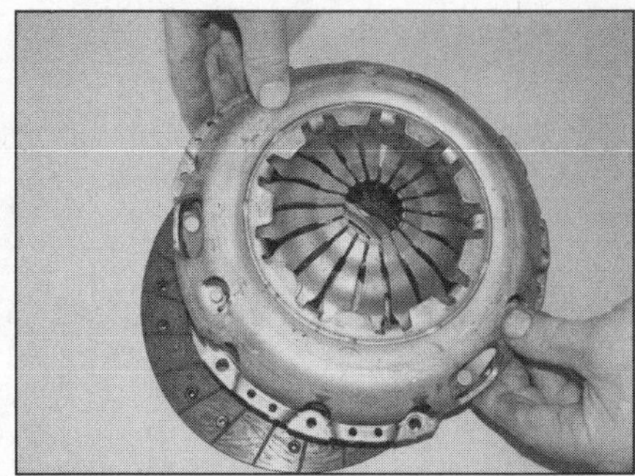

6.17 **Locate the friction disc on the pressure plate, making sure it is the correct way round . . .**

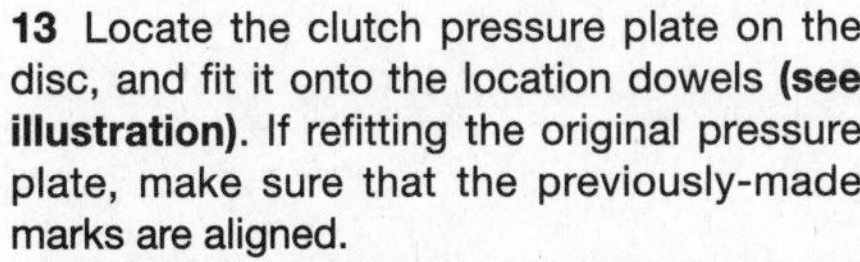

13 Locate the clutch pressure plate on the disc, and fit it onto the location dowels **(see illustration)**. If refitting the original pressure plate, make sure that the previously-made marks are aligned.

14 Insert the bolts finger-tight to hold the pressure plate in position.

15 The friction disc must now be centralised, to ensure correct alignment of the transmission input shaft with the spigot bearing in the crankshaft. To do this, a proprietary tool may be used, or alternatively, use a wooden mandrel made to fit inside the friction disc and flywheel spigot bearing. Insert the tool through the friction disc into the spigot bearing, and make sure that it is central.

16 Tighten the pressure plate bolts progressively and in diagonal sequence, until the specified torque setting is achieved, and then remove the centralising tool.

Centralising disc to pressure plate

17 Locate the friction disc on the pressure plate; making sure it is the correct way round **(see illustration)**.

18 Insert the tool and tighten the knob to lock it onto the disc hub, then centralise the disc with the pressure plate and tighten the knob to lock the two components together **(see illustrations)**.

19 Locate the disc and pressure plate on the flywheel and hand-tighten the retaining bolts **(see illustration)**.

20 Tighten the pressure plate bolts progressively and in diagonal sequence, until the specified torque setting is achieved, and then remove the centralising tool.

6.18a . . . insert the tool . . .

6.18b . . . and lock to the disc hub . . .

6.18c . . . then centralise the disc to the pressure plate and lock the two components together . . .

6.19 . . . and locate the disc and pressure plate on the flywheel

All methods

21 Check the release bearing in the transmission bellhousing for smooth operation, and if necessary renew it with reference to Section 5.

22 Refit the transmission with reference to Chapter 7A.

Chapter 7 Part A: Manual transmission

Contents

Degrees of difficulty

Easy, suitable for novice with little experience

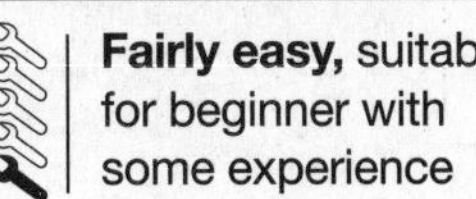

Fairly easy, suitable for beginner with some experience

Fairly difficult, suitable for competent DIY mechanic

Difficult, suitable for experienced DIY mechanic

Very difficult, suitable for expert DIY or professional

Specifications

General

Type	Transversely-mounted, front-wheel-drive layout with integral transaxle differential/final drive, 5 forward speeds and 1 reverse
Designation:	
A140	716.501, 716.503, 716.506 or 716.507
A160:	
Petrol	716.501, 716.503, 716.506, 716.507, 716.511 or 716.512
Diesel	716.504 or 716.505
A170	716.500 or 716.502
A190	716.506, 716.507, 716.511 or 716.512
A210	716.506 or 716.507

Torque wrench settings	Nm	lbf ft
Engine mounting bracket-to-transmission bolts	55	41
Gear lever mounting bracket	8	6
Reversing light switch	27	20
Right-hand driveshaft intermediate bearing to crankcase	20	15
Starter motor bolts	20	15
Transmission to engine	20	15

1 General information

The manual transmission is bolted directly to the left-hand end of the engine. This layout has the advantage of providing the shortest possible drive path to the front wheels, as well as locating the transmission in the airflow through engine bay, optimising cooling. The unit is cased in aluminium alloy.

Drive from the crankshaft is transmitted through the clutch to the gearbox input shaft, which is splined to accept the clutch friction disc.

All forward gears are fitted with synchromesh. The floor-mounted gear lever is connected to the gearbox by shift cables **(see illustration)**. Levers on the transmission actuate internal selector forks, which are connected to the synchromesh sleeves. The sleeves are locked to the gearbox shafts but can slide axially by means of splined hubs, and they press baulk rings into contact with the respective gear/pinion. The coned surfaces between the baulk rings and the pinion/gear act as a friction clutch, which progressively matches the speed of the synchromesh sleeve (and hence the gearbox shaft) with that of the gear/pinion. This allows gearchanges to be carried out smoothly.

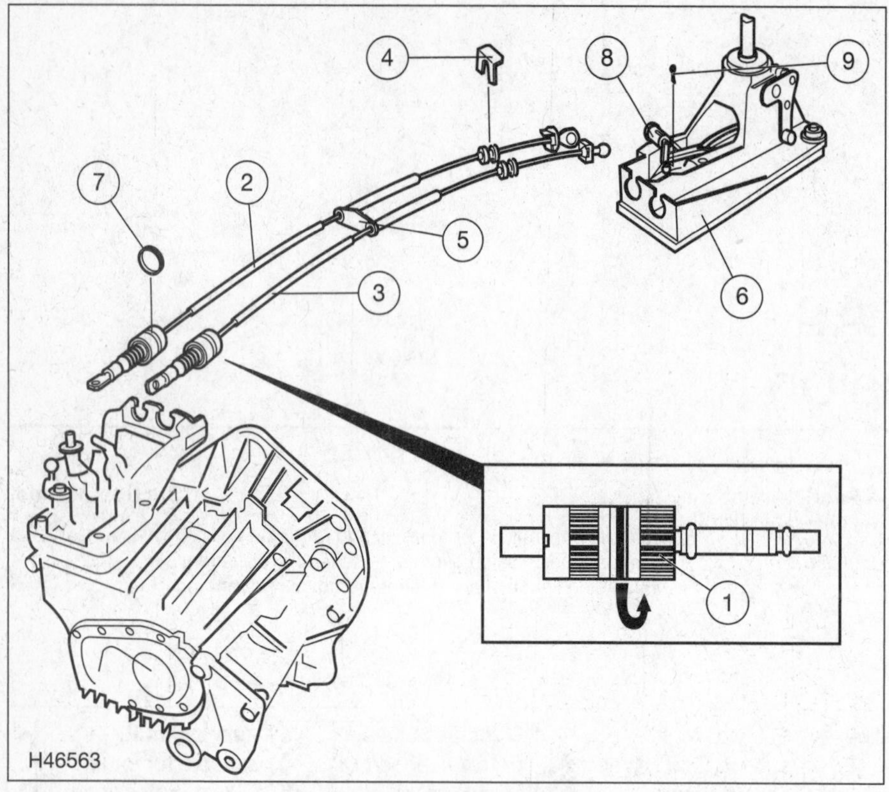

1.1 Transmission and gear linkage

1 *Locking nut*
2 *Shift cable*
3 *Selector cable*
4 *Retaining clip*
5 *Bulkhead grommet*
6 *Gear lever assembly*
7 *Spacer ring*
8 *Shift sensor (where fitted)*
9 *Cotter pin*

Drive is transmitted to the differential crownwheel, which rotates the differential case and planetary gears, thus driving the sun gears and driveshafts. The rotation of the differential planetary gears on their shaft allows the inner roadwheel to rotate at a slower speed than the outer roadwheel during cornering.

2 Gearchange linkage cables – removal, refitting and adjustment

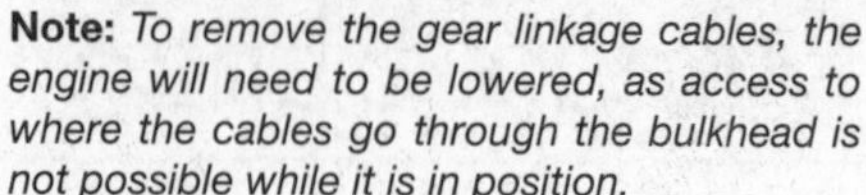

Note: *To remove the gear linkage cables, the engine will need to be lowered, as access to where the cables go through the bulkhead is not possible while it is in position.*

Removal

1 Disconnect the battery negative lead. **Note:** *Before disconnecting the battery, refer to 'Disconnecting the battery' in the Reference section at the rear of this manual.*

2 Apply the handbrake, then jack up the front of the vehicle and support it on axle stands (see *Jacking and vehicle support*). Remove the engine undertrays.

3 Lower the engine on the front subframe as described In Chapter 2C.

4 Remove the centre console as described in Chapter 11.

5 Working in the engine compartment, press down on the grey spacer ring until it is locked down in place and then turn the locking ring on the gear linkage cable anti-clockwise **(see illustration)**. Unclip the outer cable from the mounting bracket.

6 Using a pair of long nose-pliers (or similar), lever the balljoints on the end of the inner cable apart from the gear selector levers on the transmission **(see illustrations)**.

7 Working inside the vehicle, release the outer cable retaining clips and withdraw the outer cables from the gear lever mounting bracket **(see illustration).**

8 Using a pair of long-nose pliers (or similar), lever the balljoints on the end of the inner cable apart from bottom of the gear selector lever **(see illustration).**

9 Release the rubber grommet in the bulkhead and withdraw the cables from inside the vehicle **(see illustration).**

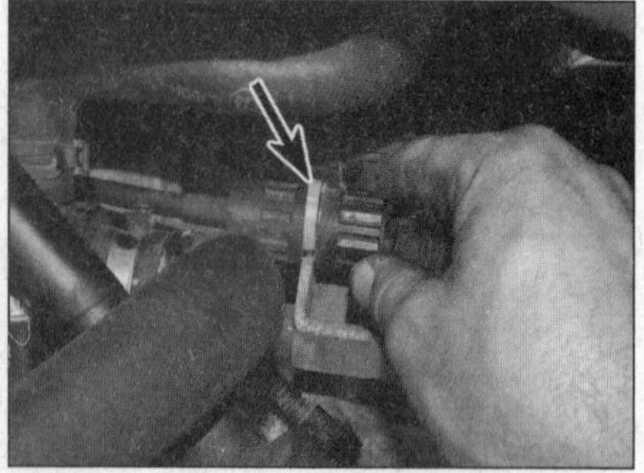

2.5 Press down the spacer (arrowed) and turn the locking ring

2.6a Using long-nose pliers . . .

2.6b . . . to disconnect the balljoints

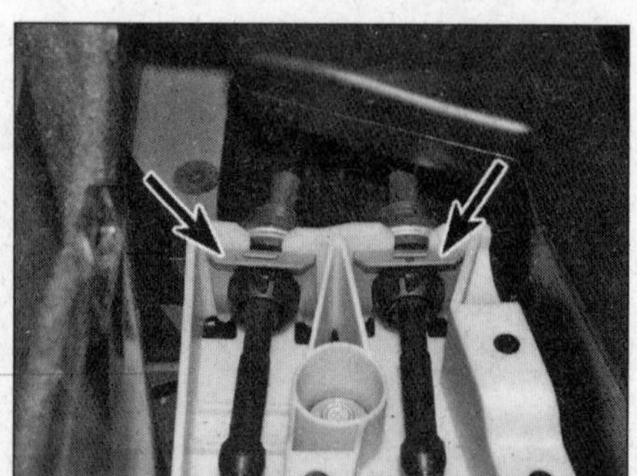

2.7 Outer cable retaining clips – arrowed

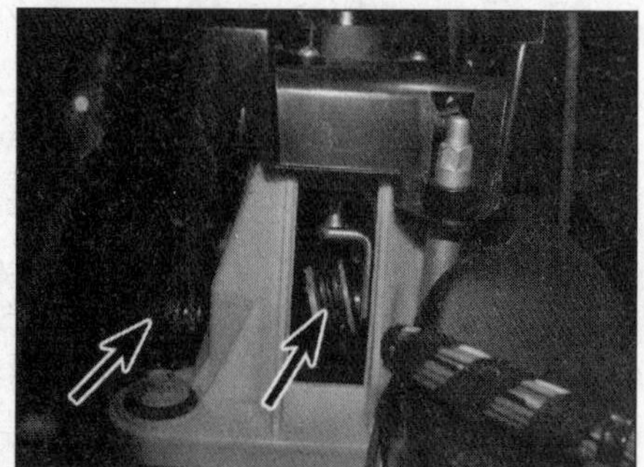

2.8 Disconnect the balljoints – arrowed

Refitting

10 Refitting is a reversal of removal, noting the following points:

a Make sure the balljoints are securely fitted, lightly grease the balljoints for refitting.

b) Make sure the grey spacer rings are in the raised position to lock the outer cables ***(see illustration)****.*

c) Refer to Chapter 2C, to refit the subframe/engine.

d) See following paragraphs, for adjusting the gearchange cables.

Adjusting

11 Mercedes-Benz technicians use a special tool to keep the gear lever in the neutral position, it is a sleeve that fits over the top of the gear lever and holds the gear lever in position. We used a large socket with a grommet in the square drive end to keep it central. Slide the socket down over the gear lever and press it down onto the lower plastic gear lever mounting **(see illustrations).**

12 Press down on the orange retaining clips to release the cable adjusters **(see illustration).**

13 Make sure that both ends of the cables are located correctly on their balljoints on the lower end of the gear lever and on the transmission.

14 With the gear lever held in the neutral position with the special tool (socket), use a screwdriver to operate the locking clips on the cable adjusters **(see illustration).**

15 With the cable adjustment set and locked in position, remove the special tool (socket) from the gear lever.

16 The centre console can now be refitted, with reference to Chapter 11, if required.

17 Check the operation of the gear lever making sure it can select all gears.

3 Manual transmission – removal and refitting

Note: *To remove the transmission, the engine will need to be removed from the vehicle complete with front subframe.*

Removal

1 Disconnect the battery negative lead. **Note:** *Before disconnecting the battery, refer to 'Disconnecting the battery' in the Reference section at the rear of this manual.*

2 Apply the handbrake, then jack up the front of the vehicle and support it on axle stands (see *Jacking and vehicle support*). Remove the engine undertrays.

3 Position a suitable container beneath the transmission, then unscrew the drain plug and drain the transmission oil.

4 Remove the engine/transmission complete with front subframe as described In Chapter 2C.

5 Undo the retaining bolts and withdraw the starter motor from the cylinder block, with reference to Chapter 5A.

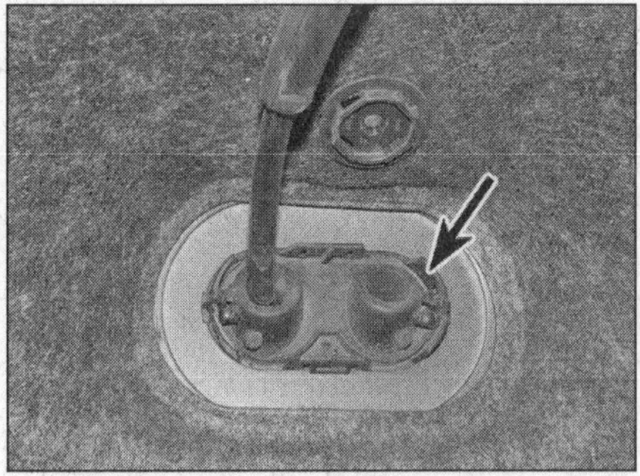

2.9 Rubber grommet in bulkhead – arrowed

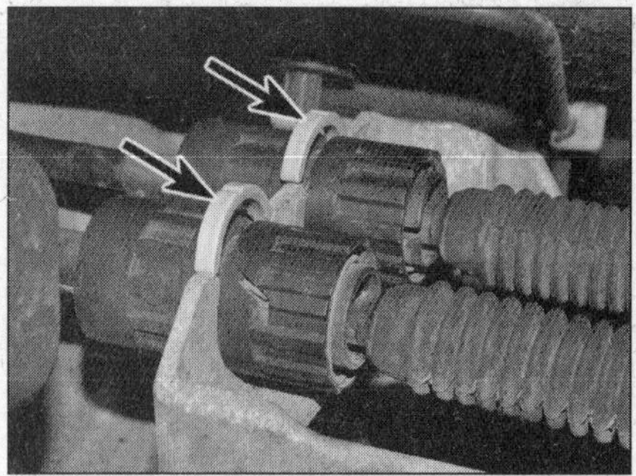

2.10 Spacer rings – arrowed

6 Remove the driveshafts with reference to Chapter 8.

7 With the engine hoist secured to the engine/transmission, undo the engine mounting bolts/nuts and lift the engine/transmission unit from the front subframe.

8 Where applicable, unscrew the bolt securing the small plate at the lower part of the engine-to-transmission.

9 Ensure that both engine and transmission are adequately supported, and then unscrew the remaining engine-to-transmission bolts, noting the location of each bolt (different lengths), and the locations of any brackets secured by the bolts.

10 Carefully withdraw the transmission from the engine, ensuring that the weight of the transmission is not allowed to hang on the input shaft while it is engaged with the clutch friction disc. A second person is helpful to pull the engine as far forwards as possible.

Refitting

11 Refitting the transmission is essentially a reversal of the removal procedure, but note the following points:

a) Apply a smear of high melting-point grease to the clutch friction disc hub splines; take care to avoid contaminating the friction surfaces.

b) In order to align the transmission with the flywheel; gently pull the engine forward as the transmission is manoeuvred into place.

c) Tighten the transmission-to-engine bolts to the specified torque.

d) Refer to the relevant part of Chapter 2C for refitting of the engine/transmission assembly.

e) Refer to Chapter 8 and tighten the driveshaft bolts to the specified torque.

f) Where applicable, have the air

2.11a Slide a large socket . . .

2.11b . . . down to the base of the gear lever

2.12 Release the cable adjuster

2.14 Push down on the locking clip

5.2 Reversing light switch location – arrowed

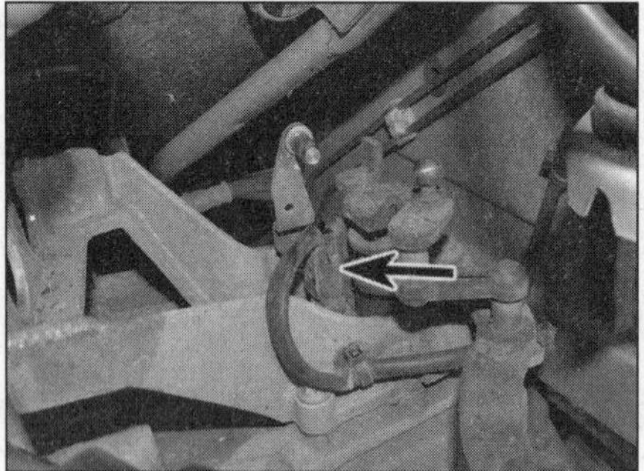
5.7 Disconnect the wiring connector – arrowed

conditioning system recharged with refrigerant by a suitably-qualified professional.

g) Refill the transmission with the correct grade and quantity of oil. Refer to 'Lubricants and fluids' and Chapter 1A or 1B, as appropriate.

4 Manual transmission overhaul – general information

The overhaul of a manual transmission is a complex (and often expensive) task for the DIY home mechanic to undertake, which requires access to specialist equipment. It involves dismantling and reassembly of many small components, measuring clearances precisely and if necessary, adjusting them by selecting shims and spacers. Internal transmission components are also often difficult to obtain and in many instances, extremely expensive. Because of this, if the transmission develops a fault or becomes noisy, the best course of action is to have the unit overhauled by a specialist repairer or to obtain an exchange reconditioned unit.

Nevertheless, it is not impossible for the more experienced mechanic to overhaul the transmission if the special tools are available and the job is carried out in a deliberate step-by-step manner, to ensure nothing is overlooked.

The tools necessary for an overhaul include internal and external circlip pliers, bearing pullers, a slide hammer, a set of pin punches, a dial test indicator and possibly a hydraulic press. In addition, a large, sturdy workbench and a vice will be required.

During dismantling of the transmission, make careful notes of how each component is fitted to make reassembly easier and accurate.

Before dismantling the transmission, it will help if you have some idea of where the problem lies. Certain problems can be closely related to specific areas in the transmission, which can make component examination and renewal easier. Refer to the *Fault finding* Section in this manual for more information.

5 Reversing light switch – testing, removal and refitting

Testing

1 Ensure that the ignition switch is turned to the OFF position.

2 Unplug the wiring harness from the reversing light switch at the connector. The switch is located on the top of the casing, below the gear linkage cables **(see illustration)**.

3 Connect the probes of a continuity tester, or multimeter set to the resistance measurement function, across the terminals of the reversing light switch.

4 The switch contacts are normally open, so with any gear other than reverse selected; the tester/meter should indicate an open circuit or infinite resistance. When reverse gear is selected, the switch contacts should close, causing the tester/meter to indicate continuity or zero resistance.

5 If the switch does not operate correctly, it should be renewed.

Removal

6 Ensure that the ignition switch is turned to the OFF position and reverse gear is selected.

7 Unplug the wiring harness from the reversing light switch at the connector. To gain better access, disconnect the gear linkage cables from the selector levers **(see illustration)**, with reference to Section 2.

8 Unscrew the switch from the transmission casing, and recover the sealing ring.

Refitting

9 Refitting is a reversal of removal, noting the following points:

a) Check the condition of the sealing ring, and renew if required.

b) Tighten the switch to the specified torque setting.

c) Refer to Section 2 for refitting or adjusting the gearchange cables.

6 Driveshaft oil seals – renewal

1 Apply the handbrake, then jack up the front of the vehicle and support it on axle stands (see *Jacking and vehicle support*). Remove the engine undertrays.

2 Position a suitable container beneath the transmission, then unscrew the drain plug and drain the transmission oil.

3 Remove the appropriate front roadwheel, and then remove the driveshaft as described in Chapter 8.

4 Note the correct fitted depth of the seal in its housing then carefully prise it out of position using a large flat-bladed screwdriver **(see illustration)**.

5 Remove all traces of dirt from the area around the oil seal aperture, then apply a smear of grease to the outer lip of the new oil seal. Ensure the seal is correctly positioned, with its sealing lip facing inwards, and tap it squarely into position. Use either a suitable tubular drift (such as a socket), which bears only on the hard outer edge of the seal, or a drift working your way around the edge of the seal **(see illustration)**. Ensure the seal is fitted at the same depth in its housing that the original was.

6 Refit the driveshaft as described in Chapter 8.

7 If the transmission was drained, refill the transmission with the specified type and amount of oil. If the oil was not drained top-up the transmission oil level and check as described in the appropriate part of Chapter 1.

6.4 Prise the oil seal from the housing

6.5 Using a drift to tap the seal into place

Chapter 7 Part B: Automatic transmission

Contents

Degrees of difficulty

Easy, suitable for novice with little experience 	**Fairly easy,** suitable for beginner with some experience	**Fairly difficult,** suitable for competent DIY mechanic	**Difficult,** suitable for experienced DIY mechanic	**Very difficult,** suitable for expert DIY or professional 

Specifications

General

Description	Computer-controlled gearbox providing five forward speeds and one reverse speed. Drive transmitted through torque converter
Designation:	
A140	722.700 or 722.703
A160:	
Petrol	722.703
Diesel	722.701
A170	722.701
A190	722.700 or 722.703
A210	722.702
Vaneo	722.750 or 722.751

Torque wrench settings

Torque wrench settings	Nm	lbf ft
Engine mounting bracket to transmission bolts	55	41
Oil drain plug	22	16
Right-hand driveshaft intermediate bearing to crankcase	20	15
Selector cable bracket to transmission	8	6
Starter motor bolts	20	15
Torque converter-to-driveplate bolts	42	31
Transmission to engine	20	15

1 General information

The Mercedes-Benz type 722 automatic transmission has five forward speeds and one reverse. The automatic gearchanges are electro-hydraulically controlled and the electronic control module (ECM) has a 'self diagnosis' facility. The engine control module gives information to the transmission control module and exchanges signals with other control units. Some of the signals exchanged are engine speed, engine torque, throttle position, kickdown, ignition timing and cruise control. Any faults are stored in the memory and the transmission will remain in an emergency running mode. If a problem occurs, consult a Mercedes-Benz dealer or transmission specialist to test the electrical/electronic controls.

The transmission consists of three main assemblies, these being the torque converter, which is directly coupled to the engine; the final drive unit, which incorporates the differential unit; and the planetary gearbox, with its multidisc clutches and brake bands. The transmission is lubricated with automatic transmission fluid (ATF).

A starter inhibitor relay is fitted, to prevent starter motor operation unless the transmission is in P or N. A fault diagnosis system is integrated into the control unit, but analysis can only be undertaken with specialised equipment. It is important that any transmission fault be identified and rectified at the earliest possible opportunity. A Mercedes-Benz dealer can 'interrogate' the ECM fault memory for stored fault codes, enabling them to pinpoint the fault quickly. Once the fault has been corrected and any fault codes have been cleared, normal transmission operation is restored.

Because of the need for special test equipment, the complexity of some of the parts, and the need for scrupulous cleanliness when servicing automatic transmissions, the work which the owner can do is limited. Most major repairs and overhaul operations should be left to a Mercedes-Benz dealer (or specialist), who will be equipped with the necessary equipment for fault diagnosis and repair. The information in this Chapter is therefore limited to a description of the removal and refitting of the transmission as a complete unit. The removal, refitting and adjustment of the selector cable is also described.

In the event of a transmission problem occurring, consult a Mercedes-Benz dealer or transmission specialist before removing the transmission from the vehicle, since the majority of fault diagnosis is carried out with the transmission *in situ*.

2.8a Remove the cover . . .

2.8b . . . and remove the bolts

2.12 Use a bolt and metal strap to hold torque converter in place

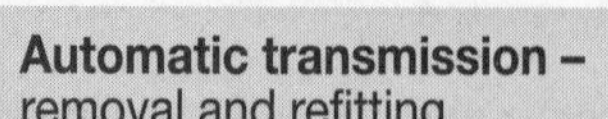

2 Automatic transmission – removal and refitting

Note: *To remove the transmission, the engine will need to be removed from the vehicle complete with front subframe.*

Removal

1 Disconnect the battery negative lead. **Note:** *Before disconnecting the battery, refer to 'Disconnecting the battery' in the Reference section at the rear of this manual.*

2 Apply the handbrake, then jack up the front of the vehicle and support it on axle stands (see *Jacking and vehicle support*). Remove the engine undertrays.

3 Position a suitable container beneath the transmission, then unscrew the drain plug and drain the transmission oil.

4 Remove the engine/transmission complete with front subframe as described in Chapter 2C.

5 Undo the retaining bolts and withdraw the starter motor from the cylinder block, with reference to Chapter 5A.

6 Remove the driveshafts with reference to Chapter 8.

7 With the engine hoist secured to the engine/transmission, undo the engine mounting bolts/nuts and lift the engine/transmission unit from the front subframe.

8 Prise out the torque converter bolts cover in the transmission casing **(see illustrations)**. Turn the crankshaft to position one of the torque converter-to-driveplate bolts in the access aperture. Unscrew and remove the bolts whilst preventing the engine from turning using a wide-bladed screwdriver engaged with the ring gear teeth on the driveplate.

9 Using the same method described in the previous paragraph, unscrew the remaining torque converter-to-driveplate bolts, turning the crankshaft a third-of-a-turn at a time to locate them.

10 Ensure that both engine and transmission are adequately supported, and then unscrew the engine-to-transmission bolts, noting the location of each bolt (different lengths), and the locations of any brackets secured by the bolts.

11 Carefully withdraw the transmission from the engine (take care – the transmission is heavy), making sure that the torque converter remains fully engaged with the transmission input shaft. If necessary, use a lever to release the torque converter from the driveplate. Recover the engine-to-transmission plate.

12 Once the transmission has been separated from the engine, strap a restraining bar across the front of the bellhousing to keep the torque converter in position **(see illustration)**.

Refitting

13 Reconnection and refitting are a reversal of removal, bearing in mind the following points:

a) *When fitting the torque converter, make sure that it engages correctly.*

b) *Where applicable, tighten retaining bolts to their specified torque wrench settings.*

c) *Reconnect and adjust the selector cable, as described in Section 4.*

d) *On completion, check and if necessary top-up the automatic transmission fluid level as described in Chapter 1A or 1B.*

e) *If a new transmission unit has been fitted, it may be necessary to have the transmission ECM 'matched' to the engine management ECM electronically, to ensure correct operation – seek the advice of your Mercedes-Benz dealer.*

3 Automatic transmission overhaul – general information

In the event of a fault occurring, it will be necessary to establish whether the fault is electrical, mechanical or hydraulic in nature, before repair work can be contemplated. Diagnosis requires detailed knowledge of the transmission's operation and construction, as well as access to specialised test equipment, and so is deemed to be beyond the scope of this manual. It is therefore essential that problems with the automatic transmission be referred to a Mercedes-Benz dealer for assessment.

Note that a faulty transmission should not be removed before the vehicle has been assessed by a dealer, as fault diagnosis is carried out with the transmission *in situ*.

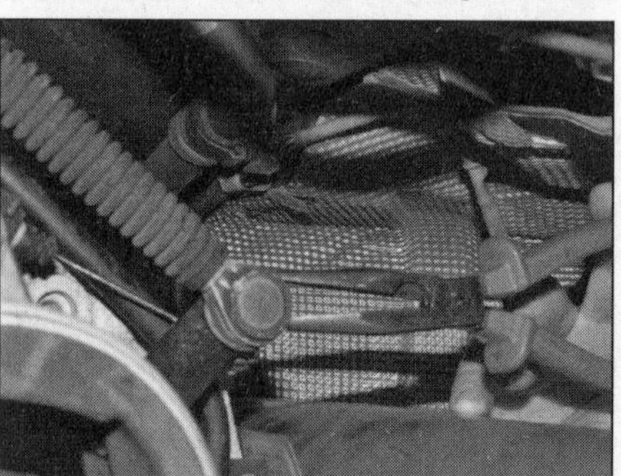

4.6a Using long-nose pliers . . .

4 Selector cable – removal, refitting and adjustment

Note: *To remove the gear linkage cables, the engine will need to be lowered, as access to where the cables go through the bulkhead is not possible while it is in position.*

Removal

1 Disconnect the battery negative lead. **Note:** *Before disconnecting the battery, refer to 'Disconnecting the battery' in the Reference section at the rear of this manual.*

2 Apply the handbrake, then jack up the front of the vehicle and support it on axle stands (see *Jacking and vehicle support*). Remove the engine undertrays.

3 Lower the engine on the front subframe as described in Chapter 2C.

4 Remove the centre console as described in Chapter 11.

5 Move the selector lever into the P (Park) position.

6 Working under the vehicle, use a pair of long-nose pliers (or similar), and lever the balljoint on the end of the inner cable apart from the gear selector lever on the transmission **(see illustrations)**.

7 Working inside the engine compartment, undo the gear selector cable mounting bracket bolt and withdraw the cable and mounting bracket from down the back of the transmission housing **(see illustrations)**.

8 Working inside the vehicle, release the outer

4.6b . . . to disconnect the balljoints

4.7a Undo the retaining bolt . . .

4.7b . . . and withdraw the cable mounting bracket

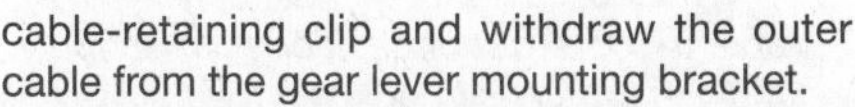

cable-retaining clip and withdraw the outer cable from the gear lever mounting bracket.

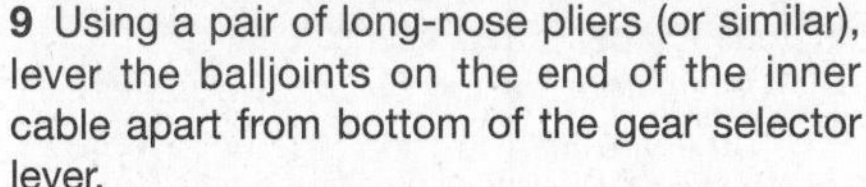

9 Using a pair of long-nose pliers (or similar), lever the balljoints on the end of the inner cable apart from bottom of the gear selector lever.

10 Release the rubber grommet in the bulkhead and withdraw the cable from inside the vehicle **(see illustration)**.

Refitting

11 Refitting is a reversal of removal, noting the following points:

a) Make sure the balljoints are securely fitted, lightly grease the balljoints for refitting.

b) Refer to Chapter 2C to refit the subframe/ engine.

c) See the following paragraphs for adjusting the gear selector cable.

Adjusting

12 The gear lever needs to be in position D.

13 Make sure that both ends of the cable are located correctly on their balljoints on the lower end of the gear lever and on the transmission.

14 Press down on the orange retaining clip to release the cable adjuster.

15 With the gear lever held in the D position, use a screwdriver to operate the locking clip on the cable adjuster **(see illustration)**. The cable adjustment should be set and locked in position.

16 The centre console can now be refitted, with reference to Chapter 11, if required.

17 Check the operation of the gear lever making sure it can select all gears.

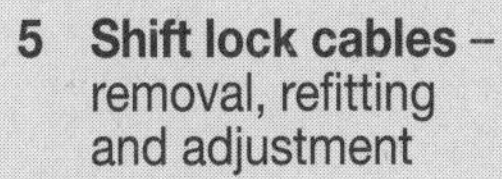

5 Shift lock cables – removal, refitting and adjustment

Removal

Brake shift lock cable

1 Disconnect the battery negative lead. **Note:** *Before disconnecting the battery, refer to 'Disconnecting the battery' in the Reference section at the rear of this manual.*

2 Apply the handbrake, then jack up the front of the vehicle and support it on axle stands (see *Jacking and vehicle support*). Remove the engine undertrays.

3 Remove the lower facia trim panel from the driver's side of the vehicle, as described in Chapter 11.

4 Working under the vehicle, use a small screwdriver to release the retaining clip and withdraw the inner cable from the selector lever on the transmission **(see illustrations)**.

5 Release the outer cable from the rubber grommet, and then unclip it from the transmission housing **(see illustrations)**.

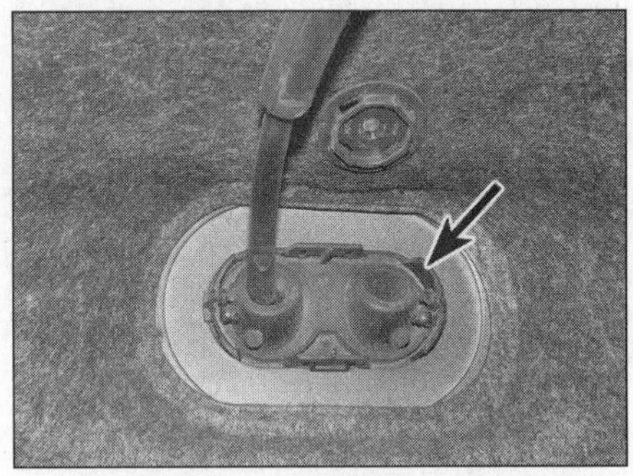

4.10 Rubber grommet in bulkhead – arrowed

4.15 Locking clip for cable adjuster – arrowed

5.4a Release the retaining clip . . .

5.4b . . . and remove the inner cable

5.5a Pull the outer cable from the grommet . . .

5.5b . . . and remove the grommet from the casing

6 Working inside the vehicle, release the cable-retaining clip and withdraw the shift lock cable from the brake pedal bearing bracket.
7 Release the rubber grommet in the bulkhead and withdraw the cable from inside the vehicle.

Ignition shift lock cable (models up to 09/01/01)

Note: *The cable goes from the ignition switch to the transmission shift lever.*
8 Disconnect the battery negative lead. **Note:** *Before disconnecting the battery, refer to 'Disconnecting the battery' in the Reference section at the rear of this manual.*
9 Apply the handbrake, then jack up the front of the vehicle and support it on axle stands (see *Jacking and vehicle support*). Remove the engine undertrays.
10 Remove the steering column cowling as described in Chapter 11.
11 Working under the vehicle, use a small screwdriver to release the retaining clip and withdraw the inner cable from the selector lever on the transmission **(see illustrations 5.4a and 5.4b)**.
12 Release the outer cable from the rubber grommet, and then unclip it from the transmission housing **(see illustration 5.5a and 5.5b)**.
13 Working inside the vehicle, release the connection to the lower part of the ignition switch and disconnect the cable.
14 Release the rubber grommet in the bulkhead and withdraw the cable from inside the vehicle.

Ignition shift lock cable (models from 10/01/01)

Note: *The cable goes from the ignition switch to the brake pedal bearing bracket.*
15 Disconnect the battery negative lead. **Note:** *Before disconnecting the battery, refer to 'Disconnecting the battery' in the Reference section at the rear of this manual.*
16 Remove the lower facia trim panel and steering column cowling from the driver's side of the vehicle, as described in Chapter 11.
17 Working inside the vehicle, release the connection to the lower part of the ignition switch and disconnect the cable.
18 Release the other end of the cable from the brake pedal bearing bracket, release the retaining clip and withdraw the shift lock cable.

Refitting

19 Refitting is a reversal of removal, noting the following points:
a) Make sure the cables are connected securely.
b) Refer to Chapter 11, to refit the trim panels.
c) See following paragraphs, for adjusting the gear selector cable.

Adjusting

Note: *On models from 10/01/01, the ignition shift lock cable that goes from the ignition switch to the brake pedal bearing bracket is not adjustable.*
20 First make sure the gear lever selector cable is adjusted correctly, as described in Section 4.
21 Turn the ignition switch to position 0
22 Move the selector lever into the P (Park) position.
23 Working in the engine compartment, locate the adjuster halfway up the length of the shift cable.
24 While pushing the two parts of the cable inwards towards the adjuster, press the adjuster to take up any slack. Then while still keeping the pressure on the two parts of the cable, release the adjuster and it will lock into position.
25 Check the operation of the cables by:
a) The gear selector lever must only be able to move out of position P when the ignition switch is in position 2 and the brake pedal is depressed.
b) The ignition key can only be withdrawn from the ignition when the gear selector lever is in P.
26 Repeat the adjustment if these functions are not fulfilled.

6 Manual gear range selector

At the time of writing there was no information about the manual +/- gear selector.

The W/S switch removal and refitting is covered in Chapter 12, Section4.

Chapter 8
Driveshafts

Contents

Degrees of difficulty

Easy, suitable for novice with little experience	**Fairly easy,** suitable for beginner with some experience	**Fairly difficult,** suitable for competent DIY mechanic	**Difficult,** suitable for experienced DIY mechanic	**Very difficult,** suitable for expert DIY or professional

Specifications

General

Driveshaft type	Steel shafts with outer constant velocity joints and inner tripod or constant velocity joints (according to type). The right-hand shaft has an intermediate bearing supporting the inner part of the shaft

Lubrication

Overhaul and repair	Long-life grease (NLGI grade 2) – or grease supplied in sachets with gaiter/overhaul kits; joints are otherwise prepacked with grease and sealed
Joint grease type	
Mercedes-Benz	MB 266.2 long-life grease 000 989 63 51 or 001 989 88 51
Other options	Castrol Olistamoly or Shell Stamina 0233B
Joint grease quantity	
Outer joint	100 g
Inner joint	120 g

Torque wrench settings

Torque wrench settings	Nm	lbf ft
Brake pipe connection to brake hose	14	10
Driveshaft hub nut:*		
Stage 1	180	133
Stage 2	Slacken fully	
Stage 3	80	59
Stage 4	Angle-tighten a further 45°	
Intermediate shaft bearing-to-crankcase bolts*	20	15
Lower arm-to-balljoint nuts:*		
Stage 1	20	15
Stage 2	Angle-tighten a further 45°	
Lower wishbone to subframe bolts	105	77
Strut-to-steering knuckle nut	100	74
Track-rod arm self-locking nut:*		
Stage 1	30	22
Stage 2	Angle-tighten a further 90°	
Wheel bolts	110	81

** Use new bolt/nuts*

2.4 Removing the hub nut

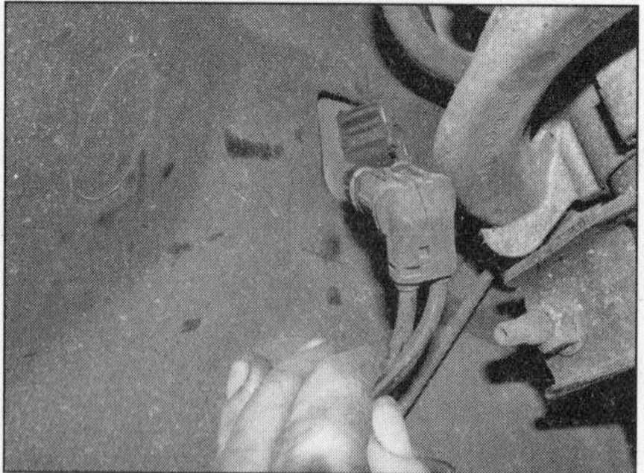

2.5 Disconnecting the speed sensor and brake warning light wiring

2.9 Undo the mounting bolts – arrowed

1 General information

Drive is transmitted from the differential to the front wheels by means of two steel driveshafts of either solid or hollow construction (depending on model). Both driveshafts are splined at their outer ends, to accept the wheel hubs, and are secured to the hub by a large nut. The inner end of each driveshaft is splined directly into the differential sun gear. This model is fitted with an intermediate driveshaft, with its own support bearing, between the transmission and right-hand driveshaft.

Ball-bearing type constant velocity (CV) joints are fitted to the outer ends of each driveshaft, to ensure the smooth and efficient transmission of drive at all the angles possible as the roadwheels move up-and-down with the suspension, and as they turn from side-to-side under steering. The inner joints are a tripod type or CV joint, which are able to move in-and-out to allow for lengthening and shortening of the shaft as the suspension moves up-and-down.

Rubber/plastic gaiters are fitted over both all joints with steel clips. The gaiters contain the grease, which lubricates the joints, and also protect the joints from the entry of dirt and debris.

2 Driveshafts – removal and refitting

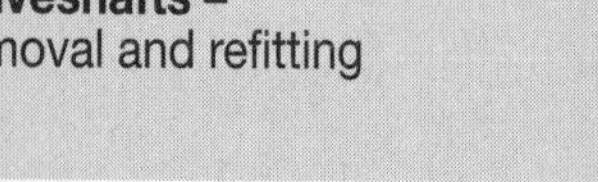

Note: *New hub nuts will be required on refitting.*

Removal

1 Remove the wheel trim/hub cap (as applicable) then apply the handbrake, and partially unscrew, by a maximum of 90°, the relevant hub nut with the vehicle resting on its wheels – note that the nut is very tight, and a suitable extension bar will probably be required to aid unscrewing. Also unscrew the roadwheel securing bolts.

Caution: Do not loosen the bolt more than 90° with the vehicle standing on the ground, as the wheel bearings may be damaged.

2 Chock the rear wheels of the car, firmly apply the handbrake, and then jack up the front of the vehicle and support it on axle stands (see *Jacking and vehicle support*). Remove the appropriate front roadwheel.

3 Remove the retaining screws and/or clips, and remove the undertray from beneath the engine/transmission unit to gain access to the driveshafts.

4 Unscrew and remove the hub nut **(see illustration)**. **Note:** *Discard the bolt and obtain a new one.*

5 Disconnect the wiring connectors for the speed sensor and brake pad warning light (right-hand side only) from under the wheel arch **(see illustration)**.

6 Unscrew the two bolts securing the brake caliper assembly to the swivel hub, and slide the caliper assembly off the disc. Using a piece of wire or string, tie the caliper to the front suspension coil spring, to avoid placing any strain on the hydraulic brake hose.

7 Slacken and remove the nut securing the steering gear track rod end balljoint to the swivel hub. Release the balljoint tapered shank using a universal balljoint separator.

8 Slacken and remove the two nuts from the bolts securing the swivel hub to the suspension strut, noting that the nuts are positioned on the front side of the strut. Withdraw the upper bolt, but leave the lower bolt in position at this stage.

9 For right-hand driveshaft, unscrew the two bolts securing the driveshaft support bearing to the engine cylinder block **(see illustration)**.

10 Position a container beneath the transmission to catch any spilt oil when the driveshafts are withdrawn. On refitting, top-up transmission oil, if required.

2.11 Removing the driveshaft from the hub

11 Remove the lower bolt securing the swivel hub to the suspension strut. Taking care not to damage the driveshaft gaiters, release the outer constant velocity joint from the hub and remove the driveshaft. Note that it is likely the joint will be a tight fit in the hub splines. Try tapping the joint out of position using a hammer and a soft metal drift, whilst an assistant supports the hub assembly. If this fails to move the joint, a suitable puller/extractor will be required to draw the hub assembly off the driveshaft end **(see illustration)**. Whilst the driveshaft is removed, support the hub assembly by refitting the bolts to the base of the strut.

Caution: Support the driveshaft by suspending it with wire or string – do not allow it to hang under its own weight, or the joint may be damaged.

Refitting

12 Where applicable, check the condition of the circlip on the inner end of the driveshaft, and if necessary, renew it.

13 As applicable, clean the splines on each end of the driveshaft and in the hub and apply a little oil, and where applicable wipe clean the oil seal in the transmission casing. Check the oil seal and if necessary renew it as described in Chapter 7A or 7B. Smear a little oil on the lips of the oil seal before fitting the driveshaft.

14 Manoeuvre the driveshaft into position, and locate the inner end of the driveshaft into the transmission – turn the driveshaft as necessary to engage the splines. Press in the driveshaft until the internal circlip (where fitted) engages the groove.

15 Ensure both the hub and driveshaft outer constant velocity joint splines are clean and dry, and apply a light coat of grease.

16 Move the top of the swivel hub inwards, at the same time engaging the driveshaft with the hub.

17 Slide the hub fully onto the driveshaft splines, then insert the two suspension strut mounting bolts from the rear side of the strut. Refit the nuts to the front of the bolts, and tighten them to the specified torque setting.

18 Fit the new driveshaft hub-retaining nut, tightening it by hand only at this stage.

3.2 Release the joint gaiter clip

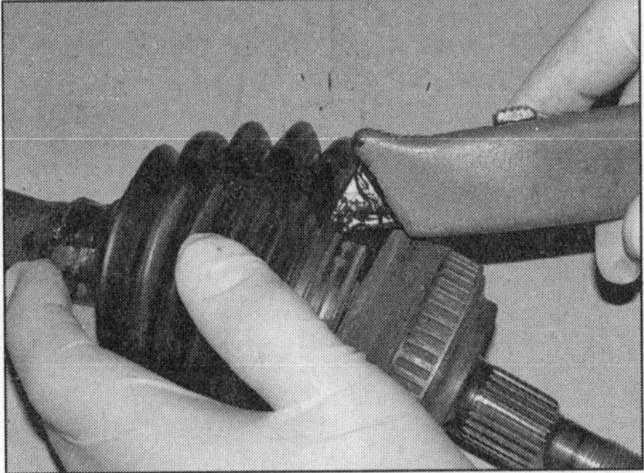

3.3 Cutting the old gaiter off the joint

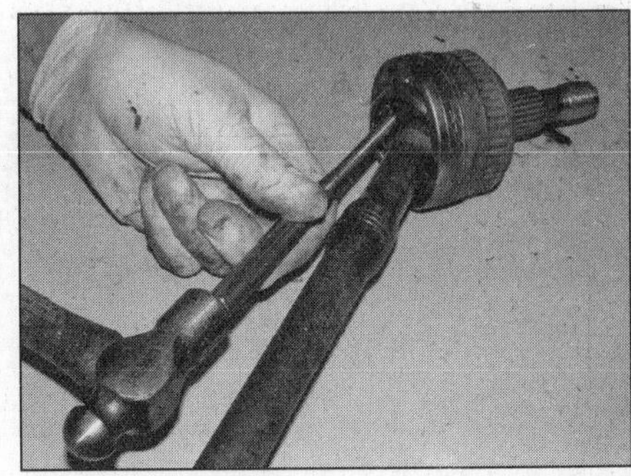

3.4 Using a drift to remove the outer joint

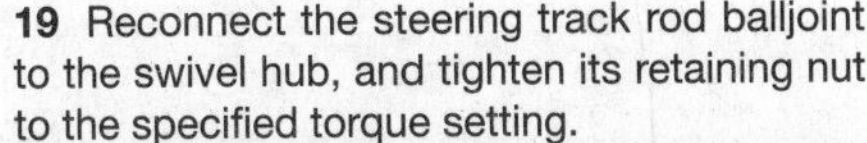

19 Reconnect the steering track rod balljoint to the swivel hub, and tighten its retaining nut to the specified torque setting.

20 Slide the caliper into position, making sure the pads pass either side of the disc, and tighten the caliper bracket bolts to the specified torque setting (see Chapter 9 Specifications).

21 Using the method employed during removal to prevent the hub from rotating, tighten a new driveshaft hub retaining nut to the specified torque. Alternatively, lightly tighten the nut at this stage, and tighten it to the specified torque once the vehicle is resting on its wheels again.

22 Reconnect the wiring connectors for the speed sensor and brake pad warning light (right-hand side only) to the connectors under the wheel arch.

23 Refit the engine undershields

24 Refit the roadwheel. Lower the car to the ground and tighten the roadwheel bolts to the specified torque. If not already done, also tighten the driveshaft hub retaining nut to the specified torque.

25 If required, refill the transmission with the specified type and amount of oil, and check the level using the information given in Chapter 1A or 1B.

3 Driveshaft rubber gaiters – renewal

1 Remove the driveshaft from the car, as described in Section 2. Continue as described under the relevant sub-heading.

Outer joint gaiter

2 Secure the driveshaft in a vice equipped with soft jaws, and release the two outer joint gaiter retaining clips **(see illustration)**. If necessary, the retaining clips can be cut to release them.

3 Cut off the rubber gaiter and discard it, scoop out all the old dirty grease **(see illustration)**.

4 Using a drift against the inner star part of the joint, carefully tap the joint off the end of the driveshaft, taking care not to damage the joint or splines **(see illustration)**.

5 Withdraw the joint from the end of the shaft and remove the circlip from the driveshaft groove **(see illustrations)**.

6 Thoroughly clean the constant velocity joint(s) using paraffin, or a suitable solvent, and dry thoroughly. Carry out a visual inspection as follows.

7 Move the inner splined driving member from side-to-side to expose each ball in turn at the top of its track. Examine the balls for cracks, flat spots or signs of surface pitting.

8 Inspect the ball tracks on the inner and outer members. If the tracks have widened, the balls will no longer be a tight fit. At the same time, check the ball cage windows for wear or cracking between the windows.

9 If on inspection any of the constant velocity joint components are found to be worn, or damaged, it will be necessary to renew the complete joint assembly. If the joint is in satisfactory condition, obtain a new gaiter and retaining clips, a constant velocity joint circlip and the correct type of grease. Grease is often supplied with the joint repair kit – if not, use good-quality molybdenum disulphide grease.

10 Slide the new gaiter complete with inner retaining clip onto the end of the driveshaft **(see illustration)**.

11 Pack the joint with the specified type of grease. Work the grease well into the bearing tracks whilst twisting the joint, until it is full **(see illustration)**.

12 Fit a new circlip to the driveshaft, then tap the joint onto the driveshaft until the circlip engages in its groove **(see illustrations)**. Make sure that the joint is securely retained by the circlip.

13 Fill the rubber gaiter with the remaining half of the grease **(see illustration)**.

14 Ease the gaiter over the joint, and ensure that the gaiter lips are correctly located on both the driveshaft and constant velocity joint.

3.5a Slide the joint off the splines . . .

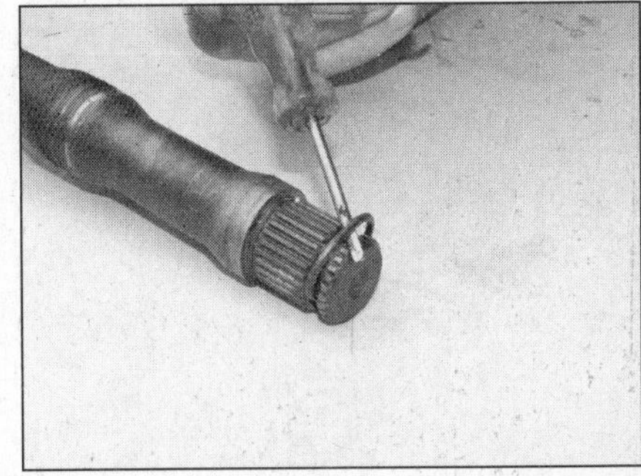

3.5b . . . and remove the circlip

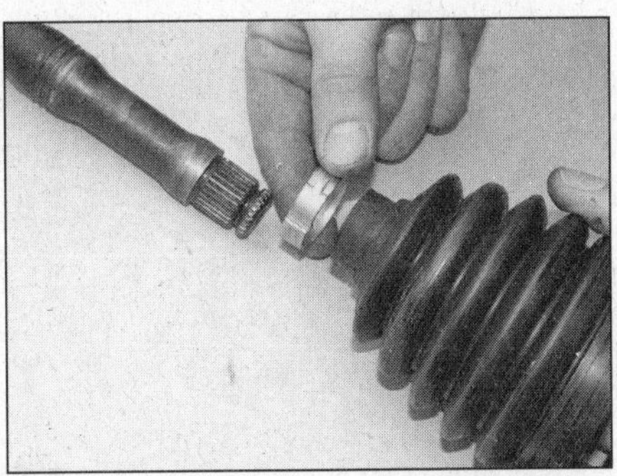

3.10 Slide the small clip and gaiter onto the driveshaft

3.11 Fill the joint with grease

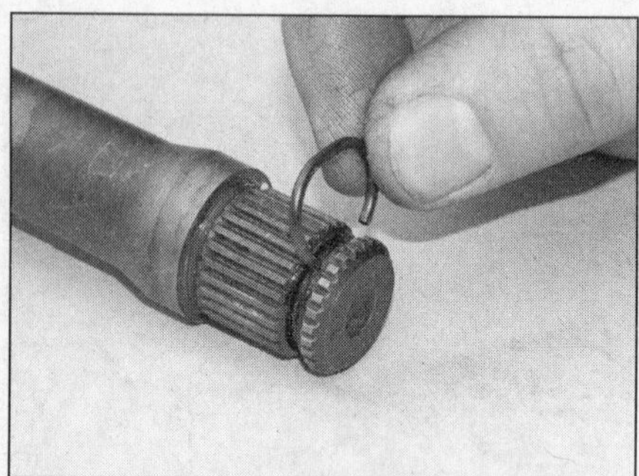
3.12a Fit the new circlip in position . . .

3.12b . . . and tap the joint onto the shaft

3.13 Squeeze the remaining grease into the gaiter

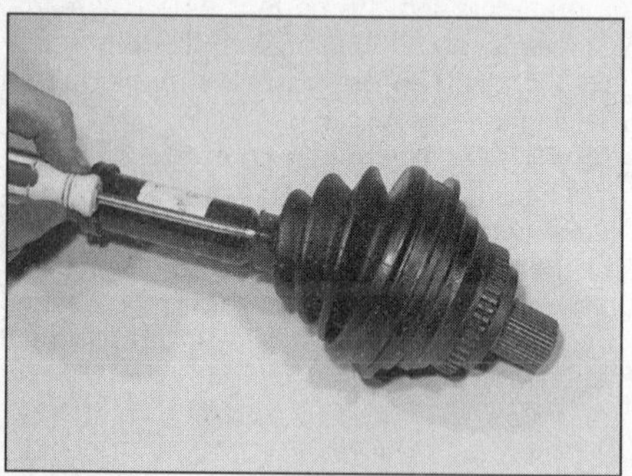
3.14 Lift the gaiter to equalise the air pressure

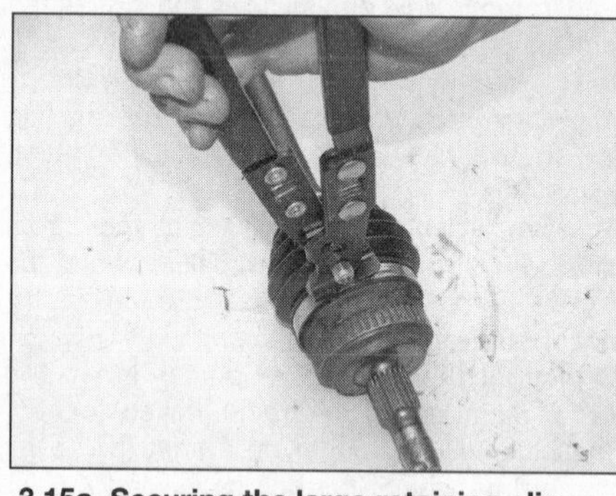
3.15a Securing the large retaining clip . . .

3.15b . . . and the small retaining clip, using special pliers

Lift the sealing lip of the gaiter to equalise air pressure within the gaiter **(see illustration)**.

15 Fit the large metal retaining clip to the gaiter. Pull the clip as tight as possible, and locate the hooks on the clip in their slots. Remove any slack in the gaiter-retaining clip by carefully compressing the raised section of the clip. In the absence of the special tool, a pair of side-cutters may be used, taking care not to cut the clip **(see illustrations)**. Secure the small retaining clip using the same procedure.

16 Check the constant velocity joint moves freely in all directions, then refit the driveshaft to the vehicle, as described in Section 2.

Inner joint gaiter

17 Release the two inner joint gaiter retaining clips **(see illustrations)**. If necessary, the retaining clips can be cut to release them. Slide the rubber gaiter down the shaft, away from the joint outer member. Be prepared to catch the grease as the gaiter is removed.

18 Mark the outer side of the shaft and housing to make sure that it is refitted in the same position. Slide the shaft with the bearing tripod out from the inner part of the shaft **(see illustration)**, and clean out any remaining grease.

19 Using a small screwdriver release the circlip from the end of the shaft **(see illustration)**.

20 Mark the side of the shaft and tripod bearing to make sure that it is refitted in the

3.17a Using a small chisel . . .

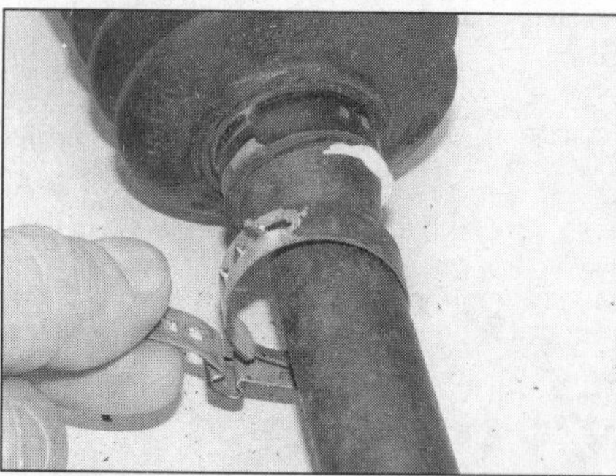
3.17b . . . to release the retaining clip

3.18 Slide the tripod out from the outer joint

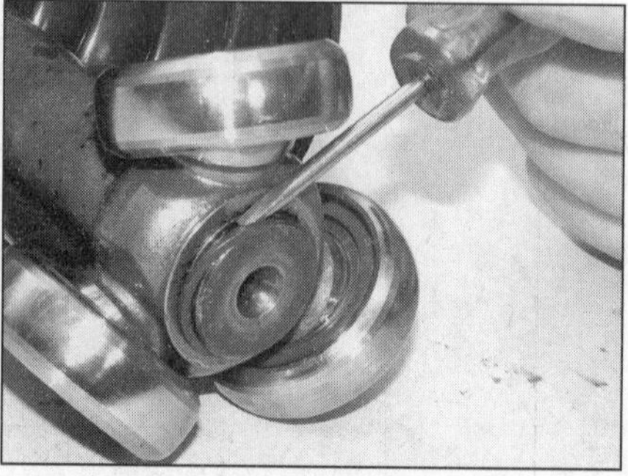
3.19 Releasing the circlip from the end of the shaft

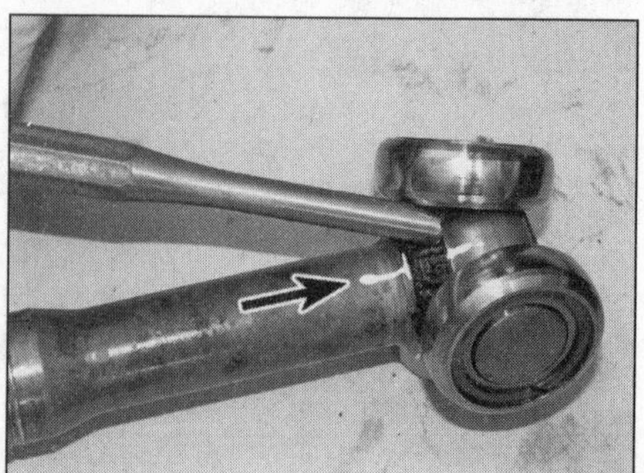
3.20 Mark the shaft (arrowed) and joint for refitting

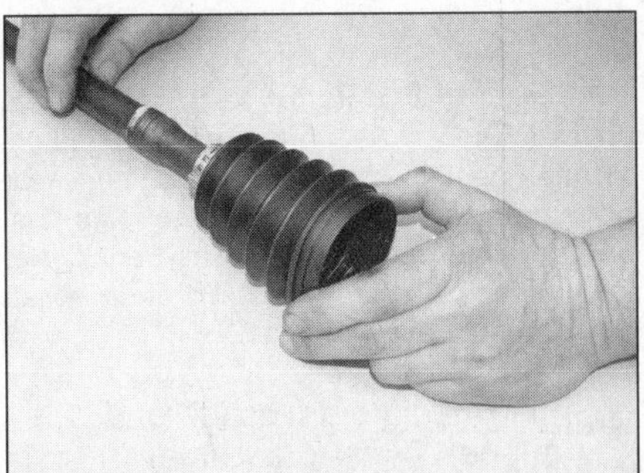

3.22 Slide the gaiter and small clip onto the driveshaft

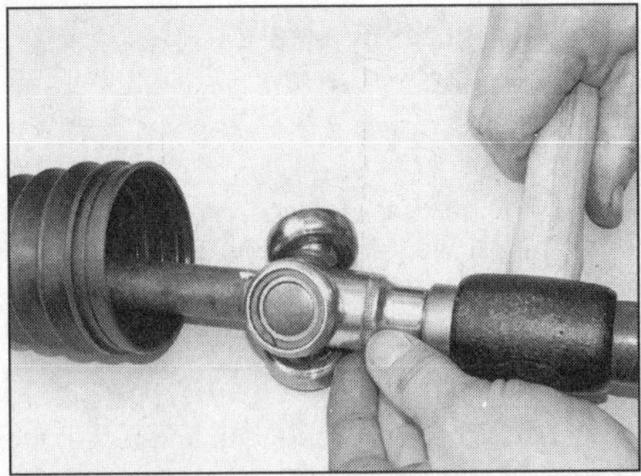

3.23a Using a socket to tap on the joint . . .

3.23b . . . and then fit the circlip

3.24 Squeeze grease into the outer part of the joint

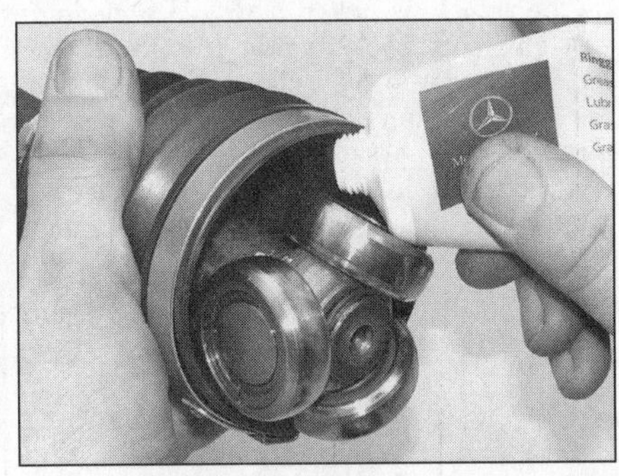

3.25 Squeeze the remaining grease into the gaiter

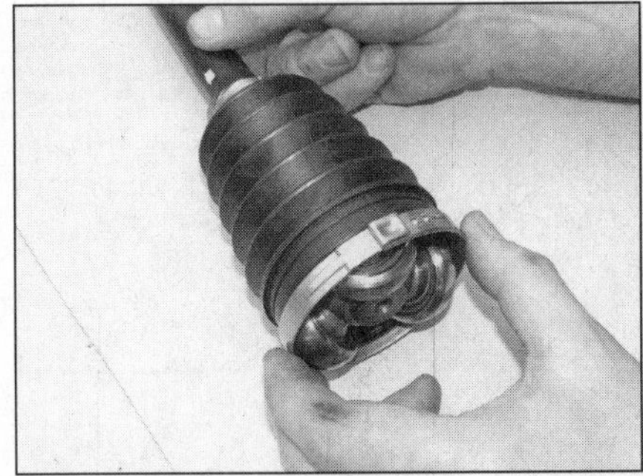

3.26a Fit the large retaining clip onto the gaiter

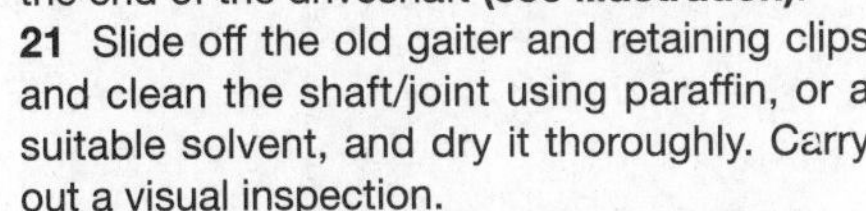

same position. Using a drift, tap the joint off the end of the driveshaft **(see illustration).**

21 Slide off the old gaiter and retaining clips and clean the shaft/joint using paraffin, or a suitable solvent, and dry it thoroughly. Carry out a visual inspection.

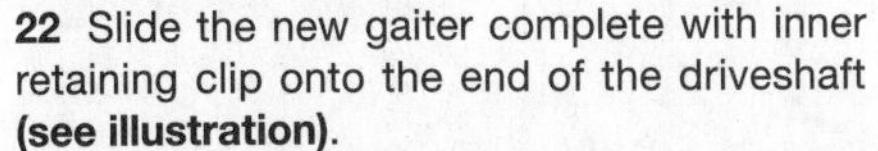

22 Slide the new gaiter complete with inner retaining clip onto the end of the driveshaft **(see illustration).**

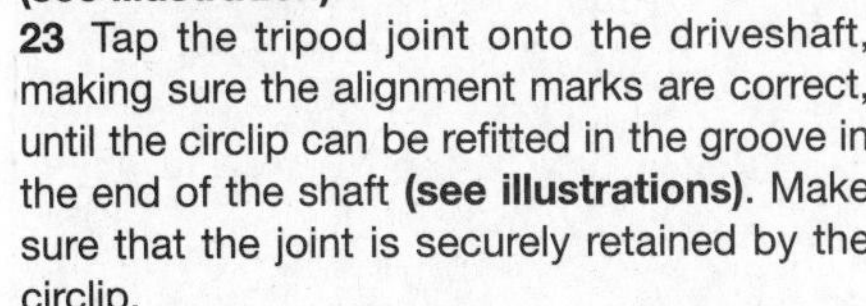

23 Tap the tripod joint onto the driveshaft, making sure the alignment marks are correct, until the circlip can be refitted in the groove in the end of the shaft **(see illustrations).** Make sure that the joint is securely retained by the circlip.

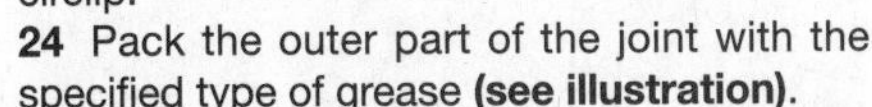

24 Pack the outer part of the joint with the specified type of grease **(see illustration).**

25 Fill the rubber gaiter with the remaining half of the grease **(see illustration).**

26 Fit the new retaining clip over the large end of the gaiter, and slide the tripod bearing into the outer part of the joint **(see illustrations).**

27 Before tightening the gaiter retaining clips, use a small screwdriver to lift the outer sealing lip of the gaiter to equalise air pressure within the gaiter **(see illustration).** Then slide the joint together until the measurement from the transmission end of the joint to the small end of the rubber gaiter is 159 mm **(see illustration).**

28 With the gaiter in position, remove any slack in the gaiter-retaining clips by carefully compressing the raised section of the clips. In the absence of the special tool, a pair of side-cutters may be used, taking care not to cut the clip **(see illustration).**

3.26b Align the marks (arrowed) made on removal

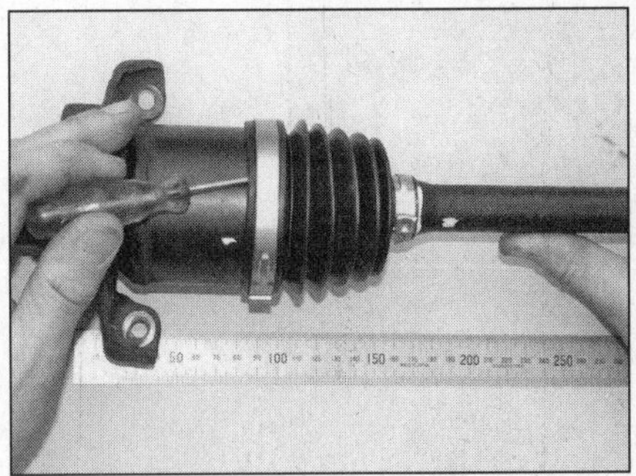

3.27a Use a screwdriver to lift the gaiter to equalise the air pressure

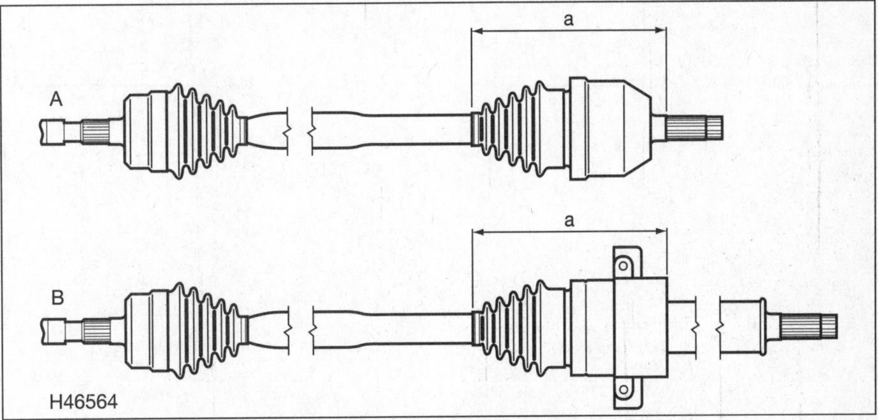

3.27b Measurement for gaiter

A Left driveshaft *B Right driveshaft*

a = 159 mm before tightening clips

3.28 Securing the large retaining clip

29 Check the constant velocity joint moves freely in all directions, then refit the driveshaft to the vehicle, as described in Section 2.

4 Driveshaft overhaul – general information

If any of the checks described in Chapter 1A or 1B reveal wear in any driveshaft joint, first remove the roadwheel trim or centre cap (as applicable) and check that the hub nut is tight. If the nut is loose, obtain a new one, and tighten it to the specified torque (see Section 2). If the nut is tight, refit the centre cap/trim, and repeat the check on the other hub nut.

Road test the vehicle, and listen for a metallic clicking from the front of the vehicle as the vehicle is driven slowly in a circle on full-lock. If a clicking noise is heard, this indicates wear in the outer constant velocity joint; this means that the joint must be renewed.

If vibration consistent with roadspeed is felt through the car when accelerating, there is a possibility of wear in the inner constant velocity joints.

To check the joints for wear, remove the driveshafts (see Section 2), then dismantle them as described in Section 3. If any wear or free play is found, the affected joint must be renewed. Refer to a Mercedes-Benz dealer for information on the availability of driveshaft components.

5 Intermediate driveshaft and support bearing assembly – general information

The intermediate shaft is part of the right-hand driveshaft and can be removed as described In Section 2. At the time of writing there was no information on removing the support bearing from the driveshaft. Refer to a Mercedes-Benz dealer for information on the availability of the driveshaft support bearing.

Chapter 9
Braking system

Contents

Degrees of difficulty

Easy, suitable for novice with little experience 	**Fairly easy,** suitable for beginner with some experience	**Fairly difficult,** suitable for competent DIY mechanic	**Difficult,** suitable for experienced DIY mechanic	**Very difficult,** suitable for expert DIY or professional 

Specifications

Front brakes

Caliper type	Single piston, sliding caliper
Disc diameter:	
All models except 1.9 and 2.1 litre	260 mm
1.9 and 2.1 litre models	276 mm
Disc thickness.	
Vented disc:	
New	22.0 mm
Wear service limit	20.0 mm
Solid disc:	
New	12.0 mm
Wear service limit	10.0 mm
Maximum disc run-out	0.1 mm
Brake pad lining thickness:	
New (including backplate)	16.0 mm
Wear limit (including backplate)	7.0 mm
Minimum (wear indicator activated)	2.0 mm

Rear disc brakes

Caliper type	Single piston, sliding caliper
Disc diameter	258 mm
Disc thickness:	
New	8.0 mm
Wear service limit	7.0 mm
Maximum disc run-out	0.1 mm
Brake pad lining thickness (including backplate):	
New	14.0 mm
Wear limit	6.0 mm

Rear drum brakes

Drum diameter:	
New	180.0 to 180.2 mm
Wear limit	181.2 mm
Brake lining thickness:	
New (leading shoe)	4.5 mm
New (trailing shoe)	3.5 mm
Wear limit	2.0 mm

Torque wrench settings

	Nm	lbf ft
ABS wheel speed sensor retaining bolts	8	6
Front brake caliper:		
Guide pin bolts*	30	22
Mounting bracket bolts	115	85
Handbrake mounting bolts	20	15
Hydraulic brake hose to caliper	18	13
Hydraulic brake line to ABS unit	14	10
Hydraulic brake line to master cylinder	16	12
Hydraulic brake line union nuts	14	10
Master cylinder mounting nuts	20	15
Rear brake cylinder retaining bolt	15	11
Rear disc retaining screw*	10	7
Rear drum retaining screw*	10	7
Rear brake caliper:		
Guide pin bolts*	30	22
Mounting bracket bolts	55	41
Roadwheel bolts	110	81
Vacuum pump (diesel models)	14	10
Servo unit mounting nuts	25	18

** Use new bolts*

1 General information and precautions

General information

The braking system is of servo-assisted, diagonal dual-circuit hydraulic type. The arrangement of the hydraulic system is such that each circuit operates one front and one rear brake from a tandem master cylinder. Under normal circumstances, both circuits operate in unison, but, if there is hydraulic failure in one circuit, full braking force will still be available at two wheels. On petrol engines, vacuum for the servo unit is supplied from the inlet manifold; however, on diesel engines a vacuum pump is driven off the end of the camshaft.

ABS is fitted as standard to all models (refer to Section 19 for further information on ABS operation).

The front and rear disc brakes are actuated by single-piston sliding type calipers, which ensure that equal pressure is applied to each disc pad.

The rear discs also incorporate rear brake shoes inside the centre hub of the disc for the mechanical handbrake operation.

Precautions

• When servicing any part of the system, work carefully and methodically; also observe scrupulous cleanliness when overhauling any part of the hydraulic system. Always renew components in axle sets (where applicable) if in doubt about their condition, and use only genuine Mercedes-Benz parts, or at least those of known good quality. Note the warnings given in *Safety first!* and at relevant points in this Chapter concerning the dangers of asbestos dust and hydraulic fluid.

2 Hydraulic system – bleeding

Warning: Hydraulic fluid is poisonous; wash off immediately and thoroughly in the case of skin contact, and seek immediate medical advice if any fluid is swallowed or gets into the eyes. Certain types of hydraulic fluid are flammable, and may ignite when allowed into contact with hot components; when servicing any hydraulic system, it is safest to assume that the fluid is flammable, and to take precautions against the risk of fire as though it is petrol that is being handled. Hydraulic fluid is also an effective paint stripper, and will attack plastics: if any is spilt, it should be washed off immediately, using copious quantities of fresh water. Finally, it is hygroscopic (it absorbs moisture from the air) – old fluid may be contaminated and unfit for further use. When topping-up or renewing the fluid, always use the recommended type, and ensure that it comes from a freshly-opened, sealed container.

General

1 The correct operation of any hydraulic system is only possible after removing all air from the components and circuit; this is achieved by bleeding the system. Since the clutch hydraulic system also uses fluid from the brake system reservoir, it should also be bled at the same time by referring to Chapter 6.

2 During the bleeding procedure, add only clean, unused hydraulic fluid of the recommended type; never re-use fluid that has already been bled from the system. Ensure that sufficient fluid is available before starting work.

3 If there is any possibility of incorrect fluid being already in the system, the brake components and circuit must be flushed completely with uncontaminated, correct fluid, and new seals should be fitted to the various components.

4 If hydraulic fluid has been lost from the system, or air has entered because of a leak, ensure that the fault is cured before continuing further.

5 Park the vehicle on level ground, then chock the wheels and release the handbrake.

6 Check that all pipes and hoses are secure, unions tight and bleed screws closed. Clean any dirt from around the bleed screws.

7 Unscrew the master cylinder reservoir cap, and top the reservoir up to the MAX level line; refit the cap loosely, and remember to maintain the fluid level at least above the MIN level line throughout the procedure, or there is a risk of further air entering the system.

8 There is a number of one-man, do-it-yourself brake bleeding kits currently available from motor accessory shops. It is recommended that one of these kits is used whenever possible, as they greatly simplify the bleeding operation, and reduce the risk of expelled air and fluid being drawn back into the system. If such a kit is not available, the basic (two-man) method must be used, which is described in detail below.

9 If a kit is to be used, prepare the vehicle as described previously, and follow the kit manufacturer's instructions, as the procedure may vary slightly according to the type being used; generally, they are as outlined below in the relevant sub-section.

10 Whichever method is used, the same sequence must be followed (paragraph 12) to ensure the removal of all air from the system.

Bleeding sequence

11 If the system has been only partially disconnected, and suitable precautions were taken to minimise fluid loss, it should be necessary only to bleed that part of the system.

12 If the complete system is to be bled, then it should be done working in the following sequence:

RHD models

a) Right-hand front brake.
b) Left-hand front brake.
c) Right-hand rear brake.
d) Left-hand rear brake.

LHD models

a) Left-hand front brake.
b) Right-hand front brake.
c) Left-hand rear brake.
d) Right-hand rear brake.

Bleeding

Basic (two-man) method

13 Collect together a clean glass jar of reasonable size, a suitable length of plastic or rubber tubing which is a tight fit over the bleed screw, and a ring spanner to fit the screw. The help of an assistant will also be required.

14 Remove the dust cap from the first bleed screw in the sequence **(see illustration)**. Fit the spanner and tube to the screw, place the other end of the tube in the jar, and pour in sufficient fluid to cover the end of the tube.

15 Ensure that the master cylinder reservoir fluid level is maintained at least above the MIN level line throughout the procedure.

16 Have the assistant fully depress the brake pedal several times to build-up pressure, and then maintain it on the final downstroke.

17 While pedal pressure is maintained, unscrew the bleed screw (approximately one turn) and allow the compressed fluid and air to flow into the jar. The assistant should maintain pedal pressure, following it down to the floor if necessary, and should not release it until instructed to do so. When the flow stops, tighten the bleed screw again, have the assistant release the pedal slowly, and recheck the reservoir fluid level.

18 Repeat the steps given in paragraphs 16 and 17 until the fluid emerging from the bleed screw is free from air bubbles. If the master cylinder has been drained and refilled, and air is being bled from the first screw in the sequence, allow approximately five seconds between cycles for the master cylinder passages to refill.

19 When no more air bubbles appear, tighten the bleed screw securely, remove the tube and spanner, and refit the dust cap. Do not overtighten the bleed screw.

20 Repeat the procedure on the remaining screws in the sequence, until all air is removed from the system and the brake pedal feels firm again.

Using a one-way valve kit

21 As their name implies, these kits consist of a length of tubing with a one-way valve fitted, to prevent expelled air and fluid being drawn back into the system; some kits include a translucent container, which can be positioned so that the air bubbles can be more easily seen flowing from the end of the tube.

22 The kit is connected to the bleed screw, which is then opened. The user returns to the driver's seat, depresses the brake pedal with a smooth, steady stroke, and slowly releases it; this is repeated until the expelled fluid is clear of air bubbles **(see illustration)**.

23 Note that these kits simplify work so much that it is easy to forget the master cylinder reservoir fluid level; ensure that this is maintained at least above the MIN level line at all times.

Using a pressure-bleeding kit

24 These kits are usually operated by the reservoir of pressurised air contained in the spare tyre. However, note that it will be probably necessary to reduce the pressure to less than 1.0 bar (14.5 psi); refer to the instructions supplied with the kit.

25 By connecting a pressurised, fluid-filled container to the master cylinder reservoir, bleeding can be carried out simply by opening each screw in turn (in the specified sequence), and allowing the fluid to flow out until no more air bubbles can be seen in the expelled fluid.

26 This method has the advantage that the large reservoir of fluid provides an additional safeguard against air being drawn into the system during bleeding.

27 Pressure-bleeding is particularly effective when bleeding 'difficult' systems, or when bleeding the complete system at the time of routine fluid renewal.

All methods

28 When bleeding is complete, and firm pedal feel is restored, wash off any spilt fluid, tighten the bleed screws securely, and refit their dust caps.

29 Check the hydraulic fluid level in the master cylinder reservoir, and top-up if necessary (see *Weekly checks*).

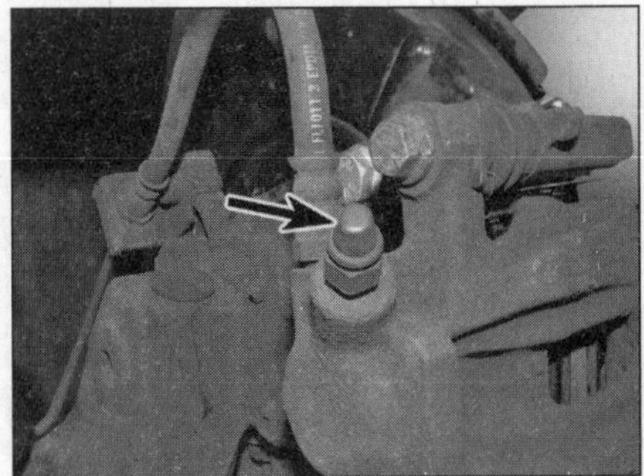

2.14 Bleed screw dust cap – arrowed

30 Discard any hydraulic fluid that has been bled from the system; it will not be fit for re-use.

31 Check the feel of the brake pedal. If it feels at all spongy, air must still be present in the system, and further bleeding is required. Failure to bleed satisfactorily after a reasonable repetition of the bleeding procedure may be due to worn master cylinder seals.

3 Hydraulic pipes and hoses – renewal

Note: *Refer to the note in Section 2 concerning the dangers of hydraulic fluid.*

1 If any pipe or hose is to be renewed, minimise fluid loss by first removing the master cylinder reservoir cap, then tightening it down onto a piece of polythene to obtain an airtight seal. Alternatively, flexible hoses can be sealed, if required, using a proprietary brake hose clamp; metal brake pipe unions can be plugged (if care is taken not to allow dirt into the system) or capped immediately they are disconnected. Place a wad of rag under any union that is to be disconnected, to catch any spilt fluid.

2 If a flexible hose is to be disconnected, where applicable unscrew the brake pipe union nut before removing the spring clip which secures the hose to its mounting bracket.

3 To unscrew the union nuts, it is preferable to obtain a brake pipe spanner of the correct size; these are available from most large motor

2.22 Bleeding a brake using a one-way vaive kit

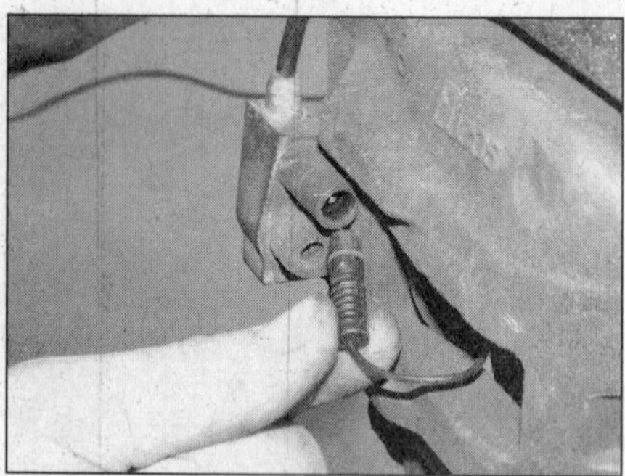

4.2 Disconnect the brake pad wiring connector

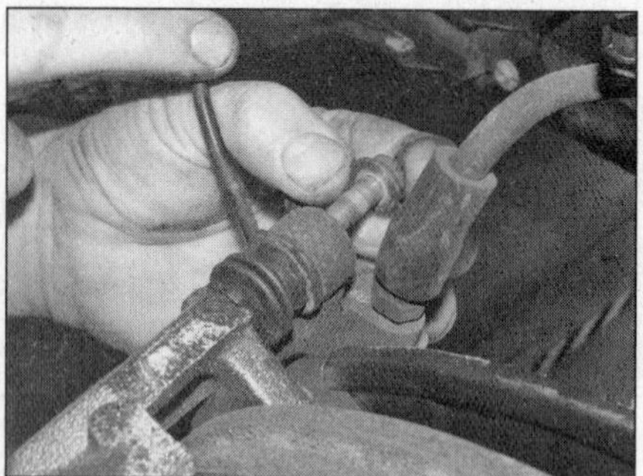

4.3 Remove the guide pin bolts

4.4 Removing the brake pads

accessory shops. Failing this, a close-fitting open-ended spanner will be required, though if the nuts are tight or corroded, their flats may be rounded-off if the spanner slips. In such a case, a self-locking wrench is often the only way to unscrew a stubborn union, but it follows that the pipe and the damaged nuts must be renewed on reassembly. Always clean a union and surrounding area before disconnecting it. If disconnecting a component with more than one union, make a careful note of the connections before disturbing any of them.

4 If a brake pipe is to be renewed, it can be obtained, cut to length and with the union nuts and end flares in place, from Mercedes-Benz dealers or brake specialist. All that is then necessary is to bend it to shape, following the line of the original, before fitting it to the car. Alternatively, most motor accessory shops can make up brake pipes from kits, but this requires very careful measurement of the original, to ensure that the new pipe is of the correct length. The safest answer is usually to take the original to the shop as a pattern.

5 On refitting, do not overtighten the union nuts. It is not necessary to exercise brute force to obtain a sound joint.

6 Ensure that the pipes and hoses are correctly routed, with no kinks, and that they are secured in the clips or brackets provided. After fitting, remove the polythene from the reservoir, and bleed the hydraulic system as described in Section 2. Wash off any spilt fluid, and check all the brake line connections carefully for fluid leaks.

4.5 Unclip the springs from the mounting bracket

4 Front brake pads – removal, inspection and refitting

Warning: Renew both sets of brake pads at the same time – never renew the pads on only one wheel, as uneven braking may result. Note that the dust created by wear of the pads may contain asbestos, which is a health hazard. Never blow it out with compressed air, and do not inhale any of it. An approved filtering mask should be worn when working on the brakes. DO NOT use petrol or petroleum-based solvents to clean brake parts; use brake cleaner or methylated spirit only.

Removal

1 Apply the handbrake, then jack up the front of the vehicle and support it on axle stands (see *Jacking and vehicle support*). Remove the front roadwheels.

2 Trace the brake pad wear sensor wiring (right-hand side only) to the pads, and disconnect it from the wiring connector **(see illustration)**. Note the routing of the wiring, and free it from any relevant retaining clips.

3 Slacken and remove the two caliper guide pin bolts from the caliper **(see illustration)**. Then lift the caliper, away from the hub carrier, and tie it to the suspension strut using a suitable piece of wire. Do not allow the caliper to hang unsupported on the flexible brake hose.

4.9 Open the bleed nipple as the piston is pushed back into the caliper

4 Remove the two brake pads from the caliper mounting bracket **(see illustration)**. If the original pads are to be refitted, mark them so that they can be refitted in their original positions.

5 Unclip the upper and lower spring clips from the mounting bracket, noting their fitted position **(see illustration)**.

Inspection

6 First measure the thickness of each brake pad. If either pad is worn at any point to the specified minimum thickness or less, all four pads must be renewed. Also, the pads should be renewed if any are fouled with oil or grease; there is no satisfactory way of degreasing friction material, once contaminated. If any of the brake pads are worn unevenly, or are fouled with oil or grease, trace and rectify the cause before reassembly. New brake pad kits are available from Mercedes-Benz dealers.

7 If the brake pads are still serviceable, carefully clean them using a clean, fine wire brush or similar, paying particular attention to the sides and back of the metal backing. Clean out the grooves in the friction material (where applicable), and pick out any large embedded particles of dirt or debris. Carefully clean the pad locations in the caliper body/ mounting bracket.

8 Prior to fitting the pads, check that the guide pins are free to slide easily in the caliper body bushes, and are a reasonably tight fit. Brush the dust and dirt from the caliper and piston, but *do not* inhale it, as it is injurious to health. Inspect the dust seal around the piston for damage, and the piston for evidence of fluid leaks, corrosion or damage. If attention to any of these components is necessary, refer to Section 5.

Refitting

9 If new brake pads are to be fitted, the caliper piston must be pushed back into the cylinder to make room for them. Either use a G-clamp or similar tool, or use suitable pieces of wood as levers. To avoid any dirt entering the ABS solenoid valves, connect a pipe to the bleed nipple and, as the piston is pushed back, open the nipple and allow the displaced fluid to flow through the pipe into a suitable container **(see illustration)**.

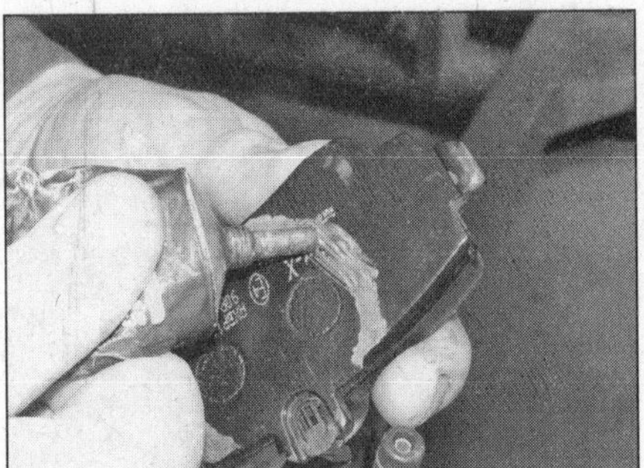

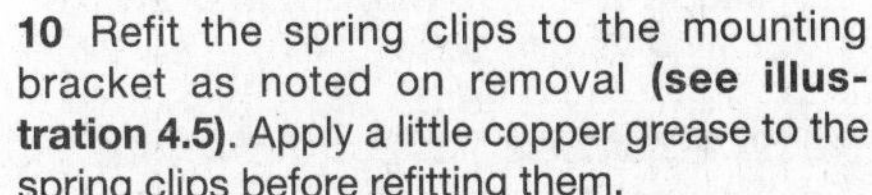

4.11a Apply copper grease to the rear of the pads . . .

10 Refit the spring clips to the mounting bracket as noted on removal **(see illustration 4.5)**. Apply a little copper grease to the spring clips before refitting them.

11 Apply a little copper grease to the metal backplates of the brake pads before refitting them, and then fit the new brake pads into the mounting bracket **(see illustrations)**.

12 Position the caliper over the brake disc **(see illustration)**, and pass the pad-warning sensor wiring (where fitted) through the caliper aperture.

13 Position the caliper until it is possible to install the new caliper guide pin bolts. Apply a little copper grease to the bolts before refitting them, and tighten them to the specified torque. **Note:** *Do not exert excess pressure on the caliper, as this will deform the pad springs, resulting in noisy operation of the brakes.*

14 Where applicable, reconnect the brake pad wear sensor wiring connectors, ensuring that the wiring is correctly routed.

15 Depress the brake pedal repeatedly, until the pads are pressed into firm contact with the brake disc, and normal (non-assisted) pedal pressure is restored.

16 Repeat the above procedure on the remaining front brake caliper.

17 Refit the roadwheels, then lower the vehicle to the ground and tighten the roadwheel bolts to the specified torque.

Caution: New pads will not give full braking efficiency until they have bedded-in. Be prepared for this, and avoid hard braking as far as possible for the first hundred miles or so after pad renewal.

5 Front brake caliper – removal, overhaul and refitting

Note: *Before starting work, refer to the note at the beginning of Section 2 concerning the dangers of hydraulic fluid, and to the warning at the beginning of Section 4 concerning the dangers of asbestos dust.*

Removal

1 Apply the handbrake, then jack up the front of the vehicle and support it on axle stands (see *Jacking and vehicle support*). Remove the appropriate roadwheel.

4.11b . . . and fit them into the mounting bracket

2 Minimise fluid loss by first removing the master cylinder reservoir cap, and then tightening it down onto a piece of polythene, to obtain an airtight seal. Alternatively, use a brake hose clamp, a G-clamp or a similar tool to clamp the flexible hose.

3 Clean the area around the union, and then loosen the brake hose union nut.

4 Lift the caliper from the brake pads as described in Section 4.

5 Unscrew the caliper from the end of the brake hose and remove it from the vehicle.

Overhaul

6 At the time of writing, no parts where available to overhaul the calipers. Consequently, if the calipers are faulty, they must be renewed. It may be possible to get exchange units, check with your local Mercedes-Benz dealer or brake specialist.

Refitting

7 Screw the caliper fully onto the flexible hose union.

8 Refit the caliper over brake pads as described in Section 4.

9 Securely tighten the brake pipe union nut, checking that the brake hose it not twisted.

10 Remove the brake hose clamp or polythene, as applicable, and bleed the hydraulic system as described in Section 2. Note that, providing the precautions described were taken to minimise brake fluid loss, it should only be necessary to bleed the relevant front brake.

11 Refit the roadwheel, then lower the vehicle to the ground and tighten the roadwheel bolts to the specified torque.

6.4 Using a DTI gauge to measure disc run-out

4.12 Fit the brake caliper over the brake pads

6 Brake disc – inspection, removal and refitting

Note: *Before starting work, refer to the note at the beginning of Section 4 concerning the dangers of asbestos dust.*

Note: *If either disc requires renewal, BOTH should be renewed at the same time, to ensure even and consistent braking. New brake pads should also be fitted.*

Front brake disc

Inspection

1 Apply the handbrake, then jack up the front of the car and support it on axle stands (see *Jacking and vehicle support*). Remove the appropriate front roadwheel.

2 Slowly rotate the brake disc so that the full area of both sides can be checked; remove the brake pads if better access is required to the inboard surface. Light scoring is normal in the area swept by the brake pads, but if heavy scoring or cracks are found, the disc must be renewed.

3 It is normal to find a lip of rust and brake dust around the perimeter of the disc; this can be scraped off if required. If, however, a lip has formed due to excessive wear of the brake pad swept area, then the disc thickness must be measured using a micrometer. Take measurements at several places around the disc, at the inside and outside of the pad swept area; if the disc has worn at any point to the specified minimum thickness or less, the disc must be renewed.

4 If the disc is thought to be warped, it can be checked for run-out. Either use a dial gauge mounted on any convenient fixed point, while the disc is slowly rotated, or use feeler blades to measure (at several points all around the disc) the clearance between the disc and a fixed point, such as the caliper mounting bracket. If the measurements obtained are at the specified maximum or beyond, the disc is excessively warped, and must be renewed; however, it is worth checking first that the hub bearing is in good condition. If the run-out is excessive, the disc must be renewed **(see illustration)**.

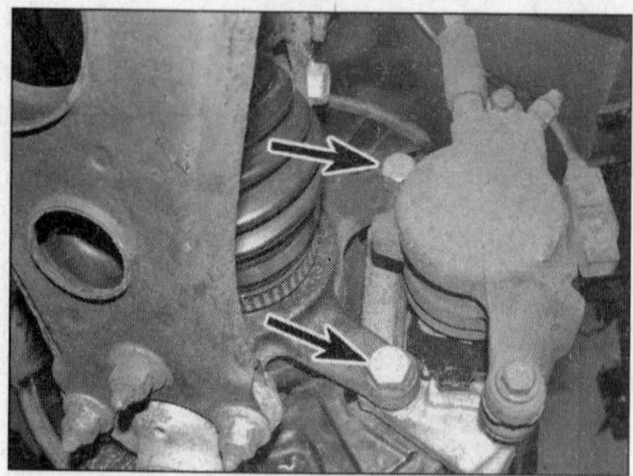
6.6 Front caliper mounting bracket bolts – arrowed

6.7a Remove the securing screw . . .

6.7b . . . and withdraw the brake disc

5 Check the disc for cracks, especially around the wheel bolt holes, and any other wear or damage, and renew if necessary.

Removal

6 Unscrew the two bolts **(see illustration)** securing the brake caliper mounting bracket to the hub carrier, then slide the caliper assembly off the disc. Using a piece of wire or string, tie the caliper to the front suspension coil spring, to avoid placing any strain on the brake hose.

7 Remove the screw securing the brake disc to the hub, and remove the disc **(see illustrations)**. If it is tight, apply penetrating fluid, and tap its rear face gently with a hide or plastic mallet. The use of excessive force could cause the disc to be damaged.

Refitting

8 Refitting is the reverse of the removal procedure, noting the following points:

a) *Ensure that the mating surfaces of the disc and hub are clean and flat.*
b) *Align (if applicable) the marks made on removal, and securely tighten the disc retaining screw.*
c) *If a new disc has been fitted, use a suitable solvent to wipe any preservative coating from the disc, before refitting the caliper.*
d) *Slide the caliper into position over the disc, making sure the pads pass either side of the disc. Tighten the caliper bracket mounting bolts to the specified torque.*
e) *Refit the roadwheel, then lower the vehicle to the ground and tighten the roadwheel bolts to the specified torque. On completion, repeatedly depress the brake pedal until normal (non-assisted) pedal pressure returns.*

Rear brake disc

Inspection

9 Firmly chock the front wheels, then jack up the rear of the car and support it on axle stands. Remove the appropriate rear roadwheel.

10 Inspect the disc as described in paragraphs 2 to 5.

Removal

11 Unscrew the two bolts securing the brake caliper mounting bracket in position **(see illustration)**, and then slide the caliper assembly off the disc. Using a piece of wire or string, tie the caliper to the rear suspension coil spring, to avoid placing any strain on the hydraulic brake hose.

12 Use chalk or paint to mark the relationship of the disc to the hub, then remove the screw securing the brake disc to the hub, and remove the disc **(see illustrations)**. If it is tight, apply penetrating fluid, and tap its rear face gently with a hide or plastic mallet. The use of excessive force could cause the disc to be damaged.

Refitting

13 Refitting is a reversal of the removal procedure, noting the following points:

a) *Ensure that the mating surfaces of the disc and hub are clean and flat.*
b) *Align (if applicable) the marks made on removal, and securely tighten the disc retaining screw.*
c) *If a new disc has been fitted, use a suitable solvent to wipe any preservative coating from the disc, before refitting the caliper.*
d) *Slide the caliper into position over the disc, making sure the pads pass either side of the disc. Tighten the caliper bracket mounting bolts to the specified torque. If new discs have been fitted and there is insufficient clearance between the pads to accommodate the new, thicker disc, it may be necessary to push the piston back into the caliper body as described in Section 8.*
e) *Refit the roadwheel, then lower the vehicle to the ground and tighten the roadwheel bolts to the specified torque. On completion, repeatedly depress the brake pedal until normal (non-assisted) pedal pressure returns.*

7 Rear brake cylinder – removal and refitting

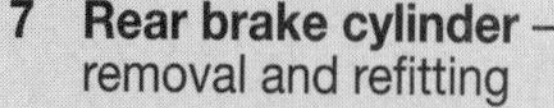

Removal

1 Chock the front wheels, then jack up the rear of the vehicle and support on axle stands (see *Jacking and vehicle support*). Remove the relevant rear wheel.

2 Minimise fluid loss by first removing the master cylinder reservoir cap, and then tightening it down onto a piece of polythene, to obtain an airtight seal. Alternatively, use a brake hose clamp, a G-clamp or a similar tool to clamp the flexible hose.

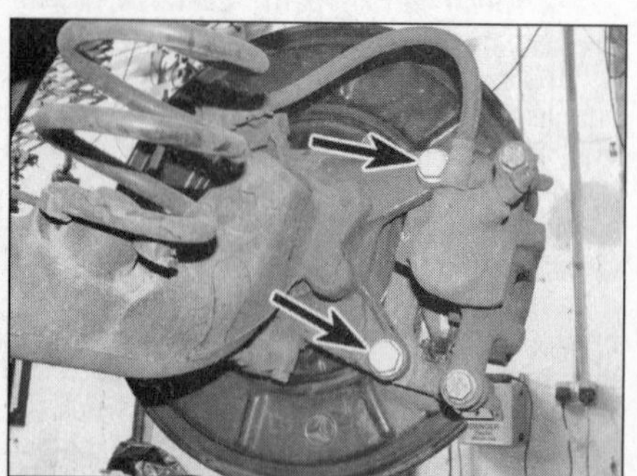
6.11 Rear caliper mounting bracket bolts – arrowed

6.12a Undo the securing screw . . .

6.12b . . . and remove the brake disc

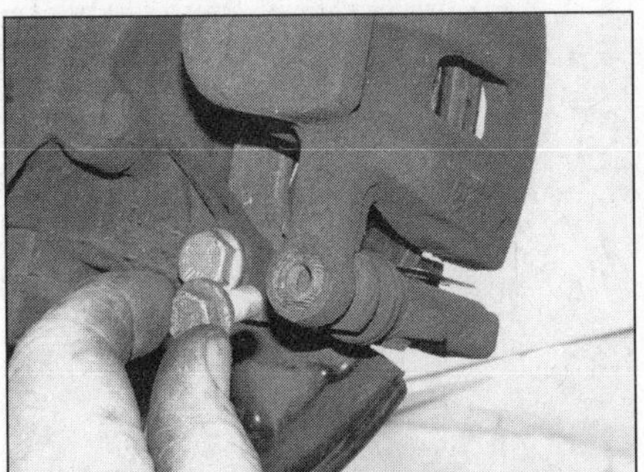

8.2 Remove the caliper guide pin bolts

8.3 Remove the brake pads

8.8 Open the bleed nipple as the piston is pushed back into the caliper

3 Remove the brake shoes as described in Section 17.

4 Clean the area around the union on the rear of the brake cylinder, and then loosen the brake pipe nut.

5 Unscrew the retaining bolt from the rear of the brake cylinder and remove it from the backplate.

Refitting

6 Refitting is a reversal of removal, noting the following points:

a) Tighten the cylinder retaining bolts to the specified torque.

b) Refit the brake shoes as described in Section 17.

c) Securely tighten the brake pipe union nut.

d) Bleed the hydraulic system as described in Section 2.

e) Refit the roadwheel, then lower the vehicle to the ground and tighten the roadwheel bolts to the specified torque.

f) On completion, check the hydraulic fluid level as described in 'Weekly checks'.

8 Rear brake pads – removal, inspection and refitting

Warning: Renew both sets of brake pads at the same time – never renew the pads on only one wheel, as uneven braking may result. Note that the dust created by wear of the pads may contain asbestos, which is a health hazard. Never blow it out with compressed air, and do not inhale any of it. An approved filtering mask should be worn when working on the brakes. DO NOT use petrol or petroleum-based solvents to clean brake parts; use brake cleaner or methylated spirit only.

Removal

1 Apply the handbrake, then jack up the rear of the vehicle and support it on axle stands (see *Jacking and vehicle support*). Remove the rear roadwheels.

2 Slacken and remove the two, caliper guide pin bolts from the caliper **(see illustration)**. Then lift the caliper, away from the hub carrier, and tie it to the suspension strut using a suitable piece of wire. Do not allow the caliper to hang unsupported on the flexible brake hose.

3 Remove the two brake pads from the caliper mounting bracket **(see illustration)**. If the original pads are to be refitted, mark them so that they can be refitted in their original positions.

4 If required, unclip the upper and lower spring clips from the mounting bracket, noting their fitted position.

Inspection

5 First measure the thickness of each brake pad. If either pad is worn at any point to the specified minimum thickness or less, all four pads must be renewed. Also, the pads should be renewed if any are fouled with oil or grease; there is no satisfactory way of degreasing friction material, once contaminated. If any of the brake pads are worn unevenly, or are fouled with oil or grease, trace and rectify the cause before reassembly. New brake pad kits are available from Mercedes-Benz dealers.

6 If the brake pads are still serviceable, carefully clean them using a clean, fine wire brush or similar, paying particular attention to the sides and back of the metal backing. Clean out the grooves in the friction material (where applicable), and pick out any large embedded particles of dirt or debris. Carefully clean the pad locations in the caliper body/ mounting bracket.

7 Prior to fitting the pads, check that the guide pins are free to slide easily in the caliper body bushes, and are a reasonably tight fit. Brush the dust and dirt from the caliper and piston, but *do not* inhale it, as it is injurious to health. Inspect the dust seal around the piston for damage, and the piston for evidence of fluid leaks, corrosion or damage. If attention to any of these components is necessary, refer to Section 9.

Refitting

8 If new brake pads are to be fitted, the caliper piston must be pushed back into the cylinder to make room for them. Either use a G-clamp or similar tool, or use suitable pieces of wood as levers.

9 To avoid any dirt entering the ABS solenoid valves, connect a pipe to the bleed nipple and, as the piston is pushed back, open the nipple and allow the displaced fluid to flow through the pipe into a suitable container **(see illustration)**.

10 Refit the spring clips to the mounting bracket as noted on removal. Apply a little copper grease to the spring clips before refitting them.

11 Apply a little copper grease to the metal backplates of the brake pads before refitting them, and then fit the new brake pads into the mounting bracket **(see illustrations)**.

12 Position the caliper until it is possible to install the new caliper guide pin bolts. Apply a little copper grease to the bolts before refitting them, and tighten them to the specified torque. **Note:** *Do not exert excess pressure on the caliper, as this will deform the pad springs, resulting in noisy operation of the brakes.*

13 Depress the brake pedal repeatedly, until the pads are pressed into firm contact with the brake disc, and normal (non-assisted) pedal pressure is restored.

8.11a Fit the brake pads . . .

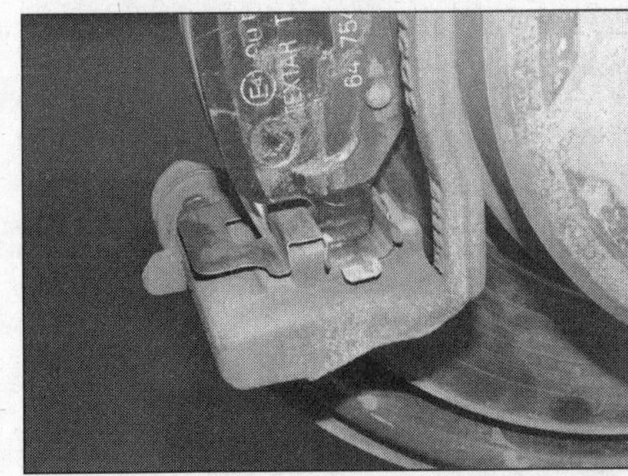

8.11b . . . making sure they are located in the spring clips

10.3 Brake pedal return spring – arrowed

10.4 Twist the brake light switch to remove

10.5 Release the retaining clip – arrowed

14 Repeat the above procedure on the remaining rear brake caliper.
15 Refit the roadwheels, then lower the vehicle to the ground and tighten the roadwheel bolts to the specified torque.
Caution: New pads will not give full braking efficiency until they have bedded-in. Be prepared for this, and avoid hard braking as far as possible for the first hundred miles or so after pad renewal.

9 Rear brake caliper – removal, overhaul and refitting

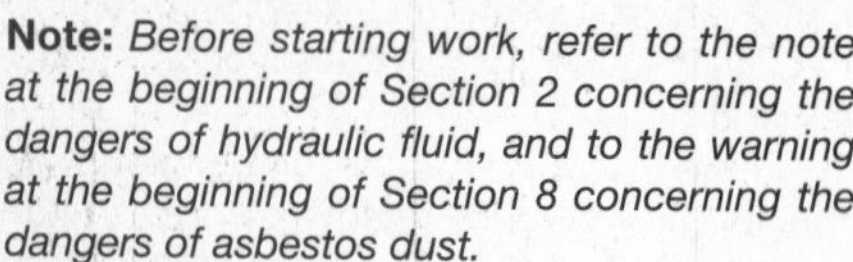

Note: *Before starting work, refer to the note at the beginning of Section 2 concerning the dangers of hydraulic fluid, and to the warning at the beginning of Section 8 concerning the dangers of asbestos dust.*

Removal

1 Chock the front wheels, then jack up the rear of the vehicle and support on axle stands (see *Jacking and vehicle support*). Remove the relevant rear wheel.
2 Minimise fluid loss by first removing the master cylinder reservoir cap, and then tightening it down onto a piece of polythene, to obtain an airtight seal. Alternatively, use a brake hose clamp, a G-clamp or a similar tool to clamp the flexible hose.
3 Clean the area around the union on the caliper, and then loosen the brake hose union nut.
4 Lift the caliper from the brake pads as described in Section 8.
5 Unscrew the caliper from the end of the flexible hose and remove it from the vehicle.

Overhaul

6 At the time of writing, no parts where available to overhaul the calipers. Consequently, if the calipers are faulty, they must be renewed. It may be possible to get exchange units, check with your local Mercedes-Benz dealer or brake specialist.

Refitting

7 Screw the caliper fully onto the flexible hose union.
8 Refit the caliper over the brake pads as described in Section 8.
9 Securely tighten the brake pipe union nut.
10 Remove the brake hose clamp or remove the polythene from the fluid reservoir, as applicable, and bleed the hydraulic system as described in Section 2. Note that, providing the precautions described were taken to minimise brake fluid loss, it should only be necessary to bleed the relevant rear brake.
11 Refit the roadwheel, then lower the vehicle to the ground and tighten the roadwheel bolts to the specified torque. On completion, check the hydraulic fluid level as described in *Weekly checks*.

10 Brake pedal – removal and refitting

Removal

1 Disconnect the battery negative lead. **Note:** *Before disconnecting the battery, refer to 'Disconnecting the battery' in the reference section at the rear of this manual.*
2 With reference to Chapter 11, remove the driver's side lower facia trim panels.
3 Unhook the return spring from the brake pedal **(see illustration)**.
4 Turn the brake light switch and remove it from the mounting bracket **(see illustration)**.
5 Release the retaining clip and withdraw the actuating linkage pin from through the pedal **(see illustration)**.
6 On automatic transmission models, disconnect the shift lock cable from the brake pedal unit, see Chapter 7B.

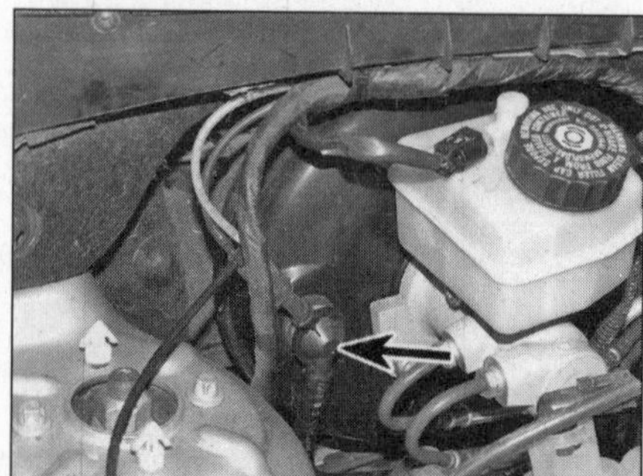
11.5 Disconnect the vacuum pipe – arrowed

7 Withdraw the inner part of the pivot tube out from the top of the brake pedal, and then push the outer part of the pivot tube out through the other side.
8 Remove the pedal and recover the pivot bush, check the condition of the pivot bushes and renew if required.
9 Carefully clean all components, and renew any that are worn or damaged.

Refitting

10 Refitting is a reversal of removal. Prior to refitting, apply a smear of multipurpose grease to the pivot shaft tube and pedal bearing surfaces. Refit the facia trim panels as described in Chapter 11.

11 Servo unit – testing, removal and refitting

Testing

1 To test the operation of the servo unit, depress the footbrake several times to exhaust the vacuum, then start the engine whilst keeping the pedal firmly depressed. As the engine starts, there should be a noticeable 'give' in the brake pedal as the vacuum builds-up. Allow the engine to run for at least two minutes, and then switch it off. If the brake pedal is now depressed, it should feel normal, but further applications should result in the pedal feeling firmer, with the pedal stroke decreasing with each application.
2 If the servo does not operate as described, first inspect the servo unit non-return valve as described in Section 12. On diesel models, also check the operation of the vacuum pump as described in Section 21.
3 If the servo unit still fails to operate satisfactorily, the fault lies within the unit itself. Repairs to the unit are not possible – if faulty, the servo unit must be renewed.

Removal

4 Remove the master cylinder as described in Section 13.
5 Disconnect the vacuum hose from the brake servo/booster unit **(see illustration)**.
6 Where applicable, disconnect the wiring connector(s) from the brake servo unit. This is

11.11 Brake servo mounting bolts – arrowed

for a travel sensor and solenoid valve that is fitted on models up to 28/02/01.

7 On left-hand drive models, disconnect the brake lines from the top of the ABS unit, to allow for the removal of the servo unit. Plug the ends of the brake lines to prevent dirt ingress.

8 On right-hand drive models, remove the air intake housing as described in Chapter 4A or 4B. To make access easier, depending on model, it may be necessary to remove the inlet manifold as described in Chapter 4A or 4B, to allow for removal.

9 With reference to Chapter 11, remove the driver's side lower facia trim panels.

10 Working inside the vehicle, release the retaining clip and withdraw the actuating linkage pin from through the pedal **(see illustration 10.5)**.

11 Again working in the footwell, undo the nuts securing the servo unit to the bulkhead **(see illustration)**, then return to the engine compartment and manoeuvre the servo unit out of position, and recover the gasket where fitted.

Refitting

12 Check the servo unit vacuum hose sealing grommet for signs of damage or deterioration, and renew if necessary.

13 Where applicable, fit a new gasket to the rear of the servo unit, and then reposition the unit in the engine compartment.

14 From inside the vehicle, ensure that the servo unit pushrod is correctly engaged with the brake pedal. Refit the pivot pin through the pedal and pushrod, and then fit the retaining clip to secure it in place.

15 Refit the servo unit mounting nuts and tighten them to the specified torque.

16 Refit the facia trim panels, with reference to Chapter 11.

17 Carefully ease the vacuum hose back into position in the servo, taking great care not to displace the sealing grommet.

18 Where applicable, refit the wiring connectors to the sensor and solenoid valve.

19 Where applicable on RHD models, refit the intake housing and inlet manifold as described in Chapter 4A or 4B.

20 On LHD models, refit the brake lines to the ABS unit and bleed the brake system as described in Section 2.

21 Refit the master cylinder as described in Section 13 of this Chapter.

22 On completion, start the engine and check for air leaks at the vacuum hose-to-servo unit connection; check the operation of the braking system.

12 Servo non-return valve – testing, removal and refitting

1 The non-return valve is located in the vacuum hose leading from the inlet manifold or vacuum pump to the brake servo.

Removal

2 Ease the vacuum hose out of the servo unit **(see illustration)**, taking care not to displace the grommet.

3 Note the routing of the hose, then slacken the retaining clip(s) and disconnect the opposite end of the hose assembly from the manifold/pump/hose, and remove it from the car.

Testing

4 Examine the check valve and vacuum hose for signs of damage, and renew if necessary.

5 The non-return valve may be tested by blowing through it in both directions; air should flow through the valve in one direction only; when blown through from the servo unit end of the valve. Renew the valve if this is not the case.

6 Examine the servo unit rubber sealing grommet for signs of damage or deterioration, and renew as necessary.

Refitting

7 Ensure that the sealing grommet is correctly fitted to the servo unit.

8 Ease the hose union into position in the servo, taking great care not to displace or damage the grommet.

9 Ensure that the hose is correctly routed, and connect it to the inlet manifold/pump/hose, ensuring the hose is secured in the retaining clips.

10 On completion, start the engine and check the valve-to-servo unit connection for signs of air leaks.

13.2 Disconnect the wiring connector – arrowed

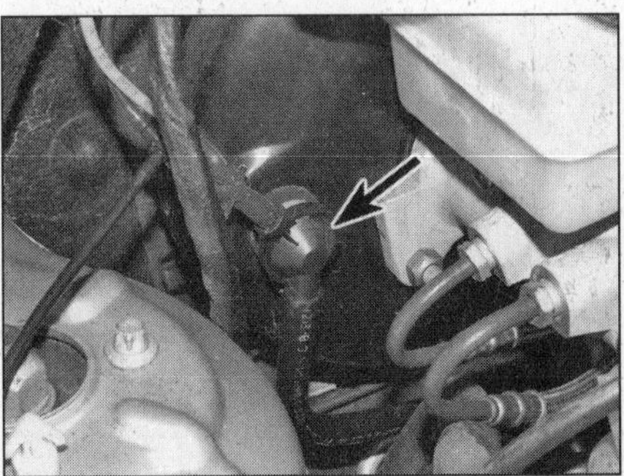

12.2 Brake servo non-return valve – arrowed

13 Master cylinder – removal, overhaul and refitting

Note: *Before starting work, refer to the warning at the beginning of Section 2 concerning the dangers of hydraulic fluid. A new master cylinder O-ring will be required on refitting.*

Removal

1 Disconnect the battery negative lead. **Note:** *Before disconnecting the battery, refer to 'Disconnecting the battery' in the Reference section at the rear of this manual.*

2 Remove the master cylinder reservoir cap (disconnect the wiring plug from the brake fluid level warning switch), and syphon the hydraulic fluid from the reservoir **(see illustration). Note:** *Do not syphon the fluid by mouth, as it is poisonous; use a syringe or an old antifreeze tester.*

3 On manual transmission models, disconnect and plug the clutch master cylinder supply hose from the brake reservoir **(see illustration)**.

4 Undo the retaining bolt **(see illustration)** and remove the hydraulic fluid reservoir from the top of the master cylinder. To do this, pull the reservoir upwards from the rubber grommets.

5 Wipe clean the area around the brake pipe unions on the side of the master cylinder, and place absorbent rags beneath the pipe unions to catch any leaking fluid. Make a note of the correct fitted positions of the unions, then unscrew the union nuts and carefully withdraw

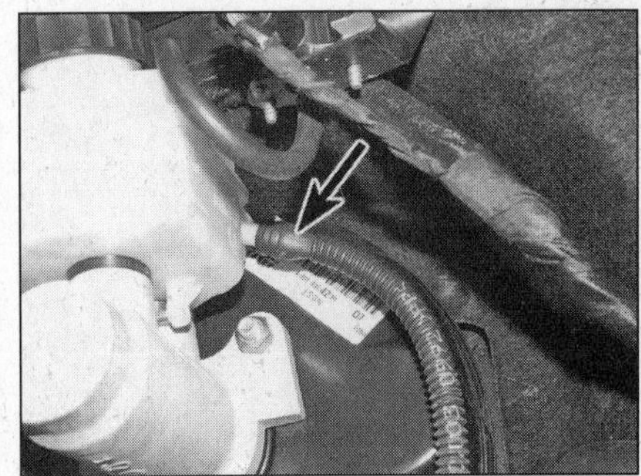

13.3 Disconnect the supply hose (arrowed) from the reservoir

13.4 Reservoir mounting bolt – arrowed

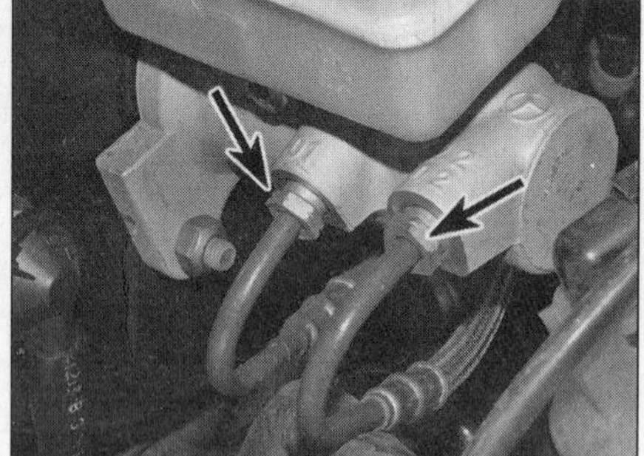
13.5 Unscrew the brake pipe union nuts – arrowed

13.6 Mounting nuts for brake master cylinder – arrowed

the pipes **(see illustration)**. Plug or tape over the pipe ends and master cylinder orifices, to minimise the loss of brake fluid, and to prevent the entry of dirt into the system. Wash off any spilt fluid immediately with cold water.

6 Unscrew and remove the two nuts and washers securing the master cylinder to the vacuum servo unit, and then withdraw the unit from the engine compartment **(see illustration)**. Remove the O-ring from the rear of the master cylinder, and discard it.

Overhaul

7 If the master cylinder is faulty, it must be renewed. Repair kits are not available from Mercedes-Benz dealer, so the cylinder must be treated as a sealed unit.

8 The only items, which can be renewed are the mounting seals for the fluid reservoir; if these show signs of deterioration, prise them out with a screwdriver. Lubricate the new seals with clean brake fluid, and press them into the master cylinder ports.

Refitting

9 Remove all traces of dirt from the master cylinder and servo unit mating surfaces, and fit a new O-ring to the groove on the master cylinder body.

10 Fit the master cylinder to the servo unit, ensuring that the servo unit pushrod enters the master cylinder bore centrally. Refit the master cylinder mounting nuts, and tighten them to the specified torque.

11 Wipe clean the brake pipe unions, then refit them to the master cylinder ports and tighten them securely.

12 Refit the hydraulic fluid reservoir, making sure it is entered correctly in the rubber grommets and tighten the securing bolt.

13 On manual transmission models, reconnect the clutch master cylinder supply hose to the reservoir.

14 Refill the master cylinder reservoir with new fluid, and bleed the complete hydraulic system as described in Section 2.

15 Reconnect the wiring to the brake level sender unit in the top of the reservoir.

16 Reconnect the battery negative lead.

17 On completion, start the engine and check the brake master cylinder for signs of leaks; check the operation of the braking system

14 Handbrake – adjustment

1 If the handbrake can be pulled up (with medium force) by more than 3 clicks, the handbrake will need to be adjusted as follows.

2 Chock the front wheels, then jack up the rear of the vehicle and support it on axle stands (see *Jacking and vehicle support*). Leaving the handbrake in the off position.

3 Remove the lower covers from under the rear of the vehicle.

4 Working under the vehicle, slacken the locknut on the cable adjuster to the rear of the fuel tank until the cable is slack **(see illustration)**.

5 Remove one wheel bolt from each of the rear wheels **(see illustration)**. If required, to make access easier, remove both the rear wheels.

6 Using a long thin screwdriver, insert it into the wheel bolt hole and feel for the teeth of the adjuster wheel **(see illustrations)**. Turn the adjuster wheel until the brake shoes are applied and the wheel can no longer be turned. Carry this procedure out on both rear brakes on the left and right-hand side of the vehicle. **Note:** *On the right-hand side of the vehicle, move the adjuster wheel from the front to the rear of the vehicle. On the left-hand side of the vehicle, move the adjuster wheel from the rear to the front of the vehicle.*

7 Now slacken both adjusters by 8 teeth and check that the both wheel can freely rotate.

8 Adjust the handbrake cable adjuster **(see**

14.4 Handbrake cable adjuster – arrowed

14.5 Remove one of the wheel bolts

14.6a Using a screwdriver . . .

14.6b . . . to rotate the adjuster wheel – arrowed

illustration) until the brake shoes are pressed firmly to the brake drum and the wheels cannot rotate. Back the cable adjuster off until the both wheels spin freely and tighten the locknut on the cable adjuster.

9 Operate the handbrake lever inside the vehicle several times to make sure it operates correctly, and then check that the wheels spin freely when the handbrake is released.

10 Once adjustment is correct, refit the wheel bolts.

11 Refit the lower covers, and then lower the vehicle to the ground. Tighten the roadwheel bolts to the specified torque.

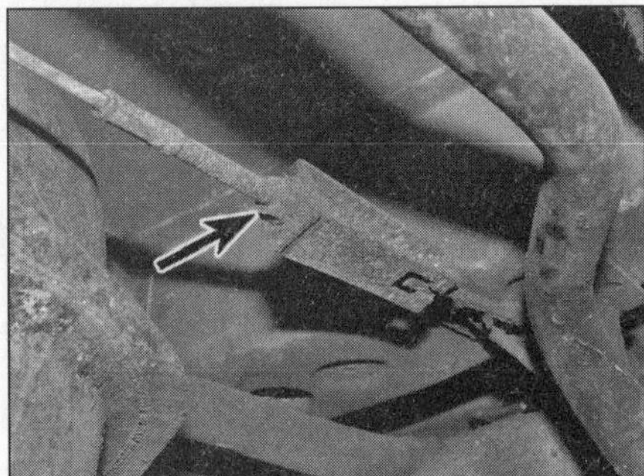

14.8 Cable adjuster locking nut - arrowed

15.1a Using a small screwdriver . . .

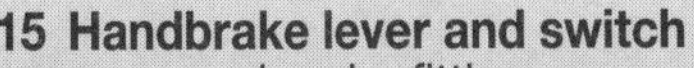

15 Handbrake lever and switch – removal and refitting

Removal

1 Using a thin screwdriver release the plastic cap, and then withdraw the locking pin from the handbrake lever **(see illustrations)**. Discard the locking pin and cap as a new one will be required for refitting.

2 Withdraw the plastic handle grip off the handbrake lever and the lower plastic surround **(see illustrations)**.

3 Remove the centre console as described in Chapter 11.

4 Chock the front wheels, then jack up the rear of the vehicle and support it on axle stands (see *Jacking and vehicle support*). Remove the lower covers from under the rear of the vehicle and slacken the locknut on the cable adjuster (to the rear of the fuel tank) until the cable is slack.

5 Press each side of the brake light switch and release it from the handbrake mounting bracket **(see illustration)**.

6 Undo the two mounting bolts and remove the handbrake lever from the mounting bracket, disconnect the brake cable from the lever as it is removed **(see illustration)**.

Refitting

7 Refitting is a reversal of removal, bearing in mind the following points.

a) Adjust the handbrake as described in Section 14.

b) Check the operation of the handbrake 'on' warning switch prior to refitting the centre console.

16 Handbrake cables – removal and refitting

Removal

1 Remove the centre console as described in Chapter 11, to gain access to the handbrake lever. The handbrake cable consists of three sections, a front section, a right rear section and a left rear section; these are linked together at the rear of the vehicle in front of the rear axle. Each section can be removed individually.

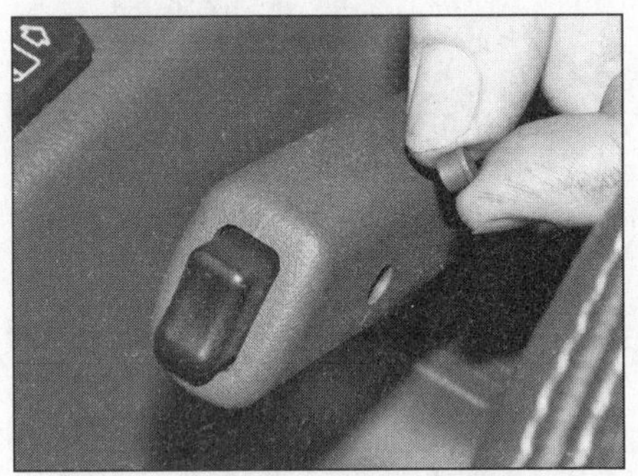

15.1b . . . to remove the plastic cap . . .

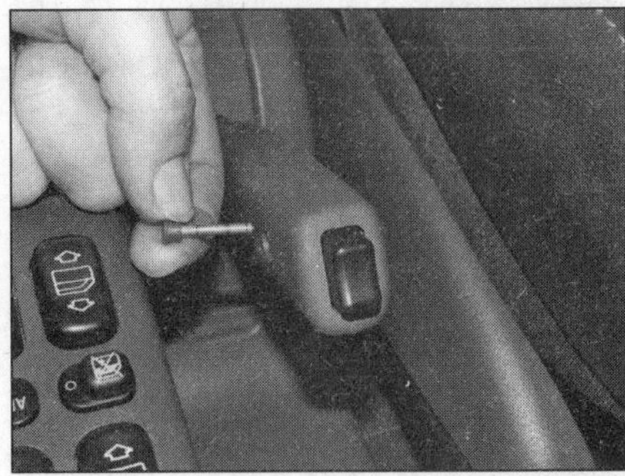

15.1c . . . and remove the locking pin

2 Chock the front wheels, then jack up the rear of the car and support it on axle stands.

3 Slacken the handbrake cable adjuster nut sufficiently to allow the ends of the cables to be disengaged from the cable adjuster and locating bracket **(see illustrations)**.

4 Working back along the length of the cable, note its correct routing and free it from all the relevant guides and retaining clips.

5 Disengage the right rear inner cable from

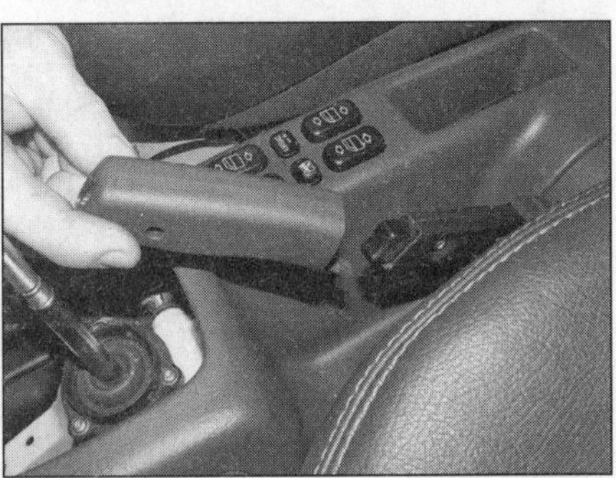

15.2a Remove the plastic handle grip . . .

15.2b . . . and the lower plastic surround

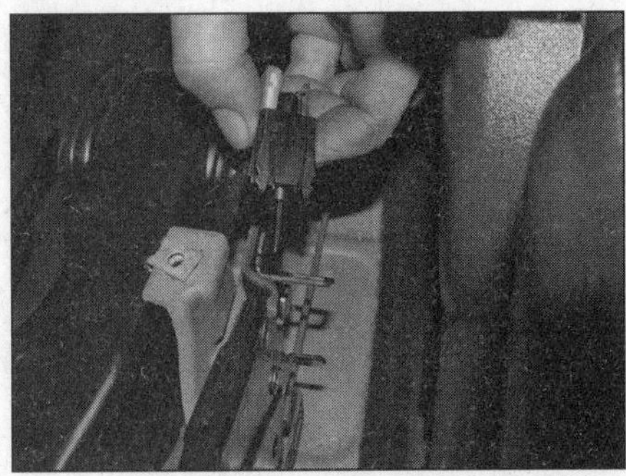

15.5 Release the switch from the mounting bracket

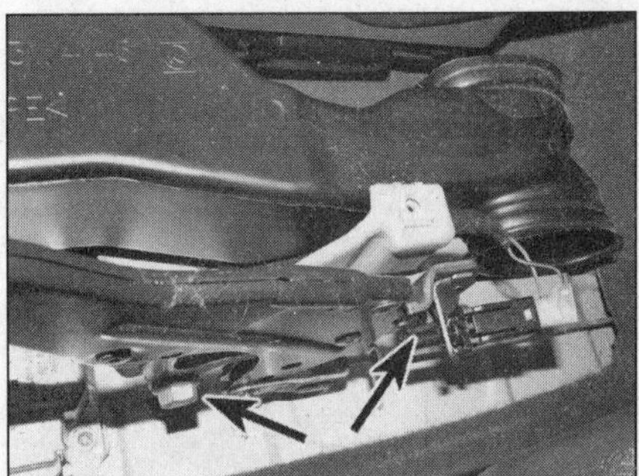

15.6 Handbrake lever mounting bolts – arrowed

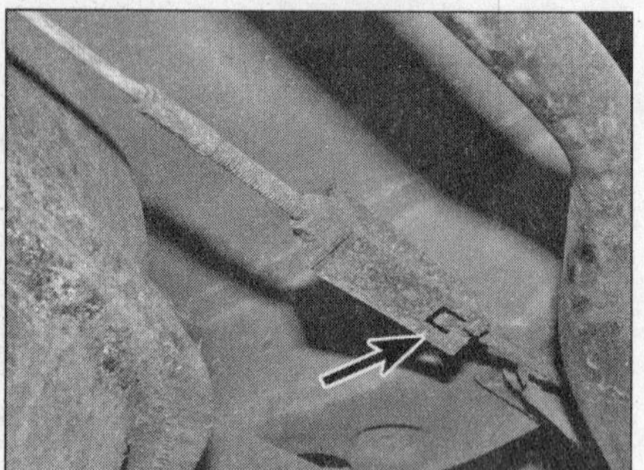

16.3a Disconnect the handbrake cable from the adjuster – arrowed . . .

the cable adjuster, then remove the left inner cable from the locating bracket on the front outer cable. **Note:** *Depending on model year, there may be a clip or a pin holding the left-hand rear inner cable in position in the bracket on the front outer cable.*

6 To remove the front handbrake cable, remove the handbrake lever as described in Section 15, and release the outer cable from the floor panel.

7 To remove the rear handbrake cables, remove the relevant rear brake shoes as described in Section 17, undo the retaining bolt and withdraw the cable from the hub **(see illustration)**.

Refitting

8 Refitting is a reversal of removal, bearing in mind the following points.

a) Make sure the handbrake cable is routed correctly and located in any retaining clips.

17.10a Using a chisel to remove the hub cap . . .

17.11 Releasing the brake shoe retaining spring

16.3b . . . and from the bracket on the other rear cable

b) Before refitting the centre console, adjust the handbrake as described in Section 14.

17 Rear brake shoes and handbrake shoes – removal and refitting

1 Chock the front wheels, then jack up the rear of the vehicle and support it on axle stands (see *Jacking and vehicle support*). Remove the rear wheels.

2 Remove the lower covers from under the rear of the vehicle and slacken the locknut on the cable adjuster (to the rear of the fuel tank), until the cable is slack.

Rear brake shoes

Removal

3 Undo the retaining screw and remove the brake drum.

17.10b . . . and then remove nut and withdraw the hub

17.12 Release the brake shoe from the adjuster

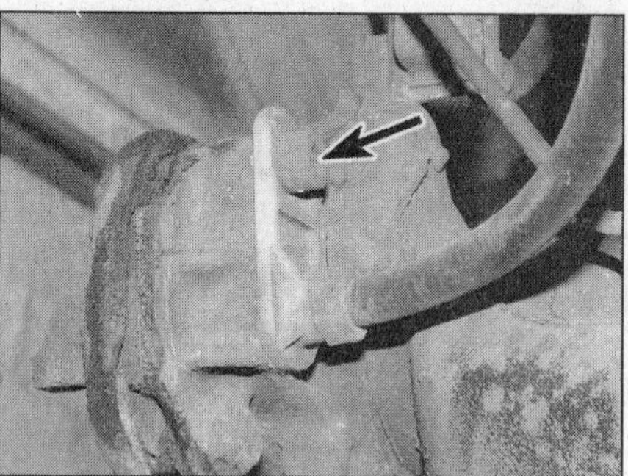

16.7 Handbrake cable retaining bolt

4 To make access easier, remove the dust cap and undo the rear hub nut. Withdraw the rear hub from the stub axle.

5 Release the brake shoe retaining clips and remove pins from the rear of the backplate.

6 Pull the brake shoe out from the backplate and release the handbrake cable from the lever.

7 If required unclip the return springs from the holes in the brake shoes, noting their fitted position.

Refitting

8 Refitting is a reversal of removal.

a) Apply a small amount of copper grease to the backplate.

b) Make sure the shoes are securely positioned on the backplate.

b) Adjust the handbrake as described in Section 14.

Handbrake shoes

Removal

9 Remove the rear brake discs as described in Section 6.

10 To make access easier, remove the dust cap and undo the rear hub nut. Withdraw the rear hub from the stub axle **(see illustrations)**.

11 Release the lower brake shoe retaining spring from the backplate **(see illustration)**.

12 Pull the lower brake shoe out from the backplate and release the adjuster from between the ends of the brake shoes **(see illustration)**.

13 Unclip the return spring from the holes in the brake shoes, noting its fitted position **(see illustration)**.

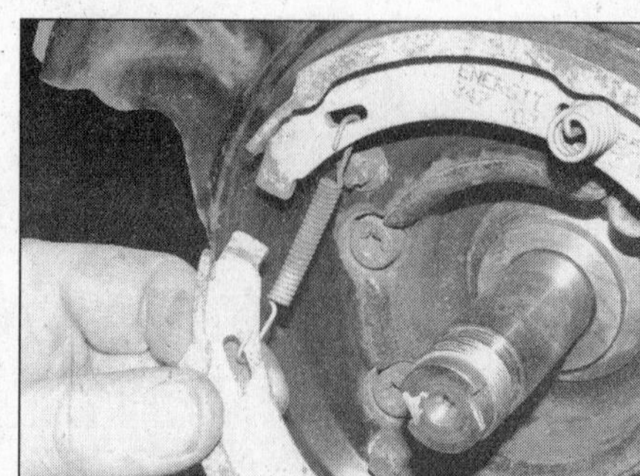

17.13 Unclip the spring from the brake shoe

17.14 Release the upper brake shoe retaining spring

14 Release the retaining spring from the upper brake shoe **(see illustration)**.

15 Remove the brake shoes by releasing them from the handbrake lever pivot and unhooking the return spring, noting its fitted position **(see illustrations)**.

Refitting

16 Refitting is a reversal of removal.

a) Apply a small amount of copper grease to the handbrake lever pivot.

b) Make sure the shoes are securely positioned on the backplate.

c) If required, adjust the handbrake as described in Section 14.

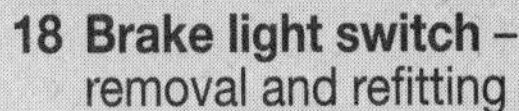

18 Brake light switch – removal and refitting

Removal

1 The brake light switch is located on the top of the pedal bracket beneath the facia panel. Disconnect the battery negative lead. **Note:** *Before disconnecting the battery, refer to 'Disconnecting the battery' in the Reference section at the rear of this manual.*

2 With reference to Chapter 11, remove the driver's side lower facia trim panels.

3 Reach up behind the facia and disconnect the wiring connector from the switch.

4 Twist the brake light switch through 90° and remove it from the mounting bracket **(see illustration)**.

Refitting

5 Prior to installation, fully extend the brake light switch plunger **(see illustration)**.

6 Fully depress and hold the brake pedal, then manoeuvre the switch into position. Make sure that it has located securely in the mounting bracket, before releasing the brake pedal.

7 Reconnect the wiring connector, and check the operation of the brake lights. The brake lights should illuminate after the brake pedal has travelled approximately 5 mm. If the switch is not functioning correctly, it is faulty and must be renewed; no adjustment is possible.

8 On completion, reconnect the battery and refit the lower facia panel with reference to Chapter 11.

17.15a Release the brake shoes from the handbrake pivot . . .

19 Anti-lock braking system (ABS) – general information and precautions

The anti-lock braking system (ABS) fitted as standard to all models, prevents wheel lock-up under heavy braking, and not only optimises stopping distances, but also improves steering control. By electronically monitoring the speed of each roadwheel in relation to the other wheels, the system can detect when a wheel is about to lock-up, before control is actually lost. The brake fluid pressure applied to that wheel's brake caliper is then decreased and restored ('modulated') several times a second until control is regained. The system components are: four wheel speed sensors, a hydraulic unit with integral Electronic Control Module (ECM), brake lines and a dashboard-mounted warning light. The four wheel sensors are mounted on the wheel hub carriers. Each wheel has a rotating toothed hub mounted on the driveshaft (front) or on the hub (rear). The wheel speed sensors are mounted in close proximity to these hubs. The teeth produce a voltage waveform whose frequency varies with the speed of the hubs. These waveforms are transmitted to the ECM, and used to calculate the rotational speed of each wheel. The ECM has a self-diagnostic facility, to inhibit the operation of the ABS if a fault is detected, lighting the dashboard-mounted warning light. The braking system will then revert to conventional, non-ABS operation. If the nature of the fault is not immediately obvious upon inspection, the vehicle *must* be taken to a Mercedes-Benz dealer, who will have

17.15b . . . and remove the brake shoes

the diagnostic equipment required to interrogate the ABS ECM electronically and pin-point the problem.

Depending on model, there are other functions fitted including a traction control system (TCS), which uses the basic ABS system, with an additional pump and valves fitted to the hydraulic actuator. If wheelspin is detected at a speed below 30 mph, one of the valves opens, to allow the pump to pressurise the relevant brake, until the spinning wheel slows to a rotational speed corresponding to the speed of the vehicle. This has the effect of transferring torque to the wheel with most traction. At the same time, the throttle plate is closed slightly, to reduce the torque from the engine.

Other versions include electronic stability programme (ESP), the system recognises critical driving conditions and stabilises the vehicle by individual wheel braking and by intervention in the engine control, which occurs independently of the position of the brake and accelerator pedals. Also an acceleration slip regulation (ASR) or brake assist system (BAS) are used on some models.

The operation of the ABS system is entirely dependent on electrical signals. To prevent the system responding to any inaccurate signals, a built-in safety circuit monitors all signals received by the ECM. If an inaccurate signal or low battery voltage is detected, the ABS system is automatically shut down, and the warning light on the instrument panel is illuminated to inform the driver that the ABS system is not operational. Normal braking will still be available, however.

18.4 Turn the switch and remove

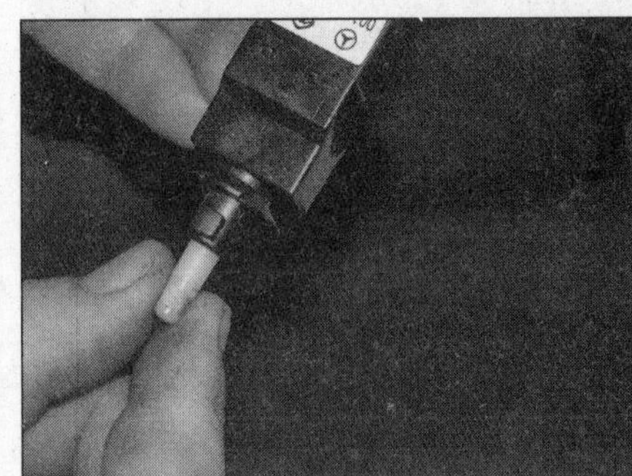

18.5 Pull out the switch plunger, before refitting

20.12 Remove the ECM cover

20.13 Disconnect the wiring connectors . . .

20.14 . . . and withdraw the ECM

If a fault does develop in the ABS system, the car must be taken to a Mercedes-Benz dealer for fault diagnosis and repair.

20 Anti-lock braking system (ABS) components - removal and refitting

Hydraulic unit

Note: *Before starting work, refer to the warning at the beginning of Section 2 concerning the dangers of hydraulic fluid. A new master cylinder O-ring will be required on refitting.*

Removal

1 Disconnect the battery negative lead. **Note:** *Before disconnecting the battery, refer to 'Disconnecting the battery' in the Reference section at the rear of this manual.*

2 Open the bonnet, release the locking clip and remove the windscreen washer reservoir from the engine compartment.

3 Disconnect the wiring connector from the ESP pressure sensor(s) on the side of the hydraulic unit. **Note:** *On models up to 28/02/01, there is one pressure sensor, on models after 01/03/01, there are two pressure sensors fitted.*

4 Disconnect the traction system wiring block connector from the hydraulic unit.

5 To minimise fluid loss, have an assistant depress and hold down the brake pedal, then attach a length of plastic hose to the bleed screw on a caliper, with the other end of the hose in a clean container. Unscrew the bleed screw a couple of turns and allow the fluid to flow into the container. As soon as the flow of fluid slows, close the bleed screw, and secure the pedal in the depressed position. This can be achieved with a proprietary pedal jack, or improvised using a length of wood (broom handle, etc) cut to the right length.

6 Clean the area around the brake unions on the hydraulic unit, noting their fitted positions, and detach the pipes from the unit. Plug or seal the openings to prevent contamination. Be prepared for some spillage.

7 Undo the mounting bolts from the base of the hydraulic unit and remove it from the engine compartment. Always keep the unit in the upright position to prevent any damage to the hydraulic unit.

8 Any further dismantling of the hydraulic unit is best entrusted to a Mercedes-Benz dealer.

Refitting

9 Refitting is a reversal of removal.

a) *Bleed the brake system as described in Section 2.*
b) *On completion, a fault diagnosis check must be performed using specialist equipment.*

Electronic control module (ECM)

Caution: Always wait at least 30 seconds after switching off the ignition before disconnecting the wiring from the ECM. When the wiring is disconnected, all the learned values are erased, although any contents of the fault memory are retained. After reconnecting the wiring, the basic settings must be reinstated by a Mercedes-Benz dealer using a special test instrument. Note also that if the ECM is renewed, it may need to be set up with diagnostic equipment by a Mercedes-Benz dealer.

10 Disconnect the battery negative lead and position it away from the terminal. **Note:** *Refer to 'Disconnecting the battery' at the rear of this manual first.*

11 The ECM is located behind a plastic panel to the left-hand end of the engine compartment bulkhead.

12 Undo the retaining screws and remove the plastic cover **(see illustration)**.

13 Release the securing clips and disconnect the wiring connectors from the electronic control module **(see illustration)**.

14 Withdraw the electronic control module from its location in the bulkhead **(see illustration)**.

15 Refitting is a reversal of removal. Noting the comments made in the *Caution* above – the ECM may need to be set at a Mercedes-Benz dealer.

Front wheel sensor

Removal

16 Chock the rear wheels, then firmly apply the handbrake, jack up the front of the car and support on axle stands (see *Jacking and vehicle support*). Remove the appropriate front roadwheel.

17 Trace the wire from the sensor and disconnect the wiring connector from the inner wing panel **(see illustration)**. Unclip the wiring from any retaining clips along its length.

18 Slacken and remove the bolts securing the sensor to the front hub carrier, and remove the sensor from the car **(see illustration)**.

Refitting

19 Ensure that the sensor and hub carrier sealing faces are clean.

20 Refit the retaining bolts and tighten them to the specified torque setting.

21 Ensure that the sensor wiring is correctly routed and retained by all the necessary clips, and reconnect the wiring connector.

22 Refit the roadwheel, then lower the car to the ground and tighten the roadwheel bolts to the specified torque.

20.17 Disconnect the wiring connectors

20.18 Remove the sensor retaining bolts

Rear wheel sensor

Removal

23 Chock the front wheels, then jack up the rear of the car and support it on axle stands (see *Jacking and vehicle support*). Remove the appropriate roadwheel.
24 Trace the wire from the sensor and remove the rubber grommet from the floor panel, and then disconnect the wiring connector. Unclip the wiring from any retaining clips along its length.
25 Slacken and remove the bolt securing the sensor to the rear hub carrier, and remove the sensor from the car **(see illustration)**.

Refitting

26 Refit the sensor as described above in paragraphs 19 to 22. Make sure the rubber grommet is located securely in the floor panel.

Front reluctor rings

27 The front reluctor rings are integral with the driveshaft **(see illustration)**, and at the time of writing could not be renewed separately. If they are damaged, see your local Mercedes-Benz dealer for the availability of parts, or renew the driveshaft. Refer to Chapter 8 for the removal and refitting procedure of the driveshaft.

Rear reluctor rings

28 The rear reluctor rings are integral with the rear hub **(see illustration)**, and can only be inspected after removal of the rear hubs. If faulty, the rear hub must be renewed as described in Chapter 10.

Yaw rate and lateral acceleration sensor

29 The sensor monitors the movement of the vehicle and gives the information to the ECM. It measures the roll from side-to-side (or skidding) and also the lateral acceleration, which then gives a signal that can be evaluated electronically.
30 The sensor is located inside the driver's footwell to the right-hand side of the heater unit, below the steering column. Pull back the carpet and disconnect the wiring connector from the sensor, undo the two retaining bolts and withdraw the sensor from the footwell **(see illustration)**.

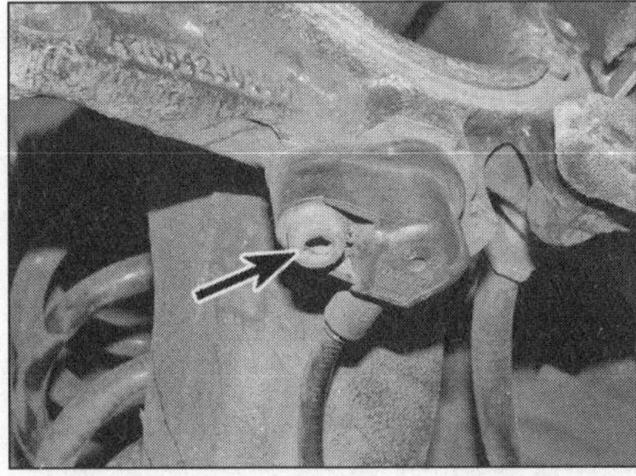
20.25 Rear sensor retaining bolt - arrowed

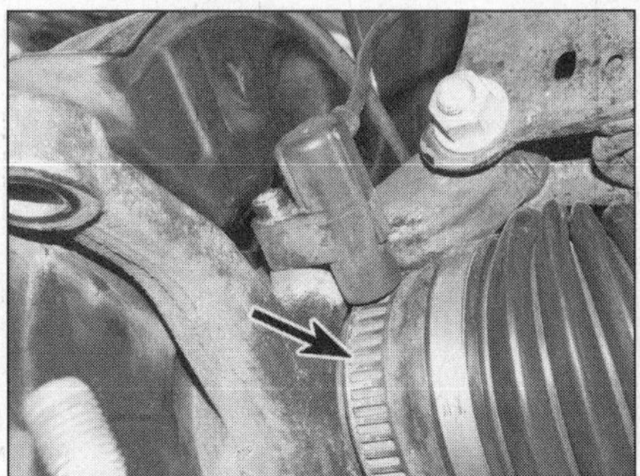
20.27 Front reluctor ring - arrowed

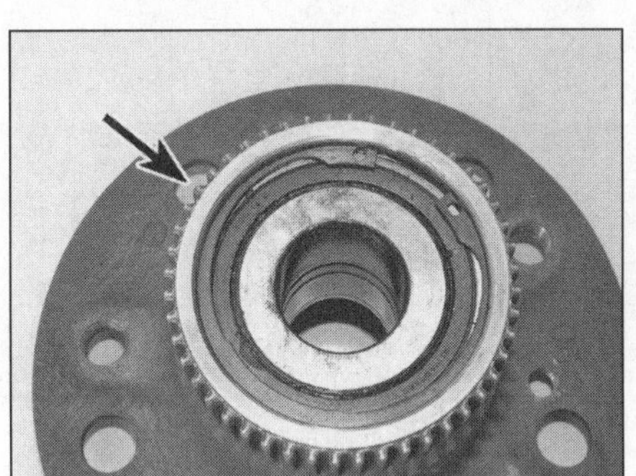
20.28 Rear hub reluctor ring - arrowed

20.30 Yaw rate and lateral acceleration sensor

21 Servo unit mechanical vacuum pump (diesel models) - testing, removal and refitting

Testing

1 The operation of the braking system vacuum pump can be checked using a vacuum gauge. The pump is located on the timing chain end of the cylinder head, driven off the inlet camshaft.
2 Disconnect the vacuum hose from the pump, and connect the gauge to the pump union using a suitable length of hose.
3 Start the engine and allow it to idle, and then measure the vacuum created by the pump. As a guide, after one minute, a minimum of approximately 500 mm Hg should be recorded. If the vacuum registered is significantly less than this, it is likely that the pump is faulty. However, seek the advice of a Mercedes-Benz dealer before condemning the pump.
4 Reconnect the vacuum hose. Overhaul of the pump is not possible, since no major parts are available separately for it. If faulty, the complete pump assembly must be renewed.

Removal

Note: *A new pump O-ring will be required on refitting.*
5 Release the retaining clip and move the coolant expansion reservoir to one side.
6 Release the retaining clip, and disconnect the vacuum hose from the top of pump **(see illustration)**.
7 Unclip the coolant hose from the securing clip, and then remove the retaining clip from the inner wing panel **(see illustration)**.
8 Unscrew the mounting bolts and withdraw the vacuum pump from the cylinder head **(see illustration)**, and recover the O-ring seal.

21.6 Disconnect the pipe from the vacuum pump

21.7 Remove the hose securing clip . . .

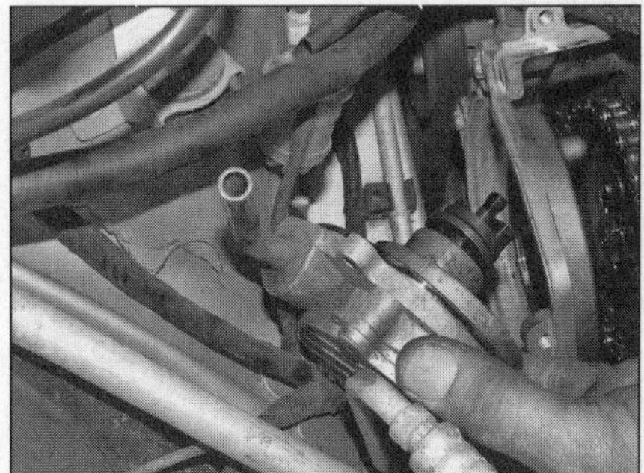
21.8 . . . and remove the vacuum pump

Discard it and obtain new ones for using on refitting.

Refitting

9 Fit the new O-ring seals to the vacuum pump, and apply a smear of oil to aid installation.

10 Manoeuvre the vacuum pump into position, making sure that the slot in the pump drive gear aligns with the slot on the camshaft.

11 Refit the pump retaining bolts, and tighten to the specified torque.

12 Refit the coolant pipe and retaining clip to the inner wing panel.

13 Reconnect the vacuum hose and secure with the retaining clip.

14 Refit the coolant expansion reservoir and check the operation of the brakes.

Chapter 10
Suspension and steering systems

Contents

Degrees of difficulty

Easy, suitable for novice with little experience	**Fairly easy,** suitable for beginner with some experience	**Fairly difficult,** suitable for competent DIY mechanic	**Difficult,** suitable for experienced DIY mechanic	**Very difficult,** suitable for expert DIY or professional

Specifications

Front suspension

Type	Independent, with MacPherson struts incorporating coil springs, telescopic shock absorbers and anti-roll bar connected to struts by connecting drop links

Rear suspension

Type	Trailing arm with multi-link transverse arms, separate gas-filled telescopic shock absorbers, coil springs and anti-roll bar

Steering

Type	Rack-and-pinion. Electro-hydraulic power assistance

Wheel alignment and steering angles*

Front wheel:	
Toe-in	0° 29' ± 10'
Camber angle:	
With 0° wheel toe (by means of steering lock)	-0° 59' ± 20'
Castor angle:	
With 0° wheel toe (by means of steering lock)	2° 11' ± 30'
Rear wheel:	
Toe setting:	
All models except Vaneo after 03/02	0° 18'
Vaneo models after 03/02	0° 55'
Camber angle:	
All models except Vaneo	-1° 30' (-1°/+0°)
Vaneo models	-2° 6' ± 27'

* *Refer to a Mercedes-Benz dealer for the latest recommendations.*

Roadwheels

Type	Aluminium alloy or steel

Tyres

Size	185/55R15, 195/50R15, 195/50R16, 205/45R16 and 205/40ZR17
Pressures	See *Weekly checks* – these can be found on the inside of the fuel filler flap

Torque wrench settings

	Nm	lbf ft
Front suspension		
Anti-roll bar link nut:		
Up to 25/08/02	45	33
From 26/08/02	60	44
Anti-roll bar to subframe	28	21
Balljoint-to-lower arm bolts:		
Stage 1	20	15
Stage 2	Angle-tighten a further 45°	
Driveshaft hub nut:*		
Stage 1	180	133
Stage 2	Slacken fully	
Stage 3	80	59
Stage 4	Angle-tighten a further 45°	
Lower arm to subframe bolts	105	77
Lower balljoint nut:*		
Stage 1	30	22
Stage 2	Angle-tighten a further 120°	
Front engine mounting to subframe	40	30
Subframe-to-underbody bolts	120	89
Suspension strut:		
Lower mounting bolts to steering knuckle	100	74
Upper mounting bolts	40	30
Upper piston rod nut	60	44
Rear suspension		
ABS speed sensor	8	6
Anti-roll bar:		
To trailing arm/shock absorber:		
Stage 1	80	59
Stage 2	Angle-tighten a further 90°	
To trailing arm:	70	52
Hub to stub axle	170	125
Shock absorber:		
Lower mounting nut and bolt:		
Stage 1	80	59
Stage 2	Angle-tighten a further 90°	
Upper mounting nut and bolt (models up to 18/02/01):		
Stage 1	40	30
Stage 2	Angle-tighten a further 45°	
Upper mounting nut and bolt (models from 19/02/01):		
Stage 1	45	33
Stage 2	Angle-tighten a further 90°	
Trailing arm:		
Mounting (outer) bolt:		
Stage 1	70	52
Stage 2	Angle-tighten a further 90°	
Threaded (inner) bush type bolt:		
Stage 1	140	103
Stage 2	Angle-tighten a further 90°	
Axle mounting bracket to underbody	95	70
Steering		
Steering column:		
Bolt to mounting bracket	20	15
Nuts to mounting bracket	20	15
Universal joint to steering gear	20	15
Steering column to subframe:		
Stage 1	45	33
Stage 2	Angle-tighten a further 60°	
Steering wheel to column*	80	59
Track rod end to steering knuckle:		
Stage 1	30	22
Stage 2	Angle-tighten a further 90°	
Track rod end to track rod locking nut	50	37
Track rod to steering rack	90	66
Roadwheels		
Roadwheel bolts	110	81

** Renew the nut/bolt every time it is removed*

1 General information

The independent front suspension is of the MacPherson strut type, incorporating coil springs and integral telescopic shock absorbers. The struts are located by transverse lower suspension arms, which use rubber inner mounting bushes, and incorporate a balljoint at the outer ends. The front wheel bearing housings/steering knuckle, which carry the wheel bearings, brake calipers and the hub/disc assemblies, are attached to the MacPherson struts by clamp bolts, and connected to the lower arms through the balljoints. A front anti-roll bar is fitted to all models. The anti-roll bar is rubber-mounted, and is connected to both lower suspension arms by short drop links.

The rear suspension consists of a trailing arm, rubber-mounted at its front end to the underbody, a wheel bearing housing, lower main transverse link and coil spring, upper transverse link, and separate shock absorber. A rear anti-roll bar is fitted to all models. The anti-roll bar is rubber-mounted on the rear subframe, and is connected to the wheel bearing housings on each side by a short connecting link.

The steering column is made up of three sections, upper section, intermediate section and lower section. The intermediate shaft is connected to the upper section by a universal joint, and it is joined to the lower section by splines. The lower section has a universal joint at the bottom, where it connects to the steering rack. The upper section of the steering column has a lever to adjust the height of the steering wheel.

The steering gear is mounted onto the front subframe, and is connected by two track rods, with balljoints at their inner and outer ends, to the steering arms projecting rearwards from the wheel bearing housings. The track rod ends are threaded to the track rods in order to allow adjustment of the front wheel toe setting. The steering gear has electro-hydraulic assistance, and incorporates an integral control unit. It is only functional when the engine is running. The steering assistance is automatically matched to the vehicle speed, steering wheel torque and steering wheel angle.

2.2a Remove the hub cap . . .

2.2b . . . and remove the retaining nut

All models are fitted with an Anti-lock Brake System (ABS), and can also be fitted with a Traction Control System (TCS) and an Electronic Stability Program (ESP). The ABS may also be referred to as including EBD (Electronic Brake Distribution), which means it adjusts the front and rear braking forces according to the weight being carried. The TCS may also be referred to as ASR (Anti Slip Regulation). The TCS system prevents the front wheels from losing traction during acceleration by reducing the engine output, it utilises the ABS system sensors to monitor the rotational speeds of the front wheels.

The ESP system extends the ABS, TCS and ESP functions to reduce wheel spin in difficult driving conditions. It does this by using highly-sensitive sensors which monitor the speed of the vehicle, lateral movement of the vehicle, the brake pressure, and the steering angle of the front wheels. If, for example, the vehicle is tending to oversteer, the brake will be applied to the front outer wheel to correct the situation. If the vehicle is tending to understeer, the brake will be applied to the rear inside wheel.

2 Front wheel bearing housing – removal and refitting

Note: *This Section describes removal of the wheel bearing housing leaving the suspension strut in position, however, if necessary it can be removed together with the suspension strut, and then separated on the bench. All self-locking nuts and bolts disturbed on removal must be renewed as a matter of course.*

Removal

1 Loosen the front wheel bolts by half a turn, then jack up the front of the vehicle and support it on axle stands (see *Jacking and vehicle support*). Remove the front roadwheel.

2 Remove the centre hubcap and remove the driveshaft retaining nut **(see illustrations)**. Have an assistant depress the brake pedal to prevent the hub from turning. Discard the nut, as a new one will be required for refitting.

3 Remove the brake disc as described in Chapter 9. This procedure includes removing the brake caliper; however **do not** disconnect the hydraulic brake hose from the caliper. Using a piece of wire or string, tie the caliper to the front suspension coil spring, to avoid placing any strain on the hydraulic brake hose.

4 Remove the ABS wheel sensor as described in Chapter 9.

5 Loosen the nut securing the steering track rod balljoint to the wheel bearing housing **(see illustration)**. Leave the nut on by a few turns to protect the threads, and then use a universal balljoint separator to release the balljoint. Remove the nut completely once the taper has been released.

6 Unscrew the front suspension strut lower retaining bolts **(see illustrations)**. Lever the wheel bearing housing down to release the driveshaft from the hub splines, if the driveshaft is tight on the splines, it may be necessary to use a puller bolted to the hub to remove it. Tie the driveshaft to one side.

2.5 Undo the track rod end retaining nut

2.6a Suspension strut lower mounting bolts – arrowed

2.6b Withdraw the driveshaft from the front hub

3.2a Insert a large bolt and nut . . .

3.2b . . . and hammer the centre . . .

3.2c . . . out from the front hub

7 Unscrew the front suspension lower balljoint-to-lower arm retaining nut, then lift the wheel bearing housing from the lower arm and remove it from the vehicle.

Refitting

8 Prior to refitting, remove all traces of metal, adhesive, rust, oil or dirt from the splines and threads of the driveshaft outer CV joint and the bearing housing mating surface on the hub carrier.

9 The remainder of the refitting procedure is a reversal of the removal procedure, but observe the following points:

a) Ensure the hub and brake disc mating faces are clean and refit the disc as described in Chapter 9.

b) A new driveshaft retaining nut should be used.

c) Make sure the ABS sensor is fitted correctly, as described in Chapter 9.

d) Tighten all nuts and bolts to the specified torque setting (see Chapter 9 for brake components)

3 Front hub bearings – renewal

Note: *The bearing is a sealed, pre-adjusted and pre-lubricated, double-row roller type, and requires no maintenance. It is a press-fit in the wheel bearing housing.*

1 Remove the front wheel bearing housing as described in Section 2.

2 Support the swivel hub securely on blocks or in a vice. Using a tubular spacer, which bears only on the inner end of the hub flange, press the hub flange out of the bearing **(see illustrations)**.

3 Extract the bearing retaining circlip from the inner end of the swivel hub assembly **(see illustration)**.

4 Using a tubular spacer, that bears only on the inner race and threaded bar, press the complete bearing assembly out of the swivel hub **(see illustration)**.

5 Thoroughly clean the hub and swivel hub, removing all traces of dirt and grease, and polish away any burrs or raised edges, which might hinder reassembly. Check both for cracks or any other signs of wear or damage, and renew them if necessary. Renew the circlip, regardless of its apparent condition.

6 On reassembly, apply a light film of oil/ grease to the bearing outer race and hub flange shaft, to aid installation of the bearing.

7 Securely support the swivel hub, and locate the bearing in the hub. Press the bearing fully into position, ensuring that it enters the hub squarely, using a tubular spacer, which bears only on the bearing outer race **(see illustrations)**.

8 Once the bearing is correctly seated, secure the bearing in position with the new circlip, ensuring that it is correctly located in the groove in the swivel hub.

9 Securely support the outer face of the hub flange, and locate the swivel hub bearing inner race over the end of the hub flange. Press the bearing onto the hub, using a tubular spacer that bears only on the inner race of the hub bearing until it seats against the hub shoulder **(see illustration)**. Check that the hub flange rotates freely, and wipe off any excess oil or grease.

10 Refit the swivel hub assembly as described in Section 2.

3.3 Remove the circlip

3.4 Press the bearing out from the hub

3.7a Locate the bearing into the hub . . .

3.7b . . . and press it back into the hub

3.9 Tighten the bearing all the way into the hub

4.2 Unclip the wiring from the strut

4.3 Drop link retaining nut - arrowed

4.4 Undo the lower strut mounting bolts

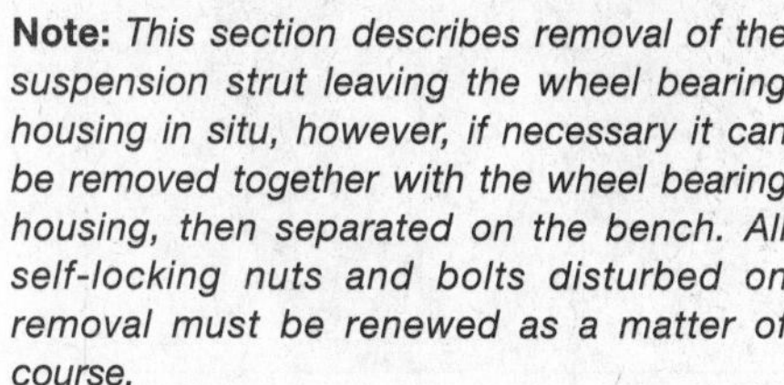

4 Front suspension strut – removal, overhaul and refitting

Note: *This section describes removal of the suspension strut leaving the wheel bearing housing in situ, however, if necessary it can be removed together with the wheel bearing housing, then separated on the bench. All self-locking nuts and bolts disturbed on removal must be renewed as a matter of course.*

Removal

1 Chock the rear wheels, apply the handbrake, and then jack up the front of the car and support on axle stands (see *Jacking and vehicle support*). Remove the appropriate roadwheel.

2 Unclip the wiring and/or hoses from the strut/body bracket from the swivel hub **(see illustration)**.

3 Unscrew the nut and disconnect the anti-roll bar link from the strut **(see illustration)**.

4 Note which way round they are fitted, then unscrew the nuts and remove the clamp bolts securing the wheel bearing housing to the bottom of the strut **(see illustration)**. Using wire or similar tie the wheel bearing housing up to the inner wing panel to prevent any strain on the driveshaft.

5 To ensure correct refitting, mark the strut upper mounting in relation to the body. If the reason for removing the strut is overhaul, loosen the upper mounting centre nut one turn, while holding the piston rod with an Allen key **(see illustration)**.

6 Support the strut, then unscrew the upper mounting bolts and lower the strut from under the wheel arch **(see illustration)**.

Overhaul

Warning: Before attempting to dismantle the suspension strut, a suitable tool to hold the coil spring in compression must be obtained. Adjustable coil spring compressors are readily available, and are recommended for this operation. Any attempt to dismantle the strut without such a tool is likely to result in damage or personal injury.

7 With the strut removed from the car, clean away all external dirt. If necessary, mount it upright in a vice during the dismantling procedure.

8 Fit the spring compressor, and compress the coil spring until all tension is relieved from the upper spring seat **(see illustrations)**.

9 Unscrew and remove the upper centre retaining nut, whilst retaining the strut piston with a suitable Allen key **(see illustrations)**.

4.5 Slacken the upper mounting bolts - arrowed

4.6 Remove the strut from under the wheel arch

4.8a Fit the spring compressor . . .

4.8b . . . and tighten the bolts

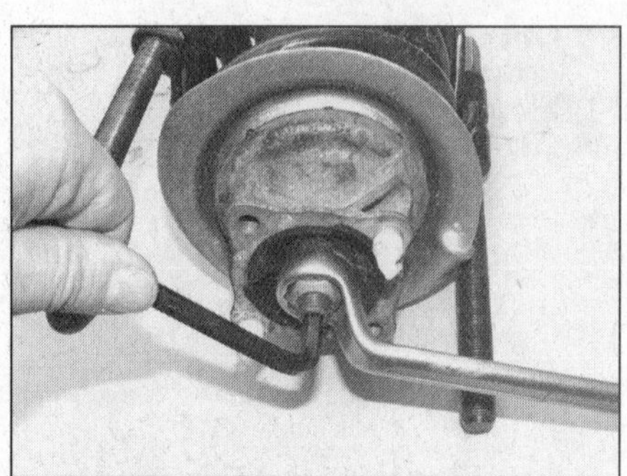

4.9a Slacken the nut while holding the piston strut with an Allen key

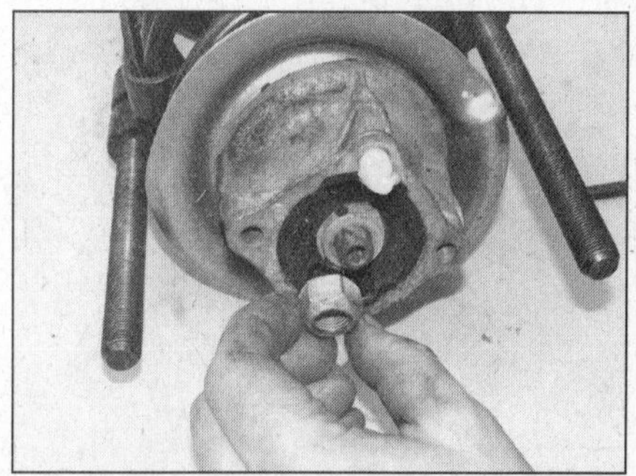

4.9b Remove the retaining nut . . .

4.9c . . . and the washer

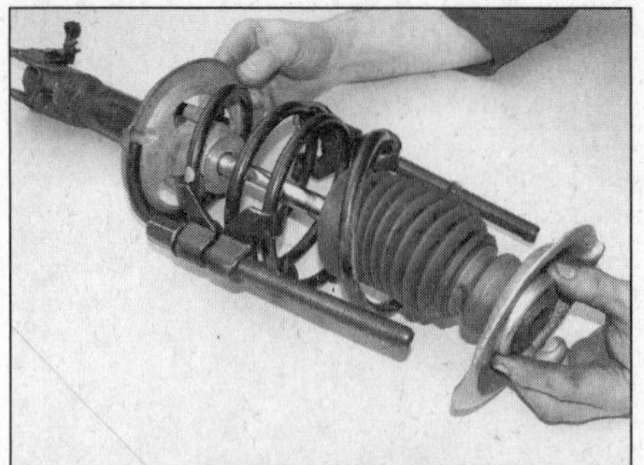

4.10 Remove the upper plate complete with protective sleeve

4.11a Withdraw the spring from the strut . . .

4.11b . . . noting its fitted position in the lower plate

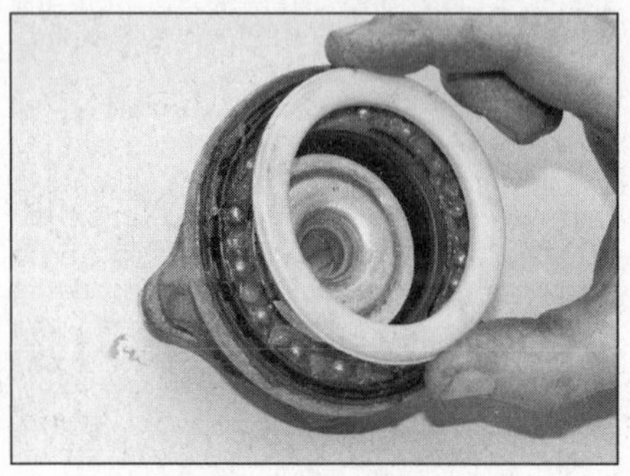

4.12a Remove the plastic cover . . .

4.12b . . . and renew the grease in the bearing

Make sure the spring is securely located in the spring compressor before removing the centre retaining nut.

10 Remove the protective sleeve and upper plate, including the bump stop from the strut **(see illustration)**.

11 Withdraw the coil spring, noting its fitted position for refitting **(see illustrations)**.

12 With the strut assembly now completely dismantled, examine all the components for wear, damage or deformation, and check the bearing for smoothness of operation. Renew any of the components as necessary and grease the upper bearing **(see illustrations)**.

13 Examine the strut for signs of fluid leakage. Check the strut piston for signs of pitting along its entire length, and check the strut body for signs of damage. While holding it in an upright position, test the operation of the strut by moving the piston through a full stroke, and then through short strokes of 50 to 100 mm. In both cases, the resistance felt should be smooth and continuous. If the resistance is jerky, or uneven, or if there is any visible sign of wear or damage to the strut, renewal is necessary.

14 If any doubt exists about the condition of the coil spring, carefully remove the spring compressors, and check the spring for distortion and signs of cracking. Renew the spring if it is damaged or distorted, or if there is any doubt as to its condition.

15 Inspect all other components for signs of damage or deterioration, and renew as necessary.

16 Assemble the bump stop to the upper mounting **(see illustrations)**, and then refit the upper bearing race and protective sleeve to the mounting. The larger diameter of the bump stop must be against the upper mounting.

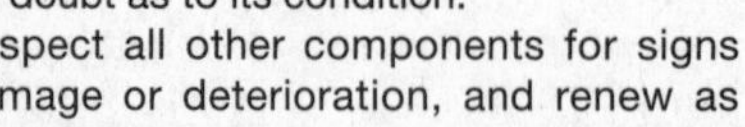

17 Fit the coil spring (together with the compressor tool) onto the strut, making sure its lower (larger diameter) end is correctly located against the spring seat stop, as noted on removal.

18 Refit the protective sleeve, bump stop, upper plate and upper bearing mounting, then screw on a new retaining nut. Tighten the nut to the specified torque while holding the piston rod with an Allen key.

Refitting

19 Manoeuvre the strut into position under the wheel arch, and locate in the suspension strut turret in the previously noted position. Insert the bolts and tighten to the specified torque.

20 Engage the wheel bearing housing with the bottom of the suspension strut, making sure that the bolt holes align. Raise the wheel bearing housing, while pressing it inwards to assist entry. When fully entered, remove the wire that was holding the bearing housing in place.

21 Insert the strut-to-wheel bearing housing bolts from the rear, and fit the retaining nuts. Tighten the nuts to the specified torque.

22 Refit the anti-roll bar link to the strut and fit new nut, tighten to the specified torque setting.

23 Clip the wiring for the ABS and brake warning light (where fitted), back into its retaining clips at the base of the strut.

24 Lower the vehicle to the ground, tighten the roadwheel bolts, and refit the wheel trim/hub cap.

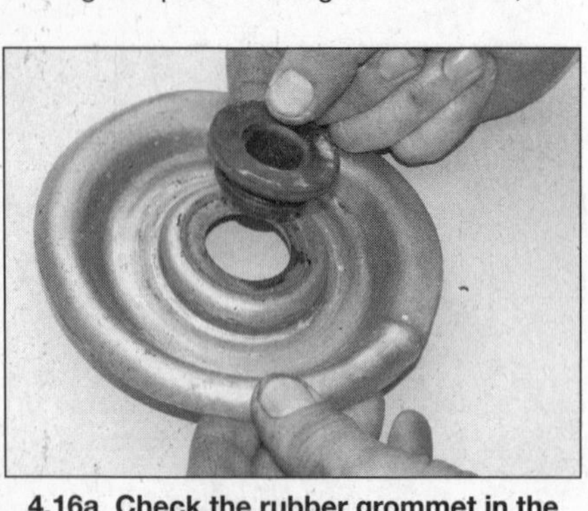

4.16a Check the rubber grommet in the upper plate . . .

4.16b . . . and refit the protective sleeve

5 Front suspension lower arm – removal, overhaul and refitting

Note: *All self-locking nuts and bolts disturbed on removal must be renewed as a matter of course.*

Removal

1 Apply the handbrake, then jack up the front of the vehicle and support it on axle stands (see *Jacking and vehicle support*). Remove the appropriate front roadwheel, and if required, the engine compartment undertray.

2 Remove the centre hubcap and remove the driveshaft retaining nut. Have an assistant depress the brake pedal to prevent the hub from turning. Discard the nut, as a new one will be required for refitting.

3 Unscrew the suspension lower balljoint-to-lower arm retaining nut **(see illustration)**, then lever down the lower arm to release the arm from the wheel bearing housing. Pull back on the hub and allow the driveshaft to slide out of the hub splines slightly, to allow more room to remove the lower arm.

4 Undo the retaining screws and remove the plastic cover from the lower part of the inner wing panel **(see illustration)**.

5 Unscrew and remove the rear lower arm mounting bolt from the front subframe **(see illustration)**.

6 Unscrew and remove the front lower arm mounting bolt from the front subframe **(see illustration)**, then remove the lower arm from beneath the car.

Overhaul

7 Thoroughly clean the lower arm, then check carefully for cracks or any other signs of wear or damage, paying particular attention to the rubber mounting bushes and the balljoint.

8 If the balljoint requires renewal, refer to Section 6 for the removal and refitting procedure.

9 If either of the two inner bushes require renewal, take the lower arm to a Mercedes-Benz dealer or suitably-equipped garage. Alternatively, a hydraulic press and suitable spacers may be used to press the bushes out of the arm, and to install the new ones. Note the position of the bushes in the lower arm for refitting. Dip the bushes in a mild solution of washing-up liquid and water. Note the following:

a) When fitting new bushes, make sure the bush is centred in its bore.

b) Make sure the bushes are installed in the correct position in the lower arm as noted on removal.

Refitting

10 Locate the lower arm on the subframe and insert the front mounting bolt loosely.

11 Insert the rear mounting bolt loosely, then position the balljoint into the lower part of the front wheel bearing housing.

5.3 Lower balljoint retaining nut – arrowed

5.5 Lower arm rear mounting bolt – arrowed

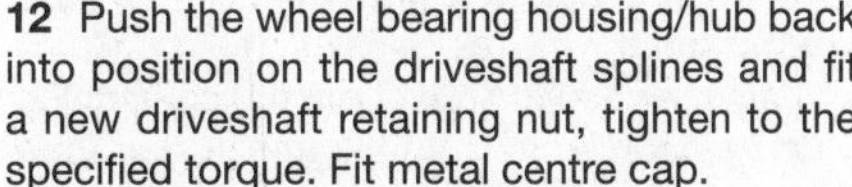

12 Push the wheel bearing housing/hub back into position on the driveshaft splines and fit a new driveshaft retaining nut, tighten to the specified torque. Fit metal centre cap.

13 Tighten the lower arm balljoint retaining nut to the specified torque.

14 Tighten the lower arm inner mounting bolts to the specified torque.

15 Refit the plastic cover to the inner wing panel.

16 Refit the roadwheel and undertray (if removed), and lower the car to the ground. Tighten the roadwheels to their specified torque setting.

6 Front suspension lower arm balljoint – removal and refitting

Note: *All self-locking nuts and bolts disturbed on removal must be renewed as a matter of course.*

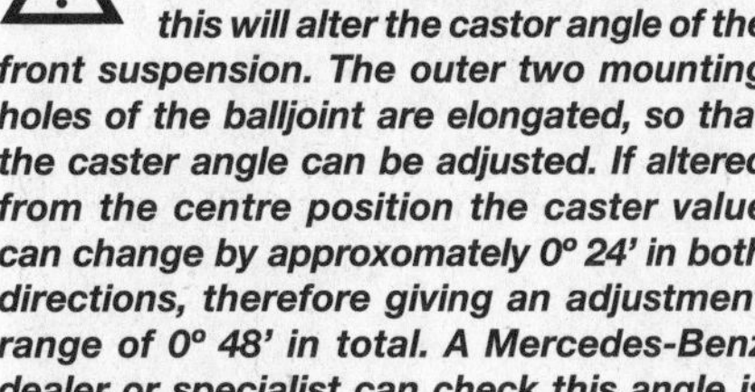

Warning: The balljoint is adjustable and can be fitted in three positions; this will alter the castor angle of the front suspension. The outer two mounting holes of the balljoint are elongated, so that the caster angle can be adjusted. If altered from the centre position the caster value can change by approxomately 0° 24' in both directions, therefore giving an adjustment range of 0° 48' in total. A Mercedes-Benz dealer or specialist can check this angle is within tolerance after the work has been carried out.

5.4 Remove the plastic inner panel

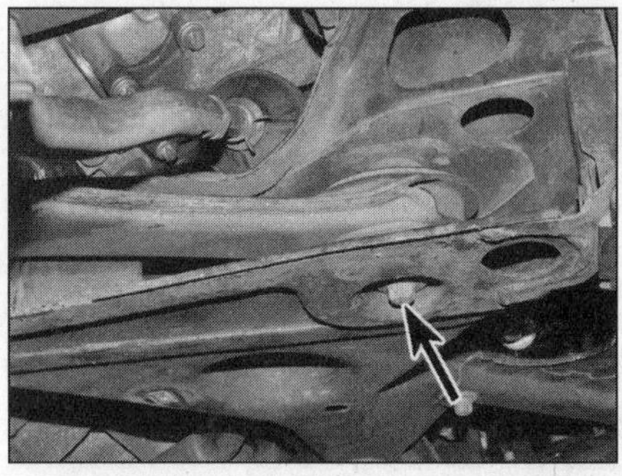

5.6 Lower arm front mounting bolt – arrowed

Removal

1 Remove the front suspension lower arm as described in Section 5.

2 Undo the three balljoint retaining bolts and remove the balljoint from the lower arm **(see illustration)**. Mark the position of the balljoint on the lower arm to aid refitting, see *Warning* at the beginning of this Section.

Refitting

3 Fit the balljoint to the suspension lower arm in the position noted on removal, and then insert the balljoint retaining bolts and tighten to the specified torque.

4 Refit the suspension lower arm with reference to Section 5.

5 If required, have the front suspension alignment checked by your local Mercedes-Benz dealer or specialist.

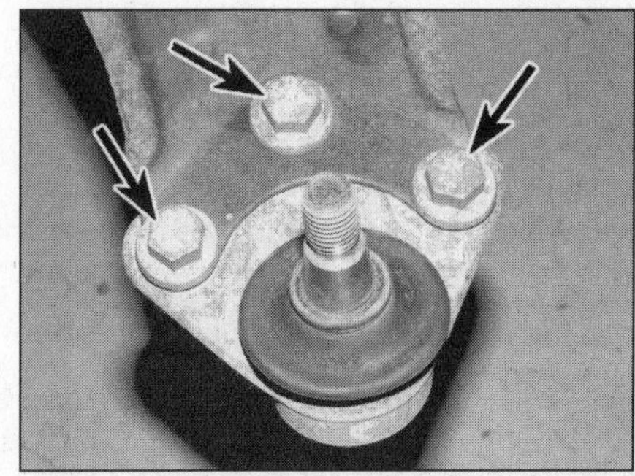

6.2 Balljoint mounting bolts to lower arm – arrowed

7.3a Front right-hand mounting . . .

7.3b . . . and front left-hand mounting

7.4 Anti-roll bar to drop link balljoint nut – arrowed

7.5 Anti-roll bar retaining clamp bolts – arrowed

7 Front anti-roll bar – removal and refitting

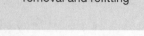

Note: *All self-locking nuts and bolts disturbed on removal must be renewed as a matter of course.*

Removal

1 Apply the handbrake, then jack up the front of the vehicle and support it on axle stands (see *Jacking and vehicle support*). Remove both front roadwheels and the engine compartment undertray.

2 Remove the air cleaner intake housing as described in Chapters 4A or 4B.

3 Use an engine hoist to support the engine (or a trolley jack and block of wood), and then undo the retaining bolts and remove the both front engine/transmission mountings **(see illustrations)**.

4 Undo the securing nuts from the connecting links at each end of the anti-roll bar **(see illustration)**.

5 Unscrew the bolts securing the anti-roll bar clamps to the subframe **(see illustration)**. Mark the anti-roll bar to indicate which way round it is fitted, and the position of the rubber mounting bushes; this will aid refitting.

6 Turn the steering fully to the right and withdraw the anti-roll bar out through the left-hand side of the vehicle. If required lift the engine slightly to allow more room, take care not to put any strain on wiring, cables, steering, exhaust ,etc.

7 Carefully examine the anti-roll bar components for signs of wear, damage or deterioration, paying particular attention to the rubber mounting bushes. Renew worn components as necessary.

Refitting

8 Refitting is a reversal of removal, but tighten all nuts and bolts to the specified torque where given. When refitting the anti-roll bar, align it with the marks made on removal.

8 Front anti-roll bar connecting link – removal and refitting

Note: *All self-locking nuts and bolts disturbed on removal must be renewed as a matter of course.*

Removal

1 Apply the handbrake, then jack up the front of the vehicle and support it on axle stands (see *Jacking and vehicle support*). Remove the relevant front roadwheel.

2 Unscrew and remove the nuts securing the link to the strut and anti-roll bar **(see illustration)**.

3 Inspect the link rubbers for signs of damage or deterioration. If evident, renew the link complete.

Refitting

4 Refitting is a reversal of removal, but tighten the nuts to the specified torque.

9 Rear stub axle – removal and refitting

Removal

1 Chock the front wheels, then jack up the rear of the vehicle and support it on axle stands (*see Jacking and vehicle support)*.

2 Remove the rear brake disc or brake drum with reference to Chapter 9.

3 Remove the dust cap from the centre of the hub using a screwdriver or cold chisel.

4 Unscrew and remove the hub nut **(see illustration 10.4)**. Note that it is tightened to a high torque and a socket extension bar may be required to loosen it. The bolt must be renewed whenever removed.

5 Withdraw the hub complete with bearing from the stub axle **(see illustration 10.5)**.

6 Remove the rear brake shoes/handbrake shoes as described in Chapter 9.

7 Undo the retaining bolts and remove the backplate from the stub axle **(see illustration)**.

8 Undo the four Torx bolts and remove the stub axle from the trailing arm **(see illustration)**.

Refitting

9 Refitting is a reversal of removal, noting the following points:

a) Where applicable, tighten the nuts/bolts to the specified torque.

b) Refer to Chapter 9, for refitting of brake shoes and discs (or drums)

8.2 Removing the drop link from the front suspension

9.7 Removing the backplate from the hub

9.8 Undo the Torx bolts – arrowed

10.3 Using a chisel to remove the hub cap

10 Rear hub/wheel bearings – removal and refitting

Note: *The bearing is a sealed, pre-adjusted and pre-lubricated, double-row roller type, and requires no maintenance. It is a press-fit in the hub.*

Removal

1 Chock the front roadwheels, then jack up the rear of the vehicle and support on axle stands (see *Jacking and vehicle support*). Release the handbrake and remove the relevant rear roadwheel.

2 Remove the rear brake disc or brake drum with reference to Chapter 9.

3 Remove the dust cap from the centre of the hub using a screwdriver or cold chisel **(see illustration)**.

4 Unscrew and remove the hub nut **(see illustration)**. Note that it is tightened to a high torque and a socket extension bar may be required to loosen it. The bolt must be renewed whenever removed.

5 Withdraw the hub complete with bearing from the stub axle **(see illustration)**.

6 Using a pair of circlip pliers remove the circlip from the hub **(see illustration)**.

7 Using a tubular spacer, that bears only on the inner race and threaded bar, press the complete bearing assembly out of the swivel hub.

Refitting

8 Thoroughly clean the hub and stub axle, removing all traces of dirt and grease, and polish away any burrs or raised edges which might hinder reassembly. Check both for cracks or any other signs of wear or damage, and renew them if necessary. Renew the circlip, regardless of its apparent condition.

9 On reassembly, apply a light film of oil/grease to the bearing outer race and hub flange shaft, to aid installation of the bearing.

10 Securely support the hub, and locate the bearing in the hub. Press the bearing fully into position, ensuring that it enters the hub squarely, using a tubular spacer, which bears only on the bearing outer race.

11 Once the bearing is correctly seated, secure the bearing in position with the new circlip, ensuring that it is correctly located in the groove in the hub.

12 Locate the hub on the stub axle and screw on the new nut and tighten it to the specified torque, use a drift to lock the nut in position **(see illustration)**.

13 Check the dust cap for damage and renew it if necessary. Use a hammer to carefully tap the cap into the hub. **Note:** *A badly fitting dust cap will allow moisture to enter the bearing, reducing its service life.*

14 Refit the brake disc or drum as described in Chapter 9.

15 Refit the roadwheel and lower the vehicle to the ground.

11 Rear axle – removal, overhaul and refitting

Note: *This following procedure is with the trailing arms removed from the axle. If required, remove the rear coil springs, shock absorbers, brake lines and handbrake cables, and remove the axle complete with trailing arms.*

10.4 Remove the rear hub nut

10.5 Withdraw the hub from the stub axle

10.6 Remove the circlip – arrowed

10.12 Using a drift to lock the hub nut in place

11.3a Front mounting bolt (arrowed) – one side shown

Removal

1 Chock the front roadwheels, then jack up the rear of the vehicle and support on axle stands (see *Jacking and vehicle support*). Remove the both roadwheels.

2 Remove both the rear trailing arms as described in Section 12.

3 Support the rear axle with a trolley jack at each side, and undo the the four mounting bolts (two at each side) **(see illustrations)**.

4 With the aid of an assistant, make sure the axle is supported safely on the trolley jacks and withdraw the four mounting bolts.

5 Lower the assembly and withdraw the rear axle from under the vehicle.

Overhaul

6 Thoroughly clean the rear axle, and the check carefully for cracks or any other signs of wear or damage, paying particular attention to the four mounting bushes.

7 If the bushes require renewal, take the axle to a Mercedes-Benz dealer or suitably-equipped garage. Alternatively, a hydraulic press and suitable spacers may be used to press the bushes out of the axle-mounting bracket, and to install new ones. When fitting the new bushes, it is important to position them as noted on removal.

Refitting

8 Refitting is a reversal of removal, noting the following points:

a) *Where applicable, tighten the nuts/bolts to the specified torque.*

b) *Refer to Section 12 for refitting of the trailing arms.*

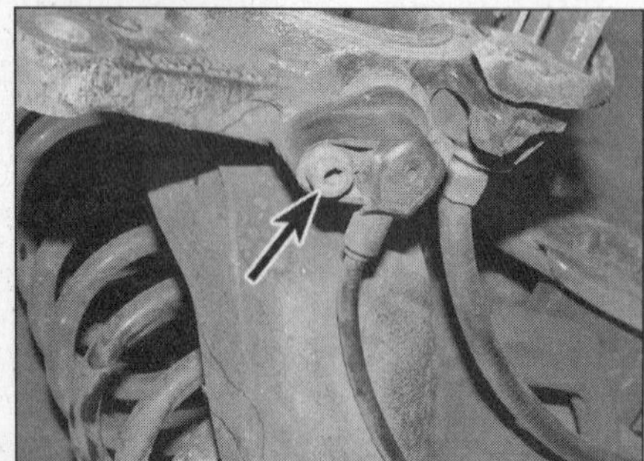

12.5 Rear wheel speed sensor retaining bolt – arrowed

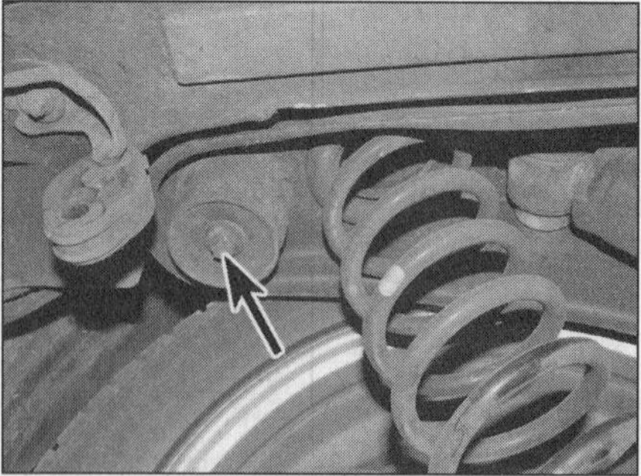

11.3b Rear mounting bolt (arrowed) – one side shown

c) *Refit the roadwheel and lower the vehicle to the ground.*

d) *If required, have the rear wheel alignment checked by a Mercedes-Benz dealer.*

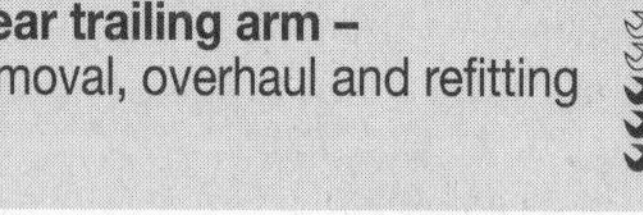

12 Rear trailing arm – removal, overhaul and refitting

Note: *All self-locking nuts and bolts disturbed on removal must be renewed as a matter of course.*

Removal

1 Chock the front roadwheels, then jack up the rear of the vehicle and support on axle stands (see *Jacking and vehicle support*). Remove the roadwheel and inner wheel arch liner.

2 Remove the rear coil spring as described in Section 13. Use trolley jack to support under the rear brake assembly.

3 Disconnect the handbrake cable from the rear brake unit as described in Chapter 9, and unclip it from the trailing arm.

4 Disconnect the anti-roll bar from the trailing arm with reference to Section 15.

5 Undo the retaining bolts and remove the wheel speed sensor from under the rear hub **(see illustration)**, unclip the wiring from along the trailing arm.

6 With reference to Chapter 9, disconnect the brake hose mounting bracket from the trailing arm and brake assembly **(see illustration)**. **Note:** *On disc brake models, there is no need to disconnect the brake line, undo the brake pipe/hose mounting bracket and move the brake caliper away from the trailing arm, taking care not to damage the brake lines.*

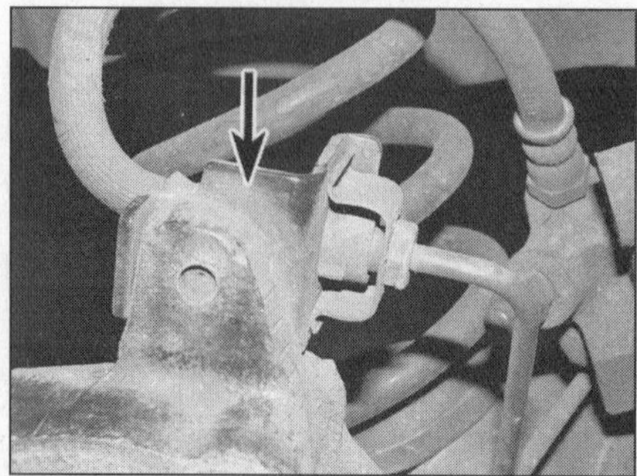

12.6 Disconnect the brake pipe mounting bracket (arrowed) from the trailing arm

7 With the trailing arm supported on a trolley jack, unscrew the front mounting bolt, lower the assembly and withdraw the rear trailing arm from under the vehicle **(see illustration)**.

Overhaul

8 Thoroughly clean the trailing arm, and the, check carefully for cracks or any other signs of wear or damage, paying particular attention to the front bearings.

9 If the bearings require renewal, take the arm to a Mercedes-Benz dealer or suitably-equipped garage. Alternatively, a hydraulic press and suitable spacers may be used to press the bearings out of the arm, and to install new ones. When fitting the new bearings to the front of the trailing arm, it is important to position them as noted on removal, and make sure the spacers in-between the bearings are seated correctly.

10 Refitting is a reversal of removal, noting the following points:

a) *Where applicable, tighten the nuts/bolts to the specified torque.*

b) *Refer to Chapter 9 for bleeding the rear brakes if required.*

c) *Refer to Section 15 for refitting of the anti-roll bar.*

d) *Refer to Section 13 for refitting of the coil spring.*

e) *Refit the roadwheel and lower the vehicle to the ground.*

f) *If required, have the rear wheel alignment checked by a Mercedes-Benz dealer.*

13 Rear coil spring – removal and refitting

Removal

1 Chock the front roadwheels, then jack up the rear of the vehicle and support on axle stands (see *Jacking and vehicle support*). Remove the relevant rear roadwheel and rear undertray.

2 Place a jack under the rear hub/drum and

12.7 Front mounting bolt – arrowed

remove the shock absorber lower mounting bolt, with reference to Section 14 **(see illustrations)**.

3 Lower the jack and withdraw the coil spring from between the body and the rear trailing arm, noting its fitted position **(see illustration)**.

4 Check and clean thoroughly the spring locations on the underbody and trailing arm.

Refitting

5 Refitting is a reversal of removal, but make sure that the spring engages correctly in the upper mounting plate, as noted on removal **(see illustration)**. Tighten the retaining bolts to their specified torque.

14 Rear shock absorber – removal and refitting

Note: *All self-locking nuts and bolts disturbed on removal must be renewed as a matter of course.*

Removal

1 Before removing the shock absorber, an idea of how effective it is can be gained by depressing the rear corner of the car. If the shock absorber is in good condition, the body should rise then settle in its normal position. If the body oscillates more than this, the shock absorber is defective. **Note:** *To ensure even rear suspension, both rear shock absorbers should be renewed at the same time.*

2 Chock the front roadwheels, then jack up the rear of the vehicle and support on axle stands (see *Jacking and vehicle support*). Remove the relevant rear roadwheel.

3 Remove the wheel arch liner.

4 Position a trolley jack and block of wood beneath the coil spring position on the trailing arm, and raise the arm so that the shock absorber is slightly compressed. **Note:** *If preferred, the rear coil spring may be removed completely at this stage, refer to Section 13.*

5 Undo the shock absorber lower mounting nut and withdraw the bolt from the trailing arm **(see illustrations)**.

6 Unscrew the upper mounting bolt and withdraw the shock absorber. An open-ended spanner will need to be inserted between the body and the trailing arm to hold the nut in place **(see illustration)**.

7 If necessary, the action of the shock absorber can be checked by mounting it upright in a vice. Fully depress the rod, and then pull it up fully. The piston rod must move smoothly over its complete length.

Refitting

8 Locate the shock absorber in the top of the rear axle carrier, and then insert the upper mounting bolt and tighten to the specified torque. Use a magnetic screwdriver or a

13.2a Place a jack under he hub . . .

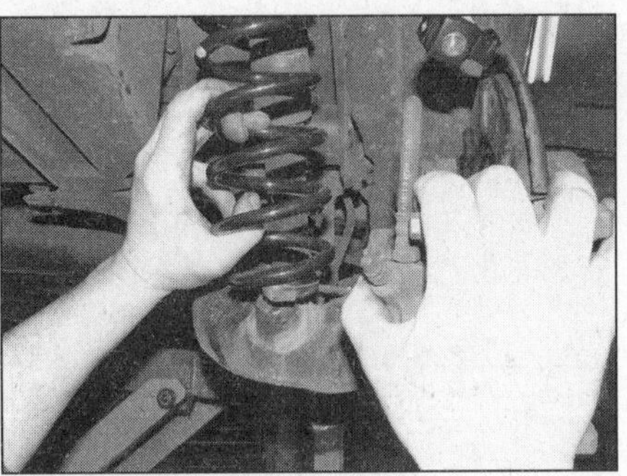

13.3 Pull down on the hub and remove the coil spring

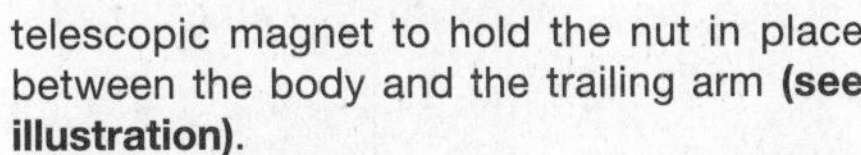

telescopic magnet to hold the nut in place between the body and the trailing arm **(see illustration)**.

9 If required, refit the rear coil spring with reference to Section 13.

10 Extend the shock absorber if necessary,

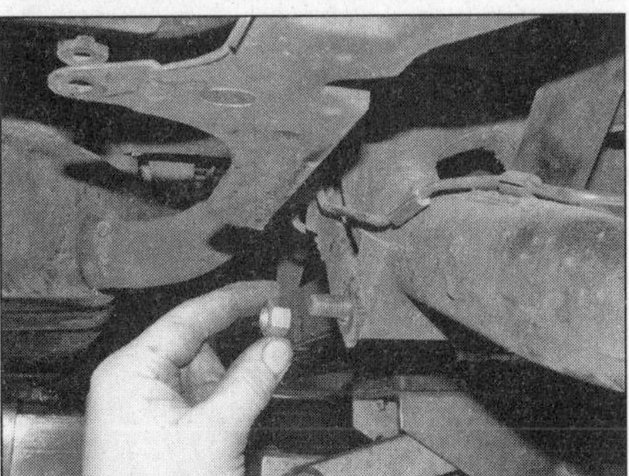

14.5a Undo the retaining nut . . .

14.6 Insert spanner to reach the upper mounting nut

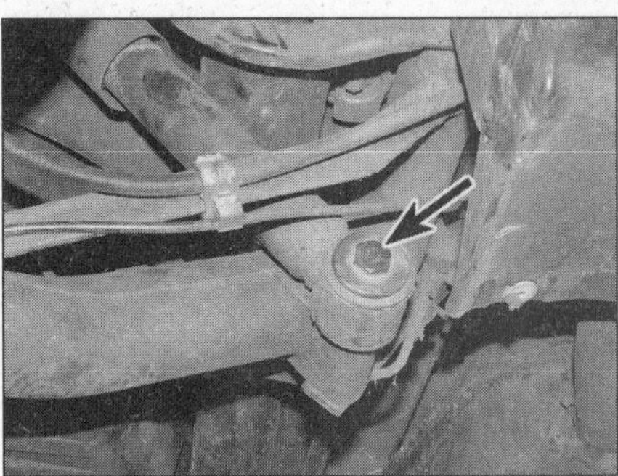

13.2b . . . and remove the lower shock absorber mounting bolt – arrowed

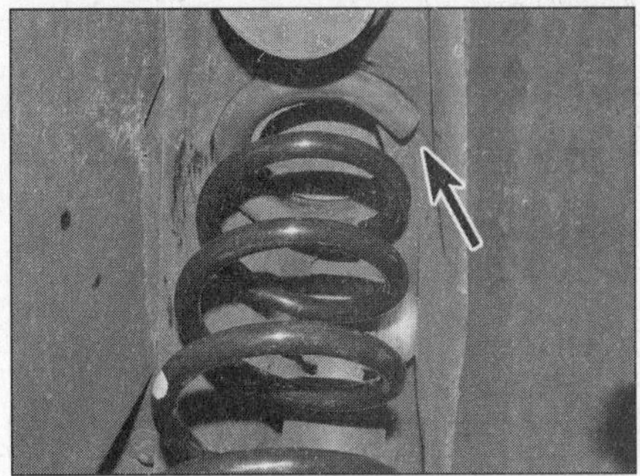

13.5 Make sure the end of the spring locates correctly

and insert the lower mounting bolt, then tighten the retaining nut.

11 Refit the wheel arch liner.

12 Refit the roadwheel and lower the vehicle to the ground. Tighten the wheel bolts to the specified torque setting.

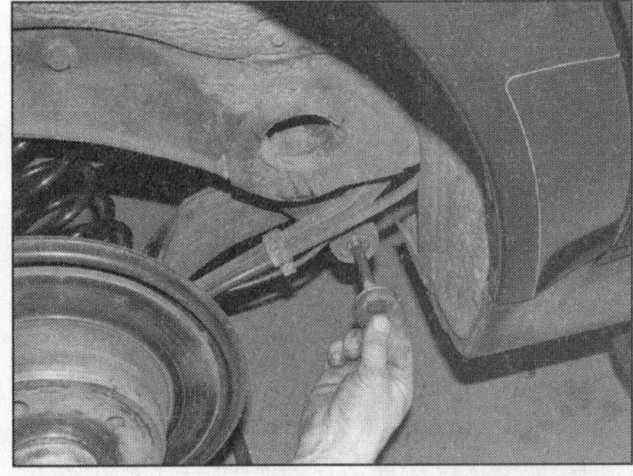

14.5b . . . and remove the lower mounting bolt

14.8 Use a magnetic screwdriver to hold nut in position

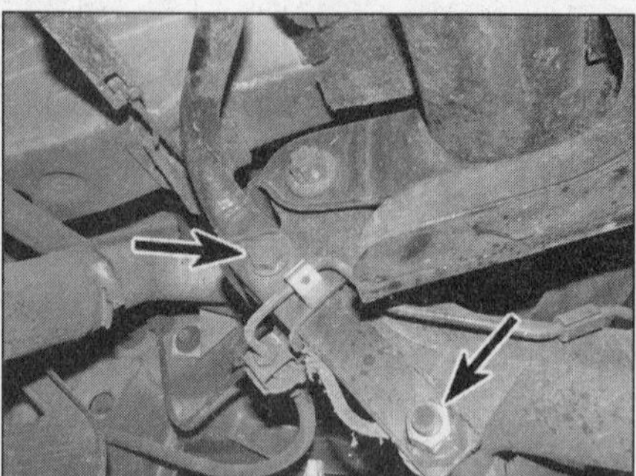
15.4 Undo the mounting bolt and nut – arrowed

15 Rear anti-roll bar – removal and refitting

Removal

1 Chock the front roadwheels, then jack up the rear of the vehicle and support on axle stands (see *Jacking and vehicle support*). Remove the rear undertrays.
2 Working on each side in turn, unscrew the nut and detach the side brackets from the trailing arms.
3 Mark the anti-roll bar to indicate which way round it is fitted; this will aid refitting.
4 Unscrew the bolts securing the side brackets to the anti-roll bar **(see illustration)**, and withdraw the anti-roll bar from the vehicle. Take care not to damage the brake line or hoses as the anti-roll bar is removed.

16.4 Remove the retaining screw from the steering wheel

Refitting

5 Refitting is a reversal of removal but tighten all nuts and bolts to the specified torque.

16 Steering wheel – removal and refitting

Warning: During the airbag removal and refitting procedures, avoid sitting in the front seats.

Removal

1 Set the front wheels in the straight-ahead position, and release the steering lock by inserting the ignition key.
2 Disconnect the battery negative (earth) lead and position it away from the terminal.
3 Remove the driver's airbag as described in Chapter 12.

16.5 Remove the steering wheel from the column

Caution: To prevent any discharge of static electricity into the airbag circuit, temporarily touch the vehicle bodywork before disconnecting the wiring.

Warning: Position the airbag in a safe and secure place, away from the work area.

4 Unscrew and remove the countersunk retaining bolt, while holding the steering wheel stationary **(see illustration). Note:** *The steering wheel retaining bolt must be discarded as a new one will be required for refitting.*
5 Check if the steering wheel is marked in relation to the column. If not, use a dab of paint to mark them, then ease the steering wheel from the column splines **(see illustration)**. Feed the wiring connector out through the steering wheel when it is removed.

Refitting

6 Locate the steering wheel on the column splines making sure that the previously-made marks are correctly aligned and the wiring connector is through the steering wheel.
7 Refit the new retaining bolt and tighten to the specified torque while holding the steering wheel stationary.
8 Refit the driver's airbag with reference to Chapter 12.
9 Reconnect the battery negative (earth) lead.

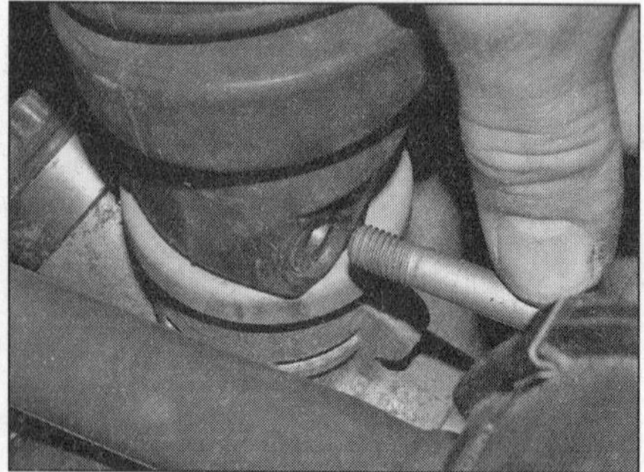
17.3 Remove the steering joint securing bolt

17.4a Remove the joint from the column . . .

17.4b . . . checking the alignment marks – arrowed

17.5a Slide the lower shaft . . .

17 Steering column – removal, inspection and refitting

Note: *All self-locking nuts and bolts disturbed on removal must be renewed as a matter of course.*

Removal

1 Disconnect the battery negative lead (see *Reference* at end of Manual), and position it away from the terminal.
2 Working under the bonnet, release the retaining clip and lift the windscreen washer reservoir to one side.
3 Turn the steering wheel until it is in the straight-ahead position and then undo and remove the retaining bolt at the bottom of the steering shaft **(see illustration)**.
4 Make sure the marking on the plastic cap is aligned with the mark on the housing and

17.5b . . . out from the engine compartment . . .

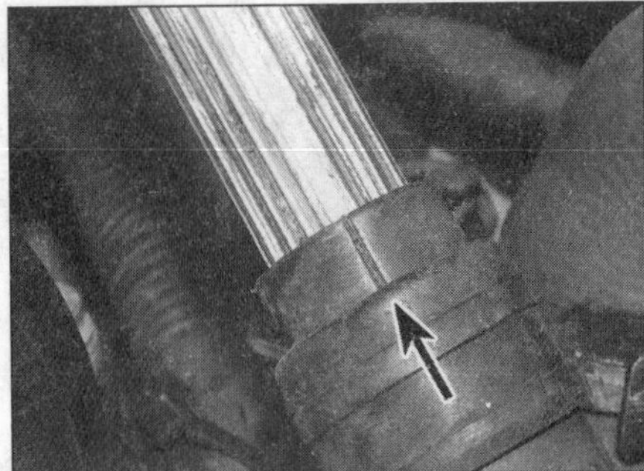

17.5c . . . noting the alignment marks/ spline – arrowed

17.14 Undo the upper mounting nuts – arrowed

17.15 Lower mounting bolts – arrowed

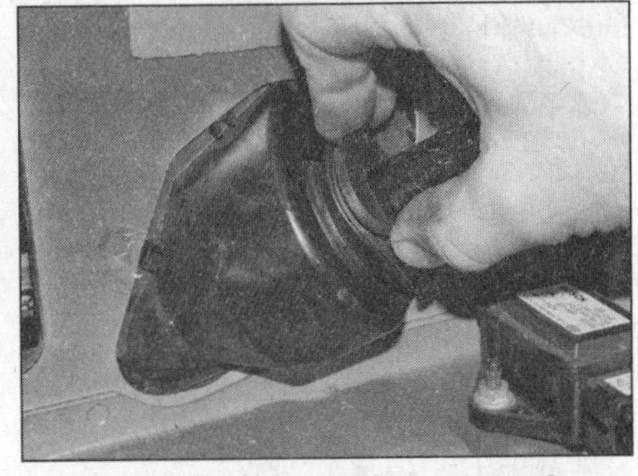

17.16a Pull out the rubber grommet . . .

17.16b . . . and withdraw the upper steering column

pull the steering joint from the steering column **(see illustrations)**.

5 Slide the lower part of the steering column from the splines on the intermediate section of the steering column and remove it from the vehicle **(see illustrations)**. Note the marking on the lower steering column shaft and the master spline on the intermediate section for refitting.

6 Working inside the vehicle, remove the steering wheel as described in Section 16, making sure the steering is in the straight-ahead position.

7 Remove the instrument panel and steering rotary switch, as described in Chapter 12.

8 Undo the securing screw and remove the handle from the column height adjuster.

9 Undo the retaining screws and remove the trim panel and steering column shrouds from below the driver's side of the facia, for more information refer to Chapter 11.

10 Disconnect the wiring connector from the ignition switch.

11 Unclip any wiring from the securing clips along the steering column.

12 On automatic transmissions, disconnect the shift lock cable from the ignition starter switch. Press the shift cable forward and pull downawards to remove the cable, making sure the steering wheel is in the 0 position. See Chapter 7B for further information.

13 Remove the cable guide from below the steering column.

14 Slacken and remove the two upper steering column mounting nuts **(see illustration)**.

15 Support the steering column and remove the two lower mounting bolts **(see illustration)**.

16 Lower the steering column and slide out the inner sleeve and withdraw the rubber gaiter from the floor panel **(see illustrations)**.

17 The upper and intermediate sections of the steering column can now be removed from inside the vehicle.

Caution: Do not carry the steering column by suspending it from the universal joint or intermediate shaft, as this will damage the universal joint and steering column bushes. Also, do not bend and force the joints.

Inspection

18 Before refitting the steering column, examine the column and mountings for signs of damage and deformation.

19 Check the inner column sections for signs of free play in the column bushes, also check the universal joint for wear on the intermediate shaft. If any damage or wear is found on any part of the shaft, then it will need to be renewed, check with your local Mercedes-Benz dealer for availability of parts.

20 The intermediate shaft can be removed from the upper part of the steering column, but a press will be required for refitting. There is a spring washer fitted between the two parts of the shaft and this has to be compressed before the bolt can be refitted **(see illustrations)**.

Refitting

21 Refitting is a reversal of removal, noting the following points:

a) Where applicable, tighten the nuts/bolts to the specified torque.

b) Make sure that all alignment marks are in position when refitting.

c) Refer to Chapter 12 for refitting the instrument panel and rotary switch.

d) Refer to Section 16 for refitting the steering wheel.

17.20a Remove the clamp bolt . . .

17.20b . . . pull the shaft apart . . .

17.20c ... remove the spring washer ...

17.20d ... and the lower bush

e) Make sure the rubber gaiter is located in the floor panel securely.

f) Refer to Chapter 7B for information on refitting the shift lock cable.

g) Reconnect the battery and check all electrics.

18 Ignition switch and steering column lock/switch carrier – removal and refitting

Ignition switch

Removal

1 Disconnect the battery negative lead (see *Reference* at end of Manual), and position it away from the terminal.

2 With the key removed from the ignition switch, carefully unclip the plastic transponder surround from the ignition barrel **(see illustration)**. Note this has wiring going to it so cannot be removed completely, let it hang down the side of the steering column.

3 Insert the key into the ignition switch and turn it to position I, holding the key in position, turn the black sleeve anti-clockwise and withdraw the key complete with ignition switch from the steering column **(see illustration)**.

Refitting

4 Refitting is a reversal of removal, making sure the ignition is in position I when refitting.

Steering column lock/ switch carrier

Note: *A new column lock assembly will be required, as it will break on removal.*

Removal

5 See Section 17, paragraphs 6 to 13, for access to the upper part of the steering column. **Note:** *There is no need to completely remove the steering column.*

6 Remove the ignition switch as described previously in this Section and disconnect the wiring block from the switch carrier **(see illustration)**.

7 Note the fitted position of the lock carrier and using a drift, drive out the retaining pin in the downward direction **(see illustration). Note:** *The lower guide of the lock carrier will break off.*

Refitting

8 Refitting is a reversal of removal, noting the following points:

a) Support the lower guides of the lock carrier, when inserting the retaining pins.

b) Keep the two parts of the lock carrier pushed together to line up the roll-pin holes.

c) Make sure the ignition is in position I for refitting.

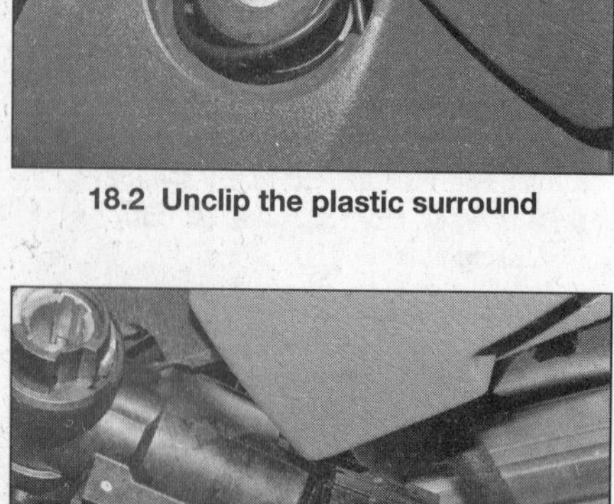

18.2 Unclip the plastic surround

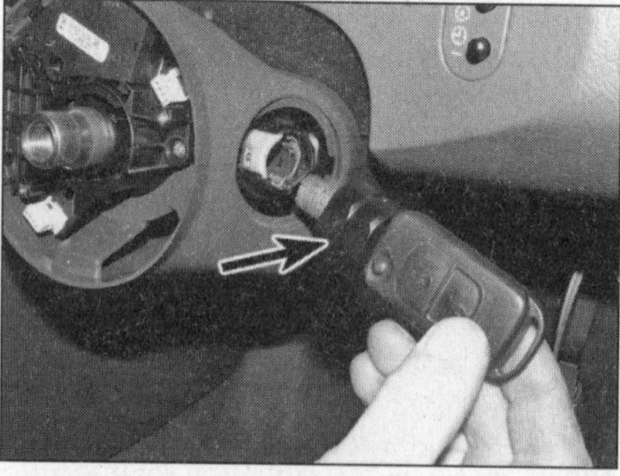

18.3 Turn sleeve (arrowed) and withdraw ignition switch

18.6 Disconnect the wiring block connector

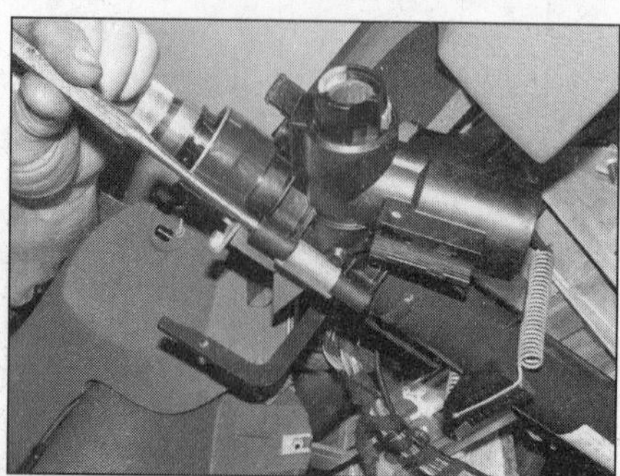

18.7 Drift out the retaining pin

19 Steering gear and pump assembly – removal, inspection and refitting

Note: *All self-locking nuts and bolts disturbed on removal must be renewed as a matter of course.*

Removal

1 Disconnect the battery negative lead (refer to *Disconnecting the battery* in the *Reference* Chapter at the end of this manual).

2 Apply the handbrake, then jack up the front of the vehicle and support it on axle stands (see *Jacking and vehicle support*). Remove both front roadwheels and the engine compartment undertray.

3 Working on each side in turn, unscrew the nuts from the track rod ends, then use a balljoint separator tool to release the ends from the steering arms on the front wheel bearing housings.

4 Working on each side in turn, unscrew the nuts securing the lower end of the anti-roll bar links to the anti-roll bar.

5 Remove the air cleaner intake housing as described in Chapters 4A or 4B.

6 Turn the steering wheel until it is in the straight-ahead position and then undo and remove the retaining bolt at the bottom of the steering shaft. Make sure the marking on the plastic cap is aligned with the mark on the housing, and then pull the steering joint from the steering column (see Section 17).

7 On petrol engines, remove the air injection pump as described in Chapter 4C.

8 Unbolt the power steering pump from the front left-hand side front of the subframe and move it to one side **(see illustration)**, do not disconnect the hydraulic pipes.

9 Use an engine hoist to support the engine (or a trolley jack and block of wood), and then undo the retaining bolts and remove the both front engine/transmission mountings and mounting brackets **(see illustrations)**.

10 Disconnect the fluid lines from the steering rack, noting their fitted position. Use

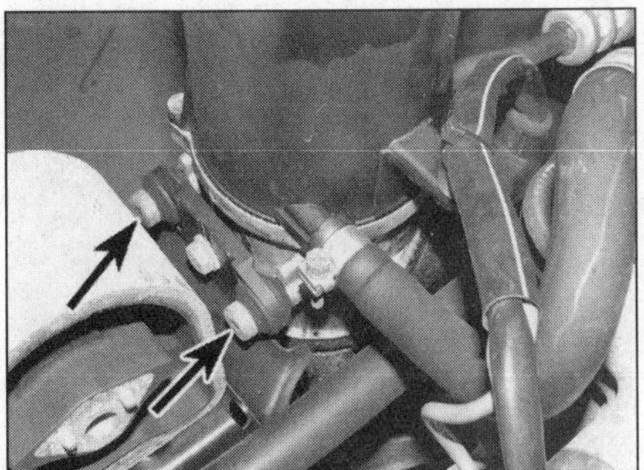
19.8 Undo the pump mounting bolts – arrowed

19.9a Front right-hand engine mounting

19.9b Front left-hand engine mounting

19.10 Undo the fluid lines – arrowed

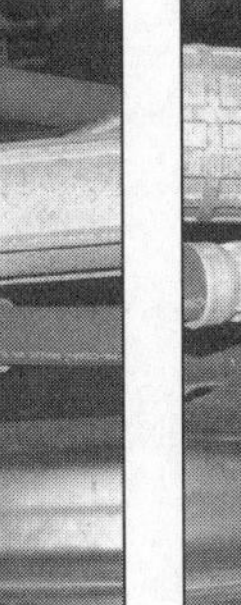
19.12a Left-hand mounting bolt – arrowed . . .

19.12b . . . and right-hand mounting bolt – arrowed

a container to catch power steering fluid as it drains from the fluid pipes **(see illustration)**. Plug the end of the fluid lines and steering rack to prevent contamination.

11 Undo the retaining bolt from under the left-hand front of the subframe, where the two parts of the subframe join together.

12 Unbolt the steering gear from the subframe **(see illustrations)**, and carefully withdraw it, out through the left-hand side of the vehicle. If required lift the engine slightly to allow more room, take care not to put any strain on wiring, cables, exhaust, etc.

13 Disconnect the wiring connectors and withdraw the power steering pump out from the engine compartment **(see illustration)**.

Inspection

14 Examine the steering gear assembly for signs of wear or damage, and check that the rack moves freely throughout the full length of its travel, with no signs of roughness or excessive free play between the steering gear pinion and rack.

15 It is not possible to overhaul the steering gear assembly housing components, and if it is faulty, the assembly must be renewed. The only components which can be renewed individually are the steering gear gaiters, the track rod end balljoints and the track rods, as described later in this Chapter.

Refitting

16 Refitting is a reversal of removal, noting the following points:

a) Tighten the mounting bolts to the specified torque setting.

b) Refer to the relevant Chapter for further information on refitting.

c) See Section 17 for refitting the steering column universal joint.

d) Reconnect the battery negative lead.

e) Have the front wheel alignment checked at the earliest opportunity.

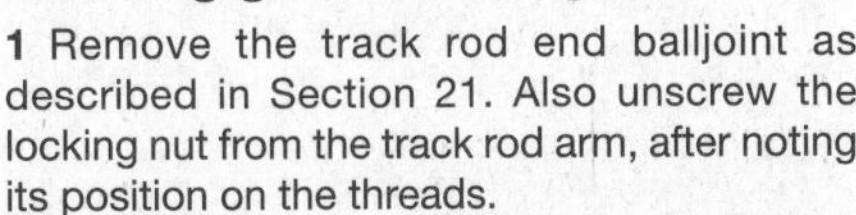

20 Steering gear rubber gaiters and track rods – renewal

Steering gear rubber gaiters

1 Remove the track rod end balljoint as described in Section 21. Also unscrew the locking nut from the track rod arm, after noting its position on the threads.

2 Wipe clean the rubber gaiter to prevent entry of dirt or moisture. Note the fitted position of the gaiter on the track rod, then release the retaining clips and slide the gaiter off the steering gear housing and track rod **(see illustration)**.

3 Wipe clean the track rod and the steering gear housing, and then apply a film of suitable grease to the surface of the rack. To do this, turn the steering wheel as necessary to fully extend the rack from the housing, then reposition it in its central position.

4 Carefully slide the new gaiter onto the track rod, and locate it on the steering gear housing. Position the gaiter as previously-noted on removal, making sure that it is not twisted, then lift the outer sealing lip of the gaiter to equalise air pressure within the gaiter.

5 Secure the gaiter in position with new retaining clips. Where crimped-type clips are used, pull the clip as tight as possible, and locate the hooks in their slots. Remove any slack in the clip by carefully compressing the raised section. In the absence of the special

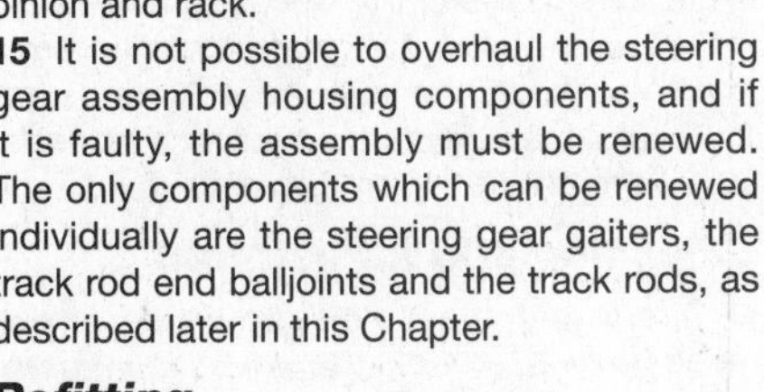
19.13 Disconnect the pump wiring connectors – arrowed

20.2 Release the retaining clip – arrowed

21.3 Slacken the track rod locknut – arrowed

21.4a Remove the retaining nut . . .

21.4b . . . and remove the balljoint from the stub axle

crimping tool, a pair of side-cutters may be used, taking care not to cut the clip.

6 Screw on the locking nut, then refit the track rod end balljoint as described in Section 21.

Track rods

7 Remove the relevant steering gear rubber gaiter as described earlier. If there is insufficient working room with the steering gear mounted in the car, remove it as described in Section 19 and hold it in a vice while renewing the track rod.

8 Hold the steering rack stationary with one spanner on the flats provided, then loosen the balljoint nut with another spanner. Fully unscrew the nut and remove the track rod from the rack.

9 Locate the new track rod on the end of the steering rack and screw on the nut. Hold the rack stationary with one spanner and tighten the balljoint nut to the specified torque. A crow's-foot adapter may be required since the track rod prevents access with a socket, and care must be taken to apply the correct torque in this situation.

10 Refit the steering gear or rubber gaiter with reference to the earlier paragraphs or Section 19. On completion check and, if necessary, adjust the front wheel alignment as described in Section 22.

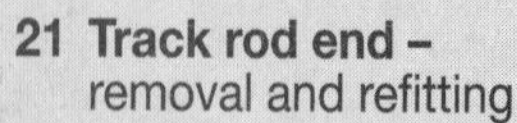

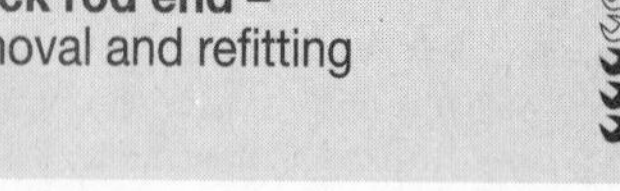

21 Track rod end – removal and refitting

Note: *A new balljoint retaining nut will be required on refitting.*

Removal

1 Apply the handbrake, then jack up the front of the vehicle and support it on axle stands (see *Jacking and vehicle support*). Remove the relevant roadwheel.

2 If the track rod end is to be re-used, mark its position in relation to the track rod to facilitate refitting.

3 Unscrew the track rod end locknut by a quarter of a turn **(see illustration)**. Do not move the locknut from this position, as it will serve as a handy reference mark on refitting.

4 Loosen and remove the nut securing the track rod end balljoint to the wheel bearing housing, and release the balljoint tapered shank using a universal balljoint separator. Note that the balljoint shank has a hexagon hole – hold the shank with an Allen key while loosening the nut **(see illustrations)**.

5 Counting the exact number of turns necessary to do so, unscrew the track rod end from the track rod.

6 Carefully clean the balljoint and the threads. Renew the balljoint if its movement is sloppy or too stiff, if excessively worn, or if damaged in any way; carefully check the stud taper and threads. If the balljoint gaiter is damaged, the complete balljoint assembly must be renewed; it is not possible to obtain the gaiter separately.

Refitting

7 Screw the track rod end onto the track rod by the number of turns noted on removal. This should bring the track rod end to within a quarter of a turn of the locknut, with the alignment marks that were made on removal (if applicable) lined up. Tighten the locknut.

8 Refit the balljoint shank to the steering arm on the wheel bearing housing, then fit a new retaining nut and tighten it to the specified torque. Hold the shank with an Allen key if necessary.

9 Refit the roadwheel, then lower the car to the ground and tighten the roadwheel bolts to the specified torque.

10 Check and, if necessary, adjust the front wheel toe setting as described in Section 22.

22 Wheel alignment and steering angles – general information

Definitions

1 A car's steering and suspension geometry is defined in three basic settings – all angles are expressed in degrees; the steering axis is defined as an imaginary line drawn through the axis of the suspension strut, extended where necessary to contact the ground.

2 Camber is the angle between each roadwheel and a vertical line drawn through its centre and tyre contact patch, when viewed from the front or rear of the car. Positive camber is when the roadwheels are tilted outwards from the vertical at the top; negative camber is when they are tilted inwards.

3 Camber angle is only adjustable by loosening the front suspension subframe mounting bolts and moving it slightly to one side. This also alters the castor angle. The camber angle can be checked using a camber checking gauge.

4 Castor is the angle between the steering axis and a vertical line drawn through each roadwheel's centre and tyre contact patch, when viewed from the side of the car. Positive castor is when the steering axis is tilted so that it contacts the ground ahead of the vertical; negative castor is when it contacts the ground behind the vertical. Slight castor angle adjustment is possible by loosening the front suspension subframe bolts and moving it slightly to one side. This also alters the camber angle.

5 Castor is not easily adjustable, and is given for reference only; while it can be checked using a castor checking gauge, if the figure obtained is significantly different from that specified, the car must be taken for careful checking by a professional, as the fault can only be caused by wear or damage to the body or suspension components.

6 Toe is the difference, viewed from above, between lines drawn through the roadwheel centres and the car's centre-line. Toe-in is when the roadwheels point inwards, towards each other at the front, while toe-out is when they splay outwards from each other at the front.

7 The front wheel toe setting is adjusted by screwing the track rod(s) in/out of the outer balljoint(s) to alter the effective length of the track rod assembly.

8 Rear wheel toe setting is not adjustable, and is given for reference only. While it can be checked, if the figure obtained is significantly different from that specified, the car must be taken for careful checking by a professional, as the fault can only be caused by wear or damage to the body or suspension components.

Checking and adjustment

9 Due to the special measuring equipment necessary to check the wheel alignment, and the skill required to use it properly, the checking and adjustment of these settings is best left to a Mercedes-Benz dealer or similar expert. Note that most tyre-fitting centres now possess sophisticated checking equipment.

Chapter 11
Bodywork and fittings

Contents

Degrees of difficulty

Easy, suitable for novice with little experience	**Fairly easy,** suitable for beginner with some experience	**Fairly difficult,** suitable for competent DIY mechanic	**Difficult,** suitable for experienced DIY mechanic	**Very difficult,** suitable for expert DIY or professional

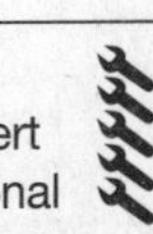

Specifications

Torque wrench settings	Nm	lbf ft
Bonnet hinge bolts	10	7
Door hinge pin nut	8	6
Door hinge-to-pillar bolts	30	22
Door lock	8	6
Front seat mounting retaining bolts	50	37
Rear seat belt buckle nut	23	17
Rear seat belt guide bolts	9	7
Seat belt and stalk anchorage bolts	35	26
Seat belt reel mounting bolt	35	26
Tailgate hinge-to-roof retaining nuts	9	7
Tailgate lock assembly retaining screws	9	7
Tailgate striker retaining screws	9	7

1 General information

The main body shell is made of pressed-steel sections, and is available in both three- and five-door Hatchback versions. It also comes in a short (SWB) and long (LWB) wheelbase versions. These components are welded together, and some use is made of structural adhesives.

Extensive use is made of plastic materials, mainly in the interior, but also in exterior components. The front wings, bonnet and rear tailgate are all made from plastic. The front and rear bumpers, and front grille, are injection-moulded from a synthetic material that is very strong and yet light. Plastic components such as wheel arch liners are fitted to the underside of the vehicle, to improve the body's resistance to corrosion.

2 Maintenance – bodywork and underframe

The general condition of a vehicle's bodywork is the one thing that significantly affects its value. Maintenance is easy, but needs to be regular. Neglect, particularly after minor damage, can lead quickly to further deterioration and costly repair bills. It is important also to keep watch on those parts of the vehicle not immediately visible, for instance the underside, inside all the wheel arches, and the lower part of the engine compartment.

The basic maintenance routine for the bodywork is washing – preferably with a lot of water, from a hose. This will remove all the loose solids, which may have stuck to the vehicle. It is important to flush these off in such a way as to prevent grit from scratching the finish. The wheel arches and underframe need washing in the same way, to remove any accumulated mud, which will retain moisture and tend to encourage rust. Paradoxically enough, the best time to clean the underframe and wheel arches is in wet weather, when the mud is thoroughly wet and soft. In very wet weather, the underframe is usually cleaned of large accumulations automatically, and this is a good time for inspection.

Periodically, except on vehicles with a wax-based underbody protective coating, it is a good idea to have the whole of the underframe of the vehicle steam-cleaned, engine compartment included, so that a thorough inspection can be carried out to see what minor repairs and renovations are necessary. Steam-cleaning is available at many garages, and is necessary for the removal of the accumulation of oily grime, which sometimes is allowed to become thick in certain areas. If steam-cleaning facilities are not available, there are some excellent grease solvents available which can be brush-applied; the dirt can then be simply hosed off. Note that these methods should not be used on vehicles with wax-based underbody protective coating, or the coating will be removed. Such vehicles should be inspected annually, preferably just prior to winter, when the underbody should be washed down, and any damage to the wax coating repaired. Ideally, a completely fresh coat should be applied. It would also be worth considering the use of such wax-based protection for injection into door panels, sills, box sections, etc, as an additional safeguard against rust damage, where such protection is not provided by the vehicle manufacturer.

After washing paintwork, wipe off with a chamois leather to give an unspotted clear finish. A coat of clear protective wax polish will give added protection against chemical pollutants in the air. If the paintwork sheen has dulled or oxidised, use a cleaner/polisher combination to restore the brilliance of the shine. This requires a little effort, but such dulling is usually caused because regular washing has been neglected. Care needs to be taken with metallic paintwork, as special non-abrasive cleaner/polisher is required to avoid damage to the finish. Always check that the door and ventilator opening drain holes and pipes are completely clear, so that water can be drained out. Brightwork should be treated in the same way as paintwork. Windscreens and windows can be kept clear of the smeary film which often appears, by the use of proprietary glass cleaner. Never use any form of wax or other body or chromium polish on glass.

3 Maintenance – upholstery and carpets

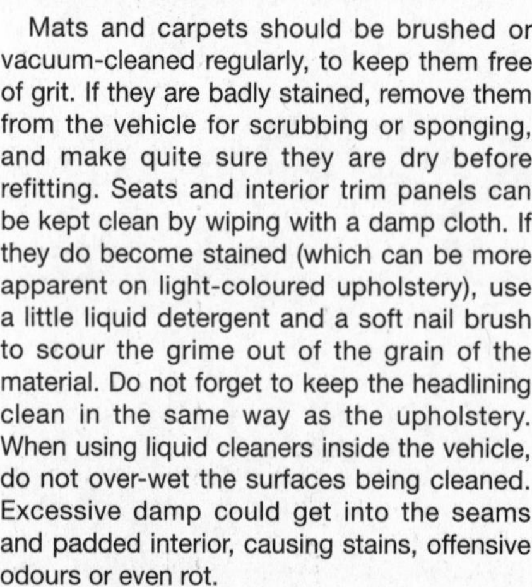

Mats and carpets should be brushed or vacuum-cleaned regularly, to keep them free of grit. If they are badly stained, remove them from the vehicle for scrubbing or sponging, and make quite sure they are dry before refitting. Seats and interior trim panels can be kept clean by wiping with a damp cloth. If they do become stained (which can be more apparent on light-coloured upholstery), use a little liquid detergent and a soft nail brush to scour the grime out of the grain of the material. Do not forget to keep the headlining clean in the same way as the upholstery. When using liquid cleaners inside the vehicle, do not over-wet the surfaces being cleaned. Excessive damp could get into the seams and padded interior, causing stains, offensive odours or even rot.

If the inside of the vehicle gets wet accidentally, it is worthwhile taking some trouble to dry it out properly, particularly where carpets are involved. Do not leave oil or electric heaters inside the vehicle for this purpose.

4 Minor body damage – repair

Scratches

If the scratch is very superficial, and does not penetrate to the metal of the bodywork, repair is very simple. Lightly rub the area of the scratch with a paintwork renovator, or a very fine cutting paste, to remove loose paint from the scratch, and to clear the surrounding bodywork of wax polish. Rinse the area with clean water.

Apply touch-up paint to the scratch using a fine paint brush; continue to apply fine layers of paint until the surface of the paint in the scratch is level with the surrounding paintwork. Allow the new paint at least two weeks to harden, and then blend it into the surrounding paintwork by rubbing the scratch area with a paintwork renovator or a very fine cutting paste. Finally, apply wax polish.

Where the scratch has penetrated right through to the metal of the bodywork, causing the metal to rust, a different repair technique is required. Remove any loose rust from the bottom of the scratch with a penknife, and then apply rust-inhibiting paint to prevent the formation of rust in the future. Using a rubber or nylon applicator, fill the scratch with bodystopper paste. If required, this paste can be mixed with cellulose thinners to provide a very thin paste that is ideal for filling narrow scratches. Before the stopper-paste in the scratch hardens, wrap a piece of smooth cotton rag around the top of a finger. Dip the finger in cellulose thinners, and quickly sweep it across the surface of the stopper-paste in the scratch; this will ensure that the surface of the stopper-paste is slightly hollowed. The scratch can now be painted over as described earlier in this Section.

Dents

When deep denting of the vehicle's bodywork has taken place, the first task is to pull the dent out, until the affected bodywork almost attains its original shape. There is little point in trying to restore the original shape completely, as the metal in the damaged area will have stretched on impact, and cannot be reshaped fully to its original contour. It is better to bring the level of the dent up to a point, which is about 3 mm below the level of the surrounding bodywork. In cases where the dent is very shallow anyway, it is not worth trying to pull it out at all. If the underside of the dent is accessible, it can be hammered out gently from behind, using a mallet with a wooden or plastic head. Whilst doing this, hold a suitable block of wood firmly against the outside of the panel, to absorb the impact from the hammer blows and thus prevent a large area of the bodywork from being 'belled-out'.

Should the dent be in a section of the

bodywork, which has a double skin, or some other factor making it inaccessible from behind, a different technique is called for. Drill several small holes through the metal inside the area – particularly in the deeper section. Then screw long self-tapping screws into the holes, just sufficiently for them to gain a good purchase in the metal. Now the dent can be pulled out by pulling on the protruding heads of the screws with a pair of pliers.

The next stage of the repair is the removal of the paint from the damaged area, and from an inch or so of the surrounding 'sound' bodywork. This is accomplished most easily by using a wire brush or abrasive pad on a power drill, although it can be done just as effectively by hand, using sheets of abrasive paper. To complete the preparation for filling, score the surface of the bare metal with a screwdriver or the tang of a file, or alternatively, drill small holes in the affected area. This will provide a really good 'key' for the filler paste.

To complete the repair, see the Section on filling and respraying.

Rust holes or gashes

Remove all paint from the affected area, and from an inch or so of the surrounding 'sound' bodywork, using an abrasive pad or a wire brush on a power drill. If these are not available, a few sheets of abrasive paper will do the job most effectively. With the paint removed, you will be able to judge the severity of the corrosion, and therefore decide whether to renew the whole panel (if this is possible) or to repair the affected area. New body panels are not as expensive as most people think, and it is often quicker and more satisfactory to fit a new panel than to attempt to repair large areas of corrosion.

Remove all fittings from the affected area, except those, which will act as a guide to the original shape of the damaged bodywork (e.g. headlight shells etc). Then, using tin snips or a hacksaw blade, remove all loose metal and any other metal badly affected by corrosion. Hammer the edges of the hole inwards, in order to create a slight depression for the filler paste.

Wire-brush the affected area to remove the powdery rust from the surface of the remaining metal. Paint the affected area with rust-inhibiting paint, if the back of the rusted area is accessible, treat this also.

Before filling can take place, it will be necessary to block the hole in some way. This can be achieved by the use of aluminium or plastic mesh, or aluminium tape.

Aluminium or plastic mesh, or glass-fibre matting, is probably the best material to use for a large hole. Cut a piece to the approximate size and shape of the hole to be filled, then position it in the hole so that its edges are below the level of the surrounding bodywork. It can be retained in position by several blobs of filler paste around its periphery.

Aluminium tape should be used for small or very narrow holes. Pull a piece off the roll, trim it to the approximate size and shape required, then pull off the backing paper (if used) and stick the tape over the hole; it can be overlapped if the thickness of one piece is insufficient. Burnish down the edges of the tape with the handle of a screwdriver or similar, to ensure that the tape is securely attached to the metal underneath.

Filling and respraying

Before using this Section, see the Sections on dent, deep scratch, rust holes and gash repairs.

Many types of bodyfiller are available, but generally speaking, those proprietary kits, which contain a tin of filler paste and a tube of resin hardener, are best for this type of repair. A wide, flexible plastic or nylon applicator will be found invaluable for imparting a smooth and well-contoured finish to the surface of the filler.

Mix up a little filler on a clean piece of card or board – measure the hardener carefully (follow the maker's instructions on the pack), otherwise the filler will set too rapidly or too slowly. Using the applicator, apply the filler paste to the prepared area; draw the applicator across the surface of the filler to achieve the correct contour and to level the surface. As soon as a contour that approximates to the correct one is achieved, stop working the paste – if you carry on too long, the paste will become sticky and begin to 'pick-up' on the applicator. Continue to add thin layers of filler paste at 20-minute intervals, until the level of the filler is just proud of the surrounding bodywork.

Once the filler has hardened, the excess can be removed using a metal plane or file. From then on, progressively finer grades of abrasive paper should be used, starting with a 40-grade production paper, and finishing with a 400-grade wet-and-dry paper. Always wrap the abrasive paper around a flat rubber, cork, or wooden block – otherwise the surface of the filler will not be completely flat. During the smoothing of the filler surface, the wet-and-dry paper should be periodically rinsed in water. This will ensure that a very smooth finish is imparted to the filler at the final stage.

At this stage, the dent should be surrounded by a ring of bare metal, which in turn should be encircled by the finely 'feathered' edge of the good paintwork. Rinse the repair area with clean water, until all of the dust produced by the rubbing-down operation has gone.

Spray the whole area with a light coat of primer – this will show up any imperfections in the surface of the filler. Repair these imperfections with fresh filler paste or bodystopper, and once more smooth the surface with abrasive paper. Repeat this spray-and-repair procedure until you are satisfied that the surface of the filler, and the feathered edge of the paintwork, are perfect. Clean the repair area with clean water, and allow to dry fully.

The repair area is now ready for final spraying. Paint spraying must be carried out in a warm, dry, windless and dust-free atmosphere. This condition can be created artificially if you have access to a large indoor working area, but if you are forced to work in the open, you will have to pick your day very carefully. If you are working indoors, dousing the floor in the work area with water will help to settle the dust that would otherwise be in the atmosphere. If the repair area is confined to one body panel, mask off the surrounding panels; this will help to minimise the effects of a slight mis-match in paint colours. Bodywork fittings (e.g. chrome strips, door handles etc) will also need to be masked off. Use genuine masking tape, and several thicknesses of newspaper, for the masking operations.

Before commencing to spray, agitate the aerosol can thoroughly, and then spray a test area (an old tin, or similar) until the technique is mastered. Cover the repair area with a thick coat of primer; the thickness should be built up using several thin layers of paint, rather than one thick one. Using 400-grade wet-and-dry paper, rub down the surface of the primer until it is really smooth. While doing this, the work area should be thoroughly doused with water, and the wet-and-dry paper periodically rinsed in water. Allow to dry before spraying on more paint.

Spray on the top coat, again building up the thickness by using several thin layers of paint. Start spraying at one edge of the repair area, and then, using a side-to-side motion, work until the whole repair area and about 2 inches of the surrounding original paintwork is covered. Remove all masking material 10 to 15 minutes after spraying on the final coat of paint.

Allow the new paint at least two weeks to harden, then, using a paintwork renovator, or a very fine cutting paste, blend the edges of the paint into the existing paintwork. Finally, apply wax polish.

Plastic components

With the use of more and more plastic body components by the vehicle manufacturers (e.g. bumpers. spoilers, and in some cases major body panels), rectification of more serious damage to such items has become a matter of either entrusting repair work to a specialist in this field, or renewing complete components. Repair of such damage by the DIY owner is not really feasible, owing to the cost of the equipment and materials required for effecting such repairs. The basic technique involves making a groove along the line of the crack in the plastic, using a rotary burr in a power drill. The damaged part is then welded back together, using a hot-air gun to heat up and fuse a plastic filler rod into the groove. Any excess plastic is then removed, and the area rubbed down to a smooth finish. It is important that a filler rod of the correct plastic is used, as body components can be made of a variety of different types (e.g. polycarbonate, ABS, polypropylene).

6.1 Undo the screws - arrowed

6.2 Undo the two bolts from under the bumper - one shown

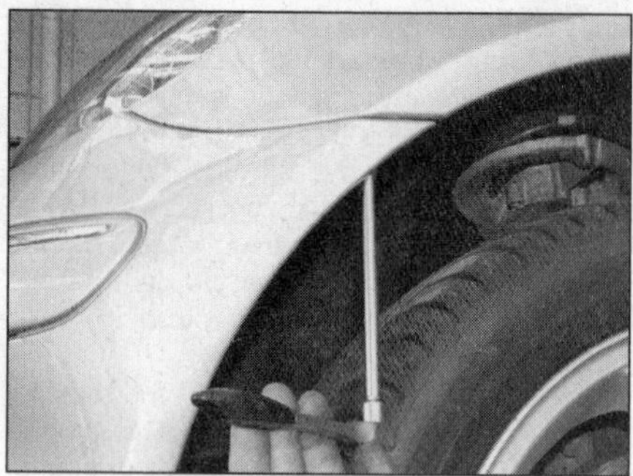
6.4 Undo the bolts at each end of the bumper

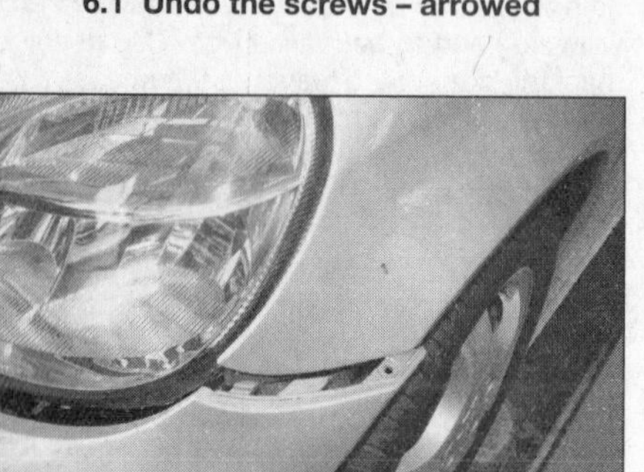
6.5a Unclip the ends of the bumper . . .

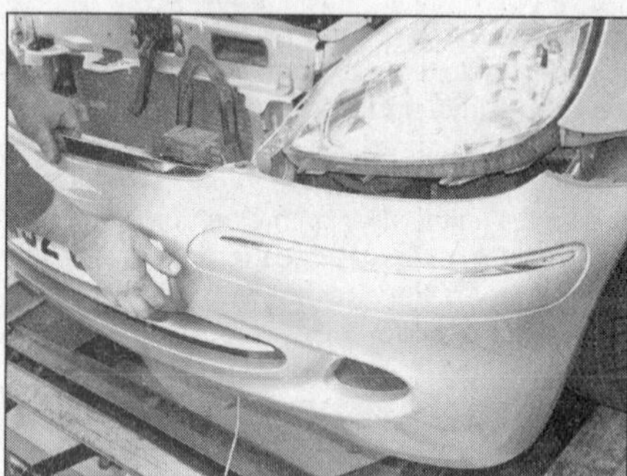
6.5b . . . and remove the bumper

Damage of a less serious nature (abrasions, minor cracks etc) can be repaired by the DIY owner using a two-part epoxy filler repair material. Once mixed in equal proportions, this is used in similar fashion to the bodywork filler used on metal panels. The filler is usually cured in twenty to thirty minutes, ready for sanding and painting.

If the owner is renewing a complete component himself, or if he has repaired it with epoxy filler, he will be left with the problem of finding a suitable paint for finishing which is compatible with the type of plastic used. At one time, the use of a universal paint was not possible, owing to the complex range of plastics encountered in body component applications. Standard paints, generally speaking, will not bond to plastic or rubber satisfactorily. However, it is now possible to obtain a plastic body parts finishing kit, which consists of a pre-primer treatment, a primer and coloured top coat. Full instructions are normally supplied with a kit, but basically, the method of use is to first apply the pre-primer to the component concerned, and allow it to dry for up to 30 minutes. Then the primer is applied, and left to dry for about an hour before finally applying the special-coloured top coat. The result is a correctly coloured component, where the paint will flex with the plastic or rubber, a property that standard paint does not normally possess.

5 Major body damage - repair

Where serious damage has occurred, or large areas need renewal due to neglect, it means that complete new panels will need welding-in, and this is best left to professionals. If the damage is due to impact, it will also be necessary to check completely the alignment of the body shell, and this can only be carried out accurately by a Mercedes-Benz dealer using special jigs. If the body is left misaligned, it is primarily dangerous, as the car will not handle properly, and secondly, uneven stresses will be imposed on the steering, suspension and possibly transmission, causing abnormal wear, or complete failure, particularly to such items as the tyres.

6 Front bumper - removal and refitting

Removal

1 Open the bonnet, and undo the two screws securing the top of the bumper to the engine compartment crossbar **(see illustration)**.

2 Undo the two lower screws from the front edge of the bumper **(see illustration)**.

3 Working on each side in turn, release the retaining clips securing the wheel arch liners to the bumper ends.

4 Pull back the wheel arch liner and undo the securing bolts (one each side) from the end of the bumper **(see illustration)**.

5 With the help of an assistant, unclip the ends of the bumper from the front wing panels, and withdraw it from the vehicle **(see illustrations)**. **Note:** *On some models, it may be necessary to disconnect the wiring from the foglights.*

Refitting

6 Refitting is a reverse of the removal procedure, ensuring that the bumper ends engage correctly with the locating guides as the bumper is refitted. New clips may be required for inner wheel arch liner.

7 Rear bumper - removal and refitting

Removal

1 Open the tailgate, and remove the four plastic covers from the rear bumper upper mounting screws **(see illustration)**.

2 Undo the four screws securing the top of the bumper to the rear crossbar **(see illustration)**.

7.1 Remove the plastic covers . . .

7.2 . . . and remove the screws

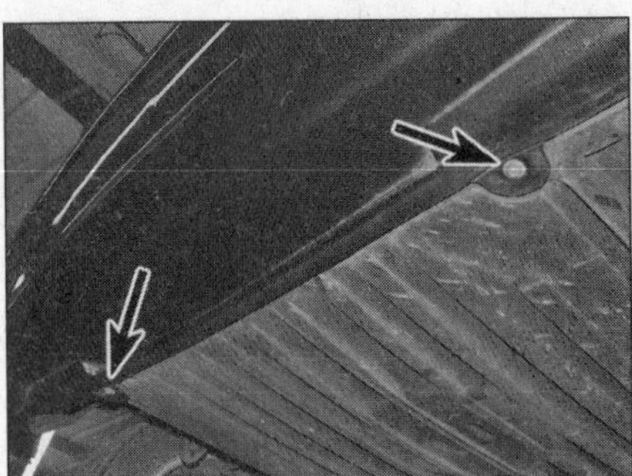
7.3 Undo the two lower screws - arrowed

7.5 Undo the bolts at each end of the bumper

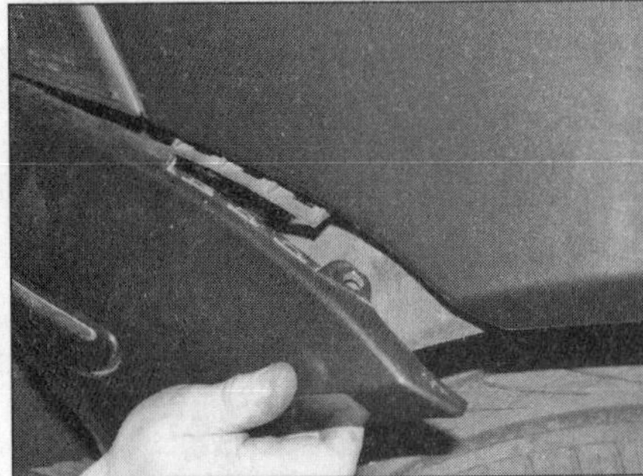
7.6 Unclip the bumper at each side

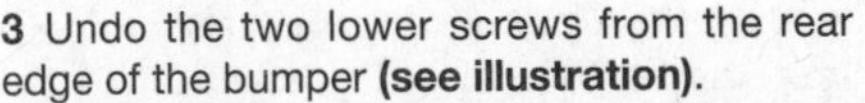
3 Undo the two lower screws from the rear edge of the bumper **(see illustration)**.

4 Working on each side in turn, release the retaining clips securing the wheel arch liners to the bumper ends.

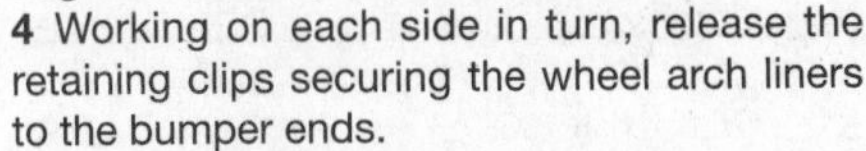
5 Pull back the wheel arch liner and undo the securing bolts (one each side) from the end of the bumper **(see illustration)**.

6 With the help of an assistant, unclip the ends of the bumper from the rear wing panels, and withdraw it from the vehicle **(see illustration)**. **Note:** *On some models, it may be necessary to disconnect the wiring from the rear parking sensors.*

Refitting

7 Refitting is a reverse of the removal procedure, ensuring that the bumper ends engage correctly with the locating guides as the bumper is refitted. New clips may be required for inner wheel arch liner.

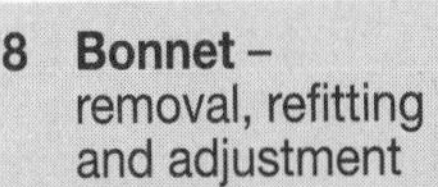
8 Bonnet - removal, refitting and adjustment

Removal

1 Open the bonnet and using a pencil or felt tip pen, mark the outline of each bonnet hinge relative to the bonnet, to use as a guide on refitting.

2 With the help of an assistant to support the bonnet, disengage the bonnet stay from the slot in the bumper.

3 Undo the bonnet retaining bolts **(see illustration)** and carefully lift the bonnet clear. Store the bonnet out of the way in a safe place.

8.3 Remove the bonnet retaining bolts

4 Inspect the bonnet hinges for signs of wear and free play at the pivots, and if necessary renew. Each hinge is secured to the body by two bolts **(see illustration)**, mark the position of the hinge on the body then undo the retaining bolts and remove it from the vehicle. On refitting, align the new hinge with the marks and tighten the retaining bolts.

Refitting and adjustment

5 Refitting is a reverse of the removal procedure. Align the hinges with the marks made on removal, and then tighten the retaining bolts securely.

6 Close the bonnet, and check for alignment with the adjacent panels. If necessary, unscrew the hinge bolts and re-align the bonnet. Once the bonnet is correctly aligned, tighten the hinge bolts. Check that the bonnet fastens and releases satisfactorily.

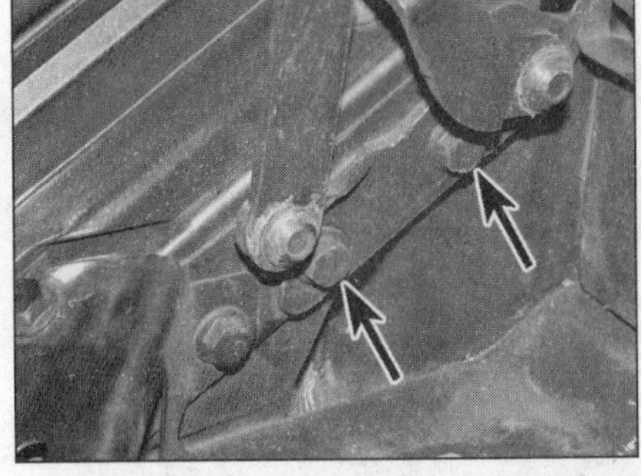
8.4 Hinge mounting bolts - arrowed

9 Bonnet release cable - removal and refitting

Removal

1 Working inside the vehicle, locate the release lever, undo the retaining screw and unclip the lever from the facia panel **(see illustrations)**.

2 Unclip the inner and outer cable from the bonnet release lever **(see illustration)**

3 Work your way along the cable and release the cable sealing grommet from the bulkhead panel.

4 Working inside the engine compartment, release the locking clip and move the windscreen washer reservoir to one side.

5 Remove the bonnet lock as described in Section 10.

6 Withdraw the release cable from inside the front crossmember.

9.1a Undo the retaining screw . . .

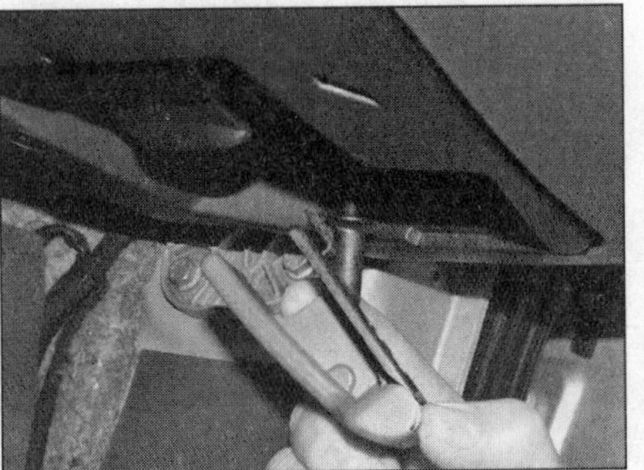
9.1b . . . and unclip lever from panel

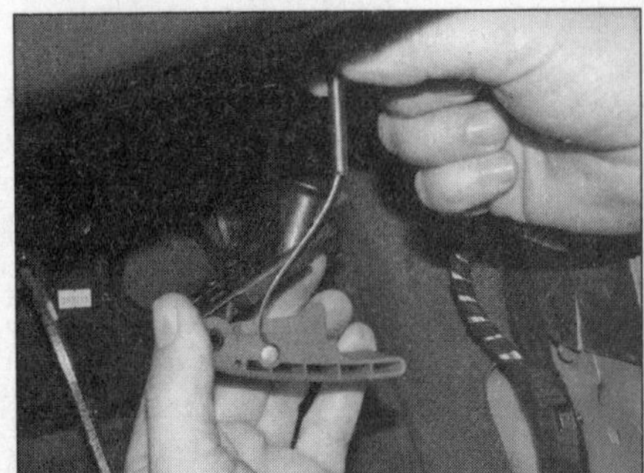
9.2 Unclip the cable from the lever

10.1 Mark around the catch for refitting

10.2 Disconnect the wiring connector

10.3 Removing the bonnet catch

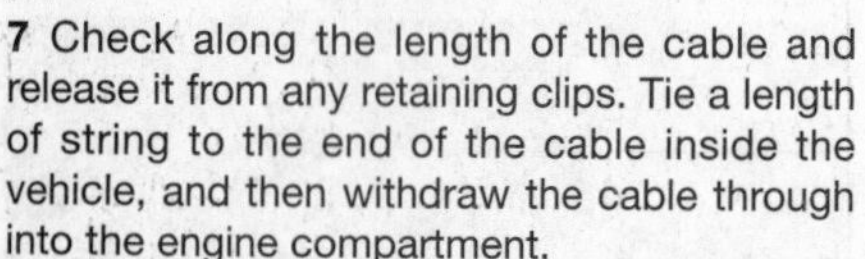

7 Check along the length of the cable and release it from any retaining clips. Tie a length of string to the end of the cable inside the vehicle, and then withdraw the cable through into the engine compartment.

8 Once the cable is free, untie the string and leave it in position in the vehicle; the string can then be used to draw the new cable back into position.

Refitting

9 Tie the inner end of the string to the end of the cable, then use the string to draw the bonnet release cable back from the engine compartment. Once the cable is through, untie the string.

10 Refitting is a reversal of the removal, noting the following points:

a) Ensure the rubber grommet in the bulkhead is fitted correctly.

b) Check the cable is correctly routed and secured to all the relevant retaining clips.

c) Before closing the bonnet, check the operation of the release lever and cable to make sure it is operating correctly.

10 Bonnet lock – removal and refitting

Removal

1 Open the bonnet, and mark the outline of the bonnet catch to the cross panel **(see illustration)** to use as a guide on refitting.

2 Disconnect the wiring connector from the rear of the bonnet catch **(see illustration)**.

3 Undo the four mounting bolts and remove the bonnet catch from the crossmember **(see illustration)**. Unclip the release cable from the bonnet catch as it is removed

Refitting

4 Refitting is a reversal of removal. Check that the bonnet fastens and releases satisfactorily. If adjustment is necessary, loosen the bonnet lock retaining bolts, and adjust the position of the lock to suit. Finally, tighten the bolts.

11 Door – removal, refitting and adjustment

Removal

1 Open the door, then disconnect the wiring and pneumatic pipe at the A- or B-pillar as applicable. To do this, on front doors, first release the rubber gaiter and turn the wiring connector in a clockwise direction to disconnect it from the door panel. On rear doors, pull back the rubber gaiter and unplug the wiring connectors and pneumatic pipe.

2 Undo the retaining bolt and disconnect the door check strap from the pillar **(see illustration)**.

3 Slacken and remove the securing nuts from the upper and lower hinge pins **(see illustration)**.

4 With the aid of an assistant, lift the door from the hinge pins and remove it from the vehicle. Make sure the door is kept in a safe place to prevent it getting damaged.

5 Examine the hinges for signs of wear or damage. If renewal is necessary, the hinges can be unbolted from the A- or B-pillar. Before removing them, accurately mark their position to ensure correct refitting.

Refitting

6 Where renewed, fit the hinges and tighten the bolts to the specified torque, where applicable.

7 With the aid of an assistant, offer up the door to the vehicle and locate it on the hinges. Refit the securing nuts and tighten to the specified torque setting.

8 Reconnect the wiring plug and secure with the locking lever.

9 Refit the rubber bellows.

Adjustment

10 Close the door and check the door alignment with the surrounding body panels (approximately 6.0 mm gap). There must be an even gap all around, and the door must be level with the surrounding body panels. Loosening the hinge bolts and moving the door can make slight adjustment. Check that the striker enters the door lock centrally as the door is closed, and if necessary adjust the position of the striker by loosening its mounting bolts **(see illustration)**. Note markings on door pillar and striker for alignment.

11.2 Door check strap mounting bolt – arrowed

11.3 Hinge securing nut – arrowed

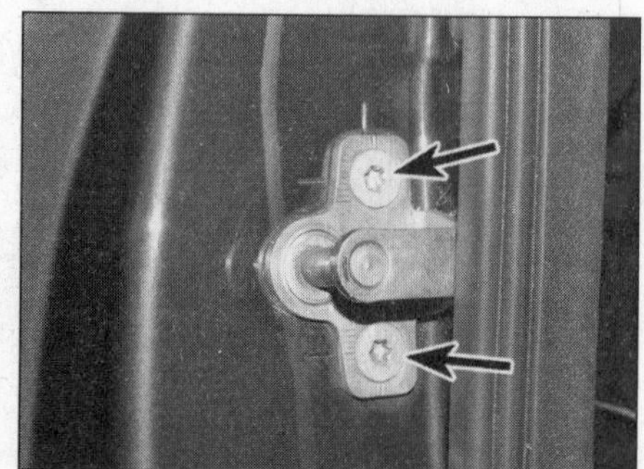

11.10 Striker plate mounting bolts – arrowed

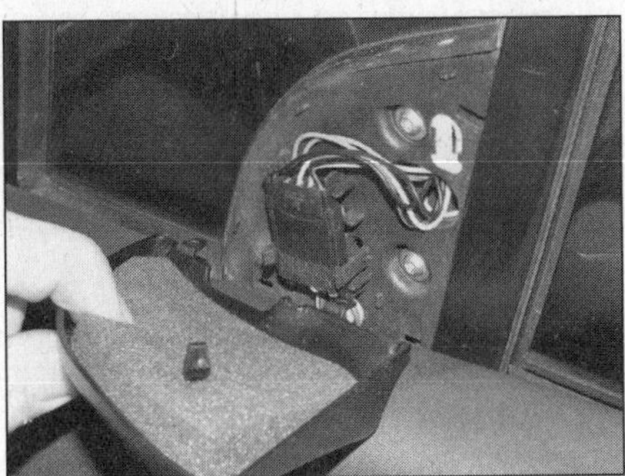
12.2 Unclip the trim panel

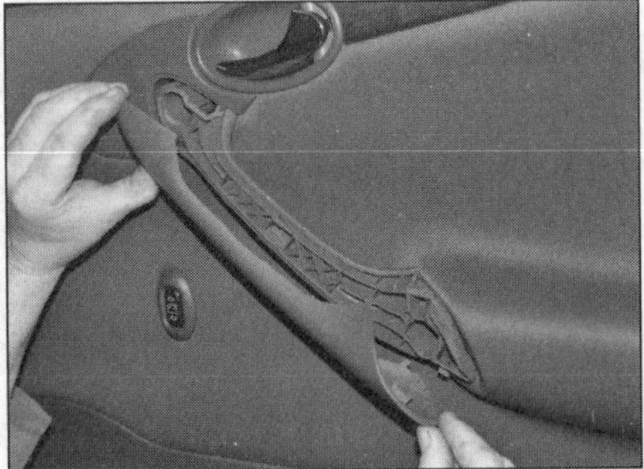
12.4a Unclip the door handle cover . . .

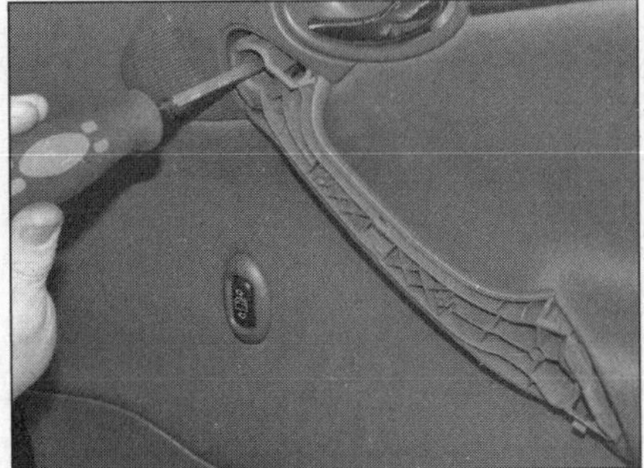
12.4b . . . and undo the retaining screws

12 Door inner trim panel – removal and refitting

Removal

Front doors

1 Open the door to be worked on and put the window in the down position.

2 Unclip the mirror inner trim panel from the top of the door panel **(see illustration)**.

3 On models up to 28/02/01, unclip the two plastic caps from the top and bottom of the door pull handle, and remove the retaining screws.

4 On models from 01/03/01, unclip the plastic cover from the door pull handle and remove the retaining screws **(see illustrations)**.

5 On models with side airbags, unclip the cover from the top rear corner of the door panel and remove the retaining screw **(see illustration)**.

6 Release the door trim panel studs, carefully levering between the panel and door with a flat-bladed lever. Work around the outside of the panel, and when all the studs are released, lift the door trim panel upwards and off the window slot.

7 Support the panel away from the door, and then release the control cable from the rear of the door catch lever **(see illustration)**. Also unclip the small speaker from the inside of the door trim panel.

8 On models with electric windows, disconnect the wiring connector from the rear of the switch **(see illustration)**.

9 Where applicable, release the securing clips and withdraw the door lock button from the top of the door trim panel **(see illustration)**.

10 The inner trim panel can now be withdrawn from the door and be kept in a safe clean place, ready for refitting.

Rear doors

11 Open the door to be worked on and put the window in the down position.

12 On models up to 28/02/01, unclip the two plastic caps from the top and bottom of the door pull handle, and remove the retaining screws.

13 On models from 01/03/01, unclip the plastic cover from the door pull handle and remove the retaining screws **(see illustrations 12.4a and 12.4b)**.

14 On models with mechanical window mechanism, release the securing clip at the rear of the winder handle and pull it off the winder mechanism.

15 Release the door trim panel studs, carefully levering between the panel and door with a flat-bladed lever. Work around the outside of the panel, and when all the studs are released, lift the door trim panel upwards and off the window slot.

16 Support the panel away from the door, and then release the control cable from the rear of the door catch lever **(see illustration 12.7)**. Also unclip the small speaker from the inside of the door trim panel.

17 On models with electric windows, disconnect the wiring connector from the rear of the switch **(see illustration 12.8)**.

18 Where applicable, release the securing clips and withdraw the door lock button from the top of the door trim panel **(see illustration 12.9)**.

19 The inner trim panel can now be withdrawn from the door and be kept in a safe clean place, ready for refitting.

Refitting

20 Before refitting, check whether any of the trim panel retaining studs, from around the outer edge of the door trim panel, were broken on removal, and renew them as necessary. Refitting of the trim panel is then a reversal of removal. Check the operation of the door electrical equipment.

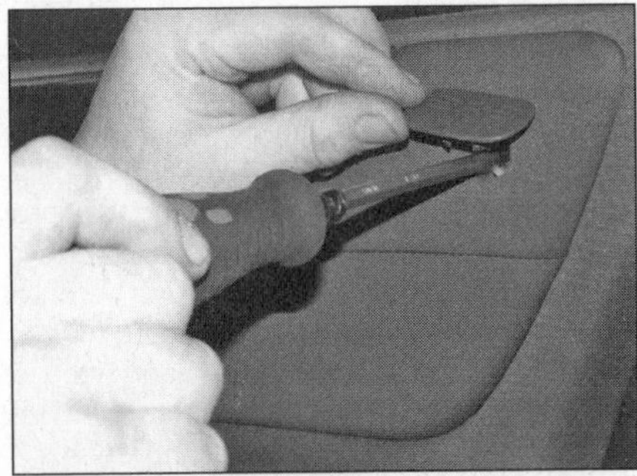
12.5 Unclip cover and undo retaining screw

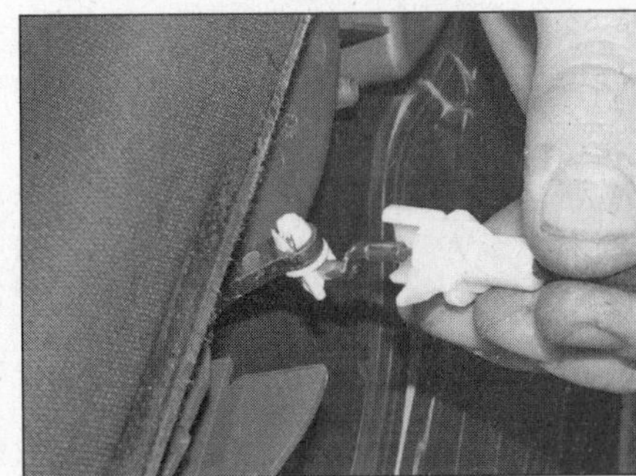
12.7 Release the control cable from the door catch

12.8 Disconnect the wiring connector

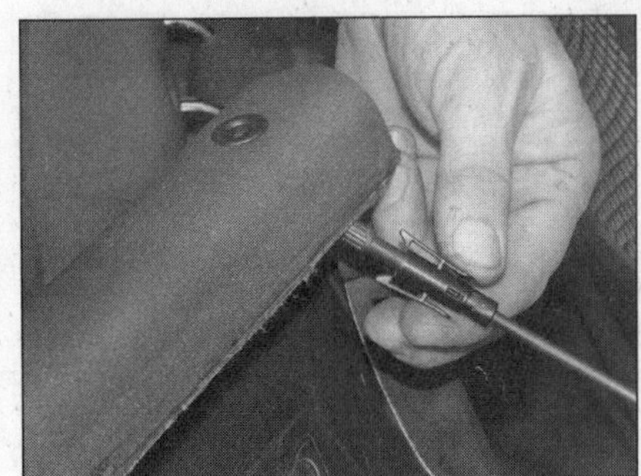
12.9 Unclip the door button from the panel

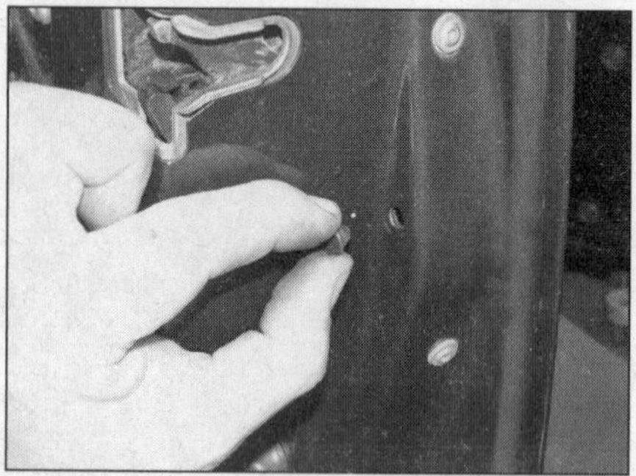
13.4a Remove plastic cap – front door

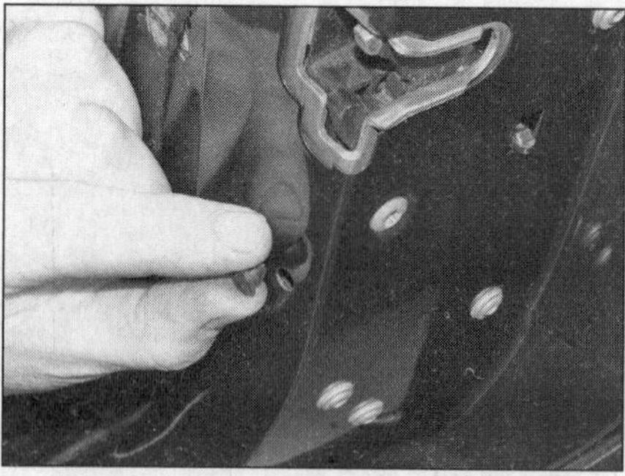
13.4b Remove plastic cap – rear door

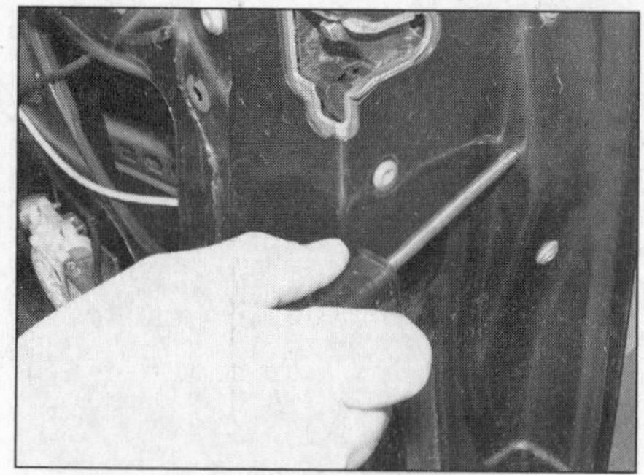
13.5a Undo the retaining screw . . .

13.5b . . . and remove the door lock cylinder

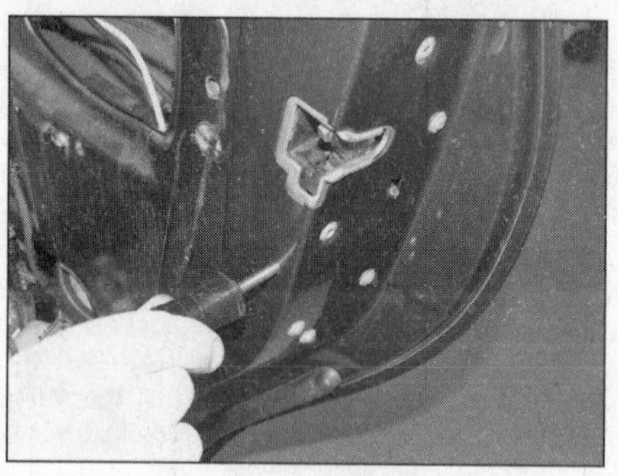
13.6a Undo the retaining screw . . .

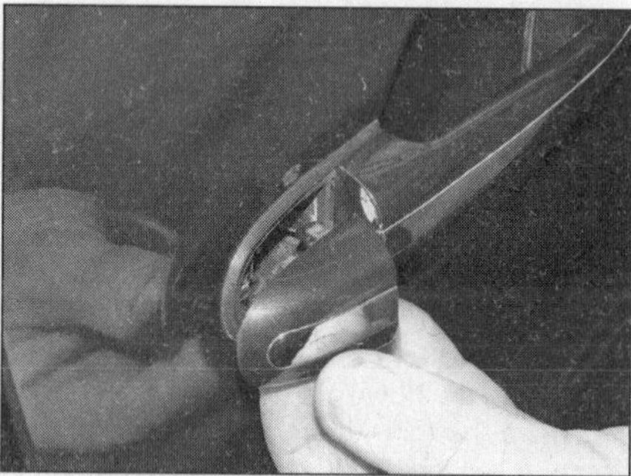
13.6b . . . and remove the handle end cap

13 Door handle and lock components – removal and refitting

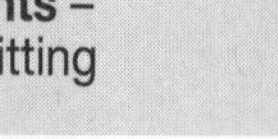

Interior door handle

1 Remove the door inner trim panel as described in Section 12.

2 Unclip the door handle from the inside of the door trim panel to remove it.

3 Refitting is a reversal of removal, making sure the door handle is secure in the trim panel.

Front door lock cylinder housing or rear door handle end cap

4 Open the door, then remove the plastic cap in the rear edge of the door to locate the retaining screw **(see illustrations)**.

5 On the front doors, slacken the retaining screw and pull the lock cylinder housing out of the door handle **(see illustrations)**.

6 On the rear doors, slacken the retaining screw and pull the end cap from the door handle **(see illustrations)**.

7 Refitting is a reversal of removal, check operation of the lock after refitting.

Exterior door handle

8 Remove the door lock cylinder housing or end cap as described in paragraphs 3 to 5.

9 Slide the door handle towards the outer edge of the door, pull it out and then unhook the front of the handle from the door. Recover the rubber gaskets **(see illustrations)**. Check rubber gaskets for damage and renew if necessary.

10 Refitting is a reversal of removal.

Door lock

11 Remove the door inner trim panel as described in Section 12.

12 Remove the exterior handle as described in paragraphs 6 and 7.

13 Carefully remove the inner door liner from the door panel by cutting around the outside of the seal **(see illustration)**. If the liner is ripped or damaged in any way, it will need to be renewed.

14 Working inside the door frame, move the plastic slide to release the linkage from the door catch **(see illustration)**.

15 Undo the lock securing bolts from the end of the door frame **(see illustration)**. Hold the lock from the inside to prevent it from falling down.

16 On the rear doors, push the door lock assembly upwards and remove the door lock

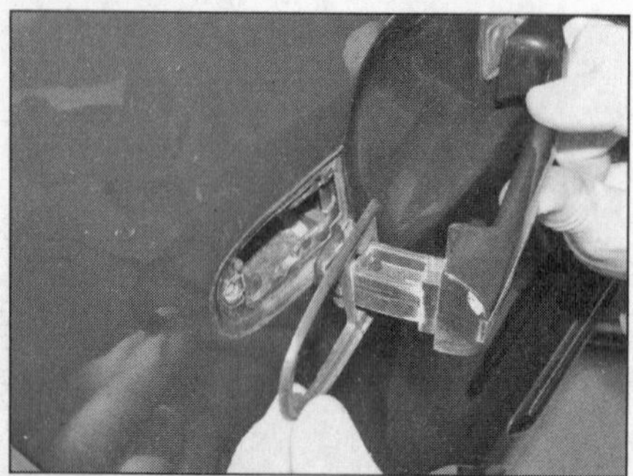
13.9a Unclip the door handle . . .

13.9b . . . and remove it from the door

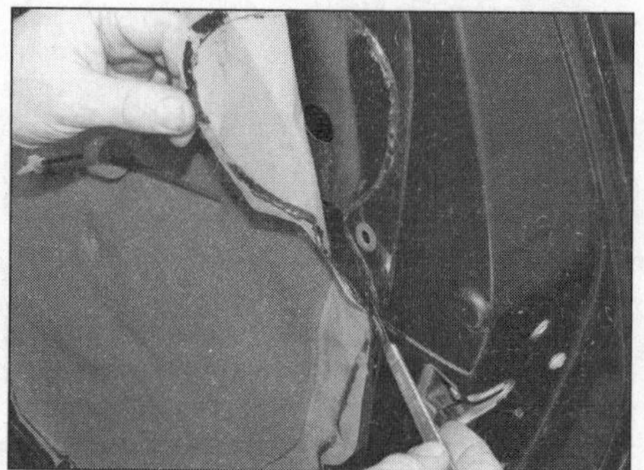
13.13 Carefully remove the door liner

13.14 Plastic slide on door catch

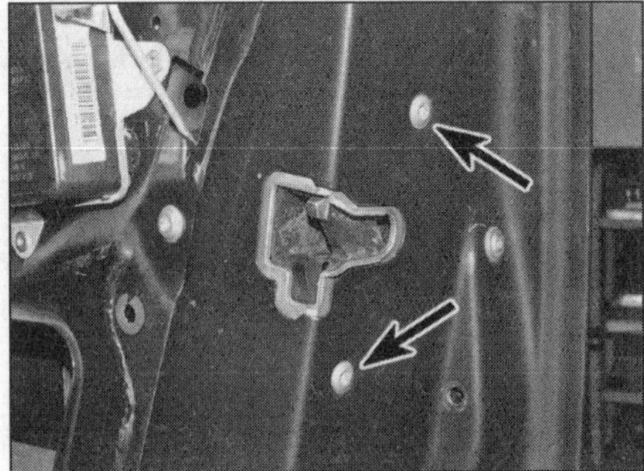
13.15 Door lock securing bolts (front) – arrowed

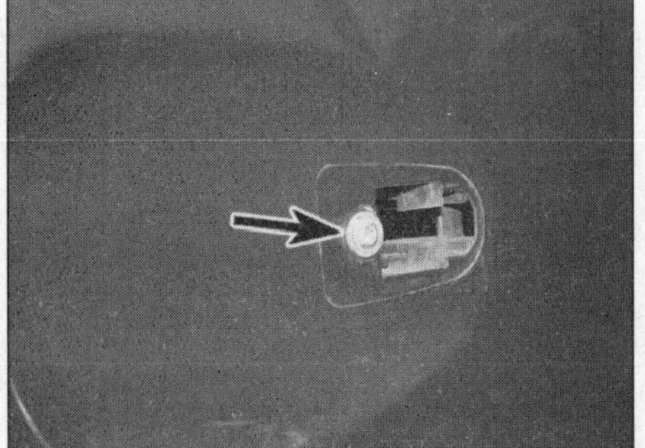
13.16 Mounting bracket retaining screw – arrowed

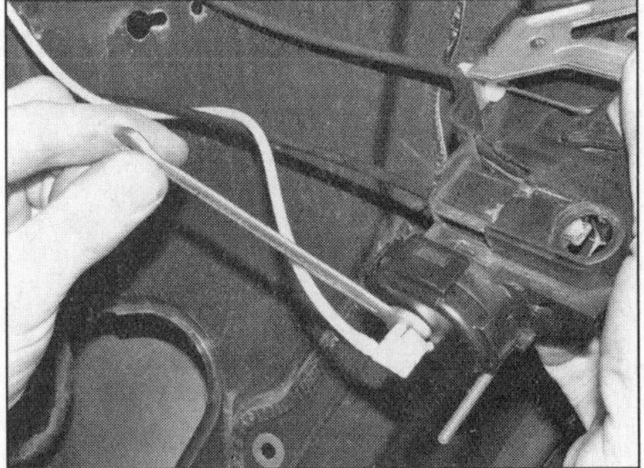
13.17a Using a spanner . . .

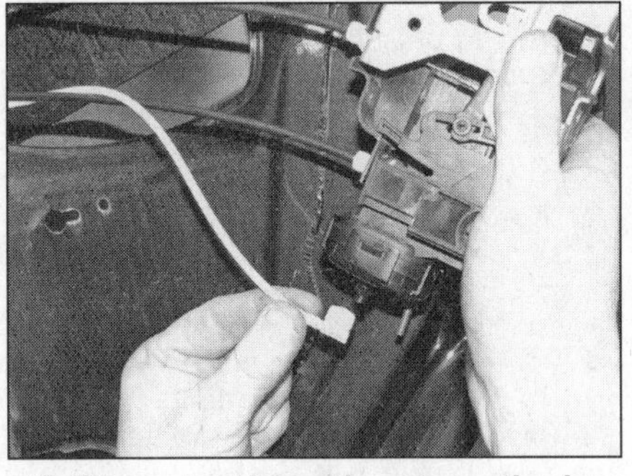
13.17b . . . to release the pneumatic pipe

13.18 Withdraw the lock assembly out from the door

mounting bracket retaining screw from the outside of the door panel **(see illustration)**. Slide the mounting bracket to the front edge of the door to remove.

17 Lower the lock from inside the door and disconnect the pneumatic pipe and wiring connector from the door lock mechanism. Use an open-ended 7 mm spanner to prise of the pneumatic pipe from the lock assembly, taking care not to damage it **(see illustrations)**.

18 Withdraw the door lock complete with operating cables out through the door aperture **(see illustration)**. Unclip the pneumatic pipe, wiring and cables from any retaining clips in the door frame.

19 The operating cables can then be unclipped from the lock linkage as required **(see illustration)**.

20 Refitting is a reversal of removal. Make sure all wiring and cables operate correctly and refer to Section 12 for refitting the door inner trim panel.

14 Door window glass and regulator – removal and refitting

Door window glass

1 Remove the door inner trim panel as described in Section 12.

2 Unclip the outer and inner sealing rails from along the top edge of the door frame **(see illustration)**.

3 Carefully remove the inner door liner from the door panel by cutting around the outside of the seal **(see illustration)**. If the liner is ripped or damaged in any way it will need to be renewed.

4 On the rear doors, remove the rear door lock as described in Section 13.

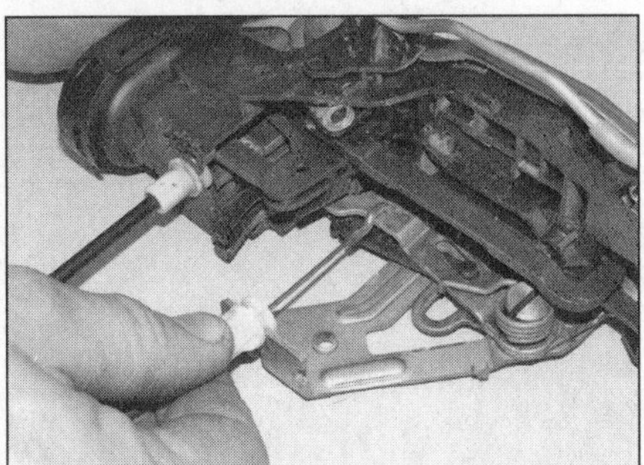
13.19 Unclip the outer cable from the bracket

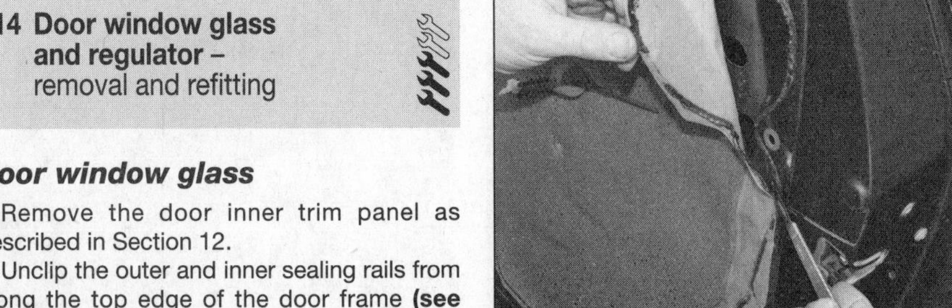
14.3 Carefully remove the door liner

5 Temporarily connect the wiring to the switches, then switch on the ignition, and lower the window glass until the bolts attaching it to the regulator are visible **(see illustration)**.

6 Remove the two bolts from the mechanism

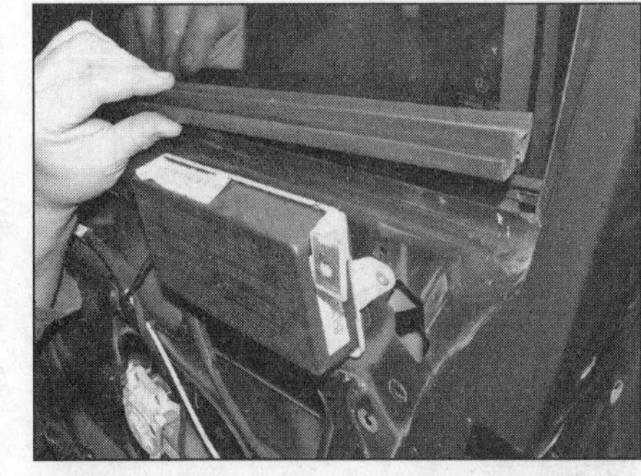
14.2 Unclipping the inner door frame seal

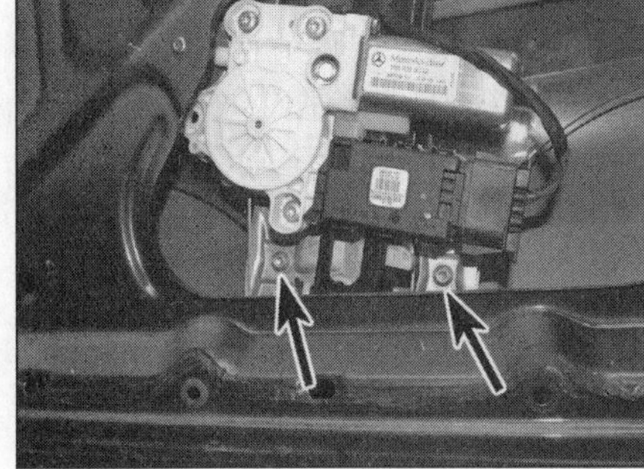
14.5 Make sure the two bolts (arrowed) are visible

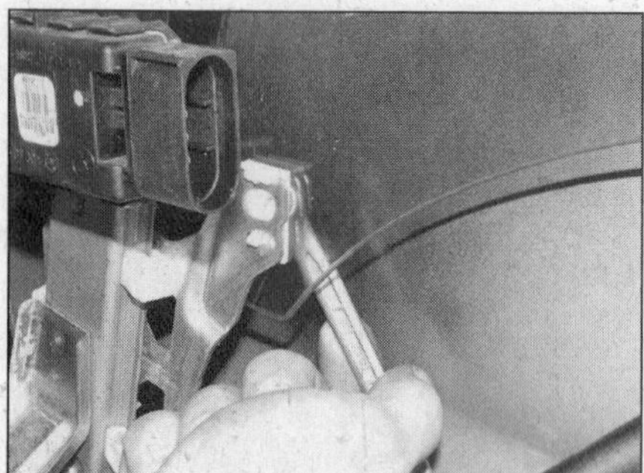
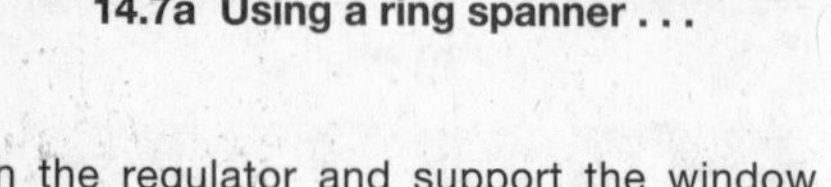

14.7a Using a ring spanner . . .

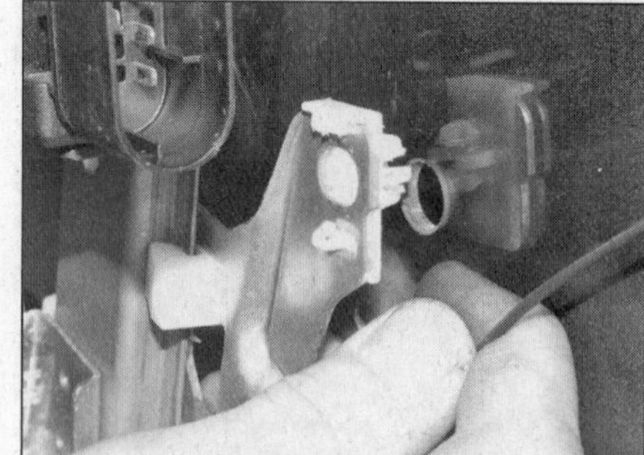

14.7b . . . to release the securing clip

14.8 Lift the window glass out from the door

on the regulator and support the window glass.

7 While supporting the window glass, use a 10 mm ring spanner to close the legs on the clips, and then push the glass to release it from the securing clips **(see illustrations)**.

8 Lift the window glass so that it is tilted, then remove it upwards and out from the door **(see illustration)**.

9 Refitting is a reversal of removal, noting the following points:

a) Carefully lower the tilted window glass into the door and engage it with the regulator retaining clips.

b) Apply light pressure to the glass to make sure it is correctly located in the channels, then tighten the retaining bolts.

c) If necessary, the window may be checked for correct operation at this stage by connecting the wiring to the switches.

d) Refit the door inner trim panel with reference to Section 12.

Front door fixed window

10 Remove the front door window glass as described in paragraphs 1 to 7.

11 Undo the retaining screws, disconnect the wiring connector and remove the mirror from the door frame **(see illustration)**.

12 Pull the window guide rubber out from the upright channel **(see illustration)**.

13 Undo the retaining screw from the top of the guide channel **(see illustration)**.

14 Undo the two retaining screws from the bottom of the mirror mounting bracket **(see illustration)**.

15 Undo the retaining screw from the lower part of the guide channel **(see illustration)**.

16 The guide channel can now be withdrawn out from the door frame.

17 Slide the fixed window out from the front of the door frame, complete with rubber seal.

18 Refitting is a reversal of removal.

Window regulator motor assembly

19 Remove the door window glass as described in paragraphs 1 to 8.

20 Disconnect the wiring connector from the window regulator motor **(see illustration)**. Unclip the wiring from the retaining clip on the regulator.

21 Drill out the rivets that are holding the window regulator in place **(see illustration)**. You only need to drill the top of the rivet off, as the inner part of the rivet will drop out.

22 The window regulator can now be removed downward out through the lower door aperture.

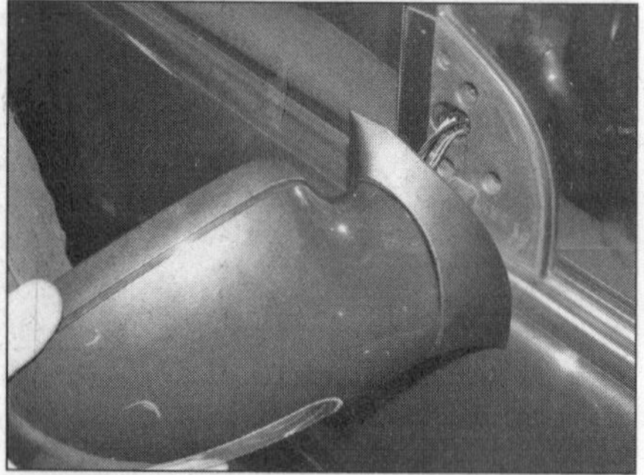

14.11 Remove the exterior mirror

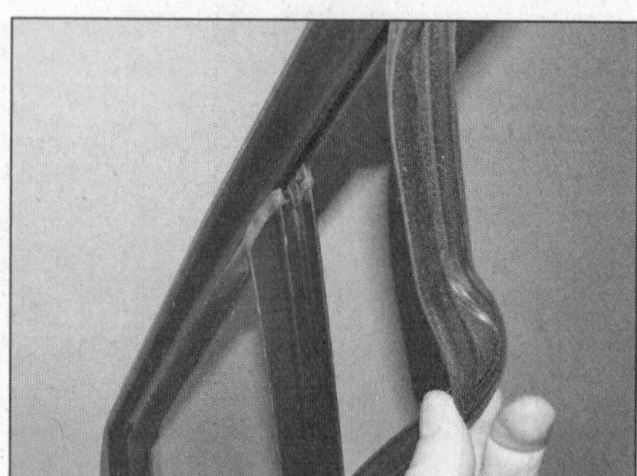

14.12 Pull the guide rubber out from the frame

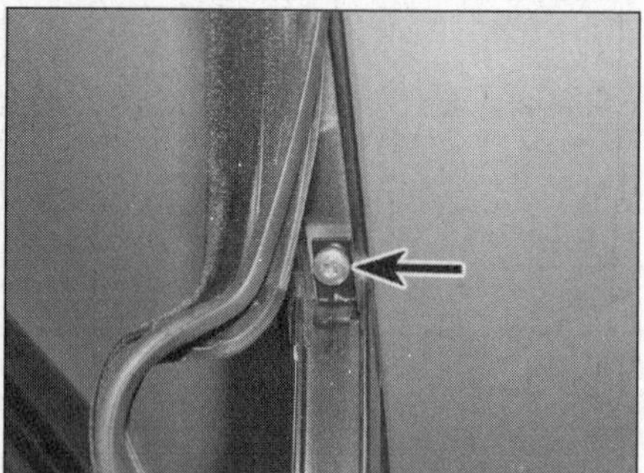

14.13 Undo the upper retaining screw – arrowed

14.14 Undo the two mounting screws – arrowed

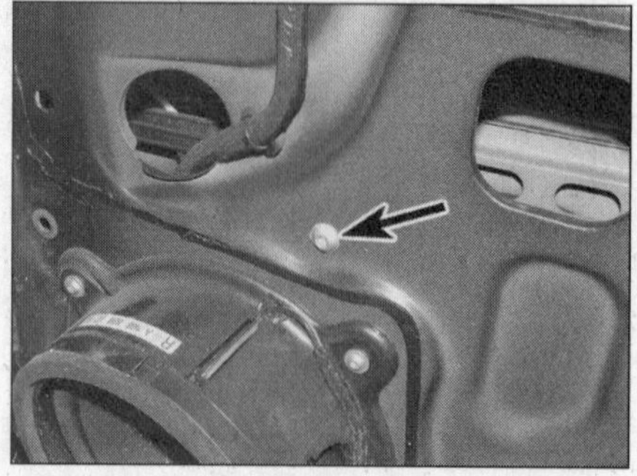

14.15 Undo the lower guide rail retaining screw – arrowed

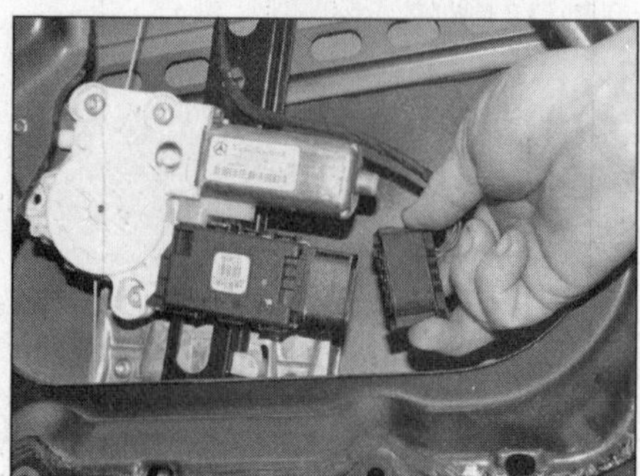

14.20 Disconnect the wiring connector

14.21 Drilling out the mounting bracket rivets

15.1a Release the retaining clips . . .

15.1b . . . and remove the trim panel

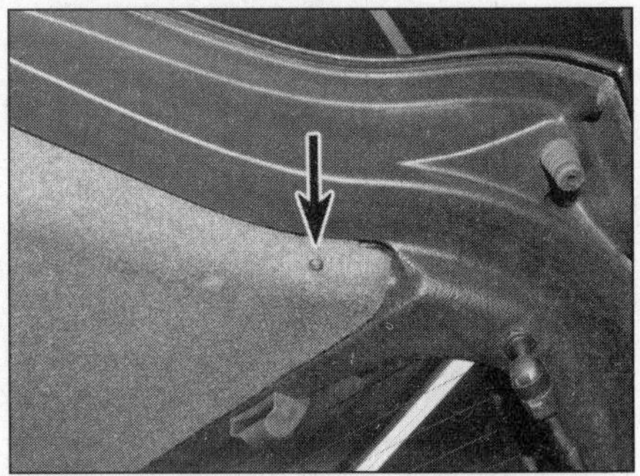

15.2 Remove the retaining screws (where fitted)

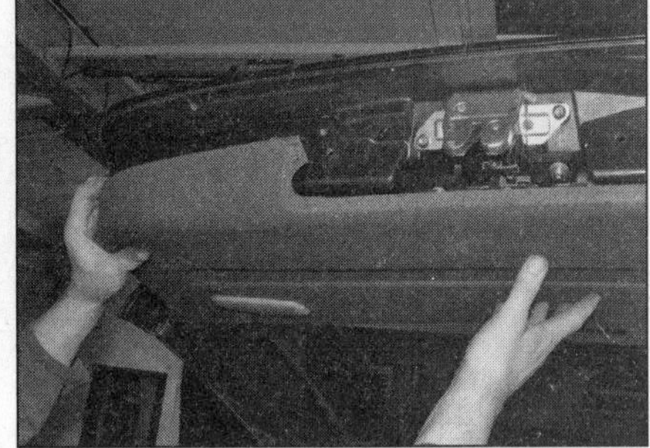

15.4a Remove the tailgate trim . . .

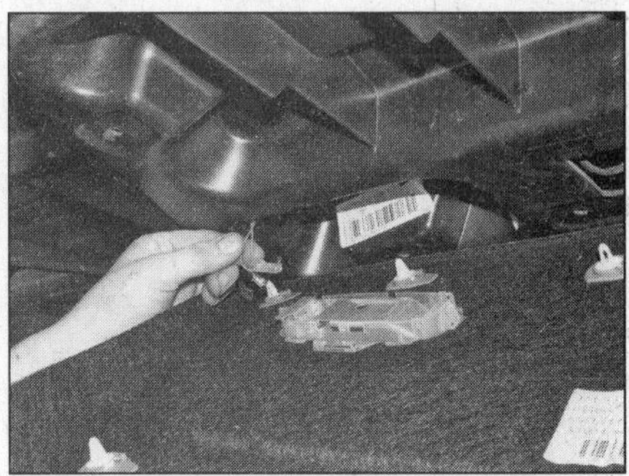

15.4b . . . and disconnect the wiring connector

23 Refitting is a reversal of removal, noting the following points:

a) Make sure the correct size rivets are used, to make sure the regulator motor assembly is secure.

b) Refit the window glass as described earlier.

15 Tailgate inner trim panel – removal and refitting

Removal

1 Open up the tailgate, remove the three retaining clips from the plastic trim panel by the tailgate catch and unclip the panel from the edge of the tailgate **(see illustrations)**.

2 On some models, remove the two screws from the outside edge of the tailgate inner trim panel **(see illustration)**.

3 Release the trim panel studs, carefully levering between the panel and tailgate with a flat-bladed lever. Work around the outside of the panel to release the plastic studs, renew any broken ones before refitting.

4 When all the studs are released, remove the trim panel from the tailgate. Where fitted, disconnect the wiring connector from the tailgate light in the panel as it is removed **(see illustrations)**.

Refitting

5 Refitting is the reverse of removal, making sure the wiring connector is refitted to the light (where applicable).

16 Tailgate and support struts – removal and refitting

Removal

Tailgate

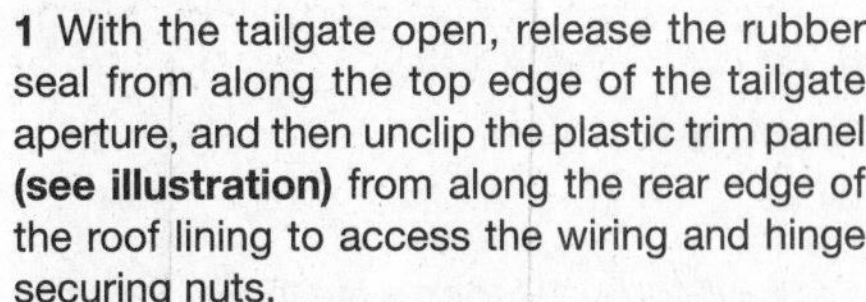

1 With the tailgate open, release the rubber seal from along the top edge of the tailgate aperture, and then unclip the plastic trim panel **(see illustration)** from along the rear edge of the roof lining to access the wiring and hinge securing nuts.

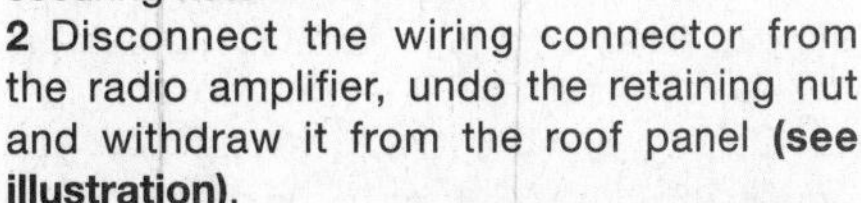

2 Disconnect the wiring connector from the radio amplifier, undo the retaining nut and withdraw it from the roof panel **(see illustration)**.

3 Disconnect the washer pipe, pneumatic pipe and wiring connectors from along the rear of the roof panel **(see illustration)**. If required, unclip the wiring and pipes from any retaining clips.

4 Unclip the rubber grommet from the roof panel **(see illustration)**.

16.1 Unclip the trim panel

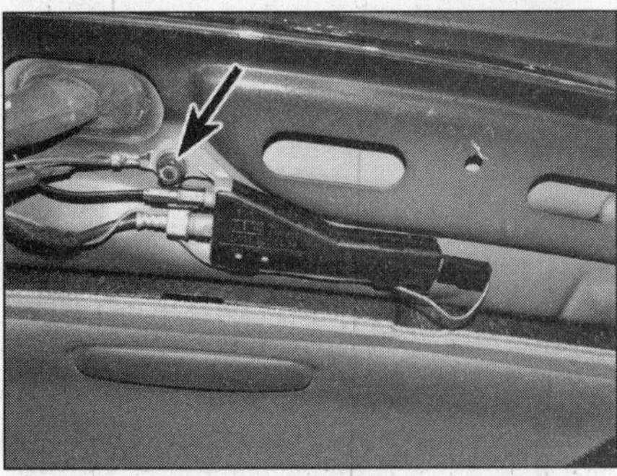

16.2 Undo the radio amplifier retaining nut – arrowed

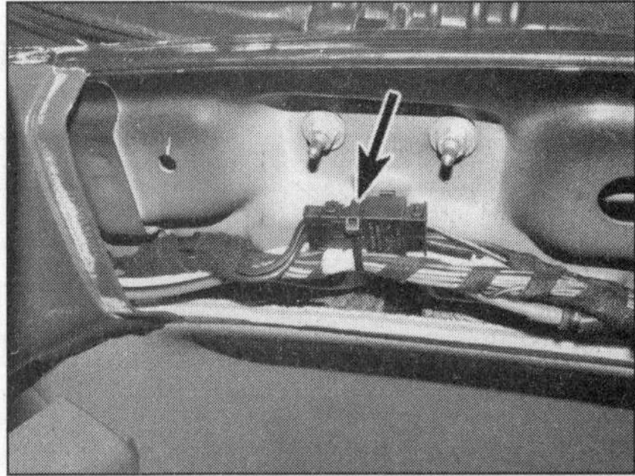

16.3 Release the wiring from the retaining clip – arrowed

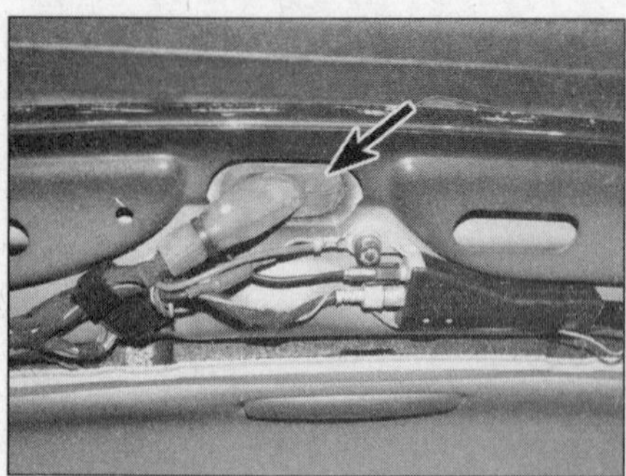
16.4 Unclip the grommet (arrowed) from the tailgate

16.6 Undo the hinge securing bolts (one side shown) – arrowed

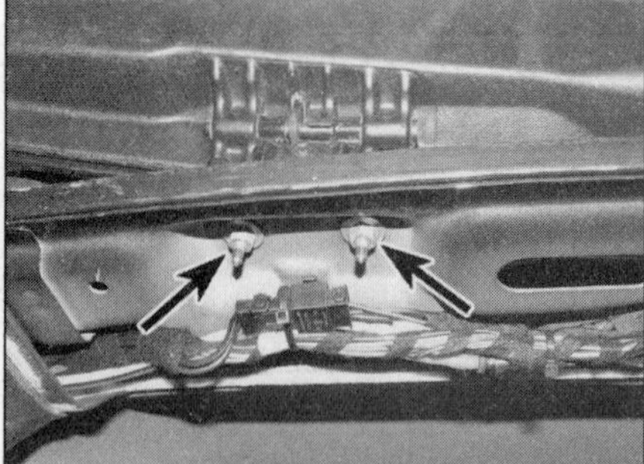
16.7 Hinge retaining nuts – arrowed

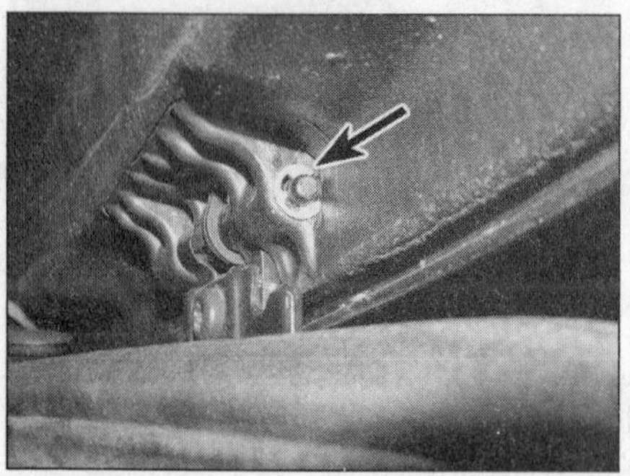
16.8 Hinge pin retaining clip – arrowed

16.10a Release the securing clip . . .

16.10b . . . and disconnect the support strut

5 With the help of an assistant to support the tailgate, remove the support struts as described below.

6 Unscrew and remove the bolts securing the hinges to the tailgate **(see illustration)**, with an assistant, remove the tailgate from the vehicle and withdraw the wiring and pipes as it is removed.

7 Inspect the hinges for signs of wear or damage and renew if necessary. The hinges are secured to the vehicle by nuts, which can be accessed from under the rear of the roof panel **(see illustration)**. Mark the position of the hinges before removing, so that they can be refitted in the same place.

8 If required, the hinge pins can be removed by releasing the retaining clip and using a drift to knock out the pin **(see illustration)**.

Support struts

Warning: The support struts are filled with a gas and must be disposed of safely.

16.13 Adjustable rubber buffer – arrowed

9 With the help of an assistant, support the tailgate in the open position.

10 Using a small flat-bladed screwdriver lift the locking clip, and pull the gas support strut off its balljoint mounting on the inner wing panel **(see illustrations)**. Repeat the procedure on the tailgate strut mounting point and remove the strut from the vehicle body. **Note:** *If the gas strut is to be re-used, the locking clip must not be taken all the way out, or the clip will be damaged.*

Refitting

Tailgate

11 Refitting is the reverse of removal, aligning the hinges and tighten the retaining bolts to the specified torque.

12 On completion, close the tailgate and check its alignment with the surrounding panels. If necessary, slight adjustment can be made by unscrewing the retaining bolts and repositioning the tailgate on its hinges. If the tailgate buffers are in need of adjustment, continue as follows.

17.2a Unclip the trim cover . . .

13 Locate the adjustment buffers on the lower corners of the tailgate. Slacken the locknut and adjust the rubber buffers evenly until they are in the right position. Tighten the locknut when the tailgate is adjusted correctly. **Note:** *On some models, the rubber buffer may be a rubber plug, which can be adjusted by winding it in or out to get the correct fitting* ***(see illustration)***. There must be an even gap all around, and the tailgate must be level with the surrounding body panels; close the tailgate and check the alignment with the surrounding body panels (approximately 6.5 mm gap).

Support struts

14 Refitting is a reverse of the removal procedure, ensuring that the strut is securely retained by its retaining clips.

17 Tailgate lock components – removal and refitting

Removal

Tailgate lock assembly

1 Open up the tailgate and remove the inner trim panel as described in Section 15.

2 On models from 21/08/00, use a plastic wedge to lever the plastic cover from the door handle on the outside of the tailgate, and then undo the four retaining screws and remove the plastic trim **(see illustrations)**.

17.2b . . . and remove the handle trim

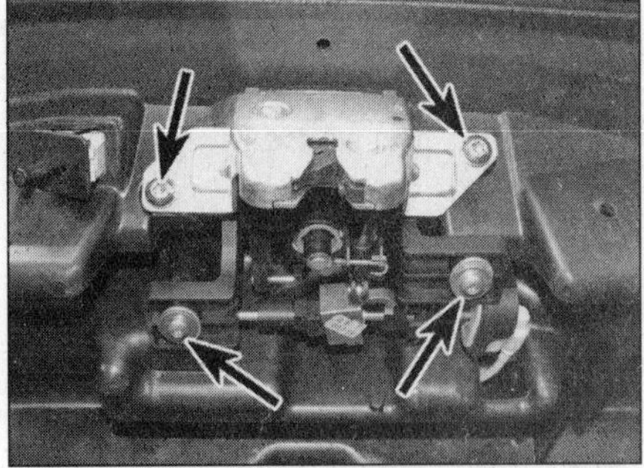

17.3a Undo the retaining screws – arrowed . . .

17.3b . . . and remove the tailgate lock

3 Working inside the tailgate, undo the four retaining screws and remove the lock assembly from the tailgate **(see illustrations)**.

4 As the lock assembly is removed from the tailgate, disconnect the pneumatic pipe from the lock assembly **(see illustration)**, and where applicable, the wiring connector.

Lock catch (tailgate)

5 To remove the catch from the lock assembly, disconnect the operating cable **(see illustration)**.

Lock catch (floor panel)

6 Using two small screwdrivers, release the securing clips and remove the trim panel from along the rear edge of the boot compartment **(see illustrations)**.

7 Remove the trim, and then mark the position of the catch mounting bracket on the rear crossmember to aid refitting, and then undo the two retaining screws and remove the catch **(see illustration)**.

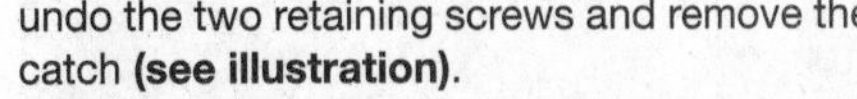

Tailgate lock barrel

8 On models from 21/08/00, with the key in the tailgate lock, use a small screwdriver to release the locking pin and withdraw the lock barrel **(see illustration)**.

Refitting

9 Refitting is a reversal of removal, however, before refitting the trim panel, check the operation of the lock components.

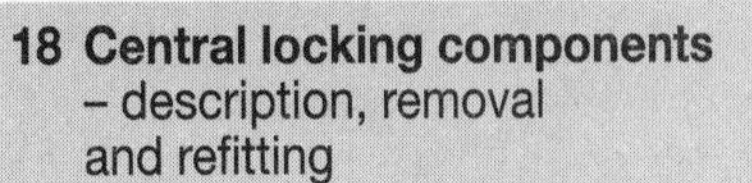

18 Central locking components - description, removal and refitting

1 The central locking system consists of the following electrical and pneumatic components, for further information on the electrical components, refer to Chapter 12.

17.4 Disconnect the pneumatic pipe from the lock

Electrical

a) Control unit on supply pump in spare wheel compartment.

17.5 Disconnecting the operating cable

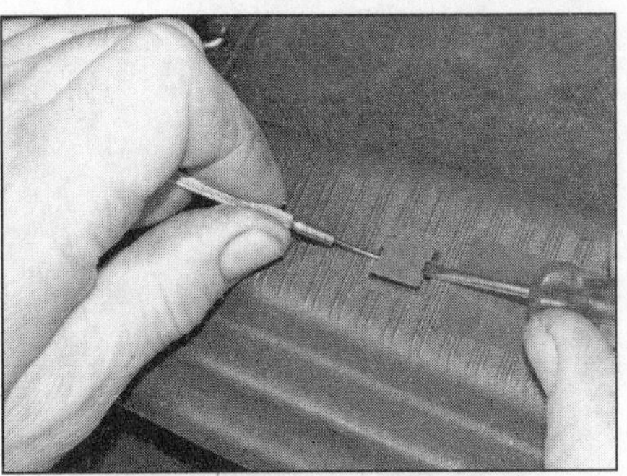

17.6a Release the centre . . .

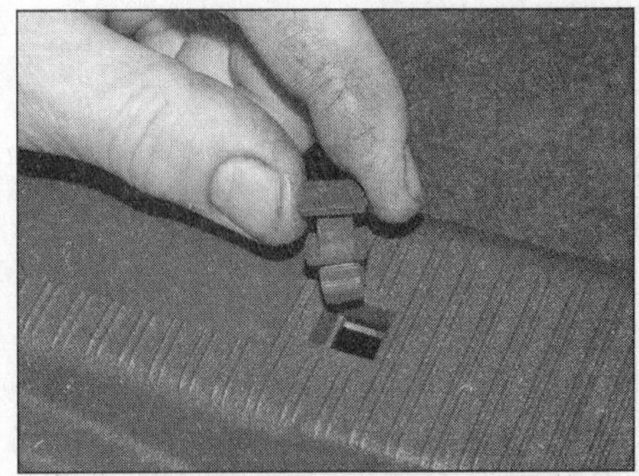

17.6b . . . withdraw the securing clip . . .

17.6c . . . and remove the trim panel

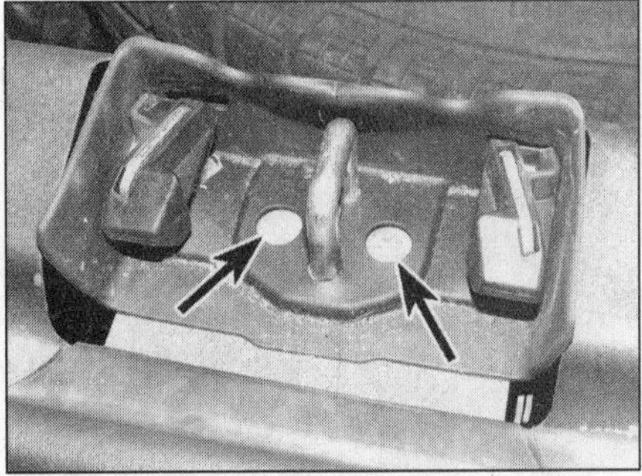

17.7 Tailgate catch mounting bolts – arrowed

17.8 Release the locking pin and withdraw the lock barrel

18.3 Lift the spare wheel cover

18.4a Lift the pump . . .

18.4b . . remove the strap . . .

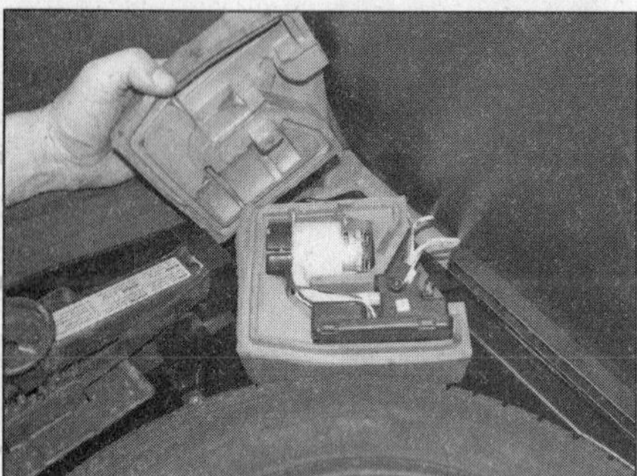
18.4c . . . and remove the foam insulation

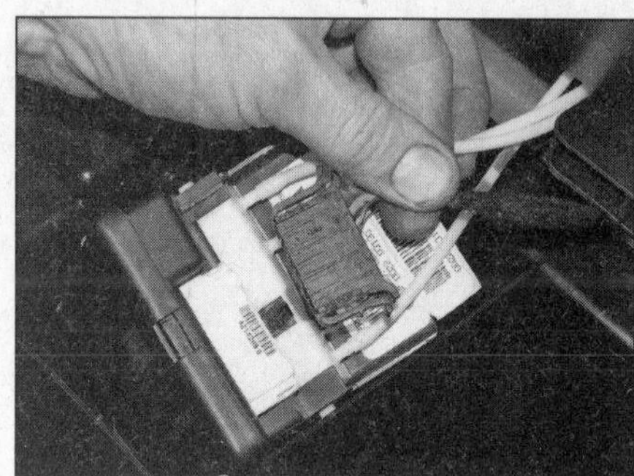
18.5 Disconnect the wiring connector

b) Central locking switch on facia panel.
c) Four door switches (interior lights).
d) Tailgate door switch (interior light).
e) Front door lock switches (driver's door only on some models).
f) Tailgate lock switch (depending on model).

Pneumatic

a) Supply pump in spare wheel compartment.

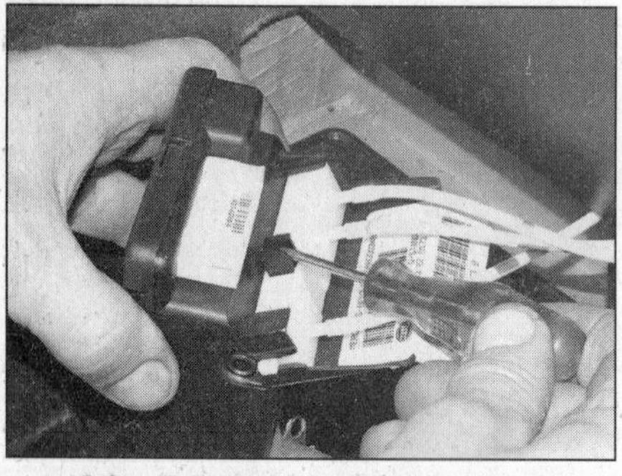
18.6a Release the securing clip . . .

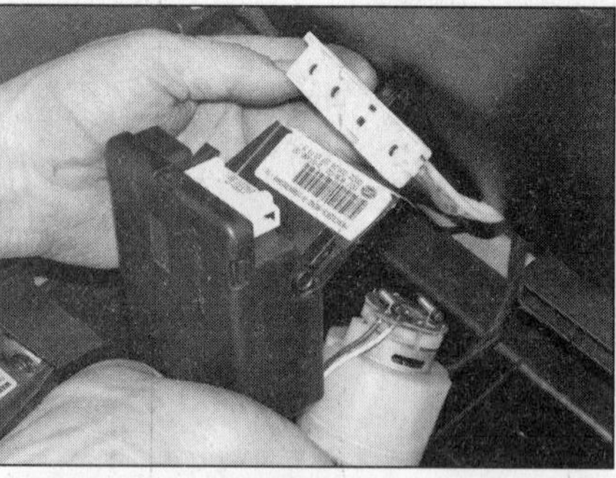
18.6b . . . and disconnect the pneumatic pipe connector

18.12a Filler flap actuator in fitted position

18.12b Remove the actuator from inside the wing panel

b) Actuator in each of the four doors.
c) Actuator in the tailgate.
d) Actuator for the fuel tank flap.
e) 4-way pipe distributor under the rear seat at the left-hand side.
f) Pipe connections at all doors including tailgate.
g) Pneumatic pipes connecting all components.

Removal and refitting

2 Disconnect the battery negative lead (refer to *Disconnecting the battery* in the *Reference* Chapter at the end of this manual).

Supply pump/control unit

3 Open the tailgate and lift up the spare wheel cover **(see illustration)**.
4 Lift the pump out from the front left-hand corner of the spare wheel compartment and remove the foam insulting cover from around the pump **(see illustrations)**.
5 Disconnect the wiring block connector from the control unit **(see illustration)**.
6 Release the securing clip and disconnect the pneumatic pipe connector from the control unit **(see illustrations)**.
7 The pump can now be removed from the vehicle.
8 Refitting is a reversal of removal. Make sure all pneumatic pipes connections are secure. On completion check the operation of the central locking system.

Door lock actuator

9 Remove the door lock as described in Section 13.

Tailgate lock actuator

10 Remove the tailgate lock assembly as described in Section 17.

Fuel tank filler flap actuator

11 Remove the right-hand trim from the luggage compartment with reference to Section 26. To make access easier, remove the right-hand rear light unit.
12 Reach up inside the right-hand rear wing panel, and release the retaining clip on the fuel flap actuator **(see illustrations)**.
13 As the actuator is removed, disconnect the pneumatic pipe **(see illustration)**.
14 Working inside the fuel filler neck aperture, twist the plastic sleeve for the actuator rod,

and remove it from the filler neck panel **(see illustration)**.

15 When refitting the actuator make sure that it locates in the plastic sleeve securely **(see illustration)**.

16 Make sure the pneumatic pipe connection is secure. On completion check the operation of the central locking system.

17 If the fuel locking actuator does not work, reach up inside the rear wing panel and pull the metal actuator rod to open the fuel filler flap.

18 To adjust the position of the rubber stop on the fuel filler flap, twist the outer rubber ring **(see illustration)**.

18.13 Disconnect the pneumatic pipe

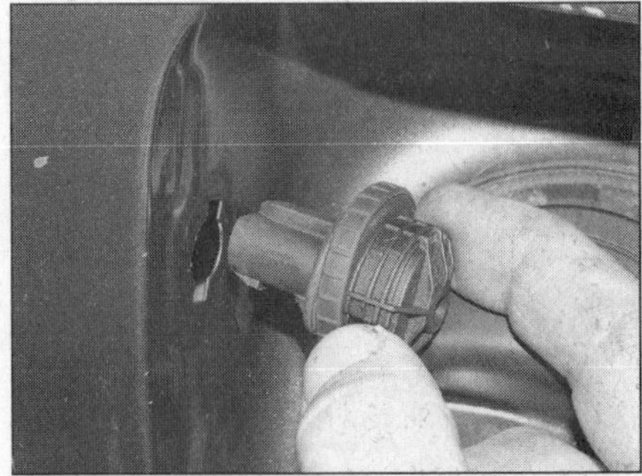

18.14 Remove the plastic sleeve

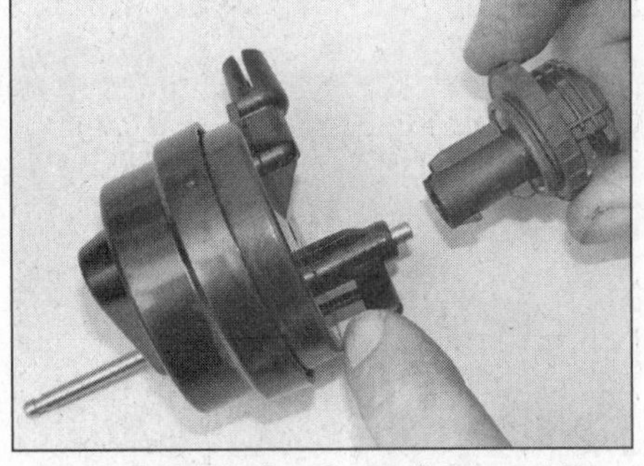

18.15 Release the clip to disengage the actuator (shown out of vehicle for clarity)

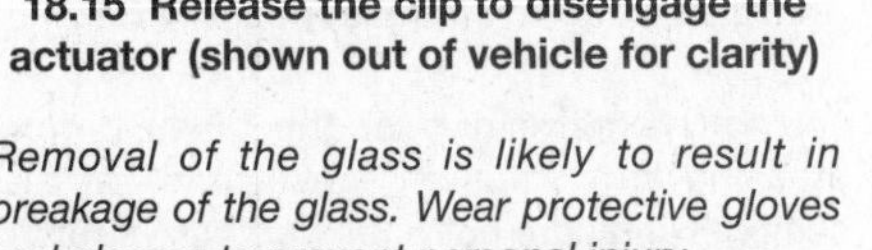

18.18 Turn the outer rubber to adjust flap

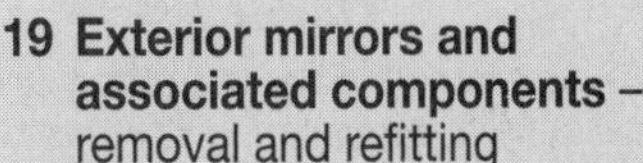

19 Exterior mirrors and associated components – removal and refitting

Removal

Exterior mirror

1 Unclip the trim panel from the inside of the window frame **(see illustration)**.

2 Release the wiring block connector from the mirror mounting bracket and disconnect it **(see illustration)**.

3 While supporting the mirror, undo the mounting screws from the inside of the window frame **(see illustration)**.

4 Withdraw the mirror from the door while guiding the wiring through the hole **(see illustration)**.

Mirror glass

Note: *The mirror glass is clipped into place. Removal of the glass is likely to result in breakage of the glass. Wear protective gloves and glasses to prevent personal injury.*

5 Press in the bottom of the mirror glass so that the top edge is furthest from the housing. Then insert a small screwdriver and release the mirror glass retaining spring clip and unclip the mirror. Take great care when removing the glass; do not use excessive force, as the glass is easily broken **(see illustrations)**.

19.1 Unclip the trim panel

19.2 Release the wiring connector and disconnect

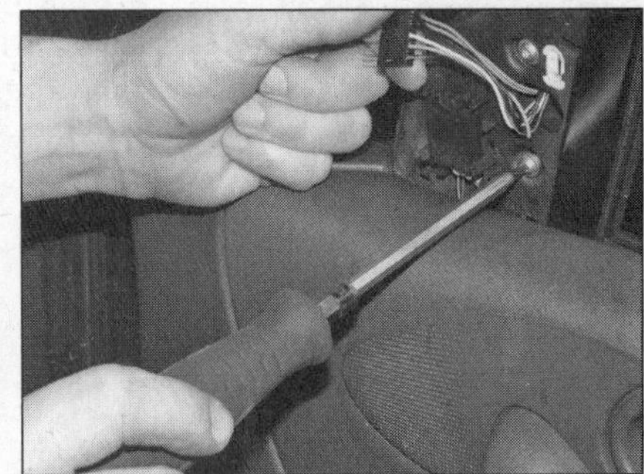

19.3 Undo the retaining screws . . .

19.4 . . . and remove the mirror

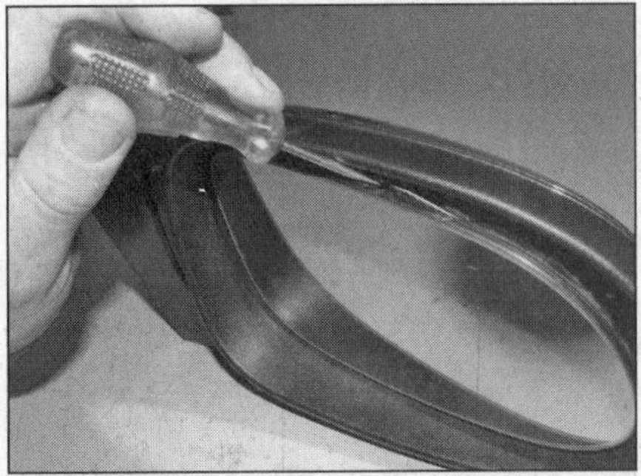

19.5a Release the securing clip . . .

19.5b . . . and unclip the mirror glass

19.6 Disconnect the wiring from the mirror glass

19.8a Undo the retaining screws – arrowed . . .

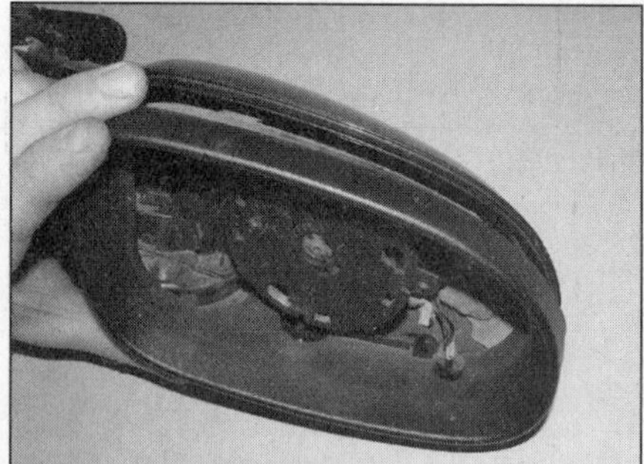
19.8b . . . and remove the mirror surround

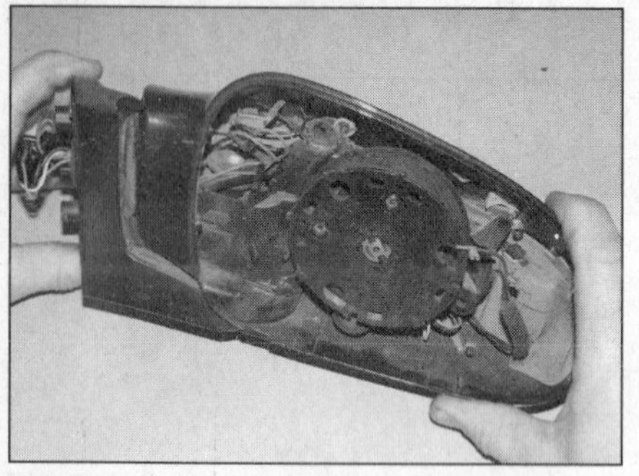
19.9a Remove the cover from the mechanism . . .

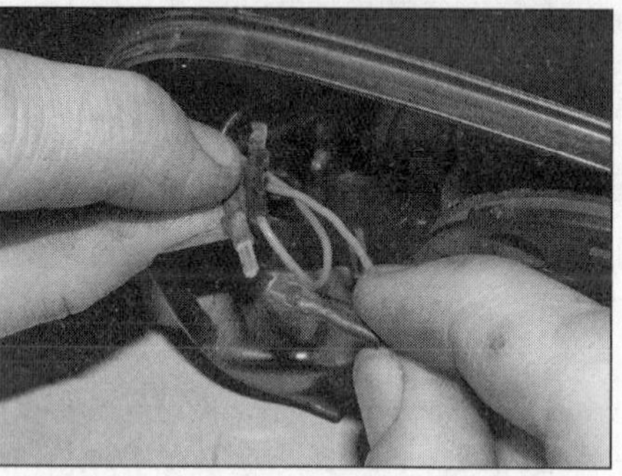
19.9b . . . and disconnect the wiring

6 Disconnect the wiring connector from the mirror heating element as the mirror glass is removed **(see illustration)**.

Mirror housing

7 Remove the mirror and mirror glass as described in paragraphs 1 to 6.

8 Undo the four retaining screws from inside the mirror glass housing and unclip the front surround from the mirror **(see illustrations)**.

9 Withdraw the cover from the mirror motor mechanism; disconnect the wiring connectors if required **(see illustrations)**.

Mirror switch

10 Refer to Chapter 12 for the removal of the mirror electrical switch.

Refitting

11 Refitting is the reverse of the relevant removal procedure. When refitting the mirror glass, make sure the spring clip is located correctly on the rear of the glass before pressing into position. Press firmly at the centre taking care not to use excessive force, as the glass is easily broken. Make wiring inside the mirror is connected securely before refitting the mirror glass.

20 Windscreen and rear window glass – general information

These areas of glass are bonded in position with a special adhesive. Renewal of such fixed glass is a difficult, messy and time-consuming task, which is beyond the scope of the home mechanic. It is difficult, unless one has plenty of practice, to obtain a secure, waterproof fit. Furthermore, the task carries a high risk of breakage; this applies especially to the laminated glass windscreen. In view of this, owners are strongly advised to have this sort of work carried out by one of the many specialist windscreen fitters.

21 Sunroof – general information

Due to the complexity of the sunroof mechanism, considerable expertise is needed to repair, renew or adjust the sunroof components successfully. Removal of the roof first requires the headlining to be removed, which is a complex and tedious operation, and not a task to be undertaken lightly. Therefore, any problems with the sunroof should be referred to a Mercedes-Benz dealer. On models with an electric sunroof, if the sunroof motor fails to operate, first check the relevant fuse. If the fault cannot be traced and rectified, the sunroof can be opened and closed manually using an Allen key to turn the motor spindle (a suitable key is supplied with the vehicle, and should be with the handbook in the glove compartment). To gain access to the motor, unclip the interior light lens and insert the Allen key fully into the motor opening **(see illustrations)**. Rotate the key to move the sunroof to the required position.

21.1a Unclip the light lens . . .

21.1b . . . and insert and Allen key into sunroof motor

22 Body exterior fittings – removal and refitting

Wheel arch liners and body under-panels

1 The various plastic covers fitted to the underside of the vehicle are secured in position by a mixture of screws, nuts and retaining clips, and removal will be fairly obvious on inspection. Work methodically around the panel removing its retaining screws and releasing its retaining clips until the panel is free and can be removed from the underside of the vehicle. Most clips used on the vehicle are simply prised out of position. Remove the wheels to ease the removal of the wheel arch liners **(see illustration)**.

2 On the driver's side front, there is a small

22.1 Remove the inner liner

22.2 Small access trim panel (driver's side front)

22.3 Disconnect the wiring connectors

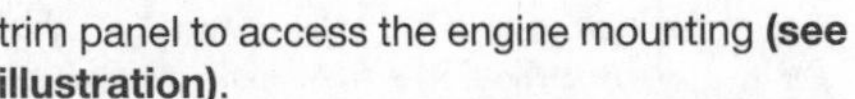

trim panel to access the engine mounting **(see illustration)**.

3 Before removing the front inner wheel arch liners, disconnect the wiring connectors for the front wheel speed sensors and brake warning light wiring (right-hand front only) **(see illustration)**.

4 On refitting, renew any retaining clips that may have been broken on removal, and ensure that the panel is securely retained by all the relevant clips and screws.

Body trim strips and badges

5 The various body trim strips and badges are held in position with a special adhesive tape and/or locating lugs. Removal requires the trim/badge to be heated to soften the adhesive, and then carefully lifted away from the surface. Due to the high risk of damage to the vehicle's paintwork during this operation, it is recommended that this task should be entrusted to a Mercedes-Benz dealer.

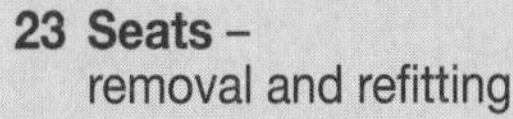

23 Seats - removal and refitting

Note: *Refer to the warnings in Chapter 12 on side airbags.*

Removal

Front seats

Note: *The amount of wiring connectors under the seat may vary depending on the vehicle specification.*

23.3b Seat right-hand front mounting bolt - arrowed

1 Disconnect the battery negative lead (refer to *Disconnecting the battery* in the *Reference* Chapter at the end of this manual).

2 Slide the seat forwards as far as possible and unscrew the rear mounting bolts **(see illustration)**.

3 Slide the seat rearwards as far as possible and unscrew the front mounting bolts **(see illustrations)**.

4 Tilt the seat backwards and disconnect the seat wiring connector **(see illustration)**.

Warning: As a precaution against unintentional electrostatic discharge into the airbag, briefly touch part of the vehicle body before disconnecting the wiring.

5 Check that the wiring harness is released from any clips, and then remove the seat from the vehicle. If necessary, have an assistant help to remove the seat as it is heavy, and surrounding trim panels may be otherwise damaged.

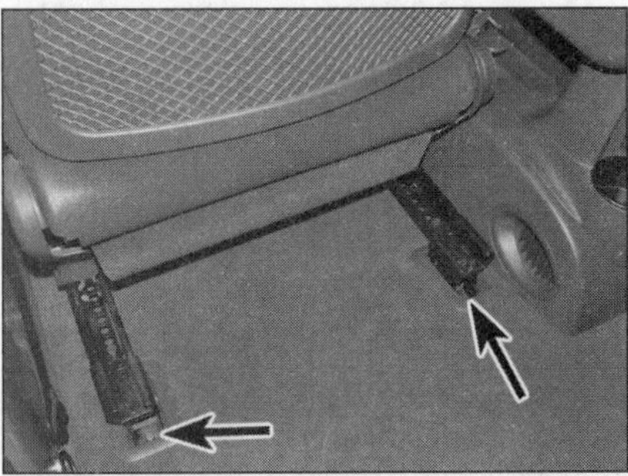

23.2 Seat rear mounting bolts - arrowed

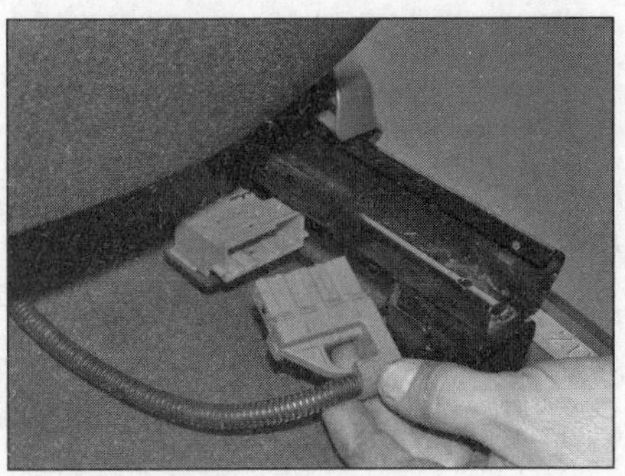

23.4 Disconnect the wiring connector

Rear seats

6 Before removing the rear seat, make sure the headrests are inserted all the way into the back of the seat, the seat is positioned as far back as it can go and the storage box under the seat (where fitted) is closed.

7 Pull the lever on the side of the seat forwards and fold the back of the seat down **(see illustration)**. Make sure the seat belt is fastened up out of the way, to the retaining bracket on the door pillar.

8 Pull the lever on the side of the seat upwards **(see illustration)**, and fold the rear of the seat forwards.

9 If the seat is to stay in this position while driving, remove the strut locking bar out from inside the lower part of the right-hand seat cover and insert it into the seat mounting bracket **(see illustrations)**.

10 To remove the rear seat completely, pull

23.3a Seat right-hand front mounting bolt - arrowed

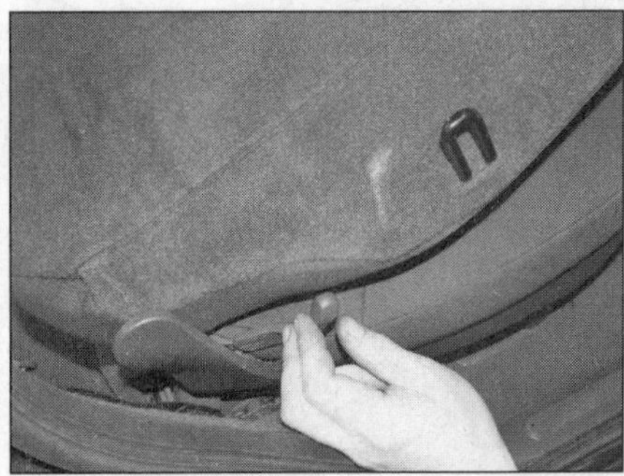

23.7 Pull lever forward to fold seat down

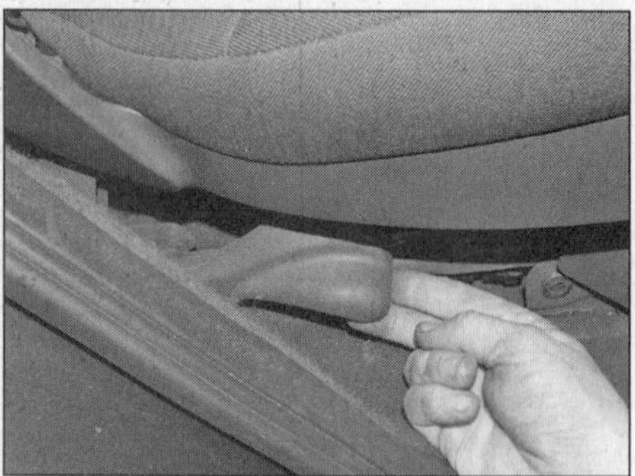
23.8 Pull lever upwards to release the seat

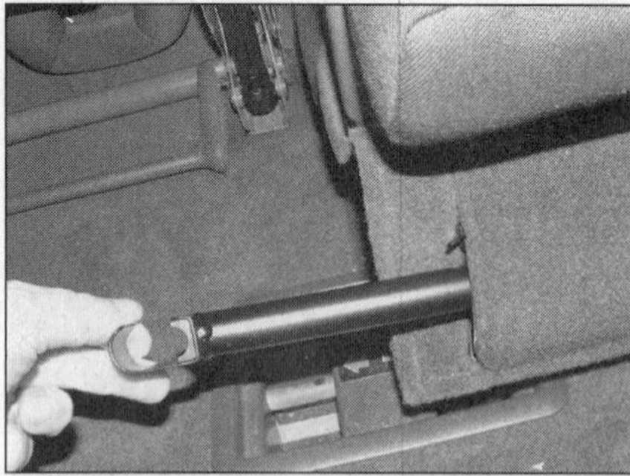
23.9a Remove the seat locking bar . . .

23.9b . . . and secure it under the seat

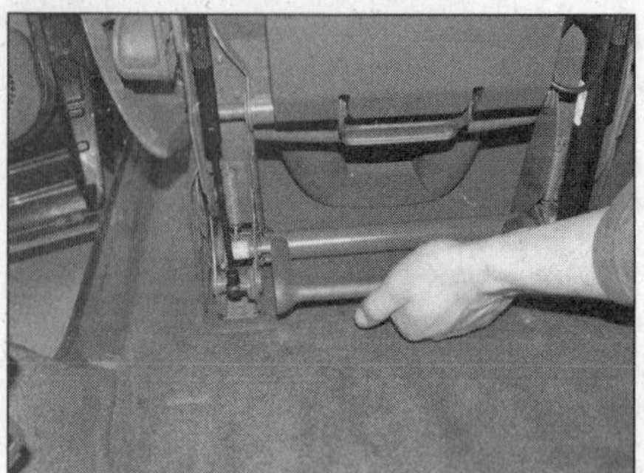
23.10a Pull the lever upwards . . .

23.10b . . . and unclip the seat from the floor

the lever bar upwards and tilt the seat forwards slightly, to disengage from the mounting bracket **(see illustrations)**.

Refitting

11 Refitting is a reversal of removal, but tighten the mounting bolts to the specified torque where given.

24 Seat belt tensioning mechanism – general information

All models covered in this manual are fitted with a front seat belt tensioner system incorporated in each of the inertia reels. Rear seat belt inertia reels with the tensioner system are only fitted to some models, other models having standard inertia reels.

The system is designed to instantaneously take up any slack in the seat belt in the case of a sudden frontal impact, therefore reducing the possibility of injury to the seat occupants. The seat belt tensioner is triggered by a frontal impact above a predetermined force. Lesser impacts, including impacts from behind, will not trigger the system.

When the system is triggered, the explosive gas in the tensioner mechanism retracts and locks the seat belt. This prevents the seat belt moving and keeps the occupant firmly in position in the seat. Once the tensioner has been triggered, the seat belt will be permanently locked and the assembly must be renewed.

There is a risk of personal injury if the system is triggered inadvertently when working on the vehicle, and it is therefore strongly recommended that any work involving the seat belt inertia reels be entrusted to a Mercedes-Benz dealer. Note the following warnings before contemplating any work on the front seat belts.

Warning: Do not expose the tensioner mechanism to temperatures in excess of 100°C.

- ***If the tensioner mechanism is dropped, it must be renewed, even it has suffered no apparent damage.***
- ***Do not allow any solvents to come into contact with the tensioner mechanism.***
- ***Do not attempt to open the tensioner mechanism as it contains explosive gas.***
- ***Tensioners must be discharged before they are disposed of, but this task should be entrusted to a Mercedes-Benz dealer.***

25 Seat belt components – removal and refitting

Warning: Refer to Section 24 before proceeding and also refer to the warnings in Chapter 12 for information on airbags.

1 Disconnect the battery negative lead (refer to *Disconnecting the battery* in the *Reference* Chapter at the end of this manual).

Removal

Front seat belt

2 Unscrew and remove the seat belt lower anchor mounting bolt and remove the belt from the floor **(see illustration)**.

3 Unclip the plastic cover, and then undo the bolt securing the seat belt upper anchor to the height adjuster on the B-pillar **(see illustrations)**.

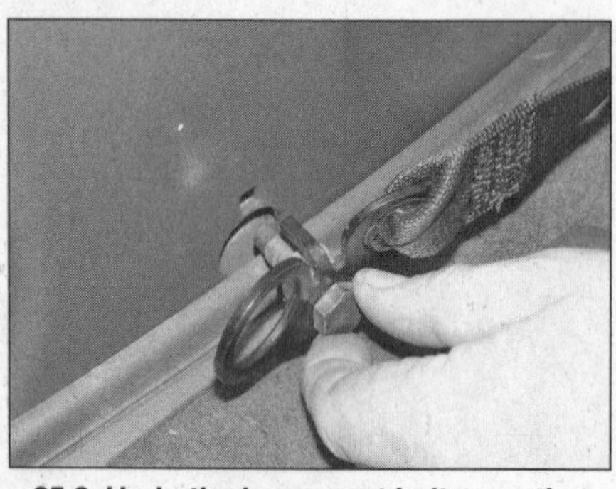
25.2 Undo the lower seat belt mounting bolt

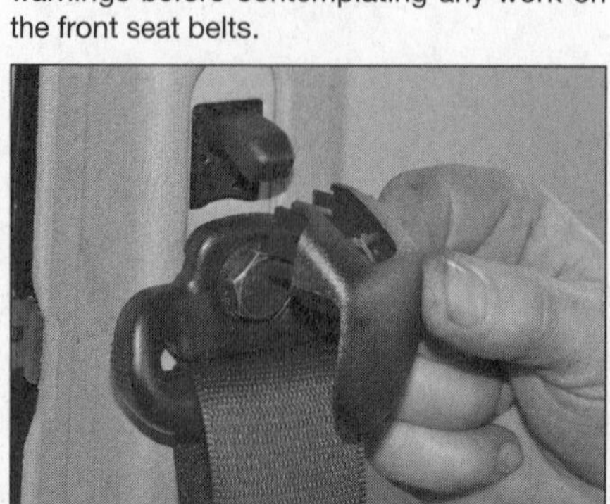
25.3a Unclip the plastic cover . . .

25.3b . . . and undo the upper mounting bolt

25.4a Use a screwdriver to remove the trim panel

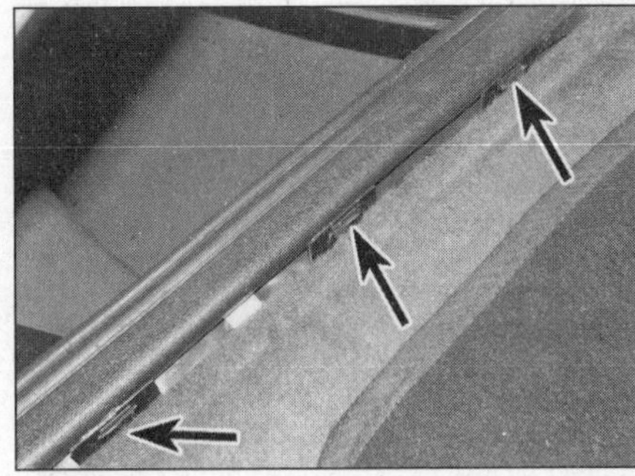

25.4b Trim panel securing clips – arrowed

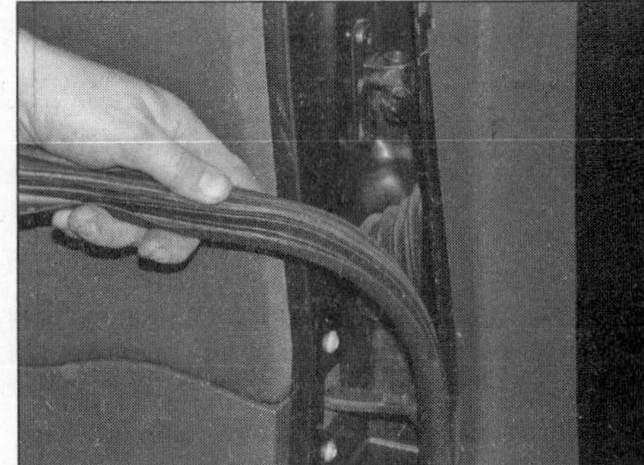

25.5a Pull back the door seal . . .

25.5b . . . and unclip the lower trim panel

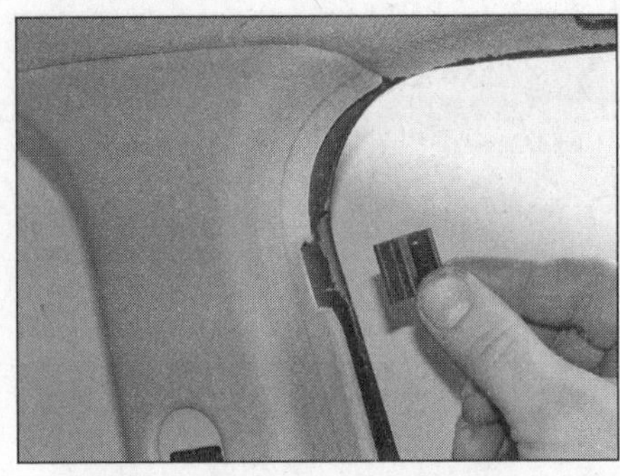

25.6a Release the securing clips . . .

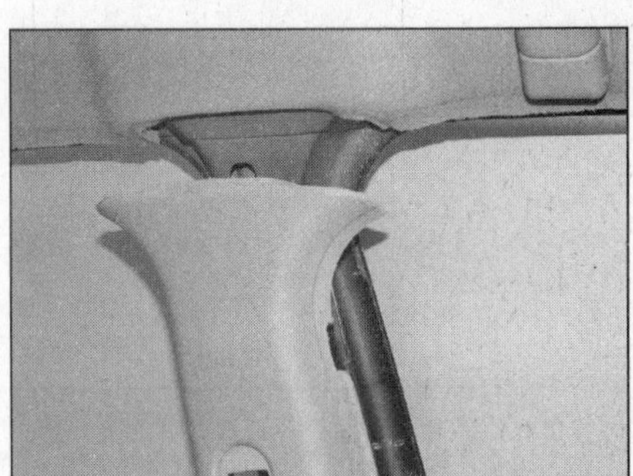

25.6b . . . and remove the upper trim panel

4 Working your way along the length of the trim, release the retaining clips and remove the door aperture lower trim panels **(see illustrations)**.

5 Carefully pull the door seal from the door pillar, and then unclip the lower trim panel from the B-pillar **(see illustrations)**.

6 Release the securing clips and remove the upper trim from the B-pillar **(see illustrations)**.

Warning: As a precaution against unintentional electrostatic discharge, briefly touch part of the vehicle body before disconnecting the wiring.

7 Unscrew the mounting bolt **(see illustration)** and remove the inertia reel from the bottom of the B-pillar. Disconnect the wiring from the inertia reel.

8 To remove the belt height adjustment, remove the securing bolt **(see illustration)**, and lift upwards from the pillar.

Front seat belt stalk

9 Remove the front seat assembly as described in Section 23.

10 Pull the seat back adjuster handle from the side of the seat **(see illustration)**.

11 Unclip the side trim panel from the lower art of the seat frame **(see illustration)**.

12 Unscrew and remove the bolt securing the stalk to the seat, and remove the stalk **(see illustration)**.

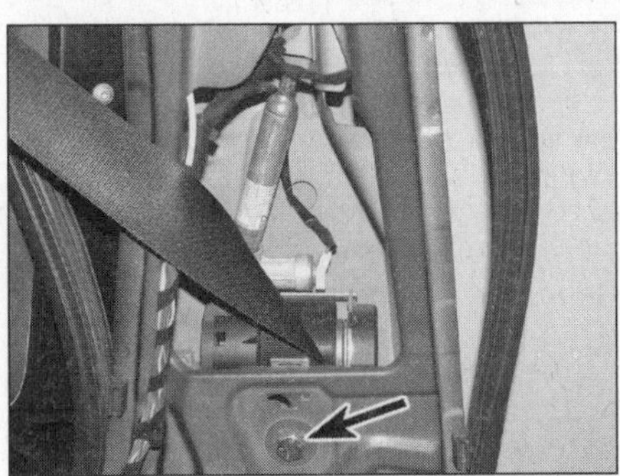

25.7 Inertia reel mounting bolt – arrowed

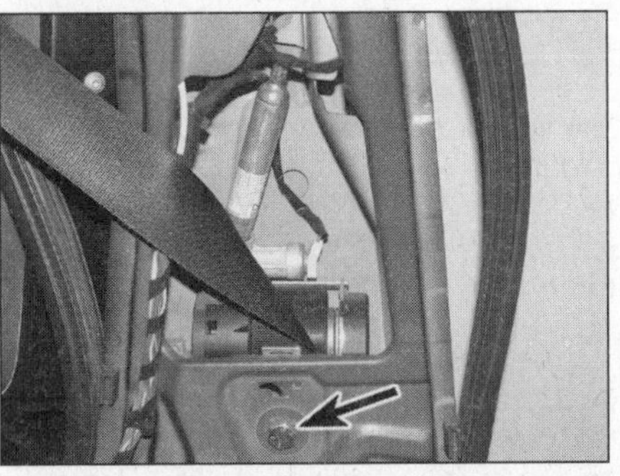

25.8 Height adjustment bar securing bolt – arrowed

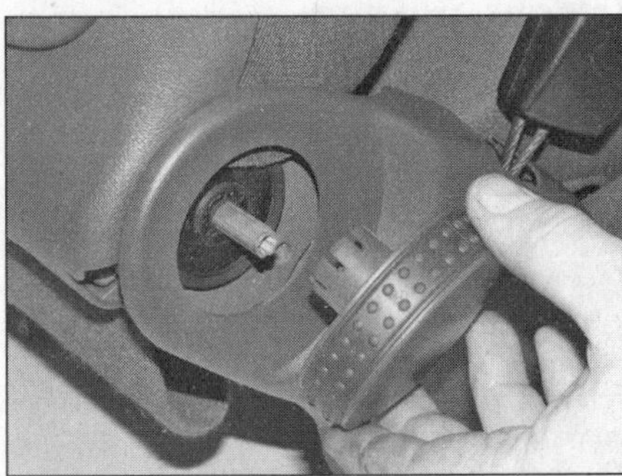

25.10 Unclip the seat adjuster from the spindle

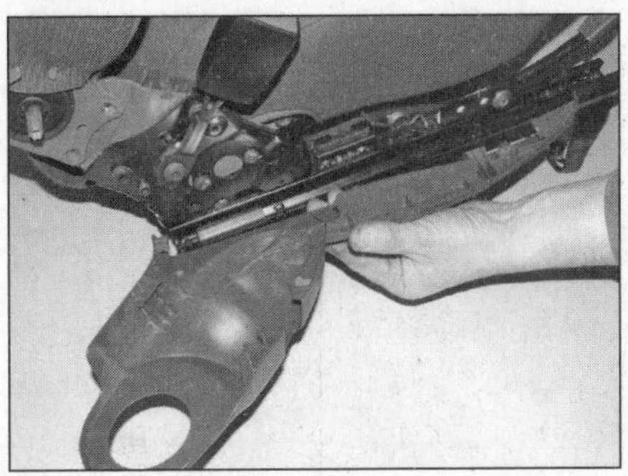

25.11 Unclip the trim panel from the side of the seat

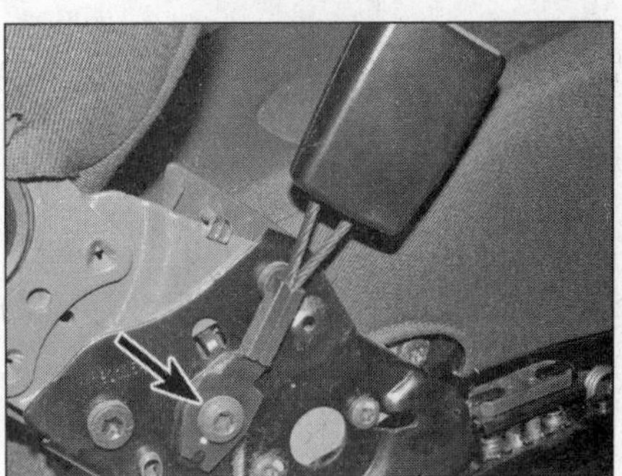

25.12 Seat belt stalk mounting bolt – arrowed

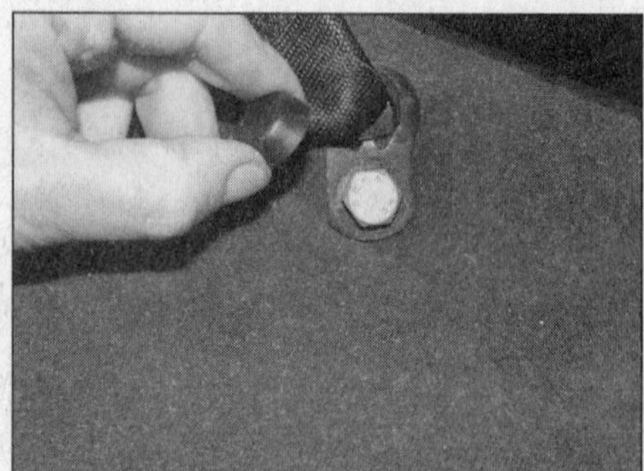
25.14 Unclip the cover and undo the retaining bolt

25.16 Pass the seat belt through the trim panel

25.17 Belt guide retaining bolts - arrowed

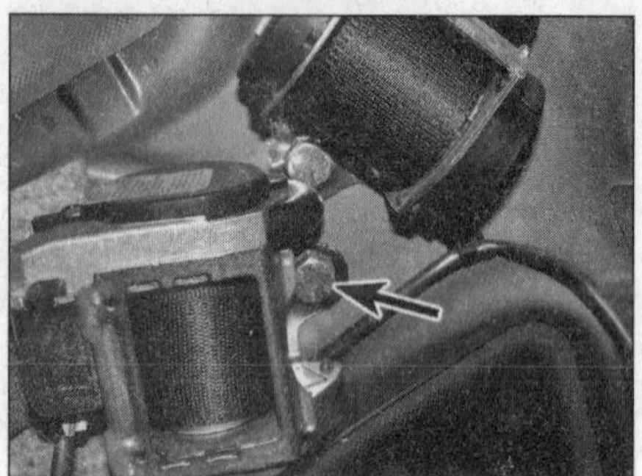
25.18 Inertia reel mounting bolt - arrowed

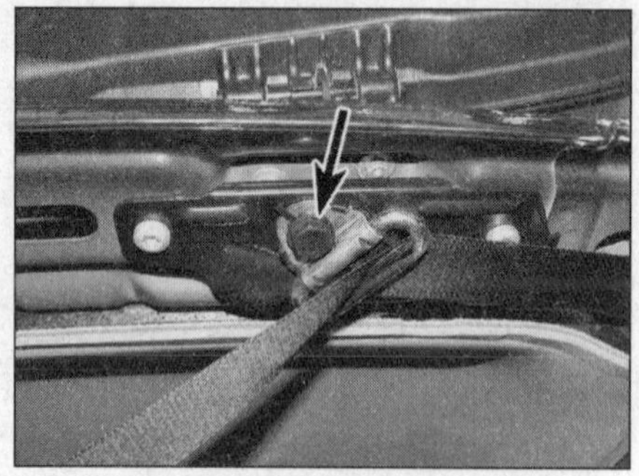
25.21 Centre belt upper mounting bolt - arrowed

25.22 Inertia reel mounting bolt - arrowed

Rear seat side inertia belt

13 To make access easier, fold the rear seats forward as described in Section 23.

14 Remove the plastic cap, and then unscrew and remove the seat belt lower anchor mounting bolt and remove the belt from the floor **(see illustration)**.

15 Remove the trim panels from the C-pillar and the plastic trim from across the rear of the roof lining, with reference to Section 26.

16 Pass the seat belt and lower anchorage bracket through the upper trim panel as it is removed **(see illustration)**

Warning: As a precaution against unintentional electrostatic discharge, briefly touch part of the vehicle body before disconnecting the wiring.

17 Disconnect the wiring connector from the inertia reel and if required unbolt the belt guide from the pillar **(see illustration)**.

18 Unscrew the mounting bolt and withdraw the inertia reel from the C-pillar **(see illustration)**.

Rear seat centre inertia belt

19 To make access easier, fold the rear seats forward as described in Section 23. **Note:** *Release the end of the centre seat belt from the seat buckle before folding the seats forward.*

20 Remove the trim panels from the C-pillar and the plastic trim from across the rear of the roof lining, with reference to Section 26. **Note:** *The upper panel has the side rear seat belt passing through it, so it can be just moved to one side without removing completely.*

21 Unscrew and remove the seat belt upper mounting bolt and remove the belt and guide from the rear of the roof panel **(see illustration)**. If required, undo the two retaining screws and remove the mounting bracket from the roof panel.

Warning: As a precaution against unintentional electrostatic discharge, briefly touch part of the vehicle body before disconnecting the wiring.

22 Unbolt and remove the inertia reel from the C-pillar **(see illustration)**.

Rear seat centre lap belt

23 With the rear seat folded forward as described in Section 23, undo the lap belt anchorage nut and bolt from the seat frame and remove the belt.

Rear seat belt stalk

24 With the rear seat folded forward as described in Section 23, undo the belt stalk anchorage nut and bolt from the seat frame and remove the stalk.

26.3a Unclip the plastic cap . . .

Refitting

25 Refitting is a reversal of the removal procedure, ensuring that all the seat belt units are located correctly and mounting bolts are securely tightened to their specified torque. Check all the trim panels are securely retained by all the relevant retaining clips, with reference to Section 26. When refitting the upper trim panels, ensure that the height adjustment levers engage correctly with the seat belt upper mounting bolt head.

26 Interior trim - removal and refitting

Interior trim panels

1 The interior trim panels are secured using either screws or various types of trim fasteners, usually studs or clips.

2 Check that there are no other panels overlapping the one to be removed; usually there is a sequence that has to be followed, and this will only become obvious on close inspection.

3 Remove all obvious fasteners, such as screws **(see illustrations)**. If the panel will not come free, it is held by hidden clips or fasteners. These are usually situated around the edge of the panel and can be prised up to release them; note, however, that they can break quite easily

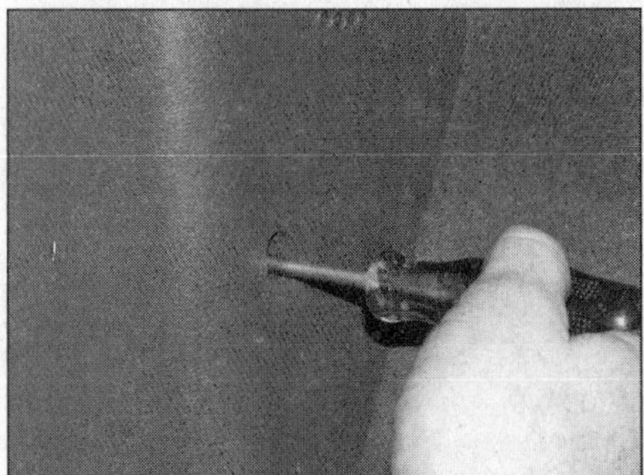
26.3b . . . and undo the securing screw

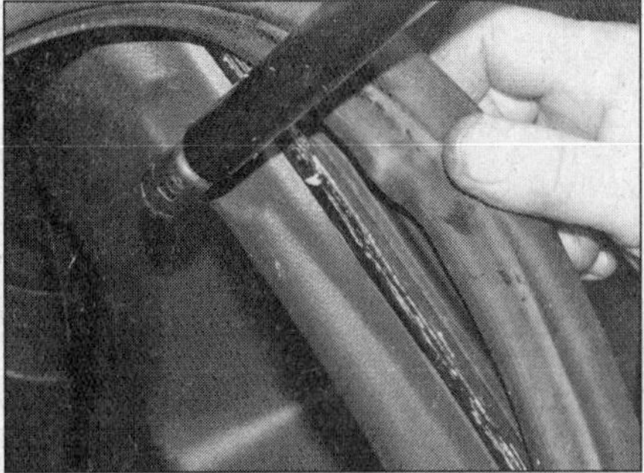
26.3c Pull back the rubber sealing strips

26.4 Disconnect the tailgate struts

so new ones should be available. The best way of releasing such clips, without the correct type of tool, is to use a large flat-bladed screwdriver. Note in many cases that the adjacent sealing strip must be prised back to release a panel **(see illustration)**.

4 When removing a panel, **never** use excessive force or the panel may be damaged; always check carefully that all fasteners or other relevant components have been removed or released before attempting to withdraw a panel **(see illustration)**.

5 Refitting is the reverse of the removal procedure; secure the fasteners by pressing them firmly into place and ensure that all disturbed components are correctly secured to prevent rattles.

Glovebox

6 Make sure the ignition switch is in the off position.

Models up to 28/02/01

7 Carefully unclip the knurled air vent knob from the left-hand side of the facia panel, and then undo the retaining screw from behind it.

8 With the glovebox lid open, undo the wire clamp retaining bolt and pull it downwards.

9 Undo the three retaining screws from under the upper part of the facia panel.

10 Slide the upper part of the facia panel towards the door and remove it from the top of the facia.

11 Close the lid of the glovebox and remove the two retaining screws from below the lid.

12 Open the lid of the glovebox and remove the two retaining screws from inside each corner of the glovebox.

13 Slide the glovebox out of position, disconnecting the wiring connector from the glovebox illumination light as it becomes accessible.

14 Refitting is the reverse of removal.

Models from 01/03/01

15 Unclip the air vent from under the left-hand side of the facia panel below the glovebox **(see illustration)**.

16 Carefully pull the door seal away from the footwell inner trim panel, remove the plastic cap and undo the retaining screw **(see illustrations)**.

17 Unclip the footwell inner trim panel from the lower part of the A-pillar **(see illustration)**.

18 Undo the three retaining screws from under the lower part of the facia panel **(see illustration)**.

19 With the glovebox lid open, undo the four retaining screws from under the upper part of the facia panel.

20 Slide the glovebox out of position, disconnecting the wiring connector from the glovebox illumination light as it becomes accessible.

21 Refitting is the reverse of removal.

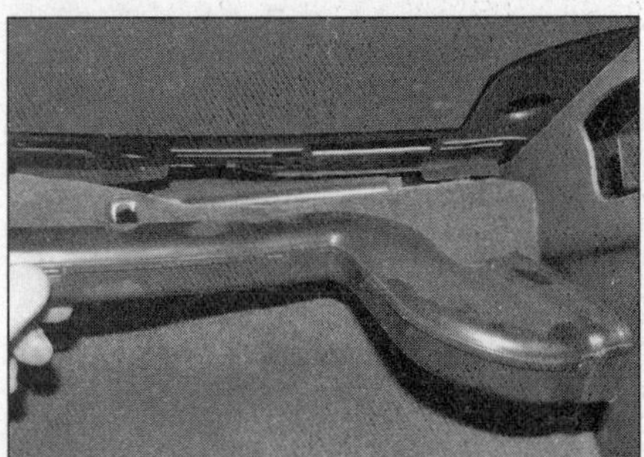
26.15 Unclip the air vent to the footwell

26.16a Pull back the door seal . . .

26.16b . . . remove the plastic cap . . .

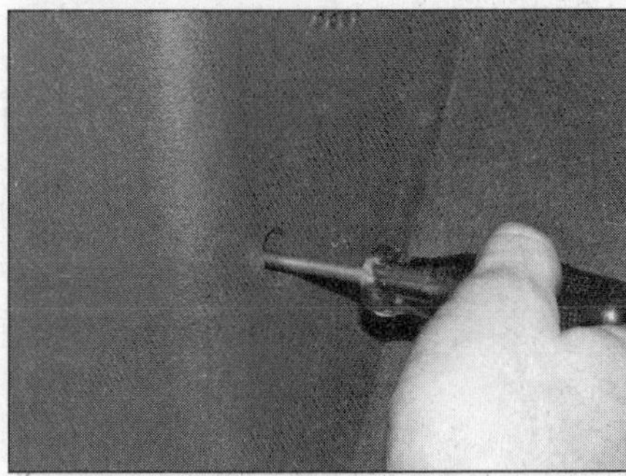
26.16c . . . and undo the retaining screw

26.17 Remove the lower trim panel

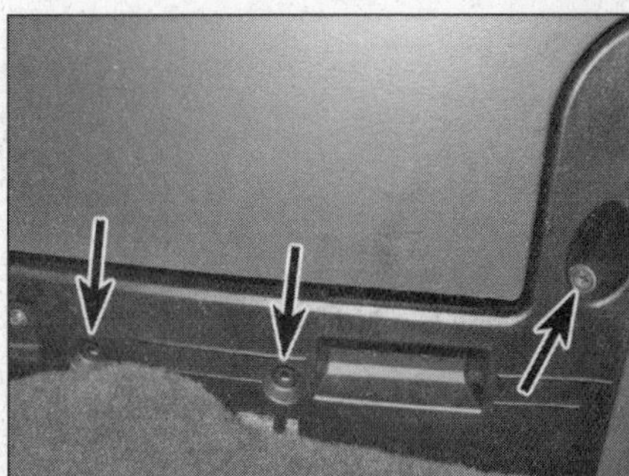
26.18 Undo the retaining screws – arrowed

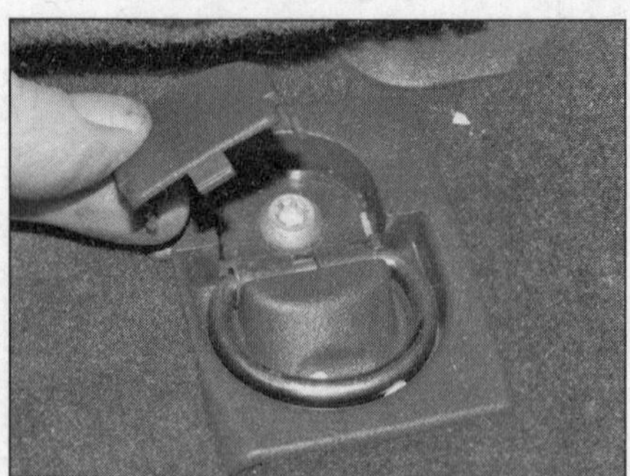
26.22 Unclip the cover to access the retaining screw

26.24a Grab handle retaining screw – arrowed

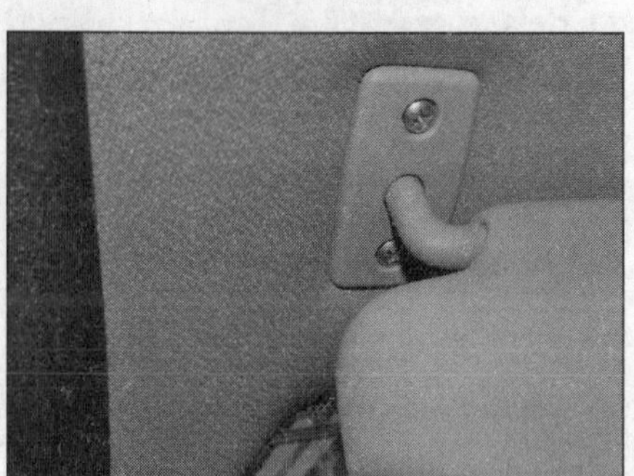
26.24b Sun visor retaining screws

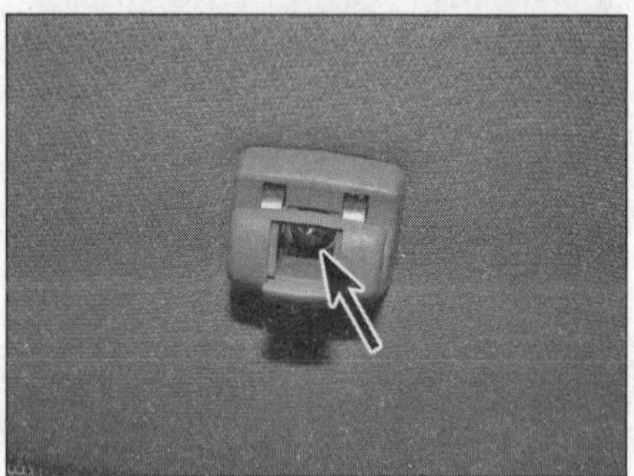
26.24c Sun visor retaining clip screw – arrowed

Carpets

22 The passenger compartment floor carpet is in one piece and is secured at its edges by screws or clips; usually the same fasteners are used to secure the various adjoining trim panels **(see illustration)**.

23 Carpet removal and refitting is reasonably straightforward but very time-consuming because all adjoining trim panels must be removed first, as must components such as the seats, the centre console and seat belt lower anchorages.

Headlining

24 The headlining is clipped to the roof and can be withdrawn only once all fittings such as the grab handles, sun visors, sunroof (if fitted), and related upper trim panels have been removed and the door, tailgate and sunroof aperture sealing strips have been prised clear. To remove the sun visors and grab handles the plastic covers have to be unclipped first, to gain access to the securing screws **(see illustrations)**.

25 Note that headlining removal requires considerable skill and experience if it is to be carried out without damage and is therefore best entrusted to an expert.

Interior mirror

26 The removal of the interior mirror is best left to a Mercedes-Benz dealer or specialist, as a special tool is used to remove the mirror from the windscreen. If the special tool is not used to remove the mirror from the mounting plate, then damage to the screen could occur.

27 On models fitted with rain sensor or automatic dimming, the trim can be unclipped from around the stem of the mirror and the wiring connectors disconnected. The mirror base is bonded to the windscreen with glass-metal adhesive.

27 Centre console – removal and refitting

Removal

1 Make sure the ignition switch is in the off position.

2 Unclip the trim panel from around the gear lever, with the gaiter lifted up, turn the gear lever knob mounting anti-clockwise and withdraw the trim and gaiter from the gear lever **(see illustrations)**. Where applicable, disconnect the wiring connector from under the trim panel as it is removed.

Models up to 28/02/01

3 Unclip the switch panel from the centre console and disconnect the wiring connector(s) as it is removed.

4 Using a thin screwdriver release the plastic cap, and then withdraw the locking pin from the handbrake lever **(see illustrations 27.14a and 27.14b)**. Discard the locking pin, as a new one will be required for refitting.

5 Withdraw the plastic handle off the handbrake lever and the lower plastic surround **(see illustrations 27.15a and 27.15b)**.

6 Where applicable, remove the cup holder from the rear of the centre console **(see illustration 27.18)**

7 On models without an armrest fitted, unclip the tray from the rear of the centre console and undo the retaining screw inside aperture.

8 On models with an armrest fitted, unclip the covers from each side of the armrest, then undo the three mounting bolts from the base of the armrest and remove it from the centre console **(illustrations 27.19a, 27.19b and 27.19c)**.

9 Move the front seats as far forward as possible and unclip the air vents from the rear of the centre console **(see illustration)**.

10 Move the seats as far backwards as possible, and unclip the front sides of the centre console from the footwell front trim panels.

11 Lift the centre console up at the rear and withdraw it from over the handbrake lever and out from the inside of the vehicle.

Models from 01/03/01

12 Unclip the ashtray cover from the front of the centre console, then slide the ashtray out

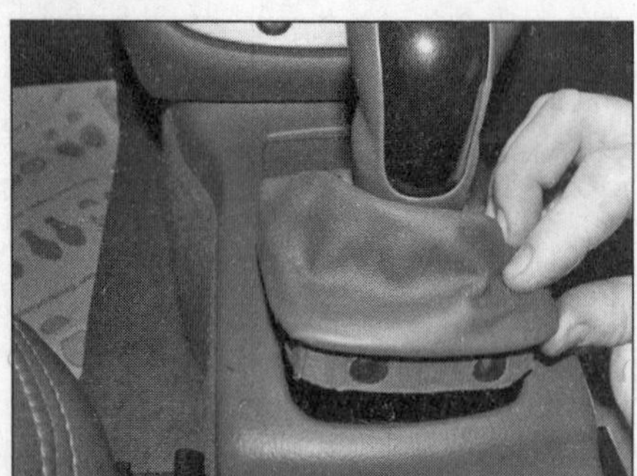
27.2a Unclip the gaiter and pull upwards . . .

27.2b . . . twist the mounting to remove the gear knob

27.9 Unclip the air vents from the console

27.12a Unclip the cover . . .

27.12b . . . slide the ashtray out . . .

27.12c . . . and disconnect the wiring connector

27.13 Undo the retaining screws – arrowed

27.14a Unclip the plastic cap . . .

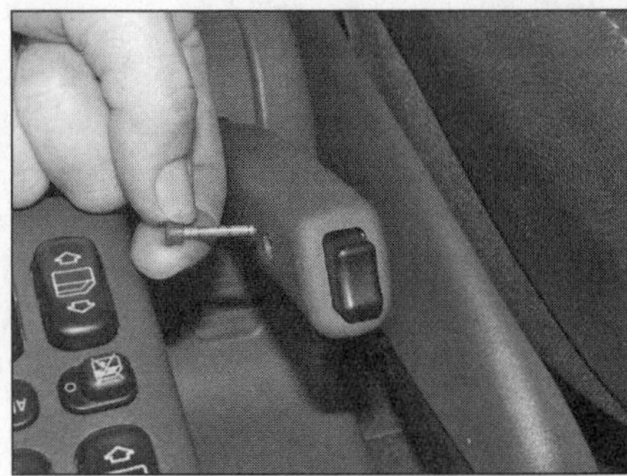
27.14b . . . and withdraw the pin

from its retaining clips and turn it a quarter of a turn and disconnect the wiring connector **(see illustrations)**.

13 Slacken and remove the two retaining screws from the front of the centre console **(see illustration)**.

14 Using a thin screwdriver release the

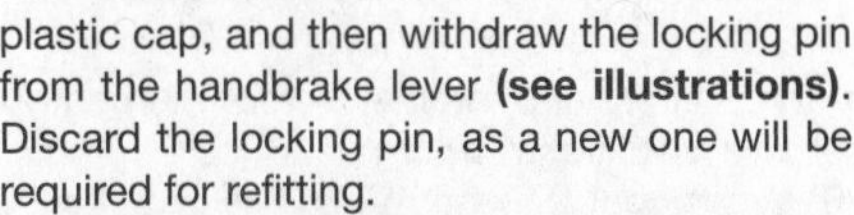
plastic cap, and then withdraw the locking pin from the handbrake lever **(see illustrations)**. Discard the locking pin, as a new one will be required for refitting.

15 Withdraw the plastic handle off the handbrake lever and the lower plastic surround **(see illustrations)**.

16 Move the front seats as far forward as possible, and unclip the air vents from the rear of the centre console **(see illustrations)**.

17 On models without an armrest fitted, lift out the rubber mat, undo the retaining screw and unclip the tray from the rear of the centre console **(see illustrations)**.

27.15a Withdraw the plastic handle . . .

27.15b . . . and the lower surround

27.16 Unclip the air vent from the console

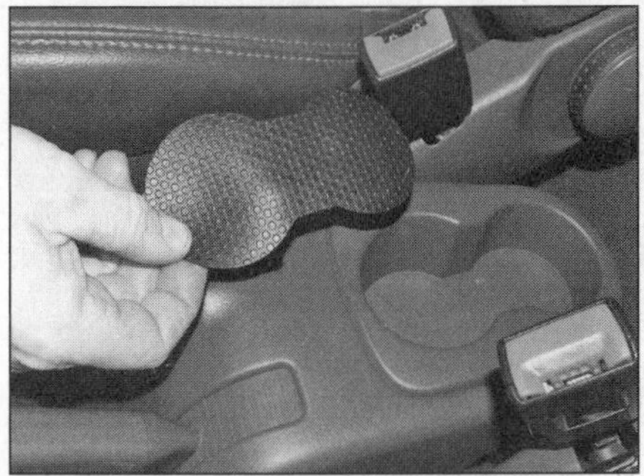
27.17a Remove the rubber mat . . .

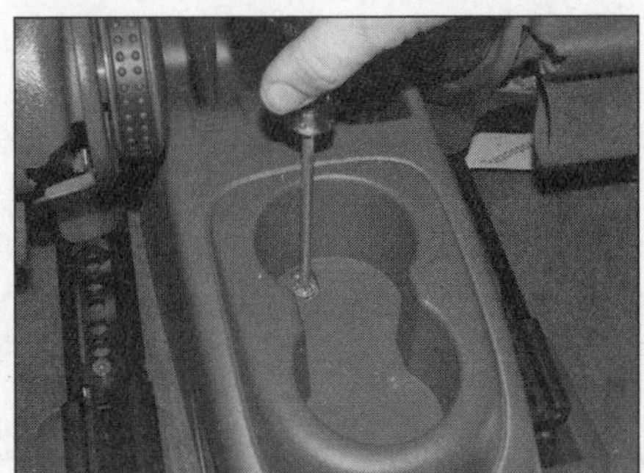
27.17b . . . undo the retaining screw . . .

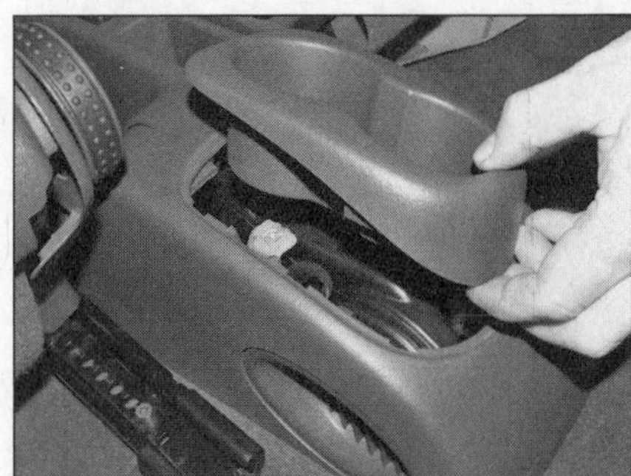
27.17c . . . and unclip the tray

27.18 Unclip the cup holder from the console

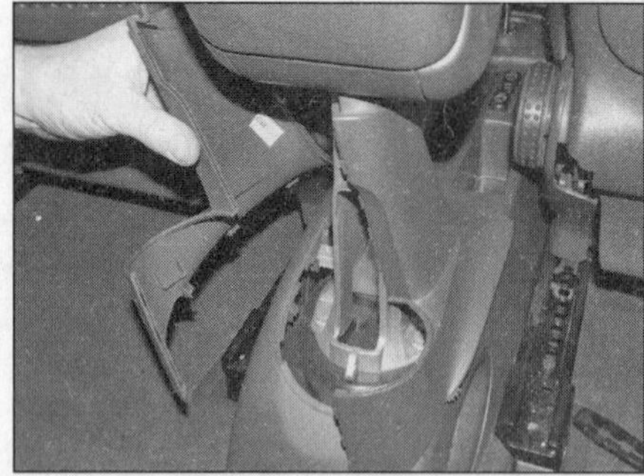
27.19a Unclip the covers . . .

27.19b . . . undo the retaining bolts . . .

27.19c . . . and remove the armrest

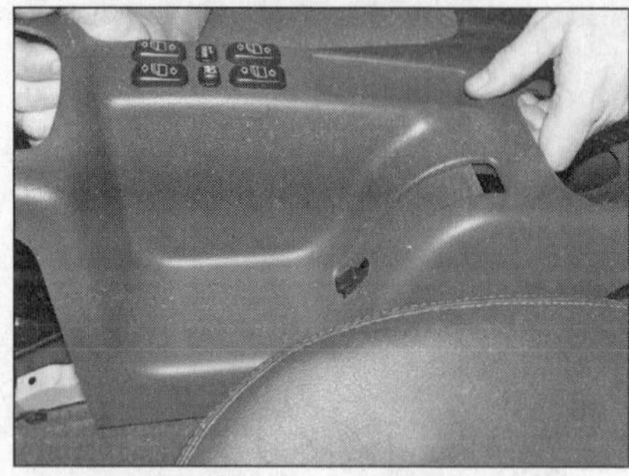
27.20a Lift the centre console out . . .

27.20b . . . disconnecting the wiring connectors – arrowed

18 On models with an armrest fitted, remove the cup holder from the rear of the centre console **(see illustration)**.

19 On models with an armrest fitted, unclip the covers from each side of the armrest, then undo the three mounting bolts from the base of the armrest and remove it from the centre console **(see illustrations)**.

20 Lift the out the centre console and reach under to disconnect the wiring connectors, and remove the centre console from inside the vehicle **(see illustrations)**.

Refitting

21 Refitting is a reversal of removal, making sure all the trim panels are correctly fitted and all wiring connectors are secure.

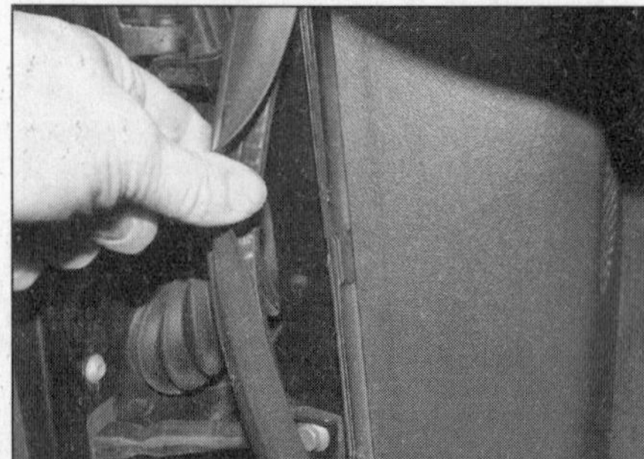
28.7 Pull back the door seals

28.8 Unclip the trim panels

28.9 Undo the upper retaining screw

28.10 Undo the left-hand retaining screw

28 Facia panels – removal and refitting

Note: *Refer to the warnings in Chapter 12 for airbags.*

Removal

1 Disconnect the battery negative lead (refer to *Disconnecting the battery* in the *Reference* Chapter at the end of this manual).

2 Remove the centre console as described in Section 27.

3 Remove the glovebox as described in Section 26.

4 Remove the instrument panel as described in Chapter 12.

5 Remove the steering wheel as described in Chapter 10.

6 Remove the heater control panel as described in Chapter 3.

7 Pull back the rubber door seals from the door apertures **(see illustration)**.

8 Unclip the upper trim panels from the top of the A-pillars **(see illustration)**.

9 Undo the retaining screw from inside the instrument panel aperture **(see illustration)**.

10 Undo the retaining screw from under the left-hand side of the upper facia trim panel **(see illustration)**.

28.11 Undo the two centre screws – arrowed

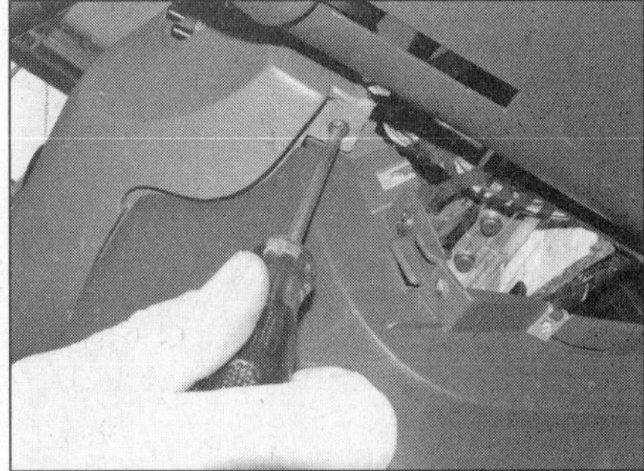

28.12 Undo the screw under the side of the steering column

28.13 Remove the upper trim panel from the vehicle

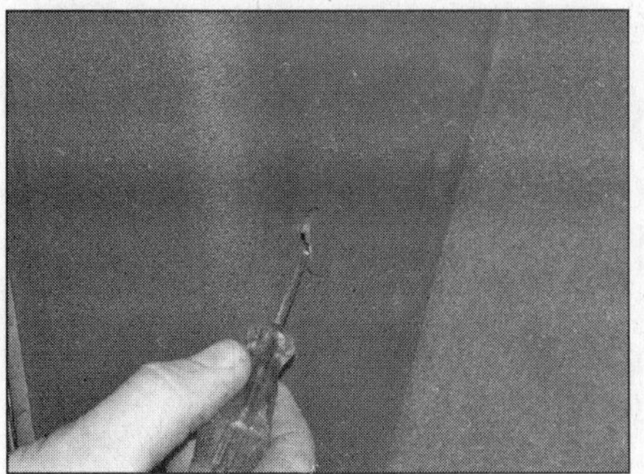

28.14a Unclip the plastic cap . . .

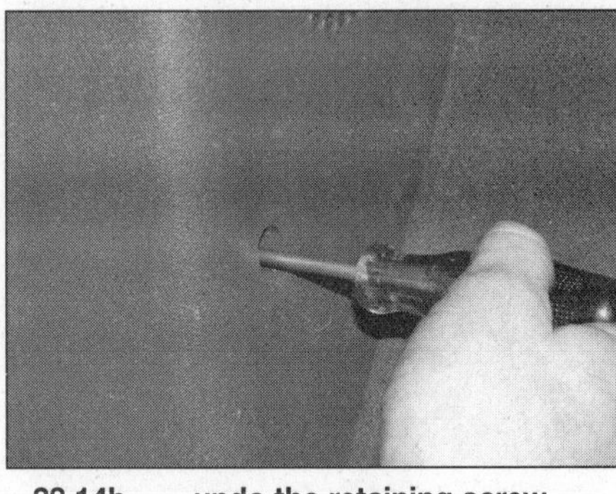

28.14b . . . undo the retaining screw . . .

28.14c . . . and remove the trim panel

11 Undo the two retaining screws from below the centre air vents **(see illustration)**.

12 Undo the retaining screw from under the upper facia trim panel next to the steering column cowling **(see illustration)**.

13 Lift the upper trim panel from the facia panel and disconnect the wiring connector as it is removed **(see illustration)**.

14 Remove the plastic cap, undo the retaining screw and unclip the footwell inner trim panel from the lower part of the A-pillar **(see illustrations)**.

15 Undo the retaining screws from each side of the facia **(see illustration)**.

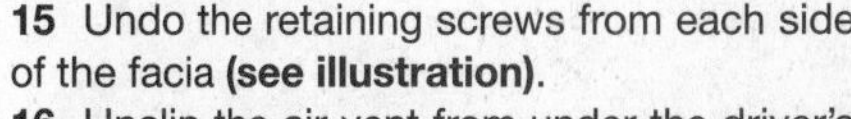

16 Unclip the air vent from under the driver's side of the facia panel below the steering column **(see illustration)**.

17 Unclip the trim from the light switch on the facia panel **(see illustration)**.

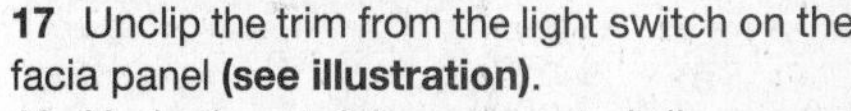

18 Undo the retaining screw and disconnect the bonnet release lever from the trim panel under the facia **(see illustration)**.

19 Undo the two retaining screws from the left-hand side of the trim panel **(see illustration)**.

20 Undo the retaining screw from above the light switch **(see illustration)**.

21 Withdraw the lower trim panel from the driver's side facia panel **(see illustration)**, disconnect the wiring connectors as the trim panel is removed.

28.15 Undo the screws from each end of the facia panel

28.16 Unclip the air vent under the facia

28.17 Unclip the light switch panel

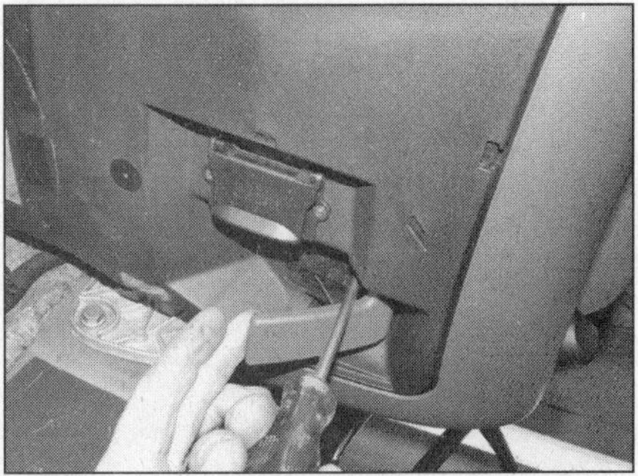

28.18 Undo the screw from the bonnet release lever

28.19 Undo the screws – arrowed

28.20 Undo the retaining screw . . .

28.21 . . . and lower the trim panel

28.22 Unclip the lower centre panel

28.23a Undo the retaining screws . . .

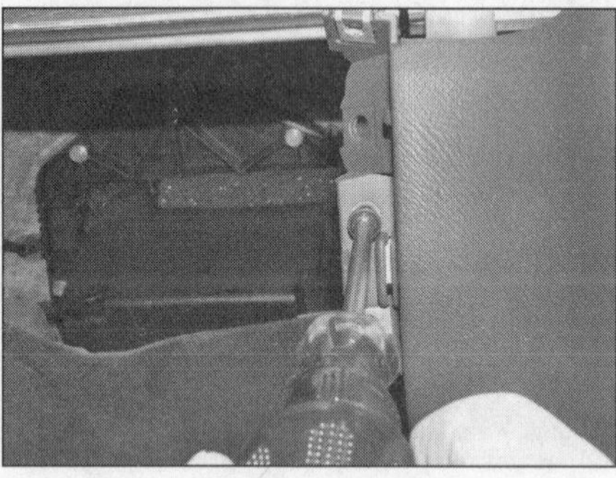
28.23b . . . at both sides of the centre console

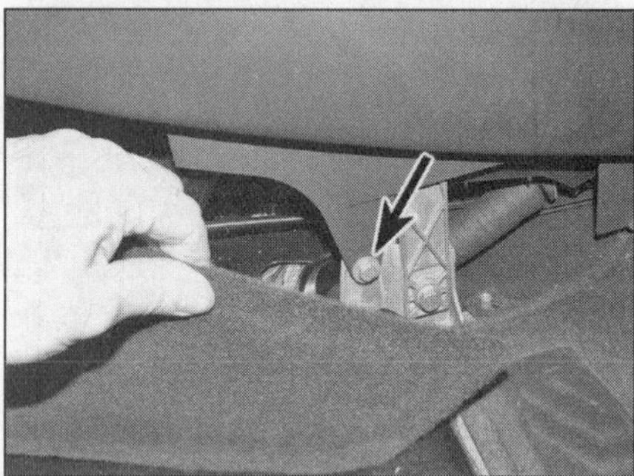
28.24 Undo the lower centre console retaining bolt - arrowed

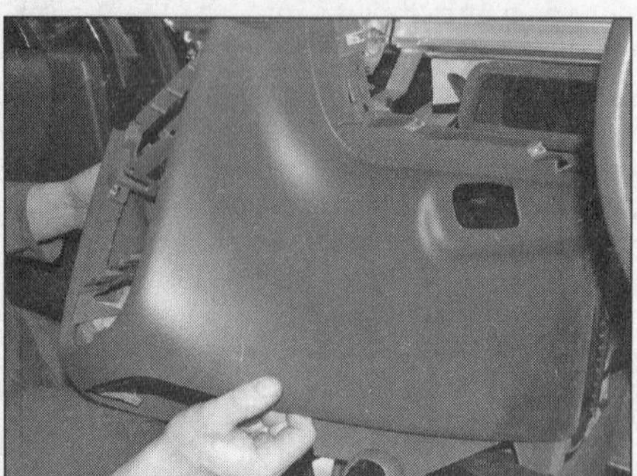
28.25 Withdraw the centre part of the facia panel

22 Unclip the trim panel from under the centre section of the facia panel **(see illustration)**.

23 Undo the retaining screws from each side of the centre section in the top corners **(see illustrations)**.

24 Undo the retaining bolts from each side of the lower part of the centre section **(see illustration)**.

25 Withdraw the centre section from the facia panel **(see illustration)**.

Refitting

26 Refitting is a reversal of the removal procedure, noting the following points:

a) *Ensure the facia panels are secure. Check that all wiring is routed as noted during removal.*

b) *On completion, reconnect the battery and check that all the electrical components and switches function correctly.*

Chapter 12
Body electrical systems

Contents

Degrees of difficulty

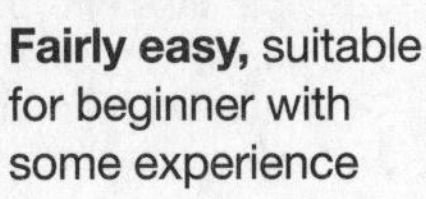

Easy, suitable for novice with little experience	**Fairly easy,** suitable for beginner with some experience	**Fairly difficult,** suitable for competent DIY mechanic	**Difficult,** suitable for experienced DIY mechanic	**Very difficult,** suitable for expert DIY or professional

Specifications

System type	12 volt negative earth	
Fuses	See *Wiring diagrams* on page 12•22	
Bulbs	**Wattage**	**Type**
Brake lights	21	Bayonet
Direction indicators	21	Bayonet
Direction indicator wing repeaters	5	Wedge
Glovebox light	10	festoon
Headlight:		
Main beam/foglights	60/55	H4
Dipped beam	55	H7
High-level brake light (x4)	5	Wedge
Interior lights	10	Festoon
Number plate light	5	Festoon
Rear fog/tail light	21/4	Bayonet
Reversing light	21	Bayonet
Sidelight	5	Wedge

Torque wrench setting	**Nm**	**lbf ft**
Passenger airbag mounting bolts	10	7

1 General information and precautions

Warning: *Before carrying out any work on the electrical system, read through the` precautions given in 'Safety first!' at the beginning of this manual, and in Chapter 5A.*

The electrical system is of 12 volt negative earth type. Power for the lights and all electrical accessories is supplied by a lead-acid type battery, which is charged by the alternator.

This Chapter covers repair and service procedures for the various electrical components not associated with the engine. Information on the battery, alternator and starter motor can be found in Chapter 5A.

It should be noted that prior to working on any component in the electrical system, the ignition and all electrical consumers must be switched off. Additionally, where stated, the battery negative lead must be disconnected, however, note the information given in *Disconnecting the battery* in the *Reference* section at the end of this manual, as special procedures have to be carried out when reconnecting the battery.

2 Electrical fault finding - general information

Note: *Refer to the precautions given in 'Safety first!' and in Chapter 5A before starting work. The following tests relate to testing of the main electrical circuits, and should not be used to test delicate electronic circuits (such as anti-lock braking systems), particularly where an electronic control module is used.*

General

1 A typical electrical circuit consists of an electrical component; any switches, relays, motors, fuses, fusible links or circuit breakers related to that component, and the wiring and connectors which link the component to both the battery and the chassis. To help to pinpoint a problem in an electrical circuit, wiring diagrams are included at the end of this Chapter. **Note:** *Many of the circuits are controlled by computerised systems, so before assuming there are faults, it is worthwhile checking if specific conditions apply.*

2 Before attempting to diagnose an electrical fault, first study the appropriate wiring diagram to obtain a complete understanding of the components included in the particular circuit concerned. The possible sources of a fault can be narrowed down by noting if other components related to the circuit are operating properly. If several components or circuits fail at one time, the problem is likely to be related to a shared fuse or earth connection.

3 Electrical problems usually stem from simple causes, such as loose or corroded connections, a faulty earth connection, a blown fuse, a melted fusible link, or a faulty relay (refer to Section 3 for details of testing relays). Visually inspect the condition of all fuses, wires and connections in a problem circuit before testing the components. Use the wiring diagrams to determine which terminal connections will need to be checked in order to pinpoint the trouble spot.

4 The basic tools required for electrical fault finding include a circuit tester or voltmeter (a 12 volt bulb with a set of test leads can also be used for certain tests); a self-powered test light (sometimes known as a continuity tester); an ohmmeter (to measure resistance); a battery and set of test leads; and a jumper wire, preferably with a circuit breaker or fuse incorporated, which can be used to bypass suspect wires or electrical components. Before attempting to locate a problem with test instruments, use the wiring diagram to determine where to make the connections.

5 To find the source of an intermittent wiring fault (usually due to a poor or dirty connection, or damaged wiring insulation), a wiggle test can be performed on the wiring. This involves wiggling the wiring by hand to see if the fault occurs as the wiring is moved. It should be possible to narrow down the source of the fault to a particular section of wiring. This method of testing can be used in conjunction with any of the tests described in the following sub-Sections.

6 Apart from problems due to poor connections, two basic types of fault can occur in an electrical circuit – open-circuit, or short-circuit.

7 Open-circuit faults are caused by a break somewhere in the circuit, which prevents current from flowing. An open-circuit fault will prevent a component from working, but will not cause the relevant circuit fuse to blow.

8 Short-circuit faults are caused by a short somewhere in the circuit, which allows the current flowing in the circuit to escape along an alternative route, usually to earth. Short-circuit faults are normally caused by a breakdown in wiring insulation, which allows a feed wire to touch either another wire, or an earthed component such as the bodyshell. A short-circuit fault will normally cause the relevant circuit fuse to blow.

Finding an open-circuit

9 To check for an open-circuit, connect one lead of a circuit tester or voltmeter to either the negative battery terminal or a known good earth.

10 Connect the other lead to a connector in the circuit being tested, preferably nearest to the battery or fuse.

11 Switch on the circuit, bearing in mind that some circuits are live only when the ignition switch is moved to a particular position.

12 If voltage is present (indicated either by the tester bulb lighting or a voltmeter reading, as applicable), this means that the section of the circuit between the relevant connector and the battery is problem-free.

13 Continue to check the remainder of the circuit in the same fashion.

14 When a point is reached at which no voltage is present, the problem must lie between that point and the previous test point with voltage. Most problems can be traced to a broken, corroded or loose connection.

Finding a short-circuit

15 To check for a short-circuit; first disconnect the load(s) from the circuit (loads are the components which draw current from a circuit, such as bulbs, motors, heating elements, etc).

16 Remove the relevant fuse from the circuit, and connect a circuit tester or voltmeter to the fuse connections.

17 Switch on the circuit, bearing in mind that some circuits are live only when the ignition switch is moved to a particular position.

18 If voltage is present (indicated either by the tester bulb lighting or a voltmeter reading, as applicable), this means that there is a short circuit.

19 If no voltage is present, but the fuse still blows with the load(s) connected, this indicates an internal fault in the load(s).

Finding an earth fault

20 The battery negative terminal is connected to earth – the metal of the engine/transmission and the car body – and most systems are wired so that they only receive a positive feed, the current returning through the metal of the car body. This means that the component mounting and the body form part of that circuit. Loose or corroded mountings can therefore cause a range of electrical faults, ranging from total failure of a circuit, to a puzzling partial fault. In particular, lights may shine dimly (especially when another circuit sharing the same earth point is in operation), motors (eg, wiper motors or the radiator cooling fan motor) may run slowly, and the operation of one circuit may have an apparently unrelated effect on another. Note that on many vehicles, earth straps are used between certain components, such as the engine/transmission and the body, usually where there is no metal-to-metal contact between components due to flexible rubber mountings, etc.

21 To check whether a component is properly earthed, disconnect the battery (refer to the warnings given in the Reference section at the rear of the manual) and connect one lead of an ohmmeter to a known good earth point. Connect the other lead to the wire or earth connection being tested. The resistance reading should be zero; if not, check the connection as follows.

22 If an earth connection is thought to be faulty, dismantle the connection and clean back to bare metal both the bodyshell and the wire terminal or the component earth connection mating surface. Be careful to remove all traces of dirt and corrosion, and then use a knife to trim away any paint, so that a clean metal-to-metal joint is made.

On reassembly, tighten the joint fasteners securely; if a wire terminal is being refitted, use serrated washers between the terminal and the bodyshell to ensure a clean and secure connection. When the connection is remade, prevent the onset of corrosion in the future by applying a coat of petroleum jelly or silicone-based grease or by spraying on (at regular intervals) a proprietary ignition sealer or a water dispersant lubricant.

3 Fuses and relays – general information

Fuses and relays

1 Fuses are designed to break a circuit when a predetermined current is reached, in order to protect the components and wiring, which could be damaged by excessive current flow. Any excessive current flow will be due to a fault in the circuit, usually a short-circuit (see Section 2).

2 The main fuses are located in the fusebox under the driver's side footwell next to the battery; open the driver's door and remove the floor panel cover to gain access to the battery and fuses **(see illustration)**.

3 The lighting fuses are located in the right-hand end of the facia panel **(see illustration)**; their locations are marked onto the rear of the fusebox cover.

4 To remove a fuse, first switch off the circuit concerned (or the ignition), and then pull the fuse out of its terminals. Mercedes-Benz supply an information sheet for the location of fuses and relays, which is located inside the battery/fuse box **(see illustration)**.

5 The wire within the fuse should be visible; if the fuse has blown it will be broken or melted.

6 Always renew a fuse with one of the correct rating; never use a fuse with a different rating from that specified.

7 Refer to the wiring diagrams for details of the fuse ratings and the circuits protected. The fuse rating is stamped on the top of the fuse; the fuses are also colour-coded as follows.

Colour	Rating
Light brown	5A
Brown	7.5A
Red	10A
Blue	15A
Yellow	20A
White or clear	25A
Green	30A
Orange	40A

8 Never renew a fuse more than once without tracing the source of the trouble. If the new fuse blows immediately, find the cause before renewing it again; a short to earth as a result of faulty insulation is most likely. Where a fuse protects more than one circuit, try to isolate the fault by switching on each circuit in turn (where possible) until the fuse blows again. Always carry a supply of spare fuses of each relevant rating on the vehicle.

3.2 Fuses and relays inside the battery box

9 Additional relays are located in the ECM storage box, which is located on the left-hand side of the engine compartment. Undo the retaining screws and remove the cover to gain access **(see illustrations)**. **Note:** *On diesel models, it will be necessary to remove the glow plug control unit from the lower part of the compartment to access the relays (see Chapter 5C).*

Relays

10 A relay is an electrically-operated switch which is used for the following reasons:

a) A relay can switch a heavy current remotely from the circuit in which the current is flowing, allowing the use of lighter-gauge wiring and switch contacts.

b) A relay can receive more than one control input, unlike a mechanical switch.

c) A relay can have a timer function – for example, the intermittent wiper relay.

11 Most of the relays are located in the battery box below the driver's side floor panel, however, additional relays are located in the engine compartment ECM storage box, see paragraph 9 in this Section.

12 Identification details of the relays are given at the start of the wiring diagrams.

13 If a circuit or system controlled by a relay develops a fault, and the relay is suspect, operate the system. If the relay is functioning, it should be possible to hear it click as it is energised. If this is the case, the fault lies with the components or wiring of the system. If the relay is not being energised, then either the relay is not receiving a main supply or a switching voltage, or the relay itself is faulty.

3.9a Remove the ECM cover . . .

3.3 Lighting fuses in end of facia

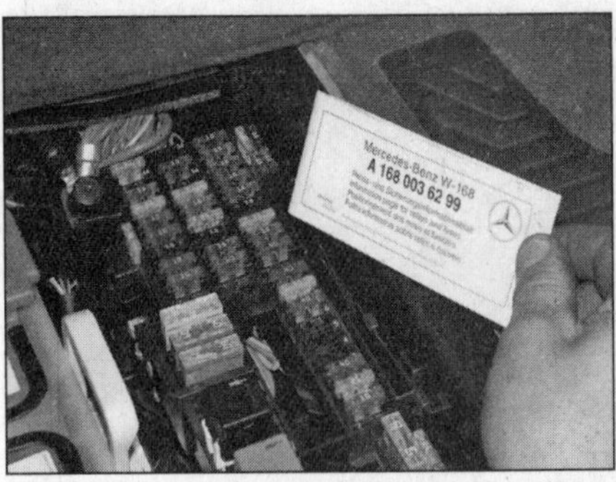

3.4 Information sheet for location of fuses and relays

Testing is by the substitution of a known good unit, but be careful – while some relays are identical in appearance and in operation, others look similar but perform different functions.

14 To remove a relay, first ensure that the relevant circuit is switched off. The relay can then simply be pulled out from the socket, and pushed back into position.

4 Switches – removal and refitting

Ignition switch

1 Refer to Chapter 10.

Wiper/indicator/main beam and cruise control switches

2 Switch off the ignition and all electrical consumers and remove the ignition key.

3.9b . . . and find relays located in the lower, rear of the compartment

4.4a Undo the retaining screws – arrowed

4.4b . . . and remove the contact unit

4.5 Remove the cruise control lever – where fitted

4.6 Undo the retaining screws and remove the switch

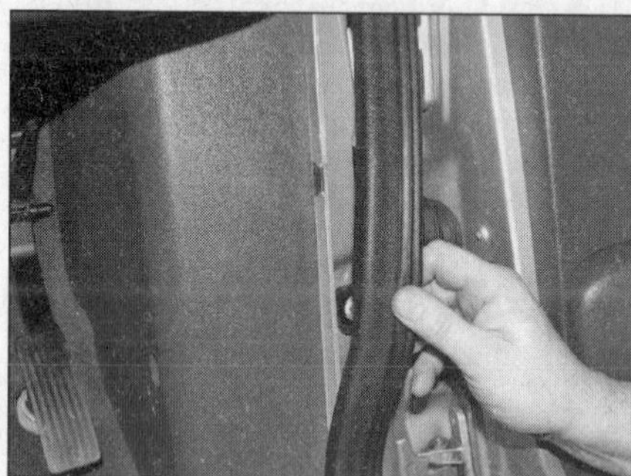
4.9 Pull the door seal back . . .

3 Check that the front wheels are pointing straight-ahead and the steering wheel is in its centre position, then remove the steering wheel as described in Chapter 10.

4 With the steering still in the straight-ahead position, slacken the two airbag contact unit retaining screws, and withdraw the unit from the steering column **(see illustrations)**. **Note:** *Do not turn the airbag contact unit, while it is off the vehicle, as it has a spring inside which will need to be refitted in the same position. See Section 24 for further information.*

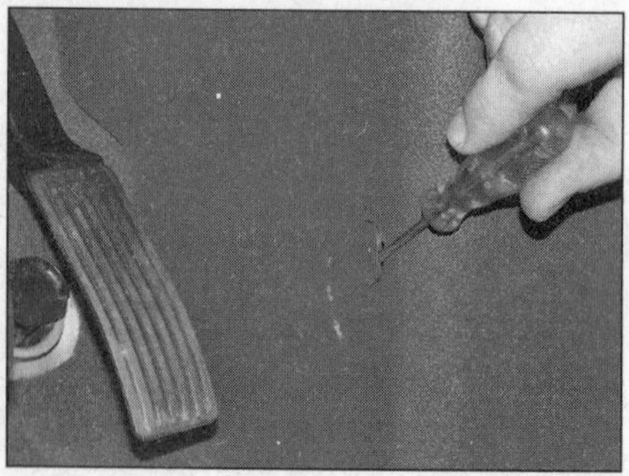
4.10a . . . unclip the plastic cap . . .

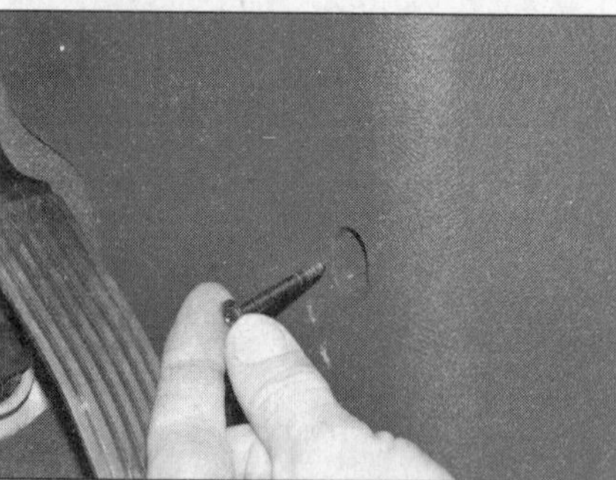
4.10b . . . and remove the retaining screw

4.16 Unclip the plastic surround

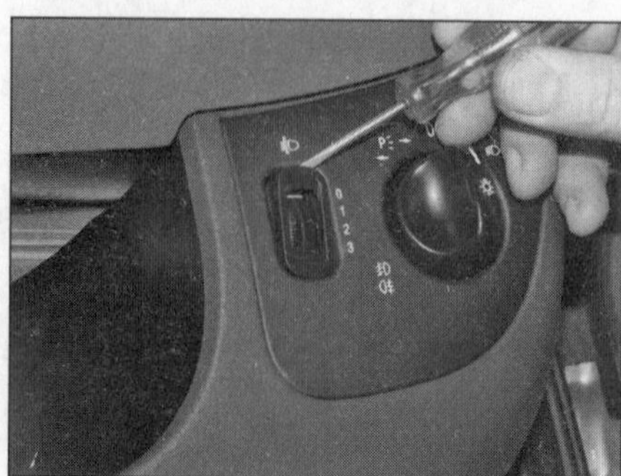
4.20 Carefully unclip the surround

5 On models with cruise control, undo the retaining screws and remove the switch lever from the top of the steering column **(see illustration)**.

6 Slacken and remove the retaining screws from the combination switch and remove it from the top of the steering column **(see illustration)**. **Note:** *The length of the screws may vary; check the length when removing, for correct refitting.*

7 Refitting is a reversal of removal.

Lighting switch

8 Release the steering wheel adjustment handle, and set it in the lowest position.

9 Carefully pull the door seal rubber from the trim panel on the driver's side of the vehicle **(see illustration)**.

10 Using a small screwdriver, unclip the plastic plug and remove the screw securing the trim panel **(see illustrations)**. Unclip and remove the trim panel from the driver's side footwell.

Models up to 28/02/01

11 Unclip the air vent adjustment wheel from the end of the facia panel.

12 Undo the two retaining screws (one each side of the steering column) in the air vent trim from under the instrument panel.

13 Unclip the air vent cover from the right-hand side of the facia and under the instrument panel, taking care not to damage the trim.

14 Undo the retaining screw from the outside edge of the facia panel, and the screw from above the light switch unit.

15 Lower the panel slightly to access the back of the switch, and disconnect the wiring connector.

16 Carefully unclip the cover from around the headlight height adjuster switch **(see illustration)**.

17 Working under the lower trim panel, undo the two retaining screws from each side of the bonnet release lever and pass it through the panel.

18 Undo the remaining screws and remove the lower trim panel from inside the vehicle.

19 Unclip the cover from around the headlight switches.

Models from 01/03/01

20 Carefully unclip the cover from around the headlight height adjuster switch **(see illustration)**.

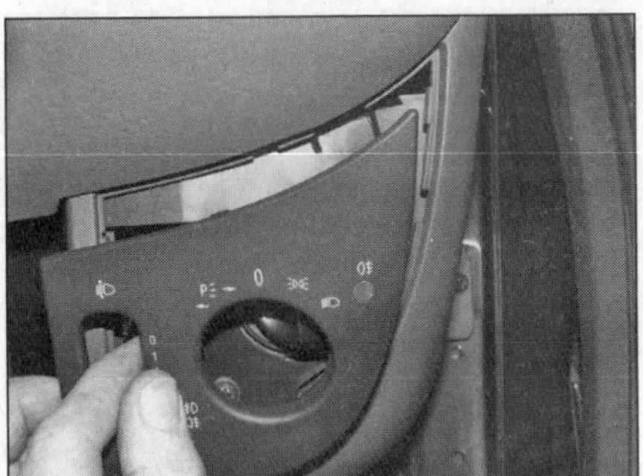
4.21a Unclip the light switch trim panel . . .

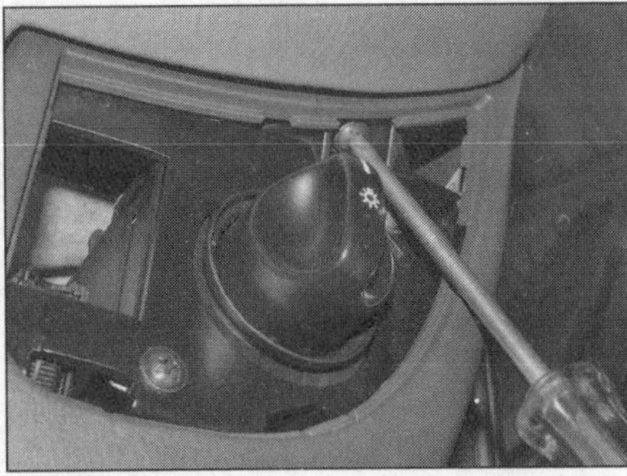
4.21b . . . and undo the retaining screw

4.22 Unclip the air duct

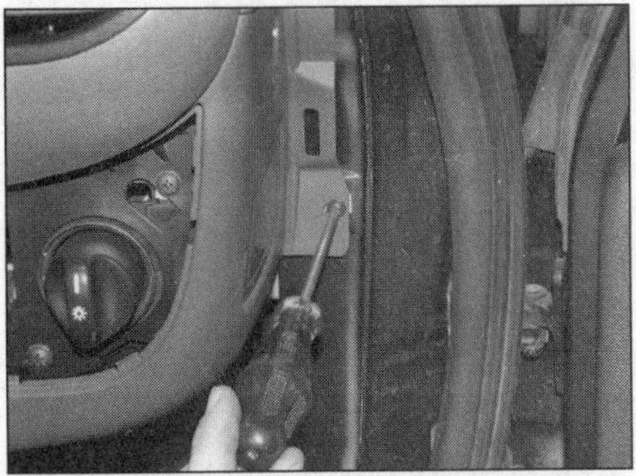
4.23 Undo the facia retaining screw

4.24a Remove trim panel retaining screws – arrowed . . .

4.24b . . . and lower the trim panel

21 Unclip the cover from around the headlight switch, and remove the retaining screw **(see illustrations)**.

22 Unclip the air duct from under the lower trim panel **(see illustration)**.

23 Undo the retaining screw from the outside edge of the facia panel **(see illustration)**.

24 Working under the lower trim panel, undo the two retaining screws from the lower trim panel **(see illustrations)**.

25 Lower the trim panel and disconnect the wiring connectors, also slide the locking lever and disconnect the diagnostic connector **(see illustrations)**.

26 Undo the retaining screw for the bonnet release lever and remove the lever from the trim panel **(see illustration)**.

All models

27 Unclip the fuse cover from the side of the facia trim panel **(see illustration)**.

28 Undo the two retaining screws and remove the light switch unit from the lower trim panel **(see illustration)**.

29 Refitting is a reversal of removal.

Headlamp range control

30 The headlamp height/range control switch is part of the main lighting switch, remove the lighting switch as described in paragraphs 8 to 28, as applicable.

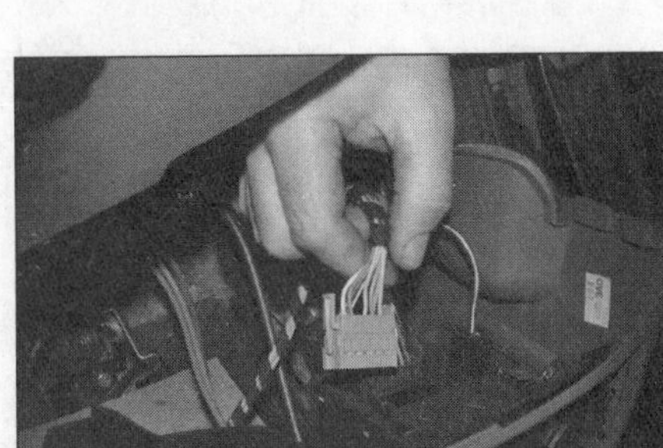

4.25a Disconnect the light switch wiring connectors . . .

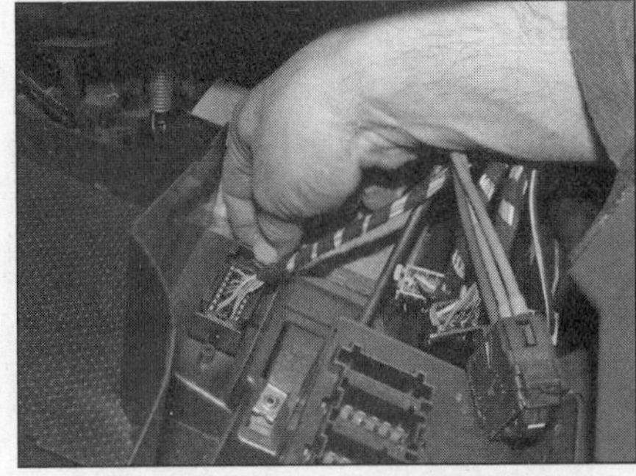
4.25b . . . and unclip the diagnostic connector wiring plug

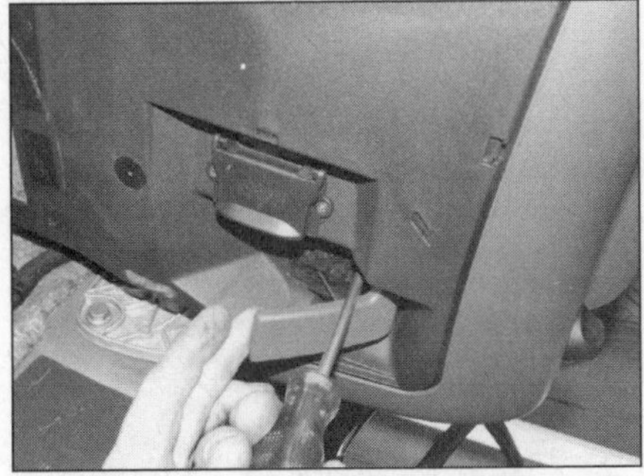
4.26 Undo the bonnet release lever retaining screw

4.27 Unclip the light fusebox cover

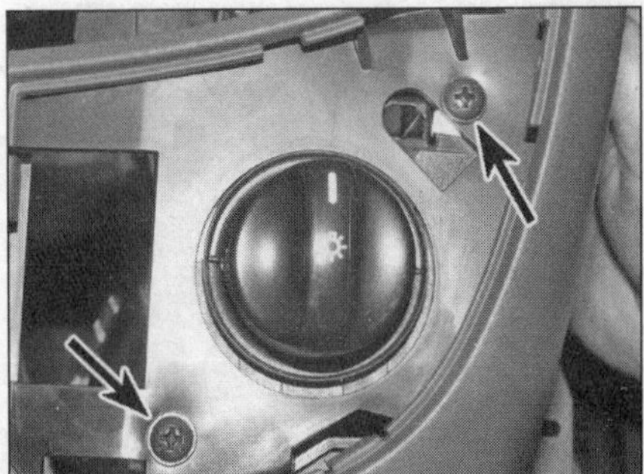
4.28 Light switch retaining screws – arrowed

4.40 Withdraw the storage compartment

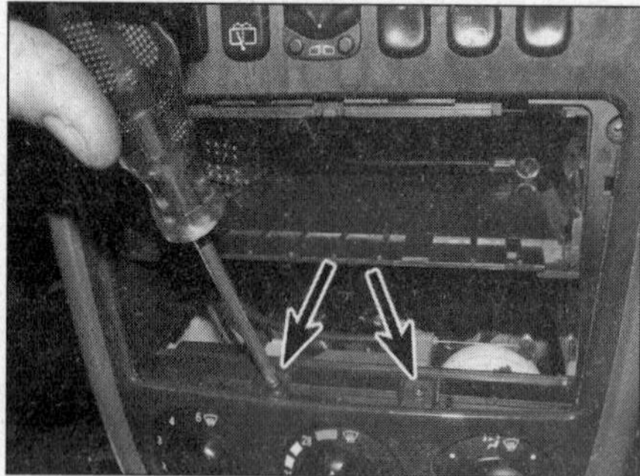
4.41a Undo the retaining screws – arrowed . . .

4.41b . . . and remove the front trim panel

Heated seat, air conditioning, rear window wiper, exterior mirrors, ESP, heated rear window and alarm motion sensor switches

31 Disconnect the battery negative lead and position it away from the terminal. **Note:** *Before disconnecting the battery, refer to 'Disconnecting the battery' in the reference section at the rear of this manual.*
32 Remove the radio as described in Section 19.

Models up to 28/02/01

33 Remove the trim panels from around the side air vents and along the facia panel with reference to Chapter 11.
34 Undo the retaining screw from inside the radio aperture, at the top centre.
35 Unclip the storage compartment, and pull it out from the facia panel.
36 Undo the four retaining screws (two at the top and two at the bottom), and remove the centre cover from the facia panel.
37 As the cover is removed, disconnect the wiring connector from the rear of the hazard warning light switch.
38 Release the retaining clips and unclip the row of switches from the rear of the cover.
39 Refitting is a reversal of removal.

Models from 01/03/01

40 Unclip the storage compartment, and pull it out from the facia panel **(see illustration)**.
41 Undo the two retaining screws from inside the aperture, at the top of the heater switch control unit **(see illustrations)**.
42 As the cover is removed, disconnect the wiring connector from the rear of the group of switches **(see illustration)**.
43 Release the retaining clips and unclip the row of switches from the rear of the cover.
44 Refitting is a reversal of removal.

4.42 Disconnect the wiring connectors from the switch panel

4.52 Unclip the switch from the door panel

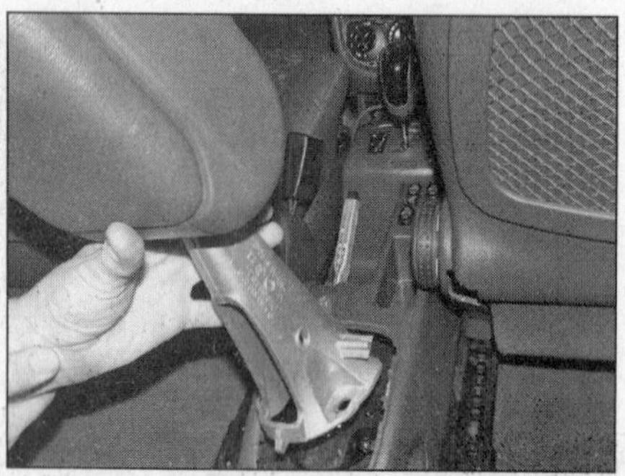
4.55 Unbolt and remove the armrest

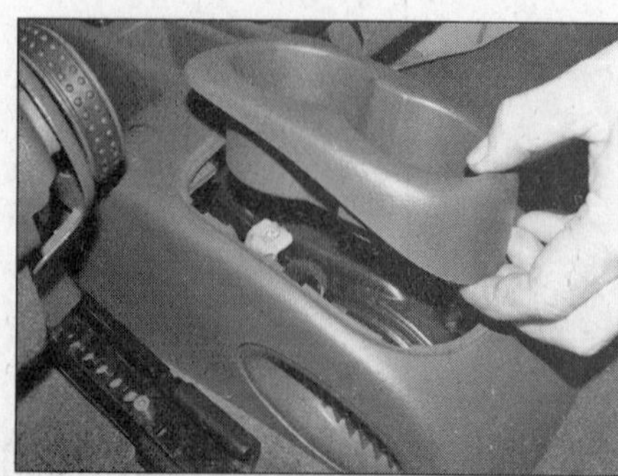
4.56 Undo the retaining screw and lift out the cup holder

Hazard warning and door locking switches

45 Remove the central switch panel as described in paragraphs 31 to 43, as applicable.
46 The switch can then be unclipped from the facia panel, and disconnect the wiring connector as it is removed
47 Refitting is a reversal of removal.

Selector W/S, electric window and door locking switches

Centre console switches

48 Remove the centre console as described in Chapter 11.
49 Release the locking lugs and remove the switches from the centre console trim panel.
50 Refitting is a reversal of removal.

Door switches

51 Remove the door trim panel as described in Chapter 11.
52 Release the locking lugs and unclip the switch from the inside of the trim panel **(see illustration)**.
53 Refitting is a reversal of removal.

Heater blower motor switch

54 The switch is integral with the heater control panel, and cannot be removed separately. Refer to Chapter 3 for details of heater control panel removal and refitting.

Handbrake 'on' warning switch

55 On models wit ah centre armrest, unclip the covers, and then undo the retaining bolts and remove the armrest from the rear of the centre console **(see illustration)**.
56 On models a without centre armrest, remove the rubber mat from the rear cup holder at the rear of the centre console, undo the retaining screw and lift out the cup holder **(see illustration)**.
57 Unclip the brake light switch from the handbrake mounting bracket and disconnect the wiring connector **(see illustration)**.
58 Refitting is a reversal of removal.

Brake light switch

59 Refer to Chapter 9.

Reversing light switch

60 Refer to Chapter 7A.

Courtesy light switches

61 Open the door and unclip the light switch from the door pillar, disconnect the wiring connector as it is removed **(see illustration)**.

Luggage area light switch

62 Open the tailgate and unclip the light switch from the lower edge of the tailgate next to the lock catch, disconnect the wiring connector as it is removed **(see illustrations)**.

Glovebox light switch

63 The light switch is part of the glovebox light unit, as the lid is opened it operates the switch. See Section 6 for the light removal and refitting procedure.

Fuel filler flap release switch

64 The fuel filler flap release is operated pneumatically; see Chapter 11, Section 18.

Rain sensor

65 Switch off the ignition and all electrical consumers and remove the ignition key.

66 Where fitted, the windscreen wipers are automatically activated when droplets of water are detected by the rain sensor, located in the front of the interior mirror base. Remove the mirror base covers, and disconnect the wiring plug.

67 Remove the interior mirror as described in Chapter 11.

5 Bulbs (exterior lights) – renewal

General

1 Whenever a bulb is renewed, note the following points:

a) Switch off the ignition and all electrical consumers before commencing work.
b) Remember that if the light has just been in use the bulb may be extremely hot.
c) Always check the bulb contacts and holder, ensuring that there is clean metal-to-metal contact. Clean off any corrosion or dirt before fitting a new bulb.
d) Wherever bayonet-type bulbs are fitted ensure that the spring-tensioned arms bear firmly against the bulb contacts.
e) Always ensure that the new bulb is of the correct rating and that it is thoroughly clean before fitting it.

2 Switch off the ignition and all electrical consumers and remove the ignition key.

Headlight main beam/foglight

Note: *Do not touch the glass envelope of the bulb if it is to be re-used. This bulb is a double filament bulb, which is for main beam and front foglight.*

3 Working in the engine compartment, remove the plastic cover from the rear of the headlight **(see illustration)**.

4 Disconnect the wiring plug from the rear of the bulb, then unhook and release the ends of the bulb retaining clip from the light unit and withdraw the bulb **(see illustrations)**.

5 When handling the new bulb, use a tissue or clean cloth to avoid touching the glass with the fingers; moisture and grease from the skin can cause blackening and rapid failure of this type of bulb. If the glass is accidentally touched, wipe it clean using methylated spirit.

6 Install the new bulb, ensuring that its

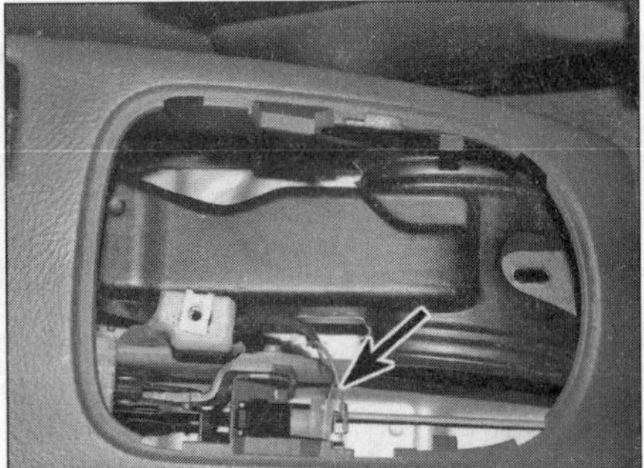

4.57 Handbrake light switch – arrowed

4.61 Disconnecting the wiring connector

4.62a Unclip the switch from the tailgate . . .

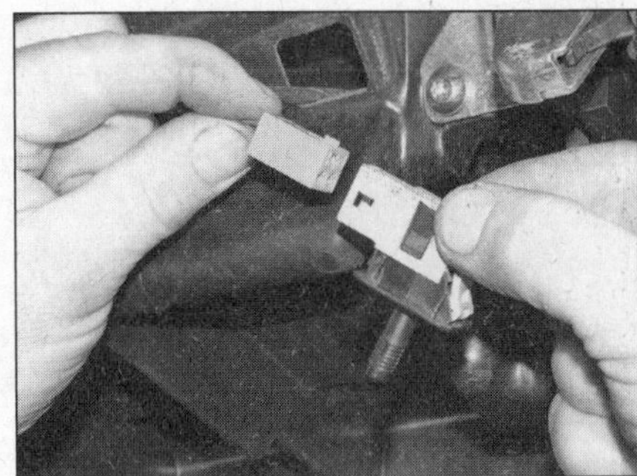

4.62b . . . and disconnect the connector

5.3 Unclip the plastic cover

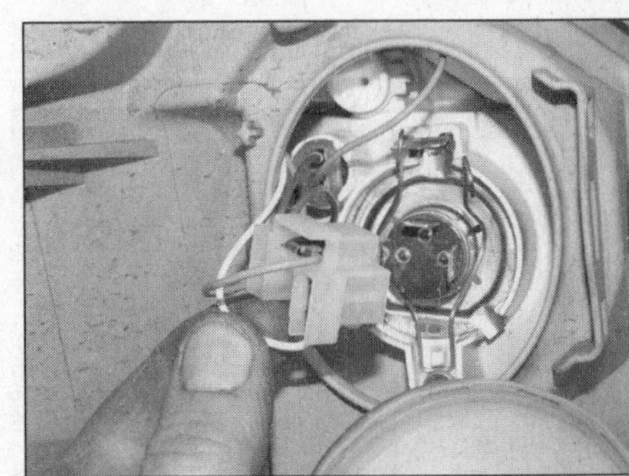

5.4a Disconnect the wiring connector . . .

5.4b . . . release the spring clip . . .

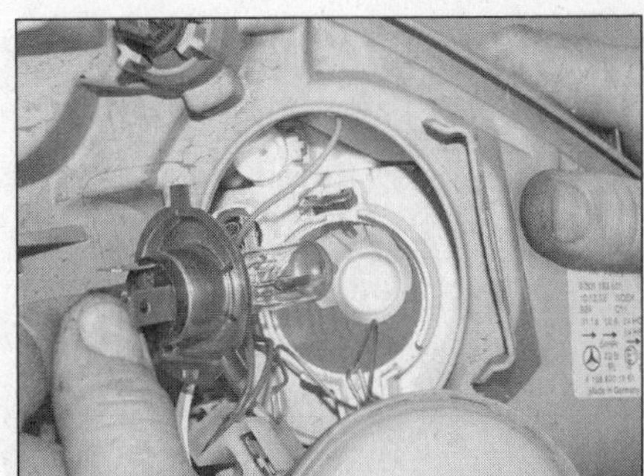

5.4c . . . and remove the bulb

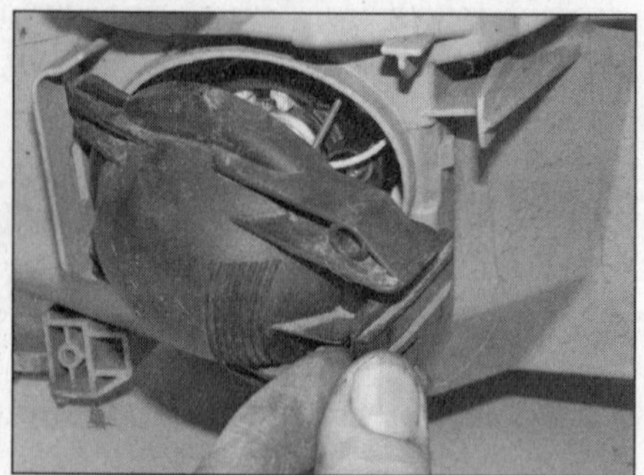
5.8 Unclip the plastic cover

5.9a Disconnect the wiring connector . . .

5.9b . . . rotate the locking ring . . .

location tabs are correctly located in the cut-outs, and secure it in position with the retaining clip.

7 Reconnect the wiring plug, and refit the headlight bulb plastic cover, making sure that it is secure.

5.15a Remove the bulbholder . . .

5.9c . . . and remove the bulb

Headlight dip beam

Note: *Do not touch the glass envelope of the bulb if it is to be re-used. This bulb is a single filament bulb, which is for dip beam only.*

8 Working in the engine compartment, remove the plastic cover from the rear of the headlight **(see illustration).**

9 Disconnect the wiring plug from the rear of the bulb, then turn the locking ring anti-clockwise and withdraw the bulb **(see illustrations).**

10 When handling the new bulb, use a tissue or clean cloth to avoid touching the glass with the fingers; moisture and grease from the skin can cause blackening and rapid failure of this type of bulb. If the glass is accidentally touched, wipe it clean using methylated spirit.

11 Fit the new bulb to the bulbholder, and turn the locking ring clockwise to lock the bulb in position.

12 Reconnect the wiring plug, and refit the headlight bulb plastic cover, making sure that it is secure.

Front foglight

13 The front foglight uses the same bulb as the headlight main beam; see paragraphs 3 to 7 for the removal and refitting procedure.

Front sidelight

14 Working in the engine compartment, remove the plastic cover from the rear of the main beam headlight bulb **(see illustration 5.3).**

15 Pull the sidelight bulbholder from the headlight unit. The bulb is a push-fit in the holder and can be removed by grasping the end of the bulb and pulling it out **(see illustrations).**

16 Refitting is a reversal of removal, making sure that the headlight bulb plastic cover is securely refitted.

Front direction indicator

17 Working in the engine compartment, disconnect the wiring connector from the rear of the indicator bulbholder **(see illustration).**

18 Turn the bulbholder and remove it from the headlight complete with bulb **(see illustration).**

19 The bulb is a bayonet-fit in the bulbholder – depress and twist the bulb to remove it **(see illustration).**

20 Fit the new bulb using a reversal of the removal procedure.

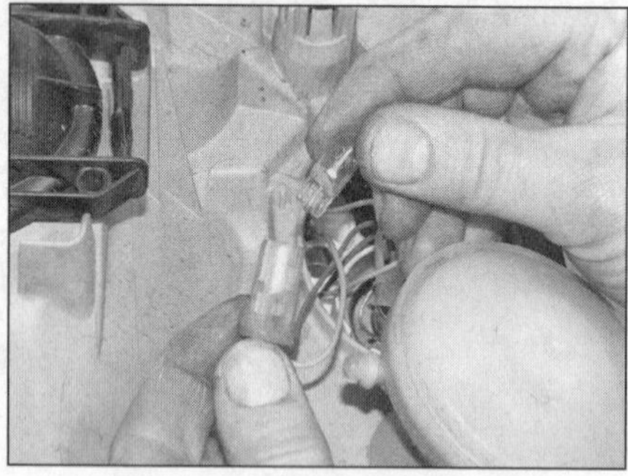
5.15b . . . and pull the bulb out

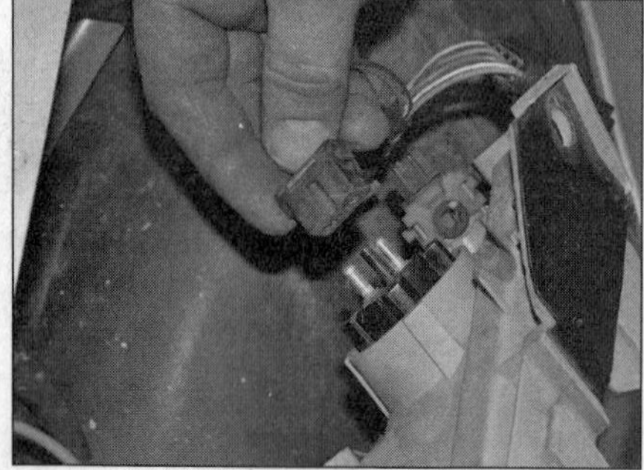
5.17 Disconnect the wiring connector – if required

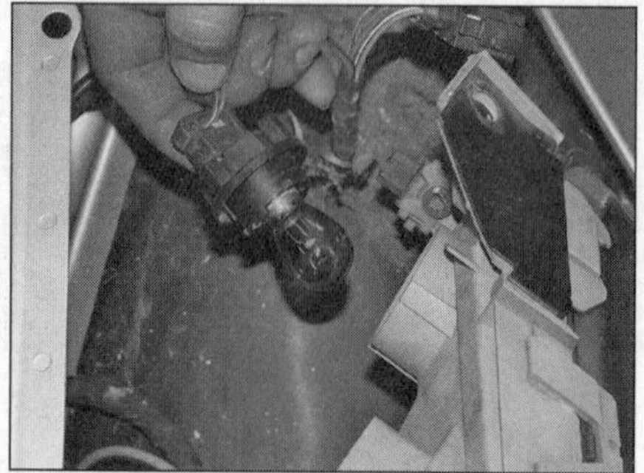
5.18 Remove bulbholder from the light unit . . .

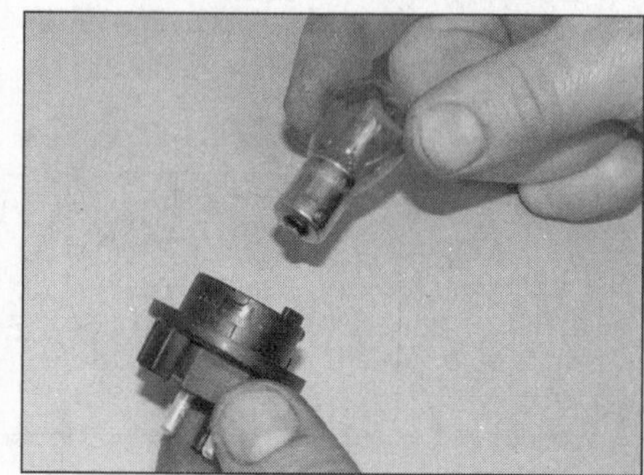
5.19 . . . and remove the bulb

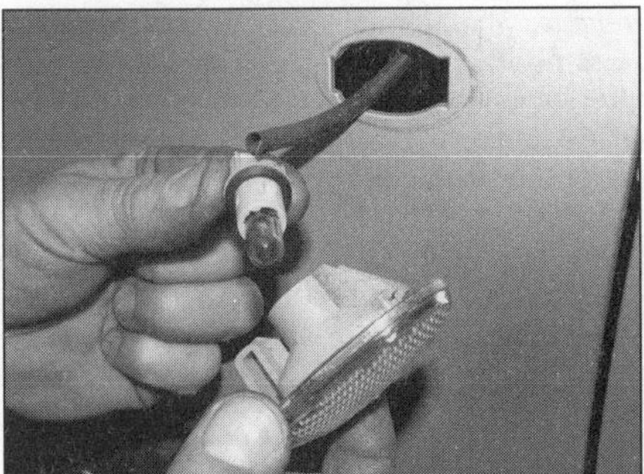

5.22 Remove the bulbholder . . .

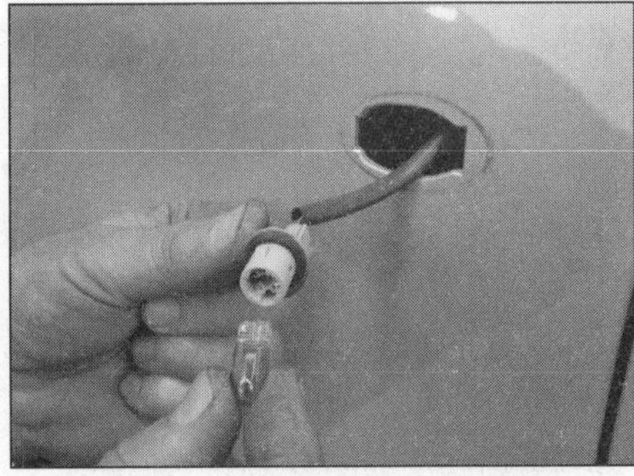

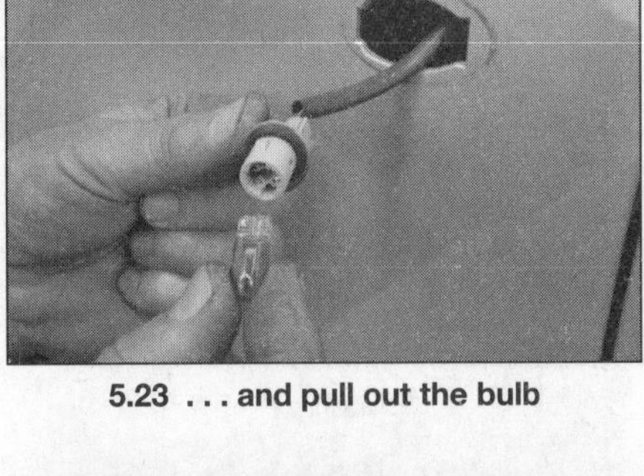

5.23 . . . and pull out the bulb

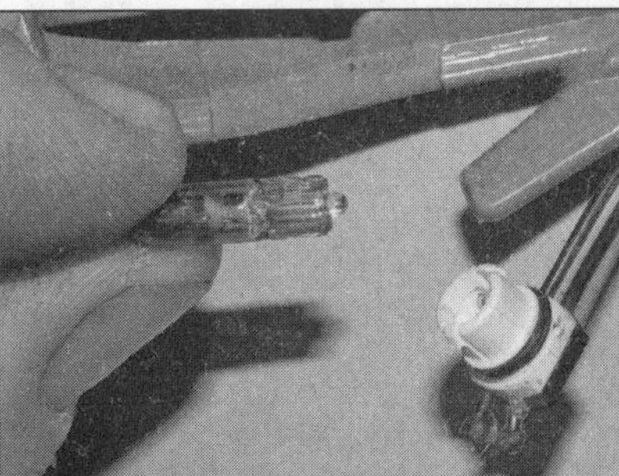

5.26 Unclip the bulbholder – arrowed

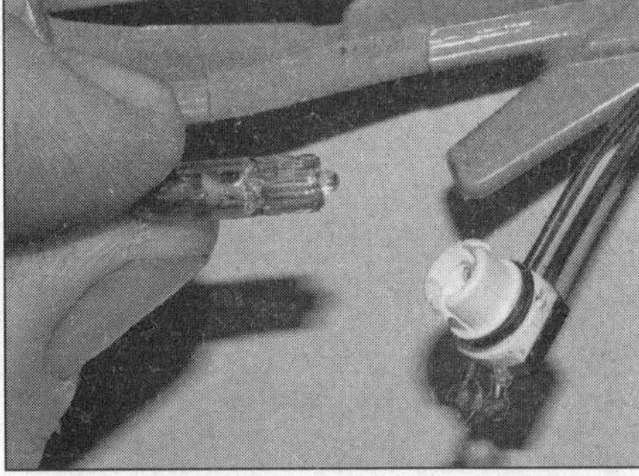

5.27 . . . and pull the bulb out of the holder

Front direction indicator repeater

In wing

21 Slide the light unit to the front of the vehicle and unclip from the front wing panel.

22 Turn the bulbholder and remove it from the light complete with bulb **(see illustration)**.

23 The bulb is a push-fit in the holder and can be removed by grasping the end of the bulb and pulling it out **(see illustration)**.

24 Refitting is a reversal of removal, making sure that the light unit is securely refitted in the wing panel.

In exterior mirror

25 Remove the exterior mirror housing as described in Chapter 11, Section 19.

26 Using a small screwdriver, unclip the relevant bulbholder from the light unit **(see illustration)**.

27 The bulb is a push-fit in the holder and can be removed by grasping the end of the bulb and pulling it out **(see illustration)**.

28 Refitting is a reversal of removal, making sure that the light unit is securely refitted in the wing panel.

Rear lights

Stop, tail, fog, indicator and reversing

29 Working in the luggage compartment, open the access panel(s) to the back of the rear lights **(see illustrations)**.

30 Release the retaining clips and withdraw the bulbholder from the light unit **(see illustration)**.

31 The bulbs are a bayonet-fit in the bulbholder – depress and twist the relevant bulb to remove it **(see illustration)**.

32 Fit the new bulb using a reversal of the removal procedure.

High-level brake light

33 Remove the inner tailgate trim panel as described in Chapter 11, Section 26.

34 Undo the two retaining screws and unclip the plastic cover from the high-level brake light unit **(see illustrations)**.

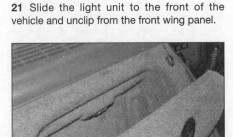

5.29a Open the compartment cover . . .

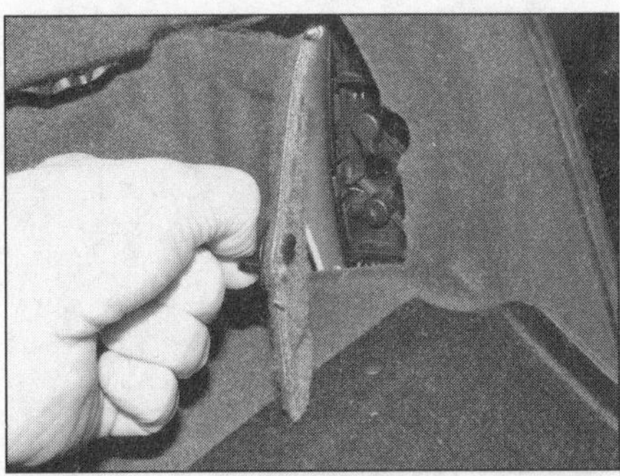

5.29b . . . and access panel to the rear lights

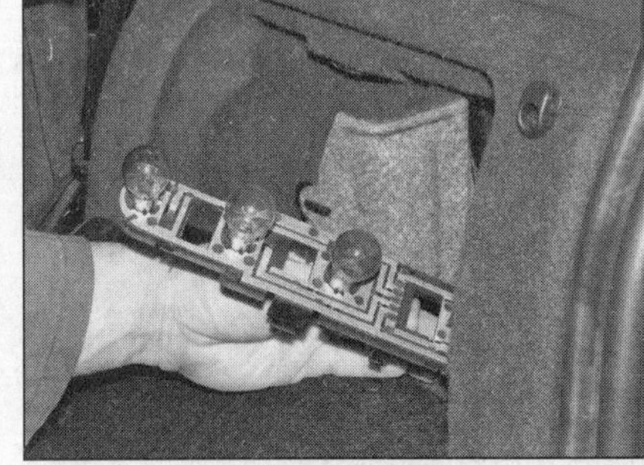

5.30 Unclip the bulbholder from the light unit

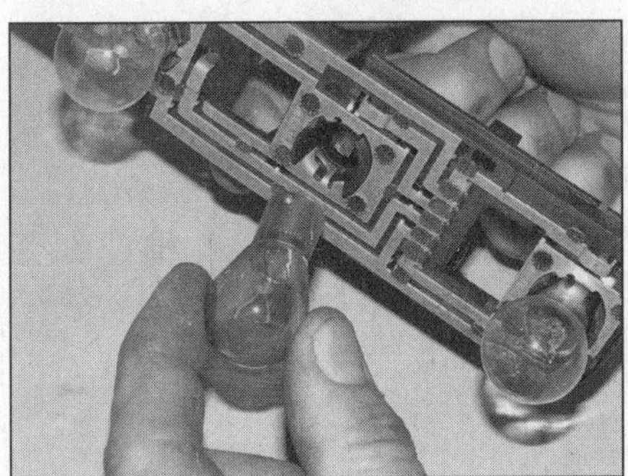

5.31 Press and twist the bulb to remove

5.34a Undo the retaining screws (one shown) . . .

5.34b . . . and remove the plastic cover

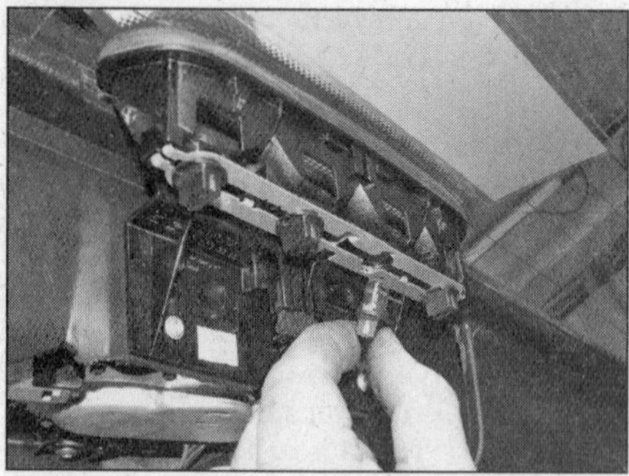

5.35 Remove the bulbholder . . .

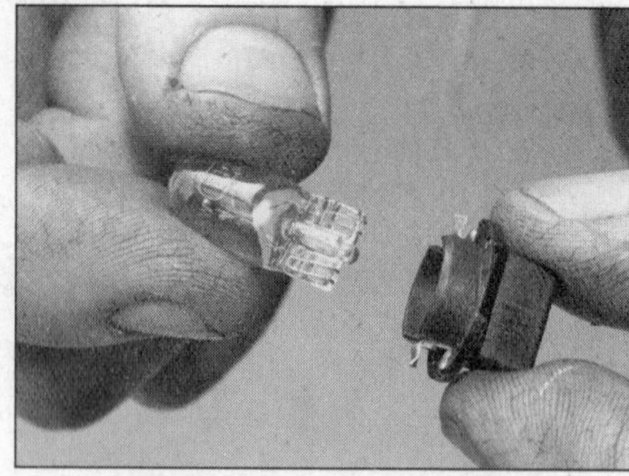

5.36 . . . and pull out the bulb

5.38a Undo the two retaining screws . . .

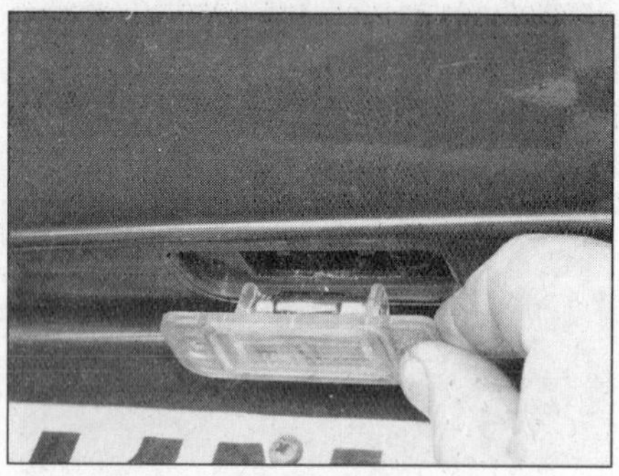

5.38b . . . and remove the light unit

35 Turn the relevant bulbholder and remove it from the light unit complete with bulb **(see illustration)**.

36 The bulb is a push-fit in the holder and can be removed by grasping the end of the bulb and pulling it out **(see illustration)**.

37 Refitting is a reversal of removal, making sure that the bulbholder is securely refitted in the light unit.

Number plate light

38 Undo the two securing screws, and withdraw the light unit from the tailgate **(see illustrations)**.

39 Unclip the festoon bulb from the light unit.

40 Fit the new bulb using a reversal of the removal procedure

6 Bulbs (interior lights) - renewal

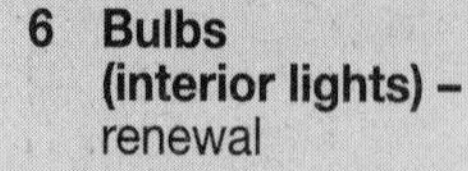

General

1 Whenever a bulb is renewed, note the following points:

a) Switch off the ignition and all electrical consumers before commencing work.

b) Remember that if the light has just been in use the bulb may be extremely hot.

c) Always check the bulb contacts and holder, ensuring that there is clean metal-to-metal contact between them. Clean off any corrosion or dirt before fitting a new bulb.

d) Wherever bayonet-type bulbs are fitted ensure that the live contact(s) bear firmly against the bulb contact.

e) Always ensure that the new bulb is of the correct rating and that it is completely clean before fitting it.

Front courtesy light

2 For access to the main courtesy light bulb, carefully prise the lens from the light unit, using a small flat-bladed screwdriver. Pull the festoon-type bulb from the spring contacts **(see illustrations)**.

3 Fit the new bulb using a reversal of the removal procedure.

Front reading light

4 For access to the reading light bulbs, remove the light unit as follows.

5 Unclip the courtesy light lenses (see paragraph 2), then undo the screws and unclip the light console from the headlining. Disconnect the wiring plug as it is removed **(see illustrations)**.

6 Using a small screwdriver unclip the bulbholder from the rear of the light unit, and then pull out the wedge-type bulb **(see illustrations)**.

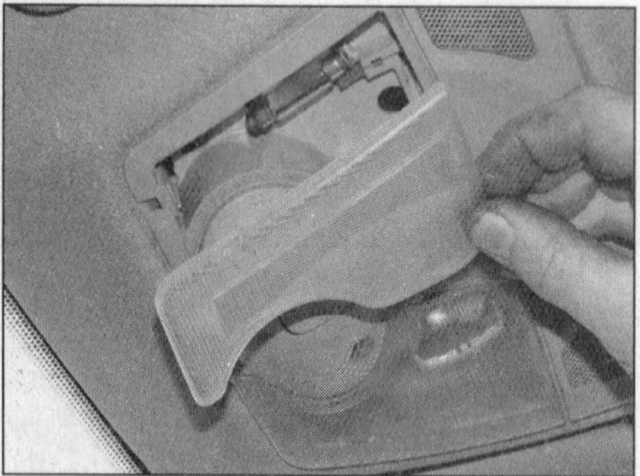

6.2a Unclip the lens . . .

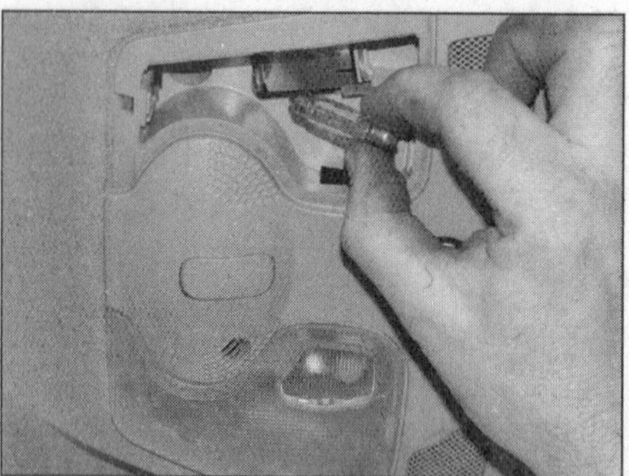

6.2b . . . and remove the bulb

6.5a Undo the retaining screws . . .

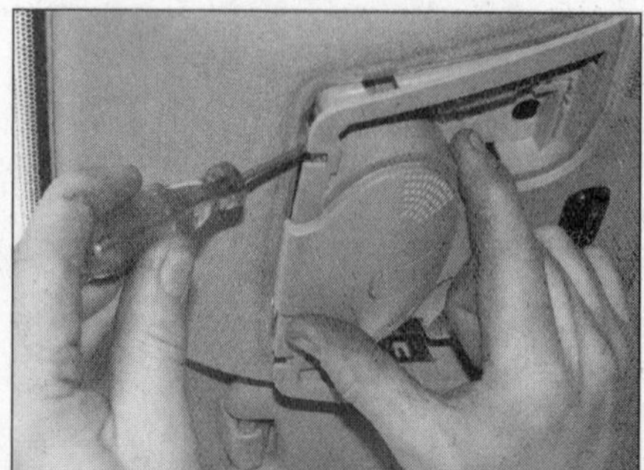

6.5b . . . unclip the light unit . . .

6.5c . . . and disconnect the wiring connectors

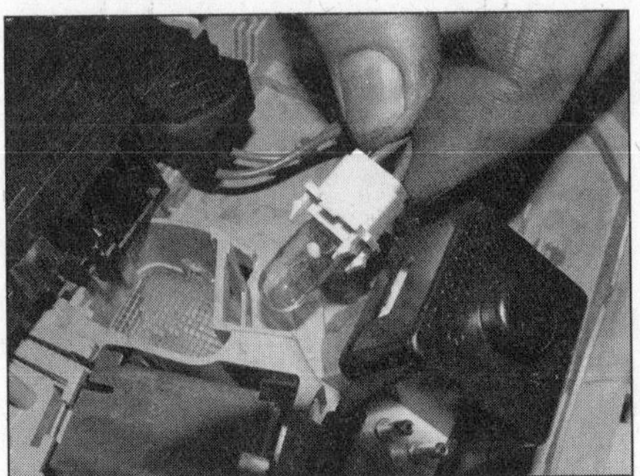
6.6a Unclip the bulbholder . . .

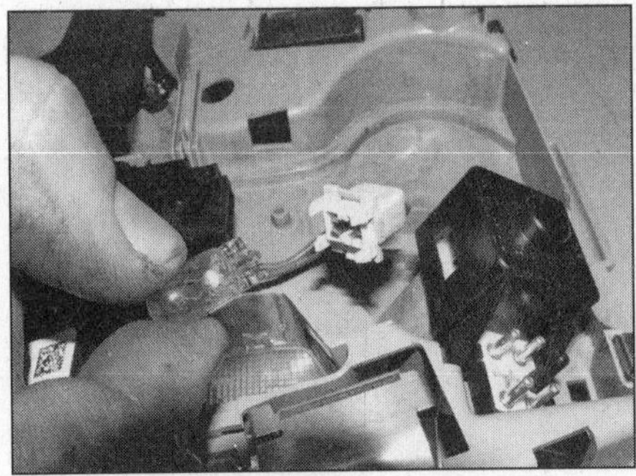
6.6b . . . and pull out the bulb

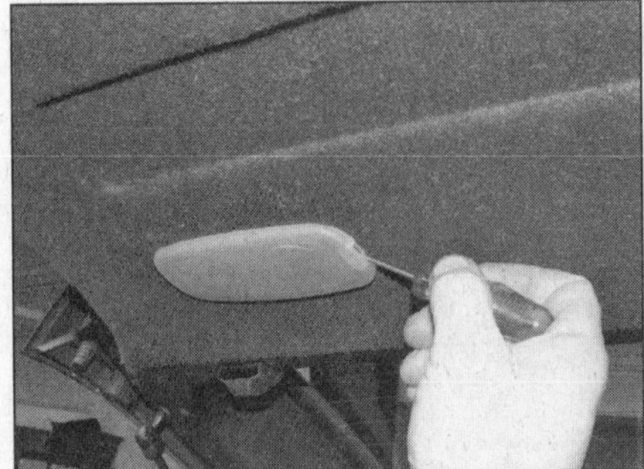
6.8 Unclip the light unit . . .

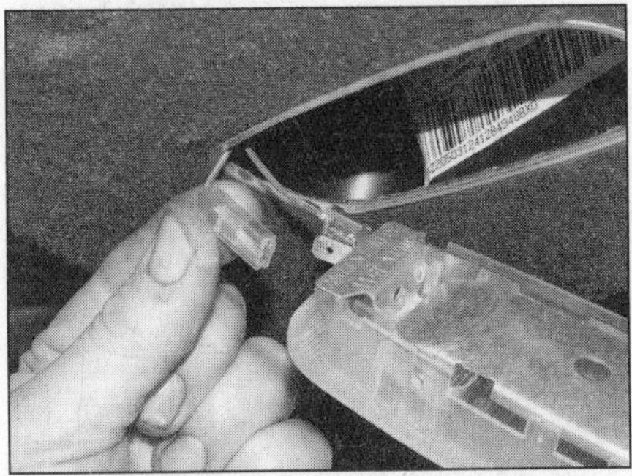
6.9 . . . and disconnect the wiring

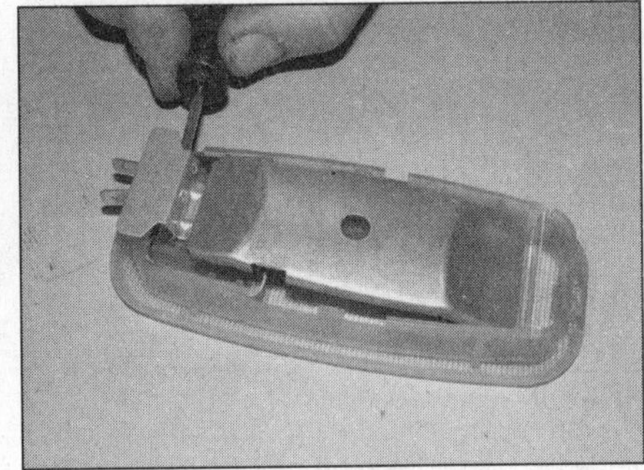
6.10a Unclip the reflector shield . . .

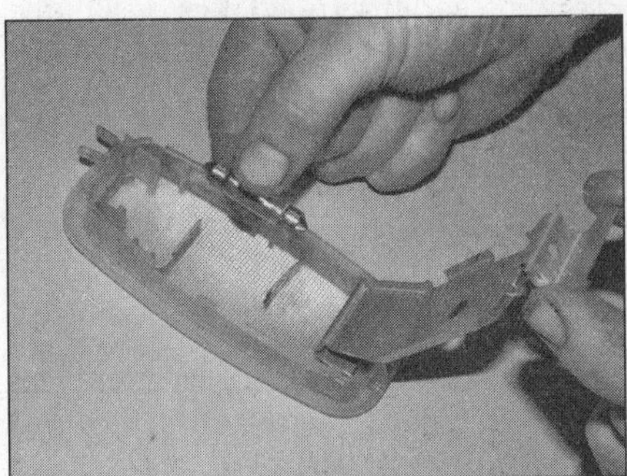
6.10b . . . and remove the bulb

7 Fit the new bulb using a reversal of the removal procedure.

Rear courtesy/ luggage compartment lights

8 Carefully prise the light unit from its location in the headlining, luggage compartment or tailgate lid **(see illustration)**.

9 Disconnect the wiring connector from the light unit as it is removed **(see illustration)**.

10 Unclip the reflector shield and remove the bulb; the festoon-type bulb is a push-fit in the spring contacts **(see illustrations)**.

11 Fit the new bulb and light unit, using a reversal of the removal procedure.

Glovebox illumination light

12 Open the glovebox, then use a screwdriver to prise out the lens. Disconnect the wiring.

13 Remove the bulb from the light unit; the festoon-type bulb is a push-fit in the spring contacts **(see illustration)**.

14 Fit the new bulb using a reversal of the removal procedure.

Instrument panel illumination/warning lights

15 Remove the instrument panel as described in Section 9.

16 Using a screwdriver turn the bulbholder anti-clockwise and remove the bulbholder complete with bulb from the rear of the instrument panel **(see illustrations)**.

17 Fit the new bulb and instrument panel, using a reversal of the removal procedure.

Cigarette lighter/ ashtray illumination

18 Unclip the cover from around the ashtray **(see illustration)**.

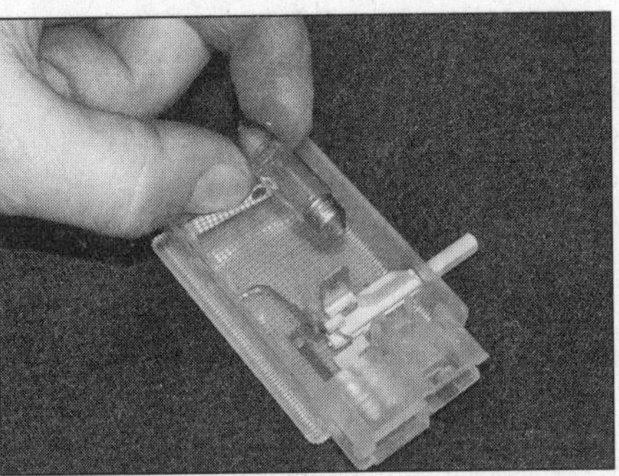
6.13 Remove the festoon bulb

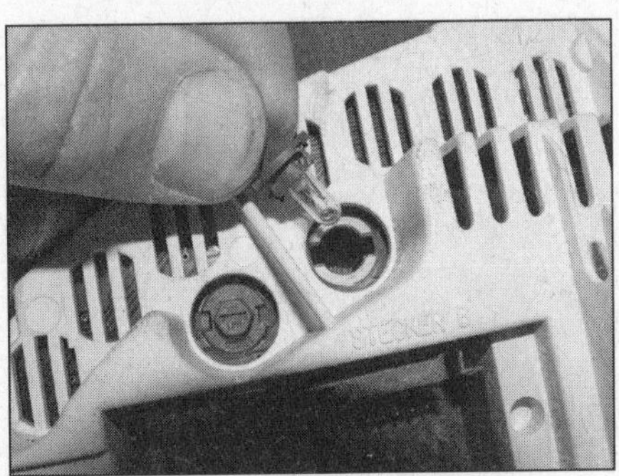
6.16b . . . and remove from panel

19 Slide the ashtray out from the front of the centre console **(see illustration)**.

20 Lift the retaining clip, and pull the bulbholder from the rear of the assembly and disconnect the wiring plug **(see illustration)**.

6.16a Turn the bulbholder . . .

6.18 Unclip the cover . . .

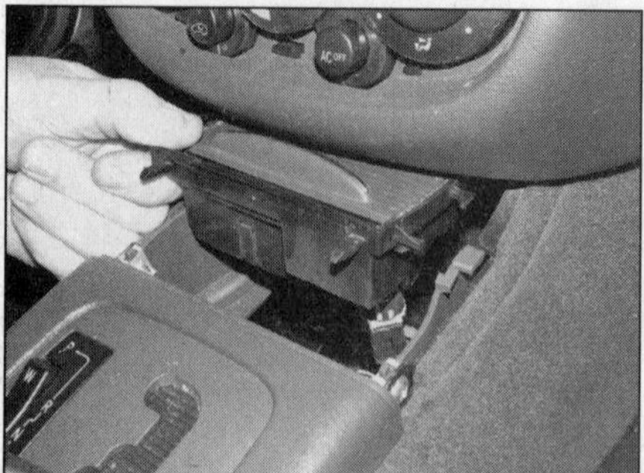
6.19 . . . slide out the ashtray . . .

6.20 . . . and disconnect the wiring connector

21 Fit the new bulb using a reversal of the removal procedure.

Switch illumination

22 The switch illumination bulbs are integral with the switches. If a bulb fails, the complete switch must be renewed.

7.3a Upper headlight mounting bolt - arrowed

7 Exterior light units - removal and refitting

Headlight unit

1 Remove the front bumper cover, as described in Chapter 11.

2 If required, release the locking clip and move the windscreen washer reservoir to one side.

3 Note the position of the mountings to ensure correct alignment on refitting, then undo the mounting bolts and pull the headlight unit slightly forward **(see illustrations)**.

4 Disconnect the wiring block connectors from the rear of the light unit **(see illustration)**.

5 Disconnect the pneumatic pipe from the headlamp adjuster on the back of the headlight unit **(see illustration)**.

6 Withdraw the headlamp forwards and out from the front of the vehicle.

7 If required, the headlight adjustment actuator can be removed from the rear of the unit. Turn it through a quarter of a turn and then unclip the balljoint from the reflector inside the light unit **(see illustration)**.

8 Refitting is a reversal of removal, but on completion, check that the actuator balljoint is located securely **(see illustration)**. If required, have the headlight alignment checked at the earliest opportunity.

Direction indicator in mirror

9 Remove the exterior mirror housing as described in Chapter 11.

10 Undo the retaining screws and withdraw the light unit out from the mirror cover **(see illustration)**.

11 Refitting is a reversal of removal.

Rear light cluster

12 Inside the rear luggage compartment, open the compartment (where applicable) and fold back the carpet liner to access the light cluster **(see illustrations)**.

13 Unscrew the three mounting nuts and withdraw the rear light cluster from the rear of the vehicle **(see illustration)**.

14 Disconnect the wiring plug from the rear of the light unit as it is removed **(see illustration)**.

15 Refitting is a reversal of removal.

7.3b Lower headlight mounting bolt - arrowed

7.4 Disconnect the wiring connector

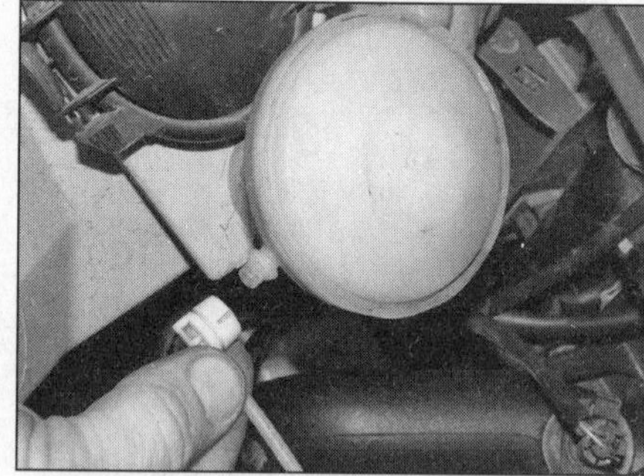
7.5 Disconnect the pneumatic pipe

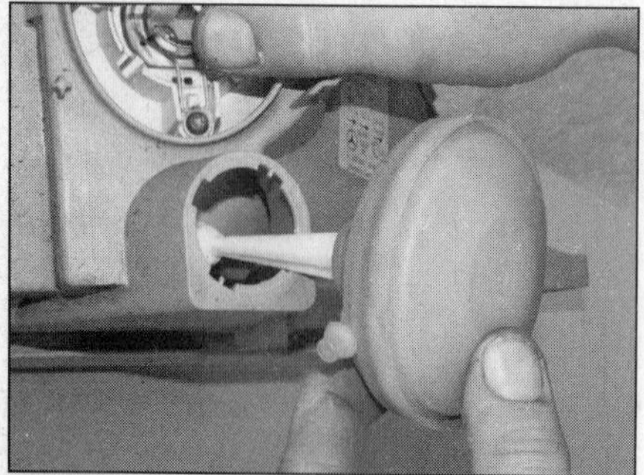
7.7 Turn and disengage the actuator from the headlight

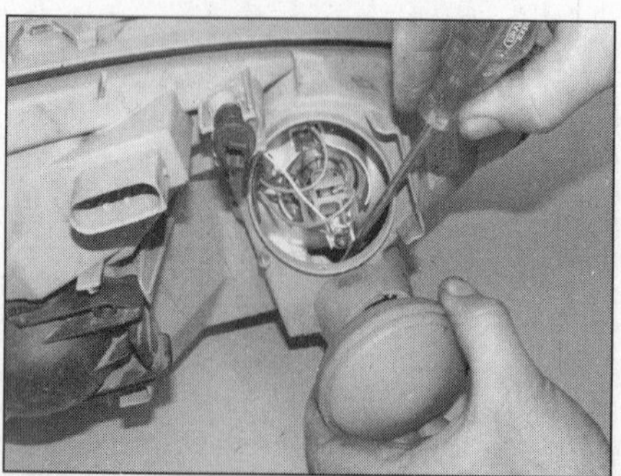
7.8 Using screwdriver to aid refitting of the actuator balljoint

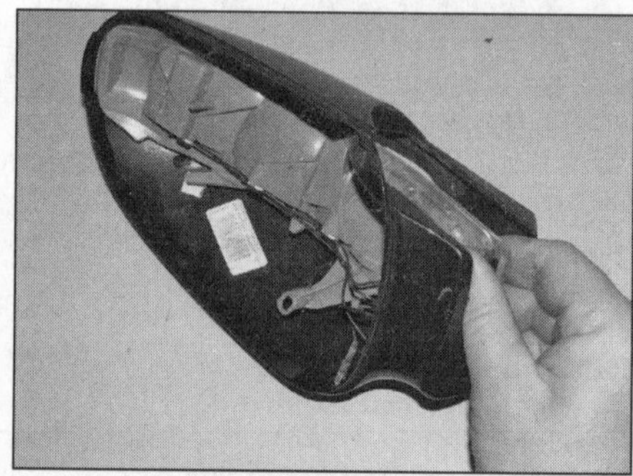
7.10 Withdraw the light unit from the mirror cover

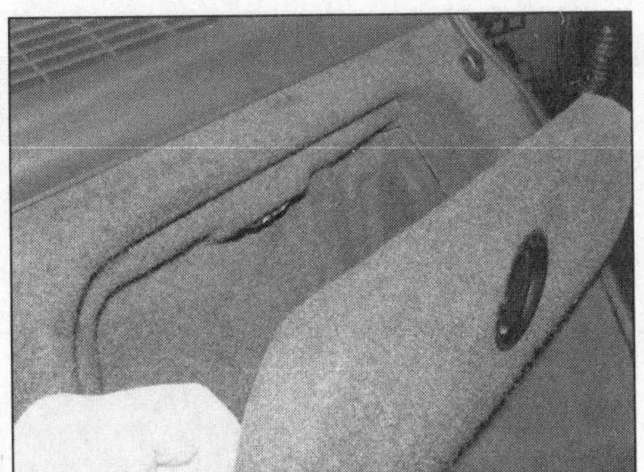

7.12a Open the luggage side compartment . . .

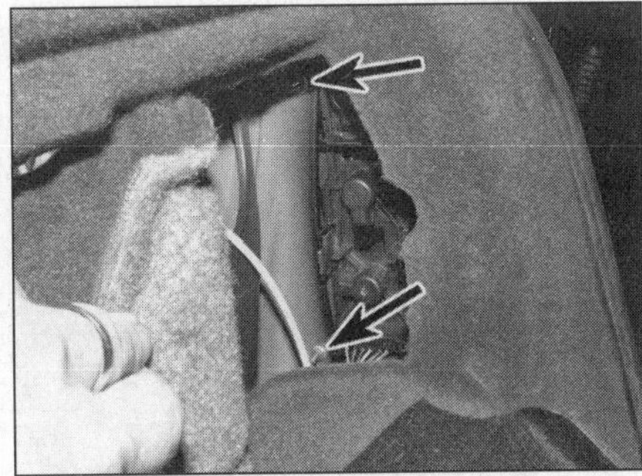

7.12b . . . and access panel, then undo retaining nuts (two shown)

7.13 Remove the rear light unit . . .

7.14 . . . and disconnect the wiring connector

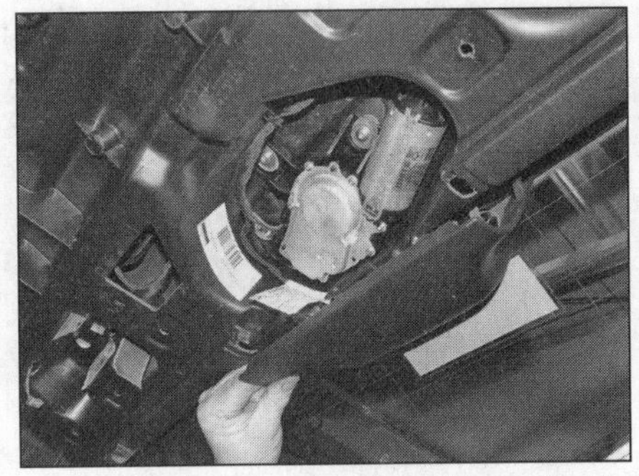

7.17 Remove the plastic cover . . .

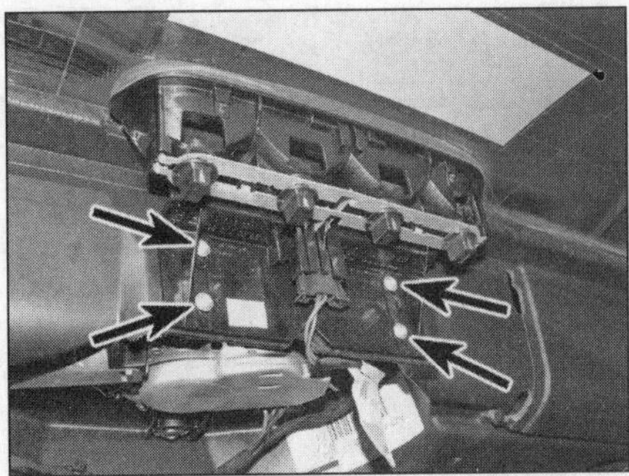

7.18 . . . and undo the retaining screws – arrowed

High-level brake light

16 Remove the tailgate inner trim panel as described in Chapter 11.

17 Undo the retaining screws and unclip the plastic cover from the high-level brake light unit **(see illustration)**.

18 Disconnect the wiring connector, then undo the retaining screws and withdraw the light unit from the tailgate **(see illustration)**.

19 Refitting is a reversal of removal.

Rear number plate light

20 The procedure is described as part of the rear number plate light bulb renewal procedure in Section 5.

Direction indicator repeater

21 The procedure is described as part of the wing repeater light bulb renewal procedure in Section 5.

8 Headlight beam alignment – general information

1 Accurate adjustment of the headlight beam is only possible using optical beam setting equipment and this work should therefore be carried out by a Mercedes-Benz dealer or suitably-equipped workshop.

2 For reference, the headlights can be adjusted using the adjuster assemblies fitted to the top of each light unit. The outer adjuster alters the lateral position of the beam whilst the inner adjuster alters the height of the beam **(see illustrations)**.

9 Instrument panel – removal and refitting

Removal

1 Switch off the ignition and all electrical consumers and remove the ignition key. Release the steering wheel adjustment handle, and set it in the lowest position.

Models up to 28/02/01

2 Undo the two retaining screws (one each side of the steering column) in the air vent trim from under the instrument panel.

3 Unclip the air vent cover from the right-hand side of the facia and under the instrument panel, taking care not to damage the trim.

4 Undo the two screws from the bottom corners of the instrument panel cover and remove the cover from the top of the instruments.

5 Undo the two screws from the lower front of the instrument panel and one screw from the rear of the instrument panel.

6 Withdraw the instrument panel upwards, and then disconnect the wiring connectors.

Models from 01/03/01

7 Using special puller hook tools (we used two bent pieces of wire), insert one in each side of the instrument panel cover, twist the special tool upwards and pull the cover from the top of the instrument panel **(see illustrations)**. **Note:** *Take care not to damage the facia panel with the pieces of wire when the cover is being removed.*

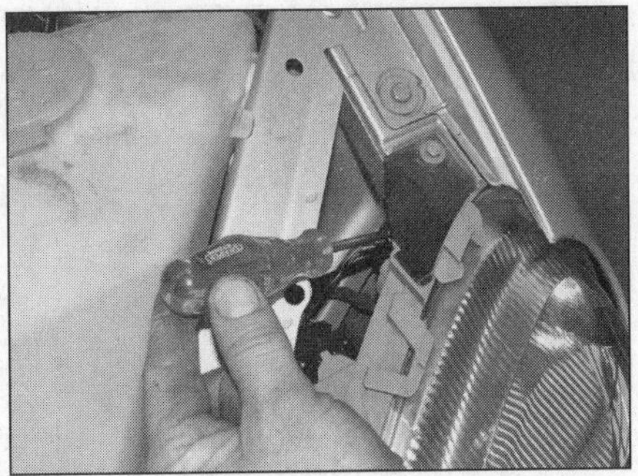

8.2a Headlight lateral adjuster . . .

8.2b . . . and height adjuster

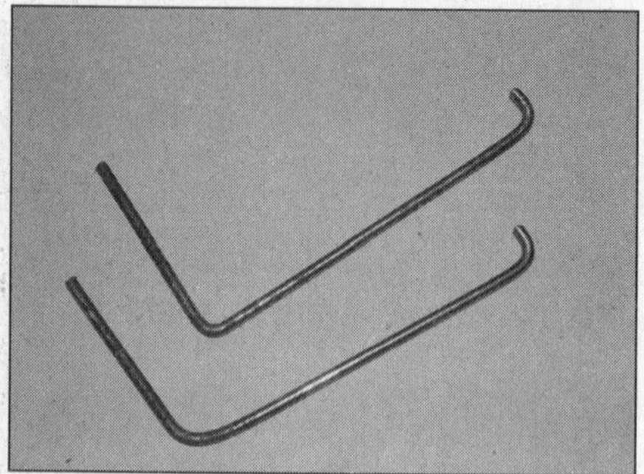
9.7a Home-made tool made out of approximately 2 mm wire

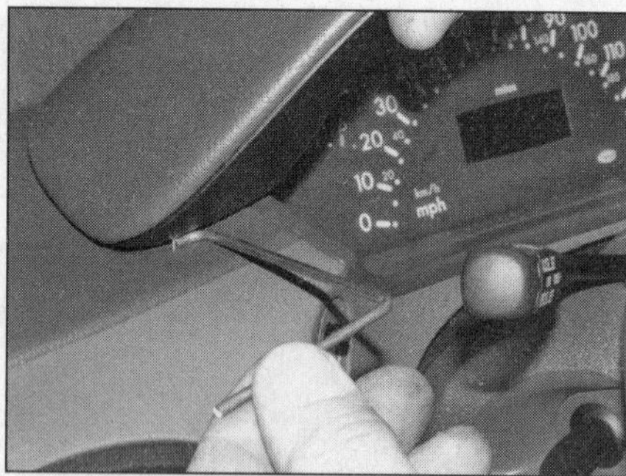
9.7b Insert the puller hook tools . . .

9.7c . . . twist the hooks upwards . . .

9.7d . . . and pull the instrument cover from the facia

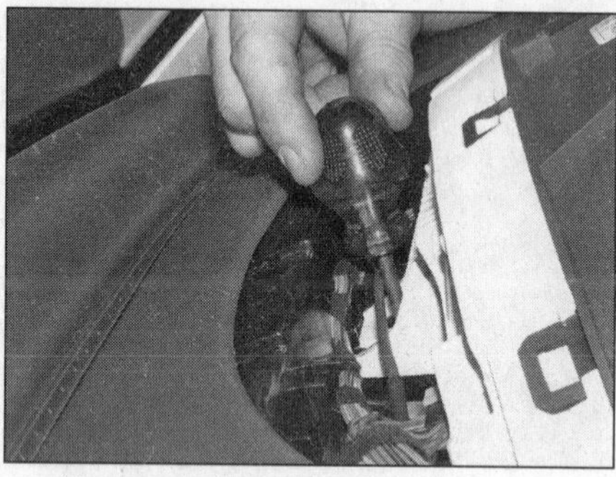
9.8a Undo the retaining screw . . .

9.8b . . . unclip the instrument cluster . . .

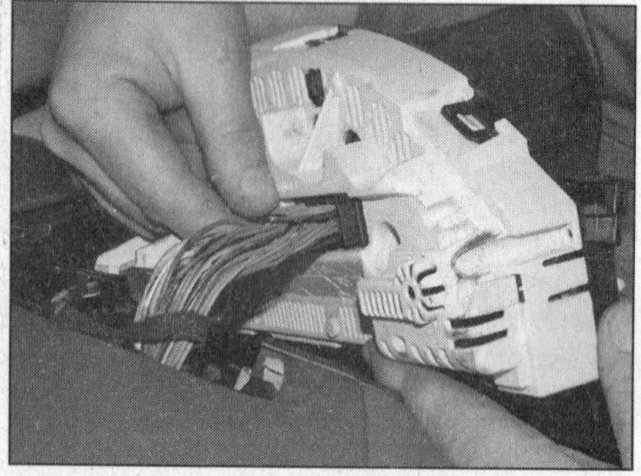
9.8c . . . and disconnect the wiring connectors

8 Undo the retaining screw from the rear of the panel, lift out the instrument panel and disconnect the wiring connectors **(see illustrations)**.

Refitting

9 Refitting is a reversal of removal.

10 Instrument panel components – removal and refitting

Renew the bulbs as described in Section 6.

It is not possible to dismantle the instrument panel further. If any of the gauges are faulty, the complete instrument panel must be renewed.

11 Clock – removal and refitting

The clock is integral with the instrument panel, and cannot be removed separately. The instrument panel is a sealed unit, and if the clock, or any other components, are faulty, the complete instrument panel must be renewed. Refer to Section 9 to remove it.

12.2 Unclip the surround . . .

12.3 . . . and slide out the ashtray

12 Cigarette lighter – removal and refitting

Removal

1 Disconnect the battery negative lead (refer to *Disconnecting the battery* in the *Reference* Chapter at the end of this manual).

2 Unclip the cover from around the ashtray **(see illustration)**.

3 Slide the ashtray out from the front of the centre console **(see illustration)**.

4 Remove the bulbholder from the ashtray as described in Section 6.

5 Push the centre element of the lighter out of the mounting and remove.

Refitting

6 Refitting is a reversal of removal.

13 Horn – removal and refitting

Note: *There are two horns fitted below the right-hand headlamp, the upper one is a high tone (500Hz) horn, and the lower one is a low tone (400Hz) horn.*

Removal

1 Switch off the ignition and all electrical consumers and remove the ignition key.

2 Remove the front bumper as described in Chapter 11.

3 Disconnect the wiring, then unscrew the mounting bolt and withdraw the horn together with the mounting bracket **(see illustration)**.
4 Unscrew the nut and remove the horn from the bracket.

Refitting

5 Refitting is a reversal of removal.

14 Speedometer sensor – general information

The vehicle speed is determined from the ABS wheel sensor signals, and processed by the engine management ECM. This measures the rotational speed of the transmission final drive and converts the information into an electronic signal, which is then sent to the speedometer module in the instrument panel. The signal is also used as an input by the engine management system ECM, and the trip meter.

15 Wiper arm – removal and refitting

Removal

1 Operate the wiper motor, then switch off so that the wiper arms return to the at-rest position.
2 Stick a piece of masking tape to the glass along the edge of the wiper blade to use as an alignment aid on refitting.
3 Undo the retaining screws from along the front edge of the trim panel and remove it from across the lower edge of the windscreen **(see illustrations)**.
4 Prise off the wiper arm spindle nut cover, then slacken but do not completely remove the spindle nut. Lift the blade off the glass and pull the wiper arm until it releases from the spindle. Remove the spindle nut **(see illustration)**. If necessary the arm can be levered off the spindle using a suitable flat-bladed screwdriver. **Note:** *If both windscreen wiper arms are to be removed at the same time mark them for identification; the arms are not interchangeable.*

Refitting

5 Ensure that the wiper arm and spindle splines are clean and dry, and then refit the arm to the spindle, aligning the wiper blade with the tape fitted on removal. Refit the spindle nut, tightening it securely, and clip the nut cover back in position.

16 Windscreen wiper motor and linkage – removal and refitting

Removal

1 Remove the wiper arms as described in Section 15.
2 Disconnect the battery negative lead (refer to *Disconnecting the battery* in the *Reference* Chapter at the end of this manual).
3 Unclip the windscreen washer pipe from along the screen lower trim panel.
4 Disconnect the heated washer jet wiring connector **(see illustration)**.
5 Working your way along the inside of the trim panel undo the retaining screws, and then unclip the panel from the lower part of the screen **(see illustrations)**.
6 Disconnect the wiring connector from the wiper motor **(see illustration)**.

13.3 Undo the horn mounting bracket – arrowed

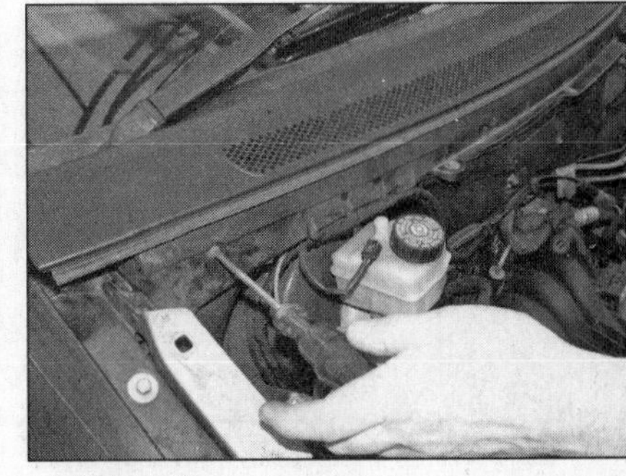

15.3a Undo the retaining screws . . .

15.3b . . . and remove the trim panel

15.4 Undo the wiper arm retaining nut

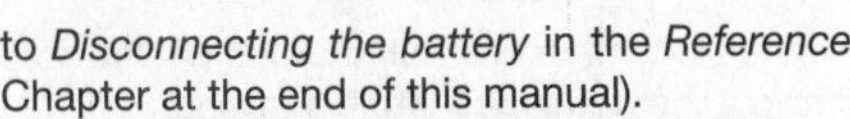

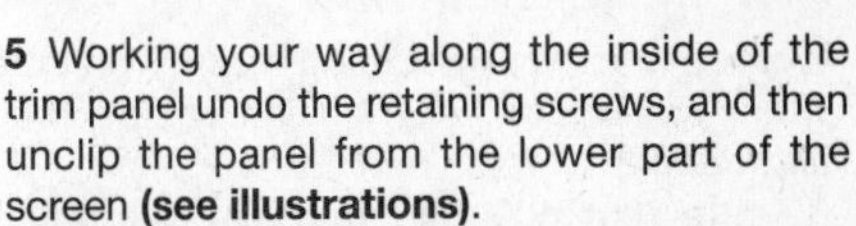

16.4 Disconnect the wiring connector

16.5a Undo the retaining screws . . .

16.5b . . . and remove the lower panel

16.6 Disconnect the wiring connector

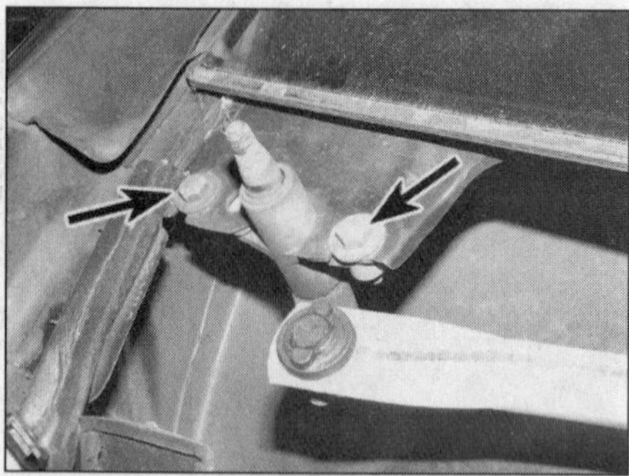

16.7 Wiper spindle mounting bolts – arrowed

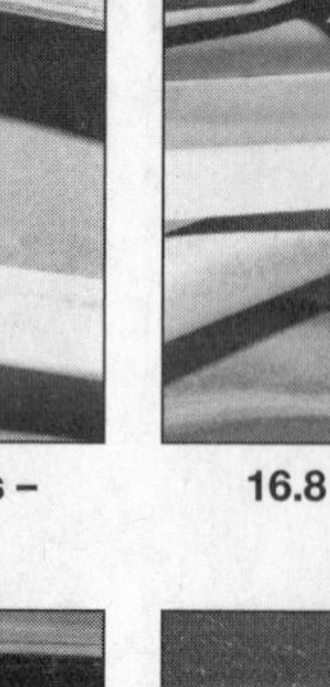

16.8 Wiper spindle mounting nut – arrowed

16.9 Wiper motor mounting bracket bolts – arrowed

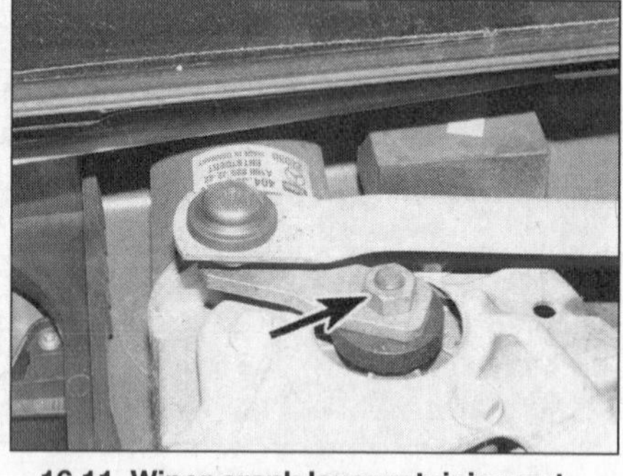

16.11 Wiper crank lever retaining nut – arrowed

7 Undo the two mounting bolts from the wiper spindle on the right-hand side **(see illustration)**.

8 Undo the mounting nut from the wiper spindle on the left-hand side **(see illustration)**.

9 Undo the mounting bolts from the wiper motor mounting bracket and manoeuvre it out from the scuttle **(see illustration)**.

10 Recover the washers and spacers from the motor mounting rubbers, noting their locations, then inspect the rubbers for signs of damage or deterioration, and renew if necessary.

17.2a Lift up the cover, undo the nut . . .

17.2b . . . and remove the wiper arm

11 To separate the motor from the linkage, proceed as follows.

a) Make alignment marks between the motor spindle and the linkage to ensure correct alignment on refitting, and note the orientation of the linkage.

*b) Unscrew the nut securing the linkage crank to the motor spindle **(see illustration)**.*

c) Unscrew the three bolts securing the motor to the mounting plate, and then withdraw the motor.

Refitting

12 Refitting is a reversal of removal, bearing in mind the following points.

a) If the motor has been separated from the linkage, ensure that the marks made on the motor spindle and linkage before removal are aligned, and ensure that the linkage is orientated as noted before removal.

b) Ensure that the washers and spacers are fitted to the motor mounting rubbers as noted before removal.

c) Do not strike the cowling to seat it in position as this could result in the windscreen cracking.

d) Refit the wiper arms as described in Section 15.

17 Rear wiper motor – removal and refitting

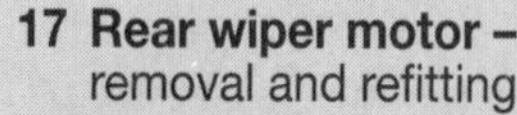

Removal

1 Stick a piece of masking tape to the glass along the edge of the wiper blade to use as an alignment aid on refitting.

2 Lift up the wiper arm spindle nut cover, then slacken but do not completely remove the spindle nut. Lift the blade off the glass and pull the wiper arm until it releases from the spindle. Remove the spindle nut **(see illustrations)**. If necessary the arm can be levered off the spindle using a suitable flat-bladed screwdriver.

3 Open the tailgate, then remove the trim panel as described in Chapter 11.

4 Undo the retaining screws and remove the plastic cover from the high-level brake light unit **(see illustration)**.

5 Disconnect the wiring connector from the wiper motor **(see illustration)**.

17.4 Remove the high-level brake light

17.5 Disconnect the wiring connector . . .

17.6 . . . and remove the rear wiper motor

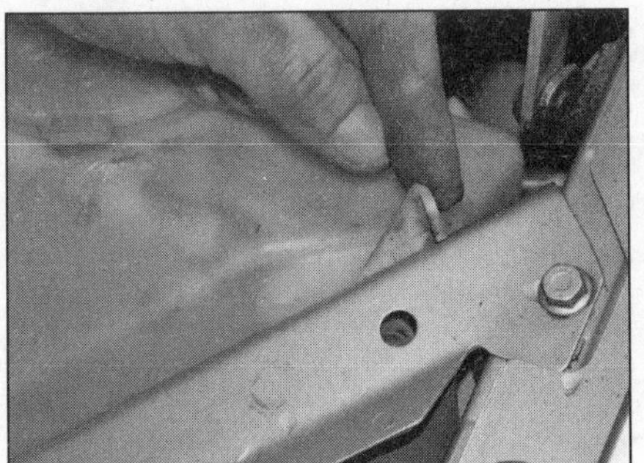
18.2a Release the locking clip . . .

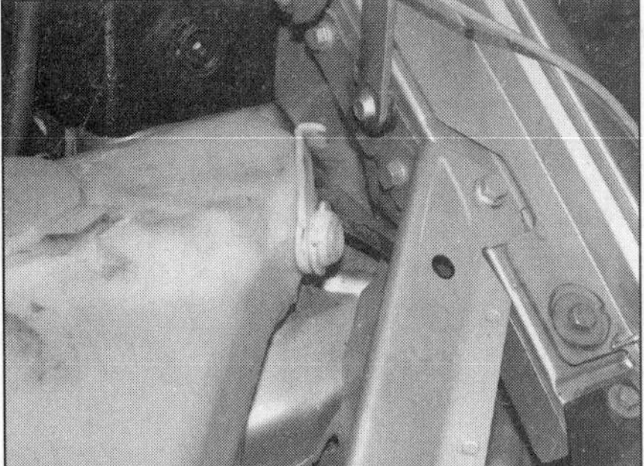
18.2b . . . and disconnect from the body panel

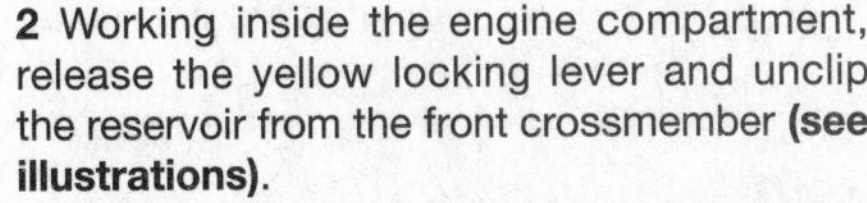

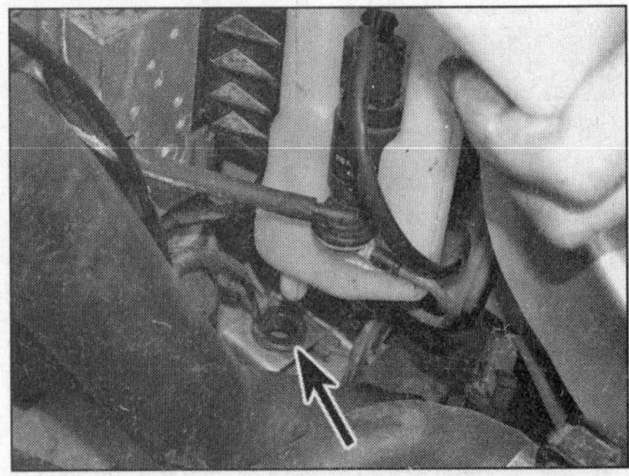
18.3 Lift the reservoir out from the lower grommet – arrowed

6 Unscrew the three screws securing the motor, and then withdraw the assembly out from the rubber grommet **(see illustration)**.

Refitting

7 Refitting is a reversal of removal, but ensure that the motor shaft rubber sealing grommet is correctly refitted to prevent water leaks, and refit the wiper arm.

18 Washer system components - removal and refitting

Fluid reservoir and pumps

Removal

1 Switch off the ignition and all electrical consumers, and remove the ignition key.

2 Working inside the engine compartment, release the yellow locking lever and unclip the reservoir from the front crossmember **(see illustrations)**.

3 Lift the reservoir to disengage it from the rubber mounting grommet in the inner wing panel **(see illustration)**.

4 Release the securing clip and disconnect the wiring connector from the washer pump **(see illustration)**.

5 Note that the hose connections to the reservoir are colour-coded to ensure correct fitment. Disconnect the hoses from the washer pump motors **(see illustration)**. **Note:** *Position a suitable container beneath the reservoir to catch spilt fluid.*

6 Pull the pump motors upwards from the reservoir and disconnect the wiring.

7 The reservoir can now be removed from the engine compartment.

Refitting

8 Refitting is a reversal of removal. Make sure that the hoses are connected securely and the reservoir is mounted correctly.

Windscreen washer jets

Removal

9 Open the bonnet, and then undo the retaining screws from along the front edge of the trim panel. Remove the trim panel from across the lower edge of the windscreen **(see illustration)**.

10 Pull the washer jet upwards out of the trim panel **(see illustration)**.

11 Disconnect the washer tube and wiring on heated jets, and then remove the jet.

Refitting

12 Refitting is a reversal of removal.

Tailgate washer jet

Removal

13 Switch off the ignition and all electrical consumers, and remove the ignition key.

14 Unclip the washer jet from the top of the tailgate, and carefully pull it out with the washer pipe still connected **(see illustration)**. Make sure the pipe remains connected, as it could become disconnected from the washer jet and drop inside the tailgate.

15 If required, the washer pipe can be located through the rubber grommet at the hinged part of the tailgate **(see illustration)**.

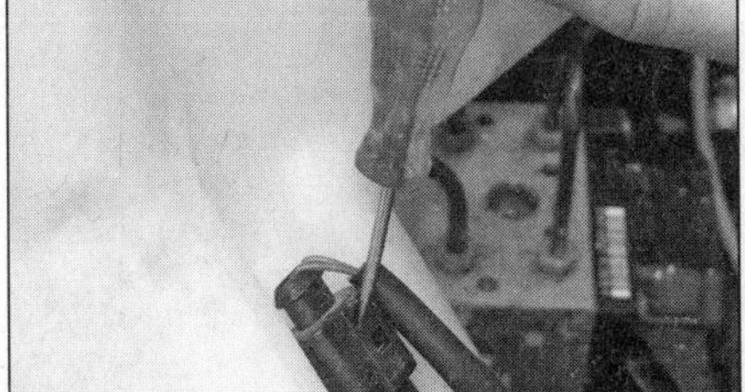
18.4 Releasing the locking clip

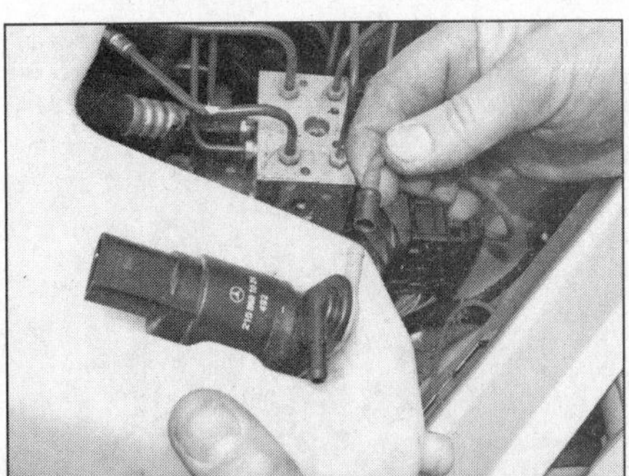
18.5 Disconnect the washer hoses

18.9 Remove the screen lower trim panel

18.10 Unclip the washer jets from the lower panel

18.14 Remove the rear washer jet

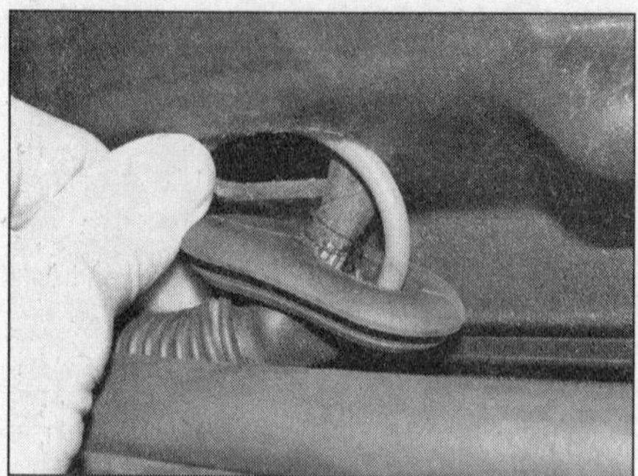

18.15 Remove the rubber grommet to access washer pipe

Refitting

16 On refitting, ensure that the jet is securely pushed into position. Check the operation of the jet. If necessary, adjust the nozzle, aiming the spray at a point slightly above the area of glass swept by the wiper blade.

19 Radio/CD player – removal and refitting

Note: *This Section only applies to standard-fit audio equipment. If the wrong code is entered incorrectly three times in succession the lettering WAIT will appear on the display, the radio will be locked then for 10 minutes, before you can try again. The radio will need to be left switched on during this 10-minute period.*

Removal

1 The radio/CD player is coded and the vehicle supplied with a 5-digit code, check the code is available for refitting. If the voltage supply to the radio is disconnected, the radio will function again once the anti-theft code has been entered.

2 Remove any CDs which may be in the unit. Switch off the ignition and all electrical consumers, and remove the ignition key.

3 Insert two keys into the lower part of the radio to release the locking clips once in place and withdraw the radio/CD player out from the facie panel **(see illustrations)**.

4 As the radio/CD player is removed, disconnect the wiring connectors and aerial lead **(see illustrations)**, and then remove it from the facia.

Refitting

5 Refitting is a reversal of removal.

20 Loudspeakers – removal and refitting

Door-mounted speakers

Removal

1 Switch off the ignition and all electrical consumers, and remove the ignition key.

2 Remove the door trim as described in Chapter 11.

3 Disconnect the speaker wiring plug from the door panel **(see illustration)**.

4 Remove the three retaining screws and withdraw the speaker from the door **(see illustration)**.

Refitting

5 Refitting is a reversal of removal.

Front door-mounted treble

Removal

6 The small loudspeaker is located on the inside of the door trim panel. First, switch off the ignition and all electrical consumers, and remove the ignition key.

7 Remove the door trim as described in Chapter 11.

8 Unclip the speaker from the inside of the door trim panel.

Refitting

9 Refitting is a reversal of removal.

21 Radio aerials and amplifier – removal and refitting

Removal

1 The radio aerial is integrated into the rear window, which is bonded in position with a special adhesive. If the aerial is faulty, a new rear window must be fitted.

2 The navigation and telephone aerial is fitted to the rear of the roof panel. First remove the trim from across the rear of the roof panel.

3 Remove the right- and left-hand upper

19.3a Insert the radio keys . . .

19.3b . . . and withdraw the radio/CD player

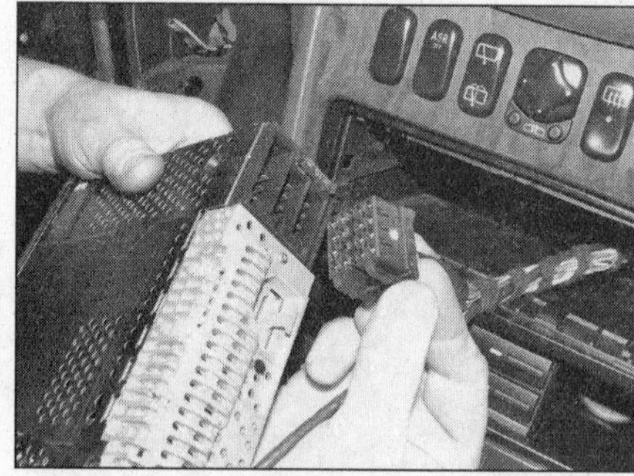

19.4a Disconnect the wiring connectors . . .

19.4b . . . and the aerial lead

20.3 Disconnect the wiring connector . . .

20.4 . . . and undo the retaining screws – arrowed

C-pillar trim panels, with reference to Chapter 11, Section 26.

4 Carefully lower the rear of the headlining and disconnect the wiring. Note the position of the connections to aid refitting.

5 Unscrew the securing nut and withdraw the aerial base from the roof. Hold the aerial base as the nut is being unscrewed to prevent the base from rotating and scratching the roof panel. Recover the rubber spacer.

6 To remove the aerial FM/AM amplifier, disconnect the wiring connector and aerial lead, then undo the retaining nut and remove the amplifier from the rear of the roof panel **(see illustration)**.

Refitting

7 Refitting is a reversal of removal, but make sure that the rubber spacer is correctly located in the aerial base.

22 Anti-theft alarm system and engine immobiliser – general information

Note: *This information is applicable only to the anti-theft alarm system fitted by Mecedes as standard equipment.*

Models in the range are fitted with an anti-theft alarm system as standard equipment. The alarm has switches on all the doors (including the tailgate), the bonnet and the ignition switch. If the tailgate, bonnet or any of the doors are opened whilst the alarm is set, the alarm horn will sound and the hazard warning lights will flash. Some models are equipped with an internal monitoring system, which will activate the alarm system if any movement in the cabin is detected.

The alarm is set using the key in the driver's or passenger's front door lock, and tailgate lock, or with the central locking remote control transmitter. The alarm system will then start to monitor its various switches approximately 30 seconds later.

All models are fitted with an immobiliser system, which is activated by the ignition switch. A transponder reading coil on the ignition switch reads a code contained within the ignition key. The system sends a signal to the engine management electronic control unit (ECM), which allows the engine to start if the code is correct. If an incorrect ignition key is used, the engine will not start.

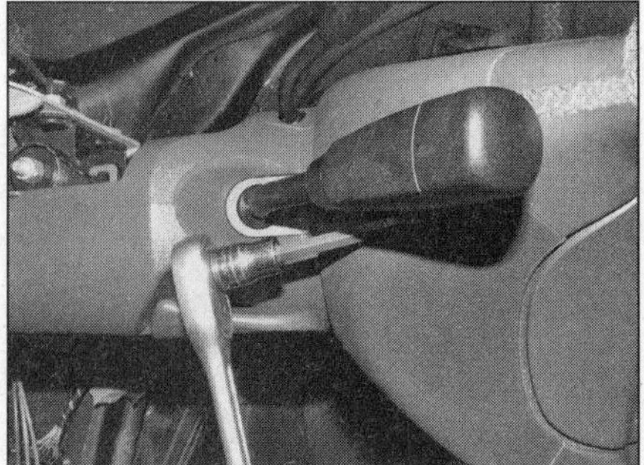

24.3 Undo the airbag retaining screws

21.6 Radio amplifier retaining nut – arrowed

If a fault is suspected with the alarm or immobiliser systems, the vehicle should be taken to a Mercedes-Benz dealer for examination. They will have access to a special diagnostic tester, which will quickly trace any fault present in the system.

23 Airbag system – general information and precautions

Warning: Before carrying out any operations on the airbag system, disconnect the battery negative terminal (refer to 'Disconnecting the battery' in the Reference section at the rear of this manual). When operations are complete, make sure no one is inside the vehicle when the battery is reconnected.

• Note that the airbags must not be subjected to temperatures in excess of 100°C. When the airbag is removed, ensure that it is stored with the pad upwards to prevent possible inflation.

• Do not allow any solvents or cleaning agents to contact the airbag assemblies. They must be cleaned using only a damp cloth.

• The airbags and control unit are both sensitive to impact. If either is dropped or damaged they should be renewed.

• The old airbags and emergency retractor units must be disposed of safely, check with your local Mercedes-Benz dealer.

A driver's airbag, passenger's airbag and side airbags are fitted as standard, certain models also have curtain airbags located behind the headlining on each side of the car. The airbag system consists of the airbag unit (complete with gas generator), which is fitted to the steering wheel (driver's side), facia (passenger's side), roof (where applicable) and front door panels, an impact sensor, the control unit and a warning light in the instrument panel.

The airbag system is triggered in the event of a heavy frontal or side impact above a predetermined force, depending on the point of impact. The airbag is inflated within milliseconds and forms a safety cushion between the driver and the steering wheel, the passenger and the facia, and in the case of side impact, between front seat occupants and the sides of the cabin. This prevents contact between the upper body and cabin interior, and therefore greatly reduces the risk of injury. The airbag then deflates almost immediately.

Every time the ignition is switched on, the airbag control unit performs a self-test. The self-test takes approximately 3 seconds and during this time the airbag warning light is illuminated. After the self-test has been completed the warning light should go out. If the warning light fails to come on, remains illuminated after the initial 3-second period or comes on at any time when the vehicle is being driven, there is a fault in the airbag system. The vehicle should then be taken to a Mercedes-Benz dealer for examination at the earliest possible opportunity.

24 Airbag system components – removal and refitting

Note: *Refer to the warnings in Section 23 before carrying out the following operations.*

1 Disconnect the battery negative lead (refer to *Disconnecting the battery* in the *Reference* Chapter at the end of this manual), then continue as described under the relevant heading.

Driver's airbag

Removal

2 Set the front wheels to the straight-ahead position, and release the steering lock by inserting the ignition key.

3 Working at the rear of the steering wheel, slacken and remove the two retaining screws **(see illustration)**.

Caution: To prevent any discharge of static electricity into the airbag circuit, temporarily touch the vehicle bodywork before disconnecting the wiring.

4 Carefully withdraw the airbag module from the steering wheel and disconnect the wiring **(see illustrations)**.

Warning: Position the airbag in a safe and secure place, away from the work area.

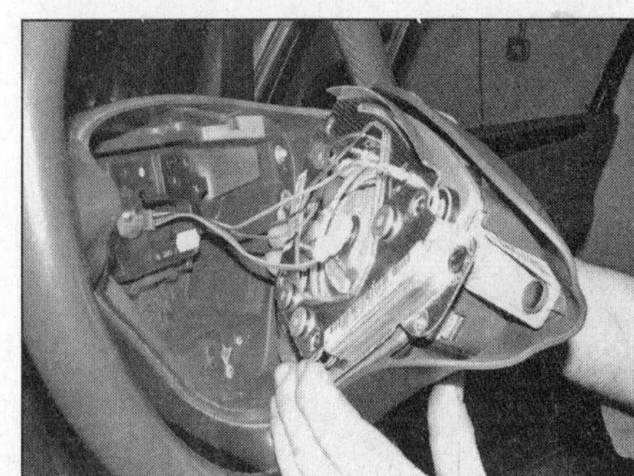

24.4a Carefully remove the airbag . . .

24.4b . . . and disconnect the wiring connector(s)

24.10 Side impact airbag – arrowed

Refitting

5 With the steering wheel in the straight-ahead position, locate the airbag module in position and reconnect the wiring, making sure it is connected securely. Reconnect the battery negative lead, ensuring that no-one is inside the vehicle as the lead is connected. **Note:** *If the airbag is being renewed after it has been deployed, the steering wheel will also need to be renewed.*

Passenger's airbag

Removal

6 Remove the passenger side glovebox and upper facia panel with reference to Chapter 11, Section 26.

Caution: To prevent any discharge of static electricity into the airbag circuit, temporarily touch the vehicle bodywork before disconnecting the wiring.

24.18 Note the direction of the arrow on the unit

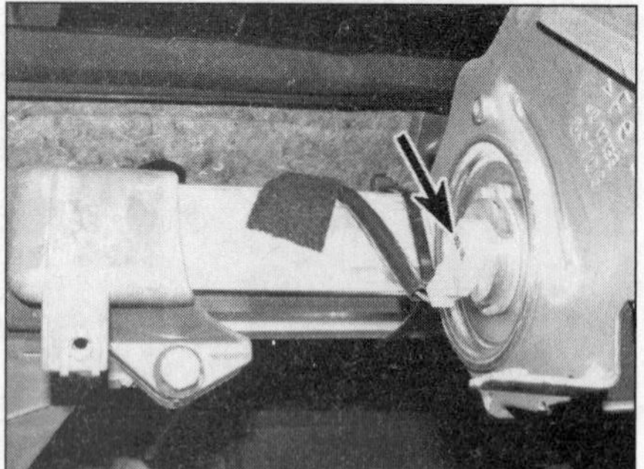

24.7 Passenger airbag wiring connector

24.14 Location of the airbag control unit – arrowed

7 Disconnect the wiring from the passenger's airbag **(see illustration)**.

8 Slacken the two mounting bolts, and slide them towards each other to release the airbag from its mounting bracket **(see illustration)**, and then withdraw from the vehicle.

Warning: Position the airbag in a safe and secure place, away from the work area.

Refitting

9 Refitting is a reversal of removal, but tighten the mounting bolts to the specified torque. Reconnect the battery negative lead, ensuring that no one is inside the vehicle as the lead is connected.

Front side impact airbags

10 The side impact air bags are fitted to the inside of the doorframe **(see illustration)**. Remove the door inner trim panels as described in Chapter 11.

24.20a Undo the retaining screws – arrowed . . .

24.8 Slacken the passenger airbag mounting bolts – arrowed

11 Disconnect the wiring from the side of the airbag unit.

12 Undo the mounting bolts, and remove the airbag from the door frame.

Roof curtain airbags

13 This work involves removing the headlining and major dismantling of interior trim panels, and is best entrusted to a Mercedes-Benz dealer.

Airbag control unit

Removal

14 The airbag control unit is located beneath the handbrake lever under the centre console, just to the rear of the gearchange assembly **(see illustration)**.

15 Remove the centre console with reference to Chapter 11.

16 Release the locking lever and disconnect the wiring from the control unit.

17 Unscrew the retaining nuts and remove the control unit from the vehicle. It may be necessary to unclip the plastic air pipe to access the retaining nuts.

Refitting

18 Refitting is the reverse of removal, making sure the wiring connector is securely reconnected and the arrow on the unit is pointing forwards **(see illustration)**. Reconnect the battery negative lead, ensuring that no one is inside the vehicle as the lead is connected.

Airbag wiring contact unit

Removal

19 Check that the front wheels are pointing straight-ahead and the steering wheel is in its centre position, then remove the steering wheel as described in Chapter 10.

20 With the steering still in the straight-ahead position, slacken the two airbag contact unit retaining screws, and withdraw the unit from the steering column **(see illustrations)**. **Note:** *Do not turn the airbag contact unit, while it is off the vehicle, as it has a spring inside which will need to be refitted in the same position.*

Refitting

21 If the contact unit has been turned while off the vehicle, before refitting the airbag

24.20b . . . and remove the contact unit

contact unit (clock spring/slip-ring), check that it is in its central position as follows:

a) Fit the contact unit, back onto the top of the steering column, and tighten the retaining screws.

b) Turn the centre of the contact unit (clock spring) anti-clockwise until a resistance is felt. DO NOT force it.

c) Then turn it back (clockwise) approximately 2.5 to 3 turns, until the mounting screws can be accessed through the openings.

d) This should then be in the central position for refitting the steering wheel.

e) The total number of turns the contact unit can make from one side to the other is approximately 5 to 6 turns.

22 The remaining procedure is a reversal of removal. Reconnect the battery negative lead, ensuring that no one is inside the vehicle as the lead is connected.

Passenger airbag isolation sensor

23 The passenger airbag will only go off if there is someone sitting in the passenger seat, as there is a sensor located inside the seat base. If there is a problem with this, it will need to be checked by your local Mercedes-Benz dealer.

Side crash sensors

Removal

24 There are sensors each side of the vehicle, under the floor panel near the centre of the sill.

25 Disconnect the battery.

26 Remove the undertrays from each side of the vehicle along the sill panels.

27 Disconnect the wiring from the crash sensor.

28 Undo the mounting screws and remove the sensor.

Refitting

29 Refitting is a reversal of removal. Make sure that nobody is inside the vehicle when first switching on the ignition.

25 Parking aid components – general information, removal and refitting

General information

1 The parking aid system is available as a standard fitment on highline models, and optional on other models. Sensors are located in the rear or front bumper and measure the distance to the closest object behind or in front of the car. They inform the driver using acoustic signals and the warning lights on the instrument panel will light up. The warning displays indicate the distance between the vehicle and the nearest obstacle. The front warning display is located above the centre air vents and the rear display is located in the rear of the roof lining.

2 The system includes a control unit, sensors and display units, in the event of a fault the vehicle should be taken to a Mercedes-Benz dealer.

Control unit

3 The parking aid control unit is located in the luggage compartment behind the right-hand trim panel. Switch off the ignition and all electrical consumers, and remove the ignition key, then remove the right-hand trim with reference to Chapter 11, Section 26.

4 Depress the locking lugs and disconnect the wiring plugs from the control unit.

5 Undo the mounting bolts and remove from the rear trim panel.

6 Refitting is a reversal of removal.

Range/distance sensor

7 Remove the front or rear bumper as described in Chapter 11.

8 Disconnect the wiring from the sensor.

9 Release the lugs and pull the sensor from the bumper.

10 Refitting is a reversal of removal. Press the sensor firmly into position until the retaining clips engage.

Display units

11 For the rear display unit, carefully prise the light/display unit from its location in the rear of the headlining and disconnect the wiring connector as it is removed.

12 For the front display unit remove the upper facia trim panel with reference to Chapter 11, and then unclip it from the facia panel.

Mercedes-Benz A-Class wiring diagrams

Diagram 1

WARNING: This vehicle is fitted with a supplemental restraint system (SRS) consisting of a combination of driver (and passenger) airbag(s), side impact protection airbags and seatbelt pre-tensioners. The use of electrical test equipment on any SRS wiring systems may cause the seatbelt pre-tensioners to abruptly retract and airbags to explosively deploy, resulting in potentially severe personal injury. Extreme care should be taken to correctly identify any circuits to be tested to avoid choosing any of the SRS wiring in error.
For further information see airbag system precautions in body electrical systems chapter.
Note: The SRS wiring harness can normally be identified by yellow and/or orange harness or harness connectors.

Key to symbols

Dashed outline denotes part of a larger item, containing in this case an electronic or solid state device. 10 denotes connector pin identification.

Solenoid actuator

Heating element

Earth point & location (E7)

Wire colour (red with yellow tracer) Rt/Ge

Bulb

Switch

Fuse/fusible link (F26)

Resistor

Variable resistor

Variable resistor

Wire splice, soldered joint, or unspecified connector

Connecting wires

Diode

Light-emitting diode

Item number (12)

Motor/pump (M)

Earth locations

E1	In passenger's compartment, in driver's footwell
E2	In engine compartment, RH inner wing
E3	In luggage compartment, above rear window
E4	In passenger's compartment, at front interior light
E5	In engine compartment, LH front inner wing
E6	In luggage compartment, near LH rear light unit
E7	In luggage compartment, on RH wheel arch

Light switch/control unit (22)

Fuse	Rating	Circuit protected
F1	7.5A	LH dip beam
F2	7.5A	RH dip beam
F3	15A	Main beam
F4	7.5A	LH side/parking light
F5	15A	RH side/parking light, number plate light, instrument cluster
F6	15A	Front and rear foglights

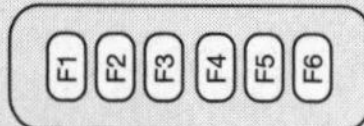

Engine relay box

R1	Washer pump
R2	Horn
R2/1	Rear interior light
R3	Starter
R4	Engine cooling fan
R5	ESP feed pump
R6	Air pump

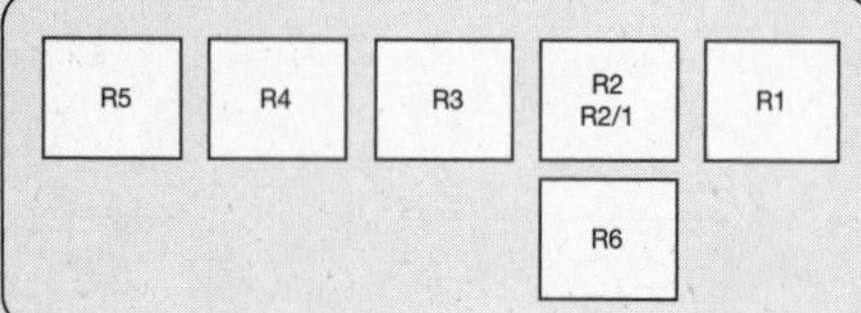

Fusebox (4)

Fuse	Rating	Circuit protected
F1	10A	Engine management
F2	15A	Engine management
F3	30A	Engine cooling fan
F4	40A	Automatic clutch
F5	7.5A	Engine management control unit
F6	30A	Fuel pump relay
F7	40A	Light switch/control unit
F8	30A	Starter relay
F9	40A	Front wiper motor
F10	40A	Rear wiper motor, sunroof
F11	15A	Wash/wipe, headlight flasher
F12	10A	Cigar lighter, rear accessory socket, audio, glovebox light
F13	30A	Electric windows
F14	15A	Instrument cluster, wash/wipe
F15	10A	Airbag
F16	15A	Heated mirrors
F17	15A	Horn
F18	10A	Instrument cluster, transponder, diagnostic connector
F19	25A	Trailer socket
F20	15A	Trailer socket
F21	15A	Trailer socket
F22	25A	Audio system
F23	7.5A	Vanity mirror light
F24	10A	Airbag
F25	15A	Front accessory socket, rear interior light
F26	-	Spare
F27	-	Spare
F28	10A	Instrument cluster, electric windows
F29	15A	Central locking
F30	7.5A	Instrument cluster, transponder
F31	25A	Heated rear window
F32	15A	Front and rear interior lights, audio
F33	30A	Electric windows
F34	-	Spare
F35	10A	Alarm
F36	25A	Heated seats
F37	10A	Heated washer nozzles
F38	10A	Air conditioning, interior mirror
F39	7.5A	Light switch/control unit, reversing lights
F40	10A	Stop lights
F41	10A	Air conditioning, diagnostic connector
F42	30A	Electric windows
F43	15A	ESP, stop light switch
F44	10A	Automatic transmission
F45	30A	Air conditioning, heater blower
F46	80A	Central securing system
F47	60A	Power steering pump
F48	60A	Engine management
F49	200A	Heater, A/C Diesel PTC

Relays

R7	Fuel pump
R8	Engine management
R9	ESP/VGS or ESP/auto. clutch
R10	Engine cooling fan

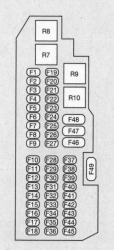

H33779

Diagram 2

Wire colours

Sw	Black	**Rs**	Pink
Br	Brown	**Rt**	Red
Bl	Blue	**Vi**	Violet
Gn	Green	**Ws**	White
Gr	Grey	**Ge**	Yellow
Nf	Neutral		

Key to items

1 Battery
2 Alternator
3 Starter motor
4 Fusebox
5 Ignition switch
6 Starter relay
7 Engine management control unit
8 Horn
9 Horn switch
10 Horn relay
11 Steering wheel clock springs
12 Power steering pump/control unit
13 Sunroof switch
14 Sunroof motor
15 Instrument cluster
16 Centre console switches
 a = heated rear window switch
17 Heated rear window relay
18 Heated rear window
19 Suppressor

H33780

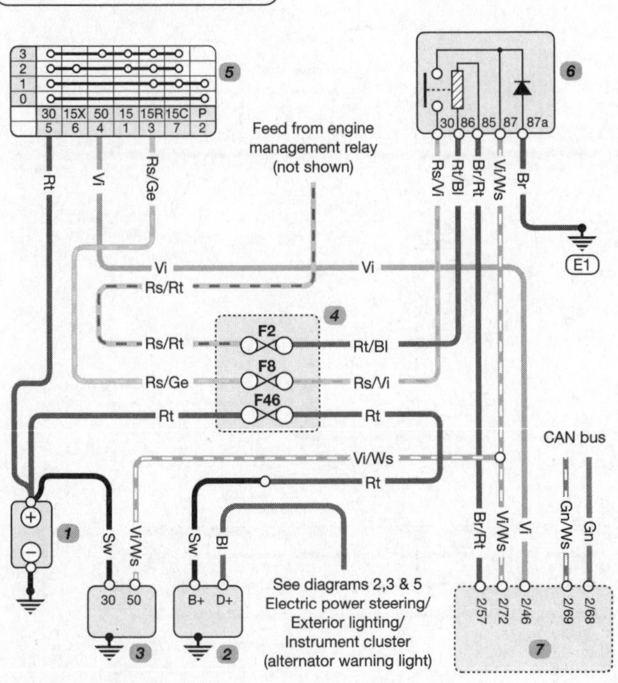

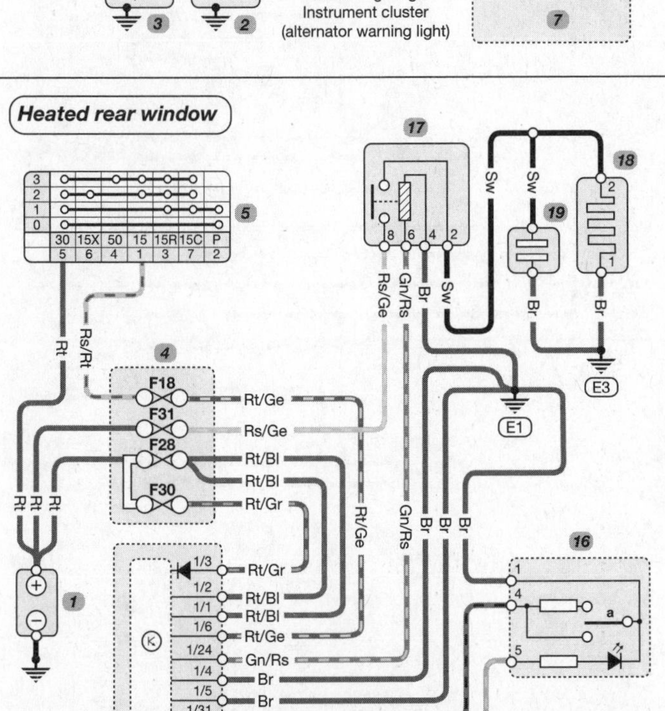

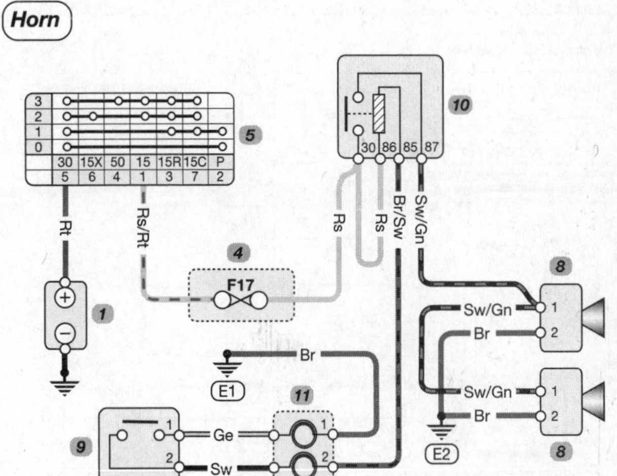

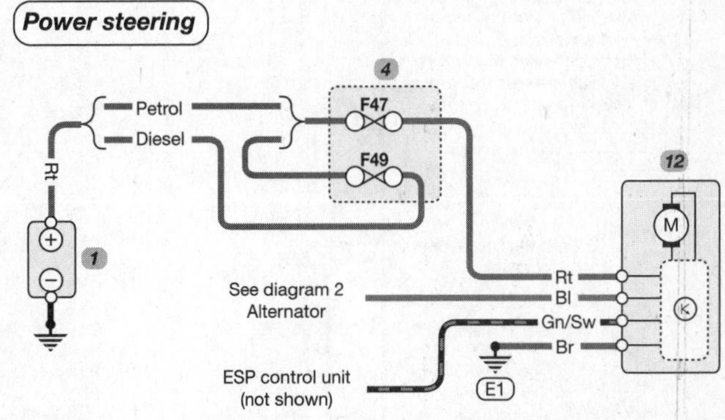

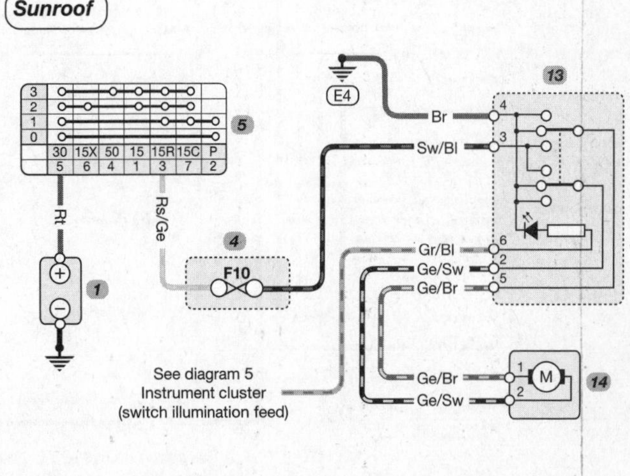

Wire colours

Sw	Black	**Rs**	Pink
Br	Brown	**Rt**	Red
Bl	Blue	**Vi**	Violet
Gn	Green	**Ws**	White
Gr	Grey	**Ge**	Yellow
Nf	Neutral		

Key to items

Diagram 3

1 Battery
4 Fusebox
5 Ignition switch
16 Centre console switches
  b = hazard warning switch
22 Lighting switch/control unit
23 Combination switch
  a = dip/main/flash
  b = indicator switch
24 Number plate light
25 LH headlight
  a = main beam
  b = dip beam
  c = side/parking light
  d = fog light
  e = direction indicator
26 RH headlight
  (as above)
27 LH rear light unit
  a = reversing light
  b = fog light
  c = stop light
  d = tail/parking light
  e = direction indicator
28 RH rear light unit
  (as above)
29 LH indicator side repeater
30 RH indicator side repeater
31 High level stop light
32 Stop light switch
33 Reversing light switch
34 Transmission control unit
35 Stop light suppressor relay

H33781

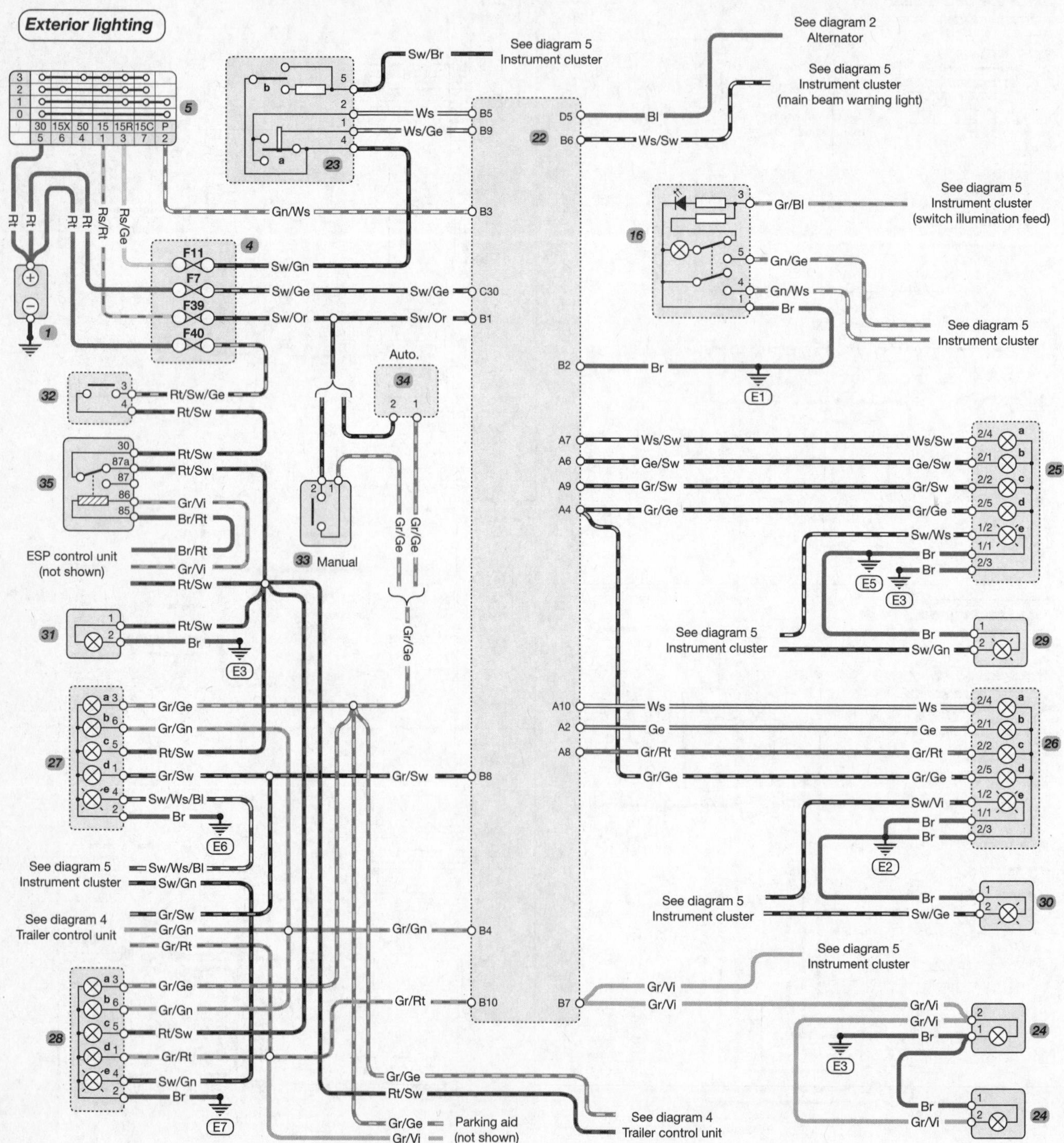

Diagram 4

Wire colours

Sw	Black	**Rs**	Pink
Br	Brown	**Rt**	Red
Bl	Blue	**Vi**	Violet
Gn	Green	**Ws**	White
Gr	Grey	**Ge**	Yellow
Nf	Neutral		

Key to items

1 Battery
4 Fusebox
5 Ignition switch
16 Centre console switches
c = rear wiper switch
23 Combination switch
c = wiper switch
d = washer switch
38 Trailer socket
39 Trailer recognition microswitch
40 Trailer control unit
41 LH vanity mirror light
42 RH vanity mirror light
43 Cigar lighter
44 Glovebox light/switch
45 Front interior light
46 Rear interior light
47 Rear wiper motor
48 Front wiper motor
49 LH heated washer nozzle
50 RH heated washer nozzle
51 Washer pump
52 Washer pump switch-over relay

H33782

Trailer socket

39
Br/Ws
Gn/Ge
Br
E1
Parking aid (not shown)
4
F20
F21
F19
Rt/Ge
Rt/Ws
Rt
1/1
1/2
40
38
See diagram 3 Exterior lighting (stop light circuit)
1
Gr/Sw 2/1
Gr/Ge 2/2
Gr/Rt 2/3
Gr/Gn 2/4
Sw/Gn 2/5
Sw/Ws 2/6
Br 1/8
E6
Rt/Sw
See diagram 3 Transmisson control unit (reversing light signal)
Gr/Ge
Rt/Sw 1/11
Gr/Gn 1/6
See diagram 3 Rear foglight
Sw/Gn/Ge 1/5
Sw/Ws/Rs 1/7
RH rear direction indicator (pin 4)
Sw/Ws/Bl 1/3
Sw/Gn 1/4
LH rear direction indicator (pin 4)
Gr/Sw 1/9
Gr/Rt 1/10
See diagram 3 Exterior lighting (direction indicators)
See diagram 3 Light switch/control unit

Interior lighting & cigar lighter

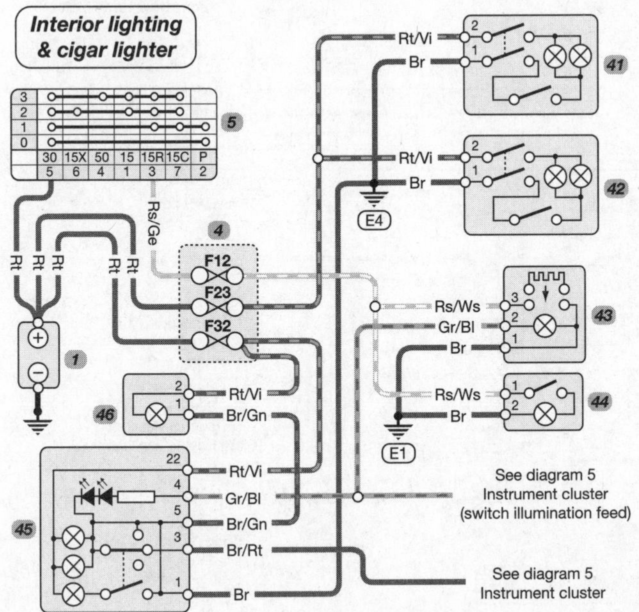

Wash/wipe

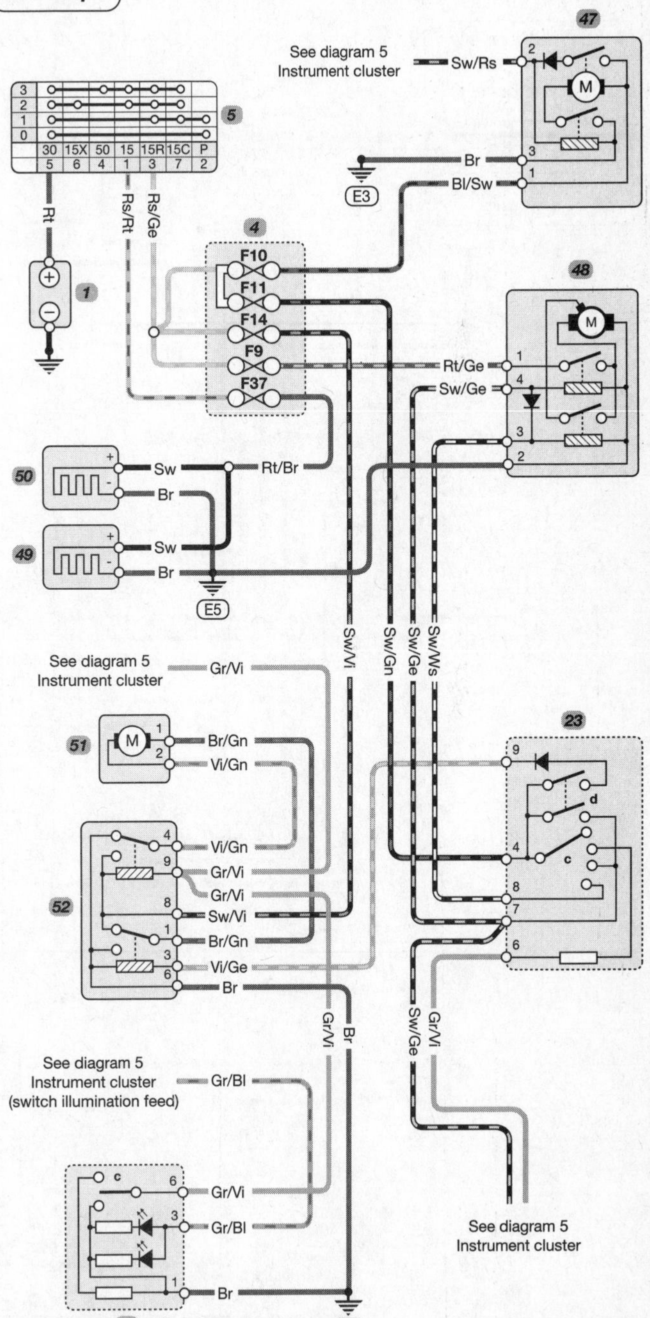

Wire colours

Sw	Black	**Rs**	Pink
Br	Brown	**Rt**	Red
Bl	Blue	**Vi**	Violet
Gn	Green	**Ws**	White
Gr	Grey	**Ge**	Yellow
Nf	Neutral		

Key to items

Diagram 5

1 Battery
4 Fusebox
5 Ignition switch
15 Instrument cluster
  a = alternator warning light
  b = main beam warning light
  c = instrument illumination
  d = illumination rheostat
  e = instrument cluster control unit
  f = LH direction indicator
  g = RH direction indicator
  h = direction indicator warning buzzer
  i = engine management warning light
  j = oil level warning light
  k = low fuel level warning light
  l = pad wear indicator warning light
  m = seatbelt reminder warning light
  n = coolant temp. warning light
  o = ASR warning light
  p = ABS warning light
  q = brake fluid/handbrake warning light
  r = SRS warning light
55 LH front door switch
56 RH front door switch
57 LH rear door switch
58 RH rear door switch
59 Luggage compartment light switch
60 Fuel gauge sender unit
61 Ambient air temp. sensor
62 Brake fluid level sensor
63 Coolant level sensor

H33783

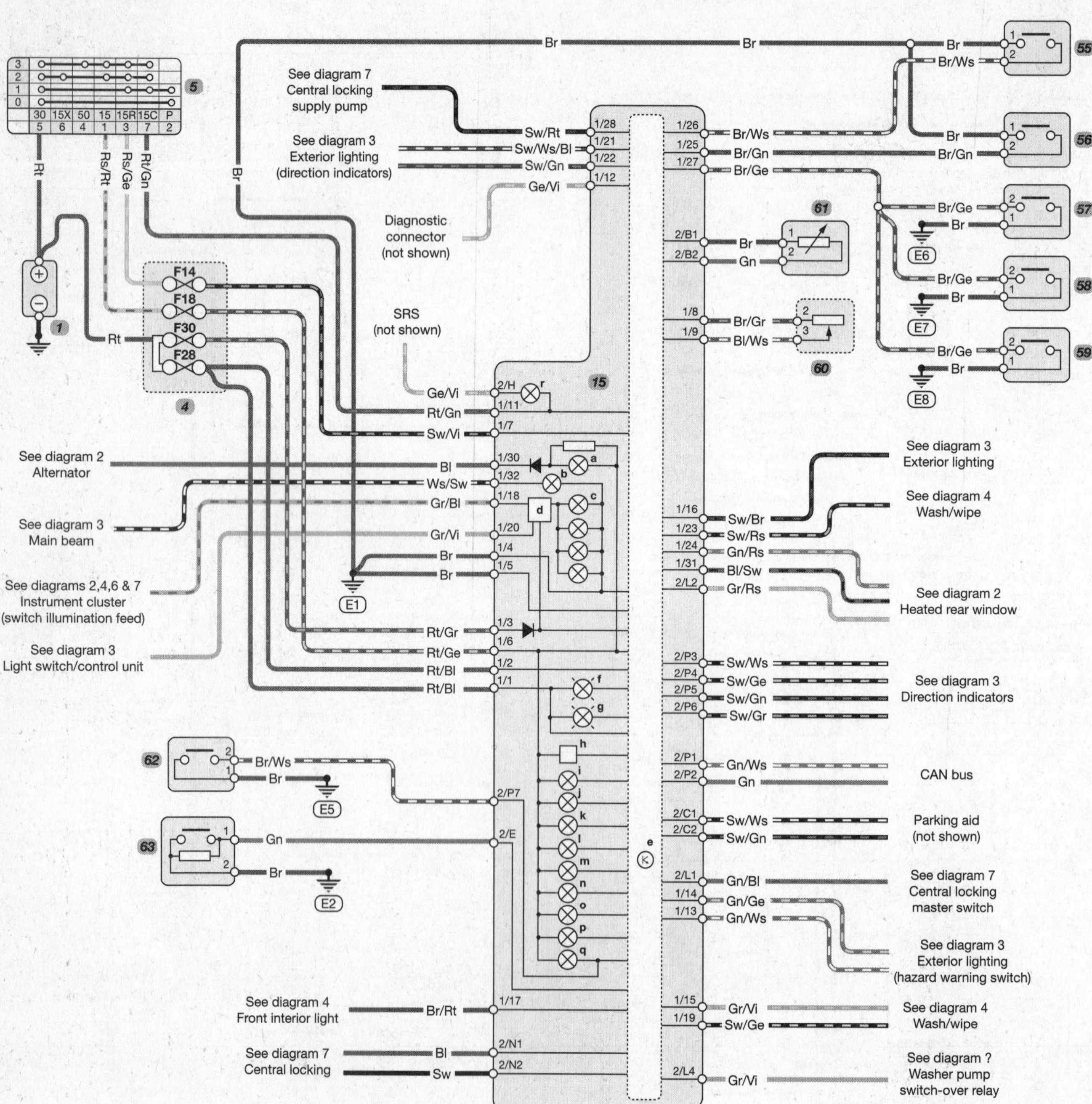

Wire colours

Sw	Black	**Rs**	Pink
Br	Brown	**Rt**	Red
Bl	Blue	**Vi**	Violet
Gn	Green	**Ws**	White
Gr	Grey	**Ge**	Yellow
Nf	Neutral		

Key to items

1 Battery
4 Fusebox
5 Ignition switch
65 Heater blower switch
66 Heater pushbutton control unit
67 Heater blower motor
68 Heater blower resistors
69 Recirculation motor
70 Audio unit
71 Aerial antenna
72 LH front door speaker
73 LH front tweeter
74 LH rear speaker
75 RH front door speaker
76 RH front tweeter
77 RH rear speaker

Diagram 6

H33784

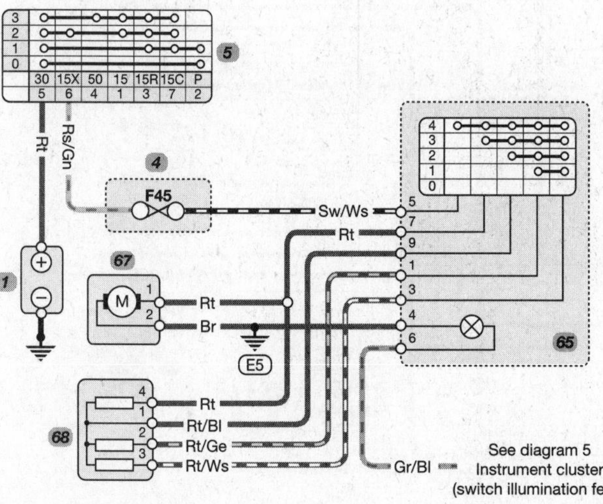

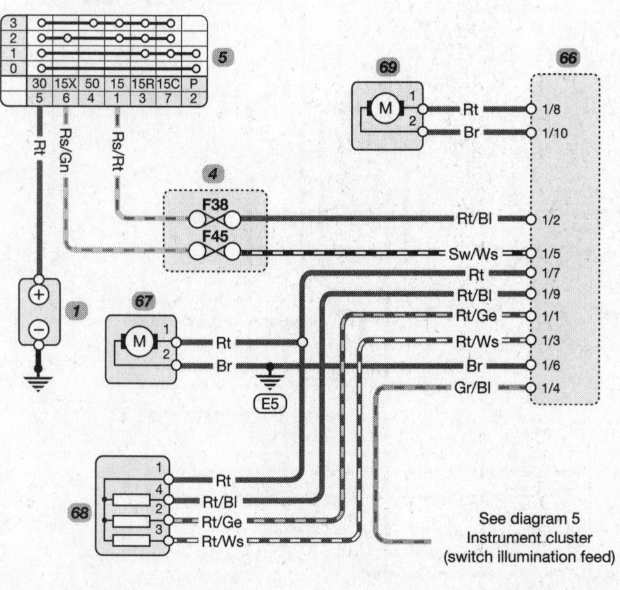

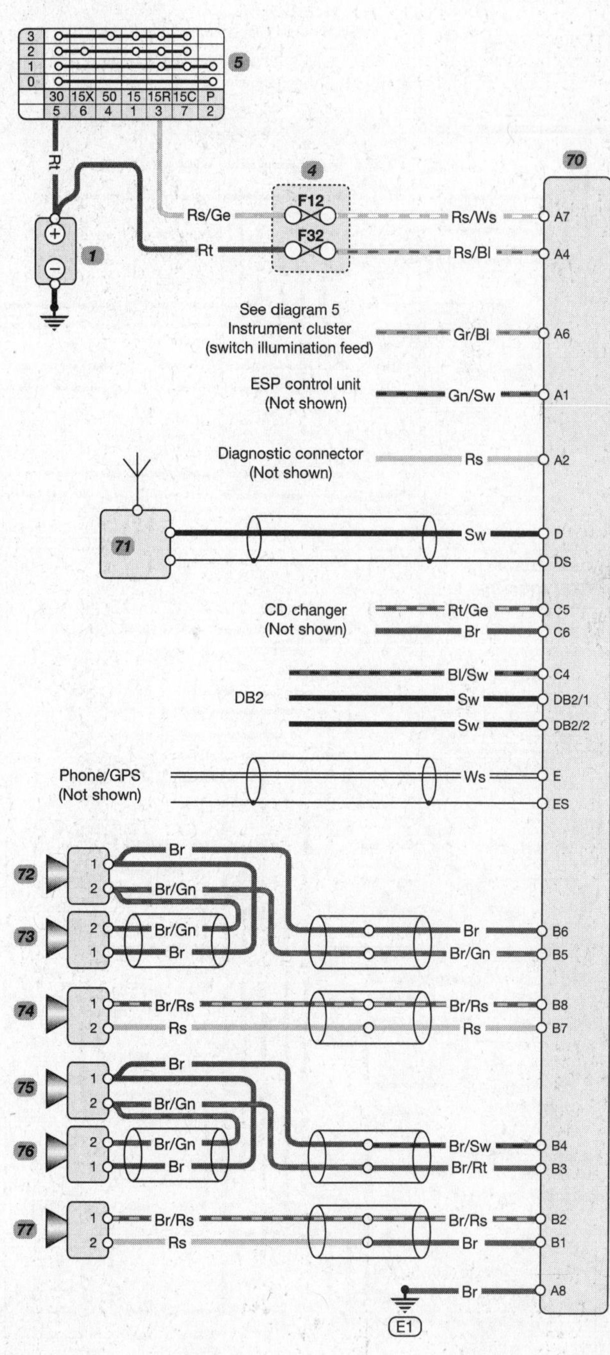

Wire colours

		Rs	Pink
Sw	Black	**Rt**	Red
Br	Brown	**Vi**	Violet
Bl	Blue	**Ws**	White
Gn	Green	**Ge**	Yellow
Gr	Grey		
Nf	Neutral		

Key to items

1 Battery
4 Fusebox
5 Ignition switch
16 Centre console switches
d = electric mirror switches
e = central locking master switch
78 Driver's door control unit
79 Passenger's door control unit
80 LH rear door control unit
81 RH rear door control unit
82 LH rear window switch
83 RH rear window switch
84 Electric window control switches
85 LH heated rear view mirror
86 RH heated rear view mirror
87 Folding mirror switch
88 Central locking transponder
89 Central locking supply pump
90 LH front door lock switch
91 RH front door lock switch
92 Tailgate lock switch

Diagram 7

H33785

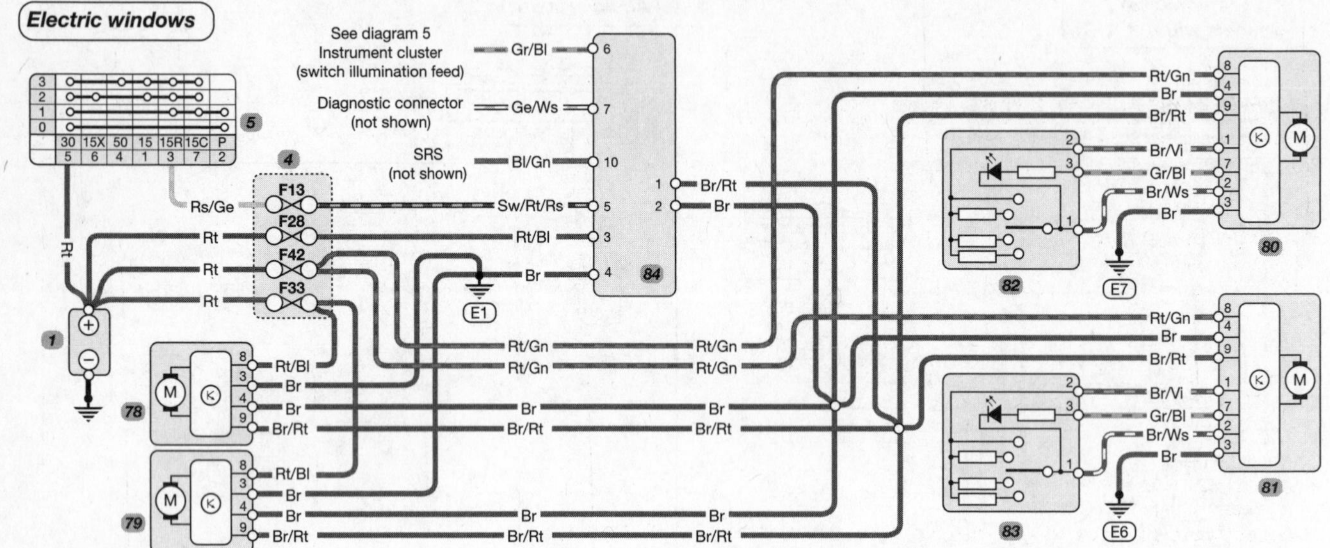

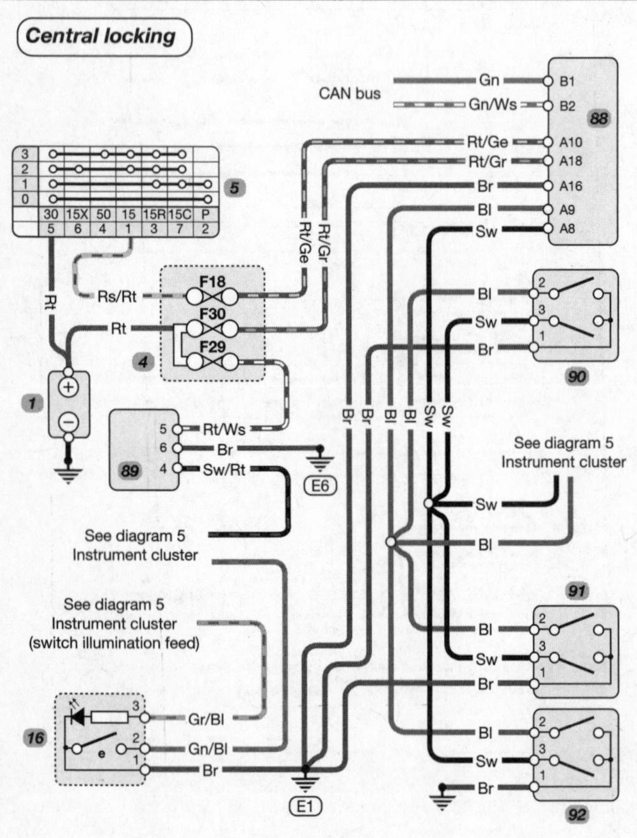

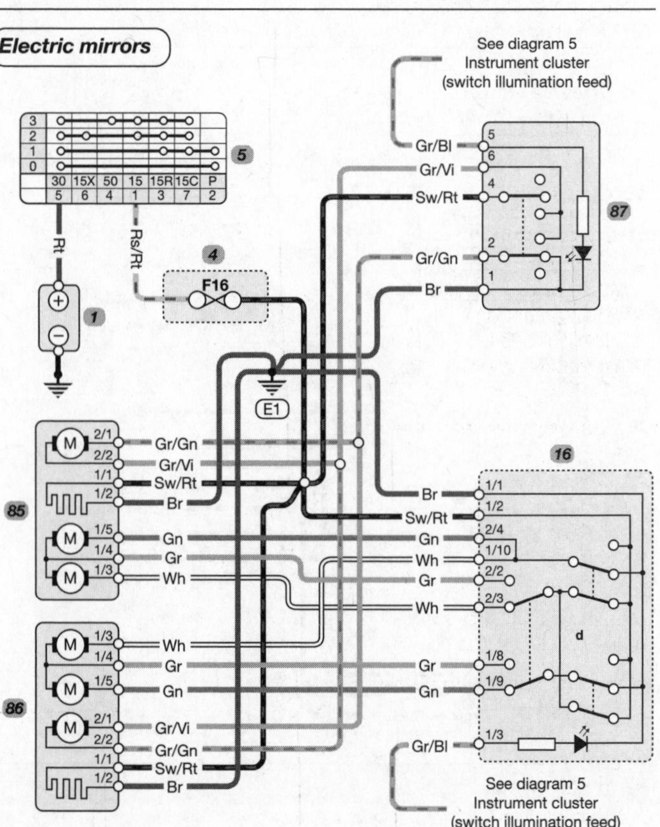

Dimensions and weights

Note: *All figures and dimensions are approximate and may vary according to model. Refer to manufacturer's data for exact figures.*

Overall length

Short wheelbase (SWB) models:	
All models except A210 Evolution	3606 mm
A210 Evolution models	3640 mm
Long wheelbase (LWB) models:	
All models except A210 Evolution	3776 mm
A210 Evolution models	3810 mm

Overall width

All models	1719 mm

Overall height (unladen)

Short wheelbase (SWB) models:	
All models except A190 and A210 petrol models	1575 mm
A190 and A210 petrol models	1587 mm
Long wheelbase (LWB) models:	
All models except A190 and A210 petrol models	1589 mm
A190 and A210 petrol models	1601 mm

Wheelbase

Short wheelbase (SWB) models	2423 mm
Long wheelbase (LWB) models	2593 mm

Weights

Unladen weight

A140 models	1030 kg
A160 models	1040 kg
A160 CDi models	1080 kg
A170 CDi models	1085 kg
A190 models	1080 kg
A210 models	1090 kg

Maximum gross vehicle weight

A140 models	1490 kg
A160 models	1500 kg
A160 CDi models	1540 kg
A170 CDi models	1545 kg
A190 models	1540 kg
A210 models	1550 kg

Maximum roof rack load

All models	50 kg

Maximum towing weights

A140 models	810 kg
A160 models	810 kg
A160 CDi models	800 kg
A170 CDi models	805 kg
A190 models	825 kg
A210 models	N/A

Conversion factors

Length (distance)

Inches (in)	x 25.4	= Millimetres (mm)	x 0.0394	= Inches (in)
Feet (ft)	x 0.305	= Metres (m)	x 3.281	= Feet (ft)
Miles	x 1.609	= Kilometres (km)	x 0.621	= Miles

Volume (capacity)

Cubic inches (cu in; in^3)	x 16.387	= Cubic centimetres (cc; cm^3)	x 0.061	= Cubic inches (cu in; in^3)
Imperial pints (Imp pt)	x 0.568	= Litres (l)	x 1.76	= Imperial pints (Imp pt)
Imperial quarts (Imp qt)	x 1.137	= Litres (l)	x 0.88	= Imperial quarts (Imp qt)
Imperial quarts (Imp qt)	x 1.201	= US quarts (US qt)	x 0.833	= Imperial quarts (Imp qt)
US quarts (US qt)	x 0.946	= Litres (l)	x 1.057	= US quarts (US qt)
Imperial gallons (Imp gal)	x 4.546	= Litres (l)	x 0.22	= Imperial gallons (Imp gal)
Imperial gallons (Imp gal)	x 1.201	= US gallons (US gal)	x 0.833	= Imperial gallons (Imp gal)
US gallons (US gal)	x 3.785	= Litres (l)	x 0.264	= US gallons (US gal)

Mass (weight)

Ounces (oz)	x 28.35	= Grams (g)	x 0.035	= Ounces (oz)
Pounds (lb)	x 0.454	= Kilograms (kg)	x 2.205	= Pounds (lb)

Force

Ounces-force (ozf; oz)	x 0.278	= Newtons (N)	x 3.6	= Ounces-force (ozf; oz)
Pounds-force (lbf; lb)	x 4.448	= Newtons (N)	x 0.225	= Pounds-force (lbf; lb)
Newtons (N)	x 0.1	= Kilograms-force (kgf; kg)	x 9.81	= Newtons (N)

Pressure

Pounds-force per square inch (psi; lbf/in^2; lb/in^2)	x 0.070	= Kilograms-force per square centimetre (kgf/cm^2; kg/cm^2)	x 14.223	= Pounds-force per square inch (psi; lbf/in^2; lb/in^2)
Pounds-force per square inch (psi; lbf/in^2; lb/in^2)	x 0.068	= Atmospheres (atm)	x 14.696	= Pounds-force per square inch (psi; lbf/in^2; lb/in^2)
Pounds-force per square inch (psi; lbf/in^2; lb/in^2)	x 0.069	= Bars	x 14.5	= Pounds-force per square inch (psi; lbf/in^2; lb/in^2)
Pounds-force per square inch (psi; lbf/in^2; lb/in^2)	x 6.895	= Kilopascals (kPa)	x 0.145	= Pounds-force per square inch (psi; lbf/in^2; lb/in^2)
Kilopascals (kPa)	x 0.01	= Kilograms-force per square centimetre (kgf/cm^2; kg/cm^2)	x 98.1	= Kilopascals (kPa)
Millibar (mbar)	x 100	= Pascals (Pa)	x 0.01	= Millibar (mbar)
Millibar (mbar)	x 0.0145	= Pounds-force per square inch (psi; lbf/in^2; lb/in^2)	x 68.947	= Millibar (mbar)
Millibar (mbar)	x 0.75	= Millimetres of mercury (mmHg)	x 1.333	= Millibar (mbar)
Millibar (mbar)	x 0.401	= Inches of water (inH_2O)	x 2.491	= Millibar (mbar)
Millimetres of mercury (mmHg)	x 0.535	= Inches of water (inH_2O)	x 1.868	= Millimetres of mercury (mmHg)
Inches of water (inH_2O)	x 0.036	= Pounds-force per square inch (psi; lbf/in^2; lb/in^2)	x 27.68	= Inches of water (inH_2O)

Torque (moment of force)

Pounds-force inches (lbf in; lb in)	x 1.152	= Kilograms-force centimetre (kgf cm; kg cm)	x 0.868	= Pounds-force inches (lbf in; lb in)
Pounds-force inches (lbf in; lb in)	x 0.113	= Newton metres (Nm)	x 8.85	= Pounds-force inches (lbf in; lb in)
Pounds-force inches (lbf in; lb in)	x 0.083	= Pounds-force feet (lbf ft; lb ft)	x 12	= Pounds-force inches (lbf in; lb in)
Pounds-force feet (lbf ft; lb ft)	x 0.138	= Kilograms-force metres (kgf m; kg m)	x 7.233	= Pounds-force feet (lbf ft; lb ft)
Pounds-force feet (lbf ft; lb ft)	x 1.356	= Newton metres (Nm)	x 0.738	= Pounds-force feet (lbf ft; lb ft)
Newton metres (Nm)	x 0.102	= Kilograms-force metres (kgf m; kg m)	x 9.804	= Newton metres (Nm)

Power

Horsepower (hp)	x 745.7	= Watts (W)	x 0.0013	= Horsepower (hp)

Velocity (speed)

Miles per hour (miles/hr; mph)	x 1.609	= Kilometres per hour (km/hr; kph)	x 0.621	= Miles per hour (miles/hr; mph)

Fuel consumption*

Miles per gallon, Imperial (mpg)	x 0.354	= Kilometres per litre (km/l)	x 2.825	= Miles per gallon, Imperial (mpg)
Miles per gallon, US (mpg)	x 0.425	= Kilometres per litre (km/l)	x 2.352	= Miles per gallon, US (mpg)

Temperature

Degrees Fahrenheit = (°C x 1.8) + 32 Degrees Celsius (Degrees Centigrade; °C) = (°F - 32) x 0.56

** It is common practice to convert from miles per gallon (mpg) to litres/100 kilometres (l/100km), where mpg x l/100 km = 282*

Spare parts are available from many sources, including maker's appointed garages, accessory shops, and motor factors. To be sure of obtaining the correct parts, it will sometimes be necessary to quote the vehicle identification number. If possible, it can also be useful to take the old parts along for positive identification. Items such as starter motors and alternators may be available under a service exchange scheme – any parts returned should be clean.

Our advice regarding spare parts is as follows.

Officially appointed garages

This is the best source of parts which are peculiar to your car, and which are not otherwise generally available (e.g. badges, interior trim, certain body panels, etc). It is also the only place at which you should buy parts if the vehicle is still under warranty.

Accessory shops

These are very good places to buy materials and components needed for the maintenance of your car (oil, air and fuel filters, light bulbs, drivebelts, greases, brake pads, touch-up paint, etc). Components of this nature sold by a reputable shop are usually of the same standard as those used by the car manufacturer.

Besides components, these shops also sell tools and general accessories, usually have convenient opening hours, charge lower prices, and can often be found close to home. Some accessory shops have parts counters where components needed for almost any repair job can be purchased or ordered.

Motor factors

Good factors will stock all the more important components, which wear out comparatively quickly, and can sometimes supply individual components needed for the overhaul of a larger assembly (e.g. brake seals and hydraulic parts, bearing shells, pistons, valves). They may also handle work such as cylinder block reboring, crankshaft regrinding, etc.

Tyre and exhaust specialists

These outlets may be independent, or members of a local or national chain. They frequently offer competitive prices when compared with a main dealer or local garage, but it will pay to obtain several quotes before making a decision. When researching prices, also ask what extras may be added – for instance fitting a new valve and balancing the wheel are both commonly charged on top of the price of a new tyre.

Other sources

Beware of parts or materials obtained from market stalls, car boot sales or similar outlets. Such items are not invariably sub-standard, but there is little chance of compensation if they do prove unsatisfactory. In the case of safety-critical components such as brake pads, there is the risk not only of financial loss, but also of an accident causing injury or death.

Second-hand components or assemblies obtained from a car breaker can be a good buy in some circumstances, but this sort of purchase is best made by the experienced DIY mechanic.

Vehicle identification numbers

Modifications are a continuing and unpublicised process in vehicle manufacture, quite apart from major model changes. Spare parts manuals and lists are compiled upon a numerical basis, the individual vehicle identification numbers being essential to correct identification of the component concerned.

When ordering spare parts, always give as much information as possible. Quote the car model, year of manufacture and registration, chassis and engine numbers as appropriate.

The *Vehicle Identification Number (VIN) plate* is visible from the outside of the vehicle, through the left-hand lower corner of the windscreen, and is also stamped on the rear bulkhead panel inside the engine compartment **(see illustrations)**.

The *Type plate* is located at the bottom of the right-hand door B-pillar, and is visible with the door open **(see illustration)**. It contains the VIN number, gross vehicle weight, front axle and rear axle weights, and paint code.

The *Engine Number* is stamped into the front lower end of the cylinder block **(see illustration)**.

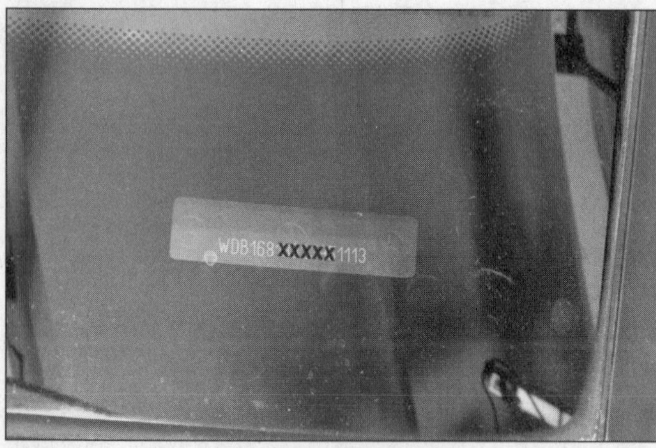

Vehicle Identification Number (VIN) located on the left-hand front edge of the windscreen

Vehicle Identification Number (VIN) located on the rear bulkhead

Vehicle type sticker located on the door pillar

Engine number located on the front lower part of the cylinder block

Vehicle identification

Petrol engines	Model code
A140 (166.940):	
Short wheelbase	168.031
Long wheelbase	168.131
A160 (166.960):	
Short wheelbase	168.033
Long wheelbase	168.133
Vaneo model	414.700
A190 (166.990):	
Short wheelbase	168.032
Long wheelbase	168.132
Vaneo model	414.700
A210 (166.995):	
Short wheelbase	168.035
Long wheelbase	168.135

Diesel engines	Model code
A160 (668.940):	
Short wheelbase	168.006
A160 (668.941):	
Short wheelbase	168.007
Vaneo model	414.700
A170 (668.940):	
Short wheelbase	168.008
Vaneo model	414.700
A170 (668.942):	
Short wheelbase	168.009
Long wheelbase	168.109
Vaneo model	414.700

Jacking and vehicle support

The jack supplied with the vehicle tool kit should only be used for changing the roadwheels – see *Wheel changing* at the front of this book. When carrying out any other kind of work, raise the vehicle using a hydraulic (or 'trolley') jack, and always supplement the jack with axle stands positioned under the vehicle jacking points. To raise the front and/or rear of the vehicle, use the jacking/support points at the front and rear ends of the door sills, indicated by the markings on the sill panel **(see illustration)**.

When using a hydraulic jack or axle stands, always position the jack head or axle stand head under one of the relevant jacking points.

Do not jack the vehicle under any other part of the sill, sump, floorpan, or any of the steering or suspension components. With the vehicle raised, an axle stand should be positioned beneath the vehicle jack location point on the sill.

Warning: Never work under, around, or near a raised car, unless it is adequately supported in at least two places.

Jacking point to lift vehicle

Disconnecting the battery

Several of the systems require battery power to be available at all times (permanent live). This is either to ensure their continued operation (such as the clock), or to maintain electronic memory settings, which would otherwise be erased. Whenever the battery is to be disconnected, first note the following points, to ensure there are no unforeseen consequences:

a) *Firstly, on any vehicle with central door locking, it is a wise precaution to remove the key from the ignition, and to keep it with you. This avoids the possibility of the key being locked inside the car, should the central locking engage when the battery is reconnected.*

b) *If a security-coded audio unit is fitted, and the unit and/or the battery is disconnected, the unit will not function until the correct security code has been entered. Therefore, if you do not know the correct security code for the radio/CD unit, **do not** disconnect either of the battery terminals, or remove the radio/CD unit from the vehicle. The code appears on a code card supplied with the car when new. Details for entering the code appear in the vehicle handbook. Should the code have been misplaced or forgotten, on production of proof of ownership, a Mercedes dealer or in-car entertainment specialist may be able to help.*

c) *The engine management system ECM is of the 'self-learning' type, meaning that, as it operates, it adapts to changes in operating conditions, and stores the optimum settings found. When the battery is disconnected, these 'learned' settings are lost, and the ECM reverts to the base factory settings. When the engine is restarted, it may idle and run roughly until the ECM has 'relearned' the best settings. If the engine does not regain its normal performance, have the system checked for faults by a Mercedes dealer.*

d) *On vehicles equipped with an original equipment anti-theft alarm system, before disconnecting the battery, de-activate the alarm system; otherwise the alarm will be triggered.*

e) *After the battery has been reconnected, the warning lights for the ESP and electro-mechanical steering will light up and stay on, they will extinguish if you drive briefly at a speed of 9 to 13 mph.*

Devices known as 'memory-savers' or 'code-savers' can be used to avoid some of the above problems. Precise details of use vary according to the device used. Typically, it is plugged into the cigarette lighter socket, and is connected by its own wiring to a spare battery; the vehicle battery is then disconnected from the electrical system, leaving the memory-saver to pass sufficient current to maintain audio unit security codes, and other memory values, and also to run permanently-live circuits such as the clock.

Warning: Some of these devices allow a considerable amount of current to pass, which can mean that many of the vehicle's systems are still operational when the main battery is disconnected. If a memory-saver is used, ensure that the circuit concerned is actually 'dead' before carrying out any work on it.

Introduction

A selection of good tools is a fundamental requirement for anyone contemplating the maintenance and repair of a motor vehicle. For the owner who does not possess any, their purchase will prove a considerable expense, offsetting some of the savings made by doing-it-yourself. However, provided that the tools purchased meet the relevant national safety standards and are of good quality, they will last for many years and prove an extremely worthwhile investment.

To help the average owner to decide which tools are needed to carry out the various tasks detailed in this manual, we have compiled three lists of tools under the following headings: *Maintenance and minor repair*, *Repair and overhaul*, and *Special*. Newcomers to practical mechanics should start off with the *Maintenance and minor repair* tool kit, and confine themselves to the simpler jobs around the vehicle. Then, as confidence and experience grow, more difficult tasks can be undertaken, with extra tools being purchased as, and when, they are needed. In this way, a *Maintenance and minor repair* tool kit can be built up into a *Repair and overhaul* tool kit over a considerable period of time, without any major cash outlays. The experienced do-it-yourselfer will have a tool kit good enough for most repair and overhaul procedures, and will add tools from the *Special* category when it is felt that the expense is justified by the amount of use to which these tools will be put.

Maintenance and minor repair tool kit

The tools given in this list should be considered as a minimum requirement if routine maintenance, servicing and minor repair operations are to be undertaken. We recommend the purchase of combination spanners (ring one end, open-ended the other); although more expensive than open-ended ones, they do give the advantages of both types of spanner.

- ☐ *Combination spanners:*
  Metric - 8 to 19 mm inclusive
- ☐ *Adjustable spanner - 35 mm jaw (approx.)*
- ☐ *Spark plug spanner (with rubber insert) - petrol models*
- ☐ *Spark plug gap adjustment tool - petrol models*
- ☐ *Set of feeler gauges*
- ☐ *Brake bleed nipple spanner*
- ☐ *Screwdrivers:*
  Flat blade - 100 mm long x 6 mm dia
  Cross blade - 100 mm long x 6 mm dia
  Torx - various sizes (not all vehicles)
- ☐ *Combination pliers*
- ☐ *Hacksaw (junior)*
- ☐ *Tyre pump*
- ☐ *Tyre pressure gauge*
- ☐ *Oil can*
- ☐ *Oil filter removal tool*
- ☐ *Fine emery cloth*
- ☐ *Wire brush (small)*
- ☐ *Funnel (medium size)*
- ☐ *Sump drain plug key (not all vehicles)*

Repair and overhaul tool kit

These tools are virtually essential for anyone undertaking any major repairs to a motor vehicle, and are additional to those given in the *Maintenance and minor repair* list. Included in this list is a comprehensive set of sockets. Although these are expensive, they will be found invaluable as they are so versatile - particularly if various drives are included in the set. We recommend the half-inch square-drive type, as this can be used with most proprietary torque wrenches.

The tools in this list will sometimes need to be supplemented by tools from the *Special* list:

- ☐ *Sockets (or box spanners) to cover range in previous list (including Torx sockets)*
- ☐ *Reversible ratchet drive (for use with sockets)*
- ☐ *Extension piece, 250 mm (for use with sockets)*
- ☐ *Universal joint (for use with sockets)*
- ☐ *Flexible handle or sliding T "breaker bar" (for use with sockets)*
- ☐ *Torque wrench (for use with sockets)*
- ☐ *Self-locking grips*
- ☐ *Ball pein hammer*
- ☐ *Soft-faced mallet (plastic or rubber)*
- ☐ *Screwdrivers:*
  Flat blade - long & sturdy, short (chubby), and narrow (electrician's) types
  Cross blade – long & sturdy, and short (chubby) types
- ☐ *Pliers:*
  Long-nosed
  Side cutters (electrician's)
  Circlip (internal and external)
- ☐ *Cold chisel - 25 mm*
- ☐ *Scriber*
- ☐ *Scraper*
- ☐ *Centre-punch*
- ☐ *Pin punch*
- ☐ *Hacksaw*
- ☐ *Brake hose clamp*
- ☐ *Brake/clutch bleeding kit*
- ☐ *Selection of twist drills*
- ☐ *Steel rule/straight-edge*
- ☐ *Allen keys (inc. splined/Torx type)*
- ☐ *Selection of files*
- ☐ *Wire brush*
- ☐ *Axle stands*
- ☐ *Jack (strong trolley or hydraulic type)*
- ☐ *Light with extension lead*
- ☐ *Universal electrical multi-meter*

Sockets and reversible ratchet drive

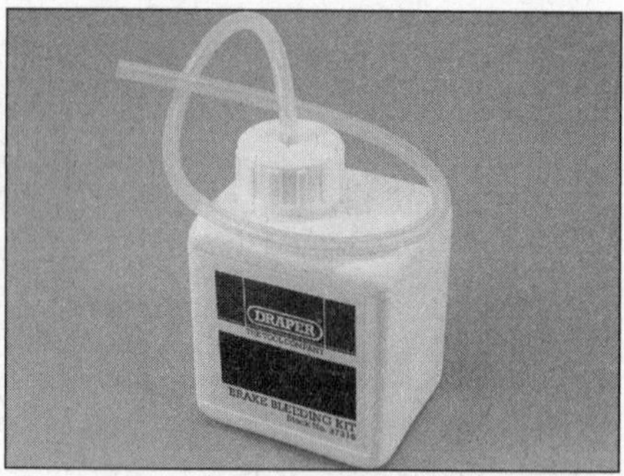

Brake bleeding kit

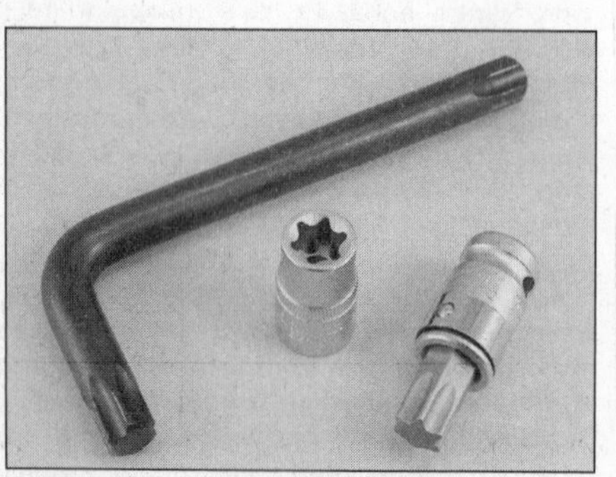

Torx key, socket and bit

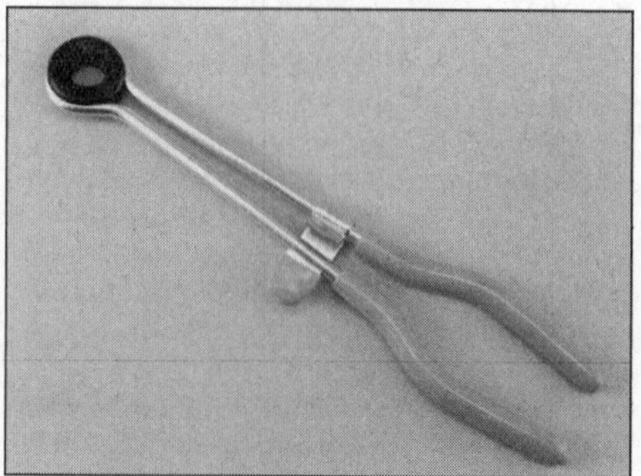

Hose clamp

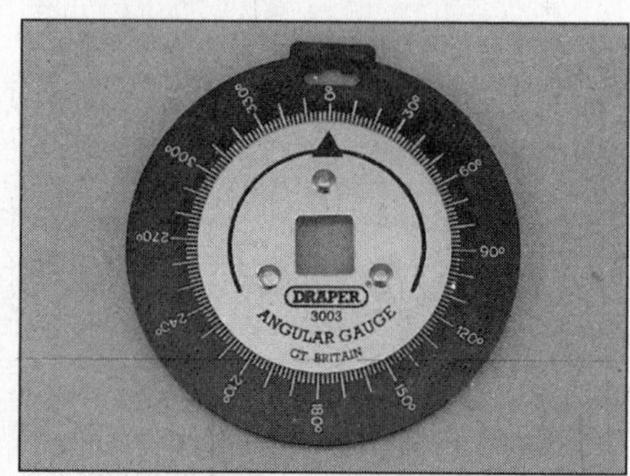

Angular-tightening gauge

Special tools

The tools in this list are those which are not used regularly, are expensive to buy, or which need to be used in accordance with their manufacturers' instructions. Unless relatively difficult mechanical jobs are undertaken frequently, it will not be economic to buy many of these tools. Where this is the case, you could consider clubbing together with friends (or joining a motorists' club) to make a joint purchase, or borrowing the tools against a deposit from a local garage or tool hire specialist. It is worth noting that many of the larger DIY superstores now carry a large range of special tools for hire at modest rates.

The following list contains only those tools and instruments freely available to the public, and not those special tools produced by the vehicle manufacturer specifically for its dealer network. You will find occasional references to these manufacturers' special tools in the text of this manual. Generally, an alternative method of doing the job without the vehicle manufacturers' special tool is given. However, sometimes there is no alternative to using them. Where this is the case and the relevant tool cannot be bought or borrowed, you will have to entrust the work to a dealer.

- ☐ *Angular-tightening gauge*
- ☐ *Valve spring compressor*
- ☐ *Valve grinding tool*
- ☐ *Piston ring compressor*
- ☐ *Piston ring removal/installation tool*
- ☐ *Cylinder bore hone*
- ☐ *Balljoint separator*
- ☐ *Coil spring compressors (where applicable)*
- ☐ *Two/three-legged hub and bearing puller*
- ☐ *Impact screwdriver*
- ☐ *Micrometer and/or vernier calipers*
- ☐ *Dial gauge*
- ☐ *Stroboscopic timing light*
- ☐ *Dwell angle meter/tachometer*
- ☐ *Fault code reader*
- ☐ *Cylinder compression gauge*
- ☐ *Hand-operated vacuum pump and gauge*
- ☐ *Clutch plate alignment set*
- ☐ *Brake shoe steady spring cup removal tool*
- ☐ *Bush and bearing removal/installation set*
- ☐ *Stud extractors*
- ☐ *Tap and die set*
- ☐ *Lifting tackle*
- ☐ *Trolley jack*

Buying tools

Reputable motor accessory shops and superstores often offer excellent quality tools at discount prices, so it pays to shop around.

Remember, you don't have to buy the most expensive items on the shelf, but it is always advisable to steer clear of the very cheap tools. Beware of 'bargains' offered on market stalls or at car boot sales. There are plenty of good tools around at reasonable prices, but always aim to purchase items which meet the relevant national safety standards. If in doubt, ask the proprietor or manager of the shop for advice before making a purchase.

Care and maintenance of tools

Having purchased a reasonable tool kit, it is necessary to keep the tools in a clean and serviceable condition. After use, always wipe off any dirt, grease and metal particles using a clean, dry cloth, before putting the tools away. Never leave them lying around after they have been used. A simple tool rack on the garage or workshop wall for items such as screwdrivers and pliers is a good idea. Store all normal spanners and sockets in a metal box. Any measuring instruments, gauges, meters, etc, must be carefully stored where they cannot be damaged or become rusty.

Take a little care when tools are used. Hammer heads inevitably become marked, and screwdrivers lose the keen edge on their blades from time to time. A little timely attention with emery cloth or a file will soon restore items like this to a good finish.

Working facilities

Not to be forgotten when discussing tools is the workshop itself. If anything more than routine maintenance is to be carried out, a suitable working area becomes essential.

It is appreciated that many an owner-mechanic is forced by circumstances to remove an engine or similar item without the benefit of a garage or workshop. Having done this, any repairs should always be done under the cover of a roof.

Wherever possible, any dismantling should be done on a clean, flat workbench or table at a suitable working height.

Any workbench needs a vice; one with a jaw opening of 100 mm is suitable for most jobs. As mentioned previously, some clean dry storage space is also required for tools, as well as for any lubricants, cleaning fluids, touch-up paints etc, which become necessary.

Another item which may be required, and which has a much more general usage, is an electric drill with a chuck capacity of at least 8 mm. This, together with a good range of twist drills, is virtually essential for fitting accessories.

Last, but not least, always keep a supply of old newspapers and clean, lint-free rags available, and try to keep any working area as clean as possible.

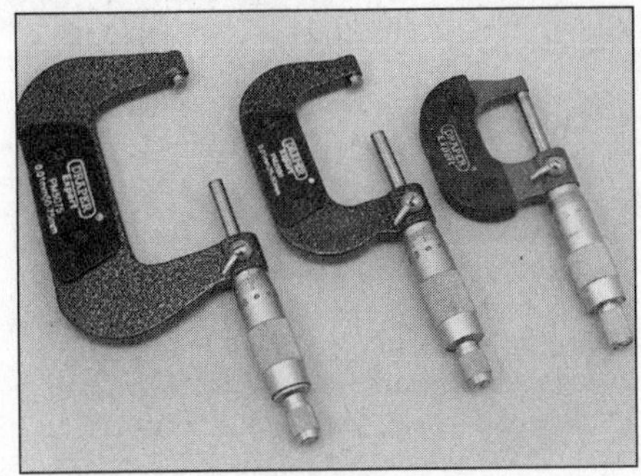

Micrometers

Dial test indicator ("dial gauge")

Strap wrench

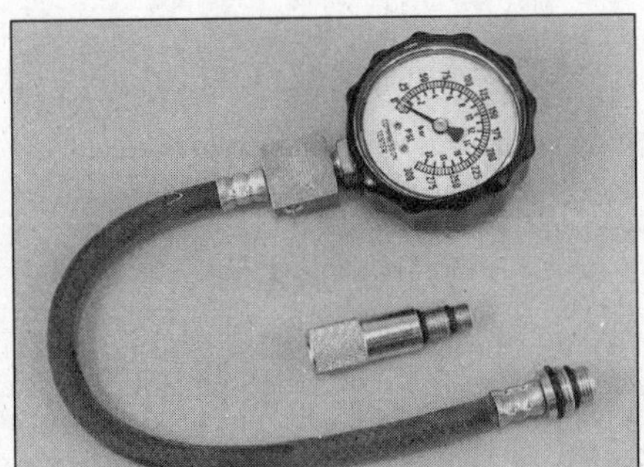

Compression tester

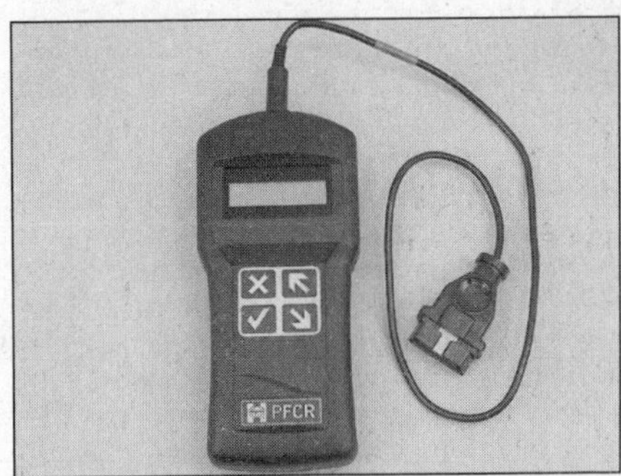

Fault code reader

MOT test checks

This is a guide to getting your vehicle through the MOT test. Obviously it will not be possible to examine the vehicle to the same standard as the professional MOT tester. However, working through the following checks will enable you to identify any problem areas before submitting the vehicle for the test.

It has only been possible to summarise the test requirements here, based on the regulations in force at the time of printing. Test standards are becoming increasingly stringent, although there are some exemptions for older vehicles.

An assistant will be needed to help carry out some of these checks.

The checks have been sub-divided into four categories, as follows:

1 Checks carried out **FROM THE DRIVER'S SEAT**

2 Checks carried out **WITH THE VEHICLE ON THE GROUND**

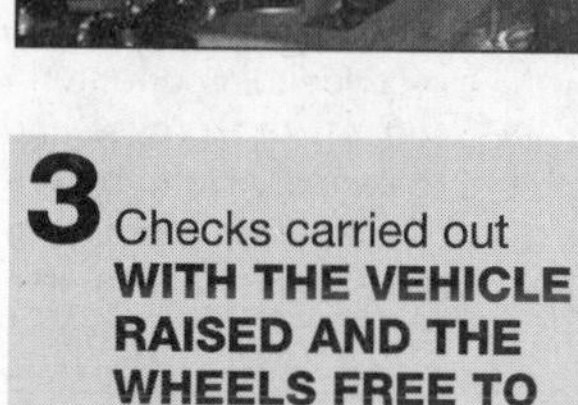

3 Checks carried out **WITH THE VEHICLE RAISED AND THE WHEELS FREE TO TURN**

4 Checks carried out on **YOUR VEHICLE'S EXHAUST EMISSION SYSTEM**

1 Checks carried out FROM THE DRIVER'S SEAT

Handbrake

☐ Test the operation of the handbrake. Excessive travel (too many clicks) indicates incorrect brake or cable adjustment.

☐ Check that the handbrake cannot be released by tapping the lever sideways. Check the security of the lever mountings.

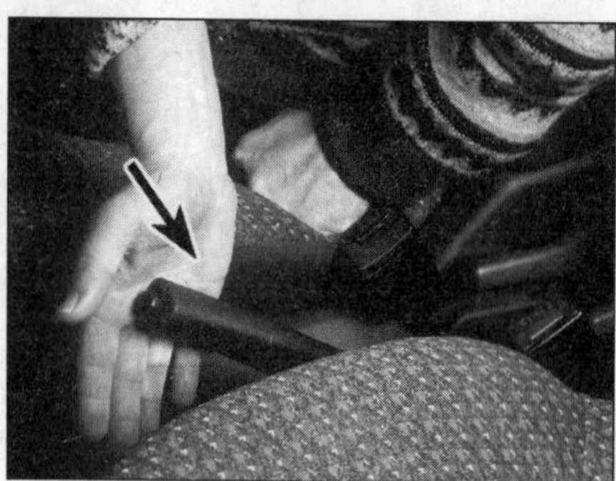

Footbrake

☐ Depress the brake pedal and check that it does not creep down to the floor, indicating a master cylinder fault. Release the pedal, wait a few seconds, then depress it again. If the pedal travels nearly to the floor before firm resistance is felt, brake adjustment or repair is necessary. If the pedal feels spongy, there is air in the hydraulic system which must be removed by bleeding.

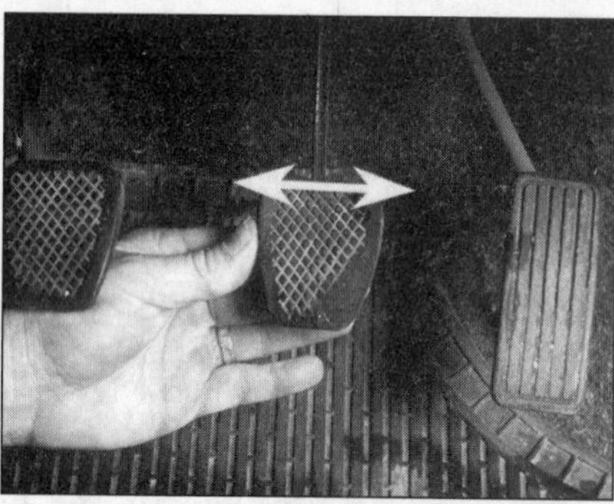

☐ Check that the brake pedal is secure and in good condition. Check also for signs of fluid leaks on the pedal, floor or carpets, which would indicate failed seals in the brake master cylinder.

☐ Check the servo unit (when applicable) by operating the brake pedal several times, then keeping the pedal depressed and starting the engine. As the engine starts, the pedal will move down slightly. If not, the vacuum hose or the servo itself may be faulty.

Steering wheel and column

☐ Examine the steering wheel for fractures or looseness of the hub, spokes or rim.

☐ Move the steering wheel from side to side and then up and down. Check that the steering wheel is not loose on the column, indicating wear or a loose retaining nut. Continue moving the steering wheel as before, but also turn it slightly from left to right.

☐ Check that the steering wheel is not loose on the column, and that there is no abnormal

movement of the steering wheel, indicating wear in the column support bearings or couplings.

Windscreen, mirrors and sunvisor

☐ The windscreen must be free of cracks or other significant damage within the driver's field of view. (Small stone chips are acceptable.) Rear view mirrors must be secure, intact, and capable of being adjusted.

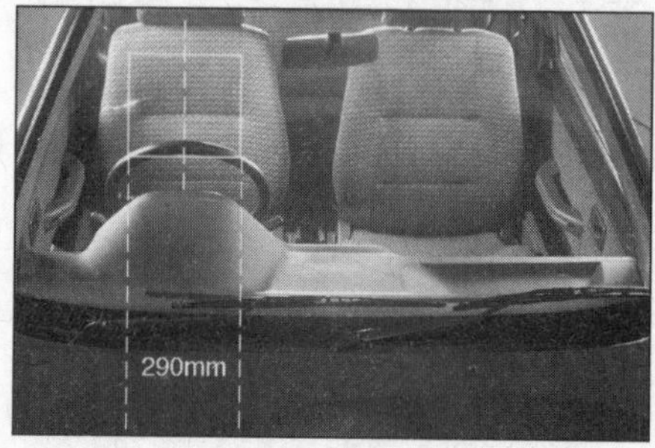

☐ The driver's sunvisor must be capable of being stored in the "up" position.

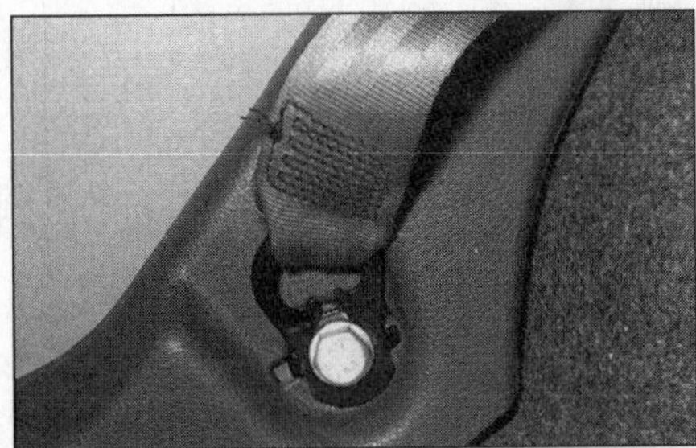

Seat belts and seats

Note: *The following checks are applicable to all seat belts, front and rear.*

☐ Examine the webbing of all the belts (including rear belts if fitted) for cuts, serious fraying or deterioration. Fasten and unfasten each belt to check the buckles. If applicable, check the retracting mechanism. Check the security of all seat belt mountings accessible from inside the vehicle.

☐ Seat belts with pre-tensioners, once activated, have a "flag" or similar showing on the seat belt stalk. This, in itself, is not a reason for test failure.

☐ The front seats themselves must be securely attached and the backrests must lock in the upright position.

Doors

☐ Both front doors must be able to be opened and closed from outside and inside, and must latch securely when closed.

2 Checks carried out WITH THE VEHICLE ON THE GROUND

Vehicle identification

☐ Number plates must be in good condition, secure and legible, with letters and numbers correctly spaced – spacing at (A) should be at least twice that at (B).

☐ The VIN plate and/or homologation plate must be legible.

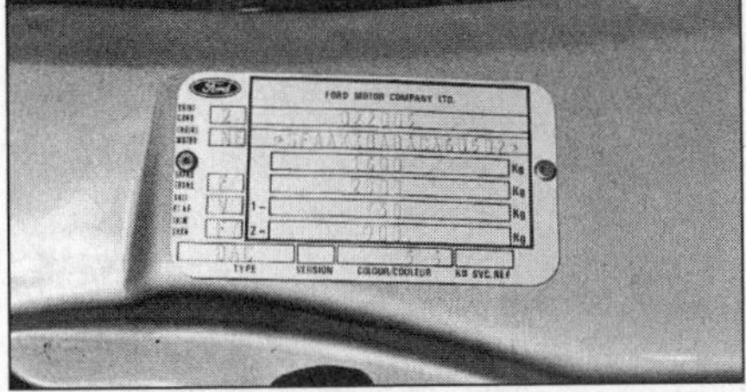

Electrical equipment

☐ Switch on the ignition and check the operation of the horn.

☐ Check the windscreen washers and wipers, examining the wiper blades; renew damaged or perished blades. Also check the operation of the stop-lights.

☐ Check the operation of the sidelights and number plate lights. The lenses and reflectors must be secure, clean and undamaged.

☐ Check the operation and alignment of the headlights. The headlight reflectors must not be tarnished and the lenses must be undamaged.

☐ Switch on the ignition and check the operation of the direction indicators (including the instrument panel tell-tale) and the hazard warning lights. Operation of the sidelights and stop-lights must not affect the indicators - if it does, the cause is usually a bad earth at the rear light cluster.

☐ Check the operation of the rear foglight(s), including the warning light on the instrument panel or in the switch.

☐ The ABS warning light must illuminate in accordance with the manufacturers' design. For most vehicles, the ABS warning light should illuminate when the ignition is switched on, and (if the system is operating properly) extinguish after a few seconds. Refer to the owner's handbook.

Footbrake

☐ Examine the master cylinder, brake pipes and servo unit for leaks, loose mountings, corrosion or other damage.

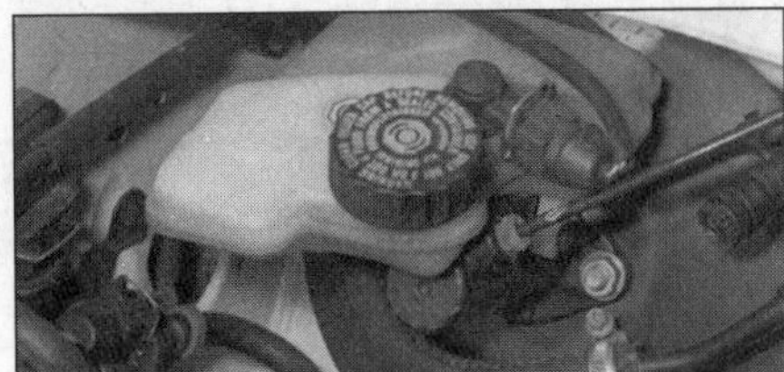

☐ The fluid reservoir must be secure and the fluid level must be between the upper (**A**) and lower (**B**) markings.

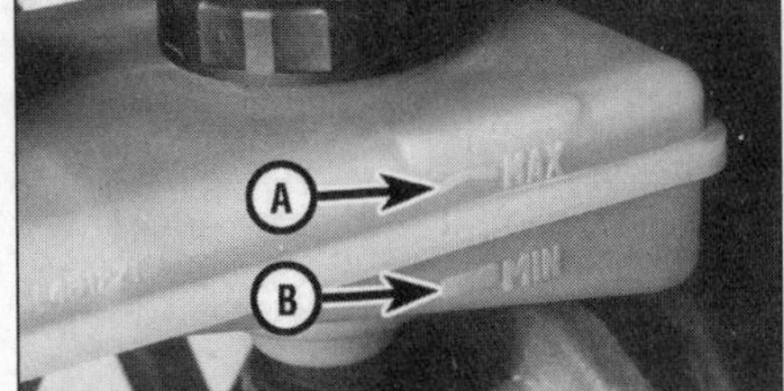

☐ Inspect both front brake flexible hoses for cracks or deterioration of the rubber. Turn the steering from lock to lock, and ensure that the hoses do not contact the wheel, tyre, or any part of the steering or suspension mechanism. With the brake pedal firmly depressed, check the hoses for bulges or leaks under pressure.

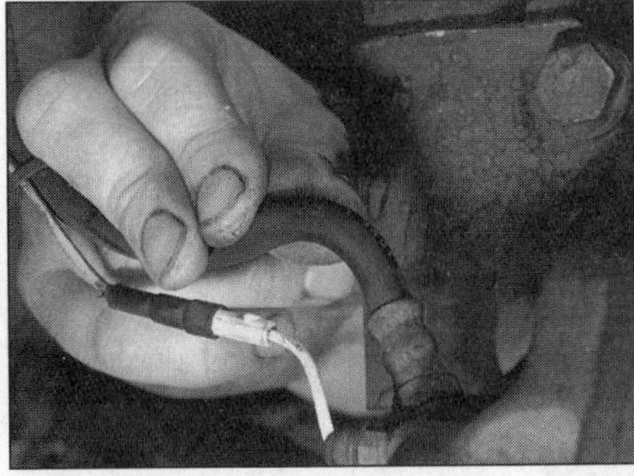

Steering and suspension

☐ Have your assistant turn the steering wheel from side to side slightly, up to the point where the steering gear just begins to transmit this movement to the roadwheels. Check for excessive free play between the steering wheel and the steering gear, indicating wear or insecurity of the steering column joints, the column-to-steering gear coupling, or the steering gear itself.

☐ Have your assistant turn the steering wheel more vigorously in each direction, so that the roadwheels just begin to turn. As this is done, examine all the steering joints, linkages, fittings and attachments. Renew any component that shows signs of wear or damage. On vehicles with power steering, check the security and condition of the steering pump, drivebelt and hoses.

☐ Check that the vehicle is standing level, and at approximately the correct ride height.

Shock absorbers

☐ Depress each corner of the vehicle in turn, then release it. The vehicle should rise and then settle in its normal position. If the vehicle continues to rise and fall, the shock absorber is defective. A shock absorber which has seized will also cause the vehicle to fail.

Exhaust system

☐ Start the engine. With your assistant holding a rag over the tailpipe, check the entire system for leaks. Repair or renew leaking sections.

3 Checks carried out WITH THE VEHICLE RAISED AND THE WHEELS FREE TO TURN

Jack up the front and rear of the vehicle, and securely support it on axle stands. Position the stands clear of the suspension assemblies. Ensure that the wheels are clear of the ground and that the steering can be turned from lock to lock.

Steering mechanism

☐ Have your assistant turn the steering from lock to lock. Check that the steering turns smoothly, and that no part of the steering mechanism, including a wheel or tyre, fouls any brake hose or pipe or any part of the body structure.

☐ Examine the steering rack rubber gaiters for damage or insecurity of the retaining clips. If power steering is fitted, check for signs of damage or leakage of the fluid hoses, pipes or connections. Also check for excessive stiffness or binding of the steering, a missing split pin or locking device, or severe corrosion of the body structure within 30 cm of any steering component attachment point.

Front and rear suspension and wheel bearings

☐ Starting at the front right-hand side, grasp the roadwheel at the 3 o'clock and 9 o'clock positions and rock gently but firmly. Check for free play or insecurity at the wheel bearings, suspension balljoints, or suspension mountings, pivots and attachments.

☐ Now grasp the wheel at the 12 o'clock and 6 o'clock positions and repeat the previous inspection. Spin the wheel, and check for roughness or tightness of the front wheel bearing.

☐ If excess free play is suspected at a component pivot point, this can be confirmed by using a large screwdriver or similar tool and levering between the mounting and the component attachment. This will confirm whether the wear is in the pivot bush, its retaining bolt, or in the mounting itself (the bolt holes can often become elongated).

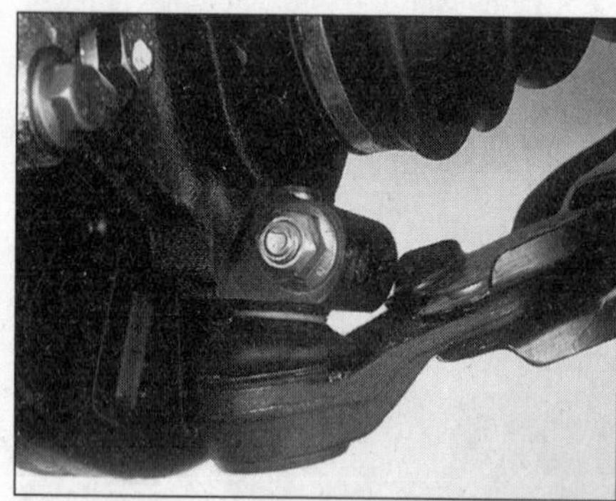

☐ Carry out all the above checks at the other front wheel, and then at both rear wheels.

Springs and shock absorbers

☐ Examine the suspension struts (when applicable) for serious fluid leakage, corrosion, or damage to the casing. Also check the security of the mounting points.

☐ If coil springs are fitted, check that the spring ends locate in their seats, and that the spring is not corroded, cracked or broken.

☐ If leaf springs are fitted, check that all leaves are intact, that the axle is securely attached to each spring, and that there is no deterioration of the spring eye mountings, bushes, and shackles.

☐ The same general checks apply to vehicles fitted with other suspension types, such as torsion bars, hydraulic displacer units, etc. Ensure that all mountings and attachments are secure, that there are no signs of excessive wear, corrosion or damage, and (on hydraulic types) that there are no fluid leaks or damaged pipes.

☐ Inspect the shock absorbers for signs of serious fluid leakage. Check for wear of the mounting bushes or attachments, or damage to the body of the unit.

Driveshafts (fwd vehicles only)

☐ Rotate each front wheel in turn and inspect the constant velocity joint gaiters for splits or damage. Also check that each driveshaft is straight and undamaged.

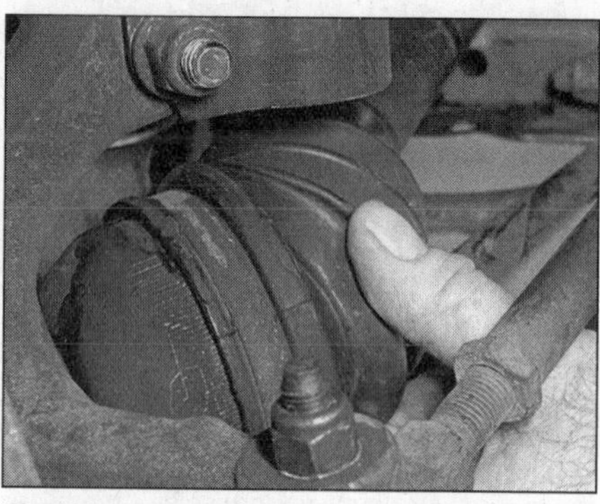

Braking system

☐ If possible without dismantling, check brake pad wear and disc condition. Ensure that the friction lining material has not worn excessively, (A) and that the discs are not fractured, pitted, scored or badly worn (B).

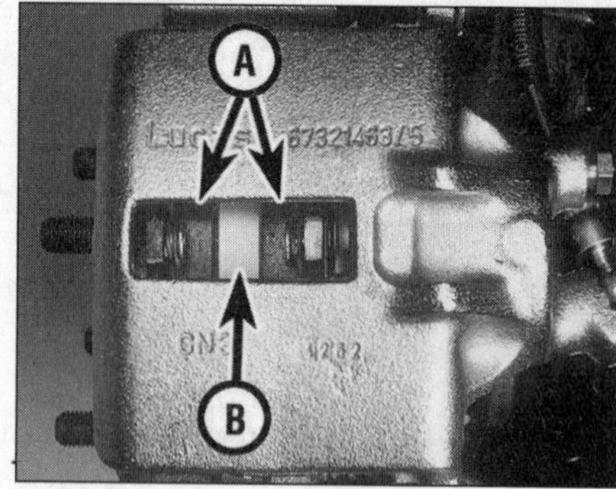

☐ Examine all the rigid brake pipes underneath the vehicle, and the flexible hose(s) at the rear. Look for corrosion, chafing or insecurity of the pipes, and for signs of bulging under pressure, chafing, splits or deterioration of the flexible hoses.

☐ Look for signs of fluid leaks at the brake calipers or on the brake backplates. Repair or renew leaking components.

☐ Slowly spin each wheel, while your assistant depresses and releases the footbrake. Ensure that each brake is operating and does not bind when the pedal is released.

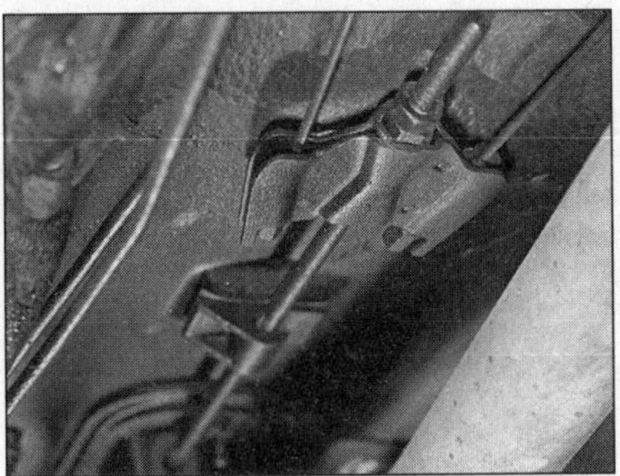

☐ Examine the handbrake mechanism, checking for frayed or broken cables, excessive corrosion, or wear or insecurity of the linkage. Check that the mechanism works on each relevant wheel, and releases fully, without binding.

☐ It is not possible to test brake efficiency without special equipment, but a road test can be carried out later to check that the vehicle pulls up in a straight line.

Fuel and exhaust systems

☐ Inspect the fuel tank (including the filler cap), fuel pipes, hoses and unions. All components must be secure and free from leaks.

☐ Examine the exhaust system over its entire length, checking for any damaged, broken or missing mountings, security of the retaining clamps and rust or corrosion.

Wheels and tyres

☐ Examine the sidewalls and tread area of each tyre in turn. Check for cuts, tears, lumps, bulges, separation of the tread, and exposure of the ply or cord due to wear or damage. Check that the tyre bead is correctly seated on the wheel rim, that the valve is sound and properly seated, and that the wheel is not distorted or damaged.

☐ Check that the tyres are of the correct size for the vehicle, that they are of the same size and type on each axle, and that the pressures are correct.

☐ Check the tyre tread depth. The legal minimum at the time of writing is 1.6 mm over at least three-quarters of the tread width. Abnormal tread wear may indicate incorrect front wheel alignment.

Body corrosion

☐ Check the condition of the entire vehicle structure for signs of corrosion in load-bearing areas. (These include chassis box sections, side sills, cross-members, pillars, and all suspension, steering, braking system and seat belt mountings and anchorages.) Any corrosion which has seriously reduced the thickness of a load-bearing area is likely to cause the vehicle to fail. In this case professional repairs are likely to be needed.

☐ Damage or corrosion which causes sharp or otherwise dangerous edges to be exposed will also cause the vehicle to fail.

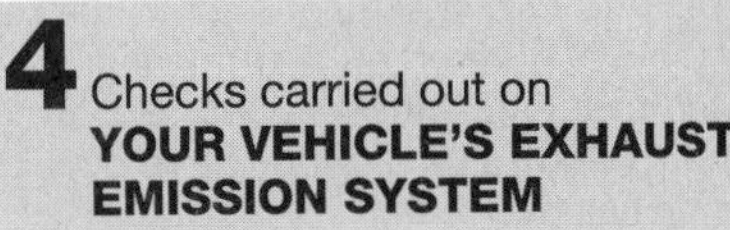

4 Checks carried out on YOUR VEHICLE'S EXHAUST EMISSION SYSTEM

Petrol models

☐ The engine should be warmed up, and running well (ignition system in good order, air filter element clean, etc).

☐ Before testing, run the engine at around 2500 rpm for 20 seconds. Let the engine drop to idle, and watch for smoke from the exhaust. If the idle speed is too high, or if dense blue or black smoke emerges for more than 5 seconds, the vehicle will fail. Typically, blue smoke signifies oil burning (engine wear); black smoke means unburnt fuel (dirty air cleaner element, or other fuel system fault).

☐ An exhaust gas analyser for measuring carbon monoxide (CO) and hydrocarbons (HC) is now needed. If one cannot be hired or borrowed, have a local garage perform the check.

CO emissions (mixture)

☐ The MOT tester has access to the CO limits for all vehicles. The CO level is measured at idle speed, and at 'fast idle' (2500 to 3000 rpm). The following limits are given as a general guide:

At idle speed – Less than 0.5% CO
At 'fast idle' – Less than 0.3% CO
Lambda reading – 0.97 to 1.03

☐ If the CO level is too high, this may point to poor maintenance, a fuel injection system problem, faulty lambda (oxygen) sensor or catalytic converter. Try an injector cleaning treatment, and check the vehicle's ECU for fault codes.

HC emissions

☐ The MOT tester has access to HC limits for all vehicles. The HC level is measured at 'fast idle' (2500 to 3000 rpm). The following limits are given as a general guide:

At 'fast idle' – Less then 200 ppm

☐ Excessive HC emissions are typically caused by oil being burnt (worn engine), or by a blocked crankcase ventilation system ('breather'). If the engine oil is old and thin, an oil change may help. If the engine is running badly, check the vehicle's ECU for fault codes.

Diesel models

☐ The only emission test for diesel engines is measuring exhaust smoke density, using a calibrated smoke meter. The test involves accelerating the engine at least 3 times to its maximum unloaded speed.

Note: *On engines with a timing belt, it is VITAL that the belt is in good condition before the test is carried out.*

☐ With the engine warmed up, it is first purged by running at around 2500 rpm for 20 seconds. A governor check is then carried out, by slowly accelerating the engine to its maximum speed. After this, the smoke meter is connected, and the engine is accelerated quickly to maximum speed three times. If the smoke density is less than the limits given below, the vehicle will pass:

Non-turbo vehicles: 2.5m-1
Turbocharged vehicles: 3.0m-1

☐ If excess smoke is produced, try fitting a new air cleaner element, or using an injector cleaning treatment. If the engine is running badly, where applicable, check the vehicle's ECU for fault codes. Also check the vehicle's EGR system, where applicable. At high mileages, the injectors may require professional attention.

Whenever servicing, repair or overhaul work is carried out on the car or its components, observe the following procedures and instructions. This will assist in carrying out the operation efficiently and to a professional standard of workmanship.

Joint mating faces and gaskets

When separating components at their mating faces, never insert screwdrivers or similar implements into the joint between the faces in order to prise them apart. This can cause severe damage which results in oil leaks, coolant leaks, etc upon reassembly. Separation is usually achieved by tapping along the joint with a soft-faced hammer in order to break the seal. However, note that this method may not be suitable where dowels are used for component location.

Where a gasket is used between the mating faces of two components, a new one must be fitted on reassembly; fit it dry unless otherwise stated in the repair procedure. Make sure that the mating faces are clean and dry, with all traces of old gasket removed. When cleaning a joint face, use a tool which is unlikely to score or damage the face, and remove any burrs or nicks with an oilstone or fine file.

Make sure that tapped holes are cleaned with a pipe cleaner, and keep them free of jointing compound, if this is being used, unless specifically instructed otherwise.

Ensure that all orifices, channels or pipes are clear, and blow through them, preferably using compressed air.

Oil seals

Oil seals can be removed by levering them out with a wide flat-bladed screwdriver or similar implement. Alternatively, a number of self-tapping screws may be screwed into the seal, and these used as a purchase for pliers or some similar device in order to pull the seal free.

Whenever an oil seal is removed from its working location, either individually or as part of an assembly, it should be renewed.

The very fine sealing lip of the seal is easily damaged, and will not seal if the surface it contacts is not completely clean and free from scratches, nicks or grooves. If the original sealing surface of the component cannot be restored, and the manufacturer has not made provision for slight relocation of the seal relative to the sealing surface, the component should be renewed.

Protect the lips of the seal from any surface which may damage them in the course of fitting. Use tape or a conical sleeve where possible. Lubricate the seal lips with oil before fitting and, on dual-lipped seals, fill the space between the lips with grease.

Unless otherwise stated, oil seals must be fitted with their sealing lips toward the lubricant to be sealed.

Use a tubular drift or block of wood of the appropriate size to install the seal and, if the seal housing is shouldered, drive the seal down to the shoulder. If the seal housing is unshouldered, the seal should be fitted with its face flush with the housing top face (unless otherwise instructed).

Screw threads and fastenings

Seized nuts, bolts and screws are quite a common occurrence where corrosion has set in, and the use of penetrating oil or releasing fluid will often overcome this problem if the offending item is soaked for a while before attempting to release it. The use of an impact driver may also provide a means of releasing such stubborn fastening devices, when used in conjunction with the appropriate screwdriver bit or socket. If none of these methods works, it may be necessary to resort to the careful application of heat, or the use of a hacksaw or nut splitter device.

Studs are usually removed by locking two nuts together on the threaded part, and then using a spanner on the lower nut to unscrew the stud. Studs or bolts which have broken off below the surface of the component in which they are mounted can sometimes be removed using a stud extractor. Always ensure that a blind tapped hole is completely free from oil, grease, water or other fluid before installing the bolt or stud. Failure to do this could cause the housing to crack due to the hydraulic action of the bolt or stud as it is screwed in.

When tightening a castellated nut to accept a split pin, tighten the nut to the specified torque, where applicable, and then tighten further to the next split pin hole. Never slacken the nut to align the split pin hole, unless stated in the repair procedure.

When checking or retightening a nut or bolt to a specified torque setting, slacken the nut or bolt by a quarter of a turn, and then retighten to the specified setting. However, this should not be attempted where angular tightening has been used.

For some screw fastenings, notably cylinder head bolts or nuts, torque wrench settings are no longer specified for the latter stages of tightening, "angle-tightening" being called up instead. Typically, a fairly low torque wrench setting will be applied to the bolts/nuts in the correct sequence, followed by one or more stages of tightening through specified angles.

Locknuts, locktabs and washers

Any fastening which will rotate against a component or housing during tightening should always have a washer between it and the relevant component or housing.

Spring or split washers should always be renewed when they are used to lock a critical component such as a big-end bearing retaining bolt or nut. Locktabs which are folded over to retain a nut or bolt should always be renewed.

Self-locking nuts can be re-used in non-critical areas, providing resistance can be felt when the locking portion passes over the bolt or stud thread. However, it should be noted that self-locking stiffnuts tend to lose their effectiveness after long periods of use, and should then be renewed as a matter of course.

Split pins must always be replaced with new ones of the correct size for the hole.

When thread-locking compound is found on the threads of a fastener which is to be re-used, it should be cleaned off with a wire brush and solvent, and fresh compound applied on reassembly.

Special tools

Some repair procedures in this manual entail the use of special tools such as a press, two or three-legged pullers, spring compressors, etc. Wherever possible, suitable readily-available alternatives to the manufacturer's special tools are described, and are shown in use. In some instances, where no alternative is possible, it has been necessary to resort to the use of a manufacturer's tool, and this has been done for reasons of safety as well as the efficient completion of the repair operation. Unless you are highly-skilled and have a thorough understanding of the procedures described, never attempt to bypass the use of any special tool when the procedure described specifies its use. Not only is there a very great risk of personal injury, but expensive damage could be caused to the components involved.

Environmental considerations

When disposing of used engine oil, brake fluid, antifreeze, etc, give due consideration to any detrimental environmental effects. Do not, for instance, pour any of the above liquids down drains into the general sewage system, or onto the ground to soak away. Many local council refuse tips provide a facility for waste oil disposal, as do some garages. If none of these facilities are available, consult your local Environmental Health Department, or the National Rivers Authority, for further advice.

With the universal tightening-up of legislation regarding the emission of environmentally-harmful substances from motor vehicles, most vehicles have tamperproof devices fitted to the main adjustment points of the fuel system. These devices are primarily designed to prevent unqualified persons from adjusting the fuel/air mixture, with the chance of a consequent increase in toxic emissions. If such devices are found during servicing or overhaul, they should, wherever possible, be renewed or refitted in accordance with the manufacturer's requirements or current legislation.

OIL CARE
FOLLOW THE CODE
OIL BANK LINE
0800 66 33 66
www.oilbankline.org.uk

Note: It is antisocial and illegal to dump oil down the drain. To find the location of your local oil recycling bank, call this number free.

Engine

- Engine fails to rotate when attempting to start
- Engine rotates, but will not start
- Engine difficult to start when cold
- Engine difficult to start when hot
- Starter motor noisy or excessively-rough in engagement
- Engine starts, but stops immediately
- Engine idles erratically
- Engine misfires at idle speed
- Engine misfires throughout the driving speed range
- Engine hesitates on acceleration
- Engine stalls
- Engine lacks power
- Engine backfires
- Oil pressure warning light illuminated with engine running
- Engine runs-on after switching off
- Engine noises

Cooling system

- Overheating
- Overcooling
- External coolant leakage
- Internal coolant leakage
- Corrosion

Fuel and exhaust systems

- Excessive fuel consumption
- Fuel leakage and/or fuel odour

Clutch

- Pedal travels to floor – no pressure or very little resistance
- Clutch fails to disengage (unable to select gears).
- Clutch slips (engine speed increases, with no increase in vehicle speed).
- Judder as clutch is engaged
- Noise when depressing or releasing clutch pedal

Manual transmission

- Noisy in neutral with engine running
- Noisy in one particular gear
- Difficulty engaging gears
- Vibration
- Jumps out of gear
- Lubricant leaks

Automatic transmission

- Fluid leakage
- General gear selection problems
- Transmission fluid brown, or has burned smell
- Transmission will not downshift (kickdown) with accelerator fully depressed
- Engine will not start in any gear, or starts in gears other than Park or Neutral
- Transmission slips, shifts roughly, is noisy, or has no drive in forward or reverse gears

Braking system

- Vehicle pulls to one side under braking
- Noise (grinding or high-pitched squeal) when brakes applied
- Brakes binding
- Excessive brake pedal travel
- Brake pedal feels spongy when depressed
- Excessive brake pedal effort required to stop vehicle
- Judder felt through brake pedal or steering wheel when braking
- Rear wheels locking under normal braking

Driveshafts

- Clicking or knocking noise on turns (at slow speed on full-lock)

Suspension and steering

- Vehicle pulls to one side
- Excessive pitching and/or rolling around corners, or during braking
- Lack of power assistance
- Wandering or general instability
- Excessively-stiff steering
- Excessive play in steering
- Wheel wobble and vibration
- Tyre wear excessive

Electrical system

- Battery will not hold a charge for more than a few days
- Ignition/no-charge warning light remains illuminated with engine running
- Ignition/no-charge warning light fails to come on
- Lights inoperative
- Instrument readings inaccurate or erratic
- Horn inoperative, or unsatisfactory in operation
- Windscreen wipers inoperative, or unsatisfactory in operation
- Windscreen washers inoperative, or unsatisfactory in operation
- Electric windows inoperative, or unsatisfactory in operation
- Central locking system inoperative, or unsatisfactory in operation

Introduction

The vehicle owner who does his or her own maintenance according to the recommended service schedules should not have to use this section of the manual very often. Modern component reliability is such that, provided those items subject to wear or deterioration are inspected or renewed at the specified intervals, sudden failure is comparatively rare. Faults do not usually just happen as a result of sudden failure, but develop over a period of time. Major mechanical failures in particular are usually preceded by characteristic symptoms over hundreds or even thousands of miles. Those components that do occasionally fail without warning are often small and easily carried in the vehicle.

With any fault-finding, the first step is to decide where to begin investigations. Sometimes this is obvious, but on other occasions, a little detective work will be necessary. The owner who makes half a dozen haphazard adjustments or component renewals may be successful in curing a fault (or its symptoms). However, will be none the wiser if the fault recurs, and ultimately may have spent more time and money than was necessary. A calm and logical approach will be found to be more satisfactory in the long run. Always take into account any warning signs or abnormalities that may have been noticed in the period preceding the fault – power loss, high or low gauge readings, unusual smells, etc – and remember that failure of components such as fuses or spark plugs may only be pointers to some underlying fault.

The pages which follow provide an easy-reference guide to the more common problems which may occur during the operation of the vehicle. These problems and their possible causes are grouped under headings denoting various components or systems, such as Engine, Cooling system, etc. The general Chapter which deals with the problem is also shown in brackets; refer to the relevant part of that Chapter for system-specific information. Whatever the fault, certain basic principles apply. These are as follows:

Verify the fault. This is simply a matter of being sure that you know what the symptoms are before starting work. This is particularly important if you are investigating a fault for someone else, who may not have described it very accurately.

Do not overlook the obvious. For example, if the vehicle will not start, is there petrol in the tank? (Do not take anyone else's word on this particular point, and do not trust the fuel gauge either!) If an electrical fault is indicated, look for loose or broken wires before digging out the test gear.

Cure the disease, not the symptom. Substituting a flat battery with a fully-charged one will get you off the hard shoulder, but if the underlying cause is not attended to, the new battery will go the same way. Similarly, changing oil-fouled spark plugs for a new set will get you moving again, but remember that the reason for the fouling (if it was not simply an incorrect grade of plug) will have to be established and corrected.

Do not take anything for granted. Particularly, do not forget that a new component may itself be defective (especially if it's been rattling around in the boot for months). Also do not leave components out of a fault diagnosis sequence just because they are new or recently fitted. When you do finally diagnose a difficult fault, you will probably realise that all the evidence was there from the start.

Diesel fault diagnosis

The majority of starting problems on small diesel engines are electrical in origin. The mechanic who is familiar with petrol engines but less so with diesel may be inclined to view the diesel's injectors and pump in the same light as the spark plugs and distributor, but this is generally a mistake.

When investigating complaints of difficult starting for someone else, make sure that the correct starting procedure is understood and is being followed. Some drivers are unaware of the significance of the preheating warning light – many modern engines are sufficiently forgiving for this not to matter in mild weather, but with the onset of winter, problems begin.

As a rule of thumb, if the engine is difficult to start but runs well when it has finally got going, the problem is electrical (battery, starter motor or preheating system). If poor performance is combined with difficult starting, the problem is likely to be in the fuel system. The low-pressure (supply) side of the fuel system should be checked before suspecting the injectors and high-pressure pump. The most common fuel supply problem is air getting into the system, and any pipe from the fuel tank forwards must be scrutinised if air leakage is suspected. Normally the pump is the last item to suspect, since unless it has been tampered with, there is no reason for it to be at fault.

Engine

Engine fails to rotate when attempting to start

- ☐ Battery terminal connections loose or corroded (*Weekly checks*).
- ☐ Battery discharged or faulty (Chapter 5A).
- ☐ Broken, loose or disconnected wiring in the starting circuit (Chapter 5A).
- ☐ Defective starter solenoid or switch (Chapter 5A).
- ☐ Defective starter motor (Chapter 5A).
- ☐ Starter pinion or flywheel ring gear teeth loose or broken (Chapters 2C and 5A).
- ☐ Engine earth strap broken or disconnected (Chapter 5A).

Engine rotates, but will not start

- ☐ Fuel tank empty.
- ☐ Battery discharged (engine rotates slowly) (Chapter 5A).
- ☐ Battery terminal connections loose or corroded (*Weekly checks*).
- ☐ Ignition components damp or damaged – petrol models (Chapters 1A and 5B).
- ☐ Broken, loose or disconnected wiring in the ignition circuit – petrol models (Chapters 1A and 5B).
- ☐ Worn, faulty or incorrectly gapped spark plugs – petrol models (Chapter 1A).
- ☐ Fuel injection system fault (Chapter 4A and 4B).
- ☐ Air in fuel system – diesel models (Chapter 4B).
- ☐ Major mechanical failure (eg, timing chain) (Chapter 2A, 2B or 2C).

Engine difficult to start when cold

- ☐ Battery discharged (Chapter 5A).
- ☐ Battery terminal connections loose or corroded (*Weekly checks*).
- ☐ Worn, faulty or incorrectly gapped spark plugs – petrol models (Chapter 1A).
- ☐ Fuel injection system fault (Chapter 4A and 4B).
- ☐ Other ignition system fault – petrol models (Chapters 1A and 5B).
- ☐ Preheating system fault – diesel models (Chapter 5C).
- ☐ Low cylinder compressions (Chapter 2A or 2B).

Engine difficult to start when hot

- ☐ Air filter element dirty or clogged (Chapter 1A or 1B).
- ☐ Fuel injection system fault (Chapter 4A and 4B).
- ☐ Low cylinder compressions (Chapter 2A or 2B).

Starter motor noisy or excessively rough in engagement

- ☐ Starter pinion or flywheel ring gear teeth loose or broken (Chapters 2C and 5A).
- ☐ Starter motor mounting bolts loose or missing (Chapter 5A).
- ☐ Starter motor internal components worn or damaged (Chapter 5A).

Engine starts, but stops immediately

- ☐ Loose or faulty electrical connections in the ignition circuit – petrol models (Chapters 1A and 5B).
- ☐ Vacuum leak at the throttle body or inlet manifold – petrol models (Chapter 4A).
- ☐ Blocked injector/fuel injection system fault (Chapter 4A or 4B).
- ☐ Faulty injector(s) – diesel models (Chapter 4B).
- ☐ Air in fuel system – diesel models (Chapter 4B).

Engine idles erratically

- ☐ Air filter element clogged (Chapter 1A or 1B).
- ☐ Vacuum leak at the throttle body, inlet manifold or associated hoses – petrol models (Chapter 4A).
- ☐ Worn, faulty or incorrectly gapped spark plugs – petrol models (Chapter 1A).
- ☐ Uneven or low cylinder compressions (Chapter 2A or 2B).
- ☐ Camshaft lobes worn (Chapter 2A or 2B).
- ☐ Blocked injector/fuel injection system fault (Chapter 4A or 4B).
- ☐ Faulty injector(s) – diesel models (Chapter 4B).

Engine misfires at idle speed

- ☐ Worn, faulty or incorrectly gapped spark plugs – petrol models (Chapter 1A).
- ☐ Vacuum leak at the throttle body, inlet manifold or associated hoses (Chapter 4A or 4B).
- ☐ Blocked injector/fuel injection system fault (Chapter 4A and 4B).
- ☐ Faulty injector(s) – diesel models (Chapter 4B).
- ☐ Uneven or low cylinder compressions (Chapter 2A or 2B).
- ☐ Disconnected, leaking, or perished crankcase ventilation hoses (Chapter 4C and 4D).

Engine (continued)

Engine misfires throughout the driving speed range

- ☐ Fuel filter choked (Chapter 1A or 1B).
- ☐ Fuel pump faulty, or delivery pressure low (Chapter 4A or 4B).
- ☐ Fuel tank vent blocked, or fuel pipes restricted (Chapter 4A or 4B).
- ☐ Vacuum leak at the throttle body, inlet manifold or associated hoses – petrol models (Chapter 4A).
- ☐ Worn, faulty or incorrectly gapped spark plugs – petrol models (Chapter 1A).
- ☐ Faulty injector(s) – diesel models (Chapter 4B).
- ☐ Faulty ignition coil – petrol models (Chapter 5B).
- ☐ Uneven or low cylinder compressions (Chapter 2A or 2B).
- ☐ Blocked injector/fuel injection system fault (Chapter 4A or 4B).

Engine hesitates on acceleration

- ☐ Worn, faulty or incorrectly gapped spark plugs – petrol models (Chapter 1A).
- ☐ Vacuum leak at the throttle body, inlet manifold or associated hoses – petrol models (Chapter 4A).
- ☐ Blocked injector/fuel injection system fault (Chapter 4A or 4B).
- ☐ Faulty injector(s) – diesel models (Chapter 4B).

Engine stalls

- ☐ Vacuum leak at the throttle body, inlet manifold or associated hoses – petrol models (Chapter 4A).
- ☐ Fuel filter choked (Chapter 1A or 1B).
- ☐ Fuel pump faulty, or delivery pressure low – petrol models (Chapter 4A).
- ☐ Fuel tank vent blocked, or fuel pipes restricted (Chapter 4A or 4B).
- ☐ Blocked injector/fuel injection system fault (Chapter 4A or 4B).
- ☐ Faulty injector(s) – diesel models (Chapter 4B).
- ☐ Air in fuel system – diesel models (Chapter 4B).

Engine lacks power

- ☐ Fuel filter choked (Chapter 1A or 1B).
- ☐ Fuel pump faulty, or delivery pressure low – petrol models (Chapter 4A).
- ☐ Uneven or low cylinder compressions (Chapter 2A or 2B).
- ☐ Worn, faulty or incorrectly gapped spark plugs – petrol models (Chapter 1A).
- ☐ Vacuum leak at the throttle body, inlet manifold or associated hoses – petrol models (Chapter 4A).
- ☐ Blocked injector/fuel injection system fault (Chapter 4A or 4B).
- ☐ Brakes binding (Chapters 1A or 1B and 9).
- ☐ Clutch slipping (Chapter 6).

Engine backfires

- ☐ Vacuum leak at the throttle body, inlet manifold or associated hoses – petrol models (Chapter 4A).
- ☐ Blocked injector/fuel injection system fault (Chapter 4A or 4B).

Oil pressure warning light illuminated with engine running

- ☐ Low oil level, or incorrect oil grade (*Weekly checks*).
- ☐ Faulty oil pressure warning light switch.
- ☐ Worn engine bearings and/or oil pump (Chapter 2C).
- ☐ High engine operating temperature (Chapter 3).
- ☐ Oil pressure relief valve defective.
- ☐ Oil pick-up strainer clogged (Chapter 2C).

Engine runs-on after switching off

- ☐ Excessive carbon build-up in engine (Chapter 2C).
- ☐ High engine operating temperature (Chapter 3).
- ☐ Fuel injection system fault – petrol models (Chapter 4A).
- ☐ Faulty stop solenoid – diesel models (Chapter 4B).

Engine noises

Pre-ignition (pinking) or knocking during acceleration or under load

- ☐ Ignition system fault – petrol models (Chapters 1A and 5B).
- ☐ Incorrect grade of spark plug – petrol models (Chapter 1A).
- ☐ Incorrect grade of fuel (Chapter 4A).
- ☐ Vacuum leak at the throttle body, inlet manifold or associated hoses – petrol models (Chapter 4A).
- ☐ Excessive carbon build-up in engine (Chapter 2C).
- ☐ Blocked injector/fuel injection system fault – petrol models (Chapter 4A).

Whistling or wheezing noises

- ☐ Leaking inlet manifold or throttle body gasket – petrol models (Chapter 4A).
- ☐ Leaking exhaust manifold gasket or pipe-to-manifold joint (Chapter 4C or 4D).
- ☐ Leaking vacuum hose (Chapters 4A, 4B, 4C, 4D and 9).
- ☐ Blowing cylinder head gasket (Chapter 2A or 2B).

Tapping or rattling noises

- ☐ Worn valve gear or camshaft (Chapter 2A, 2B or 2C).
- ☐ Ancillary component fault (coolant pump, alternator, etc) (Chapters 3, 5A, etc).

Knocking or thumping noises

- ☐ Worn big-end bearings (regular heavy knocking, perhaps worsening under load) (Chapter 2C).
- ☐ Worn main bearings (rumbling and knocking, perhaps less under load) (Chapter 2C).
- ☐ Piston slap (most noticeable when cold) (Chapter 2C).
- ☐ Ancillary component fault (coolant pump, alternator, etc) (Chapters 3, 5A, etc).

Cooling system

Overheating

- ☐ Insufficient coolant in system (*Weekly checks*).
- ☐ Thermostat faulty (Chapter 3).
- ☐ Radiator core blocked, or grille restricted (Chapter 3).
- ☐ Electric cooling fan or thermoswitch faulty (Chapter 3).
- ☐ Pressure cap faulty (Chapter 3).
- ☐ Ignition system fault – petrol engines (Chapters 1A and 5B).
- ☐ Inaccurate temperature gauge sender unit (Chapter 3).
- ☐ Airlock in cooling system.

Overcooling

- ☐ Thermostat faulty (Chapter 3).
- ☐ Inaccurate temperature gauge sender unit (Chapter 3).

External coolant leakage

- ☐ Deteriorated or damaged hoses or hose clips (Chapter 1A or 1B).
- ☐ Radiator core or heater matrix leaking (Chapter 3).
- ☐ Pressure cap faulty (Chapter 3).
- ☐ Water pump seal leaking (Chapter 3).
- ☐ Boiling due to overheating (Chapter 3).
- ☐ Core plug leaking (Chapter 2C).

Internal coolant leakage

- ☐ Leaking cylinder head gasket (Chapter 2A or 2B).
- ☐ Cracked cylinder head or cylinder bore (Chapter 2C).

Corrosion

- ☐ Infrequent draining and flushing (Chapter 1A or 1B).
- ☐ Incorrect coolant mixture or inappropriate coolant type (Chapter 1A or 1B).

Fuel and exhaust systems

Excessive fuel consumption

- ☐ Air filter element dirty or clogged (Chapter 1A or 1B).
- ☐ Fuel injection system fault (Chapter 4A or 4B).
- ☐ Ignition system fault – petrol models (Chapters 1A and 5B).
- ☐ Faulty injector(s) – diesel models (Chapter 4B).
- ☐ Tyres underinflated (*Weekly checks*).

Fuel leakage and/or fuel odour

- ☐ Damaged or corroded fuel tank, pipes or connections (Chapter 4A or 4B).
- ☐ Excessive noise or fumes from exhaust system (Chapters 4C or 4D)
- ☐ Leaking exhaust system or manifold joints (Chapters 1A, 1B, 4C or 4D).
- ☐ Leaking, corroded or damaged silencers or pipe (Chapters 1A, 1B, 4C or 4D).
- ☐ Broken mountings causing body or suspension contact (Chapter 1A or 1B).

Clutch

Pedal travels to floor – no pressure or very little resistance

- ☐ Hydraulic fluid level low/air in hydraulic system (Chapter 6).
- ☐ Broken clutch release bearing (Chapter 6).
- ☐ Broken diaphragm spring in clutch pressure plate (Chapter 6).

Clutch fails to disengage (unable to select gears)

- ☐ Clutch disc sticking on transmission input shaft splines (Chapter 6).
- ☐ Clutch disc sticking to flywheel or pressure plate (Chapter 6).
- ☐ Faulty pressure plate assembly (Chapter 6).
- ☐ Clutch release mechanism worn or incorrectly assembled (Chapter 6).

Clutch slips (engine speed increases, with no increase in vehicle speed)

- ☐ Clutch disc linings excessively worn (Chapter 6).
- ☐ Clutch disc linings contaminated with oil or grease (Chapter 6).
- ☐ Faulty pressure plate or weak diaphragm spring (Chapter 6).

Judder as clutch is engaged

- ☐ Clutch disc linings contaminated with oil or grease (Chapter 6).
- ☐ Clutch disc linings excessively worn (Chapter 6).
- ☐ Faulty or distorted pressure plate or diaphragm spring (Chapter 6).
- ☐ Worn or loose engine or transmission mountings (Chapter 2A or 2B).
- ☐ Clutch disc hub or transmission input shaft splines worn (Chapter 6).

Noise when depressing or releasing clutch pedal

- ☐ Worn clutch release bearing (Chapter 6).
- ☐ Worn or dry clutch pedal bushes (Chapter 6).
- ☐ Faulty pressure plate assembly (Chapter 6).
- ☐ Pressure plate diaphragm spring broken (Chapter 6).
- ☐ Broken clutch disc cushioning springs (Chapter 6).

Manual transmission

Noisy in neutral with engine running

- ☐ Input shaft bearings worn (noise apparent with clutch pedal released, but not when depressed) (Chapter 7A).*
- ☐ Clutch release bearing worn (noise apparent with clutch pedal depressed, possibly less when released) (Chapter 6).

Noisy in one particular gear

- ☐ Worn, damaged or chipped gear teeth (Chapter 7A).*

Difficulty engaging gears

- ☐ Clutch fault (Chapter 6).
- ☐ Worn or damaged gear linkage (Chapter 7A).
- ☐ Incorrectly adjusted gear linkage (Chapter 7A).
- ☐ Worn synchroniser units (Chapter 7A).*

Vibration

- ☐ Lack of oil (Chapter 1A or 1B).
- ☐ Worn bearings (Chapter 7A).*

Jumps out of gear

- ☐ Worn or damaged gear linkage (Chapter 7A).
- ☐ Incorrectly adjusted gear linkage (Chapter 7A).
- ☐ Worn synchroniser units (Chapter 7A).*
- ☐ Worn selector forks (Chapter 7A).*

Lubricant leaks

- ☐ Leaking differential output oil seal (Chapter 7A).
- ☐ Leaking housing joint (Chapter 7A).*
- ☐ Leaking input shaft oil seal (Chapter 7A).*

** Although the corrective action necessary to remedy the symptoms described is beyond the scope of the home mechanic, the above information should be helpful in isolating the cause of the condition. This should enable the owner can communicate clearly with a professional mechanic.*

Automatic transmission

Note: *Due to the complexity of the automatic transmission, it is difficult for the home mechanic to properly diagnose and service this unit. For problems other than the following, the vehicle should be taken to a dealer service department or automatic transmission specialist. Do not be too hasty in removing the transmission if a fault is suspected, as most of the testing is carried out with the unit still fitted.*

Fluid leakage

- ☐ Automatic transmission fluid is usually dark in colour. Fluid leaks should not be confused with engine oil, which can easily be blown onto the transmission by airflow.
- ☐ To determine the source of a leak, first remove all built-up dirt and grime from the transmission housing and surrounding areas using a degreasing agent, or by steam-cleaning. Drive the vehicle at low speed, so airflow will not blow the leak far from its source. Raise and support the vehicle, and determine where the leak is coming from.

General gear selection problems

- ☐ Chapter 7B deals with checking and adjusting the selector cables on automatic transmissions. The following are common problems, which may be caused by a poorly adjusted cable:

a) Engine starting in gears other than Park or Neutral.
b) Indicator panel indicating a gear other than the one actually being used.
c) Vehicle moves when in Park or Neutral.
d) Poor gearshift quality or erratic gearchanges.

Transmission fluid brown, or has burned smell

- ☐ Transmission fluid level low (Chapter 1A or 1B). If the fluid appears to have deteriorated badly it is recommended that it is renewed.

Transmission will not downshift (kickdown) with accelerator pedal fully depressed

- ☐ Low transmission fluid level (Chapter 1A or 1B).
- ☐ Incorrect selector cable adjustment (Chapter 7B).

Engine will not start in any gear, or starts in gears other than Park or Neutral

- ☐ Incorrect selector cable adjustment (Chapter 7B).

Transmission slips, shifts roughly, is noisy, or has no drive in forward or reverse gears

- ☐ There are many probable causes for the above problems, but unless there is a very obvious reason (such as a loose or corroded wiring plug connection on or near the transmission), the car should be taken to a franchise dealer for the fault to be diagnosed. The transmission control unit incorporates a self-diagnosis facility, and any fault codes can quickly be read and interpreted by a dealer with the proper diagnostic equipment.

Braking system

Note: *Before assuming that a brake problem exists, make sure that the tyres are in good condition and correctly inflated, that the front wheel alignment is correct, and that the vehicle is not loaded with weight in an unequal manner. Apart from checking the condition of all pipe and hose connections, any faults occurring on the anti-lock braking system should be referred to a Mercedes dealer for diagnosis.*

Vehicle pulls to one side under braking

- ☐ Worn, defective, damaged or contaminated brake pads on one side (Chapter 9).
- ☐ Seized or partially seized brake caliper piston (Chapter 9).
- ☐ A mixture of brake pad lining materials fitted between sides (Chapter 9).
- ☐ Brake caliper mounting bolts loose (Chapter 9).
- ☐ Worn or damaged steering or suspension components (Chapter 10).

Noise (grinding or high-pitched squeal) when brakes applied)

- ☐ Brake pad friction lining material worn down to metal backing (Chapter 9).
- ☐ Excessive corrosion of brake disc. This may be apparent after the vehicle has been standing for some time (Chapter 9).
- ☐ Foreign object (stone chipping, etc) trapped between brake disc and shield (Chapter 9).

Brakes binding

- ☐ Seized brake caliper piston(s) (Chapter 9).
- ☐ Incorrectly adjusted handbrake mechanism (Chapter 9).
- ☐ Faulty master cylinder (Chapter 9).

Excessive brake pedal travel

- ☐ Faulty master cylinder (Chapter 9).
- ☐ Air in hydraulic system (Chapter 9).
- ☐ Faulty vacuum servo unit (Chapter 9).

Brake pedal feels spongy when depressed

- ☐ Air in hydraulic system (Chapter 9).
- ☐ Deteriorated flexible rubber brake hoses (Chapter 9).
- ☐ Master cylinder mounting nuts loose (Chapter 9).
- ☐ Faulty master cylinder (Chapter 9).

Excessive brake pedal effort required to stop the vehicle

- ☐ Faulty vacuum servo unit (Chapter 9).
- ☐ Faulty brake vacuum pump – diesel models (Chapter 9).
- ☐ Disconnected, damaged or insecure brake servo vacuum hose (Chapter 9).
- ☐ Primary or secondary hydraulic circuit failure (Chapter 9).
- ☐ Seized brake caliper piston(s) (Chapter 9).
- ☐ Brake pads incorrectly fitted (Chapter 9).
- ☐ Incorrect grade of brake pads fitted (Chapter 9).
- ☐ Brake pads contaminated (Chapter 9).

Judder felt through brake pedal or steering wheel when braking

- ☐ Excessive run-out or distortion of discs (Chapter 9).
- ☐ Brake pad worn (Chapter 9).
- ☐ Brake caliper mounting bolts loose (Chapter 9).
- ☐ Wear in suspension or steering components or mountings (Chapter 10).

Rear wheels locking under normal braking

- ☐ Rear brake pads contaminated (Chapter 9).
- ☐ ABS system fault (Chapter 9).

Driveshafts

Clicking or knocking noise on turns (at slow speed on full-lock)

- ☐ Lack of constant velocity joint lubricant, possibly due to damaged gaiter (Chapter 8).
- ☐ Worn outer constant velocity joint (Chapter 8).
- ☐ Vibration when accelerating or decelerating
- ☐ Worn inner constant velocity joint (Chapter 8).
- ☐ Bent or distorted driveshaft (Chapter 8).

Suspension and steering

Note: *Before diagnosing suspension or steering faults, be sure that the trouble is not due to incorrect tyre pressures, mixtures of tyre types, or binding brakes.*

Vehicle pulls to one side

- ☐ Defective tyre (*Weekly checks*).
- ☐ Excessive wear in suspension or steering components (Chapter 10).
- ☐ Incorrect front wheel alignment (Chapter 10).
- ☐ Accident damage to steering or suspension components (Chapter 10).

Excessive pitching and/or rolling around corners, or during braking

- ☐ Defective shock absorbers (Chapter 10).
- ☐ Broken or weak spring and/or suspension component (Chapter 10).
- ☐ Worn or damaged anti-roll bar or mountings (Chapter 10).

Lack of power assistance

- ☐ Faulty rack-and-pinion steering gear (Chapter 10).

Wandering or general instability

- ☐ Incorrect front wheel alignment (Chapter 10).
- ☐ Worn steering or suspension joints, bushes or components (Chapter 10).
- ☐ Roadwheels out of balance (Chapter 10).
- ☐ Faulty or damaged tyre (*Weekly checks*).
- ☐ Wheel bolts loose (refer to Chapters 1A or 1B and 10 for correct torque).
- ☐ Defective shock absorbers (Chapter 10).

Excessively stiff steering

- ☐ Lack of steering gear lubricant (Chapter 10).
- ☐ Seized track rod end balljoint or suspension balljoint (Chapter 10).
- ☐ Incorrect front wheel alignment (Chapter 10).
- ☐ Steering rack or column bent or damaged (Chapter 10).

Excessive play in steering

- ☐ Worn steering column intermediate shaft universal joint (Chapter 10).
- ☐ Worn steering track rod end balljoints (Chapter 10).
- ☐ Worn rack-and-pinion steering gear (Chapter 10).
- ☐ Worn steering or suspension joints, bushes or components (Chapter 10).

Wheel wobble and vibration

- ☐ Front roadwheels out of balance (vibration felt mainly through the steering wheel) (Chapter 10).
- ☐ Rear roadwheels out of balance (vibration felt throughout the vehicle) (Chapter 10).
- ☐ Roadwheels damaged or distorted (Chapter 10).
- ☐ Faulty or damaged tyre (*Weekly checks*).
- ☐ Worn steering or suspension joints, bushes or components (Chapter 10).
- ☐ Wheel bolts loose (Chapter 10).

Tyre wear excessive

Tyres worn on inside or outside edges

- ☐ Tyres under-inflated (wear on both edges) (*Weekly checks*).
- ☐ Incorrect camber or castor angles (wear on one edge only) (Chapter 10).
- ☐ Worn steering or suspension joints, bushes or components (Chapter 10).
- ☐ Excessively hard cornering.
- ☐ Accident damage.

Tyre treads exhibit feathered edges

- ☐ Incorrect toe setting (Chapter 10).

Tyres worn in centre of tread

- ☐ Tyres overinflated (*Weekly checks*).

Tyres worn on inside and outside edges

- ☐ Tyres underinflated (*Weekly checks*).

Tyres worn unevenly

- ☐ Tyres/wheels out of balance (*Weekly checks* or Chapter 10).
- ☐ Excessive wheel or tyre run-out (*Weekly checks* or Chapter 10).
- ☐ Worn shock absorbers (Chapter 10).
- ☐ Faulty tyre (*Weekly checks*).

Electrical system

Note: *For problems associated with the starting system, refer to the faults listed under 'Engine' earlier in this Section.*

Battery will not hold a charge for more than a few days

- ☐ Battery defective internally (Chapter 5A).
- ☐ Battery terminal connections loose or corroded (*Weekly checks*).
- ☐ Auxiliary drivebelt worn or incorrectly adjusted (Chapter 1A or 1B).
- ☐ Alternator not charging at correct output (Chapter 5A).
- ☐ Alternator or voltage regulator faulty (Chapter 5A).
- ☐ Short-circuit causing continual battery drain (Chapters 5A and 12).

Ignition/no-charge warning light remains illuminated with engine running

- ☐ Auxiliary drivebelt broken, worn, or incorrectly adjusted (Chapter 1A or 1B).
- ☐ Alternator brushes worn, sticking, or dirty (Chapter 5A).
- ☐ Alternator brush springs weak or broken (Chapter 5A).
- ☐ Internal fault in alternator or voltage regulator (Chapter 5A).
- ☐ Broken, disconnected, or loose wiring in charging circuit (Chapter 5A).

Electrical system (continued)

Ignition/no-charge warning light fails to come on

- ☐ Warning light defective (Chapter 12).
- ☐ Broken, disconnected, or loose wiring in warning light circuit (Chapter 12).
- ☐ Alternator faulty (Chapter 5A).

Lights inoperative

- ☐ Bulb blown or light unit faulty (Chapter 12).
- ☐ Corrosion of bulb or bulbholder contacts (Chapter 12).
- ☐ Blown fuse (Chapter 12).
- ☐ Faulty relay (Chapter 12).
- ☐ Broken, loose, or disconnected wiring (Chapter 12).
- ☐ Faulty switch (Chapter 12).

Instrument readings inaccurate or erratic

Fuel or temperature gauges give no reading

- ☐ Faulty gauge sender unit (Chapters 3, 4A or 4B).
- ☐ Wiring open-circuit (Chapter 12).
- ☐ Faulty gauge (Chapter 12).

Fuel or temperature gauges give continuous maximum reading

- ☐ Faulty gauge sender unit (Chapters 3, 4A or 4B).
- ☐ Wiring short-circuit (Chapter 12).
- ☐ Faulty gauge (Chapter 12).

Horn inoperative, or unsatisfactory in operation

Horn operates all the time

- ☐ Horn push either earthed or stuck down (Chapter 12).
- ☐ Horn cable-to-horn push earthed (Chapter 12).

Horn fails to operate

- ☐ Blown fuse (Chapter 12).
- ☐ Cable or cable connections loose, broken or disconnected (Chapter 12).
- ☐ Faulty horn (Chapter 12).

Horn emits intermittent or unsatisfactory sound

- ☐ Cable connections loose (Chapter 12).
- ☐ Horn mountings loose (Chapter 12).
- ☐ Faulty horn (Chapter 12).

Windscreen/tailgate wipers inoperative, or unsatisfactory in operation

Wipers fail to operate, or operate very slowly

- ☐ Wiper blades stuck to screen, or linkage seized or binding (*Weekly checks* and Chapter 12).
- ☐ Blown fuse (Chapter 12).
- ☐ Cable or cable connections loose, broken or disconnected (Chapter 12).
- ☐ Faulty relay (Chapter 12).
- ☐ Faulty wiper motor (Chapter 12).

Wiper blades sweep over too large or too small an area of the glass

- ☐ Wiper arms incorrectly positioned on spindles (Chapter 12).
- ☐ Excessive wear of wiper linkage (Chapter 12).
- ☐ Wiper motor or linkage mountings loose or insecure (Chapter 12).

Wiper blades fail to clean the glass effectively

- ☐ Wiper blade rubbers worn or perished (*Weekly checks*).
- ☐ Wiper arm tension springs broken, or arm pivots seized (Chapter 12).
- ☐ Insufficient windscreen washer additive to adequately remove road film (*Weekly checks*).

Windscreen/tailgate washers inoperative, or unsatisfactory in operation

One or more washer jets inoperative

- ☐ Blocked washer jet (Chapter 1A or 1B).
- ☐ Disconnected, kinked or restricted fluid hose (Chapter 12).
- ☐ Insufficient fluid in washer reservoir (Chapter 1A or 1B).

Washer pump fails to operate

- ☐ Broken or disconnected wiring or connections (Chapter 12).
- ☐ Blown fuse (Chapter 12).
- ☐ Faulty washer switch (Chapter 12).
- ☐ Faulty washer pump (Chapter 12).

Electric windows inoperative, or unsatisfactory in operation

Window glass will only move in one direction

- ☐ Faulty switch (Chapter 12).

Window glass slow to move

- ☐ Regulator seized or damaged, or in need of lubrication (Chapter 11).
- ☐ Door internal components or trim fouling regulator (Chapter 11).
- ☐ Faulty motor (Chapter 11).

Window glass fails to move

- ☐ Blown fuse (Chapter 12).
- ☐ Faulty relay (Chapter 12).
- ☐ Broken or disconnected wiring or connections (Chapter 12).
- ☐ Faulty motor (Chapter 11).

Central locking system inoperative, or unsatisfactory in operation

Complete system failure

- ☐ Blown fuse (Chapter 12).
- ☐ Faulty relay (Chapter 12).
- ☐ Broken or disconnected wiring or connections (Chapter 12).
- ☐ Faulty control unit (Chapter 11).

Latch locks but will not unlock, or unlocks but will not lock

- ☐ Faulty control unit (Chapter 11).
- ☐ Broken or disconnected latch operating rods or levers (Chapter 11).
- ☐ Faulty relay (Chapter 12).

One actuator fails to operate

- ☐ Broken or disconnected wiring or connections (Chapter 12).
- ☐ Faulty actuator (Chapter 11).
- ☐ Broken, binding or disconnected latch operating rods or levers (Chapter 11).
- ☐ Fault in door lock (Chapter 11).

A

ABS (Anti-lock brake system) A system, usually electronically controlled, that senses incipient wheel lockup during braking and relieves hydraulic pressure at wheels that are about to skid.

Air bag An inflatable bag hidden in the steering wheel (driver's side) or the dash or glovebox (passenger side). In a head-on collision, the bags inflate, preventing the driver and front passenger from being thrown forward into the steering wheel or windscreen.

Air cleaner A metal or plastic housing, containing a filter element, which removes dust and dirt from the air being drawn into the engine.

Air filter element The actual filter in an air cleaner system, usually manufactured from pleated paper and requiring renewal at regular intervals.

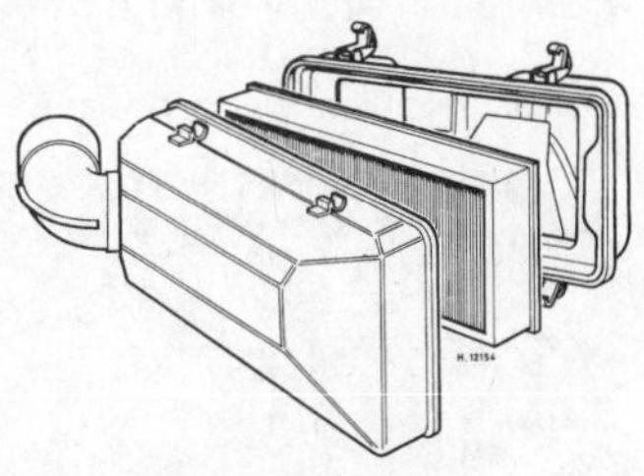

Air filter

Allen key A hexagonal wrench which fits into a recessed hexagonal hole.

Alligator clip A long-nosed spring-loaded metal clip with meshing teeth. Used to make temporary electrical connections.

Alternator A component in the electrical system which converts mechanical energy from a drivebelt into electrical energy to charge the battery and to operate the starting system, ignition system and electrical accessories.

Ampere (amp) A unit of measurement for the flow of electric current. One amp is the amount of current produced by one volt acting through a resistance of one ohm.

Anaerobic sealer A substance used to prevent bolts and screws from loosening. Anaerobic means that it does not require oxygen for activation. The Loctite brand is widely used.

Antifreeze A substance (usually ethylene glycol) mixed with water, and added to a vehicle's cooling system, to prevent freezing of the coolant in winter. Antifreeze also contains chemicals to inhibit corrosion and the formation of rust and other deposits that would tend to clog the radiator and coolant passages and reduce cooling efficiency.

Anti-seize compound A coating that reduces the risk of seizing on fasteners that are subjected to high temperatures, such as exhaust manifold bolts and nuts.

Asbestos A natural fibrous mineral with great heat resistance, commonly used in the composition of brake friction materials. Asbestos is a health hazard and the dust created by brake systems should never be inhaled or ingested.

Axle A shaft on which a wheel revolves, or which revolves with a wheel. Also, a solid beam that connects the two wheels at one end of the vehicle. An axle which also transmits power to the wheels is known as a live axle.

Axleshaft A single rotating shaft, on either side of the differential, which delivers power from the final drive assembly to the drive wheels. Also called a driveshaft or a halfshaft.

B

Ball bearing An anti-friction bearing consisting of a hardened inner and outer race with hardened steel balls between two races.

Bearing The curved surface on a shaft or in a bore, or the part assembled into either, that permits relative motion between them with minimum wear and friction.

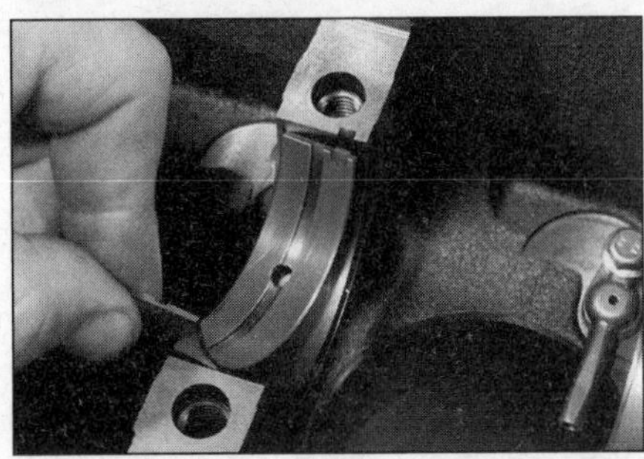

Bearing

Big-end bearing The bearing in the end of the connecting rod that's attached to the crankshaft.

Bleed nipple A valve on a brake wheel cylinder, caliper or other hydraulic component that is opened to purge the hydraulic system of air. Also called a bleed screw.

Brake bleeding Procedure for removing air from lines of a hydraulic brake system.

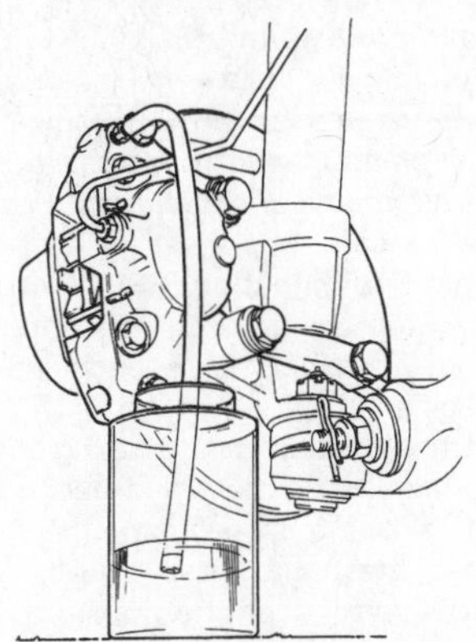

Brake bleeding

Brake disc The component of a disc brake that rotates with the wheels.

Brake drum The component of a drum brake that rotates with the wheels.

Brake linings The friction material which contacts the brake disc or drum to retard the vehicle's speed. The linings are bonded or riveted to the brake pads or shoes.

Brake pads The replaceable friction pads that pinch the brake disc when the brakes are applied. Brake pads consist of a friction material bonded or riveted to a rigid backing plate.

Brake shoe The crescent-shaped carrier to which the brake linings are mounted and which forces the lining against the rotating drum during braking.

Braking systems For more information on braking systems, consult the *Haynes Automotive Brake Manual*.

Breaker bar A long socket wrench handle providing greater leverage.

Bulkhead The insulated partition between the engine and the passenger compartment.

C

Caliper The non-rotating part of a disc-brake assembly that straddles the disc and carries the brake pads. The caliper also contains the hydraulic components that cause the pads to pinch the disc when the brakes are applied. A caliper is also a measuring tool that can be set to measure inside or outside dimensions of an object.

Camshaft A rotating shaft on which a series of cam lobes operate the valve mechanisms. The camshaft may be driven by gears, by sprockets and chain or by sprockets and a belt.

Canister A container in an evaporative emission control system; contains activated charcoal granules to trap vapours from the fuel system.

Canister

Carburettor A device which mixes fuel with air in the proper proportions to provide a desired power output from a spark ignition internal combustion engine.

Castellated Resembling the parapets along the top of a castle wall. For example, a castellated balljoint stud nut.

Castor In wheel alignment, the backward or forward tilt of the steering axis. Castor is positive when the steering axis is inclined rearward at the top.

Catalytic converter A silencer-like device in the exhaust system which converts certain pollutants in the exhaust gases into less harmful substances.

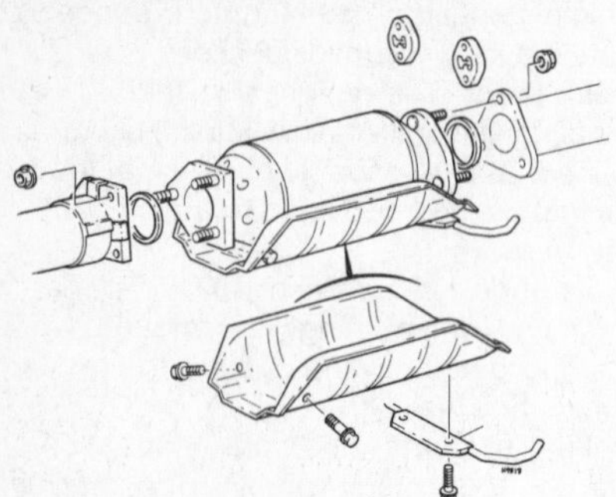

Catalytic converter

Circlip A ring-shaped clip used to prevent endwise movement of cylindrical parts and shafts. An internal circlip is installed in a groove in a housing; an external circlip fits into a groove on the outside of a cylindrical piece such as a shaft.

Clearance The amount of space between two parts. For example, between a piston and a cylinder, between a bearing and a journal, etc.

Coil spring A spiral of elastic steel found in various sizes throughout a vehicle, for example as a springing medium in the suspension and in the valve train.

Compression Reduction in volume, and increase in pressure and temperature, of a gas, caused by squeezing it into a smaller space.

Compression ratio The relationship between cylinder volume when the piston is at top dead centre and cylinder volume when the piston is at bottom dead centre.

Constant velocity (CV) joint A type of universal joint that cancels out vibrations caused by driving power being transmitted through an angle.

Core plug A disc or cup-shaped metal device inserted in a hole in a casting through which core was removed when the casting was formed. Also known as a freeze plug or expansion plug.

Crankcase The lower part of the engine block in which the crankshaft rotates.

Crankshaft The main rotating member, or shaft, running the length of the crankcase, with offset "throws" to which the connecting rods are attached.

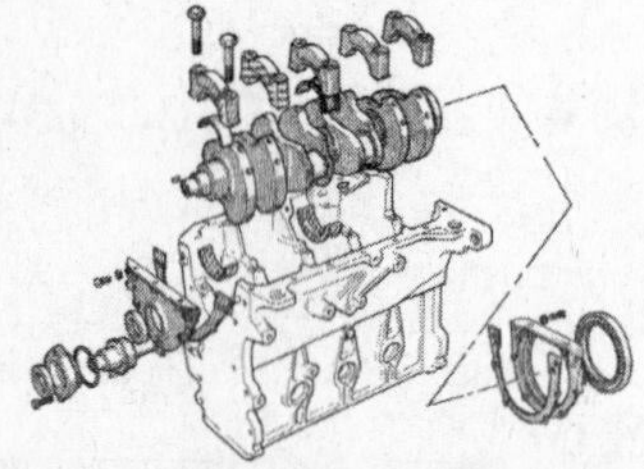

Crankshaft assembly

Crocodile clip See Alligator clip

D

Diagnostic code Code numbers obtained by accessing the diagnostic mode of an engine management computer. This code can be used to determine the area in the system where a malfunction may be located.

Disc brake A brake design incorporating a rotating disc onto which brake pads are squeezed. The resulting friction converts the energy of a moving vehicle into heat.

Double-overhead cam (DOHC) An engine that uses two overhead camshafts, usually one for the intake valves and one for the exhaust valves.

Drivebelt(s) The belt(s) used to drive accessories such as the alternator, water pump, power steering pump, air conditioning compressor, etc. off the crankshaft pulley.

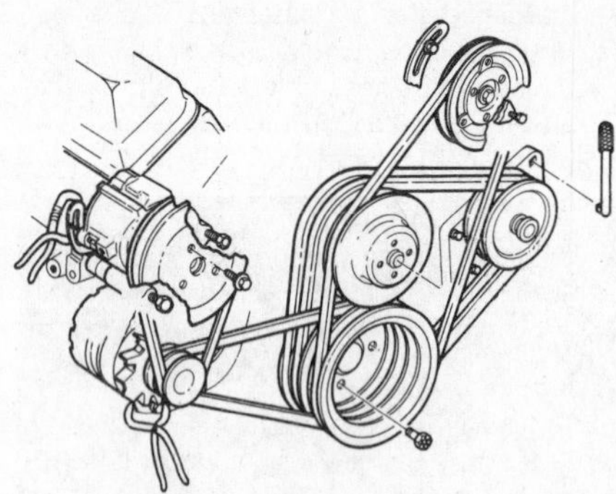

Accessory drivebelts

Driveshaft Any shaft used to transmit motion. Commonly used when referring to the axleshafts on a front wheel drive vehicle.

Drum brake A type of brake using a drum-shaped metal cylinder attached to the inner surface of the wheel. When the brake pedal is pressed, curved brake shoes with friction linings press against the inside of the drum to slow or stop the vehicle.

E

EGR valve A valve used to introduce exhaust gases into the intake air stream.

Electronic control unit (ECU) A computer which controls (for instance) ignition and fuel injection systems, or an anti-lock braking system. For more information refer to the *Haynes Automotive Electrical and Electronic Systems Manual.*

Electronic Fuel Injection (EFI) A computer controlled fuel system that distributes fuel through an injector located in each intake port of the engine.

Emergency brake A braking system, independent of the main hydraulic system, that can be used to slow or stop the vehicle if the primary brakes fail, or to hold the vehicle stationary even though the brake pedal isn't depressed. It usually consists of a hand lever that actuates either front or rear brakes mechanically through a series of cables and linkages. Also known as a handbrake or parking brake.

Endfloat The amount of lengthwise movement between two parts. As applied to a crankshaft, the distance that the crankshaft can move forward and back in the cylinder block.

Engine management system (EMS) A computer controlled system which manages the fuel injection and the ignition systems in an integrated fashion.

Exhaust manifold A part with several passages through which exhaust gases leave the engine combustion chambers and enter the exhaust pipe.

F

Fan clutch A viscous (fluid) drive coupling device which permits variable engine fan speeds in relation to engine speeds.

Feeler blade A thin strip or blade of hardened steel, ground to an exact thickness, used to check or measure clearances between parts.

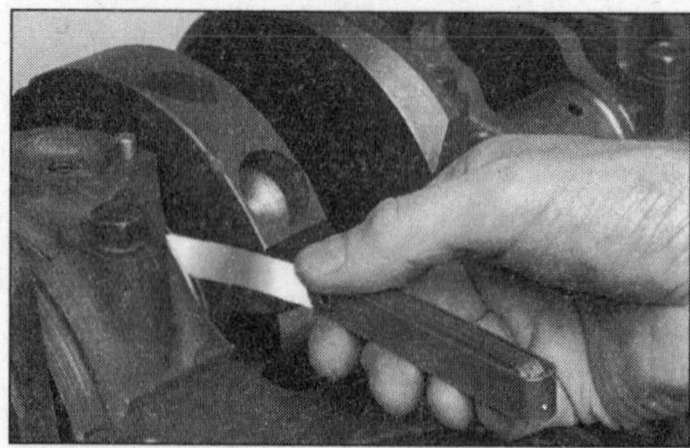

Feeler blade

Firing order The order in which the engine cylinders fire, or deliver their power strokes, beginning with the number one cylinder.

Flywheel A heavy spinning wheel in which energy is absorbed and stored by means of momentum. On cars, the flywheel is attached to the crankshaft to smooth out firing impulses.

Free play The amount of travel before any action takes place. The "looseness" in a linkage, or an assembly of parts, between the initial application of force and actual movement. For example, the distance the brake pedal moves before the pistons in the master cylinder are actuated.

Fuse An electrical device which protects a circuit against accidental overload. The typical fuse contains a soft piece of metal which is calibrated to melt at a predetermined current flow (expressed as amps) and break the circuit.

Fusible link A circuit protection device consisting of a conductor surrounded by heat-resistant insulation. The conductor is smaller than the wire it protects, so it acts as the weakest link in the circuit. Unlike a blown fuse, a failed fusible link must frequently be cut from the wire for replacement.

G

Gap The distance the spark must travel in jumping from the centre electrode to the side electrode in a spark plug. Also refers to the spacing between the points in a contact breaker assembly in a conventional points-type ignition, or to the distance between the reluctor or rotor and the pickup coil in an electronic ignition.

Adjusting spark plug gap

Gasket Any thin, soft material - usually cork, cardboard, asbestos or soft metal - installed between two metal surfaces to ensure a good seal. For instance, the cylinder head gasket seals the joint between the block and the cylinder head.

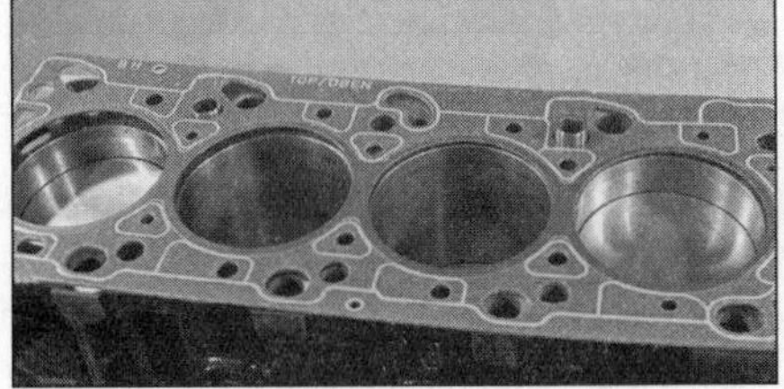

Gasket

Gauge An instrument panel display used to monitor engine conditions. A gauge with a movable pointer on a dial or a fixed scale is an analogue gauge. A gauge with a numerical readout is called a digital gauge.

H

Halfshaft A rotating shaft that transmits power from the final drive unit to a drive wheel, usually when referring to a live rear axle.

Harmonic balancer A device designed to reduce torsion or twisting vibration in the crankshaft. May be incorporated in the crankshaft pulley. Also known as a vibration damper.

Hone An abrasive tool for correcting small irregularities or differences in diameter in an engine cylinder, brake cylinder, etc.

Hydraulic tappet A tappet that utilises hydraulic pressure from the engine's lubrication system to maintain zero clearance (constant contact with both camshaft and valve stem). Automatically adjusts to variation in valve stem length. Hydraulic tappets also reduce valve noise.

I

Ignition timing The moment at which the spark plug fires, usually expressed in the number of crankshaft degrees before the piston reaches the top of its stroke.

Inlet manifold A tube or housing with passages through which flows the air-fuel mixture (carburettor vehicles and vehicles with throttle body injection) or air only (port fuel-injected vehicles) to the port openings in the cylinder head.

J

Jump start Starting the engine of a vehicle with a discharged or weak battery by attaching jump leads from the weak battery to a charged or helper battery.

L

Load Sensing Proportioning Valve (LSPV) A brake hydraulic system control valve that works like a proportioning valve, but also takes into consideration the amount of weight carried by the rear axle.

Locknut A nut used to lock an adjustment nut, or other threaded component, in place. For example, a locknut is employed to keep the adjusting nut on the rocker arm in position.

Lockwasher A form of washer designed to prevent an attaching nut from working loose.

M

MacPherson strut A type of front suspension system devised by Earle MacPherson at Ford of England. In its original form, a simple lateral link with the anti-roll bar creates the lower control arm. A long strut - an integral coil spring and shock absorber - is mounted between the body and the steering knuckle. Many modern so-called MacPherson strut systems use a conventional lower A-arm and don't rely on the anti-roll bar for location.

Multimeter An electrical test instrument with the capability to measure voltage, current and resistance.

N

NOx Oxides of Nitrogen. A common toxic pollutant emitted by petrol and diesel engines at higher temperatures.

O

Ohm The unit of electrical resistance. One volt applied to a resistance of one ohm will produce a current of one amp.

Ohmmeter An instrument for measuring electrical resistance.

O-ring A type of sealing ring made of a special rubber-like material; in use, the O-ring is compressed into a groove to provide the sealing action.

Overhead cam (ohc) engine An engine with the camshaft(s) located on top of the cylinder head(s).

Overhead valve (ohv) engine An engine with the valves located in the cylinder head, but with the camshaft located in the engine block.

Oxygen sensor A device installed in the engine exhaust manifold, which senses the oxygen content in the exhaust and converts this information into an electric current. Also called a Lambda sensor.

P

Phillips screw A type of screw head having a cross instead of a slot for a corresponding type of screwdriver.

Plastigage A thin strip of plastic thread, available in different sizes, used for measuring clearances. For example, a strip of Plastigage is laid across a bearing journal. The parts are assembled and dismantled; the width of the crushed strip indicates the clearance between journal and bearing.

Plastigage

Propeller shaft The long hollow tube with universal joints at both ends that carries power from the transmission to the differential on front-engined rear wheel drive vehicles.

Proportioning valve A hydraulic control valve which limits the amount of pressure to the rear brakes during panic stops to prevent wheel lock-up.

R

Rack-and-pinion steering A steering system with a pinion gear on the end of the steering shaft that mates with a rack (think of a geared wheel opened up and laid flat). When the steering wheel is turned, the pinion turns, moving the rack to the left or right. This movement is transmitted through the track rods to the steering arms at the wheels.

Radiator A liquid-to-air heat transfer device designed to reduce the temperature of the coolant in an internal combustion engine cooling system.

Refrigerant Any substance used as a heat transfer agent in an air-conditioning system. R-12 has been the principle refrigerant for many years; recently, however, manufacturers have begun using R-134a, a non-CFC substance that is considered less harmful to the ozone in the upper atmosphere.

Rocker arm A lever arm that rocks on a shaft or pivots on a stud. In an overhead valve engine, the rocker arm converts the upward movement of the pushrod into a downward movement to open a valve.

Rotor In a distributor, the rotating device inside the cap that connects the centre electrode and the outer terminals as it turns, distributing the high voltage from the coil secondary winding to the proper spark plug. Also, that part of an alternator which rotates inside the stator. Also, the rotating assembly of a turbocharger, including the compressor wheel, shaft and turbine wheel.
Runout The amount of wobble (in-and-out movement) of a gear or wheel as it's rotated. The amount a shaft rotates "out-of-true." The out-of-round condition of a rotating part.

S

Sealant A liquid or paste used to prevent leakage at a joint. Sometimes used in conjunction with a gasket.
Sealed beam lamp An older headlight design which integrates the reflector, lens and filaments into a hermetically-sealed one-piece unit. When a filament burns out or the lens cracks, the entire unit is simply replaced.
Serpentine drivebelt A single, long, wide accessory drivebelt that's used on some newer vehicles to drive all the accessories, instead of a series of smaller, shorter belts. Serpentine drivebelts are usually tensioned by an automatic tensioner.

Serpentine drivebelt

Shim Thin spacer, commonly used to adjust the clearance or relative positions between two parts. For example, shims inserted into or under bucket tappets control valve clearances. Clearance is adjusted by changing the thickness of the shim.
Slide hammer A special puller that screws into or hooks onto a component such as a shaft or bearing; a heavy sliding handle on the shaft bottoms against the end of the shaft to knock the component free.
Sprocket A tooth or projection on the periphery of a wheel, shaped to engage with a chain or drivebelt. Commonly used to refer to the sprocket wheel itself.
Starter inhibitor switch On vehicles with an automatic transmission, a switch that prevents starting if the vehicle is not in Neutral or Park.
Strut See MacPherson strut.

T

Tappet A cylindrical component which transmits motion from the cam to the valve stem, either directly or via a pushrod and rocker arm. Also called a cam follower.
Thermostat A heat-controlled valve that regulates the flow of coolant between the cylinder block and the radiator, so maintaining optimum engine operating temperature. A thermostat is also used in some air cleaners in which the temperature is regulated.
Thrust bearing The bearing in the clutch assembly that is moved in to the release levers by clutch pedal action to disengage the clutch. Also referred to as a release bearing.
Timing belt A toothed belt which drives the camshaft. Serious engine damage may result if it breaks in service.
Timing chain A chain which drives the camshaft.
Toe-in The amount the front wheels are closer together at the front than at the rear. On rear wheel drive vehicles, a slight amount of toe-in is usually specified to keep the front wheels running parallel on the road by offsetting other forces that tend to spread the wheels apart.
Toe-out The amount the front wheels are closer together at the rear than at the front. On front wheel drive vehicles, a slight amount of toe-out is usually specified.
Tools For full information on choosing and using tools, refer to the *Haynes Automotive Tools Manual.*
Tracer A stripe of a second colour applied to a wire insulator to distinguish that wire from another one with the same colour insulator.
Tune-up A process of accurate and careful adjustments and parts replacement to obtain the best possible engine performance.
Turbocharger A centrifugal device, driven by exhaust gases, that pressurises the intake air. Normally used to increase the power output from a given engine displacement, but can also be used primarily to reduce exhaust emissions (as on VW's "Umwelt" Diesel engine).

U

Universal joint or U-joint A double-pivoted connection for transmitting power from a driving to a driven shaft through an angle. A U-joint consists of two Y-shaped yokes and a cross-shaped member called the spider.

V

Valve A device through which the flow of liquid, gas, vacuum, or loose material in bulk may be started, stopped, or regulated by a movable part that opens, shuts, or partially obstructs one or more ports or passageways. A valve is also the movable part of such a device.
Valve clearance The clearance between the valve tip (the end of the valve stem) and the rocker arm or tappet. The valve clearance is measured when the valve is closed.
Vernier caliper A precision measuring instrument that measures inside and outside dimensions. Not quite as accurate as a micrometer, but more convenient.
Viscosity The thickness of a liquid or its resistance to flow.
Volt A unit for expressing electrical "pressure" in a circuit. One volt that will produce a current of one ampere through a resistance of one ohm.

W

Welding Various processes used to join metal items by heating the areas to be joined to a molten state and fusing them together. For more information refer to the *Haynes Automotive Welding Manual.*
Wiring diagram A drawing portraying the components and wires in a vehicle's electrical system, using standardised symbols. For more information refer to the *Haynes Automotive Electrical and Electronic Systems Manual.*

Note: *References throughout this index are in the form* **"Chapter number" • "Page number"**. *So, for example, 2C•15 refers to page 15 of Chapter 2C.*

Note: *References throughout this index are in the form* **"Chapter number" • "Page number"**. *So, for example, 2C•15 refers to page 15 of Chapter 2C.*

Note: *References throughout this index are in the form* "**Chapter number**" • "**Page number**". *So, for example, 2C•15 refers to page 15 of Chapter 2C.*

Haynes Manuals – The Complete UK Car List

Title	Book No.
ALFA ROMEO Alfasud/Sprint (74 - 88) up to F *	**0292**
Alfa Romeo Alfetta (73 - 87) up to E *	**0531**
AUDI 80, 90 & Coupe Petrol (79 - Nov 88) up to F	**0605**
Audi 80, 90 & Coupe Petrol (Oct 86 - 90) D to H	**1491**
Audi 100 & 200 Petrol (Oct 82 - 90) up to H	**0907**
Audi 100 & A6 Petrol & Diesel (May 91 - May 97) H to P	**3504**
Audi A3 Petrol & Diesel (96 - May 03) P to 03	**4253**
Audi A4 Petrol & Diesel (95 - 00) M to X	**3575**
Audi A4 Petrol & Diesel (01 - 04) X to 54	**4609**
AUSTIN A35 & A40 (56 - 67) up to F *	**0118**
Austin/MG/Rover Maestro 1.3 & 1.6 Petrol (83 - 95) up to M	**0922**
Austin/MG Metro (80 - May 90) up to G	**0718**
Austin/Rover Montego 1.3 & 1.6 Petrol (84 - 94) A to L	**1066**
Austin/MG/Rover Montego 2.0 Petrol (84 - 95) A to M	**1067**
Mini (59 - 69) up to H *	**0527**
Mini (69 - 01) up to X	**0646**
Austin/Rover 2.0 litre Diesel Engine (86 - 93) C to L	**1857**
Austin Healey 100/6 & 3000 (56 - 68) up to G *	**0049**
BEDFORD CF Petrol (69 - 87) up to E	**0163**
Bedford/Vauxhall Rascal & Suzuki Supercarry (86 - Oct 94) C to M	**3015**
BMW 316, 320 & 320i (4-cyl) (75 - Feb 83) up to Y *	**0276**
BMW 320, 320i, 323i & 325i (6-cyl) (Oct 77 - Sept 87) up to E	**0815**
BMW 3- & 5-Series Petrol (81 - 91) up to J	**1948**
BMW 3-Series Petrol (Apr 91 - 99) H to V	**3210**
BMW 3-Series Petrol (Sept 98 - 03) S to 53	**4067**
BMW 520i & 525e (Oct 81 - June 88) up to E	**1560**
BMW 525, 528 & 528i (73 - Sept 81) up to X *	**0632**
BMW 5-Series 6-cyl Petrol (April 96 - Aug 03) N to 03	**4151**
BMW 1500, 1502, 1600, 1602, 2000 & 2002 (59 - 77) up to S *	**0240**
CHRYSLER PT Cruiser Petrol (00 - 03) W to 53	**4058**
CITROËN 2CV, Ami & Dyane (67 - 90) up to H	**0196**
Citroën AX Petrol & Diesel (87 - 97) D to P	**3014**
Citroën Berlingo & Peugeot Partner Petrol & Diesel (96 - 05) P to 55	**4281**
Citroën BX Petrol (83 - 94) A to L	**0908**
Citroën C15 Van Petrol & Diesel (89 - Oct 98) F to S	**3509**
Citroën C3 Petrol & Diesel (02 - 05) 51 to 05	**4197**
Citroën CX Petrol (75 - 88) up to F	**0528**
Citroën Saxo Petrol & Diesel (96 - 04) N to 54	**3506**
Citroën Visa Petrol (79 - 88) up to F	**0620**
Citroën Xantia Petrol & Diesel (93 - 01) K to Y	**3082**
Citroën XM Petrol & Diesel (89 - 00) G to X	**3451**
Citroën Xsara Petrol & Diesel (97 - Sept 00) R to W	**3751**
Citroën Xsara Picasso Petrol & Diesel (00 - 02) W to 52	**3944**
Citroën ZX Diesel (91 - 98) J to S	**1922**
Citroën ZX Petrol (91 - 98) H to S	**1881**
Citroën 1.7 & 1.9 litre Diesel Engine (84 - 96) A to N	**1379**
FIAT 126 (73 - 87) up to E *	**0305**
Fiat 500 (57 - 73) up to M *	**0090**
Fiat Bravo & Brava Petrol (95 - 00) N to W	**3572**
Fiat Cinquecento (93 - 98) K to R	**3501**
Fiat Panda (81 - 95) up to M	**0793**
Fiat Punto Petrol & Diesel (94 - Oct 99) L to V	**3251**
Fiat Punto Petrol (Oct 99 - July 03) V to 03	**4066**
Fiat Regata Petrol (84 - 88) A to F	**1167**
Fiat Tipo Petrol (88 - 91) E to J	**1625**
Fiat Uno Petrol (83 - 95) up to M	**0923**
Fiat X1/9 (74 - 89) up to G *	**0273**
FORD Anglia (59 - 68) up to G *	**0001**
Ford Capri II (& III) 1.6 & 2.0 (74 - 87) up to E *	**0283**
Ford Capri II (& III) 2.8 & 3.0 V6 (74 - 87) up to E	**1309**
Ford Cortina Mk I & Corsair 1500 ('62 - '66) up to D*	**0214**
Ford Cortina Mk III 1300 & 1600 (70 - 76) up to P *	**0070**
Ford Escort Mk I 1100 & 1300 (68 - 74) up to N *	**0171**
Ford Escort Mk I Mexico, RS 1600 & RS 2000 (70 - 74) up to N *	**0139**
Ford Escort Mk II Mexico, RS 1800 & RS 2000 (75 - 80) up to W *	**0735**
Ford Escort (75 - Aug 80) up to V *	**0280**
Ford Escort Petrol (Sept 80 - Sept 90) up to H	**0686**
Ford Escort & Orion Petrol (Sept 90 - 00) H to X	**1737**
Ford Escort & Orion Diesel (Sept 90 - 00) H to X	**4081**
Ford Fiesta (76 - Aug 83) up to Y	**0334**
Ford Fiesta Petrol (Aug 83 - Feb 89) A to F	**1030**
Ford Fiesta Petrol (Feb 89 - Oct 95) F to N	**1595**
Ford Fiesta Petrol & Diesel (Oct 95 - Mar 02) N to 02	**3397**
Ford Fiesta Petrol & Diesel (Apr 02 - 05) 02 to 54	**4170**
Ford Focus Petrol & Diesel (98 - 01) S to Y	**3759**
Ford Focus Petrol & Diesel (Oct 01 - 05) 51 to 05	**4167**
Ford Galaxy Petrol & Diesel (95 - Aug 00) M to W	**3984**
Ford Granada Petrol (Sept 77 - Feb 85) up to B *	**0481**
Ford Granada & Scorpio Petrol (Mar 85 - 94) B to M	**1245**
Ford Ka (96 - 02) P to 52	**3570**
Ford Mondeo Petrol (93 - Sept 00) K to X	**1923**
Ford Mondeo Petrol & Diesel (Oct 00 - Jul 03) X to 03	**3990**
Ford Mondeo Petrol & Diesel (July 03 - 07) 03 to 56	**4619**
Ford Mondeo Diesel (93 - 96) L to N	**3465**
Ford Orion Petrol (83 - Sept 90) up to H	**1009**
Ford Sierra 4-cyl Petrol (82 - 93) up to K	**0903**
Ford Sierra V6 Petrol (82 - 91) up to J	**0904**
Ford Transit Petrol (Mk 2) (78 - Jan 86) up to C	**0719**
Ford Transit Petrol (Mk 3) (Feb 86 - 89) C to G	**1468**
Ford Transit Diesel (Feb 86 - 99) C to T	**3019**
Ford 1.6 & 1.8 litre Diesel Engine (84 - 96) A to N	**1172**
Ford 2.1, 2.3 & 2.5 litre Diesel Engine (77 - 90) up to H	**1606**
FREIGHT ROVER Sherpa Petrol (74 - 87) up to E	**0463**
HILLMAN Avenger (70 - 82) up to Y	**0037**
Hillman Imp (63 - 76) up to R *	**0022**
HONDA Civic (Feb 84 - Oct 87) A to E	**1226**
Honda Civic (Nov 91 - 96) J to N	**3199**
Honda Civic Petrol (Mar 95 - 00) M to X	**4050**
Honda Civic Petrol & Diesel (01 - 05) X to 55	**4611**
Honda Jazz (01 - Feb 08) 51 - 57	**4735**
HYUNDAI Pony (85 - 94) C to M	**3398**
JAGUAR E Type (61 - 72) up to L *	**0140**
Jaguar MkI & II, 240 & 340 (55 - 69) up to H *	**0098**
Jaguar XJ6, XJ & Sovereign; Daimler Sovereign (68 - Oct 86) up to D	**0242**
Jaguar XJ6 & Sovereign (Oct 86 - Sept 94) D to M	**3261**
Jaguar XJ12, XJS & Sovereign; Daimler Double Six (72 - 88) up to F	**0478**
JEEP Cherokee Petrol (93 - 96) K to N	**1943**
LADA 1200, 1300, 1500 & 1600 (74 - 91) up to J	**0413**
Lada Samara (87 - 91) D to J	**1610**
LAND ROVER 90, 110 & Defender Diesel (83 - 07) up to 56	**3017**
Land Rover Discovery Petrol & Diesel (89 - 98) G to S	**3016**
Land Rover Discovery Diesel (Nov 98 - Jul 04) S to 04	**4606**
Land Rover Freelander Petrol & Diesel (97 - Sept 03) R to 53	**3929**
Land Rover Freelander Petrol & Diesel (Oct 03 - Oct 06) 53 to 56	**4623**
Land Rover Series IIA & III Diesel (58 - 85) up to C	**0529**
Land Rover Series II, IIA & III 4-cyl Petrol (58 - 85) up to C	**0314**
MAZDA 323 (Mar 81 - Oct 89) up to G	**1608**
Mazda 323 (Oct 89 - 98) G to R	**3455**
Mazda 626 (May 83 - Sept 87) up to E	**0929**
Mazda B1600, B1800 & B2000 Pick-up Petrol (72 - 88) up to F	**0267**
Mazda RX-7 (79 - 85) up to C *	**0460**
MERCEDES-BENZ 190, 190E & 190D Petrol & Diesel (83 - 93) A to L	**3450**
Mercedes-Benz 200D, 240D, 240TD, 300D & 300TD 123 Series Diesel (Oct 76 - 85)	**1114**
Mercedes-Benz 250 & 280 (68 - 72) up to L *	**0346**
Mercedes-Benz 250 & 280 123 Series Petrol (Oct 76 - 84) up to B *	**0677**
Mercedes-Benz 124 Series Petrol & Diesel (85 - Aug 93) C to K	**3253**
Mercedes-Benz C-Class Petrol & Diesel (93 - Aug 00) L to W	**3511**
MGA (55 - 62) *	**0475**
MGB (62 - 80) up to W	**0111**
MG Midget & Austin-Healey Sprite (58 - 80) up to W *	**0265**
MINI Petrol (July 01 - 05) Y to 05	**4273**
MITSUBISHI Shogun & L200 Pick-Ups Petrol (83 - 94) up to M	**1944**
MORRIS Ital 1.3 (80 - 84) up to B	**0705**
Morris Minor 1000 (56 - 71) up to K	**0024**
NISSAN Almera Petrol (95 - Feb 00) N to V	**4053**
Nissan Almera & Tino Petrol (Feb 00 - 07) V to 56	**4612**
Nissan Bluebird (May 84 - Mar 86) A to C	**1223**
Nissan Bluebird Petrol (Mar 86 - 90) C to H	**1473**
Nissan Cherry (Sept 82 - 86) up to D	**1031**
Nissan Micra (83 - Jan 93) up to K	**0931**
Nissan Micra (93 - 02) K to 52	**3254**
Nissan Primera Petrol (90 - Aug 99) H to T	**1851**
Nissan Stanza (82 - 86) up to D	**0824**
Nissan Sunny Petrol (May 82 - Oct 86) up to D	**0895**
Nissan Sunny Petrol (Oct 86 - Mar 91) D to H	**1378**
Nissan Sunny Petrol (Apr 91 - 95) H to N	**3219**
OPEL Ascona & Manta (B Series) (Sept 75 - 88) up to F *	**0316**
Opel Ascona Petrol (81 - 88)	**3215**
Opel Astra Petrol (Oct 91 - Feb 98)	**3156**
Opel Corsa Petrol (83 - Mar 93)	**3160**
Opel Corsa Petrol (Mar 93 - 97)	**3159**
Opel Kadett Petrol (Nov 79 - Oct 84) up to B	**0634**
Opel Kadett Petrol (Oct 84 - Oct 91)	**3196**
Opel Omega & Senator Petrol (Nov 86 - 94)	**3157**
Opel Rekord Petrol (Feb 78 - Oct 86) up to D	**0543**
Opel Vectra Petrol (Oct 88 - Oct 95)	**3158**
PEUGEOT 106 Petrol & Diesel (91 - 04) J to 53	**1882**
Peugeot 205 Petrol (83 - 97) A to P	**0932**
Peugeot 206 Petrol & Diesel (98 - 01) S to X	**3757**
Peugeot 206 Petrol & Diesel (02 - 06) 51 to 06	**4613**
Peugeot 306 Petrol & Diesel (93 - 02) K to 02	**3073**
Peugeot 307 Petrol & Diesel (01 - 04) Y to 54	**4147**
Peugeot 309 Petrol (86 - 93) C to K	**1266**
Peugeot 405 Petrol (88 - 97) E to P	**1559**
Peugeot 405 Diesel (88 - 97) E to P	**3198**
Peugeot 406 Petrol & Diesel (96 - Mar 99) N to T	**3394**
Peugeot 406 Petrol & Diesel (Mar 99 - 02) T to 52	**3982**
Peugeot 505 Petrol (79 - 89) up to G	**0762**
Peugeot 1.7/1.8 & 1.9 litre Diesel Engine (82 - 96) up to N	**0950**
Peugeot 2.0, 2.1, 2.3 & 2.5 litre Diesel Engines (74 - 90) up to H	**1607**
PORSCHE 911 (65 - 85) up to C	**0264**

* Classic reprint

Title	Book No.
Porsche 924 & 924 Turbo (76 - 85) up to C	**0397**
PROTON (89 - 97) F to P	**3255**
RANGE ROVER V8 Petrol (70 - Oct 92) up to K	**0606**
RELIANT Robin & Kitten (73 - 83) up to A *	**0436**
RENAULT 4 (61 - 86) up to D *	**0072**
Renault 5 Petrol (Feb 85 - 96) B to N	**1219**
Renault 9 & 11 Petrol (82 - 89) up to F	**0822**
Renault 18 Petrol (79 - 86) up to D	**0598**
Renault 19 Petrol (89 - 96) F to N	**1646**
Renault 19 Diesel (89 - 96) F to N	**1946**
Renault 21 Petrol (86 - 94) C to M	**1397**
Renault 25 Petrol & Diesel (84 - 92) B to K	**1228**
Renault Clio Petrol (91 - May 98) H to R	**1853**
Renault Clio Diesel (91 - June 96) H to N	**3031**
Renault Clio Petrol & Diesel (May 98 - May 01) R to Y	**3906**
Renault Clio Petrol & Diesel (June '01 - '05) Y to 55	**4168**
Renault Espace Petrol & Diesel (85 - 96) C to N	**3197**
Renault Laguna Petrol & Diesel (94 - 00) L to W	**3252**
Renault Laguna Petrol & Diesel (Feb 01 - Feb 05) X to 54	**4283**
Renault Mégane & Scénic Petrol & Diesel (96 - 99) N to T	**3395**
Renault Mégane & Scénic Petrol & Diesel (Apr 99 - 02) T to 52	**3916**
Renault Megane Petrol & Diesel (Oct 02 - 05) 52 to 55	**4284**
Renault Scenic Petrol & Diesel (Sept 03 - 06) 53 to 06	**4297**
ROVER 213 & 216 (84 - 89) A to G	**1116**
Rover 214 & 414 Petrol (89 - 96) G to N	**1689**
Rover 216 & 416 Petrol (89 - 96) G to N	**1830**
Rover 211, 214, 216, 218 & 220 Petrol & Diesel (Dec 95 - 99) N to V	**3399**
Rover 25 & MG ZR Petrol & Diesel (Oct 99 - 04) V to 54	**4145**
Rover 414, 416 & 420 Petrol & Diesel (May 95 - 98) M to R	**3453**
Rover 45 / MG ZS Petrol & Diesel (99 - 05) V to 55	**4384**
Rover 618, 620 & 623 Petrol (93 - 97) K to P	**3257**
Rover 75 / MG ZT Petrol & Diesel (99 - 06) S to 06	**4292**
Rover 820, 825 & 827 Petrol (86 - 95) D to N	**1380**
Rover 3500 (76 - 87) up to E *	**0365**
Rover Metro, 111 & 114 Petrol (May 90 - 98) G to S	**1711**
SAAB 95 & 96 (66 - 76) up to R *	**0198**
Saab 90, 99 & 900 (79 - Oct 93) up to L	**0765**
Saab 900 (Oct 93 - 98) L to R	**3512**
Saab 9000 (4-cyl) (85 - 98) C to S	**1686**
Saab 9-3 Petrol & Diesel (98 - Aug 02) R to 02	**4614**
Saab 9-5 4-cyl Petrol (97 - 04) R to 54	**4156**
SEAT Ibiza & Cordoba Petrol & Diesel (Oct 93 - Oct 99) L to V	**3571**
Seat Ibiza & Malaga Petrol (85 - 92) B to K	**1609**
SKODA Estelle (77 - 89) up to G	**0604**
Skoda Fabia Petrol & Diesel (00 - 06) W to 06	**4376**
Skoda Favorit (89 - 96) F to N	**1801**
Skoda Felicia Petrol & Diesel (95 - 01) M to X	**3505**
Skoda Octavia Petrol & Diesel (98 - Apr 04) R to 04	**4285**
SUBARU 1600 & 1800 (Nov 79 - 90) up to H *	**0995**
SUNBEAM Alpine, Rapier & H120 (67 - 74) up to N *	**0051**
SUZUKI SJ Series, Samurai & Vitara (4-cyl) Petrol (82 - 97) up to P	**1942**
Suzuki Supercarry & Bedford/Vauxhall Rascal (86 - Oct 94) C to M	**3015**
TALBOT Alpine, Solara, Minx & Rapier (75 - 86) up to D	**0337**

Title	Book No.
Talbot Horizon Petrol (78 - 86) up to D	**0473**
Talbot Samba (82 - 86) up to D	**0823**
TOYOTA Avensis Petrol (98 - Jan 03) R to 52	**4264**
Toyota Carina E Petrol (May 92 - 97) J to P	**3256**
Toyota Corolla (80 - 85) up to C	**0683**
Toyota Corolla (Sept 83 - Sept 87) A to E	**1024**
Toyota Corolla (Sept 87 - Aug 92) E to K	**1683**
Toyota Corolla Petrol (Aug 92 - 97) K to P	**3259**
Toyota Corolla Petrol (July 97 - Feb 02) P to 51	**4286**
Toyota Hi-Ace & Hi-Lux Petrol (69 - Oct 83) up to A	**0304**
Toyota Yaris Petrol (99 - 05) T to 05	**4265**
TRIUMPH GT6 & Vitesse (62 - 74) up to N *	**0112**
Triumph Herald (59 - 71) up to K *	**0010**
Triumph Spitfire (62 - 81) up to X	**0113**
Triumph Stag (70 - 78) up to T *	**0441**
Triumph TR2, TR3, TR3A, TR4 & TR4A (52 - 67) up to F *	**0028**
Triumph TR5 & 6 (67 - 75) up to P *	**0031**
Triumph TR7 (75 - 82) up to Y *	**0322**
VAUXHALL Astra Petrol (80 - Oct 84) up to B	**0635**
Vauxhall Astra & Belmont Petrol (Oct 84 - Oct 91) B to J	**1136**
Vauxhall Astra Petrol (Oct 91 - Feb 98) J to R	**1832**
Vauxhall/Opel Astra & Zafira Petrol (Feb 98 - Apr 04) R to 04	**3758**
Vauxhall/Opel Astra & Zafira Diesel (Feb 98 - Apr 04) R to 04	**3797**
Vauxhall/Opel Astra Petrol (04 - 07) 04 - 07	**4732**
Vauxhall/Opel Astra Diesel (04 - 07) 04 - 07	**4733**
Vauxhall/Opel Calibra (90 - 98) G to S	**3502**
Vauxhall Carlton Petrol (Oct 78 - Oct 86) up to D	**0480**
Vauxhall Carlton & Senator Petrol (Nov 86 - 94) D to L	**1469**
Vauxhall Cavalier Petrol (81 - Oct 88) up to F	**0812**
Vauxhall Cavalier Petrol (Oct 88 - 95) F to N	**1570**
Vauxhall Chevette (75 - 84) up to B	**0285**
Vauxhall/Opel Corsa Diesel (Mar 93 - Oct 00) K to X	**4087**
Vauxhall Corsa Petrol (Mar 93 - 97) K to R	**1985**
Vauxhall/Opel Corsa Petrol (Apr 97 - Oct 00) P to X	**3921**
Vauxhall/Opel Corsa Petrol & Diesel (Oct 00 - Sept 03) X to 53	**4079**
Vauxhall/Opel Corsa Petrol & Diesel (Oct 03 - Aug 06) 53 to 06	**4617**
Vauxhall/Opel Frontera Petrol & Diesel (91 - Sept 98) J to S	**3454**
Vauxhall Nova Petrol (83 - 93) up to K	**0909**
Vauxhall/Opel Omega Petrol (94 - 99) L to T	**3510**
Vauxhall/Opel Vectra Petrol & Diesel (95 - Feb 99) N to S	**3396**
Vauxhall/Opel Vectra Petrol & Diesel (Mar 99 - May 02) T to 02	**3930**
Vauxhall/Opel Vectra Petrol & Diesel (June 02 - Sept 05) 02 to 55	**4618**
Vauxhall/Opel 1.5, 1.6 & 1.7 litre Diesel Engine (82 - 96) up to N	**1222**
VW 411 & 412 (68 - 75) up to P *	**0091**
VW Beetle 1200 (54 - 77) up to S	**0036**
VW Beetle 1300 & 1500 (65 - 75) up to P	**0039**
VW 1302 & 1302S (70 - 72) up to L *	**0110**
VW Beetle 1303, 1303S & GT (72 - 75) up to P	**0159**
VW Beetle Petrol & Diesel (Apr 99 - 01) T to 51	**3798**
VW Golf & Jetta Mk 1 Petrol 1.1 & 1.3 (74 - 84) up to A	**0716**
VW Golf, Jetta & Scirocco Mk 1 Petrol 1.5, 1.6 & 1.8 (74 - 84) up to A	**0726**

Title	Book No.
VW Golf & Jetta Mk 1 Diesel (78 - 84) up to A	**0451**
VW Golf & Jetta Mk 2 Petrol (Mar 84 - Feb 92) A to J	**1081**
VW Golf & Vento Petrol & Diesel (Feb 92 - Mar 98) J to R	**3097**
VW Golf & Bora Petrol & Diesel (April 98 - 00) R to X	**3727**
VW Golf & Bora 4-cyl Petrol & Diesel (01 - 03) X to 53	**4169**
VW Golf & Jetta Petrol & Diesel (04 - 07) 53 to 07	**4610**
VW LT Petrol Vans & Light Trucks (76 - 87) up to E	**0637**
VW Passat & Santana Petrol (Sept 81 - May 88) up to E	**0814**
VW Passat 4-cyl Petrol & Diesel (May 88 - 96) E to P	**3498**
VW Passat 4-cyl Petrol & Diesel (Dec 96 - Nov 00) P to X	**3917**
VW Passat Petrol & Diesel (Dec 00 - May 05) X to 05	**4279**
VW Polo & Derby (76 - Jan 82) up to X	**0335**
VW Polo (82 - Oct 90) up to H	**0813**
VW Polo Petrol (Nov 90 - Aug 94) H to L	**3245**
VW Polo Hatchback Petrol & Diesel (94 - 99) M to S	**3500**
VW Polo Hatchback Petrol (00 - Jan 02) V to 51	**4150**
VW Polo Petrol & Diesel (02 - May 05) 51 to 05	**4608**
VW Scirocco (82 - 90) up to H *	**1224**
VW Transporter 1600 (68 - 79) up to V	**0082**
VW Transporter 1700, 1800 & 2000 (72 - 79) up to V *	**0226**
VW Transporter (air-cooled) Petrol (79 - 82) up to Y *	**0638**
VW Transporter (water-cooled) Petrol (82 - 90) up to H	**3452**
VW Type 3 (63 - 73) up to M *	**0084**
VOLVO 120 & 130 Series (& P1800) (61 - 73) up to M *	**0203**
Volvo 142, 144 & 145 (66 - 74) up to N *	**0129**
Volvo 240 Series Petrol (74 - 93) up to K	**0270**
Volvo 262, 264 & 260/265 (75 - 85) up to C *	**0400**
Volvo 340, 343, 345 & 360 (76 - 91) up to J	**0715**
Volvo 440, 460 & 480 Petrol (87 - 97) D to P	**1691**
Volvo 740 & 760 Petrol (82 - 91) up to J	**1258**
Volvo 850 Petrol (92 - 96) J to P	**3260**
Volvo 940 petrol (90 - 98) H to R	**3249**
Volvo S40 & V40 Petrol (96 - Mar 04) N to 04	**3569**
Volvo S40 & V50 Petrol & Diesel (Mar 04 - Jun 07) 04 to 07	**4731**
Volvo S70, V70 & C70 Petrol (96 - 99) P to V	**3573**
Volvo V70 / S80 Petrol & Diesel (98 - 05) S to 55	**4263**
AUTOMOTIVE TECHBOOKS	
Automotive Electrical and Electronic Systems Manual	**3049**
Automotive Gearbox Overhaul Manual	**3473**
Automotive Service Summaries Manual	**3475**
Automotive Timing Belts Manual – Austin/Rover	**3549**
Automotive Timing Belts Manual – Ford	**3474**
Automotive Timing Belts Manual – Peugeot/Citroën	**3568**
Automotive Timing Belts Manual – Vauxhall/Opel	**3577**
DIY MANUAL SERIES	
The Haynes Air Conditioning Manual	**4192**
The Haynes Car Electrical Systems Manual	**4251**
The Haynes Manual on Bodywork	**4198**
The Haynes Manual on Brakes	**4178**
The Haynes Manual on Carburettors	**4177**
The Haynes Manual on Diesel Engines	**4174**
The Haynes Manual on Engine Management	**4199**
The Haynes Manual on Fault Codes	**4175**
The Haynes Manual on Practical Electrical Systems	**4267**
The Haynes Manual on Small Engines	**4250**
The Haynes Manual on Welding	**4176**

* Classic reprint

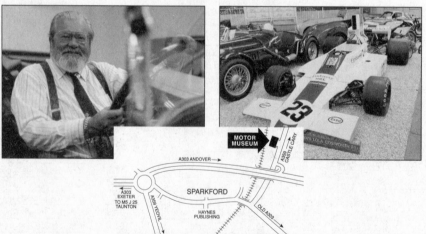